Wiley CPAexcel® Exam Review

STUDY GUIDE

2018

BUSINESS ENVIRONMENT AND CONCEPTS

Wiley CPAexcel® Exam Review

STUDY GUIDE

2018

BUSINESS ENVIRONMENT AND CONCEPTS

Allen Bizzell, Ph.D., CPA (inactive)
Robert A. Prentice, J.D.
Dan N. Stone, Ph.D., CPA (inactive)

Wiley Efficient Learning™

Cover image: © jeremykramerdesign/iStockphoto
Cover design: Wiley

Published by John Wiley & Sons, Inc., Hoboken, New Jersey.
Published simultaneously in Canada.

For general information on our other products and services or for technical support, please contact our Customer Care Department within the United States at (800) 762-2974, outside the United States at (317) 572-3993 or fax (317) 572-4002.

Wiley publishes in a variety of print and electronic formats and by print-on-demand. Some material included with standard print versions of this book may not be included in e-books or in print-on-demand. If this book refers to media such as a CD or DVD that is not included in the version you purchased, you may download this material at http://booksupport.wiley.com. For more information about Wiley products, visit www.wiley.com.

ISBN 9781119481140
ISBN 9781119481232 (ePub); ISBN 9781119481089 (ePDF)

Printed in the United States of America.

10 9 8 7 6 5 4 3 2 1

Contents

About the Authors

Wiley CPAexcel® content is authored by a team of accounting professors and CPA Exam experts from top accounting colleges such as the University of Texas at Austin (frequently ranked the #1 accounting school in the country), California State University at Sacramento, Northern Illinois University (frequently ranked in the top 10 in its peer group and top 20 overall), and the University of North Alabama.

Professor Craig Bain
CPAexcel® Author, Mentor, and Video Lecturer
Ph.D., CPA
Professor, Franke College of Business, Northern Arizona University

Professor Allen H. Bizzell
CPAexcel® Author, Mentor, and Video Lecturer
Ph.D., CPA (inactive)
Former Associate Dean and Accounting Faculty, University of Texas (Retired)
Associate Professor, Department of Accounting, Texas State University (Retired)

Professor Gregory Carnes
CPAexcel® Author, Mentor, and Video Lecturer
Ph.D., CPA
Raburn Eminent Scholar of Accounting, University of North Alabama
Former Dean, College of Business, Lipscomb University
Former Chair, Department of Accountancy, Northern Illinois University

Professor Meghann Cefaratti
CPAexcel® Author and Video Lecturer
Ph.D.
Grant Thornton Professor of Accountancy, Department of Accountancy, Northern Illinois University

Professor B. Douglas Clinton
CPAexcel® Video Lecturer
Ph.D., CPA, CMA
Alta Via Consulting Professor of Management Accountancy, Department of Accountancy, Northern Illinois University

Professor Charles J. Davis
CPAexcel® Author
Ph.D., CPA
Professor of Accounting, Department of Accounting, College of Business Administration, California State University—Sacramento

Professor Donald R. Deis Jr.
CPAexcel® Author and Video Lecturer
Ph.D., CPA, CFE
TAMUS Regents Professor and Ennis & Virginia Joslin Endowed Chair in Accounting, College of Business, Texas A&M University—Corpus Christi
Former Director, School of Accountancy, University of Missouri—Columbia
Former Professor and Director, Accounting Ph.D. Program, Louisiana State University—Baton Rouge

Professor Marianne M. Jennings
CPAexcel® Author and Video Lecturer
J.D.
Professor Emeritus of Legal and Ethical Studies, W.P. Carey School of Business, Arizona State University

Professor Robert A. Prentice
CPAexcel® Author and Video Lecturer
J.D.
Ed and Molly Smith Centennial Professor In Business Law and Distinguished Teaching Professor, J.D. McCombs School of Business, University of Texas

Professor Pam Smith
CPAexcel® Author and Video Lecturer
Ph.D., MBA, CPA
KPMG Professor of Accountancy, Department of Accountancy, Northern Illinois University

Professor Dan N. Stone
CPAexcel® Author and Video Lecturer
Ph.D., MPA, CPA (inactive)
Gatton Endowed Chair, Von Allmen School of Accountancy, University of Kentucky

Professor Donald E. Tidrick
CPAexcel® Author and Video Lecturer
Ph.D., CPA, CMA, CIA
Deloitte Professor of Accountancy, Northern Illinois University
Former Associate Chair, Department of Accounting, Director of Professional Program in Accounting and Director of the CPA Review Course, University of Texas at Austin

About the Business Professors

Professor Allen H. Bizzell has been involved with the CPA Exam for over 40 years as a researcher, developer of exam-related materials and review course instructor. He has conducted numerous CPA Exam–related studies, including several analyses of CPA Exam candidates' characteristics and performance for the Texas State Board of Public Accountancy. He has developed CPA review materials and taught review courses at both the national and local levels. Included in his innovative review materials is the use of simple network diagrams to depict the relationships between related accounting concepts/topics and the appropriate treatment for each. These diagrams are powerful tools not only for understanding accounting materials, but also for retaining the knowledge needed to pass the CPA Exam.

Several publishers have approached Dr. Bizzell to develop financial accounting textbooks incorporating his instructional methodology. According to Dr. Bizzell, he has not done so because the traditional textbook does not lend itself to using all the elements of the methodology. According to Dr. Bizzell, "The CPAexcel® approach is the first to provide the capabilities to capture and deliver to the user the benefits of the methodology."

Professor Robert A. Prentice is the Ed and Molly Smith Centennial Professor of Business Law at the University of Texas and he has taught both UT's and other CPA courses for fifteen years. He created a new course in accounting ethics and regulation that he has taught for the last decade. Professor Prentice has written several textbooks on law and ethics and many law review articles on business ethics, accountants' liability, and securities law. He has won more than 50 teaching awards.

Professor Dan N. Stone is a Gatton Endowed Chair at the University of Kentucky in the Von Allmen School of Accountancy. He is Director of the Ph.D. program for the Von Allmen School of Accountancy and of the Lewis Scholars' Program in the Lewis Honors College. His joint Ph.D. degree is in accounting and information systems from the University of Texas at Austin. Professor Stone has published over 70 academic works, including articles, essays, short stories, and poetry in a variety of journals, including the *Journal of Accounting Research, Accounting, Organizations and Society, Organizational Behavior and Human Decision Processes, and Auditing: A Journal of Theory and Practice.* His recent research investigates online deception, information technologies, mindfulness in professional accounting practice, and the effects of stress on CPA Exam candidates' performance.

Welcome to Business Environment and Concepts

Welcome to Business Environment and Concepts (BEC)! This "lesson" is an important step in your journey to CPA exam success. This series of videos will introduce you to your professors and provide guidance in the planning, application, and registration process. In addition, there are videos that provide an overview of the exam structure, time management hints, effective study strategies, and tips on how to maximize your points. Perhaps most important, the last video is a gentle reminder of how important it is to take care of you.

I. Overview

A. According to the Board of Examiners (BOE) of the AICPA, the Business Environment and Concepts (BEC) section of the exam tests:

1. Knowledge of the general business environment and concepts that candidates need to know in order to understand the underlying reasons for and accounting implications of business transactions; *and*

2. Skills needed to apply that knowledge in performing audit, attest, financial reporting, tax preparation and other professional responsibilities as certified public accountants, including skills involved in preparing written communication.

B. Content covered in this section includes knowledge of corporate governance; economic concepts essential to understanding the global business environment and its impact on an entity's business strategy and financial risk management; financial management processes; information technology; and operations management.

1. This section is patterned after the AICPA Uniform CPA Examination Blueprints provided by the BOE for the BEC section of the exam. The exam consists of multiple-choice questions, task-based simulations, and written communication tasks. Specifically, the four-hour BEC exam is structured as follows:

Testlet 1: Thirty-one multiple-choice questions
Testlet 2: Thirty-one multiple-choice questions
Testlet 3: Two task-based simulations
Testlet 4: Two task-based simulations
Testlet 5: Three written communication tasks

2. Many of the multiple-choice questions used in this section have been created by CPAexcel® authors based on the content of the material presented; *and*

3. The task-based simulations and written communication requirements have been developed based on the authors' assessments of the subject matter most likely to be examined.

C. The CPA Examination Blueprint for BEC, which is intended to identify all the topics that might be on the exam, are presented in the following area headings, together with the exam allocation for each content area:

AREA	Point Range
Corporate Governance	17%–27%
Economic Concepts and Analysis	17%–27%
Financial Management	11%–21%
Information Technology	15%–25%
Operations Management	15%–25%
TOTAL	100%

D. The material in this section of CPAexcel® covers all topics in the CPA Examination Blueprint to prepare you for success on exam day. Each of the areas covered in this material is described briefly below from the author's perspective.

II. Corporate Governance

I am responsible for but a tiny slice of the BEC material—the "Other Regulatory Frameworks and Provisions" part of the beginning section on Corporate Governance. This is essentially Sarbanes-Oxley Act (SOX) material. SOX is important in some other areas of the exam as well, but the material here relates to SOX's efforts to improve the integrity of the numbers audited by CPAs that corporations report to the SEC. Any CPA pursuing a career in the audit field should be intimately familiar with the material. Fortunately, it is pretty straight-forward and should be relatively easy to master.

~Professor Robert Prentice

III. Economic Concepts and Analysis

A. This area covers the following material:

1. Fundamental microeconomic and macroeconomic concepts and relationships that underlie an understanding of all economic activity and changes
2. Changes in economic and business cycles, including reasons for and measures of those changes
3. How the economy and markets influence business strategies
4. How globalization impacts individual companies and how it has resulted in shifts in economic power among nations
5. Various forms of risks encountered and means of mitigating those risks

B. Some of the topics covered will be familiar to you from basic economics courses, especially microeconomics and macroeconomics. Other topics may be new to you, especially if you have not taken an international economics course. Although the content specifications provided by the BOE cover a broad range of economic topics, that coverage is not particularly deep. An understanding of the material covered in this subsection should provide more than adequate preparation for this area of the exam.

IV. Financial Management

A. This area covers the following material:

1. Concepts and tools used in financial management, as well as other areas of management and accounting
2. The capital budgeting process and analytical techniques used in capital budgeting
3. Appropriate financing strategies, both short-term and long-term
4. Techniques for capital management, including the management of working capital
5. Methods for financial valuation, including the determination of fair value
6. Use of ratios and other quantitative techniques for financial management
7. Various categories of financial risk faced by a business and ways to mitigate those risks

B. As noted above, in some cases, the order of presentation in CPAexcel® is different from that in the content specifications. This has been done to present the material in a more logical sequence.

C. In studying these areas, it is important to understand the concepts and tools covered in the first set of lessons before considering the other topics listed. Those concepts and tools—including cost concepts, time value of money, interest rate concepts and calculations, financial valuation, and hedging and derivatives—are used in the subsequent topics of this area, as well as in various other topics covered on the exam.

~Professor Allen Bizzell

V. Information Technology

I am responsible for the BEC content related to information technology (IT) and corporate governance (excluding the Sarbanes-Oxley portion covered by Professor Prentice). IT content is 15% to 25% of the BEC portion of the exam, and it now mostly focuses on the effect of IT on accounting controls. Corporate Governance makes up 17%–27% of the BEC portion of the exam and focuses on corporate rights, responsibilities and authority; accounting controls and policies; and procedures for managing control-related risks. Two areas of growing CPA Exam importance on both the IT and corporate governance are the Committee of Sponsoring Organizations of the Treadway Commission (COSO) reports on internal control and Enterprise Risk Management, and, the COBIT (The Control Objectives for Information and related Technology) Framework for managing IT risks.

~Professor Dan Stone

VI. Operations Management

The BEC content related to operations management comprises approximately 15%–25% of the BEC coverage. Traditional managerial accounting topics are covered here, including cost measurement, process management, planning, and performance management. In addition, strategic market and risk analysis, as well as project management, receive significant emphasis.

Corporate Governance

Internal Control Frameworks

Introduction to COSO, Internal Control, and the COSO Cube

This chapter introduces the two most important models of accounting controls that are based in a corporate governance perspective: the Committee of Sponsoring Organizations (COSO) model and COSO Enterprise Risk Management (ERM) model.

After studying this lesson, you should be able to:

1. Apply the COSO integrated framework to identify relevant controls for risk scenarios in organizations.
2. Give examples of the goals, components, and organizational levels that are the focus of internal controls.
3. Describe the purpose and objectives of the COSO integrated internal control framework.
4. Identify the three dimensions, and the components of each dimension, in the COSO integrated framework for IC.

I. **Introduction to the Committee of Sponsoring Organizations (COSO)**

   A. In 1987, five organizations (i.e., the AICPA, the Institute of Internal Auditors, the Institute of Management Accountants, the American Accounting Association, and the Financial Executives Institute) formed COSO; their goal was to develop an integrated internal control model to guide efforts to articulate and improve accounting controls.

      1. COSO now provides guidance related to "ERM, internal control, and fraud deterrence" (COSO website). The COSO "cube" model (see below) has been widely adopted, incorporated into the structure of many organizations, and refined and expanded (e.g., the COSO ERM model). For example, a 2006 CFO magazine poll indicated that more than 80% of respondents used the COSO framework as a basis for developing and assessing the adequacy of their accounting control systems.

   B. The CPA Exam tests three areas of COSO content.

      1. In both the Auditing and Attestation and BEC sections:

         a. The COSO integrated framework

      2. In BEC:

         a. Internal Control—Integrated Framework

         b. Enterprise Risk Management (ERM)—Integrated Framework

         c. COSO elements from additional documents, relating to recent changes in IT (e.g., cloud computing) and governance

II. **Overview of Internal Control**—The Committee of Sponsoring Organizations of the Treadway Commission (COSO) defines internal control as follows:

   A. **Definition**—Internal control is a process—effected by the entity's board of directors, management, and other personnel—designed to provide reasonable assurance regarding the achievement of objectives in the following categories:

      1. Effectiveness and efficiency of **operations**

      2. Reliability of financial and nonfinancial **reporting**

      3. **Compliance** with applicable laws and regulations

B. Accordingly, internal control is closely connected to the achievement of management objectives related to operations, financial reporting, and compliance with laws and regulations (see the discussion below).

C. General Control Objectives—Several accounting pronouncements have identified the following as general objectives of internal control:

1. **Safeguard assets** of the firm.
2. **Promote efficiency** of the firm's operations.
3. **Measure compliance** with management's prescribed policies and procedures.
4. **Ensure accuracy and reliability** of accounting records and information:
   a. Identify and **record all valid transactions.**
   b. Provide **timely** information in appropriate detail to permit proper classification and financial reporting.
   c. Accurately measure the **financial value of transactions.**
   d. Accurately record transactions in the **time period** in which they occurred.

III. Internal Control—The primary areas of focus of an internal control system are:

> **Note**
> *These objectives hold regardless of whether the accounting system is manual or automated.*

A. Operations

1. Objectives related to the fundamental mission and vision of the entity.
2. Include improving financial performance, productivity, quality, environmental practices, innovation, and customer and employee satisfaction, as well as safeguarding assets (protecting and preserving assets)

B. Reporting—Objectives related to the preparation of (financial or nonfinancial) reports for use by shareholders and the organization. Reporting objectives may be for internal or external objectives.

1. **External financial reporting objectives** usually relate to, for example, annual financial statements, interim financial statements, or earnings releases. Characteristics of these reporting objectives include meeting shareholder or regulatory requirements, being prepared in accordance with external standards such as U.S. GAAP, and/or being prepared to meet regulatory, contractual, or other agreement requirements.
2. **External nonfinancial reporting objectives** usually relate to internal control reports, sustainability reports, or supply change reports. Characteristics of these external nonfinancial reporting objectives are similar to the external financial reporting characteristics (see above).
3. **Internal financial reporting objectives** usually relate to, for example, divisional financial reports, customer profitability analysis, and bank covenant calculations. These objectives may include staff or asset utilization, customer satisfaction measures, and/or health and safety measures. Reporting internal financial and nonfinancial information is necessary for management and the board to manage the business and support decisions regarding the business's strategic direction, operating plans, and expectations.

C. Compliance—Compliance objectives concern complying with external laws and regulations (as opposed to the operations objectives, which include compliance with the entity's internal policies and procedures). For example, the entity must identify any laws or regulations that must be adhered to, such as human resources, taxation, and environmental compliance, or laws that apply to operations in a foreign country.

IV. The (COSO) Integrated Framework "Cube" Model for Internal Control

A. The COSO integrated framework for designing, implementing and evaluating internal control (2013) is a cube; that is, it has three dimensions.

B. These three dimensions capture, with respect to internal control:

1. **What** is internal control (i.e., its fundamental components)
2. **Why** we have internal control (i.e., its goals or objectives)
3. **Where** we have internal control (i.e., the units of analysis where we will design, implement, and test internal control)

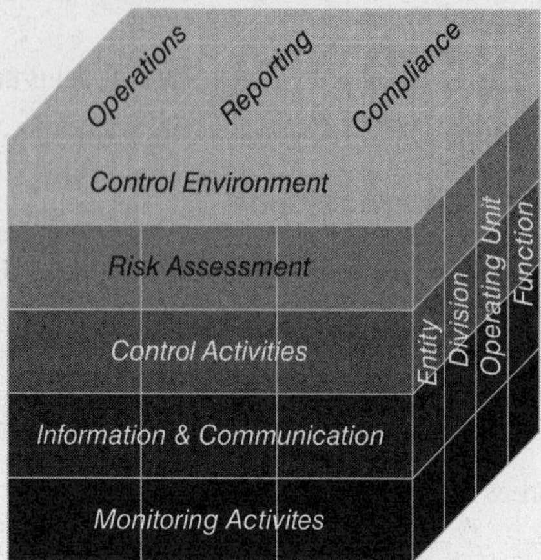

Source: COSO Internal Control—Integrated Framework

C. What is Internal Control? The Five Components—The first dimension identifies five fundamental components of an internal control system:

1. **Control (also called the internal) environment**—Management's philosophy toward controls, organizational structure, system of authority and responsibility, personnel practices, policies, and procedures. This component is the core or foundation of any system of internal control.
2. **Risk assessment**—The process of identifying, analyzing, and managing the risks involved in achieving the organization's objectives. This topic is covered in greater depth in the "Risk Management Policies and Procedures" lesson.
3. **Information and communication**—The information and communication systems that enable an organization's people to identify, process, and exchange the information needed to manage and control operations.
4. **Monitoring**—To ensure the ongoing reliability of information, it is necessary to monitor and test the system and its data.
5. **Control activities**—The policies and procedures that ensure that actions are taken to address the risks related to the achievement of management's objectives.
6. The COSO model depicts these activities in a pyramid structure.

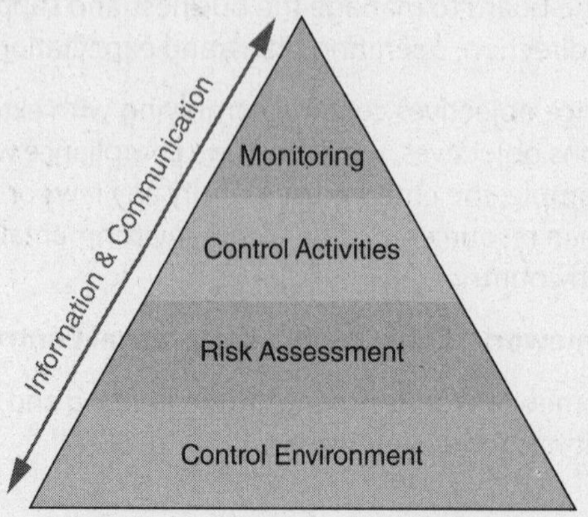

D. Why Do We Have Internal Control? The Three Objectives—The second dimension of the cube (horizontal space in the first diagram in this lesson) identifies the three fundamental objectives of a system of internal control. These are:

1. **Operations**—The effective and efficient use of an organization's resources in pursuit of its core mission
2. **Reporting**—Preparing and disseminating timely and reliable information, including financial and nonfinancial information, and internal and external reports. These four possibilities for reporting are summarized in the following figure, which includes examples of each of the four types of reporting:

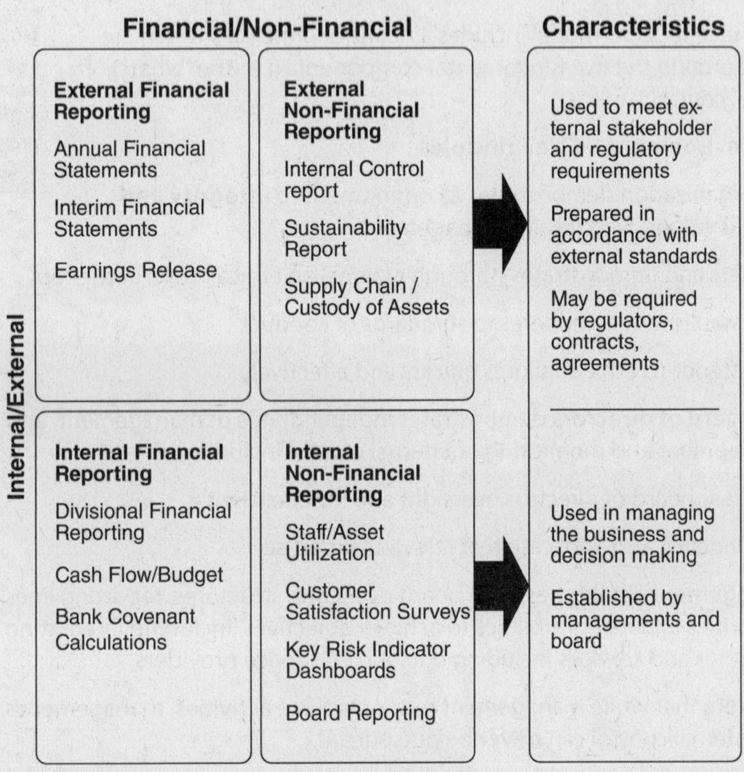

Source: COSO: Internal Control—Integrated Framework

3. **Compliance**—Complying with applicable laws and regulations
4. **Caveats and cautions about organizational objectives**—Objectives are unique to entities and their operating environments. Objectives and controls may overlap and support one another. For example, strong controls over cash are likely to increase the reliability of financial reports about cash.

E. Where Do We Have Internal Control? Units and Activities—The third dimension of the cube (depth in the first diagram in this lesson) specifies the units and activities that must be controlled within the organization.

1. For example, in a business organization, accounting controls are likely to be necessary in relation to sales, production, marketing, finance, and IT.

V. Summary—This lesson presents:

A. What is COSO? What COSO content is tested on the CPA Exam, and on which sections is it tested?

B. An introduction to the COSO integrated framework for the internal control, which describes the what, why, and where of organizational internal control

17 Principles of Internal Control

After studying this lesson, you should be able to:

1. Give examples of each of the control principles.
2. Identify and describe the 17 control principles and their related components.
3. Use the 17 control principles to assess the quality of the system of internal control in an entity.

I. COSO Internal Control Principles

> **Note**
> *Good news! As COSO notes, these principles are largely redundant with previous principles found in COSO documents.*

A. The most recent COSO model includes 17 control principles which are organized around the five fundamental components (i.e., the "what") of an internal control system.

B. **Control Environment—Five Principles**

1. The organization demonstrates a commitment to **integrity and ethical values**. Specifically, management:
    a. Sets and demonstrates (through actions) an ethical "tone at the top"
    b. Establishes and adheres to standards of conduct
    c. Attends to ethical failures quickly and effectively
2. The **board of directors** demonstrates independence of management, and oversees the development and monitoring of internal control including:
    a. Clear board of directors oversight and independence
    b. Evidence and application of relevant expertise
3. **Management** establishes, with board oversight, structures, reporting lines, and appropriate authorities and responsibilities to achieve objectives, including integrating organizational structures and services including outsourced service providers.
    a. Note that while management may outsource activities, management's responsibility for internal control can **never** be outsourced.
4. **Competence**—The organization demonstrates a commitment to attract, develop, and retain competent individuals consistent with achieving organizational objectives, including:
    a. Establishing policies and procedures to attract, develop, and retain competent individuals
    b. Assessing competencies, creating development plans to achieve needed skills and competencies, and addressing deficiencies in skills and competencies through training, hiring, or outsourcing
    c. Planning and preparing for turnover and succession
5. **Accountability**—The organization holds individuals accountable for their internal control responsibilities including:
    a. Enforcing accountability through structures, authorities, and responsibilities
    b. Establishing and evaluating performance measures, incentives, rewards, and disciplinary actions for individuals
    c. Monitoring and considering the potential for excessive performance pressures, including unrealistic performance (e.g., earnings) targets, and an excessive concern with short-term (e.g., quarterly earnings) targets

C. Risk Assessment—Four Principles. (Note that many of these principles are also found in the "Risk Management Policies and Procedures" lesson.)

1. **Objectives**—The organization specifies objectives with sufficient clarity to enable the identification and assessment of risks that threaten the achievement of objectives. In so doing, the organization should consider:
   - **a.** The precision of risk tolerance levels: for example, can we quantify the risk? To within what range?
   - **b.** Materiality in relation to risk assessment. How big of a risk poses a threat to objectives (a loss of $10,000? $100,000? $1,000,000?)?
   - **c.** Risks related to the organization's ability to comply with standards, frameworks, laws and regulations
   - **d.** Risks related to operational and financial performance goals
   - **e.** Risks in committing resources
2. **Assessment**—The organization identifies risks to the achievement of its objectives across the entity and analyzes risks as a basis for determining how the risk should be managed. In so doing, the organization should:
   - **a.** Involve appropriate levels of management in risk assessment
   - **b.** Consider and include entity, subsidiary, division, operating unit, and functional levels
   - **c.** Analyze internal and external factors
   - **d.** Estimate risk importance
   - **e.** Develop appropriate risk responses
3. **Fraud**—The organization considers the potential for fraud in assessing risks to the achievement of objectives. In so doing, it:
   - **a.** Considers fraud risk factors and threats
   - **b.** Assesses the potential fraud influences of incentives and pressures
   - **c.** Assesses opportunities that may exist in the organization for fraudsters to commit fraud
   - **d.** Assesses attitudes and potential rationalizations that might be used to justify fraudulent actions
4. **Change management**—The organization identifies and assesses changes in the external environment (regulatory, economic, and physical environment of operation), assessing changes in the business model (new or existing business lines, rapid growth, new technologies, or acquisitions/divestitures) and changes in leadership.

D. Control Activities—Three Principles

1. **Risk reduction**—Organizational control activities mitigate (i.e., reduce) the risks to the achievement of objectives to acceptable levels. In so doing, the organization:
   - **a.** Integrates controls with risk assessments
   - **b.** Uses risk reduction analyses to determine which business processes require a control focus
   - **c.** Considers how the environment, complexity, nature and scope of operations influence risk reduction and control activities
   - **d.** Evaluates a mix of potentially control activity types, including manual and automated, and preventive and detective controls
   - **e.** Segregates incompatible activities and implements alternative controls where segregation is impossible

2. **Technology controls**—The organization selects and implements general controls over technology, which support the achievement of its objectives. These activities include:
   a. Management understanding and determining the dependencies between business processes, automated controls, and technology general controls
   b. Management establishing controls to ensure the completeness, accuracy, and availability of technology and processing
   c. Restricting technology access rights to authorized users
   d. Establishing relevant security management process controls
   e. Establishing relevant technology acquisition, development, and maintenance process controls
3. **Policies**—The organization deploys control activities through policies and procedures that establish stakeholder expectations. Established procedures ensure the implementation of these policies. These activities include:
   a. Establishing policies and procedures that support the achievement of management's directives
   b. Establishing responsibility and accountability for executing policies and procedures
   c. Employing competent personnel to perform control activities in a timely manner and to take corrective action to investigate and act on control problems and issues
   d. Management periodically reassessing and revising policies and procedures to address changing conditions.

E. Information and Communication—Three Principles

1. **Quality**—Relevant, high-quality information supports the internal control processes. Organizational processes to ensure that high-quality information supports internal control processes should:
   a. Identify the information required to support internal control processes.
   b. Capture internal and external courses of data.
   c. Transform relevant data into information.
   d. Produce information that is relevant, timely, current, accurate, verifiable, protected, and retained.
   e. Consider the costs and benefits of information in relation to organizational objectives.
2. **Internal**—Internal communication supports internal control processes. This includes:
   a. Organizational processes communicate required information to enable all personnel to understand and execute their internal control responsibilities.
   b. Communication between management and the board of directors supports the achievement of organizational objectives.
   c. Separate communication lines, such as a whistle-blower hotline, exist as a fail-safe mechanism to enable anonymous, confidential communication.
   d. Internal communication methods are sensitive to the timing, audience, and nature of the communication.

Example
A large governmental agency created a toll-free hotline, an email account, and a website to enable anonymous reporting of fraud, waste, and abuse. The agency's general counsel includes a forensic audit team that investigates credible reports.

3. **External**—Communication with outsiders supports internal control processes. Organizational processes:

   a. Communicate relevant and timely information to external parties, including shareholders, partners, owners, regulators, customers, financial analysts, and others.

   b. Enable inbound communications. Communication channels support the receipt of information from customers, suppliers, external auditors, regulators, financial analysts and others.

   c. Separate communication lines, such as a whistle-blower hotline, exist as fail-safe mechanisms to enable anonymous, confidential communication

   d. Communicate relevant information resulting from assessments conducted by external parties (e.g., reviews of internal control) to the board of directors

   e. Ensure that external communication methods are sensitive to the timing, audience, and nature of the communication and to legal, regulatory and fiduciary requirements

F. Monitoring Activities—Two Principles

1. **Ongoing and periodic**—Ongoing and separate evaluations evaluate internal control functioning. These activities include:

   a. Considering the mix of ongoing and separate evaluations

   b. Benchmarking—considering the design and state of the existing system of internal control to establish a baseline understanding for ongoing and separate evaluations

   c. Developing and selecting ongoing and separate evaluations through management consideration of the rate of change of business activities and processes

   d. Ensuring that personnel have sufficient knowledge to conduct evaluations

   e. Integrating ongoing evaluations with business processes and adjusting, as needed, to changing conditions

   f. Providing periodic, separate evaluations for objective feedback

   g. Adjusting the scope and frequency of evaluations based on risk assessments

2. **Address deficiencies**—Parties responsible for taking corrective action, including senior management and the board of directors, receive timely communication of internal control deficiencies. These activities include:

   a. Assessment of the results of ongoing and separate evaluations, as appropriate, by management and the board of directors

   b. Communication of deficiencies to those responsible for acting upon them, and to management at least one level above the identified problem

   c. Communication of deficiencies to senior management and the board of directors, as appropriate

   d. Tracking by management whether deficiencies are corrected on a timely basis

Types and Limitations of Accounting Controls

This lesson introduces accounting controls and some useful classifications of these controls. This material is tested in the *Auditing and Attestation* section of the CPA Exam. The module "Basic Internal Control" in the Auditing and Attestation section of the CPAexcel review course covers internal control from the auditor's perspective. The BEC portion of the CPA Exam focuses on internal control from the perspective of corporate governance, although we will also consider some basic control principles that originate in the audit literature. In short, the goal of the overlapping discussion of accounting control in the *Auditing and Attestation* and *BEC* portions of CPAexcel should give you differing and complementary perspectives on this important topic.

After studying this lesson, you should be able to:

1. Give examples of each type of control discussed in the lesson.
2. Describe the inherent limitations of internal control and their implications for the achievement of organizational objectives.
3. Define and identify examples of preventive, detective, and corrective controls.
4. Define and identify examples of feedback and feed-forward controls.
5. Define and identify examples of general and application controls.
6. Link controls with the errors or frauds that they will, or will not, prevent or detect.

I. **Limitations of Internal Control**—COSO identifies the following inherent limitations in an internal control system:

   A. **The suitability of objectives established as a precondition to internal control.** Internal control is the responsibility of management (not the auditors). Management may set objectives that lead to poor controls (e.g., make earnings targets even if it means committing fraud).

   B. **Internal control depends heavily on people.** People are wonderful, fallible, imperfect creatures. Human judgment can be faulty, flawed, and biased. Breakdowns in control can occur because of humans (God love 'em).

   C. **Management may be able to, and may choose to, override internal control.** Many of the major financial reporting scandals are examples of management override, including Enron, WorldCom, and Computer Associates.

   D. **Collusion is an ever-present risk in internal control systems.** Management, employees, and/or third parties may collude to circumvent controls. The examples listed in the previous point are also relevant here.

   E. **External events beyond the organization's control may lead to control failures.** For example, the Fukushima nuclear disaster occurred due to a combination of events that created circumstances that exceeded TEPCO's risk assessment planning scenarios. Stated simply, unexpected doo doo can (and sometimes does) happen.

   F. **Inherent limitations, such as those listed above, preclude an internal control system from providing absolute assurance.** Hence, a cost-effective system of internal control provides reasonable but not absolute assurance of the achievement of organizational objectives.

II. **Deficiencies in Internal Control**

   A. An internal control deficiency is a shortcoming in a component or components and relevant principle(s) that reduces the likelihood of an entity achieving its objectives. Hence, a control deficiency occurs when the design or operation of a control does not allow management or employees, in the normal course of performing their assigned functions, to prevent or detect misstatements on a timely basis.

      1. When an organization determines that an internal control deficiency exists, management must assess the severity of that deficiency (i.e., classify it)

B. Types of Internal Control Deficiencies—According to the SEC:

a. **Control deficiency**—Defined above. The least serious of the three types of control deficiencies.

b. **Significant deficiency**—A deficiency (or combination of deficiencies) in internal control that is more serious than a control deficiency but less severe than a material weakness, yet it is important enough to merit attention by those charged with governance.

c. **Material weakness**—A deficiency (or combination of deficiencies) in internal control such that there is a reasonable possibility that a material misstatement of the entity's financial statements will not be prevented or detected and corrected on a timely basis. This is a serious, really bad problem.

III. Categories of Controls—The classifications of accounting controls discussed in this lesson are different ways of looking at controls. These classifications can be useful in developing and evaluating the benefits and limitations of these controls.

A. Preventive, Detective, and Corrective Controls—This classification focuses on the **timing of the control relative to the potential error**: that is, ***when*** the controls are applied. A well-controlled system balances preventive and detective controls and includes corrective controls as needed.

1. **Preventive controls—("before the fact") controls**—Preventive controls attempt to **stop an error or irregularity before it occurs**. They tend to be "passive" controls, that is, once established, they simply need to be activated to be effective. Examples of preventive controls include locks on buildings and doors, use of user names and password to gain access to computer resources, and building segregation of duties into the organizational structure.

2. **Detective controls—("after the fact" controls)**—Detective controls attempt to **detect an error after it has occurred**. They tend to be "active" controls: that is, they must be continually performed to be effective. Examples of detective controls include data entry edits (e.g., checks for missing data, values that are too large or too small), reconciliation of accounting records to physical assets (bank reconciliations, inventory counts), and tests of transactions to determine whether they comply with management's policies and procedures (audits).

   a. Effective detective controls, when known to the relevant constituency, often **take on preventive characteristics**. For example, surveillance cameras are fundamentally detective controls: They are designed to detect the commission of an unauthorized act. However, when it is known that surveillance cameras are in use, they also can serve to prevent unauthorized acts. The decrease in the number of drivers running red lights when drivers know that surveillance cameras are installed on traffic signals is an example of this phenomenon.

> **Note**
> **Which Type of Control Is It?**
> *The dual nature of such controls can make it difficult to properly categorize a control. Search for the fundamental, underlying nature of the control; distinguish this from the secondary effects of the control*

3. **Corrective controls are always paired with detective controls**—They attempt to reverse the effects of the observed error or irregularity. Examples of corrective controls include maintenance of backup files, disaster recovery plans, and insurance.

B. Feedback and Feed-Forward Controls—This classification of controls closely relates to the previous one. Feedback and feed-forward controls focus on changing inputs or processes to promote desirable outcomes by comparing actual results (feedback) or projected results (feed-forward) to a predetermined standard.

1. **Feedback controls**—Evaluate the results of a process and, if the results are undesirable, adjust the process to correct the results; most detective controls are also feedback controls.

2. **Feed-forward controls**—Project future results based on current and past information and, if the future results are undesirable, change the inputs to the system to prevent the outcome. Many inventory ordering systems are essentially feed-forward controls: The system projects product sales over the relevant time period, identifies the current inventory level, and orders inventory sufficient to fulfill the sales demand.

C. General Controls and Application Controls—This classification appears in many control models, including auditing standards, the COSO model, and the COBIT model (see the lessons related to these topics). Its focus is on the functional area of the control: that is, **where** the control is applied rather than **when** it is applied. The model divides information processing controls into two categories:

1. **General controls**—General controls are controls over the environment as a whole. They apply to all functions, not just specific accounting applications. General controls help ensure that data integrity is maintained.
   a. Examples of general controls include restricting physical access to computer resources, production and storage of backup files, and performing background checks of computer services personnel.
2. **Application controls**—Application controls are controls over specific **data input, data processing,** and **data output** activities. Application controls are designed to ensure the accuracy, completeness, and validity of transaction processing. As such, they have a relatively narrow focus on those accounting applications that are involved with data entry, updates, and reporting.
   a. Examples of application controls include checks to ensure that input data is complete and properly formatted (e.g., dates, dollar amounts), that account numbers are valid, and that values are reasonable (e.g., that we don't sell quantities that are greater than the quantity currently in inventory).
   b. Application controls are sometimes called "transaction controls" since they relate specifically to transaction processing.

IV. Linking Controls to Risks

Example

Linking controls to risks that the controls will, or will not, prevent or detect is an important skill for the CPA Exam. For example, imagine that a company implements a new password policy that requires users to provide longer, more complex passwords. Which of the following risks will this new policy **not** reduce?

A. Crackers using software to figure out the passwords of employees

B. Hackers gaining access to the computer system

C. Piggybacking (i.e., someone gaining unauthorized access by following an employee into the building)

In this case, the new security policy will reduce the risk of A and B but not C.

V. Summary

Summary—This lesson introduces the limitations of internal controls, categories of control deficiencies, and discusses several types of controls.

Internal Control Roles and Responsibilities

After studying this lesson, you should be able to:

1. Describe the internal control roles of the board of directors, management, support functions, and internal auditors.
2. Identify, and give examples of, the internal control responsibilities of the board of directors, management, support functions, internal auditors, and employees.

I. Internal Control Role and Responsibility Overview

A. Internal control exists partly because of the people who create, maintain, and monitor it. These people include the board of directors or equivalent oversight body, management and personnel, support (i.e., business-enabling) functions, and internal auditors. If aspects of internal control are outsourced, the service provider performs controls, but management retains responsibility.

B. Four key roles and responsibilities for internal control are:

1. The **board of directors (BOD)** is responsible for oversight of key internal control activities and the organization's enterprise-wide risk management.
2. **Management's** responsibility is for maintaining effective internal controls related to daily operations. Often their compensation is partly (or fully) based on the organization's achievement of objectives (e.g., earnings targets).
   a. Some COSO documents refer to management as the "first line of defense" in internal controls.
3. **Support (business-enabling) functions** may include legal, compliance, finance, human resources, IT, and others. Support functions clarify internal control requirements and evaluate control-related compliance with set standards. Support function compensation should not be tied directly to the achievement of organizational objectives.
   a. Support (business-enabling) functions are also called the "second line of defense" in internal controls.
4. **Internal auditors** assess and report on internal control and provide recommendations to correct or improve activities. Their compensation should be unrelated to the business areas that they review and assess.
   a. Internal auditors are also called the "third line of defense" in internal controls.

II. Internal Control Accountability: Roles and Responsibilities

A. Ultimately, internal controls are the responsibility of **all** individuals within an entity. That is, all employees play a role in the entity's control objectives. Specific responsibilities related to internal control, of course, depend on the individuals' function. This section describes some key functions in the system of internal control.

B. The board of directors and its committees, including the audit committee, are responsible for: oversight of the system of internal control; and for defining expectations about integrity and ethical values, transparency, and accountability for the performance of internal control responsibilities. The BOD:

1. Must have a working knowledge of the entity's activities and environment and commit to fulfilling their governance responsibilities. In addition, they must be objective, capable, and inquisitive.
2. Should maintain open and unrestricted communications channel with all entity personnel, internal auditors, independent auditors, external reviewers, and legal counsel.

> **Example**
> ***COSO Example: Internal Control Roles and Responsibilities***
> A small technology company created an organizational chart for its corporate accounting department to ensure the assignment of internal control responsibilities and key controls to competent employees. The internal audit and audit committees review the organizational charts and oversight responsibilities to ensure appropriate assignments.

C. COSO charges senior management, including the CEO and CFO, with ownership of the internal control system. Management's behavior sets the organizational ethical tone at the top by providing leadership. Accordingly, management:

1. Is accountable to the board of directors
2. Provides leadership and direction including shaping the entity's values, standards, expectations of competence, organizational structure, and accountability for internal control system (e.g., by specifying entity-wide objectives and policies)
3. Maintains daily oversight and control over relevant entity risks
4. Must guide and develop control activities at the entity level
5. Is responsible for delegating the design, implementation, and assessment of internal control to appropriate levels of management
6. Is responsible for communicating expectations (i.e., integrity, competence, key controls, and policies) and information requirements related to internal control
7. Must evaluate control deficiencies and the impact on the ongoing and long-term effectiveness of the system of internal control

D. **Support Personnel** (also called business-enabling) functions are personnel in law, compliance, IT, and risk management who assist in achieving effective and efficient internal control in multiple ways. Their activities include the following:

1. Provide guidance and assessments of internal control in their areas of expertise.
2. Identify known or emerging risks, and help management respond, communicate, and educate others about these risks.
3. Evaluate the effectiveness of developed control and risk assessment processes.
4. Help define effective controls to comply with laws and regulations.

E. **Other Personnel**—Internal control is the responsibility of everyone in an organization; therefore, the principles and components' objectives are, to differing extents, requirements of all employees.

1. Almost all employees produce information that is relevant to the internal control systems. These employees are responsible for communicating problems related to operations, code of conduct, or other policy violations or illegal actions.

F. Internal auditors evaluate the adequacy and effectiveness of controls and thereby contribute to their ongoing effectiveness. In addition, internal auditors often play a significant role in monitoring internal controls.

> **Example**
> ***COSO Example: Organizing the Internal Audit Function***
> The internal audit function of a large manufacturing firm is functionally and administratively independent from the CFO, CEO, and business-unit leaders. The internal audit department aligns its annual objectives with the enterprise-wide strategic objectives. As a result, the focus of the annual audit plan is consistent with the corporate strategic objectives at the corporate and business unit level.

G. External parties, such as external auditors, customers, legislators and regulators, and financial analysts, also play a significant role in contributing to the achievement of an entity's objectives. For example, the ability of external auditors to independently and objectively conduct the financial statement audit is critical to the system of internal control. These external parties often provide information that aids management and the board of directors in improving their internal controls; however, these parties are not responsible for, nor a part of, the internal control system.

Example

COSO Example: Working with the External Auditor

Senior management and the internal audit department of a small financial institution meet annually with their external auditor. At this meeting, they discuss management's approach to evaluating internal control over financial reporting and consider discuss potential modifications to that approach where doing so might increase the external auditor's ability to use the work of management and/or internal audit in the conduct of their external audit procedures. For example, internal audit decided to increase its sample size of control tests in a few key areas to provide a sufficient sample sizes to meet the external auditor's needs.

Example

COSO Example: Using External Specialists

An international manufacturer uses external experts to evaluate controls in some organizational units. Management chooses to use control specialists based on (1) the results of the annual risk assessment process (i.e., for key risks); (2) considering the external auditor's need to reply on these specialists in conducting its audit; and (3) the capabilities, and limitations, of the organization's internal audit staff. Results and issues identified by these specialists are reported and tracked internally.

Internal Control Monitoring—Purpose and Terminology

This lesson introduces the purpose and terminology of the COSO principles for, and guidance on, monitoring internal control. It is based on the COSO pronouncement, *Guidance on Monitoring Internal Control Systems* (COSO 2009).

After studying this lesson, you should be able to:

1. Explain why monitoring internal controls is critical to successful corporate governance.
2. Explain how control monitoring fits into the establishment of organizational goals and the related processes of establishing and evaluating internal control systems.
3. Describe the terminology of, including the qualitative characteristics of evidence related to, the assessments of internal control.
4. Give examples that illustrate how monitoring improves internal control.

I. How Does Monitoring Benefit Corporate Governance?

A. Monitoring is the core, underlying control component in the COSO ERM model. Its position at the foundation is not accidental and reflects the importance of monitoring to achieving strong internal control and effective risk management.

B. Why is control monitoring important?

1. People forget, quit jobs, get lazy, or come to work hung over; machines fail. Over time, controls deteriorate. This deterioration is called "entropy."
2. Advances in technology and management techniques demand that internal control and related monitoring processes continually evolve and improve.

C. Well-designed control monitoring helps lessen the negative effects of entropy and ensure that:

1. Management identifies internal control problems on a timely basis, meaning before they create crises, and addresses them proactively, rather than reactively.
2. Decision makers receive more timely and accurate information.
3. Financial statements are timely, reliable and accurate.
4. Certifications of internal control, e.g., as required by SOX Section 404, occur on a timely basis.
5. Organizational efficiencies are maximized and costs are reduced.

II. The Terminology of Control Monitoring

A. Who evaluates controls? **Evaluators** monitor internal control. Evaluators must have the skills, knowledge, and authority to enable them to (1) understand the risks that can materially affect the organization's objectives, (2) identify critical controls related to managing or mitigating those risks, and (3) conduct and/or oversee the monitoring of appropriately persuasive information about the effectiveness of the internal control system. Two primary attributes of effective evaluators are **competence** and **objectivity**.

1. **Competence**—The evaluator's knowledge of the controls and related processes, including how controls should operate and what constitutes a control deficiency.
2. **Objectivity**—This concerns the extent to which the evaluator may be influenced by personal or vested interests in the outcome of the evaluation. For example, having a financial or personal interest (e.g., the CEO's son works in the unit that she is evaluating) would likely inappropriately influence an evaluator due to their loss of objectivity.

B. Levels of Monitoring

1. **Board monitoring**—Control monitoring by the board, its committees, or others charged with overseeing management conduct. Includes evaluating management's own monitoring process and should include an assessment of the risk of management override of controls.
2. **Self-assessment** occurs when persons responsible for a particular unit or function determine the effectiveness of controls for their activities. The term is often used to describe assessments made by the personnel who operate the control (i.e., self-review), but may also refer to peer or supervisory review within the same unit that the control was created.
3. **Self-review** refers to the review of one's own work. It represents the least objective type of "self-assessment" described above.

Example
Self-Assessment and Self-Review
A financial services organization encourages departments to monitor their own internal control systems and self-report possible control deficiencies. This includes a policy that gives departments credit, in the internal audit grading system, for self-reported deficiencies. Deficiencies that are identified through an internal audit examination, rather than through a department's self-monitoring efforts, are counted against the score.

C. The Nature or Quality of Controls

1. **Control objectives**—Specific targets against which the effectiveness of internal control is evaluated. Typically stated in terms that describe the nature of the risk they are designed to help manage or mitigate.
2. **Compensating controls**—Controls that accomplish the same objective as another control and that can be expected to "compensate" for deficiencies in that control
3. **Deficiency or internal control deficiency**—A condition within an internal control system requiring attention. May represent a perceived, potential or real shortcoming, or an opportunity to strengthen the internal control system to provide a greater likelihood of achieving its objective.
4. **Key controls**—Those controls that are most important to monitor to support a conclusion about the internal control system's ability to manage or mitigate meaningful risks. Identifying key controls helps ensure that the organization directs monitoring resources where they can provide the most value. Key controls often have one or both of the following characteristics:
   a. Their failure might materially affect the organization's objectives, yet not reasonably be detected in a timely manner by other controls.
   b. Their effective operation might prevent other control failures or detect such failures before they have an opportunity to become material to the organization's objectives.
5. **Key performance indicators**—Metrics that reflect critical success factors. They help organizations measure progress toward goals and objectives.
6. **Key risk indicators (KRIs)**—Forward-looking metrics that seek to identify potential problems, thus enabling an organization to take timely action, if necessary.
   a. KRIs range from simple (e.g., key ratios used by the board or senior management) to elaborate (e.g., collecting and aggregating multiple indicates of risk into multidimensional risk scores that are displayed to senior managers in dashboards).
   b. KRIs measure events or causes that can prevent the achievement of performance goals.

c. Elements of well-designed key risk indicators:
   i. Are based on established practices or benchmarks
   ii. Are developed and used consistently across the organization
   iii. Provide unambiguous, intuitive view of the risk
   iv. Are comparable over time and across business units
   v. Provide opportunity for timely assessments of the performance of risk "owners"
   vi. KRIs use resources efficiently

Example

COSO Example

Executives at a medium-size manufacturing company determined that their system lacked appropriate internal ownership of risks and key controls related to financial reporting. The specific, identified deficiency was an insufficient number of competent personnel to monitor key controls related to risks related to financial reporting. Accordingly, they implemented more ongoing monitoring of internal control over financial reporting at the corporate level and reduced the frequency and scope of separate evaluations at plant locations.

D. Terms Related to Quality of Evidence in Control Monitoring and Assessment:

1. **Direct information**—Information that directly substantiates the operation of controls and is obtained by observing them in operation, reperforming them, or otherwise directly evaluating their operation. Direct information is generally highly persuasive because it provides an unobstructed view of control operation. It can be obtained from either ongoing or separate evaluations, but it must link directly to a judgment regarding the effective operation of controls.
2. **Indirect information**—Relevant information, other than direct information, for assessing whether controls are operating and an underlying risk is mitigated. Does not provide explicit evidence as to whether controls are operating effectively. In the presence of an effective monitoring structure, persuasive indirect information influences the type, timing and extent of monitoring procedures required to obtain direct information.
3. **Persuasiveness of information**—This refers to the degree to which the information provides support for conclusions. The level of persuasiveness is derived from its suitability (i.e., its relevance, reliability, and timeliness) and its sufficiency.
4. **Relevant information**—This tells the evaluator something meaningful about the operation of the underlying controls or control component. Information that directly confirms the operation of controls (see "direct information") is most relevant. Information that relates indirectly to the operation of controls (see "indirect information") can also be relevant, but is less so than direct information.
5. **Reliable information** is accurate, verifiable and from an objective source.
6. **Sufficient information**—Information is sufficient when evaluators have gathered enough of it to form a reasonable conclusion. However, in order for information to be sufficient, it must be suitable.
7. **Suitable information**—Suitable information is relevant (i.e., fit for its intended purpose), reliable (i.e., accurate, verifiable and from an objective source), and timely (i.e., produced and used in an appropriate time frame).
8. **Timely information**—Timely information is produced and used in a time frame that makes it possible to prevent or detect control deficiencies before they become material to an organization's objectives.
9. **Verifiable or verifiability**—Verifiable information is information that can be established, confirmed, or substantiated as true or accurate.

Example

COSO Example: Indirect Information

The vice president of operations at a medium-size manufacturing company uses indirect information to help assess plant controls. The company's high turnover at plant locations results in frequent additions to and terminations from plant payroll. The company has determined that the risk of material, operational (or financial reporting) problems in this area is relatively low, given the consistency and small dollar amounts involved on a per person basis and the relative simplicity of the process. As a result, the company relies on monitoring of labor variances (an indirect measure) instead of direct testing of specific controls over additions, terminations, or adjustments to payroll.

Example

COSO Example

Direct and Indirect Information—A large retailer has identified inaccurate, and improperly adjusted, store inventory balances as a key risk indicator.

What direct and indirect information should the retailer consider to gain insight into this key risk indicator?

Direct information about this key risk indicator includes store managers' triweekly and monthly inventory counts. These counts include:

1. System records detailing the date, time, and results of the store managers' inventories
2. The district managers' direct observation of store managers taking inventories
3. The results of the district managers' own monthly inventories, which would identify the failure of any given store manager's inventory count before that failure could contribute to a material error

Indirect information about this key risk indicator includes:

1. Detailed store-level metrics that show store trends and comparative metrics including product-level analyses, cost of goods sold, profitability, and so on
2. System records detailing the duration of each inventory count
3. Store-level inventory records in the system, including on-hand balances, inventory items received by the store, open purchase orders, and any needed adjustments to inventory balances based on inventory counts

Internal Control Monitoring and Change Control Processes

This lesson introduces the processes used in monitoring internal control. It is based on the COSO pronouncement, "Guidance on Monitoring Internal Control Systems" (COSO 2009).

After studying this lesson, you should be able to:

1. Describe the methods and processes used by successful companies to monitor their systems of internal control.
2. Describe the three core processes of the COSO model of control monitoring.
3. Describe the four processes in the COSO model for gaining a baseline understanding of internal control effectiveness and assessing the effects of relevant changes in controls or risks.
4. Describe an effective change control process including potential areas of change and the role of documentation in change control processes.
5. Give examples of effective and ineffective change control procedures and processes.
6. Give examples of methods and procedures for monitoring internal control.

I. Control Monitoring as an Organizational Process

A. Here is a brief description of the COSO (2006, 2008) model of control monitoring as an organizational process.

1. Internal control begins with management setting organizational objectives. This process, shown in gray in the following diagram underlies the internal control processes that are shown in colors.
2. The first four processes (risk assessment, control environment, control activities, and information and communication) are discussed in the "Introduction to COSO, Internal Control, and the COSO Cube" lesson.
3. Monitoring evaluates the internal control system's ability to manage or mitigate "meaningful risks" to organizational objectives. A meaningful risk is one with potential consequences for organizational objectives.

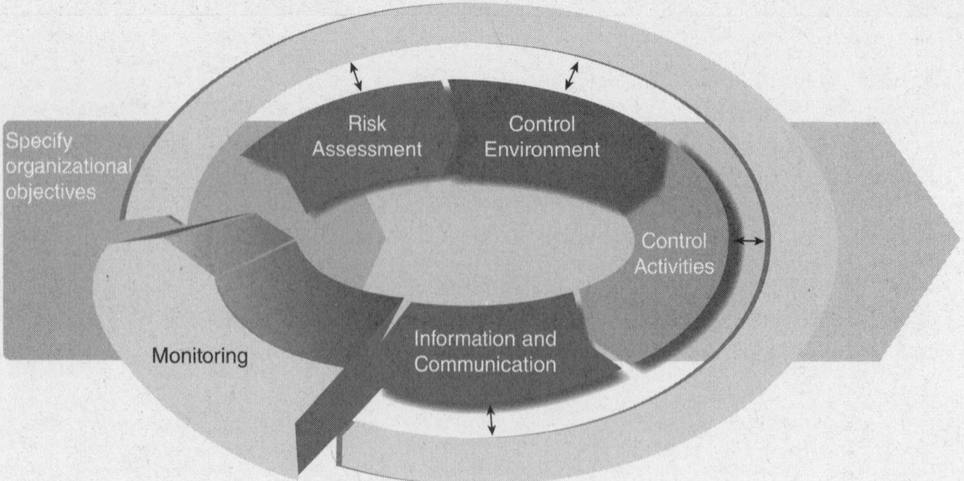

Source: COSO Guidance on Monitoring (2008)

II. Monitoring Processes

A. How do organizations monitor their control processes?

B. Monitoring should be both (a) ongoing and continuous, and (b) periodic, i.e., through separate, formally designed and designated evaluation processes.

C. Methods for reviewing control processes may include:

1. **Reviewing process** incorporating reviews of flowcharts, and risk and control documentation
2. **Benchmarking assessments** comparing organizational controls and processes with best practices in comparable functions
3. **Questionnaires** that assess the extent to which controls are operating as stipulated
4. **Focus groups and interviews** to identify concerns and surprises related to changes in the system of internal control

D. Examples of organizational processes for monitoring controls, and of control evaluators, include:

1. Periodic evaluation and testing of controls by **internal auditors** (who, to increase independence, report to the board of directors or an audit committee but not to the CFO)
2. Continuous monitoring programs built into **information systems**
3. Analysis of, and appropriate follow-up on, operating reports or metrics that identify anomalies indicating control failure (these assessments are often built into **quality control systems**)
4. **Supervisory** reviews of controls, such as reconciliation reviews
5. **Self-assessments by boards and management** regarding the tone they set in the organization and the effectiveness of their oversight functions
6. **Audit committee** inquiries of internal and external auditors
7. **Quality assurance** reviews of the internal audit department

Example

COSO Example: Monitoring Processes

Senior management of a beverage manufacturer and distributor focuses the organization's monitoring efforts by location and by risk priority. Risk considerations include areas:

- That are material or complex
- Where systems or processes have changed significantly
- Where errors or irregularities have previously occurred
- With high turnover of key personnel
- Where self-assessment has indicated previous issues

Monitoring begins with the control owners, who self-assess their key controls on a monthly, quarterly, or annual basis (depending on the control's frequency) and document the results. Management-level process owners, above the control owner, conduct supervisory reviews depends on the level of risk.

Example

COSO Example: Continuous Monitoring

Many financial institutions employ continuous control monitoring tools in areas such as:

1. Loan granting/management
2. Loan provisioning/performance
3. Money laundering
4. Counterfeit checks
5. Suspicious activity reporting (SARs) and resolution
6. Wire transfer anomalies

One financial institution developed a simple regression analysis of nonperforming loans by branch and by loan officer as one form of monitoring indirect information related to controls over loan origination.

III. COSO Model of Control Monitoring

A. **Establish a foundation for monitoring**, including (1) a positive tone at the top; (2) an effective organizational structure that assigns monitoring roles to people with appropriate capabilities, objectivity, and authority; and (3) a starting point or "baseline" of known effective internal control from which ongoing monitoring and separate evaluations can be implemented.

B. **Design and execute monitoring procedures** focused on persuasive *information* about the operation of *key controls* that address *meaningful risks* to organizational objectives.

C. **Assess and report control evaluation results,** which includes evaluating the severity of any identified deficiencies and reporting the monitoring results to the appropriate personnel and the board for timely action and follow-up if needed.

COSO Model: The Control Monitoring Process

Establish a Foundation
- Tone from the top
- Organizational structure
- Baseline understanding of internal control effectiveness

Design and Execute
- Prioritize risks
- Identify controls
- Identify persuasive information about controls
- Implement monitoring procedures

Assess and Report
- Prioritize findings
- Report results to the appropriate level
- Follow up on corrective action

Support Conclusions Regarding Control Effectiveness

Source: COSO Guidance on Monitoring (2008)

> **Example**
> ***COSO Example: Reporting on Control Deficiencies***
> The internal audit department at a medium-size manufacturer logs and tracks all identified control deficiencies and assesses their impact on the organization. They report these control deficiencies to the management team responsible for the audited business unit. An individual within the business unit is responsible for remediating the control deficiencies. Internal audit assigns a remediation time frame for each identified control deficiency based on that specific deficiency's ranking.

IV. Conceptual Model—Baseline Understanding of Internal Control Effectiveness

A. As part of establishing a foundation for monitoring, COSO specifies a conceptual four-stage process for moving from an initial understanding of control effectiveness to a revised and enhanced understanding of control effectiveness, including an assessment of the presence and effects of changes in controls or risks. The following figure illustrates this process, which is called the "monitoring-for-change continuum."

1. **Establish a control baseline**—Begin with an area in which controls on risk are well understood, or do extensive initial assessment to gain an understanding of controls and risk within a specific area of the organization. This baseline understanding of control effectiveness provides a starting point for enhanced monitoring.
2. **Identify changes**—Identify changes in the operations or design of controls or in related risks. Often includes ongoing and separate evaluations to identify, and address the potential changes in, internal control effectiveness.
3. **Manage changes**—When changes occur, verify that controls remain effective despite identified changes in controls and/or risks. Establishes a new control baseline for the modified controls.
4. **Revalidate control baseline**
   a. Ideally, ongoing monitoring procedures will use highly **persuasive information**. If this is the case, they can routinely revalidate the conclusion that controls are effective, thus maintaining a continuous control baseline.
   b. When ongoing monitoring uses less-persuasive information, or when the level of risk warrants, monitoring will need to revalidate control operation through separate evaluations using appropriately persuasive information.

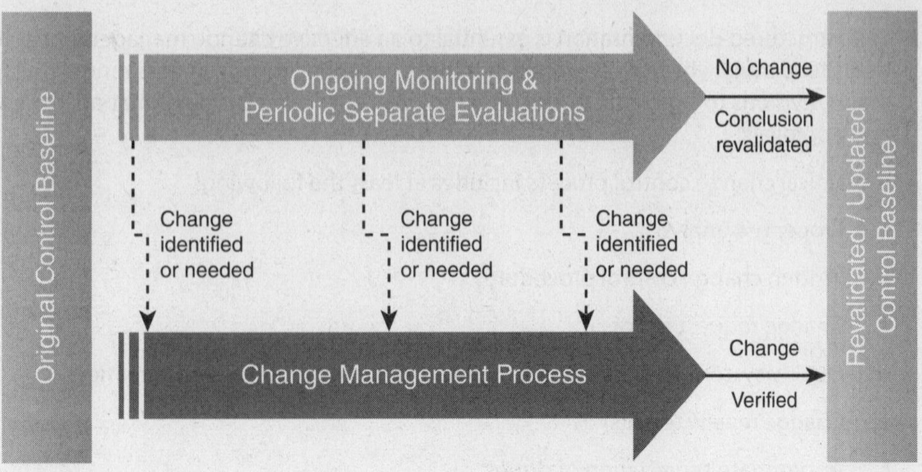

Example

COSO Example: Control Monitoring

A beverage distributor's process of internal control monitoring begins with benchmarking the key internal controls—that is, conducting a thorough review of the design and operating effectiveness of the controls to establish a baseline of effective control. After prioritizing risks and establishing the level of benchmark controls, management (with help from internal auditing) identifies controls that can be monitored through more efficient techniques, such as using indirect information or self- assessments coupled with supervisor review. At a frequency determined by the level of risk, internal audit performs periodic separate evaluations of key controls, thus reconfirming the benchmark and the effectiveness of the ongoing monitoring procedures.

V. Everything Changes Yet Control Remains the Same—Effective change control processes

A. Entity operations constantly evolve. Internal control processes must anticipate and promptly react to these changes. To identify conditions that create change, entities often create information systems to capture and report on these activities.

1. The French expression "*Plus ça change, plus c'est la même chose*" is translated as "The more things change, the more they stay the same." When this expression is applied to internal control, it means that, even though the entity and its risks are always changing, internal control should remain effective and efficient despite these changes.
2. According to the COSO internal control framework, risks change over time; management must determine whether and how the entity's internal control system can address future risks.
3. Therefore, management's ongoing monitoring activities should carefully assess whether the entity reconsiders the design of controls when risks change. This process must also verify the continued operation of existing controls that have been designed to reduce these risks to an acceptably low level.
4. Accordingly, COSO emphasizes:
   a. Monitoring as a fundamental process for analyzing risks and
   b. An understanding of how controls may or may not manage or mitigate these risks

These processes facilitate correcting control deficiencies before they impact the achievement of the entity's objectives.

B. Change control is the process used to request, review, specify, plan, approve, implement, and monitor changes to a system. Change control processes and policies ensure that implemented changes are structured, planned, and managed.

1. Well-structured documentation is essential to an effective change management system and helps to identify what can be improved. These potential improvements range in scope from major revisions to simple fixes. Documentation also ensures proper initiation, reviews, tests, and approvals.
2. A practical change control process includes at least the following:
   a. Proper risk analysis
   b. Written change control procedures
   c. Change request forms
   d. Quality system methodologies to ensure business requirements are met
   e. Change review team(s)
   f. Appropriate segregation of duties
   g. Appropriate permissions model

h. Implementation and test teams
i. Retention of applicable documentation

C. Change management should be part of the entity's risk assessment to identity potential areas of fraud, the effectiveness of the controls, and their likelihood for failure. Specific types of changes should include:

1. **Changes in operations**—A divestiture, acquisition, restructuring, or regulatory change can result in increased risks.
2. **Personnel change**—Increase in turnover or new senior management can cause significant impacts on the entity's controls.
3. **Changing technologies or information systems**—New technologies can cause control failures during the transitional period. As a practical example, consider how the Internet, mobile phones, tablet PCs, and wearable computing have and will affect internal control risks.
4. **Rapid, unexpected growth**—Current controls may be unable to keep pace with sudden growth.

D. As always, control change management must consider costs versus benefits. Specifically, modifying information systems to address changes should be done conceptually to the point where the marginal dollar spent on the systems earns less than a dollar in return.

Example
COSO Example: Monitoring and Change Controls
A small electronics research and development company recognizes that many of its financial statement risks derive from the selection and application of accounting estimates. As a result, it conducted an initial risk assessment of estimates such as the determination of allowances for uncollectible accounts, inventory obsolescence, and deferred tax assets. After the initial risk assessment, the organization conducted periodic reviews of factors that could change these risks. For example, the company closed a major plant during one fiscal year. Because of this identified change, management considered the related risks and decided to evaluate controls associated with accounting for discontinued operations, including the process for capturing all costs associated with the closed facility.

VI. **Summary**—This lesson discusses how entities monitor systems of internal control in the face of ever-evolving risks. A set of core processes is foundational to control monitoring. In addition, change control processes help in identifying potential areas of change and in structuring the process of managing changes in the system of internal control.

Enterprise Risk Management Frameworks

The COSO ERM Model

After studying this lesson, you should be able to:

1. Describe the purpose of the COSO ERM model.
2. Identify the three dimensions, and the components of each dimension, in the COSO ERM model.
3. Give examples of methods and procedures for monitoring internal control.
4. Give examples of the objectives, controls components, and areas of focus of the ERM model.

I. The COSO ERM Model

A. Introduction

1. Following the high-profile business scandals and failures in the early 2000s, COSO created (in 2004) a model that facilitated a broader understanding of the entity's overall strategies and goals, and the threats to those strategies and goals. The resulting ERM model expands on, rather than replaces, the earlier integrated framework for internal control. Similar to the integrated framework model, the ERM model is concerned with "what," "why," and "where" questions related to ERM.
2. According to COSO, ERM is (underlines added)
   - a. "a process, effected by the entity's board of directors, management, and other personnel,
   - b. applied in strategy-setting and across the enterprise,
   - c. designed to identify potential events that may affect the entity, and
   - d. manage risk to be within its risk appetite,
   - e. to provide reasonable assurance regarding the achievement of objectives."
3. What is the relationship of organizational governance, ERM, and internal control? As the figure below illustrates, organizational governance (the oval) is the broadest, most inclusive of the three constructs. ERM (the triangle) is concerned with managing risks within the context of organizational governance. And internal control is concerned with a subset of the objectives that we address in ERM. Specifically, internal control is concerned with operational, reporting, and compliance objectives. ERM is also concerned with strategic objectives.

Relationship of Organization Governance, Internal Control, and ERM

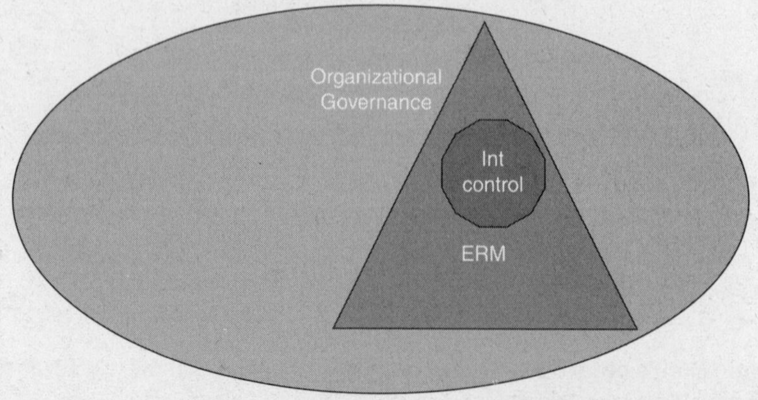

4. ERM establishes a risk management philosophy and culture. It distinguishes risks from opportunities. ERM systems can be implemented in very different ways, depending on an organization's needs of the firm. Characteristics that may vary across systems include the level of sophistication, timeliness of information, and the level of integration of risk analysis.
5. Here is the COSO ERM model, which we could call a "cube—ERM" (i.e., a cube that illustrates ERM principles):

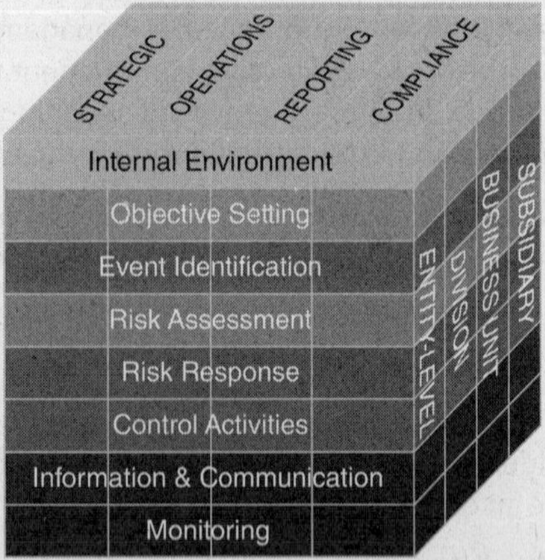

6. The COSO ERM model has the following components:
   a. **Why** manage risk? Four elements on the horizontal, representing the objectives of managing enterprise risk: strategic, operations, reporting, and compliance
   b. **What** will we manage? Eight control components (expanded from five in the original COSO model)—shown in rows
   c. **Where** will we manage risk? Four organizational levels, indicated in the third dimension (depth)

Example

COSO Example: Enterprise—Wide Risk Assessment

A large retailer conducts an annual, comprehensive, enterprise-wide risk assessment that includes senior management and business unit leaders. The focus of this risk assessment is identifying the effect and probability (sometimes referred to as "significance and likelihood") of financial, operational, and compliance risks at the store (i.e., operations) and corporate levels. Risks are scored numerically from a low of "1" to a high of "5". Once prioritized, the risks are broken down into their causes to help indicate how the risks might manifest.

B. **Why Manage Risk? Risk Management Objectives**—Organizational objectives impact the design and implementation of control systems. For example, an organization that wants to foster creativity and independence may not want to implement rigid work schedules.
   1. **COSO ERM specifies four types of objectives:**
      a. **Strategic objectives**—High-level goals that support the overall mission of the organization
      b. **Operations objectives**—Goals that deal with the day-to-day operating activities of the organization (sales activities, warehousing, manufacturing, etc.)
      c. **Reporting objectives**—Information system goals related to the accuracy, completeness, timeliness, and reliability of internal and external reporting
      d. **Compliance objectives**—Goals designed to ensure that the organization meets all legal and regulatory requirements

C. **Where Will We Manage Risk? Organizational Levels**—Risks and objectives differ depending on the specified organizational level; accordingly, four business levels are included in the model: entity-level, division, subsidiary, and business unit.

D. **What Will We Manage? Additional Control Components**—The ERM model adds three components to the five components of internal control specified by the integrated framework model. Hence, the (now) eight components in the framework are:

1. **Control environment** (called "internal" environment in the ERM model)—The most important component for ERM and internal control. Includes management's philosophy, operating style, and risk appetite; the board of directors; commitment to integrity, ethical values, and competence; organizational structure; methods of assigning authority and responsibility; human resource standards; and external influences on the entity.
2. **Objective setting**—Ensures that the company establishes objectives at each of the four specified levels (strategic, operational, reporting, and compliance)
3. **Event identification**—Events that might affect—either positively or negatively—the organization's ability to meet its objectives
4. **Risk assessment**—In assessing risk, consider inherent (before management does anything to address it) and residual (risk that remains after controls are implemented) risks. Risk assessment should be an ongoing and periodic process that adapts to changing conditions.
5. **Risk response**—Depending on management's appetite for risk, observed risks may be avoided, reduced, shared, or accepted.
6. **Control activities**—Policies and procedures that provide reasonable assurance that management's control objectives are met and their risk responses are carried out. Include the following activities, all of which are discussed in other lessons:
   - **a.** Proper authorization of transactions and activities
   - **b.** Segregation of duties
   - **c.** Project development and acquisition controls
   - **d.** Change management controls
   - **e.** Design and use of documents and records
   - **f.** Safeguarding assets, records, and data
   - **g.** Independent checks on performance to ensure correct transaction processing
7. **Information and communication**—Controls to identify, capture, and communicate information about the ERM components. This also facilitates an audit trail from the transaction to the financial statements (and vice versa).
8. **Monitoring**—Includes, but it is not limited to evaluations, supervision, periodic audits, security procedures, and fraud hotlines, and attempts to ensure proper reporting and response to deficiencies. See separate lessons on this topic.

E. **What Will We Manage?**—A second perspective: risk categories. The categories of risk that must be managed (following from COSO's objectives) include financial, operational, strategic, and compliance.

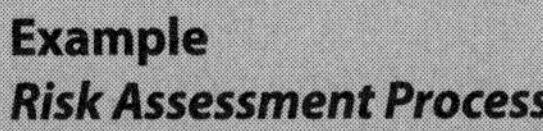

Example

Risk Assessment Process

A securities brokerage firm created a Corporate Risk Committee (CRC) that facilitates the enterprise risk management process. One of the key tasks of the CRC is an Annual Enterprise Risk Assessment using the COSO ERM Framework. CRC members identify, assess, and evaluate risks across all strategic, operational, reporting, and compliance activities. Business unit leaders, who participate in the risk assessment process, are then assigned ownership for managing or mitigating the risks within their area of responsibility. The process includes ensuring that internal control over the identified risks is designed and operating effectively (i.e., monitoring). The business unit leaders have established monitoring procedures that are linked to the prioritized risks. The results of those procedures are reported to senior management on a regular basis. If risks change, the business unit leaders are responsible for making any necessary modifications to internal control and related monitoring procedures.

Example

Risk Assessment

Senior managers in a financial trading unit at a large power company review all trading policy violations and assign a level of severity for each violation based on criteria defined in their "Trading Risk Policy" document. An automated reporting system that is integrated with the trading platform ensures that identified issues reported appropriately and ultimately cleared.

II. What Is Risk Appetite?

A. The Concept of Risk Appetite—The amount of risk that an organization is willing to accept in pursuit of its goals is central to ERM. The figure illustrates the determinants of, or influences on, risk appetite that are discussed in this lesson.

Determinants of Risk Appetite

- Current levels and distribution of risks across the entity
- Amount of risk an entity can support in pursuit of its objectives
- Acceptable levels of variation an entity will accept in pursuit of its objectives
- Stakeholder attitudes towards risk, growth, and return

1. Assessing risk appetite is essential to an organization's strategy. Organizations can set strategy only with a full consideration of the risk exposures associated with that strategy.
2. Risk appetite can be articulated in numbers or words and in ranges or exact amounts. Defining the risk appetite (i.e., the levels of acceptable risk) is more difficult than is articulating a risk management philosophy. It requires, for example, stating whether a company chooses to pursue a high-risk and high-return strategy or a more conservative and predictable strategy.

3. Elements of, and influences on, risk appetite (see figure on previous page)—
   a. **Existing risk profile**—What are the existing levels and distributions of risk across risk categories (e.g., financial, market, operational, technological, reputational)
   b. **Risk capacity**—The maximum risk that an organization may bear and remain operational
      i. Usually stated in terms of capital, liquid assets, and borrowing capacity
      ii. Obviously, risk capacity will be greater than risk appetite. In most cases, risk appetite will be far below risk capacity.
   c. **Risk tolerance**—The amount of variation that an organization is willing to allow around specific objectives. Risk appetite and risk tolerance are related but different concepts. Risk appetite is a broader, and risk tolerance a narrower, construct. Specifically:
      i. Risk appetite is a broadly conceived description (or metric) of the level of risk that an entity assumes in pursuit of its mission.
      ii. Risk tolerance is the acceptable variation that an entity will accept related to specific measures.
4. **Attitudes toward risk**—Stakeholders' objectives and attitudes toward growth and risk. May rank from desiring high growth and risk to desiring low growth and risk.

B. ERM requires a portfolio approach. That is, every level and unit of an organization engages in value-adding activities that influence risks. An effective ERM approach creates an entity-level view and assessment I of this portfolio of value-adding activities and risks.
   1. One approach to assessing such risks is to plot them on a grid where the horizontal axis is the likelihood of the event and the vertical axis is the impact. In such a figure, events in the upper left-hand corner are sometimes called "tail events" or "black swans." These are very rare but extremely consequential events (e.g., the TEPCO nuclear reactor incident in Japan).

III. ERM for Strategic Advantage

A. Effective ERM is both strategic and value-adding. It makes visible the risks associated with management's strategy. ERM without strategy is potentially a bureaucratic exercise in compliance. Strategy without ERM is potentially reckless, ill-informed, and ungrounded.

B. In 2009, COSO released guidance on how to integrate ERM into strategic initiatives. This document recommends that senior executives and boards of directors focus on four areas to better integrate ERM into strategy:
   1. **Discuss risk management philosophy and risk appetite.** Senior management and the board must reach a shared understanding of the acceptable risks that the organization will undertake.
   2. **Understand risk management practices.** Effective risk management activities are formal, holistic, and explicit. Informal, ad hoc, and implicit practices will result in inadequate risk assessments and responses.
   3. **Review portfolio risks in relation to risk appetite.** Risks do not exist in isolation; they result from a portfolio of activities that influence organizational objectives. Hence, the organization's risk focus must truly be organization-wide.
   4. **Know the organization's most significant risks and related responses.** The evolving nature of risks requires active participation in monitoring key performance indicators. These key indicators should relate to significant risks that can impact an organization's ability to achieve key objectives.

Example

The responsibilities of the board of directors at a manufacturing company include oversight of key risk areas. For example, the Board of Directors recently determined that contract compliance was a high-risk area that warranted board oversight. Accordingly, they implemented a requirement that the board review and approve any sales contracts over $50 million or greater than five years in duration and any corporate contracts that vary from standard terms.

IV. Summary—This lesson presents the COSO ERM model, including the motivation for its creation. This model presents the what, why, and where of ERM and introduces the concept of risk appetite. It also discusses the use of ERM in an organization's strategic plan.

Risk Management Policies and Procedures

After studying this lesson, you should be able to:

1. Describe the purpose and importance of enterprise risk management.
2. Describe the importance of establishing an appropriate organizational control environment.
3. Describe the importance and methods of controlling internal control effectiveness.
4. Describe the principles of the segregation of duties in relation to the five critical organizational functions.
5. Describe the roles of change agents, user and designer communications, and management in facilitating organizational change.
6. Describe how risk may be decomposed, and how expected value is computed.
7. Give examples of appropriate and poor segregation of duties.
8. Decompose risk based on a case description of an entity.

I. **Enterprise Risk Management (ERM)**—The first lesson on COSO ERM introduced the "cube"-ERM, that is, the COSO ERM framework which is concerned with the why, what, and where of ERM. This lesson expands the discussion of ERM to consider how effective organizations manage risks. ERM concerns the identification and management of events and circumstances that may impact the ability of an entity to achieve its objectives.

   A. According to COSO ERM, the goals of risk management include:

      1. **Aligning risk appetite and strategy**—Assessing and documenting the organization's **risk appetite** improves the match between desired and chosen risk. It also permits the development of mechanisms to manage risks.
      2. **Improving risk responses**—Enterprise risk management permits better choices from among alternative risk responses—risk avoidance, reduction, sharing, and acceptance.
      3. **Reducing operational surprises and losses**—Risk identification and management enhances the capacity to identify potential events and establish responses, reducing surprises and associated costs or losses.
      4. **Identifying and managing multiple and cross-enterprise risks**—Every enterprise faces risks across the organization; ERM facilitates effective responses to the interrelated impacts as well as integrated responses to multiple related risks.
      5. **Seizing opportunities**—By considering a full range of potential events, management can better identify and proactively act on opportunities.
      6. **Improving capital deployment**—Risk information allows management to better assess capital needs and improve capital allocation.

II. **Analyzing and Decomposing Risk**

   A. Risk can be usefully analyzed, or decomposed, into its constituent elements or parts. These elements or parts include:

      1. The likelihood of a loss—How likely is a loss?
      2. The amount of a loss, should one occur

   B. The **expected value** of a loss is the likelihood of the loss, multiplied by the amount of a loss, should one occur.

Example

COSO Example: Prioritizing and Mitigating Risks

Management of a small manufacturing company prioritizes its monitoring procedures based on the significance and likelihood of risks and the relative importance of certain controls in mitigating those prioritized risks. In selecting "key controls" to monitor, management first considers whether failure of a control might lead to a material error. For example, some key controls, such as reconciliation controls over certain significant accounts, could cause an error if they fail even once. In such cases, management monitors those controls on an ongoing basis, using primarily direct information.

III. The Control Environment

A. The COSO framework identifies the control environment as the foundation of the organizational control system. The fundamental nature of the control environment recognizes that the core of any organization is its people. It is their individual attributes, including integrity, ethics, and confidence, that are primarily responsible for the organizational environment and culture. The following are among the most important components of an ethical control environment.

1. The tone at the top

a. With apologies to Jane Austen, it is a truth universally acknowledged that an organization desiring an effective internal control must have top management that is ethical and proactive in establishing such a tone and culture. Consider a counter-example: Kenneth Lay urged Enron employees to buy more Enron stock at the same time that he was selling millions of dollars in Enron stock options (called a "pump and dump" scheme).

b. Positive strategies for creating an ethical culture include management emphasizing both the critical role of ethics and integrity in organizational success and the role of mission statements and codes of conduct in promoting integrity. In addition, "leading by example" is more effective than simply "talking the talk" of ethical behavior. One example of "leading by example," in a previous CPA Exam question, is top management participation in a highly visible global information security campaign.

2. Policies and standards

a. Explicit development and communication of organizational policies and standards for managing organizational risks is also critical to establishing the desired control environment. For example, some organizations require that a designated team review major proposed projects and activities to assess their risk. Note that the creation of a risk review team is implicit in this recommendation.

Example

COSO Example—Classifying Risks and Their Implications

At an international insurance services organization, the Internal Audit Department classifies control deficiencies as minor, reportable, and significant. The reporting of deficiencies is based on their potential impact to the organization, as follows:

- Minor deficiencies—Reported, **in detail,** to the **responsible manager** at the **end of the audit.**
- Reportable deficiencies—Reported, **in detail,** to the responsible **manager** and to the **senior management team** at the **end of the audit** and **quarterly,** in summary, to the **audit committee.**
- Significant deficiencies—Reported, **in detail,** to the responsible **manager** and the **senior management team** at the **end of the audit** and **quarterly, in detail,** to the **audit committee.**

IV. Segregation of Duties (SoD) and Critical Accounting Functions

A. Designing an effective organizational system of internal control requires attention to a set of critical functions. An **event** is an economic transaction that is relevant to the accounting system. Separating responsibilities for critical actions related to events lessens the likelihood of fraud and certain types of errors. Consider four critical activities related to internal control, which should be separated to lessen fraud risk:

1. **Authorizing events**—For example, approving customer credit, authorizing payment of an invoice, approving shipping to a customer
2. **Recording events**—For example, completing source documents, such as a customer invoice or bill of lading, posting events into the general ledger
3. **Safeguarding resources related to events (custody)**—For example, maintaining the cash in a bank vault or the inventory in a store
4. **Reconciling, overseeing and auditing**—For example, board of directors' review, internal and external audits, and reconciling system logs with known system activity

B. The WorldCom scandal provides a dramatic example of the failure to segregate some of these functions. WorldCom's CEO (Bernard Ebbers) and CFO (Scott Sullivan), in a remarkable display of "efficiency," authorized and recorded falsified accounting transactions that inflated revenue by about $11 billion. WorldCom's clueless board of directors approved this system of control and these transactions (lack of oversight). This fraud earned Ebbers and Sullivan 25-year and 15-year prison terms, respectively.

C. Large organizations can and should separate these functions. However, as COSO points out, segregation of duties is less feasible, and therefore less likely, in small organizations.

D. Much of the power of automated systems is their ability to combine activities, e.g., executing and recording events into a single, automated transaction. However, **SoD software** exists, such as Symantec Security Information Manager (SSIM), to help identify SoD conflicts. This software generates matrices of activities to determine incompatible functions.

> **Example**
>
> ***COSO Example: Software Tools for Segregating Duties Controls***
>
> A beverage distributor uses segregation-of-duties software to provide continuous monitoring of SoD. This tool allows the organization to customize SoD based on established rules. The SoD tool is both a preventive and a detective tool and has enabled the organization to move accountability for SoD and system security to the business units rather than maintaining it within IT. The tool produces a report listing all SoD conflicts that meet predefined criteria. This list then is reviewed by appropriately objective personnel.

V. Managing Change in the System of Internal Control

A. **Managing Change**—toward a stronger control environment—is critical in efforts to improve control processes. Critical elements of managing internal control changes include the following:

1. **Change agents**—Change agents in this discussion promote and facilitate change related to the system of internal control. Change agents act as catalysts; they meet with system stakeholders, and coordinate resources, to ensure that changes are understood and embraced by those stakeholders.
2. **Impediments to system user and designer communication**—The relationship between the creators or designers of a system of internal control, and those who must work within the system, is critical. Examples of impediments to this relationship are that the accountants and auditors who design a system of control may use terminology that is unfamiliar to system users, or designers and users may have divergent education, priorities, and loyalties. Effective user/designer communication is critical to managing change related to internal control. Recognizing the potential impediments to this communication can be useful in facilitating it.

3. **Management commitment and support**—It is difficult to overstate the importance of management involvement in, and commitment to, proposed and implemented changes in internal control. Neglecting to obtain and sustain management's support in an important internal control change initiative is a sure path to failure.

VI. Limitations of ERM

A. ERM is a valuable, imperfect process. No matter how well designed and executed, ERM does not ensure the achievement of organizational objectives.

B. Three key limitations exist in ERM:

1. Risk relates to the future; the future is inherently uncertain.
2. Problems happen. ERM operates at multiple levels in an organization. It relates to organizational processes but cannot provide even reasonable assurance of the achievement of an organization's strategic and operational objectives. In short, stuff may happen that impairs the achievement of objectives, even if the organization does everything well.
3. ERM cannot provide absolute assurance regarding any objective. No process, even if well designed, will always produce the desired results.

Fraud Risk Management

Every organization that includes more than one person and assets includes fraud risk. This lesson defines and categorizes fraud, presents COSO's fraud risk management principles, and explores processes for managing fraud.

After studying this lesson, you should be able to:

1. Define fraud and its four categories.
2. Provide examples of each category of fraud.
3. Explain the role of IT in facilitating, detecting, and preventing fraud.
4. Provide examples of each of these three roles within each of the four categories.
5. Describe COSO's five fraud risk management principles.
6. State examples and applications of the fraud risk management principles in an organization.
7. Describe, guided by COSO's five fraud risk management principles, how to maximize the likelihood that fraud will be prevented and detected in a timely manner.
8. Provide examples and applications of a fraud risk management process in an organization.
9. Describe how data analytics can help detect and prevent fraud.
10. Provide examples of data analytic techniques and explain how these techniques can be used as a part of a fraud risk management program.

I. Introduction—What Is Fraud?

A. The Case of Jeffrey Hughes (Sad!)

1. Ever heard of an employee like Jeffrey Hughes? The bosses at the government agency where Jeffrey works described him as the perfect employee. He'd been with the agency for about 10 years and did all their accounting work, so that they could focus on "the real work" and not "that bean-counter stuff." Hughes worked long hours, including weekends, and never took a vacation. He never asked for a raise and turned down offers to work elsewhere because he, "loves and cares about the people where he works."
2. Except he didn't care about other employees; he only cared about money.
   a. According to the Tennessee Comptroller's office, Jeffery Hughes stole about $250,000 from his employer over a seven-year period.
   b. And, as usually happens (according to David L. Cotton, Cotton & Company LLP, CPAs), the same four words always precede a fraud: "It can't happen here." But it did. And, as every practicing accountant knows, eventually it does happen.
3. Takeaway—Fraud risk exists in every organization.

B. Principle #8 of COSO's 17 principles (see the "17 Principles of Internal Control" lesson) states: "The organization considers the potential for fraud in assessing risks to the achievement of objectives."

1. This lesson describes COSO's recommendations (released in 2016) for managing fraud risk.

C. Defining and Categorizing Fraud

1. COSO defines fraud as "any intentional act or omission designed to deceive others, resulting in the victim suffering a loss and/or the perpetrator achieving a gain" (COSO Executive Summary).

2. COSO identifies four categories of fraud:

   a. **Reporting fraud: financial**

      i. An intentional misstatement of accounting information

         (a) Often includes a goal of improving financial results by overstating income or assets, understanding losses or expenses, or misleading disclosures.

         (b) Alternatively, may misstate to evade or avoid taxes or smooth earnings

         (c) Example—Improper revenue recognition through **backdating agreements** (recognizing unshipped goods as sales) or **channel stuffing** (shipping more products to retailers than they request or can sell)

   b. **Reporting fraud: nonfinancial**

      i. Manipulating nonfinancial reports, including environmental, health, safety, production, quality, or customer reports

         (a) Falsifications of nonfinancial reports often result from management setting unrealistic performance targets.

         (b) For example, Volkswagen installed software that effectively falsified the information about pollution emissions from its U.S. cars.

         (c) Another example: falsifying employee credentials to improve the company's reputation (e.g., our CEO has an MBA).

   c. **Misappropriation of assets**

      i. Theft or misuse of tangible or intangible assets by employees, customers, vendors, hackers, or criminal organizations

      ii. Examples—Vendors submitting inflated or fictitious invoices, customers making false claims for damaged or returned goods, employees stealing tangible or intangible assets

   d. **Other illegal acts and corruption**

      i. Violations of laws or regulations that may have a material impact on the financial statements

         (a) Examples—bribes, kickbacks, "gratuities" (i.e., gifts to purchasing agents)

D. IT and Fraud

1. IT can both facilitate fraud and help prevent and detect fraud

   a. A poorly designed accounting system increases fraud risk.

2. **Examples of IT fraud risks:**

   a. **Reporting fraud: financial**

      i. Hackers or employees may gain unauthorized access to accounting applications and change financial information.

         (a) System controls may include fail-safe mechanisms that can be overridden in some circumstances. These fail-safe mechanisms can, in some situations, facilitate inappropriate access to systems, resulting in changes to financial data.

   b. **Reporting fraud: nonfinancial**

      i. As the Volkswagen fraud illustrates, employees may override controls, including system controls, to falsify nonfinancial reports

c. Misappropriation of assets

i. Theft or misuse of assets

ii. E.g., access to both the accounting records and to assets creates many opportunities for theft (e.g., creating fictitious vendors and "paying" falsified invoices).

d. Other illegal acts and corruption

i. Data theft and abuse is an increasing problem (e.g., North Korean theft and hack of Sony video content, which was motivated by revenge and not financial gain).

II. Fraud Risk Management Principles

A. COSO's five fraud risk management principles (see diagrams below illustrating these principles).

1. These link to COSO's five components of internal control (i.e., the rows in the cube below). To review COSO's basic model see the "Introduction to COSO, Internal Control, and the COSO Cube" lesson.

COSO's Five Risk Management Principles

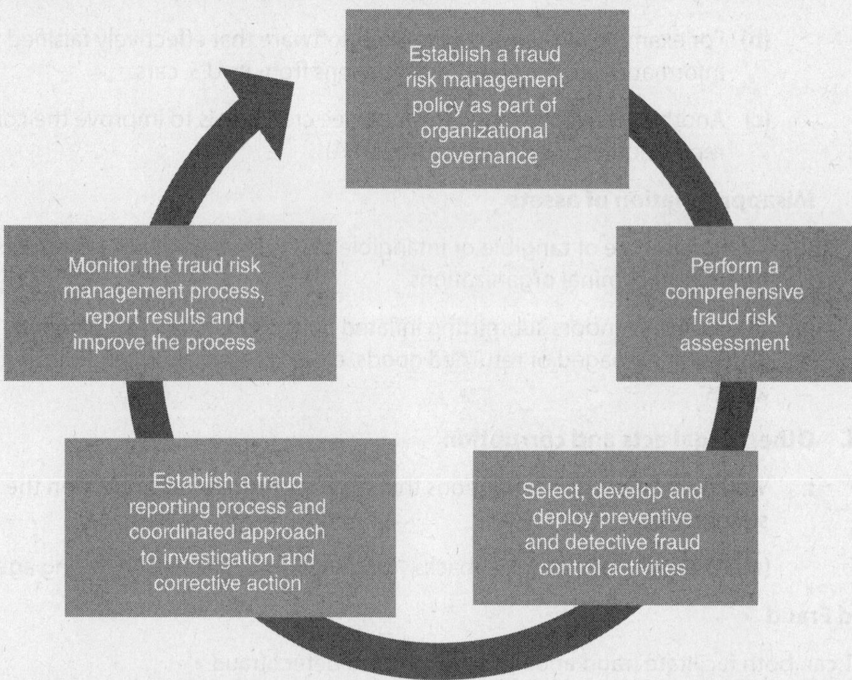

Relationship of COSO's 17 Principles and 5 Fraud Risk Management Principles

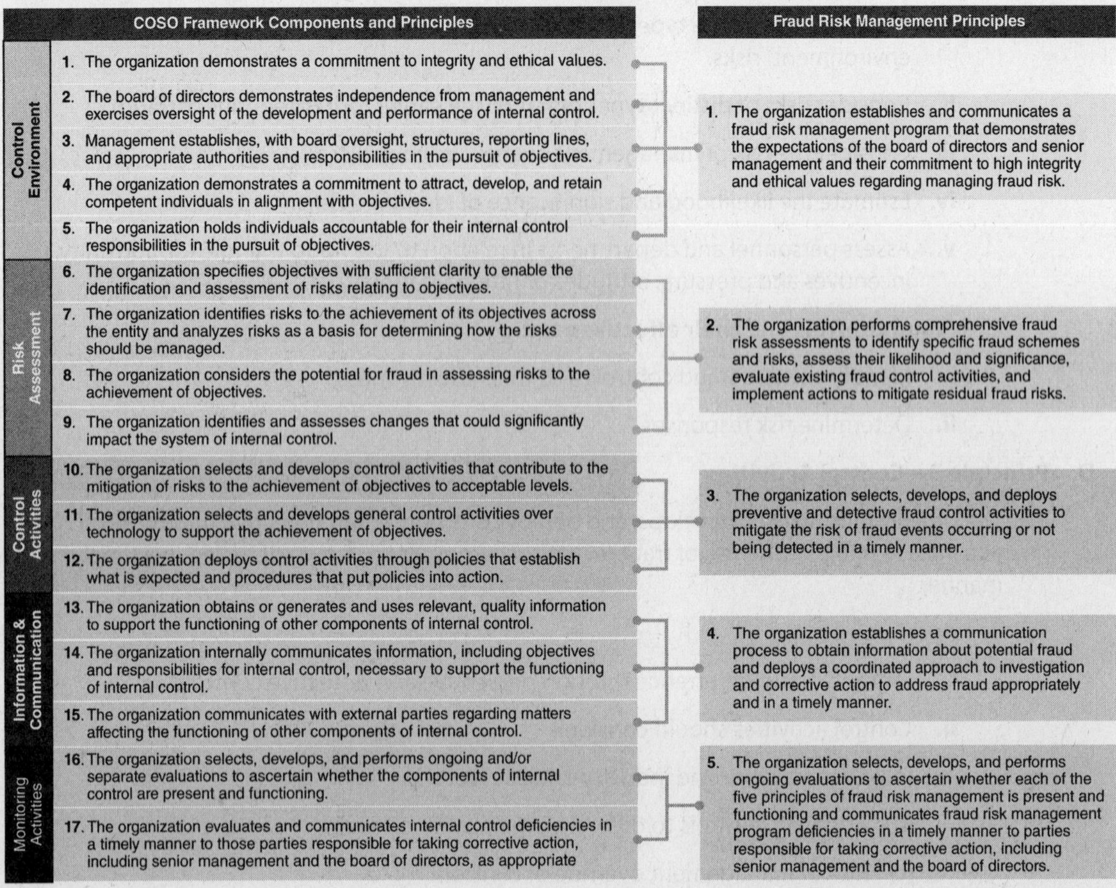

B. Principle 1—Control Environment

1. The organization establishes and communicates a fraud risk management program that demonstrates the expectations of the board of directors and senior management and their commitment to high integrity and ethical values regarding managing fraud risk.
2. Focal points include:
   - **a.** Map fraud risk program to organizations' goals and risks.
   - **b.** Establish fraud risk governance roles and responsibilities throughout the organization.
   - **c.** Document program and communicate throughout organization.

C. Principle 2—Risk Assessment

1. The organization performs comprehensive fraud risk assessments to identify specific fraud schemes and risks, assess their likelihood and significance, evaluate existing fraud control activities, and implement actions to mitigate residual fraud risks.
2. Focal points for the risk assessment include:
   - **a.** **Managing the risk assessment process:**
     - **i.** Involve appropriate management, including all organizational management levels and functions.
     - **ii.** Use data analytics to assess risks and evaluate responses.
     - **iii.** Periodically reassess fraud risk.
     - **iv.** Document risk assessment.

b. **Risk assessments:**

   i. Analyze internal (i.e., types of activities) and external (customers, vendors, environment) risks.

   ii. Consider risks of distinct types of fraud (see earlier four categories of fraud).

   iii. Consider the risk of management override of controls.

   iv. Estimate the likelihood and significance of identified risks.

   v. Assess personnel and departments in relation to the fraud triangle (opportunity, incentives and pressure, attitudes or rationalizations).

c. **Fraud controls and their effectiveness:**

   i. Identify existing fraud controls and their effectiveness.

   ii. Determine risk responses.

D. Principle 3—Control Activities

1. The organization selects, develops, and deploys preventive and detective fraud control activities to mitigate the risk of fraud events occurring or not being detected in a timely manner.

   a. **Focal points:**

      i. Promote fraud deterrence through preventive and detective controls.

      ii. Control activities should consider

         (a) Organization- and industry-specific factors.

         (b) Applying controls to differing organizational levels.

         (c) Risk of management override of controls.

         (d) Integration with fraud risk assessments.

         (e) Multiple, synergistic fraud control activities (e.g., a defense-in-depth strategy).

         (f) Proactive data analytics procedures, such as identification of anomalous transactions.

         (g) Control through policies and procedures.

E. Principle 4—Information and Communication

1. The organization establishes a communication process to obtain information about potential fraud and deploys a coordinated approach to investigation and corrective action to address fraud.

2. **Focal points:**

   a. Establish fraud investigation and response protocols.

   b. Conduct and document investigations.

   c. Communicate investigation results.

   d. Implement corrective actions.

   e. Evaluate investigation performance.

F. Principle 5—Monitoring Activities

1. The organization selects, develops, and performs ongoing evaluations to ascertain presence of the five principles of fraud risk management and functioning and communicates fraud risk management program deficiencies in a timely manner to parties responsible for taking corrective action, including senior management and the board of directors.

2. **Focal points:**
   a. Consider:
      i. Ongoing and separate evaluation.
      ii. Influences on scope and frequency of monitoring (e.g., changing fraud risks, personnel changes).
      iii. Known and emerging fraud cases.
   b. Establish appropriate management criteria.
   c. Evaluate, communicate, and remediate deficiencies identified through monitoring.

III. The Fraud Risk Management Process

A. Examples and Applications of Fraud Risk Management

1. **Managing revenue recognition fraud risk**—Revenue recognition is among the most frequent financial reporting frauds (e.g., see https://www.accountingweb.com/community-voice/blogs/admin/watch-out-for-fraudulent-revenue-recognition). Relevant questions in undertaking a program to manage revenue recognition fraud would include:
   a. What are the main sources and drivers of company revenue?
   b. Are revenues primarily from sales of many homogeneous products (e.g., consumer goods) or a small number of large transactions (e.g., large heavy equipment sales)?
   c. Are revenue transactions primarily automated (e.g., from a website feed) or manual?
   d. What are the industry-specific fraud risks of revenue?
   e. What are revenue recognition incentives or pressures in the organization? (Bonuses? Penalties?)
   f. What revenue recognition data are used by external stakeholders (e.g., financial analysts, bank loan officers)?
2. **Managing fraud risk through HR procedures**—Many HR procedures help manage fraud risk including:
   a. **Background, credit, and criminal checks** (where allowed by law)—of employees, suppliers, and business partners
   b. **Fraud risk management training**—to identify and manage entity and industry-specific risks (e.g., in financial services)
   c. **Evaluating performance and compensation programs**—e.g., do bonus programs incentivize fraud risks by offering large, short-term bonuses for sales or earnings targets?
   d. **Annual employee surveys**—including assessments of ethical tone, observed misconduct, knowledge of how to report concerns or misbehavior
   e. **Exit interviews**—including discussion of possible fraud and misconduct in the organization
   f. **Segregation of duties** (discussed in the "Risk Management Policies and Procedures" lesson)
   g. **Transaction-level controls** (discussed in the "Logical and Physical Access Controls" module)—e.g., data entry tests authorization approvals)
   h. **Implementation of a whistleblower system**—mandated for SEC registrations by SOX Act of 2002

B. The COSO fraud risk management framework includes a framework for using data analytics to prevent, detect, and investigate fraud. Data analytics can address all aspects of the fraud triangle:

1. **Incentive and pressure**—Data analytics can help identify management practices and business processes that encourage employees to bypass or circumvent controls including risks of rogue behavior and excessive spending.
2. **Opportunity**—Data analytics can help prevent fraud through monitoring (i.e., confirmation of) key controls. Continuous auditing of key controls is often possible through data analytic tools.
3. **Attitudes and rationalization**—Data analytics can deter fraud by causing mountebanks (fraudsters) to not engage in fraud because they know of monitoring programs, and, by detecting communications that indicate fraudulent activity.

C. A Data Analytics Plan to Support Fraud Risk Management

1. **Analytics design**—Assess fraud risk (described previously); map risks to data sources and data availability; create work plan, timeline, and deliverables.
2. **Data collection**—Map data to planned analytics tests, validate data.
3. **Data organization and calculation**—Execute work plan; adapt analytics to available data;, consider using advanced analytics including text mining, statistical analysis, and pattern analysis.
4. **Data analysis**—Evaluate analytics results. Develop and implement scoring models to prioritize risks. Adapt and tune the model to improve relevance and accuracy of results.
5. **Findings, observations, and remediation**—Request supporting documents to assist in making results actionable. Determine triage and escalation procedures to determine report levels (lower level, mid-level, top management?), develop remediation plan for identified issues.

D. Data Analytics Tools to Support Fraud Risk Management

1. **Data stratification**—Sort or categorize data, including payments, journal entries, surveys, or employee data.
2. **Risk scoring**—Weight, aggregate, and compare fraud risk factors.
3. **Data visualization**—Detect changes and trends, e.g., a fraud risk assessment heat map, a fraud dashboard.
4. **Trend analysis**—Analyze data over time and across locations (e.g., ratio analysis over time or across locations).
5. **Fluctuation analysis**—Detect anomalies (e.g., unusual transactions, missing but expected transactions).
6. **Statistical analysis and predictive modeling**—Often used with continuous auditing and monitoring systems.
7. **Integrating external data sources**—e.g., emerging fraud risks, industry trends, regulatory actions, economic indicators (e.g., the Consumer Price Index).

Sources

AccountingWeb. "Watch Out for Fraudulent Revenue Recognition!" 2010. https://www.accountingweb.com/community-voice/blogs/admin/watch-out-for-fraudulent-revenue-recognition

Cotton, D., "Fraud Risk Management & COSO: Past, Present & Future." Presentation to Baltimore Association of Governmental Accountants, 2017. http://agabaltimore.org/wp-content/uploads/2015/09/Cotton-Presentation.pdf

COSO. "Fraud Risk Management Guide: Executive Summary." Durham, NC:COSO, 2016. https://www.coso.org/Documents/COSO-Fraud-Risk-Management-Guide-Executive-Summary.pdf

Other Regulatory Frameworks and Provisions

After studying this lesson, you should be able to:

1. Identify and explain key corporate governance provisions of the Sarbanes-Oxley Act (SOX) of 2002.

I. Introduction

A. Because large corporations feature separation of ownership (shareholders) from control (officers and directors), an agency problem arises making corporate governance a topic of extreme importance to our economy. That importance has grown as a series of corporate scandals (e.g., the Enron-era debacles and the subprime scandals) occurred in the not-too-distant past.

B. Basic corporate law sets up a three-part pyramid, with the shareholders at the bottom, the directors in the middle, and the officers on top. The shareholders' right to vote to elect directors and right to vote on certain major structural changes, such as a merger proposal, constitute their primary input into corporate control. Directors are responsible for "big-picture" corporate policy. They also select, compensate, and remove corporate officers, who are at the top of the pyramid and are responsible for the day-to-day operations of the firm. It is important to emphasize that shareholders vote on directors but have no direct input regarding officers, a point frequently tested over the years. Officers execute their responsibilities through employees who are acting within the scope of their authority when they follow the directions of superiors or otherwise take actions in the best interests of their employers. These basic corporate principles are covered in detail in the "Business Structures" section of the Business Law topics covered in the Regulation (REG) section of the course.

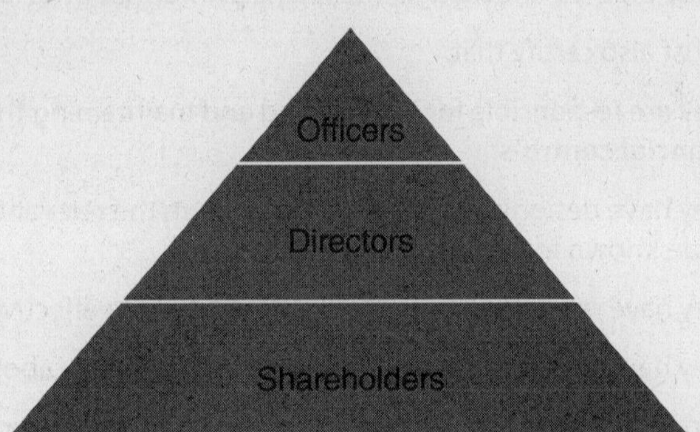

C. This lesson addresses key corporate governance provisions of the Sarbanes-Oxley Act of 2002 (SOX), which was enacted in response to the Enron-era scandals, and related regulatory pronouncements. SOX represents a big intrusion by federal law into what had previously been the entirely state-law domain of corporate governance. Remember that most (but not all) SOX provisions apply only to publicly traded companies, including all their wholly-owned subsidiaries, and all publicly traded non-U.S. companies doing business in the U.S.

II. Corporate Responsibility

A. Studies indicate that CEOs and CFOs are often involved in companies' financial wrongdoing, so it is natural that Sarbanes-Oxley's Title III contains several provisions dealing with responsible corporate governance that have an important impact upon the accuracy of firms' financial reporting. These include:

1. **Audit committees**—Audit committees have long monitored the internal audit function and overseen the financial reporting processes and annual financial statement audit. But SOX created a much larger role for public company audit committees and changed their composition. Before SOX, the same CEOs and CFOs who were often involved in financial tomfoolery selected, compensated, and terminated their company's outside auditor. To

strengthen corporate governance by reducing the control of CEOs and CFOs, SOX's Section 301 requires public companies to create audit committees that will choose, compensate, oversee, and terminate their company's auditors. Audit reports are now addressed to the audit committee rather than to corporate management.

a. **Independent directors**—Importantly, SOX requires audit committees to be composed entirely of **independent** directors—people who are neither officers of the company nor consultants or advisors who collect significant fees from the company or its affiliates. Also, as discussed below, at least one of the audit committee members must be a "financial expert."

b. **Whistleblowers**—Audit committees must establish procedures for receiving, retaining, and treating complaints by whistleblowers about accounting procedures and internal controls and protecting the confidentiality of those complainants.

c. **Engaging advisers**—In order to ensure that audit committees can be as effective as possible, SOX grants each audit committee authority to hire independent legal counsel and other advisers "as it determines necessary to carry out its duties."

2. **Officer certification of financial statements**—To impose accountability for the accuracy of firms' **financial statements**, SOX's Section 302 requires:

a. Each public company's CEO and CFO must certify that:

i. They have reviewed the quarterly and annual reports that their companies must file with the SEC;

ii. To their knowledge, the reports do not contain any materially untrue statements or half-truths; *and*

iii. Based on their knowledge, the financial information is fairly presented.

b. They must also certify that:

i. They are responsible for establishing and maintaining their company's **internal financial controls**.

ii. They have designed such controls to ensure the relevant material information is made known to them.

iii. They have recently (within 90 days) evaluated the effectiveness of the internal controls.

iv. They have presented in the report their conclusions about the controls' effectiveness.

c. Additionally, CEOs and CFOs must certify that they have reported to the auditors and the audit committee regarding all significant deficiencies and material weaknesses in the controls and any fraud, whether or not material, that involves management or other employees playing a significant role in the internal controls.

d. Finally, the CEO and CFO must indicate whether or not there have been any significant postevaluation changes in the controls that could significantly affect the controls.

3. **Misleading auditors**—SOX Section 303 makes it a crime for any officer, director, or person acting under their direction to violate SEC rules by fraudulently influencing, coercing, manipulating, or misleading an auditor for the purpose of rendering financial statements misleading.

4. **Clawbacks**—Section 304 provides that if an issuer must materially restate its financial statements as a result of "misconduct," which apparently need not be intentional, the CEO and CFO shall reimburse the company for bonuses received due to the misstatement and for any profits they realized from sale of the company's stock during that period.

III. Enhanced Financial Disclosures

A. SOX's Title IV contains provisions that even more directly impact financial reporting practices:

1. **Financial statement shenanigans**—SOX's Section 401 contained several provisions to limit financial monkey business:

a. **Off-balance sheet transactions**—SOX requires that quarterly and annual financial reports filed with the SEC disclose all material off-balance sheet transactions, arrangements, obligations, and other relationships with unconsolidated entities that might have a material impact on the financial statement. It also instructed the SEC to figure out how to reduce the use of "special purpose entities" to facilitate misleading off-balance sheet transactions. The rules that the SEC issued focus on ensuring that transactions are motivated primarily by economics rather than by accounting and reporting concerns.

b. **Pro forma financial statements**—To limit the abuse of pro forma financial statements, SOX also authorized the SEC to issue rules requiring that pro forma financial statements (those using non-GAAP financial measures) be presented in a manner that does not contain a material misstatement or half-truth and be reconciled with the financial conditions and results of operations under GAAP so that investors can readily detect the differences. In response, the SEC issued Regulation G, which does not eliminate use of pro forma results but does impose a broad range of limitations upon the use of pro forma results, including a requirement that public companies disclosing such results include the most directly comparable GAAP financial measures and a reconciliation of the two. Management must also explain why the pro formas will provide valuable information to shareholders.

2. **Improper loans**—SOX Section 402 prohibits (with some exceptions) public companies from making personal loans to their top officers and directors. Such loans are now permitted only if they are made:

   a. On market terms

   b. In the ordinary course of business

   c. Available to the public as well as to insiders

3. **Auditing internal financial controls**—Complementing Section 302's requirement for executive certification, Section 404 requires that each annual report contain an "internal control report" stating the responsibility of management for establishing and maintaining an adequate internal control structure so that accurate financial statements can be produced. The report must also contain an assessment, as of the end of the most recent fiscal year, of the effectiveness of the internal control structure and procedures. Importantly, Section 404 also requires outside auditors to evaluate the internal control assessment of the company as well as the financial statements. Thus, outside auditors of public companies audit both the financial statements and the internal financial reporting process that creates them.

4. **CFO code of ethics**—SOX Section 406 requires public companies to disclose in their filings with the SEC whether or not they have adopted a code of ethics for senior financial officers (CFOs, comptrollers, principal accounting officers, and others performing similar functions) and, if not, the reasons why not. The code is to address such matters as conflicts of interest, accurate financial reporting, and compliance with governmental rules and regulations. The goal of the disclosure requirement is to embarrass firms into adopting such codes.

5. **Financial expert**—Because boards of directors during the Enron era often were not up to the task of detecting even massive accounting frauds, SOX's Section 407 requires that at least one member of the audit committee be a "financial expert." The SEC has issued rules defining an "audit committee financial expert" to means someone with the following attributes:

   a. An understanding of GAAP and financial statements

   b. An ability to assess the general application of these principles in connection with accounting for estimates, accruals, and reserves

   c. Experience preparing, auditing, analyzing, or evaluating financial statements that present a breadth and level of complexity comparable to those presented by the issuer's financial statements, or experience actively supervising persons engaged in such activities

   d. An understanding of internal controls and procedures for financial reporting

   e. An understanding of audit committee functions

6. According to the SEC, a person may gain these aforementioned attributes of a "financial expert" through:
    a. Education and experience as a principal financial officer, principal accounting officer, controller, public accountant or auditor, or experience in one or more positions that involve the performance of similar functions;
    b. Experience actively supervising such a person; or
    c. Other relevant experience.

IV. Corporate and Criminal Fraud Accountability

A. SOX contained several provisions to increase criminal penalties and other forms of accountability for financial fraud and other wrongdoing. Many of those were contained in Title VIII.

1. Section 802 responded directly to the decision of accounting firm Arthur Andersen to shred two tons of Enron documents once it learned that it was being investigated by the SEC for potential wrongdoing in connection with its audits of Enron. This resulted in two new criminal statutes.
    a. **Destruction, alteration, or falsification of records in federal investigations and bankruptcy**—One statute subjects to fine and/or imprisonment of not more than 20 years anyone who "knowingly alters, destroys, mutilates, conceals, covers up, falsifies, or makes a false entry in any record, document, or tangible object with the intent to impede, obstruct, or influence the investigation or proper administration of any matter within the jurisdiction of any agency or department of the United States" or in any bankruptcy case filed under Chapter 11. Obviously, this provision punishes obstruction of justice beyond just SEC proceedings.
    b. **Destruction of corporate audit documents**—The second statute is narrower, requiring "any accountant" who audits a public company to "maintain all audit or review workpapers" for **five** years after the conclusion of the audit. Willful violation subjects a person to a fine, imprisonment for not more than 10 years, or both. (Note that Section 103 of SOX requires the SEC to issue rules requiring auditors to maintain audit workpapers for not less than seven years,)
2. Supplementing the requirement that audit committees set up procedures for handling whistleblower complaints, Section 806 of SOX provides a civil damages action for public company whistleblowers who are retaliated against (via demotion, suspension, harassment, etc.) for providing information in an investigation or participating as a witness or otherwise in a proceeding involving federal securities law violations or other frauds that might damages shareholders. The provision covers investigations conducted by federal agencies, members of Congress or their staffs, or any person with supervisory authority over the employee. Whistleblowers are similarly protected when they file or assist in the filing of proceedings alleging a violation of these provisions forbidding fraud against shareholders. Whistleblowers are protected from retaliation if their belief that legal violations have occurred is reasonable, even if mistaken.
3. Note that in 2010 the Dodd-Frank Act incentivized whistleblowers involving securities law violations by authorizing judges to award them between 10% and 30% of monetary sanctions imposed on wrongdoers as a result of their tips when those sanctions exceeded $1 million.

V. White-Collar Crime Penalty Enhancements

A. The key provision in Title IX of SOX complements Section 302 (which required CEOs and CFOs to personally certify the financial statements they signed and internal controls they created) and Section 404 (which required those internal controls to be audited). That provision is Section 906, which imposes criminal punishments upon those officers who "intentionally" certify SEC filings containing inaccurate financial statements. Punishments can run as high as up to $5 million in fines and 20 years in jail.

B. Other Title IX provisions increase punishments for conspiracy to commit securities fraud, for committing mail and wire fraud, and for criminally violating the Employee Retirement Income Security Act (ERISA).

VI. Corporate Fraud Accountability

A. Complementing Section 301 (requiring audit committees to set up procedures to protect whistleblower confidentiality) and Section 806 (enabling a whistleblower suffering retaliation to sue for damages), Article XI's Section 1107 makes it a crime to retaliate against an informant providing truthful information relating to the commission of any federal crime to law enforcement officers. Maximum potential punishment is a fine and/or up to 10 years in prison.

SOX Whistleblower Provisions
Section 301—Audit committees must set up procedures to protect whistleblower confidentiality.
Section 806—Whistleblowers may sue civilly if retaliated against.
Section 1107—Those who retaliate against whistleblowers commit a federal crime.

Economic Concepts and Analysis

Introduction to Economic Concepts

Economics is a social science concerned with the study of the allocation of scarce economic resources among alternative uses, usually to achieve desired objectives. This introductory lesson (1) provides an overview of the material covered in the Economic Concepts subsection, (2) defines economics and identifies the areas of economic study, (3) summarizes the use of graphs in economics, and (4) distinguishes between free-market and command economic systems.

After studying this lesson, you should be able to:

1. Identify and describe the three general areas of economics.
2. Identity and describe the components of graphs and the nature of relationships depicted by graphs.
3. Describe the command and market forms of economic systems.
4. Understand and apply the basic equation for plotting a straight line on a graph.

I. **Content Coverage**—Economics is the study of the allocation of scarce economic resources among alternative uses. From a business perspective, economics is concerned with studying the production, distribution and consumption of goods and services, generally so as to maximize desired outcomes.

   A. **Economic Concepts** covers material concerned with:

      1. The factors that determine economic activity, including demand and supply, for individual firms, industries and entire nations, and the effects of changes in those factors on economic activity
      2. The characteristics of major economic environments (called "market structures") in which firms operate and the effects of market structure on the short-term and long-term operations of an entity
      3. Measures of national economic activity and the factors and actions that change that activity, including business cycles, inflation/deflation and government policy
      4. Why international economic activity occurs and the issues that result from that activity at both the national and entity levels, including the role of exchange rates and international transfer prices
      5. The reasons for and nature of globalization of business and economic activity, including globalization of trade, production, and capital markets, and the shifts in economic power that have occurred and continue to occur as a result of globalization
      6. The processes by which an entity can analyze its economic environment and the relationship between that environment and the internal characteristics of the entity

II. **Economics Defined**

Definition
Economics: The study of the allocation of scarce economic resources among alternative uses.

   A. The field can be divided into three general areas for study purposes: microeconomics, macroeconomics, and international economics.

      1. **Microeconomics**—Studies the economic activities of distinct decision-making entities, including individuals, households, and business firms. Major areas of interest include demand and supply, prices and outputs, and the effects of external forces on the economic activities of these individual decision makers.
      2. **Macroeconomics**—Studies the economic activities and outcomes of a group of entities taken together, typically of an entire nation or major sectors of a national economy. Major areas of interest include aggregate output, aggregate demand and supply, price and employment levels, national income, governmental policies and regulation, and international implications.

3. **International economics**—Studies economic activities that occur between nations and outcomes that result from these activities. Major areas of concern include reasons for international economic activity, socioeconomic issues, balance of payments accounts, currency exchange rates, international transfer pricing, and globalization, which is a consequence of widespread international economic activity.

B. Each of these general areas of economic study is covered in the next three sections of the study text.

III. Use of Graphs

A. Many economic concepts and relationships are depicted using graphs. These graphs often show the relationship between two variables, an independent variable and a dependent variable.

B. In most cases, in economics, the independent variable is shown on the vertical axis (called the Y-axis) and the dependent variable is shown on the horizontal axis (called the X-axis). Thus, the variable plotted using values on the X (horizontal) axis (the dependent variable) depends on the value shown on the Y (vertical) axis (the independent variable). The point at which the plotted relationship (i.e., the "graphed line") intersects the Y-axis (at the left end of the X-axis) is called the "intercept."

Note: In other uses, graphs may plot the independent variable on the horizontal (X) axis and the dependent variable on the vertical (Y) axis.

C. By historic convention, in economics, price is plotted (measured) on the vertical axis and quantity on the horizontal axis. Thus, a conventional graph that plots price and quantity would show the following:

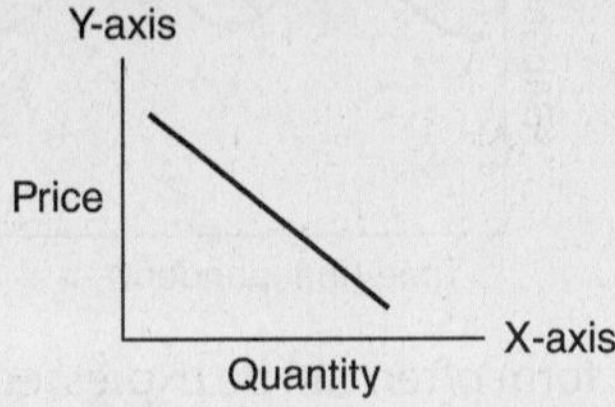

D. The graph shows that the higher the price, the lower the quantity, or vice versa.

IV. In economics, any influence that other variables (other than the one shown on the graph) may have on the dependent variable is assumed to be held constant, a concept referred to in economics as *ceteris paribus*.

V. The relationship between variables may be positive, negative, or neutral, as shown in the following graphs:

1. **Positive**—The dependent variable moves in the same direction as the independent variable.

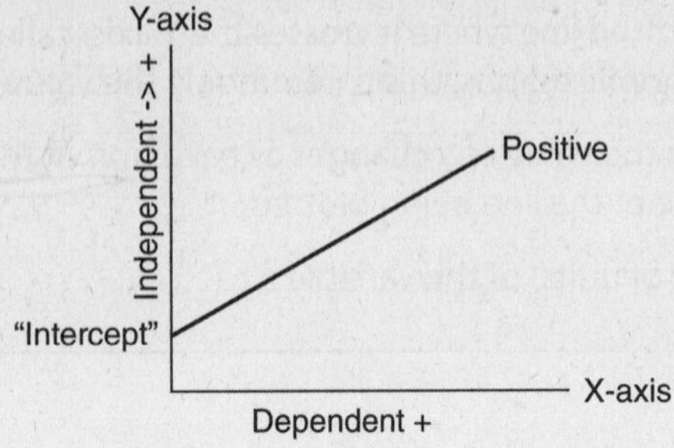

2. **Negative**—The dependent variable moves in the opposite direction from the independent variable.

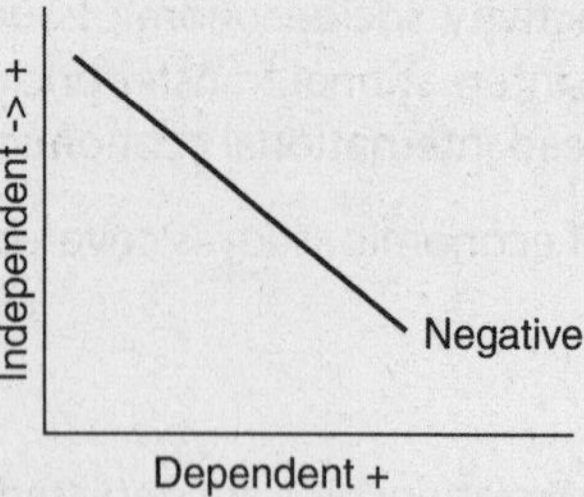

3. **Neutral**—One variable does not change as the other variable changes. (This indicates that the variables are not interdependent.)

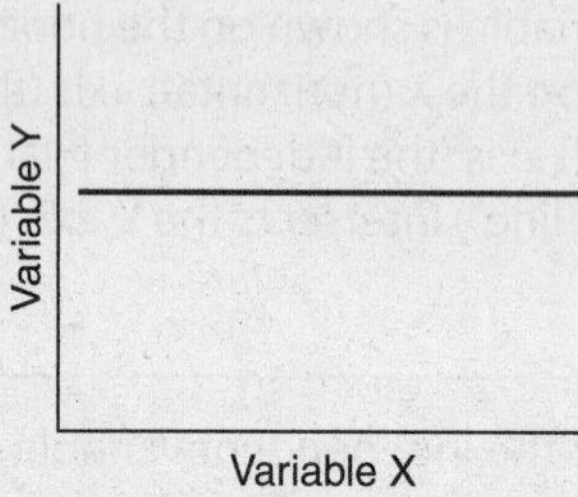

4. When the independent variable is time, the vertical axis shows the behavior of the dependent variable over time and is called a "time series graph." Such a graph might take the following form:

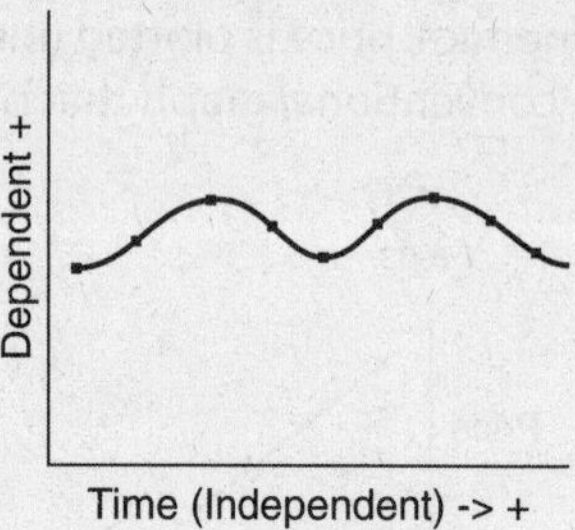

5. Relationships shown in graphic form often can be expressed as mathematical formulas. Such formulas provide quantitative expressions of the relationships between variables and are basic to making economic projections.

    1. The basic equation for a straight-line plot on a graph can be expressed as:

U = y + q (x)

Where:

U = unknown value of the variable y being determined and/or plotted.

y = the value of the plotted line where it crosses the Y'axis; called the "intercept" (or "Y-intercept"). In economic graphs, this is commonly the value of Y where X = 0.

q = the value by which the value of y changes as each unit of the x variable changes; this expresses the slope of the line being plotted.

x = the value (number of units) of the variable x.

Note: Any letters can be used to represent the two variables being plotted, and the expression can be rearranged. For example, the same formula could be, and sometimes is, written as:

Y = mx + b

Where:

Y = unknown value of Y.

m = slope of the plotted line.

x = value of the variable x.

b = Y-intercept.

Example

A common accounting example would include the determination of total cost for various levels of production using fixed cost and variable cost; it could be expressed as:

TC = FC + VC (Units)

Where:

TC = total cost.

FC = fixed cost (incurred independent of the level of production; the Y-intercept).

VC = variable cost per unit of variable X produced; the change in total cost as the number of units of variable X are produced (also, the slope of the total cost line).

Units = number of units of the variable X produced.

a. If the value of FC and VC are known, TC can be computed and plotted for any number of levels of production (units).

VI. Economic Systems—Command and Market Economies—The nature of economic activity, at the microeconomic, macroeconomic, and international levels, depends on the political environment (or economic system) within which the economic activity takes place. The two major economic systems can be found at opposite ends of a continuum of economic systems. They are:

A. Command Economic System—A system in which the government largely determines the production, distribution, and consumption of goods and services. Communism and socialism are prime examples of command economic systems.

B. Market (Free-Enterprise) Economic System—A system in which individuals, businesses, and other distinct entities determine production, distribution, and consumption in an open (free) market. Capitalism is the prime example of a market economic system.

Note

The material in this area of study assumes a free market economic system as it operates in the United States.

Microeconomics

Introduction and Free-Market Model

In a free-market or capitalist economy, resources are privately owned and economic decisions are made primarily by individual decision-making entities, including individuals and business firms. This lesson describes the flow of resources and payments between individuals and businesses in a two-sector free-market economy; in addition, it describes the characteristics of that flow.

After studying this lesson, you should be able to:

1. Describe the structure and flow of resources and payments in a two-sector free-market economy.
2. Identify the factors that are transferred in a free-market model.
3. Describe the major implications of the relationships depicted in a free-market model.

I. Flow Model

A. In a free-market economy, economic decisions are made by individual decision-making entities, including individuals and business firms.

B. The roles and relationships of these decision-making entities (individuals and business firms) are depicted in the following two-sector model:

Free-Market Flow Model

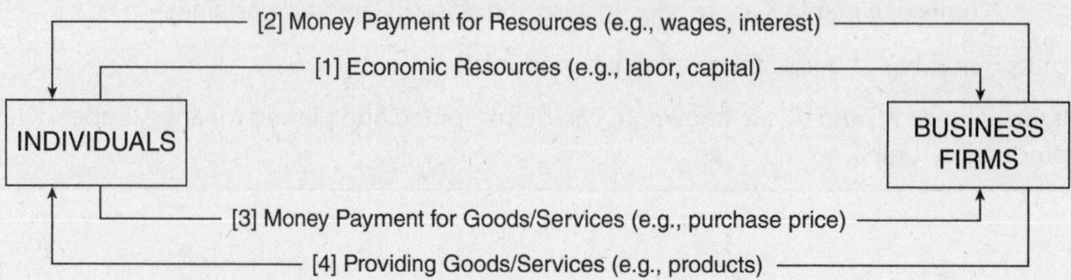

C. In the top half of the model (flow lines [1] and [2]):

1. [1]—Business firms acquire economic resources from individuals, including:
   - **a.** **Labor**—human work, skills, and similar human effort
   - **b.** **Capital**—financial resources (e.g., savings) and man-made resources (e.g., equipment, buildings, etc.)
   - **c.** **Natural resources**—land, minerals, timber, water, etc.
   - **d.** These resources are essential to the production of (other) goods and services, and they are scarce.
2. [2]—Individuals receive compensation from business firms for the use of those individuals' resources, including:
   - **a.** Wages, salaries, and profit sharing for labor
   - **b.** Interest, dividends, rental and lease payments for capital
   - **c.** Rental, lease, and royalty payments for natural resources

D. Because of the reciprocal relationship (in the top half of the model) between the economic resources provided by individuals and the compensation received for those resources, the cost of production (price of economic recourses) to business firms is equal to the money compensation (income) of individuals.

E. In the bottom half of the model (flow lines [3] and [4]):

1. [3]—Individuals use the compensation received for their economic resources to pay for goods and services acquired from business firms.
2. [4]—Business firms produce goods and services, which are purchased by individuals.

F. As a consequence of the reciprocal relationship (in the bottom half of the model) between goods and services produced by business firms and the payment for those goods and services by individuals, the cost of purchasing (price of goods and services) to individuals is equal to the money income of business firms.

II. Characteristics of Free-Market Economy

A. The relationships in the model show, among other things, that, in a true free-market economy:

1. There is an interdependent relationship between individuals and business firms. Individuals depend on business firms for money (income) to use in the purchase of goods and services provided by the business firms. Business firms depend on individuals for economic resources to carry out production and for the money (purchase price) individuals pay for goods and services provided by the firms.
2. What gets produced by business firms and how those goods and services are distributed depends on the preferences (needs and wants) of individuals who have the ability (money resources) to pay for those goods and services.
3. How goods and services get produced by business firms depends on the availability of economic resources (labor, capital, and natural resources), the level of technology available, and how business firms choose to use available resources and technology.
4. Business firms will produce goods and services only if the price at which those goods and services are sold to individuals is equal to or greater than the cost (price) of the economic resources acquired from individuals.
5. The dollar value of flows provides a means of measuring the level of activity in the economy. For example, the flows in the model, when supplemented by the effects of government (taxes, spending, etc.), financial institutions (savings, investments, etc.), and foreign exchange (imports, exports, etc.) provide a basis for measuring the gross domestic product (GDP) of the economy. These aggregate measures are covered in detail in the section on macroeconomics.

B. Central to the relationships in the free-market model is the role of price. The prices of economic resources and of goods and services produced are determined by demand and supply in the market.

Demand

Demand is the desire, willingness, and ability to acquire a commodity. It can be measured and analyzed for an individual decision-maker, for a market (e.g., a particular good or service), or for a multi-market economy. This lesson considers demand at the individual and market levels; aggregate (or economy) demand is considered in the macroeconomics subsection.

After studying this lesson, you should be able to:

1. Define demand.
2. Define a demand schedule and a demand curve at both the individual and market levels.
3. Construct a demand curve at both the individual and market levels for a given set of quantities and prices.
4. Identify and describe the factors that change a market demand curve.
5. Distinguish between a change in quantity demanded and a change in demand.

I. **Existence of Demand**—Demand is the desire, willingness, and ability to acquire a commodity. Thus, the existence of demand depends on not only having needs and wants, but also on having the financial ability to act on those needs and wants in the market. Because demand depends on having the financial ability to acquire a commodity (good or service), the quantity of a commodity for which there will be demand (quantity demanded) will be negatively associated with the price of the commodity. If other influences are held constant, the higher the price, the lower quantity demanded and the lower the price, the higher the quantity demanded.

II. **Individual Demand**—A demand schedule for an individual shows the quantity of a commodity that will be demanded at various prices during a specified time, *ceteris paribus* (holding variables other than price constant). The graphic representation of a demand schedule presents a demand curve with a negative slope.

Individual Demand Curve

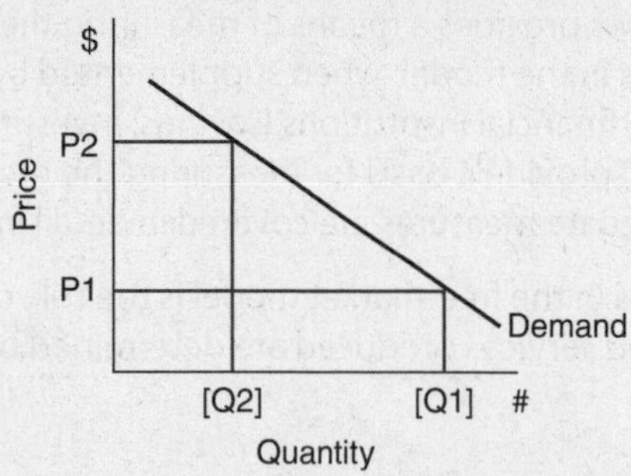

A. At P1, the lower price, the quantity demanded (Q1) is greater than the quantity demanded (Q2) at P2, the higher price. Two factors account for an increase in individual demand at lower prices:

1. **Income effect**—A given amount of income can buy more units at a lower price.
2. **Substitution effect**—Lower-priced items are purchased as substitutions for higher-priced items.

III. **Market Demand**—A market demand schedule shows the quantity of a commodity that will be demanded by all individuals (and other entities) in the market at various prices during a specified time, *ceteris paribus*. A market demand curve, like an individual demand curve, is negatively sloped.

Market Demand Curves

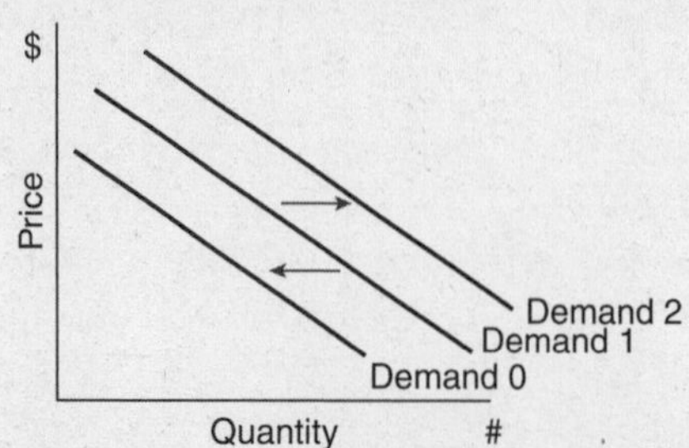

A. As the market demand curve D1 shows, holding other variables constant, as price falls, aggregate demand for a commodity increases. However, if certain other variables (other than price) in the market change, aggregate demand will change and a new market demand curve will result. Changes in other market variables that may change aggregate market demand include:

1. **Size of market**—As the size of the market for a commodity changes, the demand for a commodity may change. For example, if the population of individuals in a market increases, the market demand for a commodity (e.g., bread) may increase, or vice versa. This increase in market demand will result in a new demand curve, shown as D2 in the graph.
2. **Income or wealth of market participants**—As the spendable income or level of wealth of market participants change, the demand for a commodity may change:
   - **a.** An increase in the income of individuals in the market may increase demand for normal (or preferred) goods (e.g., fresh meat) and decrease the demand for inferior (or less than preferred) goods (e.g., canned meat).
   - **b.** A decrease in the income of individuals in the market may increase demand for inferior goods and decrease the demand for normal goods.
3. **Preferences of market participants**—As the tastes of individuals in the market change, the demand for a commodity may change. The change in preference from standard two- and four-door automobiles to the SUV-type vehicle decreased market demand for automobiles but increased demand for SUVs. A market "fad" represents an extreme outward shift in market preference (demand) for a commodity. Conversely, a boycott of a good or service would cause an inward shift (reduction) in demand for that good/service.
4. **Change in prices of other goods and services**—A change in the price of other goods and services may change the demand for a particular commodity. The effect of a change in other prices depends on whether the other goods/services are substitutable for or complementary to a particular commodity.
   - **a.** Substitute commodities satisfy the same basic purpose for the consumer as another commodity. The demand for a commodity may increase when the prices of substitute commodities increase, and vice versa. For example, the demand for rice may increase as the price of potatoes (a substitute for rice) increases.
   - **b.** Complementary commodities are those that are used together. Therefore, the demand for a commodity may increase when the price of a complementary commodity decreases, or vice versa. For example, the demand for shoelaces may increase when the price of shoes decreases because consumers buy more shoes and, thus, more shoelaces.
5. **Expectations of price changes**—When individuals expect future changes in the price of a particular commodity, they may change their current demand for that commodity. For example, if prices are expected to increase in the near future, current demand may increase in anticipation of the price increase. Conversely, an anticipated price decrease may cause current demand to decrease.
6. **Organized boycott**—An organized boycott of a particular commodity will likely decrease the demand for that commodity.

IV. Important Distinction—It is important to distinguish a change in the quantity of a commodity demanded from a change in the demand for a commodity:

A. Change in quantity demanded is movement along a given demand curve (for an individual or for the market) as a result of a change in price of the commodity. Variables other than price are assumed to remain unchanged.

B. Change in demand results in a shift of the entire demand curve, which is caused by changes in variables other than price. As shown in the earlier Market Demand Curves graph, the demand curve will shift to the left and down when aggregate demand decreases (D1 to D0) and to the right and up when aggregate demand increases (D1 to D2).

V. Derived Demand—The demand for a good or service that results from the demand for another related good or service. Derived demand for a good or service is driven by changes in demand for the good or service that require that (input) good or service. For example, the demand for steel is driven by the demand for vehicles that require the use of steel.

A. The demand for most raw materials and intermediate goods is derived demand. It is the use of those raw materials and intermediate goods in the provision of other goods or services that creates the demand for them.

B. Derived demand can be conceived as a sequence of flows from the end user of a good or service backward through the entire supply chain that resulted in the final good or service.

Supply

Supply is the quantity of a commodity provided at alternative prices during a specified time. Like demand, supply can be measured and analyzed for an individual producer, for all producers of a good or service (market supply), or in the aggregate for all providers of all goods and services in an economy. This lesson considers supply at the individual producer and market levels; the macroeconomics subsection includes consideration and review of aggregate (or economy) supply.

After studying this lesson, you should be able to:

1. Define supply.
2. Define a supply schedule and a supply curve at both the individual and market levels.
3. Construct a supply curve at both the individual and market levels for a given set of quantities and prices.
4. Identify and describe the factors that change a market supply curve.
5. Distinguish between a change in quantity supplied and a change in supply.

Definition
Supply: The quantity of a commodity provided either by an individual producer or by all producers of a good or service (market supply) at alternative prices during a specified time.

I. Individual Supply

A. A supply schedule for an individual producer shows the quantity of goods or services that the producer is willing to provide (supply) at alternate prices during a specified time, *ceteris paribus*. The graphic representation of a supply schedule presents a supply curve, which normally has a positive slope.

Individual Supply Curve

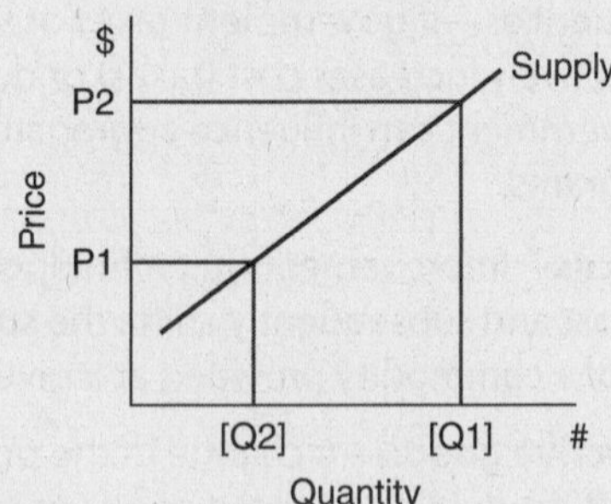

B. At P2, the higher price, the quantity supplied (Q2) is greater than the quantity supplied (Q1) at P1, the lower price. Producers normally are willing to provide higher quantities of goods and services only at higher prices because higher production costs are normally incurred in increasing production in the short run. The higher production costs (known as the principle of increasing costs) occurs because the additional resources used to increase production typically are not as efficient in producing the commodity as the resources previously used.

C. The principle of increasing costs recognizes that once the fixed factors of production are being used efficiently, increasing production (i.e., supply) will cost more than the prior average cost per unit. Therefore, increasing production (and thus increasing average cost) will occur only if that increase in average cost can be recovered through a higher sales price for the good/service. (The principle of increasing costs reflects the effects on cost as a result of the law of diminishing returns, covered in a later lesson.)

II. Market Supply

A. A market supply schedule shows the quantity of a commodity that will be supplied by all providers in the market at various prices during a specified time, *ceteris paribus*. A market supply curve, like an individual supply curve, is positively sloped.

Market Supply Curves

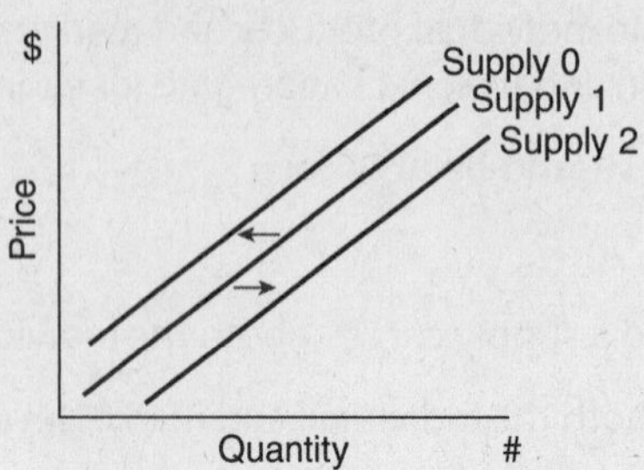

B. As the market supply curve S1 shows, holding other variables constant, as price increases, aggregate supply for a commodity (quantity) increases. However, if certain other non-price variables in the market change, aggregate supply will change and a new market supply curve will result (S2 or S0). Changes in other market variables that may change aggregate supply include:

1. **Number of providers**—As the number of providers of a commodity increase, the market supply of the commodity increases, or vice versa. An increase in market supply will result in a new supply curve, shown as S2 in the graph. The new supply curve shows more of the commodity being provided at a given price. If the number of suppliers of the product decreases, the supply curve would move (up and left) to S0, showing less of the commodity provided at a given price.
2. **Cost of inputs (economic resources) change**—As the cost of inputs to the production process changes (e.g., labor, rent, raw materials, etc.), so also will the supply curve. An increase in input prices would cause per unit cost to increase and the supply curve would shift up and to the left (S1 to S0), indicating less output at a given price. A decrease in input prices would reduce per unit cost and would shift the curve from S1 to S2, with more output at a given price.
    a. **Related commodities**—Changes in the price of other commodities that use the same inputs as a given commodity will result in more or less demand for the inputs, will change the cost of inputs for the given commodity, and, thus, will change the supply of that commodity.
    b. **Government influences**—If government taxes or subsidizes the production of a commodity, it effectively increases cost (taxes) or decreases cost (subsidizes) of the product. Thus, government can influence aggregate supply through its taxation and subsidization programs.
3. **Technological advances**—Improvements in technology for the production of a commodity reduces the per-unit cost and subsequently shifts the supply curve down and to the right (S1 to S2), showing more of a commodity provided at a given price.
4. **Prices of other productive goods**—A change in the prices of other goods and services may cause producers to shift production to those goods or services if they provide a higher return.
5. **Expectation of price changes**—When producers expect the selling price of their good or service to be higher in the future, they may increase supply in anticipation of the selling price increase. Conversely, if they expect the selling price to be lower in the future, they may decrease supply in anticipation of the selling price decrease.

III. Important Distinction—It is important to distinguish a change in the quantity of a commodity supplied from a change in supply of a commodity.

A. Change in the quantity supplied is movement along a given supply curve (for an individual provider or for the market) as a result of a change in price of the commodity. Variables other than price are assumed to remain unchanged.

B. Change in supply results in a shift of the entire supply curve that is caused by changes in variables other than price. As shown in the Market Supply Curves graph, the supply curve will shift right and down when aggregate supply increases (S1 to S2), and to the left and up when aggregate supply decreases (S1 to S0).

Market Equilibrium

Economic equilibrium occurs when, in the absence of external influences, there is no tendency for change in economic values. Market equilibrium occurs at the intersection of the market demand and market supply curves; quantity demanded equals quantity supplied. This lesson considers the determination of market equilibrium, the consequences of a price that is higher or lower than the equilibrium price, the effects of change in market demand and/or market supply on market equilibrium, and how government influences market equilibrium.

After studying this lesson, you should be able to:

1. Define market equilibrium.
2. Construct a graph showing market equilibrium.
3. Describe the effects of "artificially set" prices on a market quantity that result in shortages and surpluses.
4. Describe and graph the effect of changes in market demand and/or market supply on market equilibrium.
5. Describe the effects of government influences, including taxation and subsidization, on market equilibrium.

I. **Market Equilibrium**—The equilibrium price for a commodity is the price at which the quantity of the commodity supplied in the market is equal to the quantity of the commodity demanded in the market. Graphically, the market equilibrium price for a commodity occurs where the market demand curve and the market supply curve intersect.

Market Equilibrium

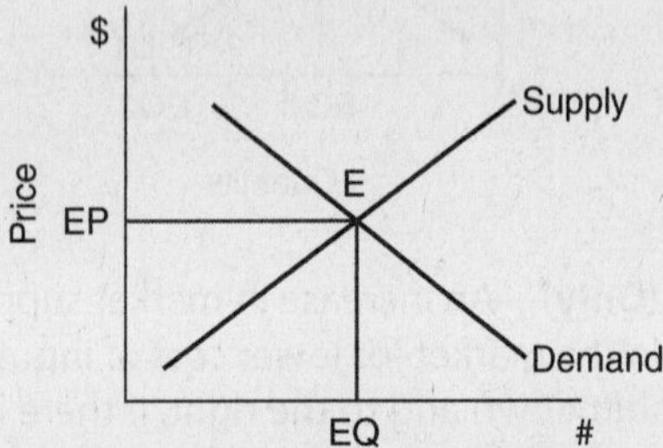

A. Equilibrium for the commodity occurs at the intersection (E) of the demand and supply curves. The equilibrium price is EP, and the equilibrium quantity is EQ. For the given supply and demand curves, at the equilibrium price (EP), the quantity of the commodity demanded (i.e., that can be sold) is exactly equal to the quantity of the commodity that will be supplied at that price. There will be no shortage or surplus of the commodity in the market.

B. Shortages and surpluses in quantity occur when the actual price (AP) of the commodity is less (shortage) or more (surplus) than the equilibrium price (EP).

Market Shortage

Market Surplus

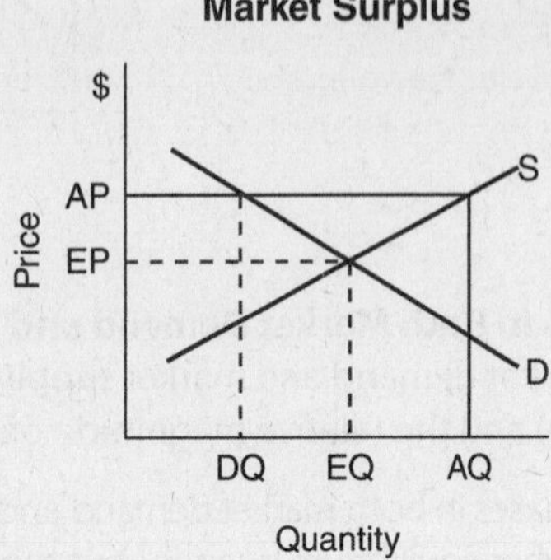

1. **Market shortage**—The actual price is less than the equilibrium price (AP less than EP); therefore, the actual quantity supplied is less than the quantity demanded at AP (AQ less than DQ). A shortage equal to DQ – AQ exists.
2. **Market surplus**—The actual price is higher than the equilibrium price (AP greater than EP); therefore, the actual quantity supplied is greater than the quantity demanded at AP (AQ greater than DQ). A surplus equal to AQ – DQ exists.

C. When attained, market equilibrium will continue until there is a change in demand for and/or supply of the commodity. The shifts in the demand and/or supply curves that result will change market equilibrium.

II. **Change in Equilibrium**—The effect of change(s) in demand and/or supply on market equilibrium depends on whether demand changes, supply changes, or both change.

A. **Change in Market Demand (Only)**—An increase in market demand D1 to D2 due to an increase in the size of the market (or increased income, changes in consumer preferences, etc.) causes the demand curve to shift up and to the right. If there is no change in market supply, the results will be an increase in both the equilibrium price (EP1 to EP2) and equilibrium quantity (EQ1 to EQ2). A decrease in market demand would cause both equilibrium price and equilibrium quantity to decrease.

Increased Demand

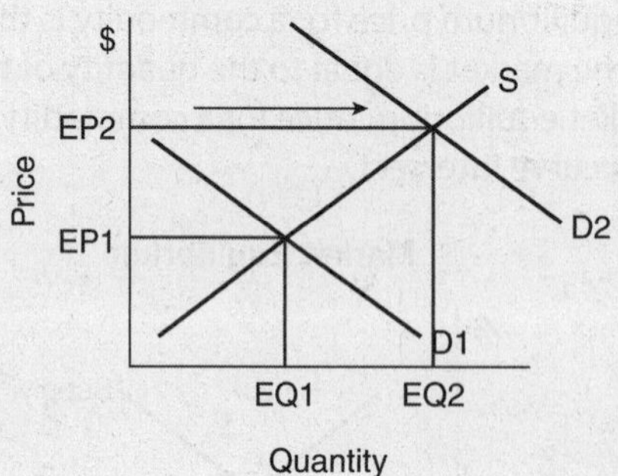

B. **Change in Market Supply (Only)**—An increase in market supply (S1 to S2) due to an increase in the number of providers in the market (or lower cost of inputs, technological advances, etc.) causes the supply curve to shift down and to the right. If there is no change in market demand, the results will be a decrease in equilibrium price (EP1 to EP0) and an increase in equilibrium quantity (EQ1 to EQ2). A decrease in market supply causes a higher equilibrium price and a lower equilibrium quantity.

Increased Supply

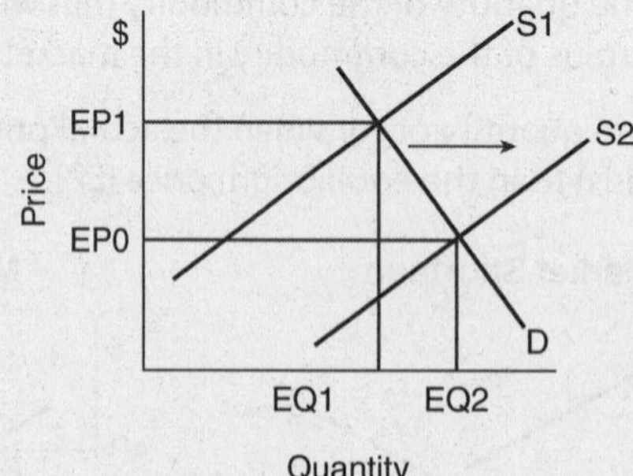

C. **Changes in Both Market Demand and Market Supply**—The effect of simultaneous changes in both market demand and market supply depends on the direction of the changes (increase or decrease) and the relative magnitude of each change.

1. Increases in both market demand and market supply will shift both curves to the right resulting in a higher equilibrium quantity, but the resulting equilibrium price will depend on the magnitude of each change. The equilibrium price could remain unchanged, increase, or decrease.

2. Decreases in both market demand and market supply will shift both curves to the left resulting in a lower equilibrium quantity, but the resulting equilibrium price will depend on the magnitude of each change.

3. The effects of a simultaneous increase in one market curve (demand or supply) and a decrease in the other market curve (supply or demand) on market price and market equilibrium can be determined only when the specific magnitude of each change is known.

III. Governmental Influences on Equilibrium

A. **Taxation and Subsidization**—As noted earlier, government taxation and subsidization have the effect of either increasing or decreasing the effective cost of production (supply). For example, a tax on a commodity at the production level increases the cost and shifts the market supply curve up and to the left. If demand remains constant, equilibrium price increases and equilibrium quantity decreases. Government subsidies have the opposite effect.

B. **Regulation**—Similarly, the imposition of government regulations on business tends to increase the cost of production (i.e., compliance costs) and shift the market supply curve up and to the left when compared with what the market supply curve would be in the absence of regulatory costs.

C. **Rationing**—By imposing a rationing system, government can change market demand and thereby equilibrium in the market. Rationing would be intended to shift the demand curve down and to the left, thus lowering equilibrium price and equilibrium quantity.

D. **Price Fiat**—Government also can affect the price of a commodity through price fiat by establishing an (artificial) price ceiling or price floor. These artificial prices result in disequilibrium in the market. An imposed market ceiling (less than free-market equilibrium price) results in market supply being less than market demand at the imposed price. Market demand and market supply are not in equilibrium. An imposed market floor (greater than free-market equilibrium price) results in market supply being more than market demand at the imposed price.

Elasticity

Elasticity measures the percentage change in a market factor (e.g., demand) because of a given percentage change in another market factor (e.g., price). This lesson defines elasticity, and it considers four major measures of elasticity and the usefulness of one of these measures (elasticity of demand) in estimating the effects on total revenue likely to result from a change in price.

After studying this lesson, you should be able to:

1. Describe the effects of a given change in price and related elasticity on demand and supply.
2. Determine the effects on total revenue using the elasticity coefficient for demand.
3. Define and calculate elasticity, including: a) elasticity of demand; b) elasticity of supply; c) cross elasticity of demand; and d) income elasticity of demand.

I. **Elasticity**—Elasticity measures the percentage change in a market factor (e.g., demand) as a result of a given percentage change in another market factor. Elasticity measures often have specific practical applications. For example, elasticity is used in estimating the change in demand (and total revenue) likely to result from a change in price.

Definition
Elasticity: Measures the percentage change in a market factor (e.g., demand) seen as a result of a given percentage change in another market factor (e.g., price).

II. **Elasticity of Demand**—Elasticity of demand (ED) measures the percentage change in quantity of a commodity demanded as a result of a given percentage change in the price of the commodity. Therefore, it is computed as:

ED = % change in quantity demanded / % change in price

This formula expresses the slope of the demand curve when showing demand graphically.

A. Expanded, the formula is:

ED = (Change in quantity demanded/Quantity demanded) / (Change in price/Price)

B. Three different values can be used as the denominators in the calculation:

1. The **prechange quantity demanded and price**—Elasticity is measured at a point on the demand curve—the original quantity and price.
2. The **average of the old and new quantity and price**—Elasticity is measured as the average of the demand curve; called the "midpoint" or "arc" method.
3. The **new quantity and price**—Elasticity is measured at a point on the demand curve—the new quantity and price.

C. Whichever values are used, the calculation will result in a negative value (called the "elasticity coefficient") because for normal goods/services, the change in quantity demanded will be the opposite of the change in price. The elasticity coefficient (value), however, is conventionally referred to as an absolute value (i.e., the negative sign is ignored).

Examples

1. Using the Prechange Values: Assume that as a result of a change in price from $1.50 to $2.00, demand decreased from 1,500 units to 1,200 units. Using the old (prechange) quantity and price, the calculation would be:

   % change in quantity: 1,500 – 1,200 = 300/1,500 = .20
   % change in price: $2.00 – $1.50 = $ .50/$1.50 = .333
   ED = .20/.333 = .60

(Alternate Calculation: ED = 300/1,500 × $1.50/$ .50 = $450/$750 = .60)

2. Using the Average Values (midpoint or arc method): Assume that as a result of a change in price from $1.50 to $2.00, demand decreased from 1,500 units to 1,200 units. Using the average of the old and new quantities and prices, the calculation would be:

   Average change in quantity = (1,500 + 1,200)/2 = 1,350
   Average change in price = ($1.50 + $2.00)/2 = $1.75

   % change in quantity: 1,500 – 1,200 = 300/1,350 = .222
   % change in price: $2.00 – $1.50 = $ .50/$1.75 = .285
   ED = .222/.285 = .778

D. In Example 1 above, a 33.3% increase in price (from $1.50 to $2.00) will result in only a 20% decrease in quantity demanded; the elasticity of demand (.20/.333) of .60 is less than 1. When elasticity of demand is less than 1, demand is inelastic— quantity demanded does not change proportionally as much as a change in price. The calculation of elasticity of demand results in the following possible outcomes:

Calculated Elasticity Coefficient	Elasticity of Demand	Meaning
Greater than 1	Elastic	% change in quantity demanded greater than % change in price
= 1	Unitary	% change in quantity demanded = % change in price
Less than 1	Inelastic	% change in quantity demanded less than % change in price

E. The effect of a change in price on total revenue can be directly estimated from the elasticity of demand coefficient. Using the data from the example above:

	Quantity	Total Revenue
Before price change	1,500	$ 2,250
After price change	1,200	$ 2,400
Change in revenue (increase)		$ 150

F. The relationship between elasticity of demand and total revenue (TR) generated can be summarized as follows:

Efficiency Coefficient	Price Increase	Price Decrease
Greater than 1 (elastic)	TR Decrease	TR Increase
Equal to 1 (unitary)	TR No Change	TR No Change
Less than 1 (inelastic)	TR Increase	TR Decrease

G. Price elasticity of demand shows the relationship between a change in price and the change in quantity demanded of a good or service. If the relationship shows that a good/service is price elastic (an elasticity coefficient greater than 1), the percentage change in demand will be greater than the percentage change in price. If the relationship shows that a good/service is price inelastic (an elasticity coefficient less than 1), the percentage change in demand will be less than the percentage change in price. The demand for some goods and services is more sensitive to a change in price than the demand for other goods and services. A number of factors can affect the elasticity of demand for a good or service, including:

1. **Availability of substitutes**—The more substitutes there are for a good/service, the more elastic the demand for that good/service will be. When there are substitutes available, consumers can switch to an alternative good/service, resulting in a more elastic demand for the good/service for which there was a price change. When there are virtually no substitutes for a good/service, demand will be inelastic. There are few substitutes for gasoline; therefore, it is price inelastic.
2. **Extent of necessity**—The more necessary a good/service, the more inelastic the demand for that good/service will be. A good/service that is highly necessary will be more insensitive to price changes than a good/service that is a luxury. Critical healthcare is necessary; therefore, it is highly price inelastic.
3. **Share of disposable income**—The larger the share of disposable income devoted to a good/service, the more elastic the demand for the goods/service will be. When a good/service consumes a large part of disposable income, consumers tend to be more sensitive to price changes, making demand more elastic.
4. **Postchange time horizon**—The longer the time following a price change for a good/service, the more elastic demand for the good/service tends to be. Over time, consumers are able to gain more information about substitute goods/services, more alternatives may become available, and constraints on consumer switching (e. g., contracts, prepayments, etc.) will expire. As a consequence, consumers may adjust their buying behavior, thus increasing the elasticity for the good/service for which there was a price change.

H. **Importance of Price Elasticity**—Price elasticity of demand is important to a firm because it indicates the extent to which a firm is likely to be able to pass on increases in its cost of inputs to its customers.

1. If demand for a good or service is inelastic, then the firm can increase its selling price with less negative financial impact.
2. On the other hand, if demand for a firm's good or service is highly elastic, it cannot increase its selling price without significant negative financial impact. Therefore, it should consider alternative ways of addressing expected increases in its cost of inputs.

Note: On the CPA Exam, most questions ask you to determine elasticity of demand (ED). However, some questions give you the ED value and ask you to determine the effect of a price change on the quantity demanded. You should note that if you have two of the three factors (ED, % change in quantity demanded, and % change in price), using the ED equation given above, you can determine the third factor using simple algebra.

Example

A firm determined that its price elasticity of demand for a given product is 1.5. If the firm plans to increase it price by 10%, the effect on quantity demanded can be determined as follows:

ED = % change in Q demanded/% change in price

% change in Q demanded = ED × % change in price

% change in Q demanded = 1.5 × 10% = 15%

Thus, a 10% increase in price would result in a 15% decrease in quantity demanded.

III. Elasticity of Supply—Elasticity of supply (ES) measures the percentage change in the quantity of a commodity supplied as a result of a given percentage change in the price of the commodity; therefore, it is computed as:

> ES = % change in quantity supplied / % change in price
>
> This formula expresses the slope of the supply curve when showing the supply graphically.

A. Expanded, the formula is:

> ES = (Change in quantity supplied / Prechange quantity supplied) / (Change in price / Prechange price)

B. As with the calculation of elasticity of demand, the above calculation can use the following as the denominator:

1. New quantity and new price
2. Average of old and new quantity and price

C. The calculation of elasticity of supply would be done in the same manner as the calculation of elasticity of demand, and the resulting outcomes could be:

Calculated Elasticity Coefficient	Elasticity of Supply	Meaning
Greater than 1	Elastic	% change in quantity supplied greater than % change in price
= 1	Unitary	% change in quantity supplied = % change in price
Less than 1	Inelastic	% change in quantity supplied less than % change in price

IV. Elasticity of Other Market Factors—In addition to measurement of elasticity of demand (and related total revenue) and elasticity of supply, other measures of elasticity include:

A. Cross Elasticity of Demand—Measures the percentage change in quantity of a commodity demanded as a result of a given percentage change in the price of another commodity.

1. The formula for cross elasticity of demand (XED) is:

> XED = % change in quantity demanded of Y / % change in price of X

Example
The effect on the quantity demanded for Coca-Cola as a result of a given change in the price of Pepsi Cola.

2. The calculation of the cross elasticity of demand results in the following possible outcomes:

XED Calculated Coefficient	Meaning
Greater than 0 (a positive coefficient)	Goods are substitutes for each other
= 0	Goods are independent of each other
Less than 0 (a negative coefficient)	Goods are complementary to each other

3. The calculated coefficient indicates both the relationship between the goods (whether substitutes or compliments) and the degree of the relationship.
4. The higher the cross elasticity of demand coefficient (whether positive or negative), the stronger the relationship between the two goods.
   a. The higher the *positive* coefficient, the more the goods are *substitutes* for each other.
   b. The higher the *negative* coefficient, the more the goods are *complementary* with each other.
5. The calculated coefficient also reflects the proportional change in the quantity of one good expected as a result of a change in the price of the other good.
6. As a result of a 10% increase in the price of laptop computers, the demand for tablets increased by 20%. Thus, the calculated XED coefficient would be:
   a. XED = .20 / .10 = 2 (a positive coefficient)
   b. Conclusions: The goods are substitutes (because the coefficient is positive), and a 10% increase in the price of laptops would result in a percentage increase in the quantity demanded for tablets that is two times the percentage increase in the price of laptops.

B. **Income Elasticity of Demand**—Measures the percentage change in quantity of a commodity demanded as a result of a given percentage change in income.

1. The formula for the income elasticity of demand (IED) is:

IED = % change in quantity demanded / % change in consumer income

Example
The effects on the quantity demanded for fresh fruit as a result of a given change in income.

2. The calculation of the income elasticity of demand results in the following possible outcomes:

IED Calculated Coefficient	Results—Assuming Increase in Income
Less than 0 (negative coefficient)	Decrease in demand ("inferior" goods)
0	No change in demand ("sticky" normal goods)
Greater than 0, less than 1	Less than proportional increase in demand ("necessary" normal goods)
1	Proportional increase in demand ("normal" normal goods)
Greater than 1	Greater than proportional increase in demand ("luxury" normal goods)

3. A decrease in income generally would result in the reverse effects on demand.
4. For all normal goods (those with a calculated coefficient of 0 or greater), the higher the non-negative IED coefficient, the greater the relative increase in demand as income increases. For inferior goods, the higher the negative IED coefficient, the greater the reduction in demand as income increases.

Example

As a result of a 25% increase in income, the demand for a good increased by 20%. Thus, the calculated IED coefficient would be:

IED = .20 / .25 = .80 (a positive coefficient value greater than 0, less than 1)

Conclusion: The good is a "normal" good (has a positive coefficient) for which demand increases less than proportional to the increase in income; the good is referred to as a "necessary" good.

Consumer Demand and Utility Theory

Consumer demand derives from the need or desire for goods and services; those goods and services provide utility to the consumer. This lesson covers the concept of utility theory and the associated indifference curves.

After studying this lesson, you should be able to:

1. Define utility, marginal utility, and the law of diminishing marginal utility.
2. Describe and calculate when an individual would maximize total utility.
3. Define indifference curves, and relate indifference curves to utility.

I. **Utility**—Consumers (individually and in the aggregate) demand a commodity because it satisfies a need or a want. In economics, the satisfaction derived from the acquisition or use of a commodity is referred to as "utility." Thus, demand for a good or service occurs because of the utility derived from that good or service. A hypothetical unit of measure called "util" is often used to assign value (or measure) an individual's utility (or satisfaction) derived from each commodity.

II. **Marginal Utility**—The more of each commodity an individual acquires during a given time, the greater total utility (or utils) the individual derives. However, while total utility increases as acquisition increases, the utility (or utils) derived from each additional unit of a commodity decreases. The last additional unit acquired is referred to as the "marginal unit," and the decreasing utility derived from each (additional) marginal unit is referred to as the "law of diminishing marginal utility." Graphically, diminishing marginal utility (MU) would be depicted as follows:

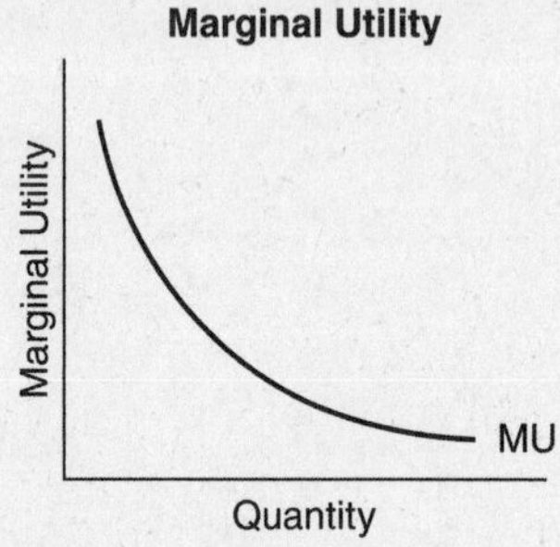

A. An individual will maximize total utility (satisfaction) for a given amount of income when the marginal utility of the last dollar spent on each and every commodity acquired is the same. Thus, total utility is maximized when:

(MU of A) / (A Price) = (MU of B) / (B Price) = (…MU of Z) / (Z Price)

B. When this condition exists, the individual is considered to be in equilibrium.

III. **Indifference Curves**—When the various quantities of two commodities that give an individual the same total utility are plotted on a graph, the result is an indifference curve. Assume, for example, that with a fixed income and given prices, an individual would be equally satisfied (have the same total utility) with the following combination of soft drinks and beer:

Soft Drinks	Beers
10	1
7	2
5	3
2	4

According to this schedule, an individual would be equally happy with 10 soft drinks and 1 beer as with 2 soft drinks and 4 beers; there is no preference for any of the shown combinations of soft drinks and beers.

A. The resulting indifference curve (I) would take the form:

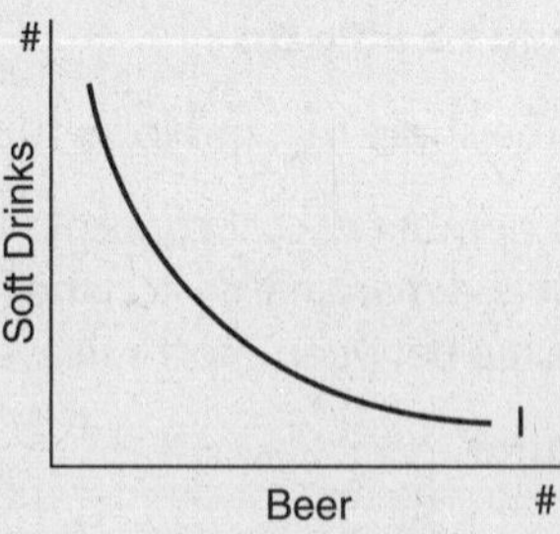

B. Along this curve, the individual would receive equal utility and therefore be indifferent to the consequent combination of soft drinks and beer.

Inputs and the Cost of Production

The costs of a firm's input factors—labor, capital, and natural resources—are the primary determinants of a firm's supply curve. For analytical purposes, a number of different ways are used to classify the costs of these factors. This lesson considers several cost concepts and how the different cost concepts apply in the economic analysis of the cost of production.

After studying this lesson, you should be able to:

1. Define and distinguish between the short-run and long-run analysis used in economics.
2. Define and graphically represent a number of cost concepts, including: a) total fixed cost, total variable cost, and total cost; b) average cost and marginal cost; c) the relationship between average costs and marginal costs; and d) the relationship between short-run average cost and long-run average cost.
3. Define the law of diminishing returns.
4. Define the concepts of economies and diseconomies of scale.

I. **Inputs**—In the free-market model, it was shown that business firms acquire economic resources in order to produce (other) goods and services. These inputs to the production process are the major determinants of a firm's supply curve. As noted in the discussion of supply, changes in the cost of inputs to the production process cause a shift in an entity's supply curve (i.e., change the quantity of goods supplied at a given price).

II. **Periods of Analysis**

A. The analysis of cost of production (and other areas of economics) distinguishes between analysis in the short run and analysis in the long run.

1. **Short-run**—The time period during which the quantity of at least one input to the production process cannot be varied; the quantity of at least one input is fixed.
2. **Long-run**—The time period during which the quantity of all inputs to the production process can be varied; no inputs are fixed.

B. Since business firms can vary all inputs in the long run and since they must nevertheless operate in the short run, analysis of production costs tends to focus on the short run.

III. **Short-Run Cost Analysis**

A. **Total Cost (TC)**—Because some costs cannot be changed in the short run, total production costs are separated into fixed costs and variable costs:

1. **Total fixed cost (FC)**—Incurred costs that cannot be changed with changes in the level of output (including no output). Examples include property taxes, contracted rent, insurance, etc.
2. **Total variable cost (VC)**—Costs incurred for variable inputs and that will vary directly with changes in the level of output. Examples include raw materials, most labor, electricity, etc.
3. **Total costs (TC)**—The sum of the total fixed and total variable costs.
4. These costs can be presented as curves in graph form as:

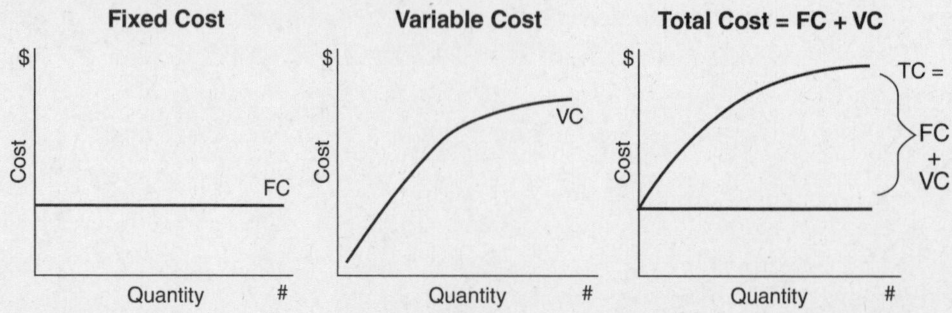

B. Average Cost—The cost per unit of commodity produced. Average fixed cost (AFC), average variable cost (AVC), and average total cost (ATC) are computed by dividing the cost (FC, VC, or TC) by the quantity of units produced. The resulting curves take the following form:

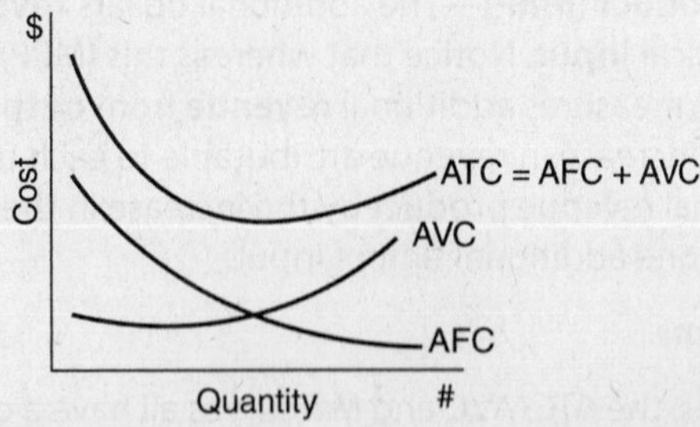

C. Marginal Cost (MC)—The dollar *cost* of producing one additional unit of physical *output*. It is computed as the difference between successive total costs or, because only variable costs change, successive total variable costs. When plotted, a marginal cost curve takes the form:

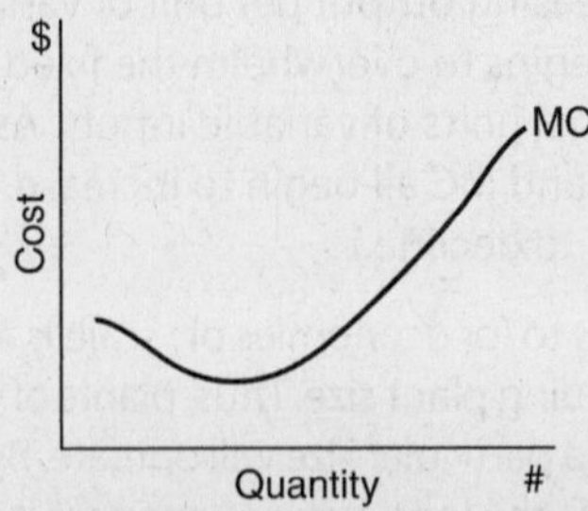

1. Related "marginal" concept—**marginal product (MP)**—The change in physical *output* that will result from one additional unit of physical *input*. Notice that this measures physical output that results from physical input; it does not measure in terms of dollars. It is computed as the change in total output that results from using one additional unit of a particular factor of production (input).

D. Average Cost and Marginal Cost—When the marginal cost curve is combined with the average cost curves, the following results:

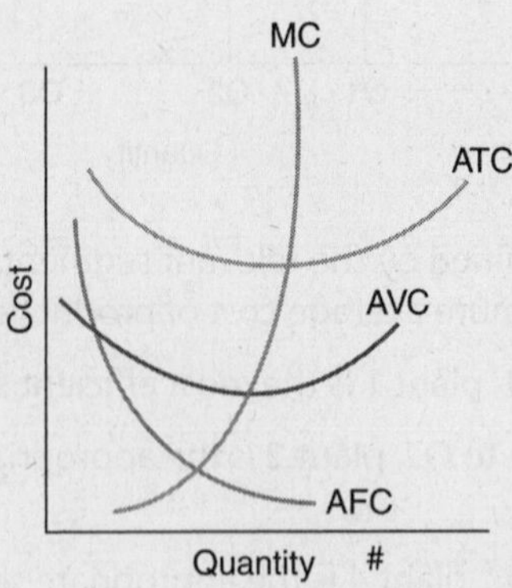

Note

The lowest MC occurs at a lower output than the lowest point on the AVC or ATC. The MC curve crosses the AVC and ATC at their respective lowest point.

IV. Revenue and Output Concepts—Costs, as described above, are incurred in order to provide goods and services (output). The benefit derived from the sale of those goods and services (output) is commonly referred to as "revenue." Revenue concepts parallel those of cost.

A. Revenue—The amount earned as a result of providing goods or services

B. Total Revenue (TR)—The total amount earned as a result of providing goods or services during a period. In the simplest context, it is the quantity provided (sold) multiplied by the price per unit sold.

C. Average Revenue (AR)—The average price (revenue) per unit for the total units sold. Average revenue is computed by dividing total revenue by the total quantity of units sold and may be expressed as AR = TR/Q.

D. Marginal Revenue (MR)—The dollar increase in **revenue** that results from the sale of one additional physical unit of **output**. Marginal revenue is computed as the change in total revenue as a result of selling one additional unit.

E. Marginal Revenue Product (MRP)—The additional dollars **revenue** that will result from one additional unit of physical **input**. Notice that whereas this (MRP) measures revenue from input, marginal revenue (MR) measures additional **revenue** from **output**. MRP per unit of input measures the average increase in revenue attributable to each unit of input added. It is computed by dividing the marginal revenue product by the increase in the number products (output) resulting from adding one additional unit of input.

V. Law of Diminishing Returns

A. In the foregoing graphs, the ATC, AVC and MC curves all have a general "U" shape. That shape is basic to each curve and occurs because of eventual diminishing returns from adding more variable inputs. In the short run, as the quantity of variable inputs increases, output initially increases, causing AC, AVC, and MC to decrease.

B. However, at some quantity of variable inputs, the addition of more units, in combination with the fixed input(s), results in decreasing output per unit of variable input. Simply put, at some point the quantity of variable inputs begins to overwhelm the fixed factor(s) resulting in inefficiencies and diminishing return on marginal units of variable inputs. As a consequence of diminishing returns as inputs increase, ATC, AVC, and MC all begin to increase. Thus, their curves are "U" shaped. (Note, however, that AFC continues to decline.)

VI. Long-Run Cost Analysis

Long-Run Cost Analysis—Returns to (or economies of) scale is a long-run concept. In the long run, all costs are considered variable, including plant size. Thus, plants of various sizes can be assumed in the long run, but in the short run, a plant of a particular size will operate. By plotting the short-run average cost (SAC) curve of plants of various sizes (1–4), the long-run average cost (LAC) curve can be constructed.

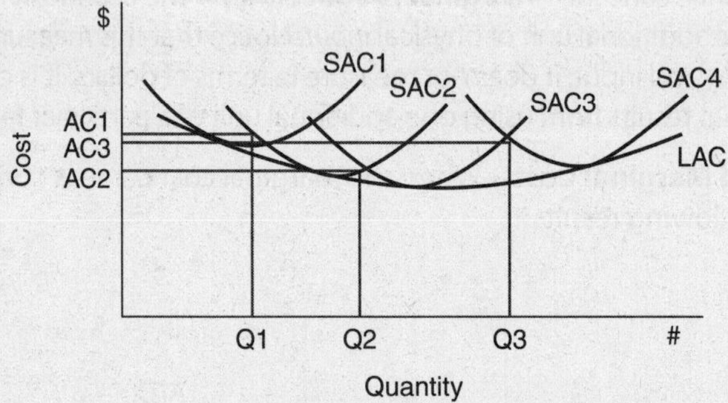

A. As shown, the LAC is determined by the relevant segments of SAC for plants 1, 2, 3, and 4. This curve (LAC) shows the minimum average cost of production with various size plants. Note that:

1. Up to the quantity at Q1, plant 1 is the most efficient size plant.
2. From the quantity at Q1 to Q2, plant 2 is the appropriate size plant, and from Q2 to Q3, plant 3 is the appropriate size.
3. Above the quantity at Q3, plant 4 is the appropriate size plant.

B. The long-run average cost curve (LAC) is also "U" shaped, reflecting that as plant size (scale) increases there are various returns to (or economics of) scale. Three possible cost outcomes exist:

1. **Economies of (or increasing return to) scale**—As shown where the LAC curve is decreasing, quantity of output increases in greater proportion than the increase in all inputs, primarily due to specialization of labor and equipment.
2. **Neither economy nor diseconomy of (constant return to) scale**—As shown at the bottom of the LAC curve, output increases in the same proportion as inputs.
3. **Diseconomies of (or decreasing return to) scale**—As shown where the LAC curve is increasing, quantity of output increases in lesser proportion than the increase in all inputs, primarily due to problems of managing very large-scale operations.

Market Structure and Firm Strategy

Introduction to Market Structure

Market structure describes the nature of the economic environment in which firms operate and economic activity occurs. Conceptually, a number of different environments or market structures can exist along a hypothetical continuum with perfect competition at one extreme and perfect monopoly at the other. This lesson identifies four of the most common market structures, each covered in detail in subsequent lessons.

After studying this lesson, you should be able to:

1. Identify the four most common market structures used for economic analysis.
2. Define a "market".
3. Define "normal profits" and "economic profits".

I. **Market Defined**—Broadly defined, a market is any facility (e.g., physical location, virtual system, etc.) that enables sellers (supply) and buyers (demand) to interact for the exchange of specific goods or services. Within a market, sellers compete with one another for buyers' demand for a particular good or service. Markets may be categorized based on the extent to which competition among sellers exists.

II. **Market Structures**

A. The extent to which competition exists, or does not exist, in an industry or market determines how prices are established, operating results at various levels of production, and other performance characteristics. Four assumptions as to market structure are considered in the following lessons:

1. Perfect Competition
2. Perfect Monopoly
3. Monopolistic Competition
4. Oligopoly

B. Analysis of factors in each of these assumed structures provides insights into real-world economic activity and outcomes, which are useful in explaining and predicting business activity. For each assumed structure, both short-term and long-term analysis is presented.

III. **Profit Concepts**—In the study of market structures, two economic concepts of profit are important to understand. These two concepts identify the extent to which a profit can be experienced by firms in a particular market. The two concepts are:

A. **Normal Profit**—Measured as just the amount of profit necessary to cover operating costs and compensate owners for their capital investment and/or managerial skills. No amount of "excess" profit is included beyond the minimum amount needed to attract and retain the owners' capital and/or managerial skills.

B. **Economic Profit**—Measured as any amount greater than that of normal profit. Unlike normal profit, the amount of economic profit is not constrained or of a limited amount. The amount of profit may be in excess of the minimum amount needed to attract and retain the owners' investment. This concept is consistent with what also is called "accounting profit."

Perfect Competition

This lesson considers the conditions that constitute a perfectly competitive market at one end of a hypothetical market structures continuum. Descriptions and illustrations include the nature of demand, revenue, costs, and profit in both the short run and long run in such a market.

After studying this lesson, you should be able to:

1. Describe the characteristics of a perfectly competitive market structure.
2. Describe the relevant cost curves and their relationships in perfect competition.
3. Identify the optimum level of output and price in a perfectly competitive market structure in both: a) short-term analysis and b) long-term analysis.
4. Describe basic firm strategy in a perfectly competitive market.

I. Characteristics

A. Perfect competition exists in industries or markets characterized by:

1. A large number of independent buyers and sellers, each of which is too small to separately, affect the price of a commodity
2. All firms sell homogeneous products or services.
3. Firms can enter or leave the market easily.
4. Resources are completely mobile.
5. Buyers and sellers have perfect information.
6. Government does not set prices.

B. A market (or industry) meeting all of these criteria is virtually impossible to identify. Nevertheless, analysis under assumed conditions of perfect competition is useful in understanding pricing, production, profit, and related elements.

C. In a perfectly competitive market, a firm is a "price taker" that must (and can) sell any quantity of its commodity at the market price. Therefore, for firms in a perfectly competitive market, the demand curve is a straight line at the market price.

D. While the demand (and marginal revenue) curve for a firm in perfect competition is a straight horizontal line at the price set by the market that cannot be affected by the individual firm, the demand curve for the entire market (market demand) is downward sloping.

1. Market demand will increase/decrease (shift) only if all suppliers lower/raise prices.
2. The characteristics of a perfectly competitive market preclude such unanimous action by all firms in the market. Therefore, firm analysis is based on the use of a horizontal demand curve at the price set by the market.

II. Short-Run Analysis

A. In the short run, a firm in a perfect competition environment will maximize profit when total revenue exceeds total costs by the greatest amount, or where its marginal revenue is equal to (rising) marginal cost. Said another way, it maximizes profit when the amount received (revenue) from the last unit sold equals the incremental (marginal) cost of producing that unit. Since, in perfect competition, each unit will be sold at the market price, marginal revenue is (the same as) market price. The relevant graph for an individual firm in a competitive market would show:

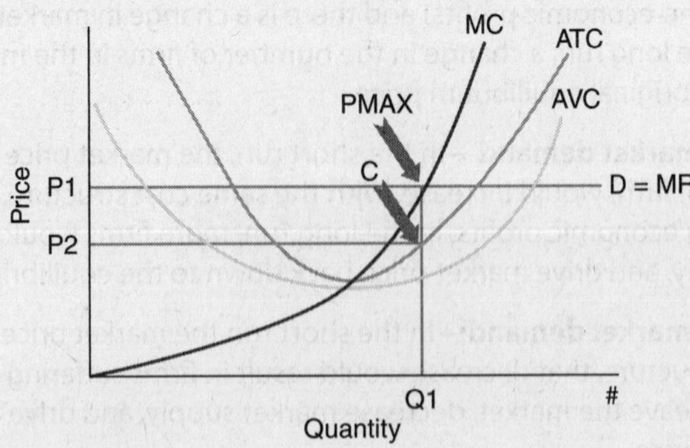

B. For the individual firm, price (P1) is set by the market; the firm must take the market price. Short-run profit would be maximized where MC intersects MR (also P1 and D), labeled PMAX at Q1 in the graph. Each unit of output up to that quantity would add more to the total revenue than to the total cost; therefore total profit would increase. Units after that quantity (Q1) would cost more to produce than the price at which the additional units could be sold; therefore, the amount of profit would decline with each additional unit greater than Q1.

C. In the above graph, total revenue would be P1 × Q1 and total cost would be P2 × Q1, which is less that P1 × Q1. Total profit would be (P1 – P2) × Q1, or on a per-unit basis PMAX – C. If, however, market demand (which is also marginal revenue and price) shifts downward, with the same cost structure, the results would be different, depending on the relationship between MR and ATC.

1. **MR = ATC**—At this level, the firm would break even (at P2 in the graph above).
2. **MR less than ATC but greater than AVC**—At this level, the firm would cover variable cost but not total cost. The excess of sales price (also D) over AVC would contribute to paying fixed cost (in the short run).
3. **MR less than AVC**—At this level, the firm would shut down because each unit it produces fails to cover the direct cost of producing the unit.

D. In the short run, when a firm in perfect competition has revenues greater than its total cost, including the required minimum return on capital invested, the firm would be earning economic profits.

III. Long-Run Analysis

A. When firms in a perfectly competitive market are making economic profit in the short run (as in the graph above), in the long run more firms will enter the market. As more firms enter the market, supply (output) increases and the market price will fall until all firms just break even. Conversely, when firms in a perfectly competitive market are suffering losses in the short run, some of the firms will exit the market, causing the market price to increase until all firms just break even. Therefore, in a perfectly competitive market, in the long run firms can earn only normal profits; there are no (economic) excess profits.

B. Because demand, price, and marginal revenue are the same, long-run equilibrium occurs where marginal revenue, marginal cost, and the lowest long-run average cost intersect.

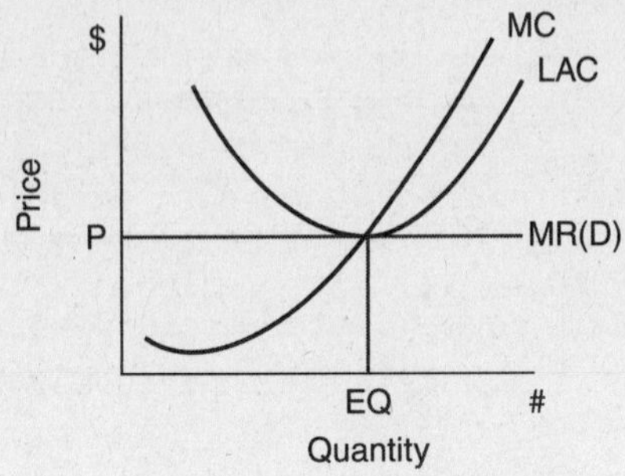

C. Thus, in the long run, at Q1, inputs are used most efficiently and price is the lowest possible.

D. If the market is in equilibrium (i.e., market supply = market demand; all firms are just breaking even—there are no economic profits) and there is a change in market demand, price will initially change, but in the long run, a change in the number of firms in the market will tend to drive the price back to the original equilibrium price.

1. **Increase in market demand**—In the short run, the market price (that must be accepted by the individual firm) would increase. With the same cost structure, that increase would result in firms earning economic profits. In the long run, more firms would enter the market, increase market supply, and drive market price back down to the equilibrium price.

2. **Decrease in market demand**—In the short run the market price would decrease. With the same cost structure, that decrease would result in firms suffering losses. In the long run firms would leave the market, decrease market supply, and drive market price back up to the equilibrium price.

E. Firm Strategy

A. In a perfectly competitive market, there is no product differentiation; all firms sell an identical product or service. Therefore, firms must focus on innovation in production, distribution, and sales processes rather than on the good or service sold.

B. Financial success depends on being the lowest-cost producer in the market.

Perfect Monopoly

This lesson considers the conditions constituting a perfectly monopolistic market, which is one end of a hypothetical market structures continuum. Example market descriptions include the nature of demand, revenue, costs, and profit in both the short-run and long-run.

After studying this lesson, you should be able to:

1. Describe the characteristics of a perfect monopoly market structure.
2. Describe the relevant cost curves and their relationships in perfect monopoly.
3. Identify the optimum level of output and price in a perfectly monopoly market structure in both: a) short-term analysis and b) long-term analysis.
4. Describe basic firm strategy in a perfectly monopolistic market.

I. Characteristics

A. Perfect monopoly exists in industries or markets characterized by:

1. A single seller
2. A commodity for which there are no close substitutes
3. Restricted entry into the market

B. A monopoly may exist as a result of:

1. Control of raw material inputs or processes (e.g., a patent)
2. Government action (e.g., a government granted franchise)
3. Increasing return to scale (or natural monopolies) (e.g., public utilities)

C. In a perfect monopoly market, a single firm is the industry. Therefore, for that firm the demand curve takes the traditional negative slope (down and to the right).

II. Short-Run Analysis

A. In the short run a monopolistic firm will maximize profit where marginal revenue is equal to (rising) marginal cost. Because the demand curve is downward sloping, in order to sell additional units, the firm must (continuously) lower its price. Therefore, the marginal revenue curve will be below the demand curve. The price charged at the point of profit maximization (MR = MC) is determined by the level of the demand curve for that quantity. These relationships are graphed as:

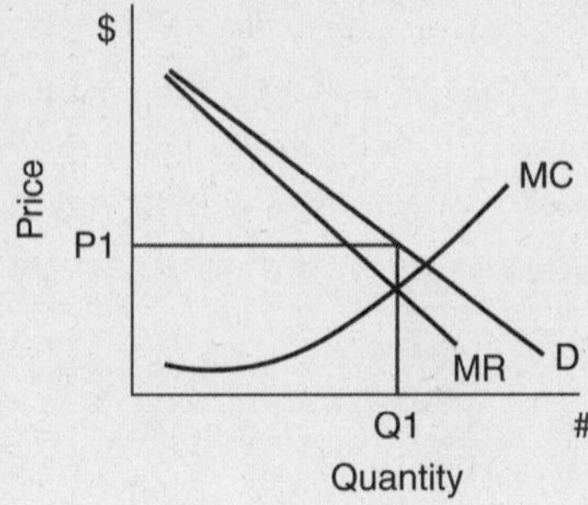

B. In the graph, the firm maximizes profit at Q1 (MR = MC) and can sell that quantity at the price level called for by demand, or P1 in the graph. Whether the monopolistic firm makes a profit depends on the average cost (AC) of producing at Q1. The following results are possible:

1. **Profit**: If AC < P1
2. **Breakeven**: If AC = P1
3. **Loss**: If AC > P1.

C. Since demand is fixed in the short run, the monopolistic firm can increase revenue only by selling at different prices to different customers, a concept known as price discrimination. For example, the firm could sell at different prices to different classes of customers or in different markets (e.g., residential customers vs. commercial customers for essentially the same service). Since some of Q1 will be sold at more than P1, total revenue and total profits will increase.

III. Long-Run Analysis

A. If a firm maintains its monopolistic position in the long run, it has two basic ways to improve its total profits:

1. Reduce its cost by changing the size of its plant so as to produce the best level of long-run production
2. Increase demand for its commodity through advertising, promotion, etc.

B. Like the firm in a perfectly competitive environment, the monopolistic firm will produce where MR = MC. In either environment, to produce at a lesser quantity (MR greater than MC) or at a greater quantity (MC greater than MR) would result in less total revenue than MR = MC. For the monopolistic firm, however, production at MR = MC results in an inefficient use of resources and a higher price than would result from a firm with the same costs under perfect competition. These less than optimum outcomes occur because for the monopolistic firm facing a downward sloping demand curve MR (at MC) is less than P, whereas for an individual firm in perfect competition MR = P (=D). (Recall that in a perfectly competitive environment the **market** demand is downward sloping, but for a **single firm** in that environment the demand curve is horizontal and the firm can sell any quantity at the market price.)

IV. Firm Strategy

A. By definition, the monopolistic firm has no competition and, therefore, there are no normal market forces on the setting of price. As a consequence, governments generally impose regulations that restrict the setting of price by a monopoly firm.

B. To lessen the degree of regulation, monopolies tend to spend more on public relations and lobbying to influence public opinion and government regulation than do firms in other markets.

C. As noted above, a monopolistic firm will focus its strategy on seeking the level of production capability that best meets its demand and on advertising to increase that demand.

Monopolistic Competition

This lesson considers monopolistic competition, the conditions that would constitute a market structure blended of competition and monopoly. Illustrative market descriptions include the nature of demand, revenue, costs, and profit in both the short-run and long-run.

After studying this lesson, you should be able to:

1. Describe the characteristics of a monopolistic competitive market structure.
2. Describe the relevant cost curves and their relationships in monopolistic competition.
3. Identify the optimum level of output and price in a monopolistic competitive market structure in both: a) short-term analysis and b) long-term analysis.
4. Describe basic firm strategy in a monopolistic competitive market.

I. Characteristics

A. Monopolistic competition exists in industries or markets characterized by:

1. A large number of sellers
2. Firms sell a differentiated product or service (similar but not perceived as identical), for which there are close substitutes
3. Firms can easily enter or leave the market

B. Thus, this market environment has elements of both perfect competition and perfect monopoly.

II. Short-Run Analysis

A. A monopolistic competitive environment has a downward sloping demand curve that is highly elastic. It is downward sloping because of product differentiation and highly elastic because there are close substitutes for the good or service. Again, optimum profit (and output) occur where MR = MC (provided P > AVC). The following graph is representative:

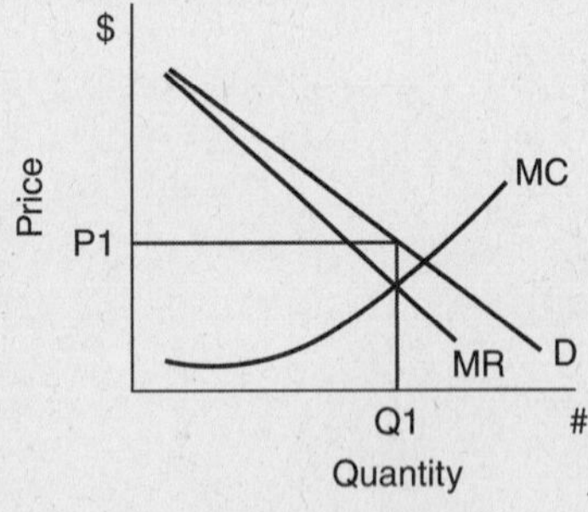

B. MR = MC at Q1 with a price of P1. Whether the firm makes a profit, breaks even, or has a loss depends on its average cost curve (AC) at Q1. The following short-run results are possible:

1. **Profit:** If AC < P1
2. **Break even:** If AC = P1
3. **Loss:** If AC > P1

III. Long-Run Analysis

A. If firms in a monopolistic competitive environment experience short-run profits, in the long run, more firms will enter the industry. More firms in the industry result in a lower demand curve for each firm. Equilibrium will result where the demand curve becomes tangential to the average cost curve and each firm just breaks even. Conversely, if firms are experiencing losses in the long run, firms will leave the industry and the demand curve will shift up so that remaining firms just break even.

B. A firm in a monopolistic competitive environment incorrectly allocates economic resources in the long run (when compared with firms in perfect competition) because the price at which it sells is greater than the marginal cost of production. Further, such firms operate with smaller-scale plants than the optimum and, consequently, more firms than would exist in perfect competition.

IV. Firm Strategy

A. Firms in a monopolistic competitive market commonly attempt to differentiate their product or service by focusing on product development and innovation.

B. To differentiate existing products/services and to develop successful new products, firms will engage in extensive market research.

C. In addition, these firms engage in extensive advertising and development of customer relations.

D. When competing online, these firms will be concerned with providing a convenient online shopping experience, providing complete and accurate product descriptions, and offering a competitive return policy.

Oligopoly

This lesson considers the final market structure, oligopoly. It describes the nature of an oligopoly market, as well as the production and profit characteristics in both the short-run and long-run in such a market.

After studying this lesson, you should be able to:

1. Describe the characteristics of an oligopoly market structure.
2. Describe the relevant cost curves and their relationships in an oligopoly market.
3. Identify the optimum level of output and price in a oligopoly market structure in both: a) short-term analysis and b) long-term analysis.
4. Describe basic firm strategy in an oligopolistic market.

I. Characteristics

A. Oligopoly exists in industries or markets characterized by:

1. A few sellers
2. Firms sell either a homogeneous product (standardized oligopoly) or a differentiated product (differentiated oligopoly).
3. Restricted entry into the market

B. Because there are few firms in an oligopolistic market, the actions of each firm are known by, and affect, other firms in the market. Therefore, if one firm lowers its price to increase its share of the market (demand), other firms in the market are likely to reduce their prices as well. In the extreme, a "price war" will result. Consequently, oligopolistic firms tend to compete on factors other than price (e.g., quality, service, distinctions, etc.).

C. In order to change prices without triggering a price war, oligopolistic firms may engage in either overt or tacit collusion. Overt collusion, in which firms (a cartel) conspire to set output, price, or profit, is illegal in the United States. The Organization of Petroleum Exporting Countries (OPEC) is an example of a cartel. Tacit collusion occurs when the firms tend to follow price changes initiated by the price leader in the market. Tacit collusion (firms do not conspire in setting output, price, or profits) is not illegal in the United States.

II. Short-Run/Long-Run Analysis

A. There is no one, universally accepted theory of an oligopoly. As a result of the observed inflexibility of prices in oligopolistic markets, the most common economic representation uses a kinked demand curve. The relevant graph would show:

Short-Run Graph in Oligopoly

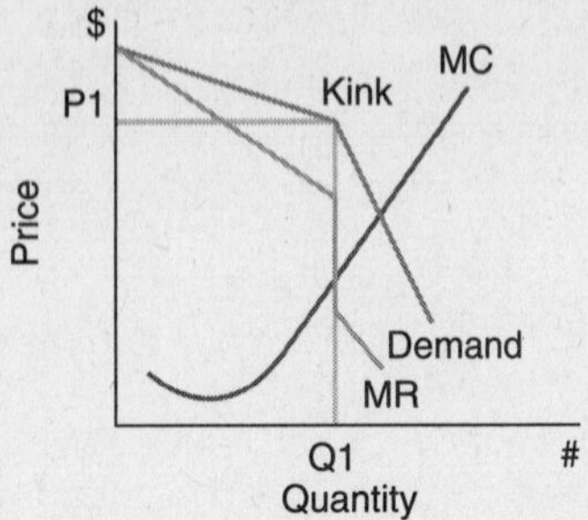

B. The kinked demand curve results from the fact that there are few firms, each of which knows and responds to the actions of other firms. If you assume from that characteristic that rival firms will lower prices if you lower your price but will not raise prices if you raise your price, the demand curve will kink at the established current price. That reflects that prices will be more elastic above the kink (if a firm raises its price, it loses a disproportionate number of customers) and more inelastic below the kink (if a firm lowers its price, others will too, so it won't gain a disproportionate number of customers).

1. With the kinked demand curve, the MR curve will have a vertical portion at the quantity of the kink.
2. If MC changes along the vertical portion of the MR curve, neither quantity nor price would change. The quantity will be at the level where MR = MC, and, because MR is vertical, there is no change in quantity (Q1 in the graph). The price will not change either; it will still be at the level of the kink in the demand curve (P1 in the graph).

C. In the short run, the oligopolistic firm will produce where MC = MR and may make a profit, break even, or have a loss, depending on the relationship between price and average cost for the quantity produced. In the long run, however, firms incurring losses (because average cost exceeds market price) will cease to operate in the industry. Further, firms operating at a profit (because average cost is less than market price) can continue to make profits in the long run because new firms are restricted from entering the market.

D. As with monopolies and monopolistically competitive firms, oligopolistic firms produce at the quantity of output where MR = MC and, therefore, where P > MC. Consequently, the oligopolistic firm under allocates resources to production and produces less, but charges more than would occur in a perfectly competitive market.

III. Firm Strategy

A. Because firms operating in an oligopoly market are interdependent, they must focus considerable strategic attention on the actions and anticipated actions of competitors, especially with respect to the setting of price.

B. In order to avoid price wars, firms tend to compete on factors other than price, including the quality of their good/service, customer relations, loyalty programs, and the like.

C. When faced with the prospect of new entrants into the industry, firms may take strategic action to discourage such entry, including developing excess capacity to provide its good/service, enhancing relationships with distributors, and engaging in extensive advertising of its good/service to make it more difficult for new entrants to penetrate the market.

Summary of Market Structure

After studying this lesson, you should be able to:

1. Recall the characteristics of four common market structures.
2. Recognize the major similarities and differences of the four major market structures.

I. A Mix of Structures

A. The U.S. economy is a mix of market economic structures. Different commodities (goods and services) and industries tend to operate in different market structures.

1. **Perfect competition**—While a perfectly competitive segment of the U.S. economy may not exist in today's sociopolitical environment, the framework of a perfectly competitive market provides a useful model for understanding fundamental economic concepts and for evaluating other market structures.
2. **Monopoly**—Exists where there is a single provider of a good or service for which there are no close substitutes. Monopolistic firms do exist in the U.S. economy. Historically, public utilities have been permitted to operate as monopolies with the justification that market demand can be fully satisfied at a lower cost by one firm than by two or more firms. To limit the economic benefits of such monopolies, governments generally impose regulations, which affect pricing, output and/or profits. Monopolies also can exist as a result of exclusive ownership of raw materials or patent rights. In most cases, however, exclusive ownership monopolies are of short duration as a result of the development of close substitutes, the expiration of rights, or government regulation.
3. **Monopolistic competition**—Common in the U.S. economy, especially in general retailing where there are many firms selling similar (but not identical) goods and services. Because their products are similar, monopolistic competitive firms engage in extensive non-price competition, including advertising, promotion, and customer service initiatives, all of which are common in the contemporary U.S. economy.
4. **Oligopoly**—Exists in markets where there are few providers of a good or service. Such markets exist for a number of industries in the U.S. The markets for many metals (steel, aluminum, copper, etc.) are oligopolistic. So also are the markets for such diverse products as automobiles, cigarettes and oil. Firms in oligopolistic markets tend to avoid price competition for fear of creating a price war, but do rely heavily on non-price competition.

B. Market Structures' Characteristics Summary

Market Characteristics Summary

Characteristic	Perfect Competition	Monopolistic Competition	Oligopoly	Perfect Monopoly
# of Firms	Very Many	Many	Few	One
Type of Product	Homogenous	Differentiated	Homogenous or Differentiated	Unique
Ease of Entry	Very Easy	Fairly Easy	Difficult	Very Difficult
Firm Price Setting Ability	None (Price Taker)	Some	Limited	Full (Price Setter)
Long-Run Profits	None	None	Possible	Possible
Economic Efficiency	High	Less Than PC	Less Than PC	None
Sample Industry	None	Fast Food, Cosmetics	Oil, Cigarettes	Some Utilities

Macroeconomics

Introduction to Macroeconomics

Macroeconomics is concerned with the economic activities and outcomes of an entire economy, typically an entire nation, or a region consisting of a set of nations. This lesson defines macroeconomics and develops a five-sector model of the major elements and flows that constitute a macroeconomy.

After studying this lesson, you should be able to:

1. Define macroeconomics.
2. Describe the five major sectors of a macro-economy and the nature of the economic relationships and flows between the sectors.

I. **Introduction**—Macroeconomics is concerned with the economic activities and outcomes of an entire economy, typically an entire nation or region comprising several nations. The most common issues considered, all of which are covered in the following lessons, relate to:

   A. Aggregate demand
   B. Aggregate supply
   C. Business cycles
   D. Inflation/deflation
   E. Gross measures of activity and status
   F. Role of government

II. **Flow Model Expanded**

   A. In the section on microeconomics we developed a two-sector free-market flow model, which showed the flows of resources and payments between individuals and business firms.
   B. For the purposes of macroeconomic analysis we need to expand that flow model to incorporate the role of additional entities in the economy, including:
      1. Government
      2. Financial sector
      3. Foreign sector

C. The following model shows the basic flows in a five-sector free-market flow model:

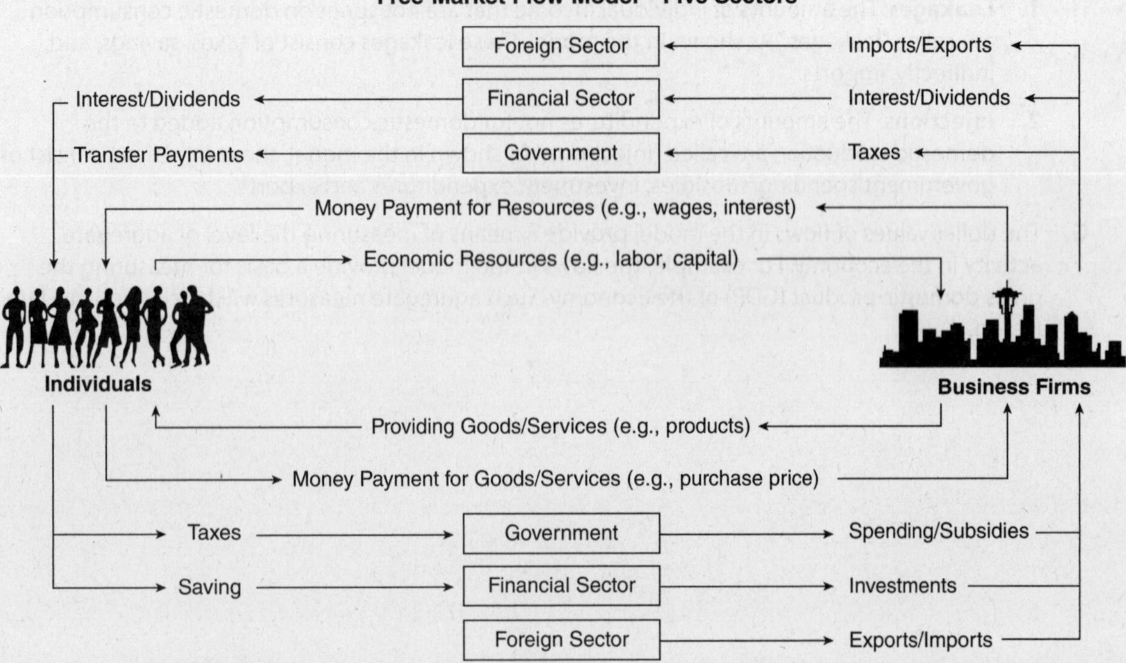

D. In the top half of the model (working from the center up):

1. The flow of economic resources from individuals to business firms and the flow of money payments for resources from business firms to individuals are shown as in the earlier two-sector model.
2. The flow of taxes (e.g., corporate income taxes) from business firms to government and the flow of payments (social security, welfare, etc.) from government to individuals are shown.
3. The flow of interest/dividends (e.g., return on investments) from business firms to the financial sector and the flow of interest/dividends (e.g., return on savings) from financial sector to individuals are shown.
4. The flow of exports from business firms as imports to foreign buyers is shown while reciprocal payment is implied.

E. In the bottom half of the model (working from the center down):

1. The flow of goods/services from business firms to individuals and the flow of money payments for goods/services from individuals to business firms are shown as in the earlier two-sector model.
2. The flow of taxes (e.g., personal income taxes) from individuals to government is shown and the flow of payments (e.g., purchases, subsidies) from the government to business firms is shown.
3. The flow of savings from individuals to the financial sector and the flow of investments from the financial sector to business firms are shown.
4. The flow of exports from the foreign sector as imports to business firms is shown; reciprocal payment is implied.

F. Because of including the additional sectors, the equality between flows to/from individuals and from/to business firms, which is assumed in the two-sector model, no longer holds.

1. **Leakages**: The amounts of individual income that are not spent on domestic consumption are called "leakages." As shown in the model, these leakages consist of taxes, savings, and, indirectly, imports.
2. **Injections**: The amounts of expenditures not for domestic consumption added to the domestic production are called "injections." As shown in the model, these injections consist of government spending/subsidies, investment expenditures and exports.

G. The dollar values of flows in the model provide a means of measuring the level of aggregate activity in the economy. For example, the flows in the model provide a basis for measuring the gross domestic product (GDP) of the economy. Such aggregate measures will be covered in a later lesson.

Aggregate Demand

At the macroeconomic (economy) level, demand measures the total spending of all entities on goods and services in an economy at different price levels. This lesson describes aggregate demand and analyzes the role of individual consumers, businesses, investment spending, governmental entities, and net foreign spending in determining aggregate demand.

After studying this lesson, you should be able to:

1. Define aggregate demand, and identify the components that constitute aggregate demand.
2. Describe the role the components of aggregate demand play in establishing the level of aggregate demand.
3. Define and calculate the average and marginal propensity to consume and to save.
4. Define discretionary fiscal policy and how it may be used to influence aggregate demand.
5. Identify and describe the factors that cause a shift in aggregate demand (and the demand curve).
6. Define the multiplier effect and its role in determining aggregate demand, and compute changes in aggregate demand using the multiplier effect.

I. Introduction

A. Aggregate Demand Curve—At the macroeconomic (economy) level, demand measures the total spending of individuals, businesses, governmental entities, and net foreign spending on goods and services at different price levels. The demand curve that results from plotting the aggregate spending (AD) is negatively sloped and can be represented as:

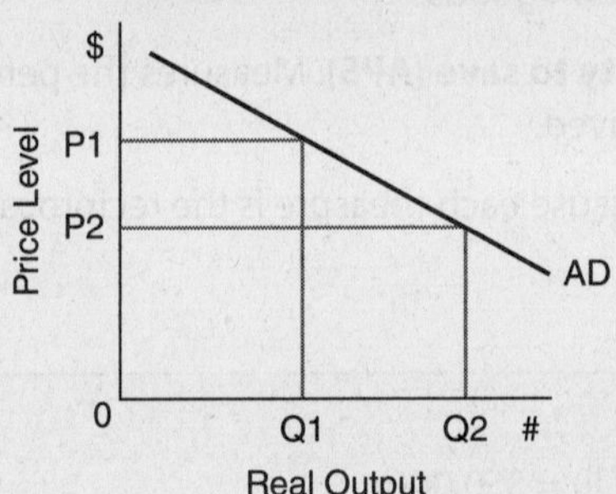

B. Like its microeconomic counterpart, the aggregate demand curve shows quantity demanded at various prices (aggregate prices = price level), assuming all other variables that affect spending are held constant (*ceteris paribus*). Thus, aggregate demand at price level P2 will be greater (Q2) than at price level P1 with demand Q1.

C. Components of Aggregate Demand—Aggregate demand is the total spending by individual consumers (*consumption* spending), businesses on *investment* goods, by *governmentalentities*, and foreign entities on *net exports*. Each is considered in the following subsections.

II. Consumer Spending—Spending on consumable goods accounts for about 70% of total spending (aggregate demand) in the United States. Personal income and the level of taxes on personal income are the most important determinants of consumption spending. Personal income less related income taxes determines individual income available for spending, called "personal disposable income." The

relationship between consumption spending (CS) and disposable income (DI) is the consumption function. Graphically, the consumption function can be plotted as a positively sloped curve.

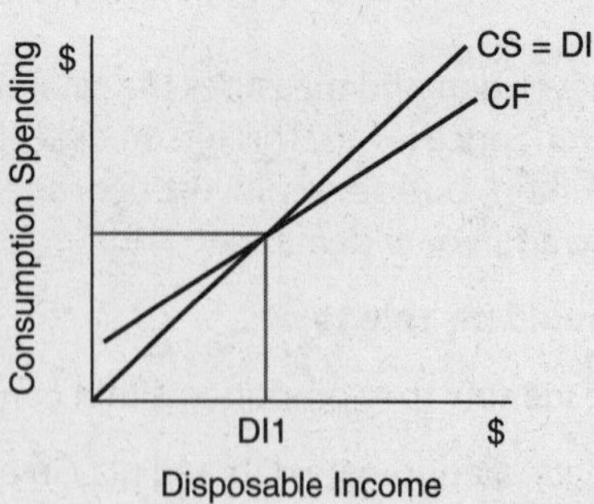

A. At the intersection of the CS = DI and CF (Consumption Function) curves on the graph, consumers are spending all of their disposable income. At other points on the CF curve, spending is either more or less than disposable income.

1. Where the CF curve is greater than the CS = DI curve (below DI1), consumer spending exceeds disposable income. This excess spending over disposable income can occur as a result of consumers spending accumulated savings or borrowing for current consumption spending.

2. Where the CF curve is less than the CS = DI curve (above DI1), consumers are not spending all available disposable income. The excess of disposable income over consumption spending is a measure of consumer savings.

B. Consumption/Saving Ratios—Several ratios are used to measure the relationship between consumption spending and disposable income:

1. **Average ratios**
   - a. **Average propensity to consume (APC)**: Measures the percentage of disposable income spent on consumption goods.
   - b. **Average propensity to save (APS)**: Measures the percentage of disposable income not spent, but rather saved.
   - c. APC + APS = 1 (because each measure is the reciprocal of the other)

Example

Disposable income (DI) = $50,000
Consumption spending (CS) = $45,000
Savings (S) = $ 5,000

APC = CS/DI = $45,000/$50,000 = .90 (90%)
APS = S/DI = $5,000/$50,000 = .10 (10%)
APC (.90) + APS (.10) = 1.00 (100%)

2. **Marginal ratios**
   - a. **Marginal propensity to consume (MPC)**: Measures the change in consumption as a percentage of a change in disposable income.
   - b. **Marginal propensity to save (MPS)**: Measures the change in savings as a percentage of a change in disposable income.
   - c. MPC + MPS = 1 (because each measure is the reciprocal of the other)

Example

		Before Change	After Change	Change (Δ) Amount
Disposable income (DI)	=	\$50,000	\$60,000	+\$10,000
Consumption spending (CS)	=	\$45,000	\$53,000	+\$8,000
Savings (S)	=	\$5,000	\$7,000	+\$2,000

MPC = ΔCS/ΔDI = \$8,000/\$10,000 = .80 (80%)
MPS = ΔS/ΔDI = \$2,000/\$10,000 = .20 (20%)
MPC (.80) + MPS (.20) = 1.00 (100%)

III. Investment

A. In the macroeconomic context, investment includes spending on:

1. Residential construction;
2. Nonresidential construction;
3. Business durable equipment; and
4. Business inventory.

B. The level of spending on these investment goods is influenced by a number of factors, including:

1. Real interest rate (nominal rate less rate of inflation)
2. Demographics (i.e., make-up of the population)
3. Consumer confidence
4. Consumer income and wealth
5. Government actions (tax rates, tax incentives, governmental spending, etc.)
6. Current vacancy rates
7. Level of capacity utilization
8. Technological advances
9. Current and expected sales levels

C. Over time, the **most significant of these factors** is the interest rate. Higher interest rates are associated with lower levels of investment spending, and lower interest rates are associated with higher levels of investment spending. The graphic representation (an investment demand [ID] curve) shows the negative relationship.

Investment Demand

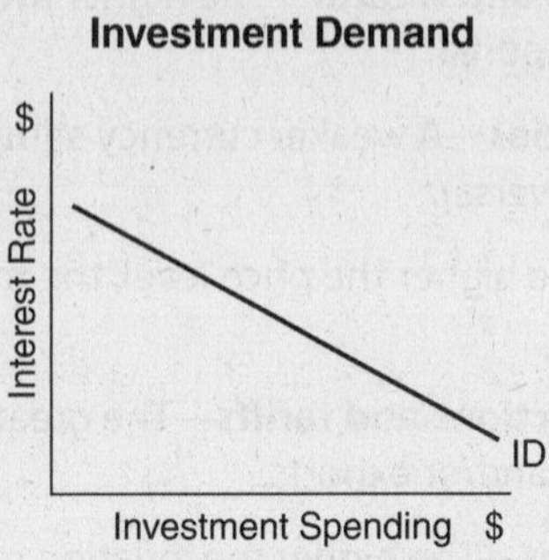

D. Investment spending is the most volatile component of aggregate spending (demand) and considered a major impetus for the business cycle. Monetary policy targets the investment component in order to moderate fluctuations of the business cycle. (See the "Business Cycles" lesson.)

IV. Government Spending and Fiscal Policy

A. Government spending increases aggregate spending (and demand) in the economy. Much of that spending comes about as a result of the reduced disposable income available to consumers due to taxes imposed to finance government spending. While taxes on income reduces aggregate demand, and government spending and transfer payments (e.g., unemployment payments, social security, etc.) increase demand, there will not be equal "offsetting" for a period because the two events—government taxing and government spending—are not absolutely interdependent, especially in the short run.

B. Consequently, government can directly affect aggregate demand by changing tax receipts, government expenditures, or both. Intentional changes by the government in its tax receipts and/or its spending, which are implemented in order to increase or decrease aggregate demand in the economy, is called **discretionary fiscal policy**.

C. The following chart summarizes possible fiscal policy initiatives to increase or decrease demand in the economy (*ceteris paribus*):

	To Increase Aggregate Demand	**To Decrease Aggregate Demand**
Government Spending	Increase	Decrease
Taxation	Decrease	Increase
Transfer Payments*	Increase	Decrease

*The spending of increased transfer payments by recipients is what increases aggregate demand; decreased transfer payments to recipients decreases their ability to spend and, therefore, decreases aggregate demand.

D. **Discretionary Fiscal Policy**—These initiatives are used to close recessionary gaps (increase demand to the full employment level) or to close inflationary gaps (reduce demand to the full employment level).

V. Net Exports/Imports

A. Exports measure foreign spending for domestic (U.S.) goods and services, while imports measure U.S. spending on foreign goods and services. Exports increase demand for domestic products; imports lower spending for domestic products. Net exports measure the excess of gross exports over gross imports.

1. When net exports are positive (exports greater than imports), aggregate demand is increased.
2. When net exports are negative (exports less than imports), aggregate demand is decreased.

B. A number of factors enter into determining a country's level of imports and exports with other countries, including:

1. **Relative levels of income and wealth**—The higher the income and wealth, the greater the spending, including on imports.
2. **Relative value of currencies**—A weaker currency stimulates exports and makes imports more expensive (and vice versa).
3. **Relative price levels**—The higher the price level, the more costly are goods/services for foreign buyers.
4. **Import and export restrictions and tariffs**—The greater the restrictions and tariffs, the lower the level of imports and/or exports.
5. **Relative inflationary rates**—The higher the inflation rate, the higher the cost of inputs, causing outputs to be more costly and less competitive in the world market.

C. During the past 20 years, the United States has been a **net import** country (negative net exports), causing a decrease in aggregate demand for U.S. goods.

VI. Aggregate Demand Curve Slope—The **aggregate demand (AD) curve,** (as shown in I. A., above) is negatively sloped because of three significant factors:

A. Interest Rate Factor—Generally, the higher the price level, the higher the interest rate. As the interest rate increases, interest-sensitive spending (e.g., new home purchases, business investment, etc.) decreases.

B. Wealth-Level Factor—As price levels (and interest rates) increase, the value of financial assets may decrease. As wealth decreases, so also may spending decrease.

C. Foreign Purchasing Power Factor—As the domestic price level increases, domestic goods become relatively more expensive than foreign goods. Therefore, spending on domestic goods decreases and spending on foreign goods increases.

VII. Aggregate Demand Curve Shift

A. If variables other than price affect total spending in the economy, aggregate demand will change and the aggregate demand curve will shift to create a new curve. The curve will shift outward (to the right) when demand increases and inward (to the left) when demand decreases. Aggregate demand typically changes as a result of the following kinds of occurrences (among others):

1. Personal taxes (e.g., income taxes)

a. Increases in personal taxes reduce personal disposable income and, therefore, reduce aggregate demand.

b. Decreases in personal taxes increase personal disposable income and, therefore, increase aggregate demand.

2. Consumer confidence

a. Increased confidence that the economy will perform favorably going forward results in consumer willingness to spend on consumer goods and services, thereby, increasing aggregate demand.

b. Decreased confidence that the economy will perform favorably going forward, or uncertainty about the future of the economy, results in consumers not being willing to spend on consumer goods and services, thereby decreasing aggregate demand.

3. Technological advances

a. New technology tends to engender increased spending by consumers and investment by business and government, resulting in increased aggregate demand.

b. The lack of new technology tends to result in deferring new investment by business and government, resulting in a decrease in aggregate demand.

4. Corporate taxes (e.g., income taxes, franchise taxes, etc.)

a. Increases in corporate taxes reduce corporate funds available for investment and distribution as dividends to shareholders, which results in decreases in both business demand and shareholder (consumer) demand.

b. Decreases in corporate taxes increase the corporate funds available to business for investment and funds available for distribution as dividends to shareholders, both of which tend to increase aggregate demand.

5. Interest rates

a. Increases in interest rates increase the cost of capital and borrowing, which results in reduced business investment and reduced consumer spending for durable goods (e.g., automobiles, major appliances, etc.), both resulting in decreased aggregate demand.

b. Decreases in interest rates decrease the cost of capital and borrowing, which results in increased business investment and increased consumer spending, both resulting in increased aggregate demand.

6. **Government spending**
   a. An increase in government spending increases aggregate demand for goods/services.
   b. A decrease in government spending decreases aggregate demand for goods/services.
7. **Exchange rates/net exports**
   a. A weakening of a country's currency relative to the currencies of other countries will cause the goods of that country to be relatively less expensive, which will cause exports to increase and imports to decrease, both of which increase net exports and increase aggregate demand.
   b. A strengthening of a country's currency relative to the currencies of other countries will cause the goods of that country to be relatively more expensive, which will cause exports to decrease and imports to increase, both of which decrease net exports and decrease aggregate demand.
8. **Wealth changes**
   a. Increases in wealth (e.g., a run-up in stock prices) foster increases in aggregate demand.
   b. Decreases in wealth foster decreases in aggregate demand.

B. Notice that government can act so as to effect increases or decreases in many of these factors (i.e., change tax rates, government spending, etc.).

C. **Multiplier Effect**

1. Factors that cause a shift in aggregate demand have a ripple effect through the economy. For example, an increase in investment spending by business results in certain increases in personal disposable income, which further spurs demand. This cascading effect on demand is called "the multiplier effect." Simply put, a change in a single factor that causes a change in aggregate demand will have a multiplied effect on aggregate demand.
2. The multiplier effect is caused by and can be calculated using the marginal propensity to consume. Recipients of additional income will spend some portion of that new income—their marginal propensity to consume a portion—which will provide income to others, a portion of which they will spend, and so on.
3. The extent of the multiplier effect can be measured as:

Multiplier Effect = Initial Change in Spending × (1/(1 − MPC))

4. Because MPC is the reciprocal of MPS, the element (1 − MPC) in the above equation is the same as (MPS). Thus, the equation can be simplified as:

Multiplier Effect = Initial Change in Spending × (1/MPS)

Example

Assume the marginal propensity to consume is .80 and that investment spending increases $10 million. While the effect of the initial spending will increase aggregate demand (output) by $10 million, it will induce additional demand so that total aggregate demand will increase $50 million, calculated as:

AD = $10 M × [1/(1 − MPC)]

AD = $10 M × [1/(1 − .80)]*

AD = $10 M × [1/.20]

AD = $10 M × 5 = $50 M

* Note: (1 − .80) is .20, the MPS.

MPC = ΔCS/ΔDI = $8,000/$10,000 = .80 (80%)

MPS = ΔS/ΔDI = $2,000/$10,000 = .20 (20%)

MPC (.80) + MPS (.20) = 1.00 (100%)

Aggregate Supply

At the macroeconomic (economy) level, supply measures the total output of goods and services in an economy at different price levels. This lesson describes aggregate supply and the three alternative supply curves used in economics: classical, Keynesian, and conventional.

After studying this lesson, you should be able to:

1. Define aggregate supply.
2. Identify and describe three alternative aggregate supply curves, including: a) classical; b) Keynesian; and c) conventional.
3. Identify and describe the factors that cause a shift in aggregate supply (and the supply curve).

I. **Three Theoretical Curves**—At the macroeconomic (economy) level, supply measures the total output of goods and services at different price levels. The exact slope of the aggregate supply curve that results from plotting the output depends on which of three theoretical curves is accepted as representing aggregate supply. These possibilities are:

   A. **Classical Aggregate Supply Curve**—This curve is completely vertical, reflecting no relationship between aggregate supply and price level.

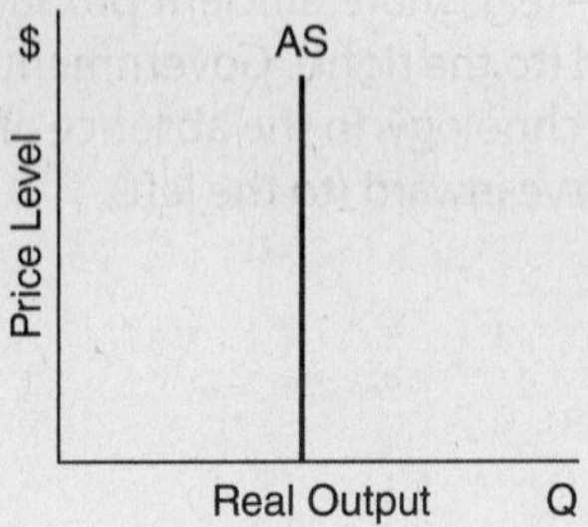

      1. This form of supply curve is sometimes associated with the nature of supply in the very short term when factors of production cannot be changed and in the long term when all inputs to the production process are fully utilized (including having full employment).

   B. **Keynesian Aggregate Supply Curve**—This curve is horizontal up to the (assumed) level of output at full employment, and then slopes upward, reflecting that output is not associated with price level until full employment is reached, at which point increased output is associated with higher price levels.

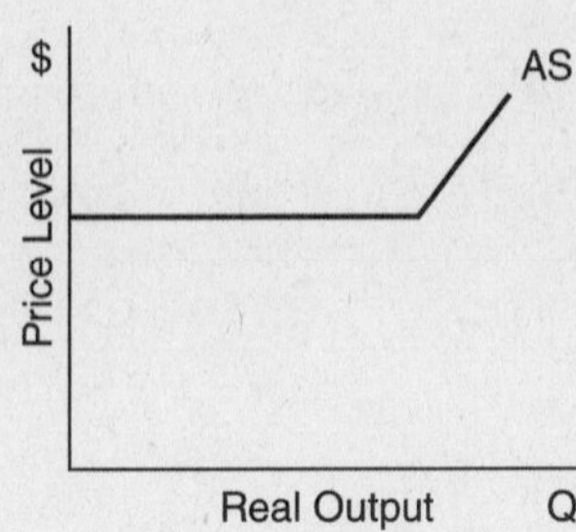

C. **Conventional Aggregate Supply Curve**—This curve has a continuously positive slope with a steeper slope beginning at the (assumed) level of output at full employment, reflecting that at full employment increased output is associated with proportionately higher increases in price levels.

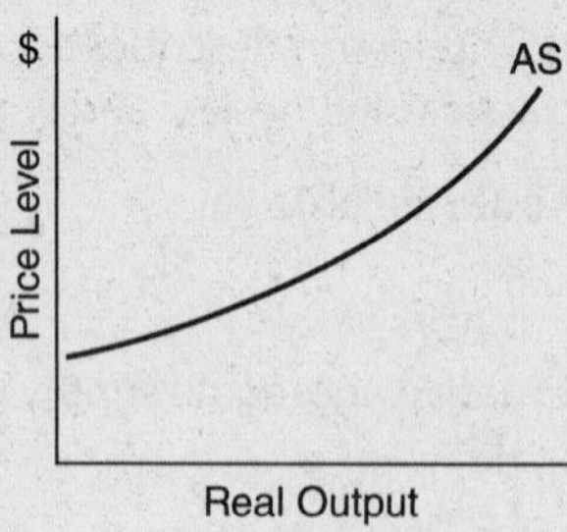

II. **Changes in Variables**—other than price level will affect aggregate supply and shift the aggregate supply curve under any of the theoretical assumptions described above. Factors that may change the position of the supply curve include:

A. **Resource Availability**—An increase in economic resources (e.g., increase in working age population) will shift the curve outward (to the right); a decrease will have the opposite effect.

B. **Resource Cost**—A decrease in the cost of economic resources (e.g., lower oil prices) will shift the curve outward (to the right); an increase would have the opposite effect.

C. **Technological Advances**—(e.g., more efficient production processes) will shift the curve outward (to the right). Government prohibitions on the use of an existing technology, in the absence of a comparable alternative, will shift the curve inward (to the left).

Note

In the remaining material, the supply curve being used will be identified.

Aggregate (Economy) Equilibrium

Aggregate equilibrium occurs when aggregate demand and aggregate supply of a multi-market economy are in balance, and in the absence of external influences, will not change. This lesson describes aggregate equilibrium and analyzes the effect on that equilibrium when externalities change aggregate demand or any of the three possible aggregate supply curve assumptions.

After studying this lesson, you should be able to:

1. Define the aggregate equilibrium of an economy.
2. Describe the effects of changes in aggregate equilibrium, assuming changes in supply and demand, when: a) shifts occur either separately or together and b) alternative supply curves are assumed.

I. Introduction

A. The equilibrium real output and price level for an economy are determined by its aggregate demand and supply curves. Graphically, equilibrium occurs where the aggregate demand and supply curves intersect. Assuming a conventional supply curve, the graph would be:

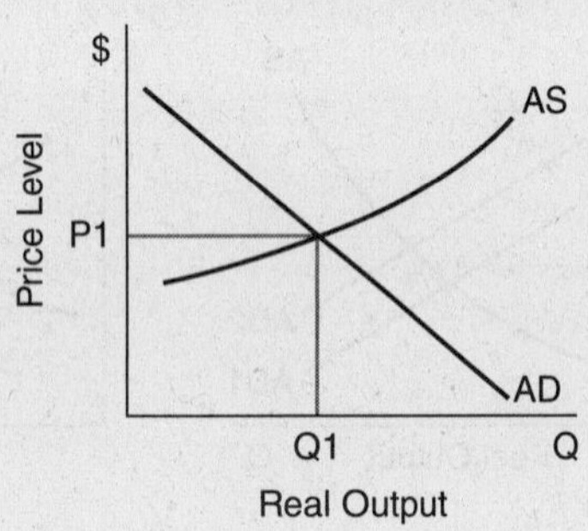

B. Equilibrium real output (real gross domestic product) would be Q1 and the price level P1. The effect of a shift in the aggregate demand and/or aggregate supply curve(s) on equilibrium output and the price level would depend on:

1. Which of the three theoretical supply curves is assumed; and
2. The degree of shift in the curve(s) relative to prechange equilibrium.

II. Classical Supply Curve

Classical Supply Curve—If the classical supply curve is assumed, an increase in aggregate demand alone results only in higher price levels. An increase in aggregate supply alone results in more output at a lower price.

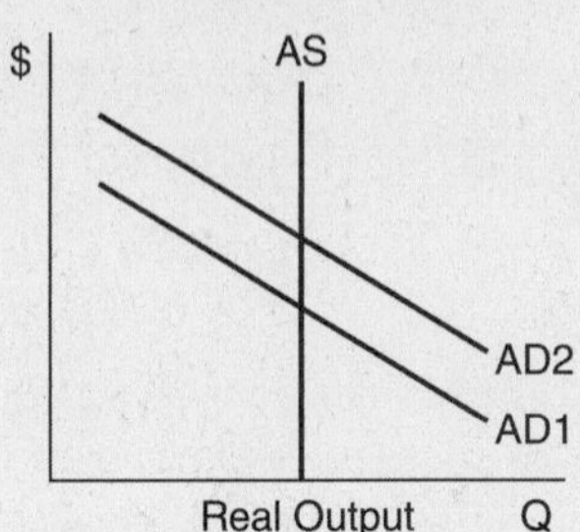

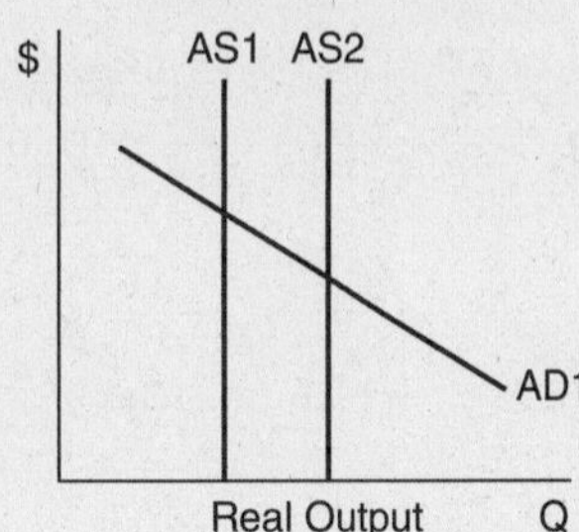

III. Keynesian Supply Curve—If the Keynesian Supply Curve is assumed, an increase in aggregate demand alone results only in more output until output at full employment, at which point output and price level each increase. An increase in supply alone will not affect either output or price level unless aggregate demand intersects supply where it is positively sloped.

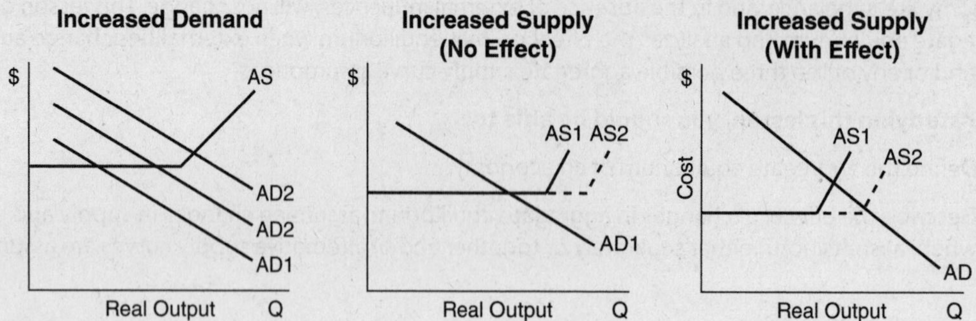

IV. Conventional Supply Curve—If the conventional supply curve is assumed, an increase in aggregate demand alone will increase both the output and the price level. An increase in supply alone will increase output, but reduce the price level.

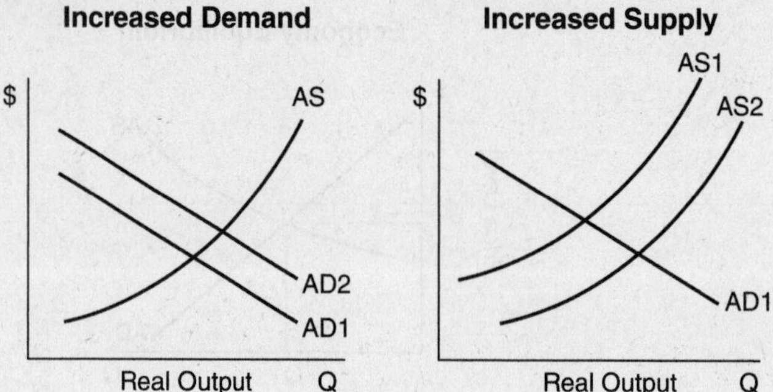

Gross Measures—Economic Activity

This lesson identifies and describes gross measures of macroeconomic activity and output, especially as they relate to the U.S. economy.

After studying this lesson, you should be able to:

1. Identify and describe the gross measures of economic activity and output, including distinguishing between: a) nominal measures and b) real measure.
2. Describe and calculate the alternative methods of computing gross domestic product.
3. Describe and graph the production-possibility frontier.

I. **Gross Measures**—Common measures of the total activity or output of the U.S. economy include:

A. **Nominal Gross Domestic Product (Nominal GDP)**—Measures the total output of final goods and services produced for exchange in the domestic market during a period (usually a year).

1. GDP does not include:

a. Goods or services that require additional processing before being sold for final use (i.e., raw materials or intermediate goods);

b. Goods produced in a prior period, but sold in the current period (those goods are included in GDP of the prior period);

c. Resale of used goods (which does not create new goods);

d. Activities for which there is no market exchange (e.g., do-it-yourself productive activities);

e. Goods or services produced in foreign countries by U.S.-owned entities (only domestically produced goods/services are included);

f. Illegal activities;

g. Transfer payments (e.g., welfare payments, social security, etc.; any effect on GDP occurs when the payments are spent on goods/services);

h. Financial transactions that simply transfer claims to existing assets (e.g., stock transactions, incurring/paying debt, etc., which in themselves do not produce a good/service); or

i. Adjustments for changing prices of goods and services over time.

2. As shown in the free-market flow model, in theory, the amount spent (expenditures) for goods and services should equal the amount received (income) for providing those goods and services. Therefore, there are two means of calculating GDP—the **expenditures approach** and the **income approach** (also called gross domestic income [GDI]).

a. **Expenditure approach**—This measures GDP using the value of final sales and is derived as the sum of the spending of:

i. **Individuals**—In the form of consumption expenditures (C) for durable and non-durable goods and for services.

ii. **Businesses**—In the form of investments (I) in residential and nonresidential (e.g., plant and equipment) construction and new inventory.

iii. **Governmental entities**—In the form of goods and services purchased by governments (G).

iv. **Foreign buyers**—In the form of net exports [exports (X) – Imports (M)] of U.S.-produced goods and services. This approach may be expressed as:

GDP = C + I + G + (X – M).

Example
U.S. 2014 GDP (actual values)

Components	Amounts in Billions
Personal consumption expenditures (C)	$11,866
Gross private domestic investment (I)	2,860
Government entities (G)	3,152
Net exports (X – M)	(530)
GROSS DOMESTIC PRODUCT (GDP)	$17,348 (Rounded)

b. **Income approach**—This measures GDP as the value of income and resource costs and is derived as the sum of:

Example
U.S. 2014 GDP (actual values)

Components	Amounts in Billions
1) Compensation to employees	$ 9,249
2) Rental income	611
3) Proprietor's income	1,347
4) Corporate profits	2,073
5) Net interest	532
6) Taxes on production and inputs	1,156
7) Depreciation (consumption of fixed capital)	2,747
8) Business transfer payments	127
Less: Government enterprise surplus	(18)
Less: Net international receipts	(263)
Less: Statistical adjustment	(212)
GROSS DOMESTIC PRODUCT (GDP)	$17,348 (Rounded)

This approach may be expressed as:

GDP (also GDI) = Wages + Self-employment income + Rent + Interest + Profits + Indirect business taxes + Depreciation + Income of foreigners

B. **Real Gross Domestic Product (Real GDP)**—Measures the total output of final goods and services produced for exchange in the domestic market during a period (usually a year) at **constant prices.**

1. **Gross domestic product (GDP) deflator**—The GDP deflator is a comprehensive measure of price levels used to derive real GDP. It relates the price paid for all new, domestically produced goods and services during a period to prices paid for goods and services in a prior reference (base) period. The specific goods and services included change from year to year based on changes in consumption and investment patterns in the economy. Using the GDP deflator, the calculation of real GDP would be:

Real GDP = (Nominal GDP/GDP Deflator) × 100

2. If the nominal GDP and the real GDP are known, the formula can be rearranged to determine the GDP deflator. That formula would be:

GDP Deflator = (Nominal GDP/Real GDP) × 100

3. Real GDP measures production in terms of prices that existed at a specific prior period; that is, it adjusts for changing prices using a price index (the GDP deflator).
4. During a period of rising prices (i.e., inflation, which is the historic norm), the application of a price index to nominal GDP can result in a real GDP that is lower than nominal GDP. A period of high inflation and a small increase in nominal GDP could result in a decrease in real GDP for the period.
5. Real GDP per capita measures the GDP per individual.
    a. Real GDP per capita is calculated as: Real GDP/Population.
    b. Real GDP per capita is a common measure of the standard of living in a country.
    c. Changes in real GDP per capita measures changes in the standard of living and, therefore, economic growth or decline.

C. **Potential Gross Domestic Product (Potential GDP)**—Measures the maximum final output that can occur in the domestic economy at a point in time without creating upward pressure on the general level of prices in the economy. The point of maximum final output will be a point on the production-possibility frontier for the economy.

1. The production-possibility frontier is the (conceptual) maximum amount of various goods and services an economy can produce at a given time with available technology and full utilization of current economic resources. It is commonly estimated by adjusting GDP for business cycle and unemployment factors.
2. A production-possibility frontier represented by a curve in a simple two-dimensional graph (assuming available inputs are totally committed to only two outputs) would be shown as:

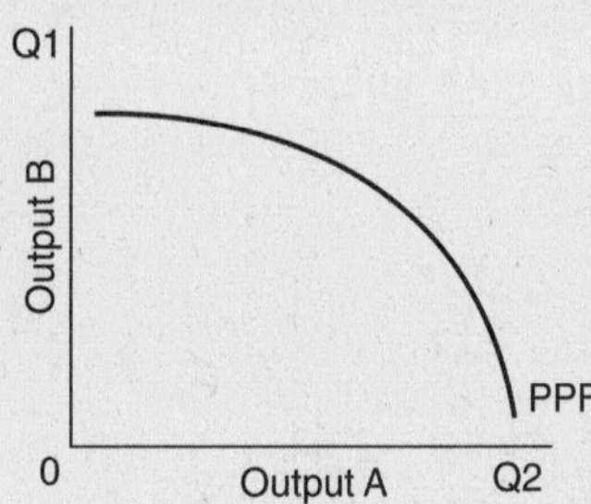

3. The curve Q1 to Q2 conceptually shows the various maximum combinations (potential production) of products A and B that could be produced with available inputs and technology.
4. If the curve Q1 to Q2 is assumed to represent all possible goods and services, then:
    a. Points on the curve represent all input resources (labor, plant capacity, etc.) used to generate maximum output. There is no inefficiency in the economy.
    b. At points within the curve actual output (i.e., real GDP) is less than potential output (potential GDP). The difference (potential GDP – real GDP) is the (negative) GDP gap, a measure of inefficiency in the economy.
    c. At points outside the curve actual output (i.e., real GDP) exceeds potential output and there is a positive GDP gap, which will result in price level increases.

D. **Net Domestic Product (NDP)**—Measures GDP less a deduction for "capital consumption" during the period—the equivalent of depreciation. Thus, NDP is GDP less the amount of capital that would be needed to replace capital consumed during the period.

E. **Gross National Product (GNP)**—Measures the total output of all goods and services produced worldwide using economic resources of U.S. entities. In 1992 GNP was replaced by GDP as the primary measure of the U.S. economy. GNP includes both the cost of replacing capital (the depreciation factor) and the cost of investment in new capital.

F. **Net National Product (NNP)**—Measures the total output of all goods and services produced worldwide using economic resources of U.S. entities, but unlike GNP, NNP includes only the cost of investment in new capital (i.e., no amount is included for depreciation).

G. **National Income**—Measures the total payments for economic resources included in the production of all goods and services, including payments for wages, rent, interest, and profits, but not indirect business taxes included in the cost of final output (sales taxes, business property taxes, etc.).

H. **Personal Income**—Measures the amount (portion) of national income, before personal income taxes, received by individuals.

I. **Personal Disposable Income**—Measures the amount of income individuals have available for spending, after taxes are deducted from total personal income.

Gross Measures—Employment/Unemployment

Employment (especially unemployment) is an important indicator of the economic performance of an economy. This lesson considers measures of employment and unemployment as carried out in the United States.

After studying this lesson, you should be able to:

1. Describe how employment and unemployment are measured in the United States.
2. Describe what constitutes the labor force.
3. Identify and describe the various categories of the unemployed, including: a) frictional unemployment; b) structural unemployment; c) seasonal unemployment; and d) cyclical unemployment.
4. Describe and calculate the unemployment rate and the natural rate of unemployment.

I. **Employment/Unemployment Measures**—Measures of the level of employment and unemployment in the U.S. economy, and associated characteristics.

   A. In the U.S., official employment/unemployment measures are determined by the Bureau of Labor Statistics (BLS), a unit of the U.S. Department of Labor. The data the BLS provides comes primarily from two different surveys, the Current Employment Survey and the Current Population Survey:

      1. **Current Employment Survey (CES):** A monthly sample survey of 160,000 businesses and government entities designed to measure employment (only), with industry and geographical details

      2. **Current Population Survey (CPS):** A monthly sample survey of approximately 60,000 households designed to measure both employment and unemployment, with demographic details

   B. In developing measures of employment/unemployment, the population is considered to be comprised of two major subsets: (1) those in the labor (or work) force, and (2) those not in the labor force. The (civilian) labor force consists of those individuals at least 16 years old who are working (excluding those on active military duty) or who are seeking work; all others are not considered part of the labor force (including those who previously were seeking employment but have become discouraged and are no longer looking for work). Macroeconomic employment/unemployment statistics are based almost exclusively on the size of the labor force.

   C. The labor force, in turn, is comprised of two subgroups: (1) the employed (employment), and (2) the unemployed (unemployment):

      1. **Employment measures:** While the primary focus of employment-related measures is concerned with the unemployed, measures of the employed provide information not only about the level of employment, but also details about the characteristics of the labor force. Those details include employment statistics by race, sex, age, marital status, educational attainment, class of worker (e.g., agricultural, government, private industry, self-employed, etc.) and full-time/part-time status.

      2. **Unemployment measures:** The primary focus of employment-related measures is concerned with the unemployed (i.e., measures of unemployment). In addition to statistics, which provide details similar to those provided for the employed, unemployment statistics provide information by duration of unemployment and unemployment by occupation and industry. In order to better understand unemployment, economists and policy-makers have established categories, which seek to describe the causes of and reasons for unemployment. These categories include:

         a. **Frictional unemployment:** Members of the labor force who are not employed because they are in transition or have imperfect information. For example, members of the labor force who are in search of a job that is in line with their talents (education, skills, experience, etc.) or who are moving to a different part of the country.

b. **Structural unemployment:** Members of the labor force who are not employed because their prior types of jobs have been greatly reduced or eliminated and/or because they lack the skills needed for available jobs. For example, the advent of computers and accounting software has greatly reduced the demand for bookkeepers in the economy.

c. **Seasonal unemployment:** Members of the labor force who are not employed because their work opportunity regularly and predictably varies by the season of the year. For example, schoolteachers are regularly unemployed during summer months when school is not in session. (This category sometimes is viewed as a kind of temporary structural unemployment.)

d. **Cyclical unemployment:** Members of the labor force who are not employed because a downturn in the business cycle (i.e., an economic contraction) has reduced the current need for workers.

3. **Special employment/unemployment concepts:** In considering measures of employment/unemployment, the following should be understood:

   a. The official unemployment rate is the percentage of the labor force that is not employed, not the percentage of the population that is not employed. The calculation would be:

Unemployment Rate = Unemployed (including all categories)/Size of Labor Force

   b. The natural rate of unemployment is the percentage of the labor force that is not employed as a result of frictional, structural and seasonal unemployment. The calculation would be:

Natural Rate of Unemployment = Frictional + Structural + Seasonal Unemployed/Size of Labor Force

   c. Officially, full employment is when there is no cyclical unemployment. Even with frictional, seasonal, and structural unemployment, officially, full employment can exist. Said another way, if unemployment is due solely to frictional, structural and seasonal causes (i.e., the natural rate of unemployment), the economy is in a state of full employment.

In the News—The official unemployment rate reported for November 2010 was 9.8%. But, the monthly official unemployment rate does not show the entire picture. The Bureau of Labor Statistics (BLS) segments the population in other, more inclusive ways that indicate the full scope of the (unemployment) problem.

15,100,000 people counted by the BLS as "unemployed," and the basis for the 9.8%.

But that doesn't take into account …

+ 1,300,000 "discouraged workers" who have given up looking for work because they don't think they'll find any …

+ 1,200,000 people who want a job but aren't actively looking for other reasons (family responsibilities, for example) …

+ 9,000,000 people who are underemployed (part-timers who would prefer full-time work).

= 26,600,000 American workers who are jobless or underemployed, which comes to 17% of the labor force.

(Adapted from *Bloomberg Businessweek*, December 20, 2010—January 2, 2011, p. 37.)

4. **Model of employment/unemployment elements:** The elements and categories of employment/unemployment may be summarized as follows:

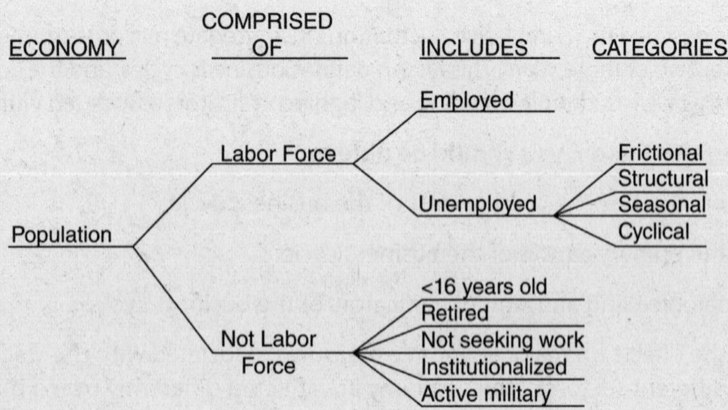

Business Cycles and Indicators

Business cycles describe the cumulative fluctuations in aggregate real gross domestic product (GDP), which generally last for two or more years. This lesson defines business cycles, and the components and causes of business cycles, as well as identifies leading and lagging indicators associated with business cycles.

After studying this lesson, you should be able to:

1. Identify and describe the components of the business cycle.
2. Describe the primary causes of the business cycle.
3. Identify major leading and lagging indicators of the business cycle.
4. Describe the effects on major economic measures associated with the stages of the business cycle and how different sectors of the economy are affected differently over a business cycle.

I. **Cyclical Economic Behavior**—"Business cycles" is the term used to describe the cumulative fluctuations (up and down) in aggregate real GDP, which generally last for two or more years.

These increases and decreases in real GDP tend to recur over time, *though with no consistent pattern of length (duration) or magnitude (intensity)*. These increases and decreases also tend to impact individual industries at somewhat different times and with different intensities. A graphic representation of generic cyclical economic behavior can be shown as:

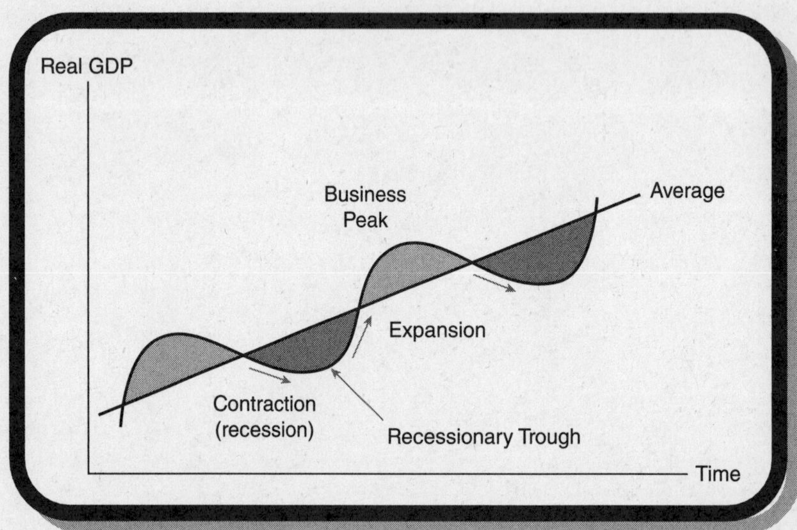

II. **Components of Business Cycle**—The following terms are used to refer to components of the business cycle:

A. **Peak**—A point in the economic cycle that marks the end of rising aggregate output and the beginning of a decline in output (the Business Peak in the graph).

B. **Trough**—A point in the economic cycle that marks the end of a decline in aggregate output and the beginning of an increase in output (the Recessionary Trough in the graph).

C. **Economic Expansion or Expansionary Period**—Periods during which aggregate output is increasing (periods from Trough to Peak in the graph); normally of longer duration than recessionary periods.

D. **Economic Contraction or Recessionary Period**—Periods during which aggregate output is decreasing (periods from Peak to Trough in the graph); normally of shorter duration than expansionary periods.

III. Business Cycles—Economic Measures and Sector Performance

A. The different stages of the economy are associated with economic measures and indicators, such as GDP, unemployment, inflation, interest rates, and inventory-to-sales ratios. These relationships are outlined in the following table:

	Boom	Contraction	Recession	Expansion
GDP growth	peak	slowing	negative/low	growing
Unemployment	lowest	rising	highest	falling
Prices	rising	slowing	falling	low
Interest rates	peak	high/falling	low	low/rising
Inventory/sales	high	falling	low	low/rising

B. Different sectors and industries in the economy perform best in different stages of the business cycle.

1. Consumer staples and utilities are two sectors that continue to perform well in the contraction and recession phases. Examples would be food, drugs, cosmetics, tobacco, liquor, electricity, gas, and water. These goods tend to be necessities or represent a low fraction of the consumer budget. Staples and utilities have very low income elasticity; that is, there is little change in demand in relation to the change in income.
2. Cyclicals and energy do well in the early expansion stage. Examples of cyclical are savings and loans, banking, advertising, apparel, retailers, and autos. Financial firms do well because interest rates are low and rising while business and consumer borrowing grows. Other sectors do well here if they have high income elasticity; that is, the demand rises with an increase in income.
3. Basic materials and technology sectors perform well as the expansion continues. These sectors include chemicals, plastics, paper, wood, metals, semiconductors, computer hardware, and communication equipment.
4. In the late expansion and boom stage, the capital goods, financial firms, and transportation sectors do well. These sectors have high income elasticity and tend to do well when durable goods replacement increases. Examples include machinery and equipment manufacturers, airlines, trucking, railroads and corporate or institutional banking.

IV. Recession and Depression

A. Recession Defined

1. There is no official quantitative definition of a recession.
2. The National Bureau of Economic Research (NBER) defines recession as "a significant decline in economic activity spread across the country, lasting more than a few months, normally visible in real GDP growth, real personal income, employment (non-farm payrolls), industrial production and wholesale-retail sales."
3. The NBER uses that definition to establish when the U.S. economy is in a recessionary period (recession).
4. Quantitative guidelines used frequently by others (but which are not official) include:
   - **a.** A period of two or more consecutive quarters in which there is a decline in real GDP growth.
   - **b.** An economic downturn in which real GDP declines by 10% or less.

B. Depression Defined

1. There is no official quantitative definition of an economic "depression."
2. The NBER does not separately identify a circumstance or time period as being a depression.
3. Economists in general refer to a depression as an economic downturn (negative GDP) that is severe and/or long term.
4. Quantitative guidelines used by economists (but which are not official) include:
   - **a.** A decline in real GDP exceeding 10%.
   - **b.** A decline in real GDP lasting two or more years.

V. Primary Cause of Business Cycles—While no single theory fully explains the causes and characteristics of business cycles, a major cause is changes in business investment spending (i.e., on plant, equipment, etc.) and consumer spending on durable goods (i.e., on goods used over multiple periods, like major appliances, automobiles, etc.). The effects of such declines in spending are shown as follows (assuming the Keynesian supply curve):

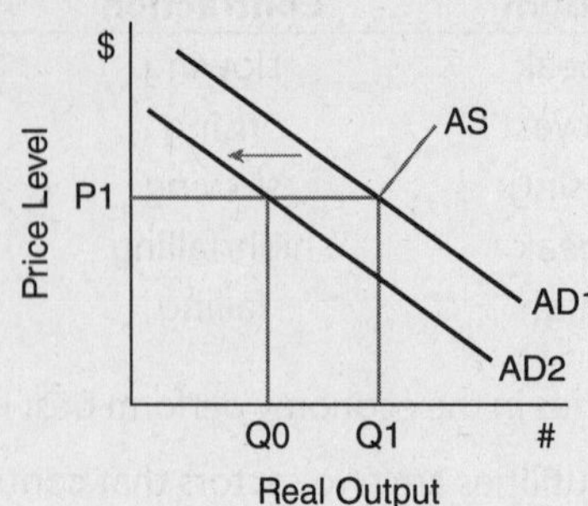

A. If the economy is in equilibrium at AD1 = AS, quantity Q1 will be produced and resources (labor, plant, and equipment, etc.) are being fully utilized. A decrease in investment and consumer spending causes demand to shift to AD2 and real output drops to Q0. The period during which output declines is recessionary and results in less than full utilization of economic resources. Unemployment will increase and plant and equipment will be underutilized.

B. As previously noted, declines in consumer and business spending may be caused by such factors as:

1. Tax increases;
2. Declining confidence in the economy; and
3. Rising interest rates and/or more difficult borrowing.

VI. Leading and Lagging Indicators of Business Cycles

A. In an effort to anticipate changes in the business cycle, economists and business groups have attempted to establish relationships between changes in the business cycle and other measures of economic activity that occur before a change in the business cycle. These measures of economic activity (which change before the aggregate business cycle) are called "leading indicators" and include measures of:

1. Consumer expectations
2. Initial claims for unemployment
3. Weekly manufacturing hours
4. Stock prices
5. Building permits
6. New orders for consumer goods
7. New order for manufactured capital goods
8. Real money supply

B. Measures of economic activity associated with changes in the business cycle, but which occur after changes in the business cycle, are called lagging or trailing indicators. These lagging indicators are used to confirm elements of business cycle timing and magnitude. Lagging indicators include measures of:

1. Changes in labor cost per unit of output
2. Ratio of inventories to sales
3. Duration of unemployment
4. Commercial loans outstanding
5. Ratio of consumer installment credit to personal income

Price Levels and Inflation/Deflation

Price is the money amount used to measure the value of goods and services. The money amounts (or prices) change over time. This lesson describes how changing prices, or different price levels, can be adjusted to a common level, how changes in the price level results in inflation or deflation, and the consequences of inflation and deflation on economic activity.

After studying this lesson, you should be able to:

1. Describe and compute certain price indexes, including: a) the Consumer Price Index and b) the gross domestic product deflator.
2. Define inflation and describe the causes of inflation, including: a) demand-induced and b) supply-induced inflation.
3. Define deflation and describe the causes of deflation.
4. Describe the consequences of inflation and deflation.

I. **Changing Prices**—Over time, changes in prices and price levels will cause changes in various measures of economic activity and economic outcomes. For example, earlier we saw that changing price levels created the need for a measure of gross domestic product (GDP) adjusted for changing price levels, called *real GDP*. Adjustments to squeeze out the effects of changing price levels on economic measures are accomplished using price indexes (or indices).

II. **Price Indexes**—Price indexes convert prices of each period to what those prices would be in terms of prices of a specific prior (or sometimes subsequent) reference period. Mathematically, the price of the reference period is set equal to 100 (100%), and the price of other periods is measured as a percentage of the reference (or base) period. Commonly used indexes prepared by the Bureau of Labor Statistics (BLS) and the Bureau of Economic Analysis (BEA) are:

   A. **Consumer Price Index (CPI-U)**—The Consumer Price Index for All Urban Consumers (published monthly) relates the prices paid by all urban consumers for a "fixed basket" of goods and services during a period to the price of the "basket" in a prior reference period. The current reference period for CPI-U is the 36-month average of prices for 1982 to 1984. The average prices in that period are taken as 100. Prices in subsequent periods are measured as percentage changes related to that base period.

      1. For example, the CPI-Us for December 2013 and 2014 were:

	CPI- U
December 2013	233.049
December 2014	234.812

      2. The December 2013 index of 233.049 indicates that prices (in the CPI-U basket) were 133.049% higher in December 2013 than they were during the 1982–1984 base period.
      3. For the period December 2013 through December 2014, the CPI-U went from 233.049 to 234.812. The change for the period is 1.763 (234.812 – 233.049), but the rate of change would be computed as (234.812 – 233.049)/233.049 = 0.00756 (or 0.756%), which is the rate of inflation (price increases) for the period December 2013 through December 2014.

   B. **Personal Consumption Expenditure Price Index (PECPI)**—Relates the average increase in prices for all domestic personal consumption using a chained index which compares one quarter's price to the previous quarter's, instead of choosing a fixed base as is done with the CPI-U (above).

1. The PECPI is benchmarked to a base of 2009 = 100.
2. The PECPI measures spending by and on hehalf of the personal sector, which includes both households and nonprofit institutions serving households. (By contrast, the CPI-U measures out-of-pocket spending by households only.)
3. The PECPI takes consumer's changing consumption patterns due to changing prices into account; the CPI-U uses a "fixed" basket of goods.

C. Purchase Price Index (PPI) (formerly Wholesale Price Index)—Measures the average change over time in the selling prices received (i.e., revenue received) by domestic producers for their output.

1. While the CPI-U includes goods and services purchased for consumption by U.S. households, the PPI includes a greater set of goods and services spanning th entire range of ouput by U.S. producers.
2. The PPI is measured by the revenue (selling price) received by producers; the CPI-U is measured by consumer expenditures.
3. The prices included in the PPI are from the first commercial transaction of producers for their domestically produced goods, services, and construction output.
4. The calculations for the PPI are done in essentially the same manner as for the CPI-U index.
5. A primary use of the PPI is to deflate revenue streams in order to measure real growth in output.

D. Gross Domestic Product (GDP) Deflator—The GDP Deflator relates nominal GDP to real GDP (both as previously defined). It is both the most comprehensive measure of price level (since GDP includes not only consumer and business spending, but also government spending and net exports) and the most contemporary measure of price level because the items included change from period to period based on changes in consumption and investment patterns in the economy.

1. The calculation is:

(Nominal GDP/Real GDP) × 100 = GDP Deflator

III. Inflation—Inflation (or inflation rate) is the annual rate of increase in the price level; deflation (or deflation rate) is the annual rate of decrease in the price level. The most common yardstick used to measure inflation or deflation in the United States is the CPI-U. Although there have been month-to-month decreases in the CPI-U (i.e., deflation), the United States has experienced annual inflation since the 1930s.

A. There are two fundamental causes of inflation, one related to demand, the other related to supply.

1. **Demand-induced (demand-pull) inflation**
   a. This results when levels of aggregate spending for goods and services exceeds the productive capacity of the economy at full employment. Consequently, the excess demand pulls up prices.

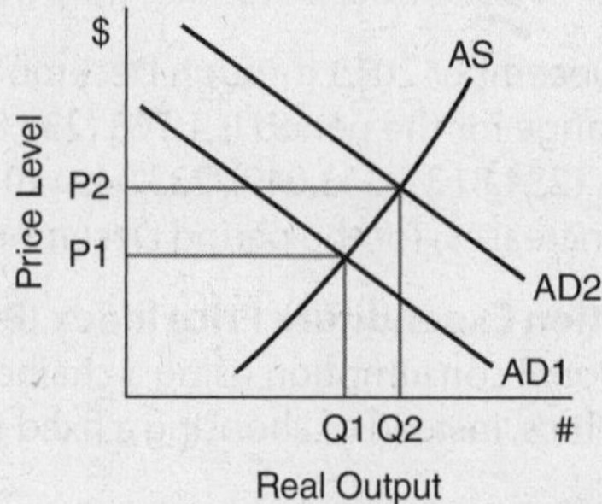

   b. If demand exceeds Q1 at price level P1, the excess demand (AD1 to AD2) increases the price level, and generally, the quantity produced (to P2 and Q2).

2. **Supply-induced (cost-push or supply-push) inflation**

   a. This results from increases in the cost of inputs to the production process—raw materials, labor, taxes, etc.—which are passed on to the final buyer in the form of higher prices. To the extent the producer absorbs the increase in cost of inputs and does not pass them on to the final buyer, inflation does not occur (or is deferred).

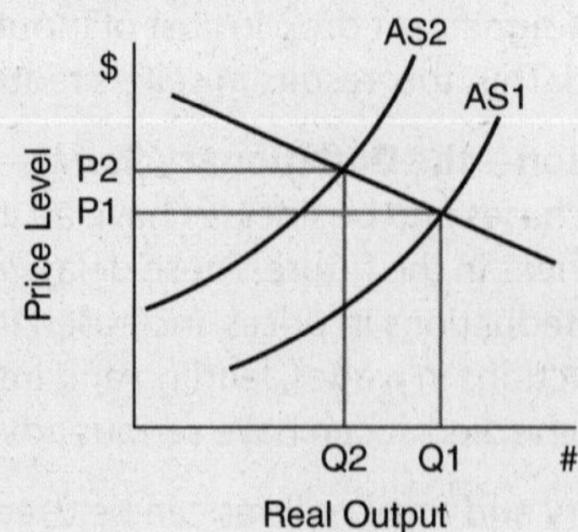

   b. An increase in the cost of inputs (say, oil) shifts aggregate supply from AS1 to AS2. As a result, the price level increases and, generally, output decreases, causing unemployment to increase.

B. Hyperinflation occurs when a country experiences a period of extremely rapid increase in the aggregate price level, resulting in extremely rapid inflation.

1. There is no formal specification of the rate of inflation that constitutes "hyperinflation."
2. Historically, the most common cause of hyperinflation has been an excessive increase in the printing of paper currency, often to fund deficit spending.

IV. Consequences of Inflation

A. The occurrence of inflation, especially when unanticipated, usually has significant economic consequences. Major consequences include:

1. **Lower current wealth and lower future real income**—Because of inflation, monetary items (those fixed in dollar amount) lose purchasing power. Consumers on fixed incomes, or those with incomes that do not keep pace with inflation, will reduce consumption. Similarly, creditors repaid with a fixed number of dollars will be able to purchase less. The effect of less consumption is a reduction in aggregate demand leading to lower output and higher unemployment.
2. **Higher interest rates**—In order to offset declines in purchasing power derived from loans, creditors increase interest rates. Higher interest rates increase the cost of borrowing, which reduces both consumer spending and business investment in capital goods. Further, lenders may tighten loan requirements, and thereby, squeeze marginal borrowers out of the market, which also would reduce spending.
3. **Uncertainty of economic measures**—The changing real value of the dollar makes it an uncertain measure for making economic decisions. Price increases create uncertainty about future costs, prices, profitability, and cash flows. Consequently, individuals and businesses are likely to postpone investments which, in turn, reduces current demand and future productive capacity.

B. Because inflation has significant adverse consequences for the economy, control of inflation is a primary economic objective of government fiscal and monetary policy.

V. Deflation—Deflation (or deflation rate) is the annual rate of decrease in the price level.

Note: Deflation is different from disinflation, which is a decline in the rate of inflation. For example, if the inflation rate was 5% in Year 1 and 4% in Year 2, prices are still increasing but at a slower rate. This is **disinflation**. This is almost always a good thing. For example, if you have a bond with a 5% return and inflation is 3%, your real return is 2%. If inflation slows to 2%, your real return is now 3%.

A. Like inflation, deflation may be caused by changes in aggregate demand and/or aggregate supply.

1. Demand changes can result in deflation when there is a significant decrease in demand (e.g., as might be caused by a significant drop in consumer confidence about the economy) which results in a widespread reduction in prices by sellers in an attempt to stimulate sales.

2. Supply changes can result in deflation when there is an increase in aggregate supply (e.g., as might be caused by a significant drop in cost of inputs) that significantly exceeds an increase in aggregate demand. This, too, results in sellers reducing prices in an effort to increase sales.

B. **Consequences of Deflation—the Deflationary Spiral**—When prices are falling, consumers have an incentive to delay purchases and businesses have an incentive to delay investments, both in anticipation of lower prices in the future. These delays create further decreases in aggregate demand, causing further reductions in prices, increased idle production capacity, increased unemployment, and reductions in wages, lending and interest rates. This cycle is called a **deflationary spiral**. If unchecked, it can have serious adverse consequence for an economy.

C. As with inflation, monetary and fiscal policies can be used to control deflation, primarily through spurring increased demand. Specifically, monetary policy would be implemented to increase the money supply through the Federal Reserve buying debt in the market (giving money for debt) and/or by reducing the federal funds rate to lower interest rates. Note, however, that historically lowering the interest rate is limited to reducing the rate to zero. Fiscal policy to control deflation would be implemented by lowering taxes and increasing government spending.

Money, Banking, and Monetary/Fiscal Policy

The use of money is central to contemporary economic activity. The management of the money supply is essential to accomplishing desired aggregate economic outcomes. This lesson describes the role of money, measures of money, and management of the money supply in the U.S. economy.

After studying this lesson, you should be able to:

1. Describe the roles of money in an economy.
2. Define the measures of money as used by the Federal Reserve System.
3. Describe the structure and operation of the Federal Reserve System, including: (a) reserve requirements; (b) open market operations; (c) discount rate; and (d) margin requirements.
4. Describe the structure and operation of the Federal Reserve System, including: (a) reserve requirements; (b) open-market operations; and (c) the discount rate.
5. Describe common bank interest rate concepts and how those rates are used, including: (a) federal funds rate; (b) federal discount rate; (c) prime interest rate; (d) London Interbank Offer Rate (LIBOR); and (e) negative interest rate.
6. Summarize the means by which the government carries out fiscal and monetary policy.

I. Overview—As shown in the free-market model, money flows from business firms to individuals (for economic resources), and from individuals to business firms (for goods and services), as well as between the government, financial and foreign sectors (for savings, payment of taxes, interest and dividends, receipt/payments for imports/exports, and for other purposes). Thus, money is central to economic activity. In the United States, the Federal Reserve System (the Fed) manages the money supply and regulates the banking system. Through its management of the money supply, and related activities, the Fed can exercise significant influence over elements of the economy.

II. Money

A. Money serves multiple functions in the economy, including as:

1. A **medium of exchange**. Money is accepted as a means of payment by buyers and sellers in exchanges of goods and services.
2. A **measure of value**. Money is a common denominator for assigning value to diverse goods and services and, therefore, for measuring economic activity.
3. A **store of value**. Money retains value over time (although often with some loss of purchasing power), therefore it can be saved for use in the future.

B. Conventionally, money is considered to consist of paper currency and coins. For economic purposes, however, money is comprised of a variety of financial items. The Federal Reserve System provides definitions and measures of money for the U.S. economy, including the following:

1. **M1**—Includes paper and coin currency held outside banks and check-writing deposits. This is the narrowest definition of money and is based on including instruments used for transactions.
   - **a.** U.S. paper currency takes the form of Federal Reserve notes. These notes ("dollar" bills of various denomination) have no intrinsic value in that they do not represent a claim to any specific commodity (e.g., gold). Rather, their value derives from the good faith and credit of the U.S. government.
   - **b.** Check-writing deposits are amounts held by banks, savings and loans, and credit unions for which ownership can be transferred by writing a check.
2. **M2**—Includes M1 items plus savings deposits, money-market deposit accounts, certificates of deposit (less than $100,000), individual-owned money-market mutual funds, and certain other deposits. This measure of money is the primary focus of Fed actions to influence the economy.

3. **M3**—Includes M2 items plus certificates of deposit (greater than $100,000), institutional-owned money-market mutual funds and certain other deposits (the FRS no longer provides a measure of M3).

4. **MZM (Money Zero Maturity)**—Includes highly liquid items that are readily available for spending at par value and consists of currency and coins, checking accounts, savings accounts, and all money market accounts. It is usually computed as M2 less time deposits (e.g., certificates of deposit) plus institutional-owned money market funds.

III. Banking System

A. The United States does not have a central bank but rather a central banking system, the Federal Reserve System, which consists of:

1. **Board of governors**—The seven-member policy-making body of the Federal Reserve System

2. **Federal open market committee**—The 12-member body responsible for implementing monetary policy through open-market operations to affect the money supply (M1)

3. **Federal reserve banks**—The 12 district banks, each responsible for a specific geographical area of the United States. Within their area, each federal bank supervises, regulates, and examines member institutions; provides currency to and clears checks for those institutions; and holds reserves and lends to those institutions. The Federal Reserve Banks are owned by their member institutions, but they operate under uniform policies of the Federal Reserve System. Member institutions, which function as financial intermediaries, include:

a. Commercial banks

b. Savings and loan associations

c. Mutual savings banks

d. Credit unions

B. Individuals, business firms, and other entities deal with these financial intermediaries, but not directly with the Federal Reserve Banks.

IV. Monetary Policy

A. Monetary policy is concerned with managing the money supply to achieve national economic objectives, including economic growth and price level stability. The Federal Reserve System can regulate the money supply (exercise monetary policy) in a number of ways:

1. **Reserve-requirement changes**—A bank's ability to issue check-writing deposits is limited by a reserve-requirement by the Fed on check-writing deposits. Simply put, loans made by banks are paid to borrowers by checks drawn on the lending bank. For every dollar of such checks issued as loans, the bank must have a required amount held as a reserve, either at the bank or on deposit at a Federal Reserve Bank.

Example

Assume the reserve requirement established by the Fed is 10% (a real reserve–requirement in recent years). A bank would be required to have $1.00 in reserves for every $10.00 it loans. By changing the reserve requirement, the Fed can greatly influence the check-writing deposits by banks.

a. By decreasing (or increasing) the reserve requirement on check-writing deposits the Fed enables banks to increase (or requires them to decrease) the amount of loans the bank can make using check-writing deposits, and thus increase (or decrease) M1 money supply. Decreasing the requirement would affect monetary easing; increasing the requirement would affect monetary tightening.

2. **Open-market operations**—The Fed engages in open-market operations by purchasing and selling U.S. Treasury debt obligations (e.g., Treasury Bonds) from/to banks. The effect of purchasing Treasury obligations is to replace debt held by banks with additional reserves for the banks. The increase in reserves permits additional check-writing deposits (i.e., lending ability) by the banks. Sale of Treasury obligations has the opposite effect. Thus, open-market purchasing implements monetary easing, while open-market sales implements monetary tightening.

   a. The open-market operations function is one of the preferred methods of changing the money supply because it permits changes of various degrees.

3. **Discount rate**—The rate of interest banks pay when they borrow from a Federal Reserve Bank in order to maintain reserve requirements is called the "discount rate." Borrowing from a Fed bank increases a bank's reserves with the Fed because the borrowing is credited to the banks reserve with the Fed, not withdrawn from the Fed bank. As a result of increased reserves, banks are able to increase loans. By decreasing or increasing the discount rate, the Fed encourages or discourages borrowing from the Fed and, thereby, eases or tightens the money supply.

   a. The Fed's intent in making changes in the discount rate is to keep it at an appropriate "spread" below other rates available to banks. Therefore, changes in the discount rate usually follow changes in the short-term rate of interest in the broad market. Consequently, changes in the discount rate, which are widely publicized, signal Fed expectations about interest rates. For example, if the Fed increases the discount rate to maintain an appropriate spread with rising rates in the market, this tends to confirm that the Fed expects general interest rates to remain at the higher level.

4. **Margin requirement**—The percentage of the cost of an investment in qualified (marginable) securities that an investor must pay for with his/her own funds; the percentage cost of such an investment for which the investor cannot use funds borrowed from a broker-dealer, bank, or other institution to purchase the securities.

   a. The margin requirement is set by the Fed, but enforced by the SEC.

   b. Theoretically, the higher the margin requirement, the lower the investment in securities because investors must pay a larger amount of the initial cost of the securities.

   c. Practically, however, the margin requirement currently has little effect on the level of investment because investors can borrow funds from other sources (credit cards, home equity loans, etc.) in lieu of using margin credit.

B. **Changes in the Money Supply (M1),** especially when accomplished through open-market operations, will affect short-term interest rates (*ceteris paribus*). For example, if other factors are held constant, an increase in the M1 money supply will lower the short-term interest rate in the market. This can be shown as follows:

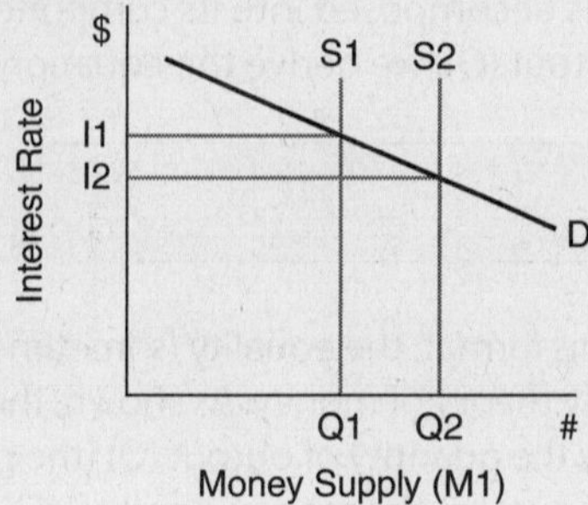

1. D represents the demand for money. If the supply of money increases from Q1 to Q2, the interest rate drops from I1 to I2. At a lower interest rate, individuals and businesses are more likely to borrow to finance purchase of high cost items (e.g., cars, houses, property, plant and equipment, etc.). The increase in demand (supported by more borrowing) will spur production, increase employment and raise GDP.

2. Similarly, if the demand for money increases, the interest rate will tend to increase. For example, large borrowings by the government will increase the demand for money and put pressure on interest rates to increase.

C. Velocity of Money

1. The velocity of money (technically, the income velocity of money) is a measure of the rate at which money in circulation is used for purchasing new, domestically produced goods and services. It measures the average rate or frequency at which the money supply "changes hands," or turns over in exchange transactions for goods and services during a period.

   a. The classical formula for computing the velocity of money (VM) is:

> VM = GDP / MS
>
> where: GDP = Gross domestic product (nominal)
> MS = Money supply (as measured by either M1 or M2)

Example
U.S. GDP (Q4, 2016) $18,860.8 billion
U.S. M2 (Q4, 2016) $13,184.8 billion
VM = $18,860.8 B/$13,184.8 billion = 1.43

Explanation: Every dollar in the money supply was used on average 1.43 times during the fourth quarter of 2016.

   b. Rearranged, the velocity of money formula would show the computation of GDP for an economy as:

> GDP = MS × VM

   c. Notice that in this equation GDP is not a function of the supply of money alone, but of the combination of the money supply and the velocity with which that money changes hands for goods and services.

   d. And, since GDP can be measured by expenditures, another version of the equation, called the "equation of exchange" would reflect that:

> MS × VM = Spending

   e. Alternatively, if GDP is decomposed into its components, the price level (P) and the real level (quantity) of output (Q), we derive the equation:

> $P \times Q \equiv MS \times VM$

   When expressed in this format, the equality (sometimes called the Fisher equation) expresses the quantity theory of money. As shown, the Fisher equation says that the price level (P) multiplied by the quantity of output (Q) (the product of which constitutes nominal GDP) is the same as (equal to) the money supply (MS) multiplied by the velocity of money (VM). Or, simply put, the sales value of final goods and services (GDP) is equal to (is the same as) the number of times the money supply is transacted to pay for those goods and service.

2. Proponents of the quantity theory of money (monetarists) hold that there is a direct relationship between the level of the money supply (MS) and the level of prices (P) in an economy. Specifically, their theory posits that if the amount of money in the economy changes, the level of prices for goods and services will change proportionately in the same direction. Thus, for example, if the supply of money increases, the price level will increase proportionately and result in inflation.

3. Conceptually, the velocity of money is useful in measuring the level of economic activity in an economy and in determining inflation. Practically, however, empirical data shows that the relationship between the velocity of money and inflation is highly variable and in some time periods has been negative. After plotting the relationship between the velocity of money (measured using M2) and the Consumer Price Index (CPI) for the 55-year period 1959 through 2014, the Fed concluded: "[W]e see no clear relationship between these variables" (FRED Economic Data, 2014). Nevertheless, an analysis of the velocity of money is useful for understanding certain macroeconomic and monetary policy concepts.

V. Fiscal Policy

A. Fiscal policy is the use of government taxation, spending, and transfer payments to achieve economic objectives. Unlike monetary policy which is implemented by the Federal Reserve at the national level, fiscal policy is implemented by legislative action and can occur not only at the national level, but it also can be implemented at the state and local levels.

1. Transfer payments are government payments to individuals or businesses for which no good or service is received in return. Primary examples are unemployment benefits, social security payments, welfare and veterans' benefits, and subsidies.

B. Taken alone, an increase in government spending, a reduction in taxes, or an increase in transfer payments would be initiated to increase aggregate demand and, thus, stimulate economic activity. Conversely, taken alone, a decrease in government spending, an increase in taxes, or a reduction in transfer payments would be initiated to decrease aggregate demand and, thus, dampen economic activity.

C. Taken together, government fiscal policy actions are considered to be of three types (or stances):

1. **Expansionary**—Undertaken to stimulate economic activity and typically involves government spending exceeding taxes collected, resulting in a deficit.
2. **Neutral**—No change in fiscal policy action because the economy is in equilibrium with government spending and tax collections in balance.
3. **Contractionary**—Undertaken to dampen economic activity and typically involves government spending lower than tax collections, resulting in a surplus.

VI. Fiscal and Monetary Policy Summary

A. Both fiscal and monetary policy provide means for the government to influence aggregate spending (demand). Fiscal policy is implemented through changes in government spending and/or taxes. Monetary policy is implemented primarily through control of the money supply.

Thus, for example, governmental efforts to increase aggregate spending (and reduce unemployment, increase GDP, etc.) would include:

Action	Policy Type
Increase government spending	Fiscal
Reduce taxes	Fiscal
Increase money supply	Monetary

B. To rein in aggregate spending the reverse types of action would be implemented. While the general effect of each type of policy action is known, the timing and net effects of the alternative forms of action are less certain.

1. **Lag-time element**—There are differences in how quickly the alternative forms of policy can be implemented and how quickly economic activity will be affected. Changes of significant magnitude in fiscal policy generally require congressional or legislative approval and may be delayed (or never approved) if there is not agreement by members of Congress or other legislators. However, once approved, changes in government spending can be implemented quickly and with an almost immediate impact on demand. Changes in tax rates, once approved, have a less immediate impact and a less certain magnitude of influence.

2. Generally, changes in monetary policy can be made more quickly than fiscal policy because monetary policy is changed by the Federal Reserve Board, not by legislative action. Once approved, monetary policy has an almost immediate effect on the interest rate, but the full effect on spending may not occur immediately because of the time lags inherent in ramping-up (or ramping-down) large-scale projects commonly sensitive to changes in the interest rate.
3. Of the two approaches, monetary policy has been the primary approach to achieving economic objectives. Changes can be approved more quickly to respond to changing economic circumstances and monetary policy changes have fewer artificial influences on the economy. Fiscal policy, on the other hand, causes a redistribution of output and income.

VII. Bank Rate Concepts Summary—The following provides a summary of common and important bank rate concepts:

A. **Federal (Fed) Funds Rate**—The interest rate at which a depository institution lends funds maintained at the Federal Reserve to another depository institution overnight without requiring collateral. The federal funds rate is generally applicable only to the most creditworthy institutions when they borrow and lend overnight funds to each other to satisfy reserve requirement shortages. When one depository institution has funds in excess of its reserve requirement needs, it may loan those funds to other institutions that have a reserve requirement shortage. The interest rate charged on those loans is the Federal Funds Rate.

B. **Federal (Bank) Discount Rate**—The interest rate the Federal Reserve charges on loans made by the regional Federal Reserve Banks to eligible commercial banks and other depository institutions. Banks whose reserves fall below the Fed's reserve requirement may borrow directly from the regional Federal Reserve Bank to correct their shortage. The rate charged for such borrowings is the (federal) discount rate.

C. **Prime (Interest) Rate**—The interest rate commercial banks charge their most creditworthy borrowers, usually large, financially sound corporations. It is one of the most widely used market lagging indicators, is a major benchmark for mortgage and credit card rates, and is often the basis for adjustable-rate loans.

D. **London Interbank Offer Rate (LIBOR)**—The average interest rate participating banks offer other banks for loans on the London market. LIBOR is the world's most widely-used benchmark for short-term interest rates. In addition, it is used as a benchmark for other transactions, including derivative instruments and foreign currency transactions.

E. **Negative Interest Rates**—A negative interest rate is one that is below zero (i.e., $< 0.0\%$). When policy or instrument terms provide for a negative interest rate, a financial institution **charges** depositors to hold their money on deposit rather than paying them interest on those deposits.

1. When a central bank (e.g., Federal Reserve, European Central Bank, etc.) adopts a negative interest rate policy, the central bank charges member banks for funds left on deposit with the central bank. Similarly, if negative interest rates are adopted by member banks, those banks would charge their business and individual customers for holding their deposits.
2. The purpose (in theory) of a negative interest rate monetary policy is to encourage businesses and individuals to spend, lend, or invest their funds rather than pay to have those funds held by a financial institution.
3. As of March, 2016, the European Central Bank (EEUECB) and the Bank of Japan, among other central banks (but *not* the U.S. Fed), had adopted a negative interest rate policy. For example, at that time, the ECB charged member banks .004 (0.4%) to hold cash for those banks.
4. Because the use of negative interest rates as a monetary policy tool is new, the practical effects are uncertain. In any case, the use of such a policy tool is not without risks, including:
   a. **Decrease in cash in circulation**—A negative interest rate at the commercial and personal level may result in cash being taken out of circulation (hoarded in a safe or under the mattress) rather than being deposited. This would reduce the funds held by financial institutions for making business and personal loans.

b. **Reduce bank profits**—Some banks that have to pay a negative interest rate (e.g., to the Fed or other financial institution) may not be able to charge their customers a negative interest rate. In such cases, banks' profits would decrease as a result of the difference between lending and deposit rates.

c. **Unintended consequences**—There may be unknown unintended consequences on the economic system as a result of the long-term use of negative interest rates.

International Economics

Introduction and Reasons for International Activity

Economic activity occurs not only at the individual, market, and national levels, but also at the international level. This lesson addresses the reasons for international economic activity.

After studying this lesson, you should be able to:

1. Identify major reasons for international economic business activity.
2. Define absolute advantage and comparative advantage.
3. Compute comparative advantage and determine the existence of a comparative advantage.
4. Identify and describe Porter's four attributes, which promote or impede the creation of competitive advantage.

I. **Introduction**—The U.S. economy (and that of most other nations) is not a closed system, but rather is connected (open) to the economies of many other nations through trade, investment, and other financial activities. These international economic relationships provide important benefits to, and create challenges not only for the national economy, but also for entities engaged in international economic activities.

II. **Reasons for International Activity**—There are a number of reasons nations and entities seek to benefit from international economic activities. Among the most important are the following:

   A. To develop new markets for the sale of goods and services abroad. Exports increase domestic demand, which raises output, revenues and employment, thus benefiting both entities engaged in export activities and national economic measures.

   B. To obtain commodities not otherwise available domestically (e.g., in the United States), or available only in limited supply. Certain raw materials, like tin, tungsten, and tea, are available only from foreign (i.e., non-U.S.) sources. Other important goods, like oil, are available domestically only in limited supply which must be supplemented with substantial imports. To obtain these economic resources in the quantity needed, entities must import commodities from other countries (economies).

   C. To obtain goods and services at lower costs than available domestically. Although certain goods and services may be available domestically, they cost more than if acquired in a foreign country. Thus, in a completely open worldwide economic system, entities will acquire economic resources from the lowest cost provider, wherever located.

III. **Absolute and Comparative Advantage**

   A. **Absolute Advantage**—From an international economic perspective, absolute advantage exists when a country, business, individual or other entity (hereafter referred to as "entity") can produce a particular good or service more efficiently (with fewer resources) than another entity. When an entity has an absolute advantage, it uses fewer resources to produce a particular good or service than another entity.

   B. **Comparative Advantage**—Comparative advantage exists when one entity has the ability to produce a good or service at a lower opportunity cost than the opportunity cost of the good or service for another entity.

      1. **Opportunity cost**—Is the money value of benefits lost from the next best opportunity as the result of choosing another opportunity. If you choose to do one thing, the opportunity cost is the value of the benefit lost by not doing another thing that would have provided the next best benefit.

      2. Comparative advantage in the providing of goods or services derives from differences, among other things, in the availability of economic resources, including natural resources, labor and technology, among entities.

3. Entities should specialize in the goods or services they produce at the least opportunity cost.
4. Entities should trade with other entities for goods and services for which they **do not have** a comparative advantage.
5. **Principle of comparative advantage**—The total output of two or more entities will be greatest when each produces the goods or services for which it has the lowest opportunity cost.

Note
The topic of "opportunity cost" is covered in greater detail in the Financial Management area in the "Cost Concepts" and "Time Value of Money Tools" lessons.

C. **Absolute and Comparative Advantage Illustrated**—The following illustrates the concepts of absolute and comparative advantage.

Assume the following relationship between a good and a service provided in both the U.S. and China in terms of the output per unit of input for televisions and financial services (the values are strictly assumed for this analysis):

	Televisions	Financial Services
U.S.	20	60
CHINA	100	80

1. For one unit of input, a U.S. entity can produce 20 televisions or 60 financial services; a Chinese entity can produce 100 televisions or 80 financial services.
2. Absolute advantage: The Chinese entity has an absolute advantage in providing both televisions (100:20) and financial services (80:60).
3. Comparative advantage analysis
   a. To produce 1 television the U.S. entity must give up 3 financial services (60/20). Therefore, 1 financial service has an opportunity cost of .33 televisions (1.00/3.00).
   b. To produce 1 television, the Chinese entity must give up .80 financial services (80/100). Therefore, 1 financial service has an opportunity cost of 1.25 televisions (1.00/.80).
   c. Financial services have a lower opportunity cost to the U.S. entity and televisions have a lower opportunity cost to the Chinese entity.
   d. Therefore:
      1. Financial services should be provided by the U.S. entity because it has a comparative advantage (versus televisions) over the Chinese entity.
      2. Televisions should be provided by the Chinese entity because it has a comparative advantage (versus financial services) over the U.S. entity.

IV. Porter's Four Factors

A. Absolute and comparative advantage are based largely on differences in the availability of traditional economic resources, including natural resources, labor, and technology.

B. In 1990, Michael Porter proposed that four broad national attributes, including but not limited to the traditional factors of production, promoted or impeded the creation of competitive advantage. The four attributes are:

1. **Factor conditions**—The extent to which a country has a relative advantage in factors of production, including infrastructure and skilled labor. Through investment and innovation, a country can enhance its factor conditions.

2. **Demand conditions**—The nature of the domestic demand for an industry's product or service. A strong domestic demand enables firms to devote more attention to a good or service than can firms in countries without a strong domestic demand.
3. **Related and supporting industries**—The extent to which supplier industries and related industries are internationally competitive. When related and supporting industries are highly developed, a country will have a comparative advantage over countries with less highly developed related and supporting industries.
4. **Firm strategy, structure, and rivalry**—The conditions governing how companies are created, organized and managed and the nature of domestic rivalry. When a country has companies with well-developed strategies, different organizational structures, and intense domestic rivalry, that country tends to have a competitive advantage.

C. Porter also proposed that chance and government policies play a role in the nature of the competitive environment.

D. Porter summarized his analysis in the form of a diamond to represent the determinants of national competitive advantage. That diamond is depicted as:

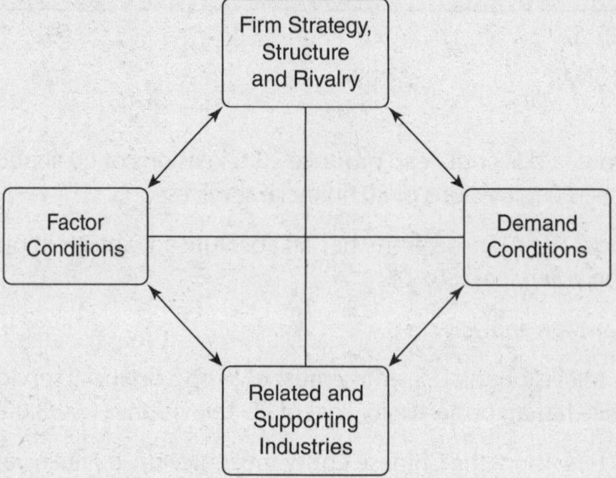

E. According to Porter, the diamond elements, taken together, affect four factors that lead to a national competitive advantage. Those factors are:

1. The availability of resources and skills
2. The information that firms use to decide which opportunities to pursue with those resources and skills
3. The goals of the individuals within the firms
4. The pressure on firms to innovate and invest

Issues at the National Level

While international economic activity benefits the national economy, it also creates issues for the national economy. This lesson considers matters that revolve around sociopolitical issues and balance of payment issues.

After studying this lesson, you should be able to:

1. Identify and describe the socio-political issues occasioned by international economic activity and the common responses to those issues.
2. Describe the effect of exchange rates on the level of a nation's imports/exports.
3. Describe the components of a nation's balance of payments accounting.
4. Describe "dumping" and its potential consequences.

I. Sociopolitical Issues

A. It is often argued that international trade causes or exacerbates certain domestic social and economic problems, including:

1. Unemployment resulting from the direct or indirect use of "cheap" foreign labor
2. Loss of certain basic manufacturing capabilities
3. Reduction of industries essential to national defense
4. Lack of domestic protection for start-up industries

B. Political responses to such concerns often result in protectionism in the form of:

1. Import quotas, which restrict the quantity of goods that can be imported
2. Import tariffs, which tax imported goods and thereby increase their cost
3. Embargo, which is a partial or complete ban on trade (imports/exports) or other commercial activity with one or more other countries
4. Foreign exchange controls, which are government controls on the purchase or sale of foreign currencies by residents and/or on the purchase or sale of the domestic currency by nonresidents, including:
    - **a.** Barring the use of foreign currencies in the country
    - **b.** Barring the possession of foreign currencies by residents
    - **c.** Restricting currency exchange to government-run or government-approved exchanges
    - **d.** Government imposed fixed exchange rates

C. **Protectionism**—Such forms of protectionism benefit some parties while harming others:

1. **Parties benefited**
    - **a.** Domestic producers—Retain market and can charge higher prices
    - **b.** Federal government—Obtains revenue through tariffs
2. **Parties harmed**
    - **a.** Domestic consumers—Pay higher prices and may have less choice of goods
    - **b.** Foreign producers—Loss of market

D. Such forms of protectionism are generally inappropriate because they are based on economic misconceptions or because there are more appropriate fiscal and monetary policy responses.

II. Exchange Rate Issue (Imports/Exports)

A. An exchange rate is the price of one unit of a country's currency expressed in units of another country's currency.

1. Example: $1.25 = 1 euro

B. Exchange rates are important in determining the level of imports and exports for a country.

1. The lower the cost of a foreign currency in terms of a domestic currency, the cheaper the foreign goods and services of that currency in the domestic market.

a. Assume the following alternate exchange rates:

$1.10 = 1 euro ("stronger" dollar than $1.25 = 1 euro)

$1.25 = 1 euro ("weaker" dollar than $1.10 = 1 euro)

b. When the exchange rate is $1.10 = 1.00 euro, U.S. consumers can buy more foreign (euro) goods than when the exchange rate is $1.25 = 1.00 euro.

c. Consequently, imports of euro goods would be higher at the lower exchange rate (stronger dollar).

2. Conversely, the lower the cost of a foreign currency in terms of a domestic currency, the higher the cost of domestic goods and services to foreign buyers resulting in lower exports.

C. Since the exchange rate directly affects the level of imports and exports for both goods and services, it directly affects the balance of trade of a country.

1. Balance of trade is the difference between the monetary value of imports and exports, which is a part of a country's current accounting in its balance-of-payments accounts. (See IV below.)

a. Trade surplus = Exports > Imports

b. Trade deficit = Exports < Imports

D. The next lesson considers the nature and determinants of exchange rates and how governments can influence the level of those rates.

III. Dumping Issue

A. In the context of international economics, "dumping" is the sale of a product in a foreign market at a lower price than is charged in the domestic market.

B. Dumping may have an adverse effect on the producers of the good that is dumped in the country that receives the good because the price charged for dumped goods may be less than the cost of production in the import country.

C. Under World Trade Organization (WTO) policy, dumping is not considered illegal competition unless the importing country can demonstrate the negative effects on domestic producers.

D. Importing nations often counter dumping by imposing quotas and/or tariffs on the dumped product, which has the effect of limiting the quantity or increasing the cost of the dumped good.

IV. Balance of Payments Issues

A. The U.S. balance of payments is a summary accounting of all U.S. transactions with all other nations for a calendar year. The U.S. reports international activity in three main accounts:

1. Current account—Reports the dollar value of amounts earned from the export of goods and services, amounts spent on import of goods and services, income from investments, government grants to foreign entities, and the resulting net (export or import) balance.

2. **Capital account**—Reports the dollar amount of capital transfers and the acquisition and disposal of non-produced, non-financial assets. Thus, it includes inflows from investments and loans by foreign entities, outflows from investments and loans U.S. entities made abroad, and the resulting net balance. Examples include funds transferred in the purchase or sale of fixed assets, natural resources and intangible assets.

3. **Financial account**—Reports the dollar amount of U.S.-owned assets abroad, foreign-owned assets in the United States, and the resulting net balance. It includes both government assets and private assets, and both monetary items (e.g., gold, foreign securities) and non-monetary items (e.g., direct foreign investments in property, plants and equipment).

B. The net effects of the amounts reported by the current account, capital account, and financial account can be summarized as:

1. When the sum of earnings and inflows exceeds the sum of spending and outflows, a balance of payment surplus exists. This surplus would result in an increase in U.S. reserves of foreign currency or in a decrease in foreign government holdings of U.S. currency.

2. When the sum of spending and outflows exceeds the sum of earnings and inflows, a balance of payment deficit exits. This deficit would result in a decrease in U.S. holding of foreign currency reserves or in an increase in foreign government holdings of U.S. currency.

C. A deficit in the U.S. balance of payments means that U.S. entities have a combined amount of imports and investments made abroad that exceeds the combined amount of exports and investments made in the U.S. by foreign entities. Consequently, the U.S. demand for foreign currencies will exceed the amount of foreign currencies provided by U.S. exports and foreign investment in the United States and (other things remaining equal) with free-floating exchange rates, the exchange rates between the dollar and other currencies will rise (i.e., the value of the dollar relative to other currencies will fall).

1. Such a decline in the dollar would make imports more expensive and exports cheaper for foreign buyers.

2. A decrease in imports and an increase in exports would, in turn, move the balance of payments back toward equilibrium.

3. Thus, free-floating exchange rates help maintain balance of payment equilibrium.

Role of Exchange Rates

Currency exchange rates are important to both nations and business entities that engage in international economic activity. This lesson defines currency exchange rates, describes the factors that determine those rates, and describes how currency exchange rates can impact a domestic economy.

After studying this lesson, you should be able to:

1. Define currency exchange rates, including the difference between: a) direct exchange rate and b) indirect exchange rate.
2. Identify and describe the factors that affect exchange rates.
3. Describe how a government can influence the exchange rate between its currency and that of other countries.
4. Describe the effect of currency exchange rates on a domestic economy.
5. Define "spot rates" and "forward rates," and calculate the premium or discount between the two rates.

I. **Currency and Currency Exchange Rates**—As a store of value (and medium of exchange), currency has characteristics of a commodity, the value of which can be measured by the rate at which one currency will exchange for another currency. Such exchange rates play a central role for both nations and individual entities in the conduct and consequences of international economic activity.

A. **Exchange Rates Defined**

Definition
Currency Exchange Rate: The exchange rate is the price of one unit of a country's currency expressed in units of another country's currency.

1. The currency exchange rate may be expressed as:
   a. **Direct exchange rate**—the domestic price of one unit of a foreign currency. For example: 1 euro = $1.10.
   b. **Indirect exchange rate**—the foreign price of one domestic unit of currency. For example: $1.00 = .909 euro ($1.00/$1.10).
2. **Exchange rate concepts**
   a. **Spot exchange rate**—The exchange rate between currencies for immediate delivery (exchange); the rate "on the spot."
   b. **Forward exchange rate**—The exchange rate between currencies existing at the present for future delivery (exchange).
   c. **Exchange rate discount or premium**—The difference at a point in time between the spot exchange rate and the forward exchange rate for two currencies. The discount or premium is computed as:

      [(Forward rate – Spot rate)/Spot rate] ×
      [Months or days in year/Months in forward period]

Example

Assume the spot rate for buying euros with dollars is $1.25 and the 180-day forward rate is $1.256. The forward rate premium would be:

[($1.256 – $1.250)/$1.250] × [360/180] =
[.006/1.250] × 2 = .0048 × 2 = .0096 (premium)

i. The result is a premium because the forward rate is higher than the spot rate. This premium indicates that the market assessment is that the value of the dollar relative to the euro will decline (weaken).

ii. If the forward rate is lower than the spot rate, a discount would result. A discount indicates tha the market believes that the value of the dollar relative to the euro will increase (strengthen).

B. Exchange Rate Determination

1. **Background**—In 1944, delegates from 45 nations meeting in Bretton Woods, New Hampshire reached agreement (Bretton Woods Agreement) to establish a post-war international monetary system, including fixed currency exchange rates. The fixed exchange rate system remained in operation until 1973, when it was abandoned and replaced by a system of floating exchange rates. The worldwide exchange system in operation today is not completely free-floating because monetary authorities in one country can and do intervene in exchange markets of other countries so as to influence exchange rates. Nevertheless, the current exchange system is largely determined by aggregate demand and supply for currency.

2. **Currency demand**—A number of factors play a role in determining the demand for a country's currency and, therefore, in determining a country's exchange rate with the currencies of other countries. Five of the major factors are:

   a. **Political and economic environment**—Currencies of countries that are politically stable and economically strong are more desirable than the currencies of countries with political turmoil and a risky economic environment. For example, investors are more likely to make investments in a politically stable country with a history of strong economic performance than a country with political unrest and a fragile economy. Consequently, there will be greater demand for the currency of the better political and economic environment.

   b. **Relative interest rates**—The interest rates in a country relative to the rates in other countries will influence the exchange rates between the currency of that country and the currencies of other countries. If the interest rate in one country is higher than the rate in another country, foreign capital will flow into the country with the higher interest rate to earn the higher return. The demand for the currency of the country with the higher interest will be greater than the demand for the currency of the country with the lower interest rate and its exchange rate would be relatively higher. For example, if higher interest rates were available in the European Economic Union (EEU), U.S. investors would invest more heavily in the EEU, which would increase the demand for the euro and increase the value of the euro relative to the dollar.

   c. **Relative inflation**—The inflation rate in one country relative to the rates in other countries will influence the exchange rates between the currency of that country and the currencies of other countries. If the inflation rate in one country is consistently lower than the rate in another country, the purchasing power in the country with the lower inflation rate will be higher relative to the purchasing power in the other country. The currency that better retains its purchasing power tends to increase in value relative to currencies of economies with higher inflation. For example, higher inflation rates in the U.S. than in the EEU would result in U.S. consumers buying more relatively less expensive EEU goods, thus increasing the demand for euros and increasing its value relative to the dollar.

   d. **Public debt level**—The level of deficit spending and the resulting level of public debt of a country influence the exchange rate between the currency of that country and the currencies of other countries. A country with a high level of public debt is likely to experience inflation, which will deter foreign investment and, thereby, weaken the country's currency relative to other currencies. Further, if government services its debt by increasing the money supply (called "monetizing debt"), even higher inflation will occur, causing a further decline in the country's currency exchange rate with other currencies.

e. **Current account balance**—The current account balance (in the balance of payments measure) of a country influences the exchange rate between the currency of that country and the currencies of other countries. A deficit in the current account of a country shows that it is spending more on foreign trade and related payments than it is receiving from foreign trading partners. This excess spending means that the country has a greater demand for foreign currencies than is demanded for the domestic currency by foreign parties. This excess demand for foreign currencies will lower the county's exchange rate with countries that have a favorable (net positive) current account balance with the domestic country.

f. **Other factors**—In addition to the five major factors identified above, other generally less important factors including consumer preferences, relative incomes, and speculation play a role in determining demand for a currency and, therefore, its exchange rate with other currencies.

g. Over time, all of these factors are both interrelated and of varying relative importance. Therefore, the exact role of each often is difficult to measure at any particular time.

3. **Currency supply**—The supply of a country's currency is determined by the country's fiscal and monetary policies. In the United States, the Federal Reserve Board (the "Fed") primarily determines the supply of currency through its control of monetary policy.

4. **Management of currency exchange rates**

a. To the extent a government can influence or determine the demand and supply factors which establish currency exchange rates, it can determine those rates.

b. In the U.S. the Fed can directly affect interest rates (a demand factor) and the supply of money.

i. To increase the value of the dollar (relative to other currencies), the Fed could buy dollars on the open market using foreign currency reserves. That results in fewer dollars in circulation (less supply) and more foreign currency in circulation (more supply).

ii. To increase the value of the dollar, the Fed could increase the interest rate in the U.S. That results in added demand for U.S. investment instruments and the dollars needed to acquire those investments (increased demand).

iii. To decrease the value of the dollar, the Fed could buy foreign currencies in the open market using dollars. That results in more dollars in circulation (more supply) and less foreign currency in circulation (less supply).

iv. To decrease the value of the dollar, the Fed could decrease the interest rate in the U.S. That results in less demand for U.S. investment instruments and the dollars needed to acquire those investments (decrease demand).

II. Exchange Rates and Domestic Economy

Exchange Rates and Domestic Economy—The exchange rate between the domestic currency (i.e., dollar) and other currencies has an impact on the domestic economy. As currency exchange rates change, the effect of a currency becoming stronger (appreciating) or weaker (depreciating) relative to other currencies likely will have a number of effects on the domestic economy.

A. Terminology

1. When a currency becomes stronger—or appreciates—the value of a currency has increased relative to another currency; it takes less of that currency to buy another currency (or more of another currency to buy that currency).

2. When a currency becomes weaker—or depreciates—the value of a currency has decreased relative to another currency; it takes more of that currency to buy another currency (or less of another currency to buy that currency).

B. Consequences of Changing Currency Value

1. When a currency appreciates (becomes stronger):

   a. Foreign goods become cheaper, providing consumers access to a wider array of goods at lower prices.

   b. Domestic producers maintain lower prices, thus encouraging efficiency and putting downward pressure on inflation (price increases).

   c. Domestic producers have more difficulty in competing in both domestic markets and foreign markets.

2. When a currency depreciates (becomes weaker):

   a. Domestic goods become cheaper relative to foreign goods, thus increasing export demand.

   b. Increased export demand increases domestic employment.

   c. Imported goods become more expensive, which drives up the cost of imported inputs (i.e., raw materials, components, etc.).

Issues at Entity Level

Currency Exchange Rate Issue

Currency exchange rates are important to both nations and business entities that engage in international economic activity. This lesson defines currency exchange rates, describes the factors that determine those rates, and describes how currency exchange rates can impact a domestic economy.

After studying this lesson, you should be able to:

1. Define currency exchange rates, including the difference between: a) direct exchange rate and b) indirect exchange rate.
2. Define "spot rates" and "forward rates," and calculate the premium or discount between the two rates.
3. Identify and describe the factors that affect exchange rates.
4. Describe how a government can influence the exchange rate between its currency and that of other countries.
5. Describe the effect of currency exchange rates on a domestic economy.

I. **Exchange Rate**—While exchange rates create issues for the national economy, for individual entities engaged in international trade and investment activities, exchange rates are central in determining the success or failure of their international activities.

   A. Entities that engage in foreign trade, investments, and/or operations face the risk associated with changes in the exchange rate, a risk not encountered in domestic transactions. This risk manifests itself in three forms:

      1. **Transaction risk**—The possible unfavorable impact of changes in currency exchange rates on transactions denominated in a foreign currency, including accounts receivable, accounts payable, and other monetary accounts to be settled in a foreign currency.
      2. **Translation risk**—The possible unfavorable impact of changes in currency exchange rates on the financial statements of an entity when those statements are converted from one currency to another. Changes in exchange rates directly affect the translated value of income statement and balance sheet items.
      3. **Economic risk**—The possible unfavorable impact of changes in currency exchange rates on a firm's future international earning power; for example, on future costs, prices, and sales. Exchange rate changes affect the price competitiveness of entities in countries for which the exchange rate changes.

   B. Each of these forms of currency exchange risk is discussed below, together with ways each may be eliminated or mitigated.

II. **Transaction Currency Exchange Risk**

   A. Foreign currency transactions may be in the form of:

      1. Importing (buying)
      2. Exporting (selling)
      3. Borrowing or lending with a foreign entity
      4. Investing in the securities of a foreign entity

   B. When an entity engages in these types of transactions, it will record the transactions on its books in terms of the domestic currency (U.S. dollar). But, if the transactions are to be settled (denominated) at a later date in a foreign currency, the number of dollars (the dollar amount) received or paid will change as the exchange rate between the currencies changes. A change in exchange rate may have a positive (gain) or negative (loss) effect on financial results, which should be recognized in the period of the change in exchange rate.

C. Import Illustration

1. Assume: On 10/15 a U.S. entity purchases goods (an import transaction) from a foreign supplier for 500,000 units of the foreign currency with terms of net 60. The relevant exchange rates between the dollar and the foreign currency (FC) are:

> 10/15 1 FC = $.75
>
> 12/14 1 FC = $.72

2. If the goods had been paid for at the date of purchase, 10/15, the dollar cost would have been 500,000 FC × $.75 = $375,000. However, because the U.S. entity deferred payment (had a payable) and the exchange rate changed from $.75 to $.72 per FC unit, the dollar cost at date of payment (12/14) was 500,000 FC × $.72 = $360,000. In this case, the exchange rate change resulted in a benefit of $15,000, because the dollar strengthened relative to the foreign currency.

D. Export Illustration

1. Assume: On 9/18 a U.S. entity sells merchandise (an export transaction) to a foreign buyer for 300,000 units of the foreign currency with terms net 90. The relevant exchange rates between the dollar and the foreign currency (FC) are:

> 9/18 1 FC = $1.18
>
> 12/17 1 FC = $1.10

2. If the U.S. entity had sold the goods for cash, it would have collected 300,000 FC × $1.18 = $354,000. However, because the U.S. entity extended payment terms (had a receivable) and the exchange rate changed from $1.18 to $1.10, the dollars received at date of collection (12/17) was 300,000 FC × $1.10 = $330,000. In this case, the exchange rate change resulted in a loss of $24,000 because the dollar strengthened relative to the foreign currency.

E. Investment Illustration

1. Assume: On 4/1 a U.S. entity purchases shares of a foreign company's securities as an investment for 1,500,000 units of the foreign currency. The U.S. entity sells the investment 11/14 for 1,600,000 units of the foreign currency. The relevant exchange rates between the dollar and the foreign currency (FC) are:

> 4/1 1 FC = $.95
>
> 11/14 1 FC = $.90

2. The dollar cost of the investment on 4/1 was 1,500,000 FC × $.95 = $1,425,000 (excluding any transaction costs). The investment was sold on 11/14 for 1,600,000 FC, a gain of 100,000 FC units. However, because the exchange rate changed from $.95 to $.90, the dollar amount received from the sale is 1,600,000 FC × $.90 = $1,440,000, resulting in a dollar net gain of only $15,000 (i.e., $1,440,000 – $1,425,000). That $15,000 is composed of an investment gain ($90,000) and a foreign exchange (FX) loss ($75,000), computed as:

> Investment gain = 100,000 FC investment gain × $.90 FX rate at settlement date = $90,000
>
> FX loss = 1,500,000 FC original investment × .05 reduction in FX rate = $75,000
>
> Net gain = $90,000 investment gain – $75,000 FX loss = $15,000

F. Eliminating or Mitigating Transaction Risk

1. An entity can avoid the risk associated with changing exchange rates by engaging only in dollar-denominated transactions. The international nature of business, however, requires that firms of any significant size conduct business with foreign entities, often in terms of a foreign currency. Therefore, rather than avoid currency risk entirely, firms seek to minimize the degree of risk associated with such activity.
2. The risk associated with a change in exchange rates on foreign currency denominated transaction balances can be mitigated internally by using:
   a. **Matching**—Incurring equal amounts of receivables and payable in a foreign currency, thus resulting in a loss on either of the balances being offset by a concurrent gain on the other of the balances.
   b. Leading and lagging receivables or payables involve collecting receivables and paying obligations either earlier or later than would normally be required.
      i. When a foreign currency is expected to strengthen against the domestic currency, the domestic entity would seek to pay an obligation early or delay collecting a receivable.
      ii. When a foreign currency is expected to weaken against the domestic currency, the domestic entity would seek to collect a receivable early or delay paying a liability.
3. The risk associated with a change in exchange rates on foreign currency denominated transaction balances can be mitigated with hedging using forward exchange, futures, or option contracts, currency swaps, and the like.
   a. Hedging is a risk management strategy, which involves using offsetting (or contra) transactions so that a loss on one transaction would be offset (at least in part) by a gain on another transaction (or vice versa).
   b. You would "hedge a bet" by offsetting a possible loss from betting on one team to win by also betting on the other team to win.
   c. You would hedge against a possible loss in the dollar value of a foreign currency to be received in the future, for example, by entering into a forward contract to sell that foreign currency now at a specified rate for delivery when you receive it in the future.
   d. You would hedge against a possible loss in the dollar amount of a foreign currency to be paid in the future, for example, by entering into a forward contract to buy that foreign currency now at a specified rate for delivery when you need to pay the foreign currency.

> **Note**
> Hedging is covered in detail in the next section, "Financial Management."

III. Translation Currency Exchange Risk

A. A foreign currency translation risk occurs when a domestic entity has a direct investment in a foreign operation and must convert (translate) the financial statements of the foreign entity expressed in a foreign currency into their domestic (dollar) equivalents.

B. The financial statements expressed in the foreign currency could be those of the domestic entity's:
   1. Branch
   2. Joint venture
   3. Partnership
   4. Equity investee
   5. Subsidiary

C. The translation of the financial statements may be needed in order to:
   1. Apply the equity method by a domestic (U.S.) investor

2. Combine with other entities
3. Consolidate with a domestic (U.S.) parent (and, possibly, other subsidiaries)

D. Translation of financial statements from one currency to another currency is accomplished by the use of exchange rates.

1. The specific rate used depends on the form of conversion being used, whether translation or remeasurement, and the specific financial statement item being converted.
2. Possible rates used for conversion include:
   a. Spot (or current) exchange rate at the balance sheet date
   b. Specific exchange rate that existed when a transaction or event occurred during the reporting period
   c. Average exchange rate for a period, when it is not significantly different from exchange rates that existed during the period
   d. Historic exchange rate that existed when a transaction or event occurred in the past
3. The use of changing spot (or current) exchange rates to convert certain assets and liabilities exposes those items to currency exchange rate gains and/or losses.
4. The use of the historic (or specific) exchange rate to convert certain assets and liabilities does not expose those items to currency exchange rate gains and/or losses.

E. The risk associated with a change in exchange rates on the translation of foreign currency denominated financial statements can be mitigated in three ways:

1. Reduce the amount of assets and liabilities to be converted using spot (or current) exchange rates.
   a. Since only assets and liabilities converted using a (changing) spot exchange rate results in gain or loss, minimizing the amount of such assets and liabilities will reduce the recognized gain or loss.
   b. Increase the amount of foreign-based assets likely to appreciate in value (hard currency assets) and decrease the amount of foreign-based assets likely to depreciate in value (soft-currency assets), or vice versa for foreign-based liabilities.
2. Create offsetting assets or liabilities so that a gain or loss on one item will be offset by a loss or gain on another item.
3. Borrowing in the foreign currency in an amount that approximates the net translation exposure (net asset) so that a gain or loss on the translation exposure will be offset by a loss or gain on the borrowing (liability), resulting in a minimum net gain/loss.

IV. Economic Currency Exchange Risk

A. An economic currency exchange risk occurs when exchange rate changes alter the value of future revenues and costs.

1. Exchange rate changes may make future foreign revenues convert to fewer units of a domestic currency (or other currency) or make future costs convert to more units of a domestic currency (or other currency).
2. These types of changes may reduce the financial viability of future transactions between entities for which the currency exchange rate has changed.

B. The risk associated with changes in exchange rates on future transactions (economic exposure) can be mitigated by:

1. Distributing an entity's productive assets in various countries with different currencies and shifting the sources of revenues and costs to different locations so that the future effects of the exchange rate changes are minimized.

2. These changes may involve, among other things:
   a. Increasing or decreasing dependency on suppliers in certain foreign countries
   b. Establishing or eliminating production facilities in certain foreign countries
   c. Increasing or decreasing sales in certain foreign markets
   d. Increasing or decreasing the level of debt in certain foreign countries

V. Other Hedgeable Risks

A. In addition to hedging foreign currency–denominated transaction risks and foreign currency–denominated translation risks, accounting permits the hedging of two other foreign currency risks:

1. **Forecasted foreign currency–denominated transactions**—The risk being hedged is the possibility that exchange rate changes will have an unfavorable effect on the cash flows associated with nonfirm but planned transactions to be settled in a foreign currency.
   a. For example, the dollar value of royalty revenue forecasted to be received in a foreign currency from a foreign entity.
   b. Accounting permits the cash flows from the expected transaction to be hedged using forward, futures, or option contracts.
2. **Unrecognized firm commitments**—The risk being hedged is the possibility that exchange rate changes will have an unfavorable effect on the fair value of a firm commitment for a future sale or purchase to be settled in a foreign currency.
   a. For example, a commitment (contract) to purchase custom-built equipment from a foreign manufacturer with payment to be made in a foreign currency.
   b. Accounting permits the cash flow or the fair value from a firm commitment to be hedged using forward, futures, or option contracts.

Note

The accounting treatments for these foreign currency hedging purposes are discussed in detail in the FAR section in "Foreign Currency Hedges."

VI. Foreign Currency Hedging Instruments

Foreign Currency Hedging Instruments—Foreign currency hedging is accomplished primarily through the use of forward and futures contracts. Forward/futures contracts are agreements (contracts) to buy or sell (or which give the right to buy or sell) a specified commodity in the future at a price (rate) determined at the time the forward contract is executed. The most important types of forward contracts are:

A. **Foreign Currency Forward Exchange Contracts (FCFX)**—Agreements to buy or sell a specified amount of a foreign currency at a specified future date at a specified (forward) rate.

1. Under an FCFX contract the obligation to buy or sell is firm; the exchange must occur.
2. This contract is an "exchange" because the contract provides for trading (exchanging) one currency for another currency. Example: A U.S. entity enters into an FCFX to pay U.S. dollars for euros.

B. **Foreign Currency Option Contracts (FCO)**—Agreements that gives the right (option) to buy (call option) or sell (put option) a specified amount of a foreign currency at a specified (forward) rate during or at the end of a specified time period.

1. Under an FCO contract, the party holding the option has the right (option) to buy (call) or sell (put), but does not have to exercise that option; the exchange will occur at the option of the option holder. *For example*: A U.S. entity acquires an option (right) to buy euros, but does not have to buy the euros.
2. If the option is exercised, there is an exchange of currencies.
3. FCO contracts usually involve fees, which make them significantly more costly to execute than FCFX contracts.

International Transfer Price Issue

A major issue for firms involved in international economic activity revolves around the use of transfer prices for activities that cross international borders. This lesson defines transfer price. In addition, it identifies factors that influence the setting of transfer prices, the tax consequences of setting transfer prices, and the methods of determining appropriate transfer prices.

After studying this lesson, you should be able to:

1. Define transfer prices and describe the role they play in international business activity.
2. Identify the factors that affect the setting of transfer prices.
3. Describe and calculate the income tax effects of alternative transfer prices.
4. Describe regulatory requirements that govern the setting of transfer prices.
5. Identify and describe alternative bases for setting transfer prices, including the advantages and disadvantages of each.

I. Introduction

A. In the international business context, transfer pricing relates to the transfer of goods and services across international borders.

B. Establishing transfer pricing policies is an important function for multinational entities because it determines, in part, the allocation of profits among affiliated units and, therefore, among different taxing jurisdictions with different tax rates.

C. By manipulating transfer prices entities can avoid taxes in countries with higher rates and thereby increased profits. In addition, transfer prices are likely to have implications for performance evaluation and related motivational issues.

Definitions

Transfer Price: The amount (price) at which goods or services are transferred between affiliated entities; the related transactions are intercompany transactions.

Examples

Goods from a parent entity to a subsidiary entity (downstream transfer).

Goods from a subsidiary entity to a parent entity (upstream transfer).

Goods from one subsidiary entity to another subsidiary entity.

II. Factors Affecting Transfer Pricing

A. Two broad factors influence the determination of international transfer prices:

1. Management's objective in setting transfer prices
2. Legal requirements governing transfer prices between countries

B. Management's objectives may be grouped into two major categories:

1. To maintain control and evaluate performance
2. To allocate and minimize costs

C. Minimizing costs focuses on total worldwide income taxes, but the minimizing of other costs may be an objective, including:

1. **Withholding of taxes**—To avoid foreign withholding taxes on cash payments for dividends, interest, and royalties by transferring cash in the form of a sales transfer price

2. **Avoiding import duties**—To minimize import duties by minimizing transfer prices
3. **Circumventing profit repatriation restrictions**—To overcome limits on profits that can be transferred out of a country in the form of dividends by moving profits through transfer prices

III. **Income Tax Effects of Setting Different Transfer Prices**—The following examples illustrate the effects of setting different transfer prices for the same goods.

A. Assume Company P, located in the U.S., owns controlling interest in Company S, located in a foreign country. The respective tax rates are:

Co. P (U.S.)	50%
Co. S (Foreign)	20%

1. Company S buys or produces goods for $100. These goods are sold (transferred) to Company P, which sells the goods to a third-party for $300. Before tax consolidated income is $200 ($300 – $100), but after tax income depends on the amount of income recognized in each of the two countries, which is determined by the price at which the goods are transferred from Company S to Company P.

a. **Example 1**—Transfer Price = $200

	Co. S Original Cost		**Co. S to Co. P Transfer Price**		**Co. P Selling Price**	**Totals**
	$100		$200		$300	
Pretax Profit		$100		$100		$200
Tax Rate		.20		.50		
Tax		$ 20		$ 50		$ 70
After Tax Profit		$ 80		$ 50		$130

b. **Example 2**—Transfer Price = $250

	Co. S Original Cost		**Co. S to Co. P Transfer Price**		**Co. P Selling Price**	**Totals**
	$100		$250		$300	
Pretax Profit		$150		$50		$200
Tax Rate		.20		.50		
Tax		$ 30		$25		$ 55
After Tax Profit		$120		$25		$145

2. As shown in the two examples above, a transfer price of $200 results in a combined income of $130, whereas a transfer price of $250 results in a combined income of $145, an increase of $15, or more than 10%. This increase was achieved without any change in operations or other procedures. It resulted from simply changing the transfer price between affiliated entities. Insofar as international entities have discretion in setting transfer prices, they can manipulate the country in which revenue is recognized and, thereby, taxes incurred and profit reported.

In the News—Fiji Water: Shutting Off the Tap?

Fiji's military government on Nov. 18 (2010) expelled David Roth, the top local manager of Fiji Water, a company owned by Los Angeles billionaires Stewart and Lynda Resnick. The move comes amid rumors that Fiji (the country) may limit access to the aquifer that supplies the water. Roth's visa was revoked following the resignation of acting Prime Minister Ratu Ganilau, who left his post citing differences with the country's ruler, Voreqe Bainimarama, "over the David Roth issue," Pacific News Agency Service reports. **Bainimarama has accused Fiji Water—which accounts for 20 percent of the island nation's exports—of selling to its U.S. parent at artificially low prices to avoid taxes, according to Agence France-Presse.** (Emphasis added.)

Source: Adapted from *Bloomberg Businessweek*, November 29–December 5, 2010

IV. Determining Transfer Price

A. In the United States, guidance on the appropriate allocation of income between entities under common control, and therefore appropriate transfer pricing, is provided by the Internal Revenue Code (Sec. 482).

1. That guidance provides that income should be allocated based on the functions performed and the risks assumed by each of the entities involved in arm's-length transactions.

2. Section 482 also gives the IRS the power to audit and adjust international transfer prices, and to impose penalties for under payment.

3. Transfer pricing guidelines also are provided by the Organization for Economic Co-operation and Development (OECD), an international body with representatives from 30-member nations. The OECD guidelines embody transfer pricing based on the principle of arm's-length transactions.

B. In practice, transfer prices are determined using a variety of methods, including:

1. Cost-based—Where the transfer price is a function of the cost to the selling unit to produce a good or provide a service.

a. Characteristics:

i. Based on variable cost, variable and certain fixed cost, or full cost

ii. Cost may be actual or standard cost

iii. Commonly used when no external market exists for the good or service

b. Advantages:

i. Relatively simple to use

ii. Less costly to implement than a negotiated price

c. Disadvantages:

i. Requires determining a cost-basis to use

ii. May encourage/facilitate inefficiencies in production of goods or provision of services

2. Market price–based—Where the transfer price is based on the price of the good or service in the market (if available).

a. Characteristics:

i. Commonly used when an external market for the good or service exists

ii. Typically a valid "arm's-length" basis for transfer pricing

- **b.** Advantage:
  - **i.** Avoids using cost-based prices, which may incorporate inefficiencies
- **c.** Disadvantage:
  - **i.** May be difficult to obtain a market-based price

3. Negotiated price—Where the transfer price is based on a negotiated agreement between buying and selling affiliates.

- **a.** Characteristic:
  - **i.** Commonly used when no external market exists for the good or service
- **b.** Advantage:
  - **i.** Preserves each manager's autonomy
- **c.** Disadvantages:
  - **i.** May be more costly to implement than a predetermined cost-based transfer price
  - **ii.** May take excessive time to negotiate a transfer price
  - **iii.** Performance measures may reflect negotiating ability, not performance

C. In addition to its role in determining the total profit of firms with multinational operations, transfer pricing also affects the profit reported by the individual affiliated units. Because unit profit is typically used to evaluate the unit's management, individual unit managers may prefer a transfer price that is different from the price that maximizes total profit to the consolidated entities. Therefore, the transfer pricing methodology used by multinational firms is important, not only to profit determination, but also to performance throughout the multinational entity.

Globalization

Introduction to Globalization

Over the last 30 or more years, business has become increasingly international in nature. A number of fundamental reasons influenced this shift and the fact that the trend continues. These reasons include the formation of global financial institutions, reductions in international trade and investment barriers, and technological advances. Despite the benefits derived from international business, entities that engage in it face challenges not encountered in a strictly domestic operation. This lesson defines globalization, describes the reasons globalization has occurred, and identifies major challenges faced by entities engaged in international business.

After studying this lesson, you should be able to:

1. Define business globalization and the globalization of markets.
2. Identify and describe the factors that have enabled or facilitated the growth in international business.
3. Describe the risks faced by entities that engage in international business.

I. Definitions (from the Business Perspective)

Definitions
Globalization: The movement toward a more integrated and interdependent world economy, evidenced by the increased mobility of goods, services, labor, technology, and capital throughout the world.

Globalization of Markets: The merging of historically separate and distinct national markets into a single, worldwide market.

- **A.** Globalization of business is often considered in three categories:
  1. Globalization of trade
  2. Globalization of production
  3. Globalization of capital markets
  4. Subsequent lessons cover each of these three areas of globalization.

II. Globalization Drivers Identified—Several macro-factors have contributed to the emergence of global economic activity. The most important of these factors fall into the following categories:

- **A.** Global institutions
- **B.** Reduction in trade and investment barriers
- **C.** Technological advances

III. Global Financial Institutions—The previously mentioned Bretton Woods Agreement, which established an international system of fixed exchange rates between currencies (which has since been replaced mostly by floating exchange rates), also established a framework for increased international commerce and finance, and founded two international institutions intended to oversee the processes of international economic activity. Those institutions are known today as:

- **A. The World Bank (formaly the International Bank for Reconstruction and Development)**—With the objective of promoting general economic development, including lending to developing countries, primarily for infrastructure, agriculture, education, and similar development needs.

B. The International Monetary Fund (IMF)—With the objective of maintaining order in the international monetary system, largely by providing funds to economies in financial crises, including:

1. **Currency crisis**—When speculation in the exchange value of a currency causes a dramatic depression in its value
2. **Banking crisis**—When a loss in confidence in the banking system of a country leads to a run on banks
3. **Financial debt crisis**—When a country cannot meet its foreign debt obligations

IV. Reduction in Trade and Investment Barriers

A. Trade Barriers—Recent declines in trade barriers can be traced to the establishment in 1947 of the General Agreement on Tariffs and Trade (GATT).

1. The original GATT and subsequent negotiated variations are multilateral agreements for the purpose of:
   - **a.** Liberalizing and encouraging trade by eliminating tariffs, subsidies, import quotas, and other trade barriers
   - **b.** Harmonizing intellectual property laws, and reducing transportation and other costs of international business as a result of group undertakings
2. The World Trade Organization (WTO) was subsequently established (1995) to encompass GATT and related international trade bodies. The WTO also serves to "police" the international trading system

B. Investment Barriers—In addition to reductions in trade barriers, there has been a move within and between countries to remove restrictions on foreign direct investment.

1. Foreign direct investment (FDI) is direct investment by an entity in facilities to manufacture and/or market goods and services in a foreign country (i.e., a country other than the investor's home country).
2. As a consequence of reduced restrictions on FDI, over the past 30 years both the annual flow and the stock (accumulated amount) of FDI has increased dramatically. In fact, the flow of FDI has grown faster than the growth in either worldwide output or worldwide trade.

V. Technological Advances—If the establishment of global institutions and reduction in trade and investment barriers helped make international business possible, advances in technology have made much of the growth of international business practical. Among those developments, advances in three areas have been particularly important.

A. Communications and Information Processing—Together, developments in communications and information processing have made possible the transmission and processing of large quantities of voice and data at a low cost. The basis for most advances has been the development of the Internet and the World Wide Web (WWW) which enable businesses to overcome certain constraints of time and location. Specifically, the Internet and the World Wide Web permit planning, communicating, coordinating, marketing, transaction processing, and other business functions to be carried out literally worldwide.

B. Transportation—Developments in transportation have made the movement of people and products faster and cheaper. Among the most important transportation developments have been:

1. Large, long-range jet aircraft have enabled people to travel and freight to be moved throughout the world in a timely and cost effective manner. The emergence of FedEx, UPS, and DHL—major air cargo carriers—reflects the importance of this development.
2. Large cargo ships, many designed to handle specific types of cargo, have enabled the economical movement of massive quantities of raw materials, large industrial equipment, and finished goods. The use of supertankers to move crude oil and container ships reflects this capability.

3. Containerization is the use of containers that can be handled by ship, by train, or by truck with standardized handling equipment. Containerization and container cargo carriers permit "start to finish" movement of goods using intermodal transportation methods in an extremely efficient manner.

VI. Challenges of Globalization

A. In its narrowest sense, an entity that imports or exports goods is engaged in international business, the most elementary form of globalization. Even in this elementary form of international business, management faces challenges not encountered in a strictly domestic operation. As the number and kinds of cross-border business activity increases, so also do the challenges.

B. Addressing the challenges of international business begins by understanding the broad macro-environment of a country, including its political, economic, and legal characteristics, and assessing the risk inherent in each.

1. **Political system**—Concerned with the system of government in a nation and the extent to which the system tends to be democratic or totalitarian.

    a. Political risk—The possibility that political forces will cause significant adverse change in a country's business environment that will have a negative effect on profits and other entity goals.

2. **Economic system**—Concerned with the extent to which the government intervenes in economic activities, and ranges from a market (free-enterprise) economy to a command economy, in which the government plays a predominant role.

    a. Economic risk—The possibility that management of an economy will cause dramatic adverse changes in a country's business environment, including such factors as inflation, adverse currency exchange rates and restrictions on transfer (repatriation) of profits out of the country.

3. **Legal system**—Concerned with the formal rules (laws) that specify behavior and the processes by which enforcement is carried out.

    a. The legal system has a direct impact on the nature of business practices, including for example, the areas of:

        i. Property rights—The recognition and enforcement of right to own and use personal property

        ii. Contract law—The specification of what is acceptable and how enforcement occurs

        iii. Intellectual property—The recognition and enforcement of intellectual property rights, including patents, trademarks, copyrights, etc.

        iv. Product safety and liability laws—The extent to which such laws exist and how they are enforced

C. The political, economic, and legal environments of a country help determine the attractiveness of the country as a market or investment location.

D. A subsequent lesson will discuss the analysis of macro-environments as a part of the strategic planning process.

Globalization of Trade

The most basic form of international business takes place in the form of international trade—the buying of goods or services from a foreign provider (importing) or the selling of goods or services to a foreign buyer (exporting). This lesson describes the reasons for undertaking international trade and the benefits of that trade. It also demonstrates the growth in international trade, with particular attention to the changes in U.S. imports and exports. Finally, this lesson identifies and describes critical cost factors to determining the viability of international trade.

After studying this lesson, you should be able to:

1. Identify and describe the reasons for and benefits of international trade.
2. Describe changes in worldwide and U.S. international trade.
3. Identify the costs incurred that are critical in assessing the prospects of international trade.

I. Definitions

Definitions

Globalization of Trade: The exchange of goods and services between and among countries.

Export: A good or service sold to a buyer in a foreign country.

Import: A good or service acquired from a seller in a foreign country.

II. Reasons for and Benefits of International Trade

A. Globalization of trade has been facilitated or enabled by (among other things):

1. Reductions in barriers to imports (and to a lesser extent, exports)
2. Increased economic integration between and among countries
3. Regional trade agreements (e.g., NAFTA, EEU, etc.), which foster international trade between participating parties
4. Internet and World Wide Web capabilities, which enable such functions as locating foreign partners and foreign buyers, and carrying out global marketing activities
5. Financial sector developments, which have, among other things, facilitated global trading by providing the mechanisms for international commercial transactions. For example, the use of letters of credit based on export contracts provides the exporter a form of guarantee from a bank that it will receive payment for exported goods.
6. Global trade enables entities, wherever they are located, to use their comparative advantage to sell goods and services worldwide. Global trade also makes a greater variety of goods available to end users and at a lower cost than would otherwise be possible. By trading internationally, both suppliers and buyers benefit.

B. Measures of International Trade

A. Worldwide Trade

During the 50-year period 1950 to 2000, the world economy grew 6-fold (six times). During that same period, global exports (trade) grew 17-fold (17 times).

During the period 2000 to 2008, the worldwide economy grew by 30%, while exports (which are also imports to another country) grew at an average annual rate of 5%; in some years the increase was close to 20%.

In 2008 and 2009, worldwide economic growth (GDP) slowed considerably, resulting in only a 1.3% increase in 2008 and a 2.6% decrease in 2009. Worldwide merchandise exports increased by 2.3% in 2008, but decreased by a 12.1% in 2009.

In 2010 and 2011, global output increased by 3.8% and 2.5%, respectively. For the same two years, global merchandise exports grew by 14% and 4.9%, respectively. Since 2011 both worldwide imports and exports have continued to grow and have more than recovered the decreases of the 2008 and 2009 global economic downturn.

Source: World Trade Organization

B. U.S. Trade

1. Aggregate imports/exports

a. The following graph shows the trend in total U.S. foreign trade (imports and exports) for the period 1994 through 2014.

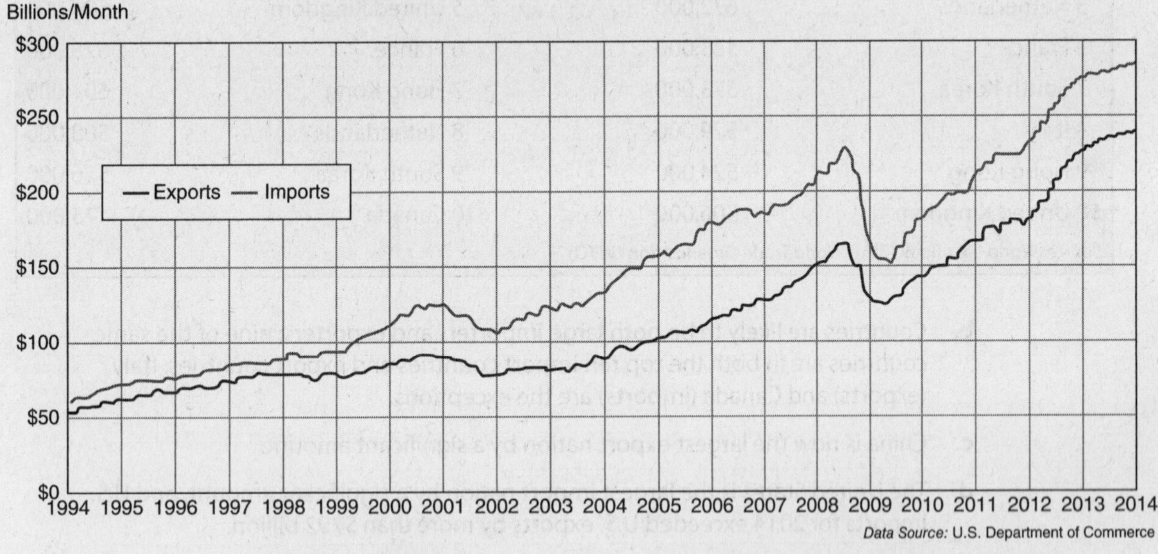

b. During the period 2000 to 2008, U.S. imports (merchandise and services) grew by 7.0%, while exports grew by 6.0%.

c. In 2009, as a result of the worldwide economic recession, U.S. imports declined about 26% and exports declined about 18%.

d. Between 2009 and the end of 2014, U.S. imports and U.S. exports increased by an average of approximately 13% annually.

2. **Share of GDP**

   a. The following table shows the change in the level of imports and exports for the U.S. as a share of gross domestic product (GDP) for selected years beginning in 1960:

	1960	1980	2000	2008	2009	2010	2011	2012	2013
Imports as % of GDP	4%	10%	15%	18%	14%	16%	18%	17%	17%
Exports as % of GDP	5%	10%	11%	13%	11%	13%	14%	14%	14%

Source: Bureau of Economic Analysis/World Bank

   b. While both U.S. imports and exports as a share of GDP reflect a significant increase since 1960, the increase in imports as a share of GDP has been greater than that of exports. Between 2011 and 2013, both imports and exports as a share of GDP leveled off at about 17% and 14%, respectively.

3. **World's largest exporters/importers**

   a. The following tables rank the world's 10 largest exporters and importers for 2014.

List of Countries by Exports—2014
(in U.S. dollars, add 000,000)

Country	Exports
1 China	$2,342,000
2 United States	1,621,000
3 Germany	1,508,000
4 Japan	683,000
5 Netherlands	672,000
6 France	583,000
7 South Korea	573,000
8 Italy	529,000
9 Hong Kong	524,000
10 United Kingdom	506,000

List of Countries by Imports—2014
(in U.S. dollars, add 000,000)

Country	Imports
1 United States	$2,413,000
2 China	1,959,000
3 Germany	1,216,000
4 Japan	822,000
5 United Kingdom	684,000
6 France	678,000
7 Hong Kong	601,000
8 Netherlands	588,000
9 South Korea	526,000
10 Canada	475,000

Source: World Fact Book (CIA) /World Trade Organization (WTO)

   b. Countries are likely to be both large importers and exporters; nine of the same countries are in both the top ten import countries and export countries. Italy (exports) and Canada (imports) are the exceptions.

   c. China is now the largest export nation by a significant amount.

   d. The United States is the largest import nation by a significant amount, and U.S. imports for 2014 exceeded U.S. exports by more than $792 billion.

   e. China is the second-largest import nation, but when the value of imports by Hong Kong, a special administrative territory of China (shown separately as number 9), is added with those of mainland China, their total imports are greater than those of the United States.

4. **Composition of imports/exports**—The composition of U.S. trade in goods and services for 2014 shows the following breakdown by end-use categories:

	Percentage of Total	
End-Use Category	**Exports**	**Imports**
Capital Goods*	24%	21%
Industrial**	22%	24%
Consumer	9%	20%
Automotive	7%	11%
Agriculture/Food	6%	4%
Other Goods	2%	3%
Services	30%	17%
TOTALS	100%	100%

*Includes machinery and equipment (except automotive)

**Includes natural resources

Source: U.S Census Bureau

C. **Summary of Measures**

1. Worldwide trade has increased dramatically in the last 50 years or so.
2. International trade by U.S. entities has continued to increase over the last 50 years or so, despite certain periods of short-term decline.
3. The U.S. has sustained a negative export (net import) position for goods and services since the mid-1970s.
4. It also should be noted that global trade in capital and industrial goods has traditionally been greater than global trade in consumer-oriented goods for which cultural differences (values, taste, etc.) play a more important role in purchase decisions.

III. Factors Affecting Costs of International Trade

A. **Transaction Costs**—The cost associated with any transaction, but which will have additional elements in international transactions, including the additional costs of negotiating with suppliers and customers, using letters of credit, currency exchange, and hedging

B. **Transportation Costs**—The cost of shipping goods from the point of production to the point of consumption, whether for goods sold (exports) or goods purchased (imports)

C. **Tariff or Other Restrictive Costs**—The direct cost of tariffs and the indirect cost of meeting standards or other requirements that may be unique to a country

D. **Time Costs**—The cost of delays due to distance and inspection and other import/export functions

Globalization of Production

Globalization of production involves the manufacturing/provision of goods or services in locations worldwide, either under a contractual arrangement with a separate provider (outsourcing) or establishing owned facilities to provide goods or services (foreign direct investment). This lesson describes outsourcing and foreign direct investment as alternative means of obtaining goods or services worldwide.

After studying this lesson, you should be able to:

1. Define and describe outsourcing, including the reasons it is used and the risk associated with its use.
2. Define and describe foreign direct investment, including the reasons it is used and the risk associated with its use.

I. **Definition**

> **Definition**
> *Globalization of Production*: The sourcing of goods and services from around the world to take advantage of differences in cost and quality of the factors of production and, thereby, gain competitive advantage.

II. **Sourcing Alternatives**—The sourcing of goods and services worldwide may be accomplished in two general ways:

   A. Outsourcing
   B. Foreign direct investment

III. **Outsourcing**—Acquiring a good or service from a separate or external provider.

   A. In the international business context, the separate provider is located in a foreign country.
   B. Goods provided may be raw materials, intermediate goods, final goods, or services (e.g., call centers, data entry, programming, design, engineering, etc.) acquired from a separate entity located anywhere worldwide.
   C. Outsourcing may be used for a number of reasons, including:
      1. Cost savings
      2. Improved quality
      3. Reduce time to delivery
      4. Enable focusing on core business
      5. Scalability
      6. Access to knowledge, talent, and best practices
   D. While outsourcing can provide significant benefits, it also presents risks, including:
      1. **Quality risk**—The possibility that the good or service will not meet the buyer's standards; in the extreme the good or service may be of such poor quality as to create liability to the buyer.
      2. **Security risk**—The possibility that the provider will misappropriate intellectual property, trade processes, data, etc.
      3. **Export/import risk**—The possibility that the home country government or the foreign government will have restrictions that prevent the transfer of inputs needed by the foreign supplier or the export/import of finished goods.

4. **Currency exchange risk**—The possibility that the exchange rate between the home country currency and the foreign currency will change such that the cost of goods or service in the domestic currency increases.

5. **Legal risk**—The possibility that a violation of either home country (e.g., Foreign Corrupt Practices Act [FCPA]) or foreign country laws (e.g., labor laws) will have an adverse impact on the entity.

E. When outsourcing in a foreign country, steps should be taken to minimize associated risks, including:

1. The use of due process in selection of providers. Determine the trustworthiness, competence, and past history of prospective suppliers.

2. Use a qualified lawyer in the foreign country for all foreign legal undertakings.

3. Determine the legal and regulatory requirements for exports/imports in both countries before entering into a contract with the foreign supplier.

4. Execute a through contract with the supplier selected that includes an arbitration clause.

5. Minimize the currency exchange risk by negotiating payment in the home country currency or, lacking that, enter into hedging arrangements (e.g., forward or option contracts) to minimize any negative effects of exchange rate changes.

6. Be knowledgeable of and have strict policies concerning relevant legal requirements in both the home and the foreign country.

IV. **Foreign Direct Investment**—Establishing owned or controlled facilities in foreign locations to produce goods or provide services through the acquisition of property, plant, equipment, and other assets in a foreign location or locations.

A. Under this approach to sourcing, an entity establishes its own production or service facilities in whatever location worldwide best meets its cost, quality, quantity, market, and other needs.

1. In a production process involving multiple stages or multiple components, each stage of production or each component produced could occur in a different country.

2. For multinational enterprises (MNEs) the use of foreign direct investment results in global production networks in which:

a. Goods are produced in a set of locations around the world.

b. Production locations are based on the advantages provided by a country's cost and the quality of the factors of production (e.g., raw materials, labor, capital, etc.).

B. The fundamental intents of establishing foreign production or service facilities may be to:

1. Lower the overall cost structure and/or improve the quality of the good or service.

2. Expand markets.

3. Increase growth potential.

C. Foreign direct investments expose the investing firm to a number of specific risks, including:

1. **Political risks**—Result from changes in the political climate or government policies that cause discontinuity or disruption to economic institutions or activity which adversely affects the foreign investment. This risk category includes, among other things, internal and external conflict, delays in granting permits, excessive red tape, corruption and bribes, and, in the extreme, expropriation.

2. **Transfer risks**—Also are mostly caused by changes in governmental policies, and result in uncertainty about or restrictions on cross-border flows of payments, capital, dividends, and other flows. For example, restrictions imposed by the foreign country could make repatriation of profits difficult or impossible.

3. **Exchange rate risks**—Result from adverse changes in the exchange rate between the foreign country's currency and the currency of the investor (or the currencies of other relevant countries). These changes could reduce revenues, profits, and asset values reported in the investor's currency.

Globalization of Capital Markets

The globalization of trade and production has been accompanied and facilitated by the globalization of capital markets. This lesson describes the nature of capital markets and international capital markets, their growth, and the benefits and risks of those markets.

After studying this lesson, you should be able to:

1. Define and describe global capital markets, including the major Eurodollar and international bond markets.
2. Describe the benefits of global financial markets, the risks of those markets, and the ways those risks can be mitigated.

I. Definitions

A. Capital Market—A market in which financial securities are traded.

1. A capital market brings together the providers of capital (investors) and the users of capital ("borrowers").
   - **a.** Providers invest to earn a return on the funds they provide.
   - **b.** Users seek funds to finance their own investments, operations or for other purposes.
   - **c.** Capital markets facilitate the interaction of providers and users of capital.
2. Generally, capital markets consist of three specific major component markets:
   - **a.** Stock market
   - **b.** Bond market
   - **c.** Money market
3. Domestic capital markets traditionally have served as the intermediary between providers and users of capital. The use of a strictly domestic capital market, however, has certain limitations even in the largest economies.
   - **a.** The pool of providers (investors) is limited by the size and wealth of domestic residents.
   - **b.** The limitations of a domestic market constrain supply, which increases the cost of capital—the rate of return that investors must be paid for the use of funds.
   - **c.** Providers are limited in the number of investment opportunities available.

B. Global Capital Market—An interconnected set of financial institutions and national markets that permit the trading of financial securities between and among investor and borrowers worldwide.

1. While many institutions make up the global capital market, there are two formal major (most important) international financial markets:
   - **a.** Eurodollar market or eurocurrency market (euromarket)
     - **i.** Eurodollars are created when a U.S. dollar deposit is made outside the United States and is maintained in U.S. dollars.
     - **ii.** Eurodollars provide short-term and intermediate-term loans, less than five years in maturity, denominated in U.S. dollars.
     - **iii.** Eurodollars provide an alternative to domestic banks for financing by international firms.
     - **iv.** Generally, the cost of borrowing in the Euromarket will be less than through a domestic bank because such lending activity is less regulated.

b. International bond market (Eurobonds)

i. Offers long-term loans outside the home country of the borrower.

ii. Bonds are offered in most major currencies.

iii. Bonds avoid most government regulation.

II. Growth in Capital Markets Flows

A. The growth in international capital markets in the past 20 years or so has been dramatic.

1. The following graph shows global trade and capital flows as a percentage of world GDP for the years 1995 to 2012:

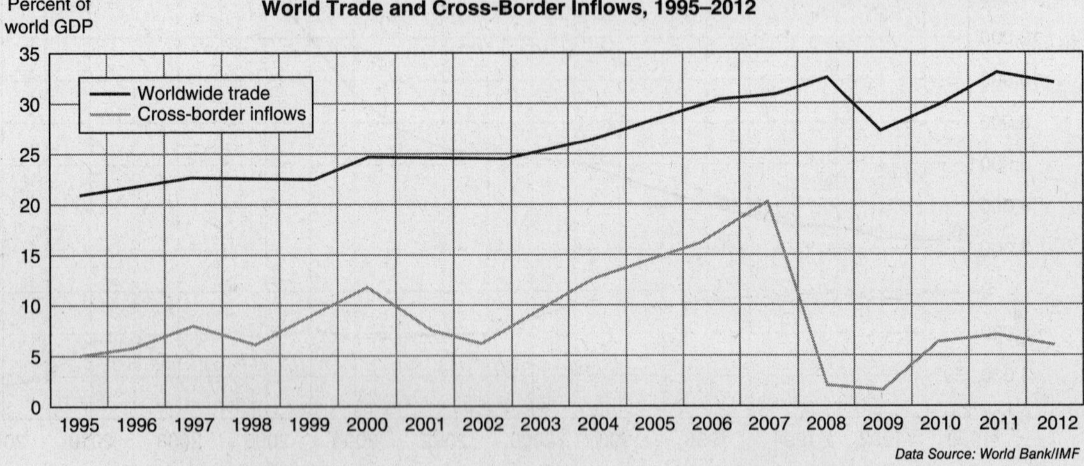

2. Charles W. L. Hill, international business author, reports that between 1990 and 2006, cross-border bank loans increased from $3,600 billion to $17,875 billion and that international equity offerings increased from $18 billion in 1990 to $377 billion in 2006.

3. Beginning with the start of the recent worldwide recession (circa August 2007), international capital flow decreased significantly (see graph, above) especially among economically developed countries and, in some periods and for some countries resulted in a reversal of flows as investors liquidated foreign holdings.

4. Beginning in 2009, cross-border flows began a rebound, but since 2010 they have leveled off.

B. There are two primary causes for the long-term increases in international capital flows:

1. Deregulation of international financial services by governments

2. Advances in communications and data processing

C. U.S. and International Investments

1. A country's net international investment position shows the difference between a country's external (foreign) assets and liabilities, including both publicly and privately held assets and debt.

2. The following chart shows the U.S. net international investment position for the 22 years 1990 through 2012:

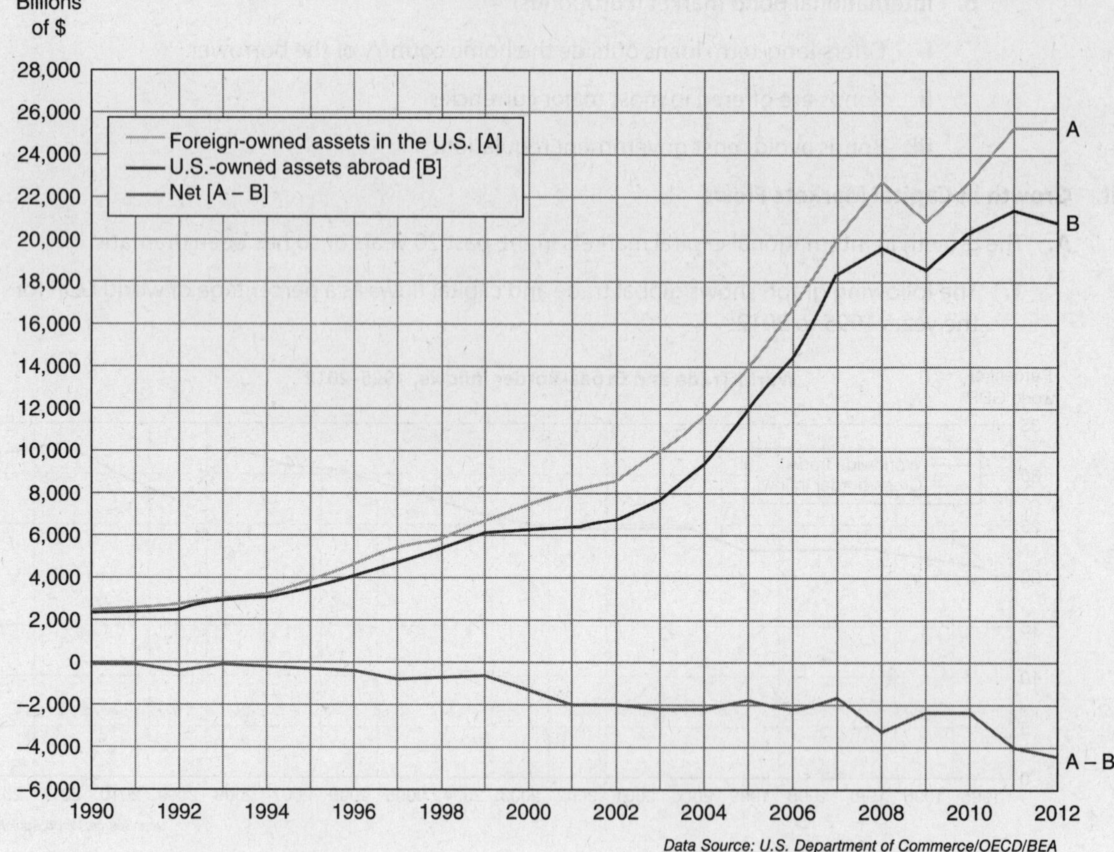

Source: Bureau of Economic Analysis

III. Benefits of Global Financial Markets

A. The globalization of capital markets, enabled by the reductions in cross-border capital transfer and transaction restrictions, permits providers to invest worldwide and enables users to seek capital from investors worldwide.

1. For investors, the range of opportunities is global, thus permitting international diversification in investment portfolios.

a. Diversifying investments abroad normally will dampen overall portfolio risk.

2. For users, the supply of funds available can be greater, while the cost of capital can be lowered.

a. A foreign subsidiary may be able to borrow in the foreign market at a lower interest rate than its parent can borrow in its home country.

b. Borrowing by a foreign subsidiary in its local foreign market for local use also will avoid the foreign currency exchange risk that its parent would encounter if it borrows in a foreign currency.

IV. Risks of Global Financial Markets

A. While global capital markets offer benefits to both investors and borrowers, international capital activity may be subject to an important risk not encountered in a domestic capital market (i.e., foreign currency exchange risk). That risk occurs if an entity engages in a transaction or has a balance to be settled in a foreign currency, in which case the domestic value of the settlement will be affected by changes in the currency exchange rate.

B. Foreign currency exchange risk is the possibility of loss resulting from changes in currency exchange rates; adverse changes in exchange rates can:

1. Reduce the domestic currency value of returns on investments.

Example
If, during the period of a foreign investment, the dollar strengthens against the foreign currency, the investment will decline in domestic currency value, even if there is no change in value in the foreign investment market.

2. Increase the domestic currency cost of borrowing.

Example
If, during the period of foreign borrowing, the dollar weakens against the foreign currency, the dollars required to service the foreign denominated debt will increase, even though the interest rate in the foreign currency remains unchanged.

C. An investor or a borrower can mitigate the risk associated with foreign currency exchange rate changes by the use of forward/futures exchange contracts, forward option contracts, or currency swap contracts.

1. An investor could hedge the foreign currency exchange risk associated with an investment by entering into a forward exchange contract or an option contract that enables the investor to convert the proceeds on the sale of the investment into a known dollar amount.
2. A borrower could hedge the foreign currency exchange risk associated with interest payments or principal repayment by entering into a forward exchange contract or option contract that enables the borrower to purchase foreign currency units at a known dollar amount.
3. An investor or a borrower (normally both would be a financial institution or a major corporation) could enter into a contract to exchange one currency for a specified amount of another currency at some future date. Such a currency swap would avoid a currency exchange rate risk at lower costs than forward, futures, and options contracts.

Globalization and Power Shifts

A shift in the economic significance of nations has accompanied the growth in international business. This lesson describes some of the major shifts in economic power among nations and regions, with special emphasis on the impact on the United States.

After studying this lesson, you should be able to:

1. Describe the worldwide shifts in nations responsible for various forms of economic activity, including: (a) output, (b) international trade, (c) services, (d) foreign direct investment, and (e) the home country of multinational entities.

I. **Introduction**—Among the most significant effects of the move to a global economy have been shifts in economic activity and economic importance among nations. These shifts have occurred in most areas of economic activity, including output (GDP), trade, services, foreign direct investment, and the home country of multinational entities.

II. **Output Shifts**

A. World output, as measured by real GDP of all countries combined, more than tripled during the period 1969–2009.

B. As late as the mid-1960s, the U.S. accounted for about 40% of worldwide economic activity as measured by GDP. By 1969 that share had dropped to slightly less than 30%. Since that time until 2007 nominal GDP of the U.S. remained within the range of 25%–35% of worldwide GDP. In 2007, the U.S. accounted for less than 25% of world GDP, but in 2012 accounted for only about 22% of world GDP. The U.S. share of world output is projected to continue to decline.

C. The following graph shows the annual share of world nominal GDP for the 10 countries with the highest nominal GDP in 2013 for the period 1980 through 2013, with projections through 2016. (The country listing in the upper-right corner is in the same order top to bottom as the country lines on the graph as of 2015.)

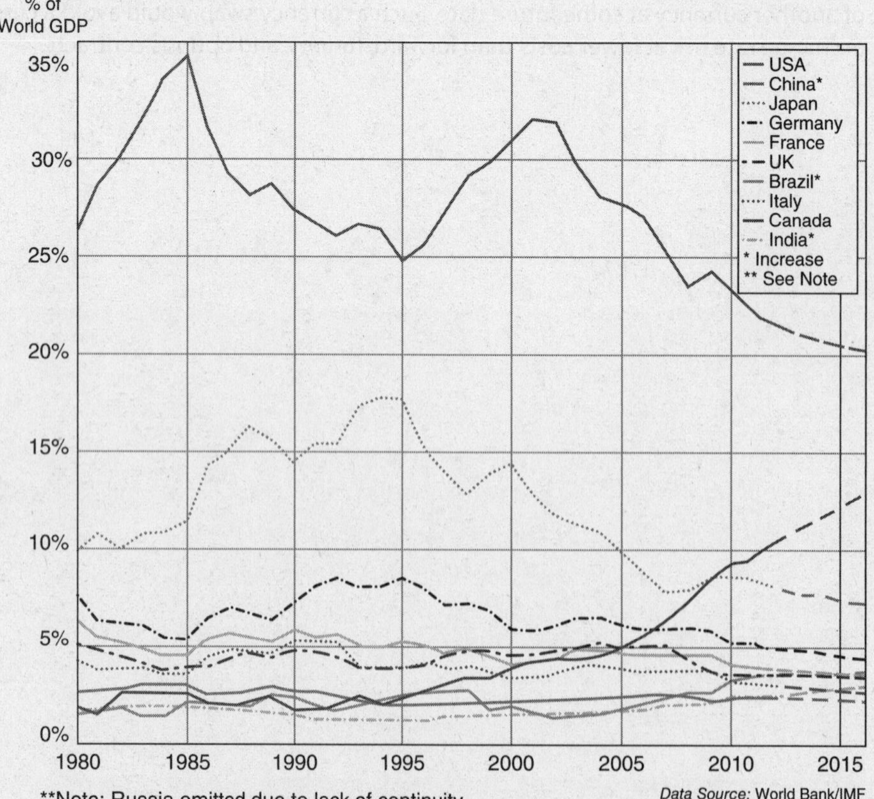

D. As the graph shows, the major change in the share of world output has occurred with the United States, Europe (Germany, France, the UK, and Italy), and Japan losing share, and China, India, and Brazil gaining share. Canada has remained fairly constant at about 3%.

E. The declines in economies that lost share were not the result of absolute decreases in economic activity of those countries, but rather the result of greater economic growth in other countries, notably in China, India, South Korea, Taiwan, and other Southeast Asian countries and in Brazil.

F. If the current trends continue, the Chinese economy will surpass the U.S. economy as the world's largest economy.

G. More significantly, however, is the expected dispersion of economic growth worldwide. The World Bank estimates that by 2020:

1. What are today considered developing nations will account for 60% of world economic activity.
2. What are today the major developed nations will account for less than 40%, down from about 55% in 2010 and about 46% in 2014.

III. Trade Shifts

A. The following graph shows the share of worldwide exports attributable to six of the largest export countries over the last 20 years or so (in the order top to bottom on the graph)—China, the United States, Germany, Japan, France, and the U.K.—for the period 1994 to 2013.

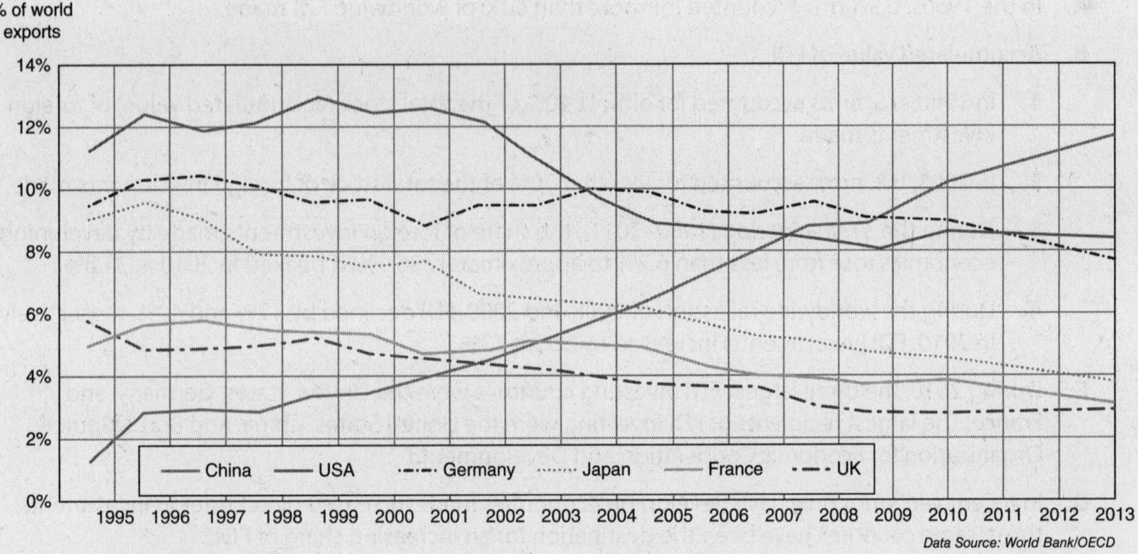

B. The share of exports attributable to these six countries has remained in the range of 40%–45% for approximately 25 years.

C. However, the relative share between the countries has changed significantly.

1. The United States has steadily lost share of world exports, from as high as 18% (in the 1950s) to 8.39% in 2013; in that year it was the number two export country. In 2013, the U.S. share of worldwide imports was 12.33%.
2. Germany gained significantly in the share of world exports from 1950 to about 1980. Between 2002 and 2008, Germany was the number one export country; in 2012, it was the number two export country, but it has since slipped back into number three behind the U.S.
3. Since 1985, China has increased its share from about 2% to about 12%, and in 2008, it became the number one export country.

D. Service Shifts—Like output and trade, there has been a shift in certain services from being provided domestically to being provided by foreign-located service providers.

- **A.** In some cases, entities are outsourcing services.
- **B.** In other cases, entities are directly establishing or acquiring service facilities in foreign countries.
  - **1.** In 2009, it was estimated that about 70% of all foreign direct investment (FDI) investments were for service industry capability.
- **C.** Two factors have been particularly important in the movement of services worldwide:
  - **1.** The Internet and global communication have enabled entities to relocate value-adding services to low-cost locations.
    - **a.** Various kinds of trade services (e.g., call centers, help lines, etc.), consulting services (IT, medical administration, etc.), development services (programming, debugging, etc.), and others can be carried out in locations where costs are low, with the benefits being realized in the firm's home country.
  - **2.** The shifts in certain forms of trade have necessitated complementary shifts or development of support services in foreign locations.

IV. Direct Investment Shifts—Shifts in other economic activities have been paralleled by shifts in foreign direct investment (FDI).

- **A.** In the 1960s, U.S. firms accounted for more than 60% of worldwide FDI made.
- **B.** Accumulated Value of FDI
  - **1.** In 1980, U.S. firms accounted for almost 40% of the total stock (accumulated value) of foreign investments made.
  - **2.** In 2005, U.S. firms accounted for less that 20% of the total stock of foreign investments made.
  - **3.** During the 31-year period (1980–2011), the share of foreign investments made by developing economies rose from less than 6.2% to approximately 26.9%. It peaked in 2010 at 31.8%.
  - **4.** During the worldwide recession of 2008 and 2009, FDI declined by 12% and 40%, respectively. In 2010, FDI (investments) increased by about 13%.
- **C.** During 2010, the three largest FDI investing countries were the United States, Germany, and France. The largest recipients of FDI investing were the United States, China, and Brazil (Source: Organization for Economic Cooperation and Development.)
- **D.** In recent years, not only have developing economies made increased direct foreign investments, those same countries have been the destination for an increasing share of FDI.
- **E.** Countries in Southeast Asia (including China and India) and Latin America, notably Mexico and Brazil, have been major recipients of recent FDI inflows.

V. Multinational Entities Shift

> **Definition**
> *Multinational Entity* (also *Multinational Enterprise or Multinational Company*): An entity that has its headquarters in one country, known as the *home country*, and operates in one or more other countries, known as *host countries*.

- **A.** Multinational firms account for a large share of global production. According to estimates of UNCTAD in its World Investment Report 2011, multinational firms account for 25 percent of global GDP and a third of international trade.
- **B.** In 1973, about 50% of the world's largest 260 multinational businesses were U.S. entities.
- **C.** In 2000, 36% of the Fortune Global 500 were headquartered in the United States.

D. In 2009, 28% of the Fortune Global 500 were headquartered in the United States.

E. By 2015, 25% of the Fortune Global 500 were headquartered in the United States.

F. During the last 40 years or so, the greatest increase in multinationals has occurred in developing countries, though there have been marginal increases in some developed nations.

G. The greatest increase in major international firms has been Asian-based, most notably in China. Between 2001 and 2012 the number of Asian-based companies in the Fortune Global 500 increased from 116 to 188. China accounted for 98 of the 188 companies.

H. While the historical statistics on the share of multinational enterprises by country are not entirely comparable, the evidence shows that there has been a relative decline in the role of U.S. multinational entities as the importance of entities from other countries has increased.

Becoming Global

An entity may engage in international business in numerous ways. This lesson identifies the primary ways and describes the advantages and disadvantages associated with each. Those advantages and disadvantages suggest the circumstances under which each method of entry may be desirable.

After studying this lesson, you should be able to:

1. Identify the primary forms of engaging in international business.
2. Describe the advantages and disadvantages of each form of international business.
3. Describe the circumstances under which one method of entry may be more desirable than others.

I. Introduction

A. An entity may engage in cross-border economic activity in a number of ways, ranging from simply buying or selling abroad, to the development of a multinational enterprise with global operations. These alternatives include:

1. Importing/exporting
2. Foreign licensing
3. Foreign franchising
4. Forming a foreign joint venture
5. Creating or acquiring a foreign subsidiary

B. Each of these alternatives is described and the advantages and disadvantages identified below.

II. Importing/Exporting

A. The most elementary form of international business involves selling abroad (exporting) and/or buying abroad (importing).

1. **Exporting**—The production of goods or services in a domestic economy (home country) and selling them in another country
2. **Importing**—The purchase of goods or services produced in another country (host country) for use in the domestic economy (home country)

B. **Advantages of Exporting**—Exporting can provide the following benefits:

1. Help an entity increase sales and domestic output and, thereby, achieve economies of scale in its home country
2. Avoid the substantial cost of establishing production facilities in a foreign country and the problems associated with such an operation, yet tap the sales potential in foreign markets
3. Provide a means for an entity to achieve experience in engaging in international business, including an understanding of differences in culture and taste, legal and administrative procedures, operating methodologies, and the like

C. **Advantages of Importing**—Importing can provide the following benefits:

1. Provide goods not otherwise available, or only available in limited quantities, in the home country (e.g., oil, precious metals, etc.)
2. Provide goods comparable to those provided in the home country, but at a lower cost due to comparative advantages in the foreign country
3. Provide goods of better quality than similar goods produced in the home country due to better technology or skills in the foreign country

D. Disadvantages of Exporting/Importing—Exporting and importing can have the following disadvantages:

1. Cost of transportation may make the total cost of importing or exporting too burdensome to warrant its use.
   a. This is particularly true of goods with a low value-to-weight ratio (i.e., they are relatively heavy for the value of the good).
   b. When the cost of transportation is added to the cost of the basic good, the good or an acceptable substitute could be produced or acquired in the domestic market at less cost.
2. Existence of trade barriers in the form of quotas or tariffs in the home country and/or the host country may constrain the extent to which importing and exporting are appropriate.
   a. If the domestic government imposes import quotas, a good may not be available or available only in inadequate limited quantities. Similarly, if a foreign government imposes export restrictions, the availability of goods may be restricted.
   b. If tariffs are imposed on imports by either the domestic government or by a foreign government, the cost of goods imported or exported is increased accordingly, which may make their total cost uncompetitive.

III. Foreign Licensing

A. Foreign licensing grants a foreign entity (the licensee) the right to use intangible property (patents, copyrights, trademarks, formulas, etc.) in return for a royalty based on sales or other agreed measure. As with other forms of foreign market entry, licensing is appropriate in many cases, but not in all cases.

B. Advantages of Foreign Licensing—Licensing can provide the following benefits:

1. Increased revenue through receipt of royalties
2. Avoid costs and risks associated with opening operations in a new foreign market
3. Avoid trade barrier issues in the foreign country

C. Disadvantages of Foreign Licensing

1. Foreign licensee may misuse access to the home entity's patents, technological processes, or other proprietary information.
2. Licensor (home country entity) may not have control over the manufacturing, marketing, distribution and customer service consistent with its standards and as needed for maximum results.
3. Licensee may not have the management and technical capabilities to fully realize the benefits of the license.

IV. Foreign Franchising

A. Franchising is a special form of licensing in which the franchisor not only sells intangible property (e.g., a trademark) to a foreign franchisee, but also mandates strict operating requirements for the franchisee.

1. Foreign franchising is used primarily in service and retail areas (e.g., hotels, restaurants, etc.).
2. Franchisor frequently provides ongoing assistance.
3. Franchisor receives royalty payment from franchisee.

B. Advantages of Foreign Franchising—Franchising can provide the following benefits, which are similar to those of foreign licensing:

1. Provide increased revenue through receipt of royalties
2. Avoid costs and risks of opening facilities in a foreign market

C. **Disadvantages of Foreign Franchising**—Franchising can have the following disadvantages:

1. Possibility of foreign franchisee misusing proprietary information
2. Quality controls of franchisee may not meet the standards of the franchisor

V. Joint Venturing

A. A joint venture is an entity that is established and jointly owned by two or more otherwise unrelated entities. In an international context, at least one of the owners is located in the foreign country in which the joint venture is established.

B. **Advantages of Joint Ventures**—Joint ventures can have the following benefits:

1. Host country co-owner (partner) has knowledge of the local customs, language, political system, business environment and competitive conditions.
2. Costs and risk associated with entering the foreign market are shared with one or more other parties.
3. Resistance from the local political system, labor, and other businesses may be less likely when there is a local stakeholder.

C. **Disadvantages of Joint Ventures**—Joint ventures can have the following disadvantages:

1. Foreign (host country) co-owner may misuse access to another partner's patents, technological processes, or other proprietorship information.
2. Domestic (home country) entity does not have absolute control over the joint venture entity, which may prevent the domestic entity from integrating the joint venture into its overall strategy.
3. Shared ownership arrangement can lead to differences over goals, objectives and strategy, and may result in conflicts and battles for control.

VI. Wholly-Owned Subsidiary

A. As the title implies, the use of a wholly-owned subsidiary involves the home country entity owning 100% of a foreign entity over which it has complete control. This may be accomplished in two ways:

1. Acquiring an entity already established in the foreign country through a legal acquisition
2. Establishing a new entity in the foreign country

B. **Acquiring an Already Existing Entity**

1. This approach would involve a business combination in which the home country entity acquires control of an existing foreign country entity in a legal and accounting acquisition.
2. Both entities would continue to exist and operate as separate legal entities, with the home country parent having control of the foreign country entity (subsidiary) through its ownership of the equity of the foreign entity.
3. Acquisition of a preexisting foreign entity may have the following advantages:
   a. It provides a quick entry into the foreign country, without the time-consuming process of establishing a new entity and developing the capital assets (e.g., property, plant, and equipment) and presence necessary for operation.
   b. There is a known level of operating results and related historic information that is not available when a new entity is established.
   c. When executed in a timely manner, it may serve to "block" or preempt competitors from seeking to enter the same foreign market by establishing a quick presence.
4. Acquisition of a preexisting foreign entity may have the following disadvantages:
   a. Lack of understanding by the acquiring home parent of the acquired foreign subsidiary's national values, culture, and business environment may result in conflict.

b. The corporate culture of the acquired foreign entity may be difficult to integrate with that of the home country parent.

c. Synergies or other benefits expected from the acquisition do not materialize, or they take longer to achieve than expected.

i. Studies by KPMG and McKenzie & Co. have reported that only about 30% of all mergers and acquisitions result in creating value for the acquiring entity.

ii. That percentage would not be expected to be higher for international acquisitions.

C. Establishing a New Entity

1. This method of obtaining a wholly-owned foreign subsidiary involves establishing a new entity in the foreign country. This approach is sometimes referred to as a "greenfield venture."

2. Establishing an entirely new entity in a foreign location may have the following advantages:

a. The foreign subsidiary can be built "from the ground up," to have the kind of corporate culture, operating style and procedures needed to integrate with the strategy established by the home country parent.

b. Home country parent is better able to transfer organizationally embedded competencies, skills, routines, and culture.

3. Establishing an entirely new entity in a foreign location may have the following disadvantages:

a. Time-consuming to establish and make operational

b. Costly to acquire the capital assets needed for operation

c. Greater risk associated with unknown future revenues, costs, and other operating aspects

D. Advantages of a Wholly-Owned Subsidiary—Whether established through acquisition or developing a new entity, a foreign wholly-owned subsidiary may have the following benefits:

1. Home country entity maintains control over patents, technological processes, and other proprietary information.

2. Provides the home country entity the ability to coordinate strategy with other operations and adapt as needed

E. Disadvantages of a Wholly-Owned Subsidiary—Whether established through acquisition or developing a new entity, a foreign wholly-owned subsidiary may have the following disadvantages:

1. Capital investment required for start-up is generally the most costly approach.

2. Greater unknowns about outcome and associated risk

3. Cost and risks are the burden of a single entity, the founding home country parent entity.

VII. Summary Conclusions—Some summary conclusions can be drawn from the forms of entry into international business activity and the advantages and disadvantages associated with each:

A. Engaging in importing/exporting provides a low-cost, low-risk means of initially pursuing international business. In addition, it may provide further insights into other aspects of engaging in international business.

B. When the protection of patents, technological processes, and other proprietary information is important, an entity should generally avoid the use of licensing and joint ventures. The use of wholly-owned subsidiaries is a better option to maintain control of proprietary elements.

C. When there is foreign opposition to the establishment of an operation in the country, use of a joint venture may avoid some of the resistance that a wholly-owned subsidiary may encounter.

D. When the home country entity is pursuing a global strategy, use of a wholly-owned subsidiary may provide the needed integration and operational control not available in other forms of entry into a foreign location.

E. When there is a need to minimize cost or risk in establishing foreign operations, the use of licensing and/or franchising may be desirable.

Business Strategy and Market Analysis

Introduction to Business Strategy and Market Analysis

Strategic planning provides purpose and direction for an entity. The development of strategic plans involves an interrelated sequence of procedures, which constitute the strategic planning process. This lesson identifies and describes the basic components of the strategic planning process and some of the analytical techniques available to carry out the process. Subsequent lessons cover analytical techniques in detail.

After studying this lesson, you should be able to:

1. Define the strategic planning process.
2. Identify and describe the sequence of procedures that make up the planning process.
3. Identify certain analytical techniques that can be used to facilitate the planning process.

I. **Planning Process**—The nature of the economic system and the economic market structure, whether domestic or foreign, define the broadest context of the economic environment within which an entity operates. Within the context of those economic characteristics an entity must carry out its activities. Central to the success of its activities, however defined, is the strategic planning process of the entity.

II. **Strategic Planning Process Defined**

A. The process of strategic planning has been defined and described in a number of ways.

Definition
Strategic Planning: The sequence of interrelated procedures for determining an entity's long-term goals and identifying the best approaches for achieving those goals.

III. **Strategic Planning Process Described**—The sequence of interrelated procedures that constitute the strategic planning process can be viewed in its basic form as consisting of the following components:

A. Establishing the entity's mission, values, and objectives:

1. **Mission statement**—An expression of the purpose and range of activities of the entity
2. **Entity values**—The underlying beliefs that govern the operations of an entity and the conduct of its relationship with other parties
3. **Objectives**—The desired outcomes or conditions an entity seeks to achieve related to such factors as profitability, growth, market share, innovation, etc.

B. Assessing the entity and the environment in which it operates, including:

1. Analyzing the external macro-environment in which the entity operates (or may operate)
   a. A variation of the PEST analysis provides a framework for this environmental analysis.
   b. PEST analysis is considered in the next lesson.
2. Analyzing the industry in which the entity operates (or may operate):
   a. The five forces framework (developed by Michael Porter) for determining the nature, operating attractiveness, and likely long-run profitability of a competitive industry may be used for this analysis.
   b. Porter's five forces framework is covered in the "Industry Analysis" lesson later in this subsection.

3. Analyzing the internal strengths and weaknesses of the entity; the external opportunities and threats present in its operating environment (or environment in which it may operate); and the relationship between the characteristics of the entity and its environment:
   a. SWOT analysis may be used to develop a profile of the entity's strengths, weaknesses, opportunities, and threats.
   b. SWOT analysis is covered in a later lesson.

C. Establishing measurable objectives that build on the entity's strengths to take advantage of identified opportunities and that build up any weaknesses and ward off threats:
   1. Establishing objectives is the process of deciding specifically what the entity wants to accomplish in order to achieve its goals.
   2. Objectives should be formulated so that they meet the SMART test; they must be:
      a. **S**pecific
      b. **M**easurable
      c. **A**ttainable
      d. **R**elevant
      e. **T**ime-bound

D. Formulating strategies, which are guidelines for achieving a competitive advantage in the market:
   1. The specific strategy formulated will be unique to the entity (or component of the entity) for which the strategy is established.
   2. Three industry-independent/entity-independent generic strategies have been identified by Michael Porter:
      a. Cost leadership
      b. Differentiation
      c. Focus

> **Note**
> *Porter's generic strategies are covered in the "Generic Strategies" lesson.*

E. Implementing strategies by initiating the programs and activities that apply the entity's resources to carry out its strategies so as to achieve its objectives and goals:
   1. Strategies provide guidelines for determining operating activities, but do not directly determine the specific operating activities to be undertaken to carry out the strategies.
   2. When an entity implements a strategy that other entities are unable to duplicate, or finds it too costly to imitate, the strategy provides a competitive advantage.

F. Evaluating and controlling strategic activities (the feedback loop):
   1. Determine performance characteristics to evaluate and measure.
   2. Establish target values for performance characteristics.
   3. Measure performance characteristics.
   4. Compare measured characteristics with target values.
   5. Implement changes in activities as needed.

IV. **Strategic Planning Process Summary**—In summary, the strategic planning process can be described as consisting of the following sequence of steps:

A. Establish the entity's mission, values, and goals.

B. Assess the entity and the environment in which it operates; also called environmental scanning.

C. Establish objectives.

D. Formulate strategies.

E. Implement strategies.

F. Evaluate and control strategic activities.

Macro-Environmental Analysis

At the broadest level, an entity will operate in the economic system of a particular country and in a particular market structure, potentially ranging from near perfect competition to near perfect monopoly. Within that context, the entity must assess the characteristics of its macro-environment. PEST analysis, and variations thereof, can be utilized to assess an entity's macro-environment. This lesson covers those methods of analysis.

After studying this lesson, you should be able to:

1. Describe macro-environmental analysis.
2. Describe the purpose and characteristics of PEST analysis and the variations of it.
3. Identify elements of the macro-environment important to an entity's strategic planning.

I. **Macro-Environmental Analysis**—Within the context of an economic system and economic market structure, an entity must carry out an assessment of the characteristics of the macro-environment in which it operates (or may operate). Such an analysis is essential to understanding the nature of the operating environment and making entity-wide decisions related to that operating environment. PEST analysis (or a variation of PEST) provides a framework for carrying out such an external macro-environmental analysis.

II. **PEST Analysis**—PEST analysis is an assessment of the **P**olitical, **E**conomic, **S**ocial and **T**echnological elements of a macro-environment. Its purpose is to provide an understanding of those elements of an environment, typically a country or region, in which a firm operates or is considering operating.

   A. **Analysis Factors**—PEST considers each of the following kinds of factors to develop a "picture" of an operating environment:

      1. **P**olitical factors—Concerned with the nature of the political environment, and the ways and the extent to which a government intervenes in its economy, including consideration of such things as:
         a. Political stability
         b. Labor laws
         c. Environmental laws
         d. Tax policy
         e. Trade restrictions, tariffs, and import quotas
      2. **E**conomic factors—Concerned with the economic characteristics of the operating environment, including such things as:
         a. Economic growth rate
         b. Interest rates
         c. Inflation rate
         d. Currency exchange rates
      3. **S**ocial factors—Concerned with the culture and values of the operating environment, including such considerations as:
         a. Population growth rate
         b. Age distribution
         c. Educational attainment and career attitudes
         d. Emphasis on health and safety

4. **T**echnology factors—Concerned with the nature and level of technology in the operating environment, including such considerations as:
    a. Level of research and development activity
    b. State of automation capability
    c. Level of technological "savvy"
    d. Rate of technological change

B. In summary, in its basic form, PEST analysis considers political, economic, social, and technological factors in assessing a macro-environment.

In the News—Severe government restrictions on certain common business practices are not limited to developing and third-world countries, as the following excerpt from the *Financial Times* (October 4, 2013, p. 1) illustrates:

Anti-Amazon Law

France passed a law aimed at online retailer Amazon that will prevent Internet booksellers from offering free delivery, to try to protect the country's traditional bookshops.

C. Variations of the basic PEST model consider other macro-environment factors:
  1. PEST **EL** adds two additional elements:
    a. **E** = **E**nvironmental factors, which include such things as:
      i. Weather
      ii. Climate and climate change
      iii. Water and air quality
    b. **L** = **L**egal factors, which include such things as:
      i. Discrimination law
      ii. Consumer law
      iii. Employment law
      iv. Antitrust law
      v. Health and safety law
  2. STEER, another variation, which identifies the same kinds of factors as other macro-environmental models—**S**ocio-cultural, **T**echnological, **E**conomic, **E**cological, and **R**egulator factors.

D. **Importance of Macro-Environmental Factors**
  1. The importance of the factors assessed in PEST analysis (or a variation thereof) will be unique to each analysis.
  2. PEST, or comparable analysis, is particularly important in considering the establishment of operations in a new foreign location.
  3. The outcome of a PEST-type analysis can provide inputs for SWOT analysis (considered in a later lesson).

Industry Analysis

In addition to an analysis of its macro-environment, an entity must develop a detailed understanding of the industry in which it operates or may operate. This micro-environment analysis can be conducted using the five forces model. This lesson covers that model.

After studying this lesson, you should be able to:

1. Describe micro-environmental analysis as it relates to an industry.
2. Define an industry for the purposes of analysis.
3. Describe the purpose and characteristics of five forces analysis.
4. Analyze elements of an industry that make that industry attractive (or not) as an operating environment.

I. **Industry Analysis**—Within the context of an economic system and an economic market structure, and with an understanding of the characteristics of the macro-environment in which an entity operates or may operate, an entity must assess the nature of the competition it faces (or would face) in its industry—that is, from its most direct competition. Michael Porter's five forces model provides a means of carrying out such a micro-environmental analysis.

II. **Industry Defined**—An industry may be defined as the group of entities that produce goods or provide services which are close substitutes and which compete for the same customers.

III. **Five Forces Analysis**—The five forces model identifies factors that determine the operating attractiveness and likely long-run profitability of an industry. Those five forces are:

A. **Threat of Entry into the Market by New Competition**—New entrants into an industry increase the level of competition, and thereby, reduce the attractiveness of the operating environment for that industry.

1. The likelihood of new entrants mostly depends on the barriers to entry into the industry, including:
   a. Capital investment required
   b. Access to raw materials, technology and/or suppliers
   c. Economies of scale
   d. Customer loyalty and their cost of switching providers
   e. Access to distribution channels
   f. Regulatory or other governmental impediments to entry
   g. Potential retaliation by existing firms in the industry
2. The easier it is for firms to enter the market, the greater the potential for competition within the market.

B. **Threat of Substitute Goods or Services**—The presence of substitute goods or services, or the possibility of the development of new substitutes, reduces an entity's ability to raise prices, and therefore, may affect its profitability.

1. The level of threat posed by substitutes depends on such factors as:
   a. Availability of substitutes
   b. Relative price and performance of substitutes
   c. Ease of substitution

   - **d.** Buyer's brand loyalty
   - **e.** Cost to buyers of switching to substitutes

2. Low levels of perceived differentiation, low switching costs and substitute costs, and little difference in performance significantly increases the threat of substitute products or services to a firm.

C. Bargaining Power of Buyers (Customers) of the Industry Good or Service—The bargaining power of buyers influences the ability of a provider to determine product or service characteristics and the price it can charge.

1. Bargaining power of customers is greatest when, among other things:
   - **a.** Products are standardized.
   - **b.** There are a large number of suppliers.
   - **c.** There are a few dominant buyers that account for a large part of sales.
   - **d.** Information about goods or services as provided by multiple suppliers is widely available.
   - **e.** Cost of buyers switching to other suppliers is low.
2. In general, environments in which there are relatively few customers, where alternative products are available, where the cost of switching to alternative products is low, and/or where high-volume purchases are common tend to favor the customer and create a more difficult competitive market.

D. Bargaining Power of Suppliers of the Inputs Used in the Industry—The bargaining power of suppliers influences the availability and cost of inputs used in the industry, and therefore, can affect operations and profitability.

1. Bargaining power of suppliers is greatest when, among other things:
   - **a.** There are few substitute inputs.
   - **b.** There are many users and few suppliers.
   - **c.** Suppliers are in a position to move downstream in the distribution channel.
   - **d.** Employees are unionized.
2. When there are relatively few suppliers, and few alternative goods or services, and/or when the cost of switching to an alternative is high, the supplier has an advantage over the buyer; the buyer's inability to negotiate effectively limits the competitive options available to the firm.

E. Intensity of Rivalry—The intensity of rivalry within the industry affects various operating factors (e.g., marketing/advertising, research and development, etc.) and pricing strategy.

1. The level of rivalry depends on such factors as:
   - **a. Structure of competition**—The relative size of competitors in the industry.
     - **i.** Many small or equal-size entities tend to engender more intense rivalry.
     - **ii.** The presence of a market leader in the industry tends to lessen rivalry.
   - **b. Degree of product differentiation**—Markets with undifferentiated products or services (e.g., commodities) tend to have greater rivalry than markets with differentiated products.
   - **c. Industry cost structure**—Industries with high fixed costs tend to have greater price rivalry as entities seek to operate at full capacity by cutting prices.
   - **d. Entities' strategic objectives**—When entities in an industry pursue aggressive growth strategies, rivalry is more intense than when the entities operate in a mature industry.

e. **Customer switching costs**—When customers incur a high cost of switching to an alternate supplier, less rivalry tends to exist than when there is little or no cost of making the change.

f. **Exit barriers**—When leaving an industry is difficult and/or costly (e.g., when there are affiliated entities to consider or a high shut-down cost), greater rivalry tends to exist than when there are few impediments to exiting the industry, since owners seek to avoid the legal, financial, and other costs associated with ceasing operations.

2. The existence of a large number of diverse competitors, high barriers to exit, and/or a low growth rate for the market make it much more difficult for a firm to compete.

IV. **Summary**—In summary, analysis of the five factors identified above provides significant insight into the nature of competition that is likely to be faced in a particular industry or market.

Entity/Environment Relationship Analysis

At the most detailed level, an entity must assess its internal characteristics and the relationship between those characteristics and the external environment in which it may or may not operate. The SWOT analysis provides a methodology, covered in this lesson, for conducting this assessment.

After studying this lesson, you should be able to:

1. Describe the analysis of an entity/environment relationship.
2. Describe the purpose and characteristics of SWOT analysis.
3. Identify factors that may represent the strengths and weaknesses of an entity and opportunities or threats to an entity.
4. Evaluate the broad types of strategies that would be appropriate for entity's strengths and weaknesses and the opportunities and threats in its environment.

I. Entity and Environment Assessment—Within the context of an economic system and an economic market structure, and with an understanding of the characteristics of the macro-environment and the industry in which an entity operates or may operate, an entity must assess the relationship between its external environment and its internal characteristics. Such an analysis is essential if an entity is to understand the possibilities, or lack thereof, of operating in the environment. A SWOT analysis provides a framework for carrying out such an assessment of the relationship between an entity and an operating environment.

II. SWOT Analysis—A SWOT analysis develops a profile of the internal Strengths and Weaknesses of an entity, and the Opportunities and Threats faced by an entity in the external environment.

- **A.** SWOT analysis facilitates matching an entity's strengths to the competitive environment in which it operates.
  - **1.** Strengths are the resources and capabilities that provide the entity a relative competitive advantage in the market, and might include, for example:
    - **a.** Favorable reputation with customers and prospective customers
    - **b.** Patents, copyrights, etc.
    - **c.** Cost advantages provided by proprietary processes
    - **d.** Exclusive access to natural resources
    - **e.** Highly desirable location
  - **2.** Weaknesses are the shortcomings of an entity that place the entity at a relative competitive disadvantage in the market. Weaknesses may be viewed as the absence of strengths, such as those noted above, as well as other factors.
  - **3.** Opportunities are the chances to benefit from external new or unmet demand, or from markets which provide the possibility for profit, growth or other desired outcomes and might include, for example:
    - **a.** Unmet market needs
    - **b.** Development or employment of new technology or processes
    - **c.** Reduction in regulations or other legal constraints
    - **d.** Reduction of international quotas, tariffs or other barriers to trade

4. Threats are the chance of adverse consequences to an entity as a result of external forces and might include, for example:
    a. Development of new substitute products or services
    b. Changes in customer preferences for goods or services
    c. Increases in regulation or other legal constraints
    d. Increases in international quotas, tariffs or other barriers to trade

B. **SWOT Matrix**—The identification of strengths, weaknesses, opportunities, and threats provides the basis for constructing a matrix useful in developing an entity's strategic plans. Such a SWOT matrix takes the form:

SWOT Matrix

	Strengths	**Weaknesses**
Opportunities	S/O Strategies	W/O Strategies
Threats	S/T Strategies	W/T Strategies

1. S/O strategies utilize the entity's strengths to take advantage of opportunities in the environment.
2. W/O strategies pursue opportunities to overcome weaknesses.
3. S/T strategies utilize the entity's strengths to reduce the entity's susceptibility to external threats.
4. W/T strategies pursue ways to prevent the entity's weaknesses from being overcome by external threats.

C. In summary, SWOT provides a framework for identifying an entity's internal strengths and weaknesses and its location-specific external opportunities and threats, and to relate those characteristics in the formulation of strategies intended to provide the entity with a competitive advantage in its environment.

Generic Strategies

The analysis of an operating environment and of an entity provides the basis for an entity to formulate its strategy. While every strategy will be unique, a set of generic strategies can be used to guide development of a particular strategy. This lesson identifies and describes certain generic strategies that can be useful for that purpose.

After studying this lesson, you should be able to:

1. Describe factors that come into play in formulating strategy.
2. Identify and describe three generic strategies that are independent of an industry or an entity.
3. Describe how each of the generic strategies may be achieved, the characteristics of each, and the risk inherent in each.

I. Introduction—Within the context of an economic system and an economic market structure, and with an understanding of (a) the characteristics of the macro-environment, (b) the industry in which an entity operates or may operate, and (c) the relationship between an entity and its external environment, an entity can formulate its basic strategy. That strategy will seek to leverage the entity's strengths in order to achieve objectives and goals established in the strategic planning process. While the specific strategy formulated will be unique to the entity (or component of the entity) and the environment, Michael Porter has identified three industry-independent/entity-independent generic strategies that identify, at a high level, the possible strengths of entities.

II. Generic Strategies

A. The two basic generic strategies that provide competitive advantage identified by Porter are:

1. Cost leadership
2. Differentiation

By considering these basic strategies as they relate to both a broad industry and more discrete market segments within an industry, Porter develops a third strategy based on competitive scope:

3. Focus

B. Cost Leadership Strategy

1. Under this strategy, an entity will seek to be the low cost provider in an industry for a given level of output.
2. An entity will sell its product or service either at the average industry price and earn a profit higher than that of other competitors in the industry or below the average industry price so as to gain market share.
3. Entities acquire or maintain cost advantages by:
   - **a.** Identifying and avoiding unnecessary costs
   - **b.** Improving process efficiency
   - **c.** Gaining exclusive access to lower cost inputs
   - **d.** Using outsourcing in an optimal manner
   - **e.** Pursuing vertical integration—moving up or down in the supply chain
4. **Characteristics of cost leadership entities**—Entities that successfully carry out the cost leadership strategy typically have the following kinds of strength:
   - **a.** Significant capital to invest in production and logistical assets to keep cost low
   - **b.** High levels of expertise in manufacturing processes

c. High levels of skill in designing products for efficient manufacturing

d. Efficient channels for the distribution of products

5. **Techniques for achieving cost leadership**—Firms seeking to achieve and maintain cost leadership may use a number of processes aimed at lowering costs and reducing time to delivery of its goods or services, including:

   a. **Lean manufacturing**—The identification and elimination of waste in the production process. The focus is on improving product design, increasing production flexibility, and reducing production time, defects, and inventory quantity so as to reduce costs.

   b. **Supply chain management**—Improving the flow of goods, services, and information along the entire supply chain, from the basic raw material to delivery of the final good or service to the end user. Supply chain management requires coordination and information sharing among all entities in the entire supply chain.

   c. **Process reengineering**—A critical evaluation and major redesign of existing process to achieve breakthrough improvement in performance and cost reduction.

6. **Risks to cost leadership strategy**—Entities that adopt the cost leadership strategy face certain risks, including:

   a. The possibility that other entities will be successful in adopting a cost leadership strategy and meet or beat the cost of the entity.

   b. The possibility that technology will improve such that other firms may be able to produce at equally low cost or be able to apply new technologies to produce at an even lower cost.

   c. The possibility that a number of firms may focus on segments of the industry and be able to separately achieve lower costs in each of those segments so that as a group they are able to control a significant portion of the industry.

C. Differentiation Strategy

1. Under this strategy, an entity will seek to develop a product or service that offers unique features that are valued by customers and that those customers perceive to be better than or different from the products of competitors in the industry.

2. An entity expects that the value added by the quality or uniqueness of the product or service will allow the entity to charge a premium price which will more than cover the extra cost of providing the good or service.

3. An entity may acquire or maintain differentiation by providing goods or services that have special or unique:

   a. Features

   b. Functionality

   c. Durability

   d. Service support

4. **Characteristics of entities following a differentiation strategy**—Entities that successfully carry out the differentiation strategy typically have the following kinds of strengths:

   a. Highly creative and skilled product/service development personnel

   b. Leading-edge scientific and market research capabilities

   c. Strong and dedicated marketing and sales personnel capable of conveying the strengths of the product or service

   d. A reputation for innovation, quality, and service.

5. **Techniques for achieving differentitation**—Firms seeking to achieve differentiation may pursue a number of processes to help achieve and maintain differentiation of its goods or services, including:
   - **a.** Market research, so as to understand not only its customers and potential customers, but also its competitors
   - **b.** New product development
   - **c.** Continuous improvement of its products and processes
   - **d.** Strict quality control
   - **e.** Customer-oriented services (e.g., delivery, financing, problem resolution, etc.)
   - **f.** High level of employee training and development
6. **Risks to differentiation strategy**—Entities that adopt the differentiation strategy face certain risks, including:
   - **a.** Changes in customer preferences or economic status
   - **b.** Imitation by competitors, including the threat of "knock-offs"
   - **c.** The possibility that a number of firms may focus on segments of the industry and be able to separately achieve greater differentiation in each of those segments so that as a group they are able to capture a significant portion of the industry

D. Focus Strategy

1. Under this strategy, an entity will focus on a narrow segment of an industry (a "niche") and within that segment seek to achieve either a cost advantage or differentiation.
   - **a.** An entity seeks to identify a distinct subgroup within an industry and focus on providing goods or services that meet the distinctive needs of that subgroup.
   - **b.** An entity also may pursue a "quick response approach," which focuses on either being the first to bring a product to market (think "as seen on TV" products) or on providing quick delivery of the good or service to the customer. Both of these approaches are variations of focus strategy.
2. **Characteristics of entities following a focus strategy**—Entities that successfully carry out the focus strategy typically have the following kinds of strengths:
   - **a.** Outstanding market research and understanding, especially of the target subgroup
   - **b.** Ability to tailor product or service development strength to the target subgroup
   - **c.** High degree of customer satisfaction and loyalty
3. **Risks to focus strategy**—Entities that adopt the focus strategy face certain risks, including:
   - **a.** Typically, smaller size, lower volume, and less bargaining power with suppliers
   - **b.** Imitation by competitors
   - **c.** Changes in targeted customers' preferences or economic status
   - **d.** The possibility of an industry cost leader adapting its products or services so as to compete in the focus market
   - **e.** The possibility that other entities may focus on and carve out subgroups of the targeted focus group

III. Generic Strategies Matrix

A. By combining the alternative advantages of low cost strategies and differentiation strategies together with the alternative of a broad (industry wide) or a narrow (market segment) focus, a generic strategies matrix can be developed. That matrix takes the form of:

Generic Strategies Matrix

	Strategic Advantages	
Scope	**Low Cost**	**Differentiation**
Broad industry-wide	Cost leadership strategy	Product uniqueness strategy
Narrow ("niche") market-segment	Focus strategy (low cost)	Focus strategy (differentiation)

B. These generic strategies—cost leadership, differentiation, and niche market focus—describe strategic objectives at a fundamental level.

Summary and Extensions

This lesson provides a summary of the strategic planning process and the analytical techniques, available for use in carrying out that process. A graphic model illustrates the elements of the planning process, their relationships, and where in the process the identified analytical techniques apply. An alternative model is also presented.

After studying this lesson, you should be able to:

1. Summarize the steps in the strategic planning process.
2. Identify the steps in the planning process for which certain analytical techniques can be used.
3. Describe the resources-based model as an alternative approach to strategic planning.

I. Summary

A. The strategic planning process is comprised of the interrelated procedures for determining an entity's long-term goals and identifying the best approaches for achieving those goals. The strategy adopted by an entity, including a component of a larger entity, determines at a basic level how an entity operates and, ultimately, its success or failure.

B. The strategic planning process can be summarized as consisting of the following requirements:

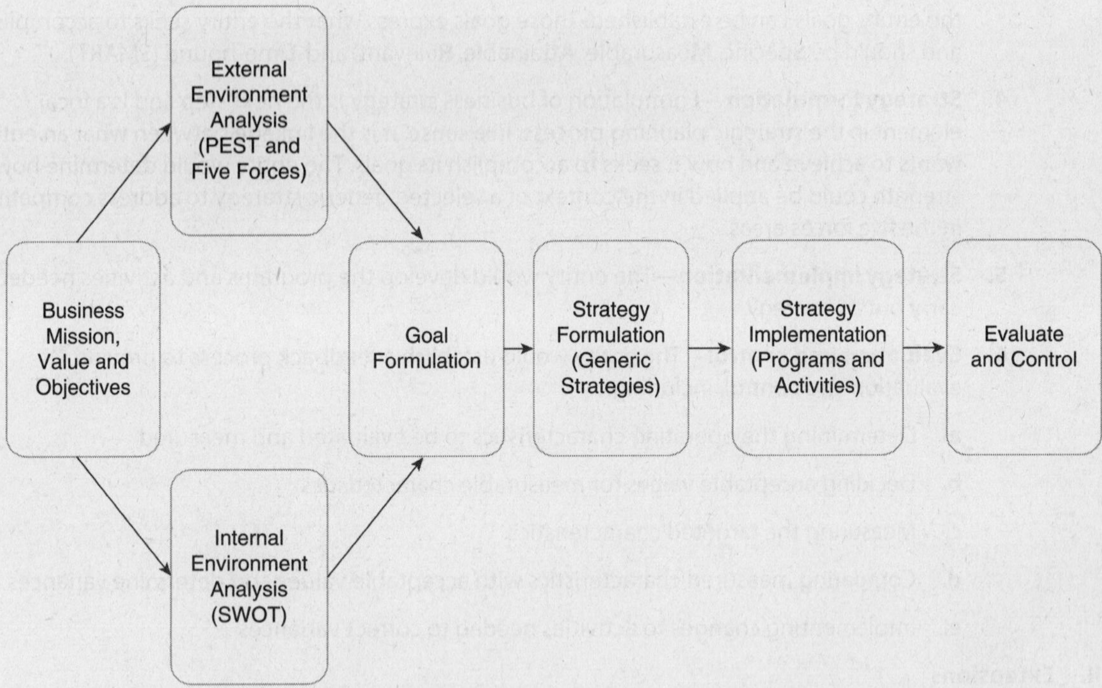

C. Requirements Summarized

1. **Mission, values, and objectives**—The cornerstone of strategic planning is the definition of the entity's vision, values, and objectives. Those elements provide direction and boundaries for the undertakings of the entity.
2. **Environmental scanning**—Analyzing the external and internal environments is the next step in an entity's planning process. That analysis takes place within the context of the economic system of a country (ranging from command economy to free-market economy) and the economic market structure of the industry within that country (ranging from perfect competition to perfect monopoly).

> **Note**
> *These elements of analysis—economic system, economic market structure, and industry analysis—are particularly useful in considering "where" an entity should locate.*

a. External analysis is concerned with an assessment of the macro-environment in which the entity operates or will operate and the nature of the industry of concern in that macro-environment. External analysis may be carried out using:

   i. **PEST**—A methodology for assessing and understanding the **P**olitical, **E**conomic, **S**ocial and **T**echnological elements of the macro-environment.

   ii. **Five forces analysis**—Provides a framework for assessing and understanding the industry of interest.

b. Internal analysis is concerned with an assessment of the micro-environment of the entity and the relationship between the entity and the macro-environment.

   i. SWOT can be used to develop a profile of the internal strengths and weaknesses of the entity and the external opportunities and threats that would be faced by the entity in a particular environment. This entity-level analysis focuses on characteristics internal to the entity and the relationship between those characteristics and the operating environment.

   ii. The results of the SWOT analysis provide insight into the generic strategy—cost leadership, differentiation, or niche market—for the entity or planned entity.

> **Note**
> *These considerations provide insight into "how" an entity should operate.*

3. **Setting goals**—With an understanding of the external environment and the characteristics of the entity, goals can be established. Those goals express what the entity seeks to accomplish and should be **S**pecific, **M**easurable, **A**ttainable, **R**elevant, and **T**ime-bound (SMART).

4. **Strategy formulation**—Formulation of business strategy is the next step and is a focal element in the strategic planning process. In a sense, it is the linkage between what an entity wants to achieve and how it seeks to accomplish its goals. The entity would determine how its strength could be applied in the context of a selected generic strategy to address competition in the five forces areas.

5. **Strategy implementation**—The entity would develop the programs and activities needed to carry out its strategy.

6. **Evaluation and control**—The entity would establish a feedback process to provide evaluation and control, including:

   a. Determining the operating characteristics to be evaluated and measured

   b. Deciding acceptable values for measurable characteristics

   c. Measuring the targeted characteristics

   d. Comparing measured characteristics with acceptable values and determine variances

   e. Implementing changes to activities needed to correct variances

II. Extensions

A. **Resources-Based Model**—An alternative variation of the strategic planning process, especially as it relates to strategy formulation, is the resources-based model (RBM).

1. RBM assesses an entity as a unique collection of resources and capabilities. The uniqueness of the set of resources and capabilities is the basis on which an entity should develop its strategy.

2. Using the RBM approach, the following set of interrelated activities would be carried out in developing an entity's strategy:

   a. Identify the entity's resources and its strengths and weaknesses.

   b. Determine the entity's capabilities; that is, what can the entity do better than its competitors?

c. Determine the potential of the entity's resources and capabilities in terms of competitive advantage(s).

d. Locate an attractive industry or market.

e. Select a strategy that best allows the entity to use its resources and capabilities to take advantage of opportunities in the industry or market.

B. **Specific Strategy Caveat**—The various forms of analysis described here, as well as similar and complementary forms of analysis, provide valuable insights and guidance in the formulation of the strategy of an entity.

1. By themselves, the analysis described here and similar methods do not provide a comprehensive methodology for establishing strategy in a particular case.
2. The actual strategy formulated and implemented in a specific case would consider the particular characteristics of the operating environment—its nature, challenges, opportunities, etc.—as well as the specific characteristics of the entity.
3. Furthermore, the actual strategy formulated and implemented in a specific case would address issues of financing, organization, production, marketing, and other "operating-level" matters.

Financial Management

Introduction to Financial Management

This lesson defines financial management and provides a summary of the material covered in the Financial Management subsection of CPAexcel.

After studying this lesson, you should be able to:

1. Define financial management.
2. Describe the major functions of financial management.

I. **Definition**—Financial management is the identification and implementation of strategies designed to maximize a firm's value; it includes:
   A. Managing the capital and financial structure of an entity, including the sources and uses of funds;
   B. Planning, allocating and controlling an entity's financial resources;
   C. Identifying and managing financial risks.

II. **Content Coverage**
   A. The Financial Management area accounts for 11% to 21% of the Business Environment and Concepts (BEC) section of the CPA Exam.
   B. This BEC area of CPAexcel will cover the following topics:
      1. Concepts and tools which are especially appropriate to financial management, including:
         a. Concepts of cost
         b. Time value of money concepts and calculations
         c. Interest rate concepts and calculations
         d. Financial valuation and valuation techniques
         e. Hedging and derivatives
      2. Financial modeling applications, especially as applied to capital budgeting decisions
      3. Alternatives for short-term and long-term financing and appropriate financing strategies, including consideration of related risk-reward trade-offs and the cost of capital
      4. Techniques for working capital management
      5. Use of ratios and other measures to assess working capital management effectiveness
      6. Summary description of various kinds of risks faced in carrying out the financial management function
   C. The focus throughout Financial Management is on the terms, concepts, applications, calculations, and risk issues that are common on the CPA Exam.

Concepts and Tools

Cost Concepts

The accounting concept of cost is as a measure of the money amount given up or the obligation incurred to acquire a resource. For economic and finance purposes, there are various other concepts of cost. In this lesson, different concepts of cost are identified, described, and illustrated.

After studying this lesson, you should be able to:

1. Describe the difference between accounting cost and accounting expense.
2. Define and describe various alternative cost concepts, including: a) sunk costs; b) opportunity cost; c) differential cost; and d) the cost of capital.
3. Calculate the weighted-average cost of capital.

I. Overview—Cost is the monetary measure of a resource; it is the money amount paid or obligation incurred for a good or service. Many different types and classifications of cost are distinguished and used for business purposes. Certain of these distinctions are especially important for financial management.

II. Cost versus Expense

A. Cost and expense are not the same concept. While cost is the amount paid for a resource (or asset), expense is the portion of cost that relates to the portion of the resource (or asset) that has been used up. As described in the FASB Statement of Concepts No. 6, " … the value of cash or other resources given up (or the present value of an obligation incurred) in exchange for a resource measures the cost of the resource acquired." Expenses result from using up acquired resources and are measured as the portion of the cost of a resource that has been used up.

B. While cost and expense for a resource can occur simultaneously and be of the same amount, the two concepts are different and in the short run, their amounts can be different for the same resource. The following diagrams illustrate the differences and relationship between the concepts using assumed amounts:

C. Cost and expense occurring at different times and at different amounts within different time periods:

Cost	⇒⇒	Resource	⇒⇒	Period Expense
		(Asset)		(e.g., Depreciation)
$10,000		$10,000		$2,000

D. Cost and expense occurring simultaneously and at the same amount:

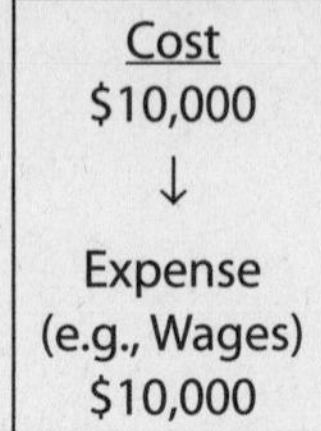

E. In the long run (over the life of a resource) cost will equal expenses, but the concepts are different and the amounts may be different within a fiscal period. The concept of cost is more important for most financial management purposes than the concept of expense.

III. Various Costs

A. **Sunk Costs**—The costs of resources incurred in the past; they cannot be changed by current or future decisions. Therefore, sunk costs are irrelevant to current and future decision making. The following examples illustrate sunk costs.

Examples

1. In making a decision concerning the replacement of equipment, the original cost (or the book carrying value) of the current equipment is a sunk cost and, therefore, not relevant in making the replacement decision. Only expected future costs (and/or future revenues and cost savings) resulting from the acquisition of the new equipment should enter into the decision of whether to replace the equipment.
2. In making a new product decision, the costs incurred in conducting technical and market research prior to making the decision of whether to introduce the product are sunk costs and, therefore, not relevant to the decision. Only expected future revenues and costs are relevant in deciding whether the product is economically justifiable.

B. **Opportunity Costs**—The discounted dollar value of benefits lost from the next best opportunity as a result of choosing another opportunity. Economic resources can normally be used in two or more economically feasible but mutually exclusive undertakings. The choice of one alternative precludes the choice of other alternatives. The revenue or other benefit, which would have been derived from the next best alternative not selected, is the opportunity costs associated with the selected alternative. Although opportunity costs do not involve actual cash transactions, they are relevant in current decision making. The following examples illustrate opportunity costs.

Examples

1. In making a decision between whether to go to school full time or go to school part time and work part time, the pay forgone by choosing to go to school full time would be an opportunity cost. Since going to school full time and working part time are mutually exclusive (an assumption in this illustration), by choosing to go to school full time, the pay that would have been received by selecting the other alternative is an opportunity cost.
2. In considering the use of vacant space or unused equipment in new production undertakings, the net revenue that would be forgone by not leasing or selling the resource (if possible) would be an opportunity cost. By using the space or equipment for its own activities, an entity gives up the opportunity to receive a net lease or sales revenue. That forgone revenue (measured at present value) is an opportunity cost that should enter into the assessment of the proposed use of the resources.

C. **Differential (or Incremental) Costs**—Those costs that are different between two or more alternatives. Cost elements that do not differ between alternatives are not relevant in making economic comparisons, but cost elements that are different between alternatives are relevant in making such comparisons. The following examples illustrate differential costs.

Examples

1. In considering whether to accept a special order for a product, only the incremental revenues and costs should be included in assessing the net benefit (profit) inherent in the order. For example, while certain variable cost elements would be different between accepting and not accepting the special order and would be relevant, fixed cost elements may not change and, because these elements would not be different between accepting and not accepting the order, would be irrelevant in making the decision.
2. In comparing two or more alternative projects, some cost elements and amounts may be the same for each project. Those costs would not be relevant in making a decision between the alternatives. Any cost elements and/or amounts that are different between the alternatives would be relevant in making an economically based decision between the alternatives.

Note

It is important to note that in the costs of financing a project, the interest and any other financing costs are NOT incremental costs in assessing the project. The discounting of these costs to their present values will account for the costs associated with the source of financing.

D. **Cost of Capital**—A firm's capital (or capital structure) is comprised of the long-term sources of funds used in financing the firm's assets. The major categories of capital elements typically include long-term debt, preferred stock, and common stock, though a variety of other instruments with various characteristics also are used. There is a cost associated with using each element of capital structure. The cost for each element identified above is defined in a similar way.

1. **Cost of debt**—The rate of return that must be earned in order to attract and retain lenders' funds. The required rate would be determined by such factors as the level of interest in the general market, the perceived default risk of the firm, perceived interest-rate and inflationary risks, and similar factors. Historically, debt has been considered less risky than equity and the required rate of return has been less than the rate required on preferred and common stock. (These risk factors and the determination of the required rate of return on debt are discussed in detail in a later lesson.)
2. **Cost of preferred stock**—The rate of return that must be earned in order to attract and retain preferred shareholders' investment. Preferred stock has characteristics of both debt (a dividend rate paid before common stock dividends) and equity (possible claim to additional dividends and claim to assets on liquidation after debt). Therefore, the required rate of return is determined by factors that enter into determining the rates for each of those securities. Normally, preferred stock is considered more risky than debt, but less risky than common stock and, consequently, the rate of return required by investors has been higher than the cost of debt, but lower than the cost of common stock. (The required rates of return on preferred stock and common stock are discussed in detail in a later lesson.)
3. **Cost of common stock**—The rate of return that must be earned in order to attract and retain common shareholders' investment. The required rate would be determined by such factors as the various perceived risks associated with the firm's common stock, as well as expected dividends and price appreciation. Historically, common stock has been considered more risky than debt or preferred stock and, as a consequence, the required rate of return has been higher than the rate on debt or preferred stock.
4. **The underlying concept**—For the cost of each of these (and other) forms of financing is that the rate of return required by all sources of financing is based on each source's opportunity cost in the capital markets.
    a. The **opportunity cost** for each source of financing is the expected rate of return that investors could earn from the best available alternative investment with perceived comparable risk. Thus, in order to attract and retain capital, an entity must earn, and be prepared to pay, a rate of return at least equal to the rate that investors could earn on investments with comparable risk elsewhere in the capital markets.

b. While the **cost of capital** can be calculated for each element of capital and these separate rates used for analytical purposes, more commonly the weighted average cost of all elements of capital is used for analytical purposes. In most cases, this is appropriate since an entity's income stream or cash flow is not determined by or attached to the separate capital elements, but rather relates to the aggregate operations of the entity. Therefore, a weighted average cost of capital is usually appropriate and used for analytical purposes. (How the cost of capital is calculated for each element of capital is discussed in later lessons.)

5. The **weighted average cost of capital (WACC)** is calculated as the required rate of return on each source of capital weighted by the proportion of total capital provided by each source, and the resulting weighted costs summed to get the total weighted average. To illustrate the weighted average cost of capital, assume the following facts and calculations:

Capital Elements	Amount	Percentage of Total	×	Cost of Capital	=	Weighted Cost
Bonds Payable	$400,000	.20		6%		1.2%
Preferred Stock	200,000	.10		10%		1.0%
Common Stock	1,400,000	.70		12%		8.4%
Totals	$2,000,000	1.00				
Weighted Average Cost of Capital =						10.6%

a. In the above illustration, the individual elements of capital have assumed costs of 6%, 10%, and 12%, but each is used to a different extent in the total financing.

b. The 6% cost of capital for bonds payable (debt) is assumed to be net of (after any) tax savings resulting from the deductibility of interest for tax purposes. If the cost of debt is before the tax savings, the cost of debt capital after tax would be computed as: pretax % cost × (1 – tax rate).

c. The amounts of capital shown for preferred stock and common stock ($200,000 and $1,400,000, respectively) are based on the book values for the share of each class of stock outstanding (book value WACC), not on the par value of shares authorized. As an alternative, the market value of shares outstanding could be used (market value WACC). The use of market values provides a better technical basis for determining the weighted average cost of capital because investors would expect a rate of return on the market value of their capital investment, not on the book value of the capital.

d. While a firm may use the weighted average cost of capital for the overall entity, there are circumstances where the use of the firm-wide weighted average cost of capital may not be the most appropriate measure. For example, if an entity has separate business units (e.g., divisions) with very different risk characteristics or if an entity considers separate projects with very different risk characteristics, the entity may consider using the cost of capital related to the business unit or specific project.

i. **Unit projects**—When an entity has more than one unit or division with different risk characteristics, the overall weighted average cost of capital for the entity may not be representative of the cost of capital for a particular unit. For a component unit with low risk characteristics, the weighted average cost for all units would be greater than necessary for its projects, causing the unit to underinvest in projects that otherwise would be economically feasible. And, for a component unit with high risk characteristics, the weighted average cost for all units would be less than necessary for its projects, causing the unit to overinvest in projects that otherwise would not be considered economically feasible. In such cases, it may be appropriate to use a unit or divisional cost of capital, which can be estimated using a capital asset pricing model (CAPM).

ii. **Separate projects**—When an entity considers a project that is considered much riskier than its typical projects, the overall weighted average cost of capital for the entity may not be the appropriate cost of capital to use for the project. Use of the overall cost of capital for highly risky projects would result in understating the cost of capital appropriate for such projects. Establishing an appropriated cost of capital for such projects will be subjective and will require the use of judgment. However, adjustments in such cases result in a more appropriate cost of capital for evaluating highly risky projects.

e. Since, as previously described, the cost of capital is the minimum rate of return that a firm must pay in order to attract and retain capital (i.e., the rate of return required by investors based on their opportunity cost), the cost of capital is also the minimum rate of return that a firm must earn on its use of capital. In order for the value of common stock to increase, a firm must earn a return greater than its cost of capital. Because the weighted average cost of capital is the minimum average rate of return that a firm must earn to fund its capital elements, the weighted average cost of capital is used as the hurdle rate when analyzing a firm's investment opportunities—if the rate of return on an investment cannot clear the hurdle rate, it is not economically feasible for the firm. The weighted average cost of capital also establishes the discount rate used in various forms of economic analysis.

IV. Conclusion—The concepts of cost identified, defined, and illustrated in this section will be used in carrying out application analysis in later lessons in this area.

Time Value of Money Tools

Money is the basic unit of measure used in finance. Nevertheless, there is a timing element or attribute to the value of money; money held today has greater value than money received in the future. Thus, there is a time value of money. This lesson considers the concepts and determinations of the value of money under different assumptions as to time. Each assumption as to time (or timing) is explained and illustrated graphically.

After studying this lesson, you should be able to:

1. Describe and calculate various time value of money concepts, including: a) present value of a single amount; b) future value of a single amount; c) present value of an ordinary annuity; d) future value of an ordinary annuity; e) present value of an annuity due; and f) future value of an annuity due; and g) present value of a perpetual annuity.
2. Determine which time value concept is appropriate in a given circumstance.
3. Apply time value of money concepts in carrying out analysis.

I. Overview

A. Virtually every area of financial management requires understanding and using time value of money concepts. While money is the unit of measure used in financial management, all money does not have the same value, in large part due to the time value associated with money. Simply put, money currently held is worth more than money to be received in the future. In order to analyze investment proposals and other opportunities, money (or dollars) that relate to different points in (or periods of) time must be adjusted to comparable values. This is accomplished by converting all dollars to their current or present value, or to a common future value. The concepts and calculations for making these conversions are covered here. Seven major circumstances will be presented.

1. Present value now of an amount to be received (or paid) at some single future date
2. Future value at some future date of a single amount invested now
3. Present value now of an ordinary annuity to be received over some future time period
4. Future value at some future time of an ordinary annuity invested over some future time period
5. Present value now of an annuity due to be received over some future time period
6. Future value at some future time of an annuity due invested over some future time period
7. Present value now of an annuity to be received indefinitely ("forever") into the future

B. A timeline graphic will illustrate the concept underlying each of these circumstances. The calculation of each value will be demonstrated using assumed facts and excerpts from relevant time value tables.

C. For each illustration, the relevant portions of time value tables are provided.

1. Those tables provide the factors used to compute the present value or future value for a given interest rate and number of periods.
2. The number of periods is not necessarily the number of years, but the number of periods to which the interest rate is applied.
   - **a.** If interest is determined on an annual basis, one period would apply for a year.
   - **b.** If interest is determined on a semi-annual basis, two periods would apply for a year.

II. Present Value of a Single Amount

A. Present Value Now of an Amount to be Received (or Paid) at Some Single Future Date—This calculation determines the value now (at the present) of a single amount to be received at some single future date. Obviously, since a dollar held now is worth more than a dollar to be received in the future, the present value of an amount is less than the future value of that amount.

B. **Illustration**—To illustrate, assume $50,000 is to be received 5 years in the future. What is the present (current) value of the future $50,000? Graphically, the circumstances can be shown as:

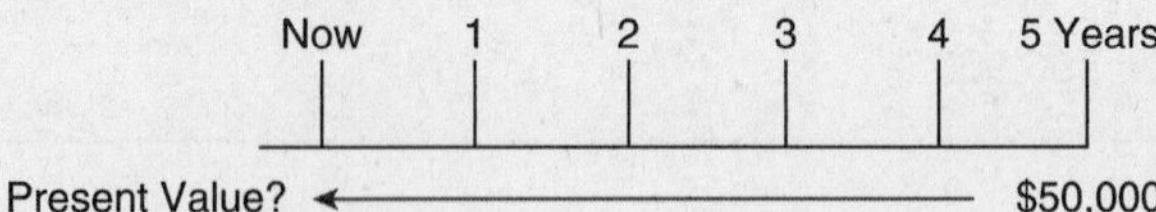

C. The future value (principal) is $50,000 and the number of periods is 5 years. In order to determine the present value, a discount (or interest) rate must be used. That rate measures the time value attached to money by the entity. Assume the appropriate rate is 6% and the related present value of $1.00 table shows the following for 5 periods:

Rate	2%	4%	6%	8%	10%
5 Periods	.906	.822	.747	.681	.621

D. The appropriate discount factor for 5 periods at 6% is .747. Therefore, the present value (PV) of 50,000 to be received in 5 years would be calculated as:

PV = $50,000 × .747 = $37,350

Or, $50,000 to be received in 5 years with a discount rate of 6% is worth $37,350 now.

E. The calculation of present value of a single future amount is frequently used in assessing investment opportunities for which a portion of the cash flows relate to a single amount to be received (or paid) in the future. For example, it is used to determine the present value of the disposal value of an asset when disposal will occur in the future (e.g., the end of the life of the project).

III. Future Value of a Single Amount

A. **Future Value at Some Future Date of a Single Amount Invested Now**—This calculation determines the value at some future date of a single amount invested now. The future value is the amount that will have accumulated as of some future date as a result of earning interest on the amount invested at the present and, over multiple periods, the compounding of interest (i.e., earning interest on interest). Obviously, as a result of interest earned, the future value will be greater than the present value of the investment.

B. **Illustration**—To illustrate, assume $50,000 invested now will earn a 6% annual interest compounded annually. What is the future value of the investment at the end of 5 years? Graphically, the circumstances can be shown as:

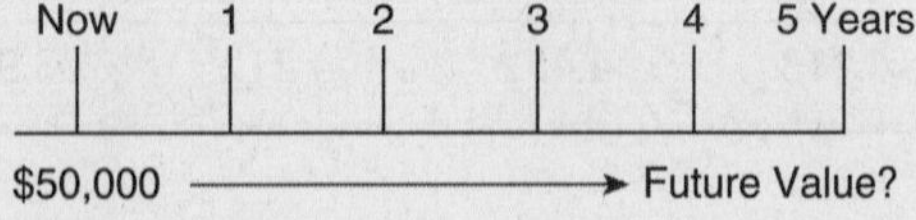

C. The present value (principal) is $50,000 and the number of periods is 5 years. The principal will earn 6% per year compounded annually. The related future value of $1.00 table shows the following for 5 periods:

Rate	2%	4%	6%	8%	10%
5 Periods	1.104	1.217	1.338	1.469	1.611

D. The appropriate future value factor for 5 periods at 6% is 1.338. Therefore, the future value (FV) of $50,000 invested for 5 years at 6% compounded annually would be calculated as:

FV = $50,000 × 1.338 = $66,900

Or, $50,000 invested now for 5 years at 6% compounded annually would accumulate to $66,900.

E. In those situations where interest compounds more often than once a year, the number of periods used is the number of compounding periods and the interest rate is the annual rate divided by the number of compounding periods within each year. For example, if interest in the above example is compounded quarterly, the number of periods is 20 (5 years × 4 quarters) and the related rate is 1.5% (6%/4 quarters = 1.5% per quarter). The future value would be $67,343.

IV. Present Value of an Ordinary Annuity (also Called an "Annuity in Arrears")

A. Present Value Now of an Ordinary Annuity to be Received Over Some Future Time Period—This calculation determines the value now (at the present) of a series of equal amounts to be received (or paid) at equal intervals over some future period of time. An annuity is, by definition, a series of equal dollar amounts. An ordinary annuity (as compared to an annuity due) means that the series of equal amounts is received (or paid) at the end of each period. In an annuity due the series of equal amounts is received (or paid) at the beginning of each period. The present value of the series of amounts to be received (or paid) in the future will be less than the sum of the future nominal values of those amounts.

B. Illustration—To illustrate, assume $5,000 is to be received at the end of each of the next 5 years. What is the present value of the $25,000 to be received over the next 5 years? Graphically, the circumstances can be shown as:

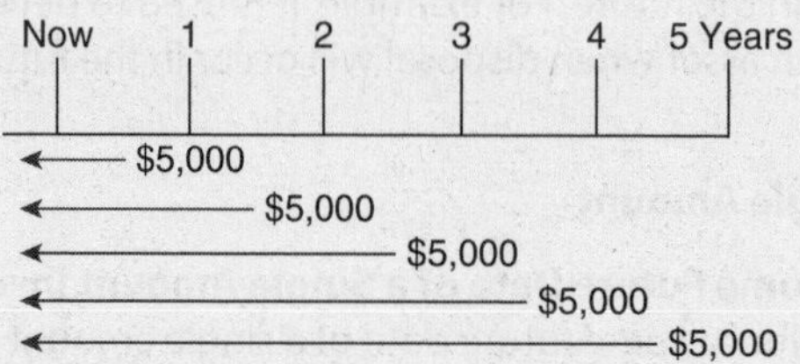

C. The annuity is $5,000 and the number of periods is 5 years. Assume the appropriate discount rate (interest rate) is 6% and the related present value of an ordinary annuity of $1.00 table shows the following for 5 periods:

Rate	2%	4%	6%	8%	10%
5 Periods	4.713	4.452	4.212	3.993	3.791

D. The appropriate discount factor for 5 periods at 6% is 4.212. Therefore, the present value (PV) of a 5-year, $5,000 ordinary annuity discount at 6% would be calculated as:

PV = $5,000 × 4.212 = $21,060

Or, $5,000 to be received at the end of each of the next five years discounted at 6% is worth $21,060 now.

E. The calculation of the present value of an annuity is frequently used in assessing investment opportunities for which a series of equal amounts of revenue, cost, and/or cost savings are expected over some future period.

V. Future Value of an Ordinary Annuity

A. Future Value at Some Future Time of an Ordinary Annuity Invested Over Some Future Time Period—This calculation determines the value at some future date of a series of equal amounts to be paid (or received) at equal intervals over some future period. As an ordinary annuity, the series of equal amounts will be paid (or received) at the end of each period. The future value of the annuity will be greater than the sum of the series of payments (or receipts) as a result of interest earned on each payment (or receipt).

B. Illustration—To illustrate, assume $5,000 is to be paid at the end of each of the next 5 years and will earn interest at 6% compounded annually. What is the future value of the series of payments at the end of 5 years? Graphically, the circumstances can be shown as follows:

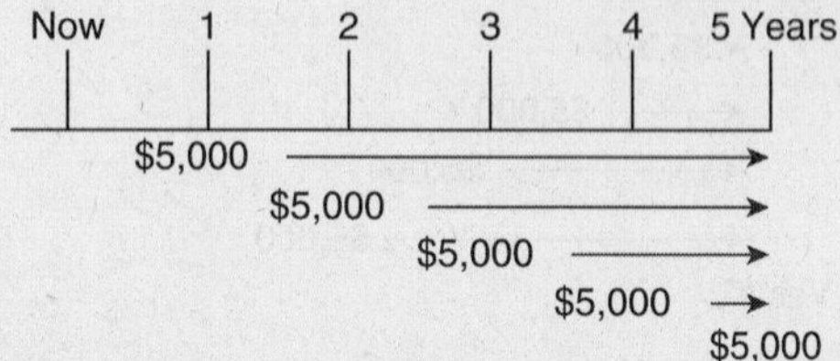

C. The annuity is $5,000 and the number of periods is 5 years. Each payment will earn 6% compounded annually. Thus, for example, the first payment made at the end of the first year will earn 6% compounded for each of the next four years. The related future value of an ordinary annuity of $1.00 table shows the following for 5 periods:

Rate	2%	4%	6%	8%	10%
5 Periods	5.204	5.416	5.637	5.867	6.105

D. The appropriate future value factor for 5 periods at 6% is 5.637. Therefore, the future value (FV) of a 5-year, $5,000 ordinary annuity at 6% would be calculated as:

$$FV = \$5,000 \times 5.637 = \$28,185$$

Or, $5,000 deposited at the end of each of the next five years earning 6% compounded annually would accumulate to $28,185.

VI. Present Value of an Annuity Due (also called Annuity in Advance)

A. Present Value Now of an Annuity Due to be Received Over Some Future Time Period (Also Called Annuity In Advance)—In an annuity due, the series of equal amounts is received (or paid) at the beginning of each period, whereas in an ordinary annuity the series of equal amounts is received (or paid) at the end of each period. The relationship between the two types of annuities is shown in the following illustration:

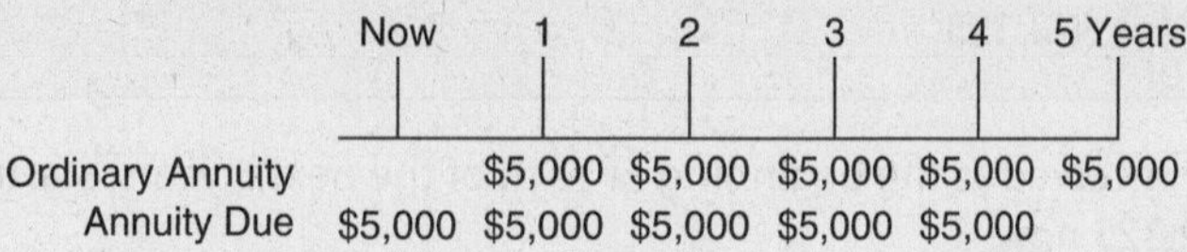

B. While each annuity is $5,000 for 5 years, the annuity due will result in a greater present value than an ordinary annuity because the first amount does not have to be discounted—its present value is $5,000. Similarly, when the future value is computed, each amount in an annuity due compounds for one additional period than in an ordinary annuity, resulting in a greater future value for an annuity due.

C. The calculation of the present value of an annuity due determines the value now (at the present) of a series of equal amounts to be received (or paid) at equal intervals over some future period of time with the amounts received (or paid) at the beginning of each period. The present value of the series of amounts to be received in the future will be less than the sum of the nominal future values of those amounts.

D. **Illustration**—To illustrate, assume $5,000 is to be received at the beginning of each of the next 5 years, with the first amount received now. What is the present value of the $25,000 to be received now and over the next 4 years? Graphically, the circumstances can be shown as:

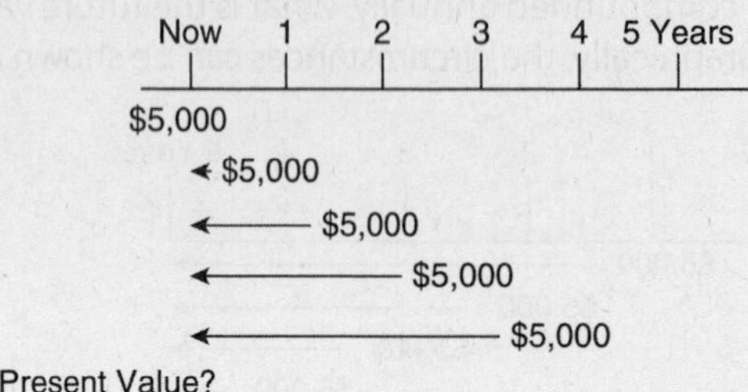

E. The annuity is $5,000 and the number of periods is 5 years. Assume the appropriate discount rate is 6% and the related present value of an ordinary annuity of $1.00 table shows the following for 4 periods and 5 periods:

Rate	2%	4%	6%	8%	10%
4 Periods	3.808	3.630	3.465	3.312	3.170
5 Periods	4.713	4.452	4.212	3.993	3.791

F. Notice that this is the present value table for an ordinary annuity, not an annuity due, and that present value factors are given for both 4 periods and 5 periods. If a present value table for an annuity due were given, you would simply use the appropriate present value factor for the number of time periods and the discount rate, as we have done in all prior illustrations. However, if only a present value table for an ordinary annuity is given, the present value of an annuity due can be determined. (Prior CPA Exams have required candidates to use ordinary annuity table values to solve for an annuity due amount.)

G. Since, as described and illustrated above, an annuity due involves the first payment (or receipt) occurring at the present, that payment does not have to be discounted. Therefore, the number of payments discounted is one less than the number of payments in the annuity and the number of periods is one less. For an annuity of 5 payments, with the first one now, only 4 payments must be discounted over 4 periods to get the present value. So, we can use the present value factor for 4 periods (3.465) and add 1.000 for the payment that is already at the present value. Our present value factor would be 3.465 + 1.000 = 4.465 and the present value (PV) of a 5-period, $5,000 annuity due at 6% would be calculated as:

$$PV = \$5,000 \times 4.465 = \$22,325$$

Or, $5,000 to be received at the beginning of each of the next 5 years, starting now, discounted at 6% is worth $22,325 now.

H. The present value of an annuity due (and annuities due, in general) is often used in accounting as well as in financial management. For example, the determination of the present value of minimum lease payments, with the first payment due at the signing of the lease, would require an annuity due calculation.

VII. Future Value of an Annuity Due

A. **Future Value at Some Future Time of an Annuity Due Invested Over Some Future Time Period**—The calculation of the future value of an annuity due determines the value at some future date of a series of equal amounts to be paid (or received) at equal intervals over some future period of time with the amounts paid (or received) at the beginning of each period. The future value will be greater than the sum of the series of amounts as a result of interest earned on each amount. Because the first amount is paid (or received) at the start of the annuity, the amount of interest earned and the amount at the end of the annuity will be greater than the future value of an ordinary annuity.

B. **Illustration**—To illustrate, assume $5,000 is to be paid at the beginning of each of the next 5 years, with the first amount paid now. What is the future value of the $25,000 to be paid starting now and over the next 4 years? Graphically, the circumstances can be shown as:

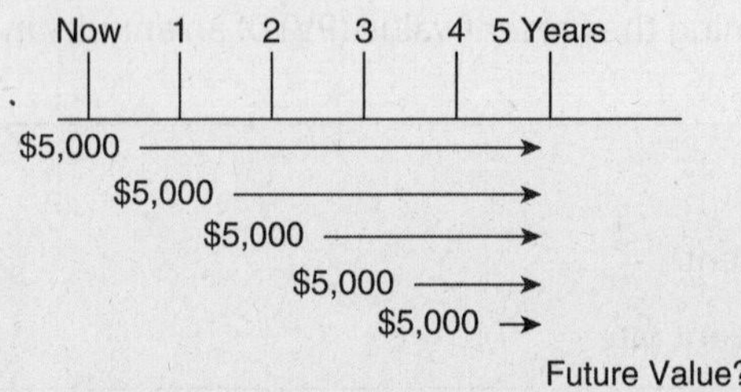

C. The annuity is $5,000 and the number of periods is 5 years. Assume the appropriate interest rate is 6% and the related future value of an ordinary annuity of $1.00 table shows the following for 5 periods and 6 periods:

Rate	2%	4%	6%	8%	10%
5 Periods	5.204	5.416	5.637	5.867	6.105
6 Periods	6.308	6.633	6.975	7.335	7.716

D. Notice that this is the future value table for an ordinary annuity, not an annuity due, and that future value factors are given for both 5 periods and 6 periods. Since an annuity due involves the first payment (or receipt) occurring at the present, that payment earns an additional period of interest. Therefore, the number of periods in which interest is earned is one more than in an ordinary annuity. Thus, for an annuity of 5 payments, with the first one now, we can use the ordinary annuity for 6 periods (6.975) and subtract 1.000 for the fact that the annuity is for 5 periods. Our future value would be 6.975 – 1.000 = 5.975 and the future value (FV) of a 5-period, $5,000 annuity due at 6% would be calculated as follows:

$$FV = \$5,000 \times 5.975 = \$29,875$$

Or, $5,000 to be paid (or received) at the beginning of each of the next 5 years, starting now, at 6% would accumulate to $29,875. (Recall that the future value of a comparable ordinary annuity was $28,185).

VIII. Present Value of a Perpetual Annuity (also called simply a "Perpetuity")

A. **Present Value Now of an Ordinary Annuity to be Received Indefinitely Into the Future**—This calculation determines the value now (at the present) of a series of equal amounts to be received (or paid) at equal intervals with no end date; the amounts continue indefinitely into the future. Such an infinite series of cash flows has a finite present value (PV) because the discounted value of far-future payments of the perpetuity decreases considerably and ultimately approaches zero.

B. Illustration—To illustrate, assume $5,000 is to be received at the end of each future year indefinitely (in perpetuity). What is the present value of that indefinite stream of cash? Graphically, the circumstances can be shown as:

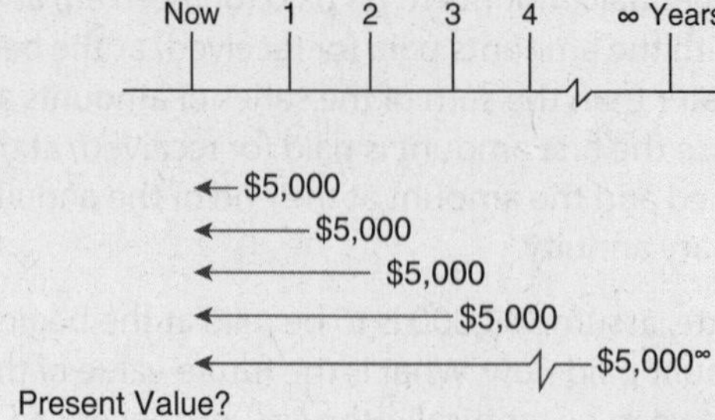

C. The formula for determining the present value (PV) of an annuity in perpetuity is:

PV = AP/R

Where: AP = Annual payment

R = Interest/Discount rate

D. Using the illustration above, the annuity is $5,000 and the number of periods is infinite (forever). Assume the appropriate discount rate (interest rate) is 10%. Using the formula, the present value of the annuity in perpetuity is:

PV = AP/R

PV = $5,000/.10 = $50,000

Consider the facts from another perspective: How many dollars would you have to invest earning 10% per year to insure $5,000 per year forever?

That can be expressed as:

PV × .10 = $5,000

PV = $5,000/.10 = $50,000

E. Perpetual Annuity Applications—The concept of a perpetual annuity currently has somewhat limited application. The primary practical applications of perpetual annuities include:

1. **United Kingdom consol bonds**—The U.K. issues undated, nonredeemable, fixed interest bonds, called consols, that pay interest in perpetuity. (In the United States, the IRS does not permit the deduction of interest payments on perpetual bonds.)
2. **Dividend discount model**—This model for the valuation of common stock assumes that the per-share value of common stock is equal to the discounted stream of all dividends indefinitely into the future and that the growth in dividends is a constant rate. (This approach to common stock valuation is covered later in the section on Financing Options.)
3. **Real estate/business valuation using a capitalization rate**—This approach to valuing real estate or an entire business assumes that the current income or cash flow from the property/business will last indefinitely into the future. (This approach to business valuation is covered later in the section on Valuation Techniques—Business Entity.)

IX. Table Factors—Underlying Concept

A. From the foregoing examples, it should be clear that computing PV or FV using table factors follows the basic formula of:

PV (or FV) = Amount × Table Factor

B. The table factor (TF) takes into account two variables—time and interest rate (as reflected by selecting a column and row from a PV or FV table). For example, a present value of $1 table shows a factor of .747 where the number of periods (time) is 5 and the interest rate is 6%. Thus, .747 represents two of the three elements (time and interest rate) needed to get the present value of a single amount to be received in 5 periods with a 6% interest (discount) rate. The third element is the amount to be received.

C. Note that if you have any two of the three elements, you can determine the third using simple algebra.

1. Basic equation for PV or FV:

PV or FV = Amount × Table Factor

2. Equation to determine amount:

Amount = PV or FV/Table Factor

Example

How much would need to be set aside each year to accumulate $12,210 to repay a loan at the end of 5 years if savings compounds at 10%?

Amount = $12,210/Table Factor (n = 5; i = 10%)

Amount = $12,210/6.105 = $2,000 per year

3. Equation to determine table factor (and, therefore, periods or interest rate):

Table Factor (TF) = PV (or FV)/Amount

Example

What interest (discount) rate was used if you have the option of receiving $3,312 now or $1,000 at the end of each of the next four years?

TF = $3,312 / $1,000 = 3.312

From a table for PV of an ordinary annuity at 4 periods, the factor 3.312 shows an interest rate of 8%, the discount rate used.

Note

The present value and future value concepts and calculations covered in this section will be used in subsequent sections in carrying out various financial management analysis and decision making.

Interest Rate Concepts and Calculations

Interest is rent for the use of money. "Interest rate" is an expression of the price or cost for the use of money. A number of interest and interest rate concepts are used in accounting and finance. This lesson considers interest and interest rate concepts and calculations.

After studying this lesson, you should be able to:

1. Define and describe different interest rate basis, including: a) fixed rate; b) variable rate; and c) variable-to-fixed rate or fixed-to-variable rate.
2. Describe and calculate a number of interest and interest rate concepts, including: a) stated interest; b) simple interest; c) compound interest; d) effective interest rate; e) annual percentage rate; and f) effective annual percentage rate; g) negative interest rate.

I. **Overview**—Interest is the money paid for the use of money. From the point of view of the borrower, it is the cost of borrowed funds; from the point of view of the lender, it is the revenue earned for lending money to another. It compensates the lender for deferring use of the funds and for the various risks inherent in making the loan. The greater the perceived risk in an investment or other undertaking, the greater the expected rate of return, or interest rate.

II. **Interest Is Expressed as a Percentage Rate**—Interest is almost always expressed as an annual percentage rate, which is applied to the principal and/or other amount to determine the dollar amount of interest. Depending on the contract in a particular situation, the rate may be fixed, variable, or a combination.

   A. **Fixed Rate**—The percentage rate of interest does not change over the life of the loan or parts of that life. For example, in a 30-year, fixed-rate mortgage, the interest rate does not change over the 30-year life of the mortgage, regardless of the changes in rates in the market during that period.

   B. **Variable Rate**—The percentage rate of interest can change over the life of the loan or part of that life. Generally, a change in the rate is triggered by a change in the general level of interest in the economy as measured by a macroeconomic indicator, such as the prime rate of interest. (The prime rate of interest is the rate banks charge to their most credit-worthy borrowers.) For example, in a 15-year adjustable rate mortgage, the interest rate may be related to changes in the prime rate of interest. If the prime rate goes up or down, so would the rate on the mortgage.

   C. **Variable-to-Fixed Rate or Fixed-to-Variable Rate**—Though less common, some loans charge one kind of rate, say variable, for a portion of the life of the loan, and a different kind of rate, say fixed, for another portion of the life of the loan. For example, a 25-year mortgage may have an adjustable rate for the first 7 years, after which it carries a fixed rate.

III. **Market Interest Rate**

   A. **Definition**

Definition
Market Interest Rate: The market rate of interest is the prevailing rate of interest paid on interest-bearing investments or charged on interest-bearing borrowings as determined by the supply and demand for funds in the market.

1. The market rate of interest (i.e., the prevailing rate of interest) can be different in different markets and change over time, depending on such factors as general economic conditions, expected inflation, the particular market, general type of instrument, government monetary policy, and similar macro-characteristics.
2. Within a given market, the rate of interest for specific instruments will depend on such factors as:
   a. Credit rating of the issuer
   b. Duration (length) of the instrument

c. Amount of the instrument

d. Liquidity (or marketability) of the instrument

e. Special covenants and features, if any

B. Determinants of Market Interest Rate for a Security

1. Generally, the nominal (or quoted) interest rate for a security is composed of a real risk-free rate of interest, plus premiums that reflect market, entity, and instrument risks and characteristics, including inflation, risk of default, length and amount of the instrument, its marketability, and special covenants and features, if any.

2. Mathematically, the nominal interest rate can be expressed as:

> Nominal (quoted) rate = Real risk-free (inflation-free) rate of interest + Inflation premium + Default risk premium + Maturity premium + Liquidity premium [+/– Special premiums / Discounts, if any].

a. Each of these elements is described in the following subsections.

3. Elements of nominal (quoted) interest rate on a security:

a. The real risk-free (inflation-free) rate of interest constitutes the interest rate that would occur if there are no risks associated with the instrument and inflation is expected to be zero.

i. Because no inflation is expected, the rate is considered a "real" rate (i.e., the rate with—or after—zero inflation).

ii. The rate of return on short-term U.S. Treasury securities assuming no inflation is commonly considered as the risk-free rate.

iii. The risk-free rate of return changes over time as economic conditions change.

b. The inflation risk premium compensates for the adverse effects of expected inflation on the security.

i. This premium is based on the average expected inflation rate over the life of the security.

ii. The higher the expected inflation rate, the higher the nominal interest rate.

iii. The market price of U.S. Treasury Bills would be the sum of the real risk-free rate of interest (which assumes no inflation) plus the inflation risk premium (often called the nominal risk-free rate or the quoted risk-free rate).

iv. Example: If the real risk-free rate is 2.5% and expected inflation for the next year is 3.0%, the quoted rate of interest on a one-year T-bill would be 2.5% + 3.0% = 5.5%.

c. The default (or credit) risk premium compensates for the possibility that the issuer of debt will not pay interest and/or principal at the contracted time and/or in the contracted amount.

i. The greater the perceived default risk, the higher the nominal interest rate.

ii. U.S. Treasury securities are assumed to have no default risk and, therefore, have the lowest interest rates for comparable taxable securities in the United States.

iii. The difference between the quoted interest rate on a U.S. T-bond and on a corporate bond with similar amount, maturity, liquidity, tax, and other features will be the amount of the default premium.

iv. Example: If T-bonds are quoted at 5.5% and otherwise comparable corporate bonds are quoted at 7.8%, the default risk premium would be 2.3% (i.e., 7.8% – 5.5% = 2.3%).

d. The maturity premium compensates for the risk that longer-term fixed-rate instruments will decline in value as a result of an increase in the market rate of interest.

i. The value of outstanding fixed-rate instruments changes inversely with changes in the market rate of interest; therefore, if over time the market rate of interest increases, the market value of outstanding comparable instruments will decline.

ii. This risk is commonly called "interest rate risk"—the risk associated with a change in the market interest rate.

iii. All long-term fixed-rate instruments, including U.S. Treasury securities, are subject to the interest rate risk and call for a maturity premium.

iv. The longer the time to maturity, the higher the maturity premium.

e. The liquidity premium (also called the marketability premium) compensates for the fact that some securities cannot be converted to cash on short notice at approximate fair market value.

i. The greater the perceived illiquidity of a security, the higher the liquidity premium.

ii. Securities of the U.S. Treasury and those of financially strong corporations that are widely traded in active markets carry little or no liquidity premium; less liquid securities of small entities are likely to carry a relatively significant liquidity premium.

f. Special premiums or discounts may attach to a particular instrument related to such factors as convertibility, call feature, seniority (priority claim over other securities), security provided, and other factors. The factors and the related premium/discount will depend on terms of the specific instrument.

C. In 1997 the U.S. Treasury began issuing inflation-indexed bonds as a security that provides investors protection against the risk of inflation. These bonds pay a stated rate of interest that is applied to a changing principal amount to offset the effects of inflation. Specifically, the principal of the bonds, initially set at $1,000, is adjusted each six months based on the inflation rate as measured by the Consumer Price Index (CPI). The stated interest rate is applied to the inflation-adjusted principal. This inflation adjustment to the principle protects against inflation risk because if inflation increases so will the bond principal and the dollar return on the bonds. As a consequence, the quoted market rate on inflation-indexed bonds should be the real risk-free rate, without the need to add an inflation premium.

IV. Interest and Interest Rate Concepts

A. While an interest rate states the cost of the use of money, not all statements of interest rate are comparable and this is primarily due to the effects of compounding. The remainder of this lesson identifies and shows the calculation of a number of different interest and interest rate concepts, including:

1. Stated interest rate
2. Simple interest
3. Compound interest
4. Effective interest rate
5. Annual percentage rate
6. Effective annual percentage rate
7. Negative interest rate

The lesson concludes with a discussion of the term structure of interest rates.

B. Understanding these interest and interest rate concepts is important to both accounting and financial management.

1. **Stated interest rate**—The stated interest rate (also called the nominal or quoted interest rate) is the annual rate specified in the loan agreement or comparable contract; it does not take into account the compounding effects of frequency of payments or the effects of inflation.

Example
The coupon rate of interest on a bond is the stated rate of interest for that bond. If the bond coupon rate is 6%, with interest paid semiannually, the stated rate of interest is 6%, even though the effective rate will be higher because interest is paid two times during a year.

a. **Nominal interest rate**—As contrasted with real interest rate, also refers to the rate of interest received before taking into account the effects of inflation.

b. **Real interest rate**—As contrasted with nominal interest rate, refers to the rate of interest after taking into account the effects of inflation on the value of funds received. The calculation of the real interest rate (RIR) is:

$$\text{RIR} = \text{Nominal interest rate} - \text{Inflation rate}$$

Example
Assume a one-year investment instrument that pays a stated (nominal) rate of interest of 8%. During the year inflation is 3%. The real interest rate (RIR) is:

$$\text{RIR} = 8\% - 3\% = 5\%$$

Therefore, while the nominal interest rate is 8%, because of inflation the real interest rate is 5%.

2. **Simple interest**—Simple interest is interest computed on the original principal only; there is no compounding in the interest computation. (See "Compound interest" below.)

Example
Assume a 2-year, $2,000 note that provides for 6% simple interest with principal and interest to be paid at the end of the 2-year period. The basic interest expression provides:

$$\begin{aligned} \text{Interest} &= \text{Principal} \times \text{Rate} \times \text{Time, or} \\ &= P \times R \times T\text{, or} \\ &= \$2{,}000 \times .06 \times 2 \text{ years} = \$240 \end{aligned}$$

Thus, at the end of the second year the borrower would repay $2,000 principal + $240 interest = $2,240.

3. **Compound interest**—Compound interest provides that interest be paid not only on the principal, but also on any amount of accumulated unpaid interest. Compound interest pays interest on interest; simple interest does not.

Example
Assume the 2-year, $2,000 note that provides 6% interest in the prior example, but terms of the note provide that interest is compounded annually with repayment at the end of the 2-year period.

$$\begin{aligned} \text{Interest Year 1} = I = P \times R \times T = \$2{,}000 \times .06 \times 1 &= \$120.00 \\ \text{Interest Year 2} = I = (\$2{,}000 + \$120) \times .06 \times 1 &= \underline{127.20} \\ \text{Total Interest} &= \$247.20 \end{aligned}$$

Thus, at the end of the second year the borrower would repay $2,000 principal + $247.20 interest = $2,247.20. As a result of paying interest on the first year's interest, the total interest is $7.20 more than under simple interest.

a. The above calculation can be done using the formula for future value (FV) of $1.00:

$$FVn = P(1+R)^n$$
Where : P = Principal
R = Interest rate per year
n = Number of years

Substituting with the facts above:

$$FVn = \$2,000(1+.06)^2$$
$$FVn = \$2,000(1.06)^2$$
$$FVn = \$2,000(1.1236)$$
$$FVn = \$2,247.20 = \$2,000 \text{ principal} + 247.20 \text{ interest}$$

b. Compound interest and future value of $1.00 calculations are performed in the same manner. Both account for interest being paid on accumulated interest. For multiple period calculations either the formula above or a future value of $1.00 table can be used.

4. **Effective interest**—The effective interest rate is the annual interest rate implicit in the relationship between the net proceeds from a loan and the dollar cost of the loan.

Example

Assume the facts above, which were a 2-year, $2,000 note with 6% interest. We saw that if the contract provided for simple interest, the dollar amount of interest was:

$$I = P \times R \times T = \$2,000 \times .06 \times 2 = \$240$$

The effective rate (EI) is 6%, which can be shown as the relationship between the cost ($240) and the proceeds ($2,000), or:

$$EI = (\$240 / \$2,000) / 2 \text{ years}$$
$$EI = .12 / 2 = .06$$

Assume the contract provides the same terms, except that the note will be discounted. In that case, the proceeds are:

$$\$2,000 - \$240 = \$1,760$$

The effective rate of interest (EI) is now:

$$EI = (\$240 / \$1,760) / 2 \text{ years}$$
$$EI = 0.1364 / 2 = 0.0682 = 6.82\%$$

a. In addition to discounting, such items as origination fees, compensating balances, and installment payments will cause the effective rate to be different from the stated rate of interest.

5. **Annual percentage rate**—The annual percentage rate (APR) is the annualized effective interest rate without compounding on loans that are for a fraction of a year. It is computed as the effective interest rate for the fraction of a year multiplied by the number of time fractions in a year (e.g., 2 if semiannual, 4 if quarterly, and 12 if monthly).

Example

Assume the facts above, which were a $2,000 note with 6% interest, but assume that the note is for 90 days (3 months = 1 quarter) and the note is discounted. The interest, proceeds, effective interest rate, and annual percentage rate will be:

$I = P \times R \times T$

$I = \$2,000 \times .06 \times 90/360$

$I = \$2,000 \times .06 \times .25 = \$30$

$\text{Proceeds} = \$2,000 - \$30 = \$1,970$

$\text{Effective Interest} = \$30 / \$1,970 = 1.52\%$

$\text{Annual Percentage Rate} = 1.52\% \times 4 \text{ quarters} = 6.08\%$

Thus, while the stated rate is 6.00%, the annual percentage rate (APR) is 6.08%. Recall that the annual percentage rate (APR) is the required basis for interest rate disclosure in the U.S.

6. **Effective annual percentage rate**—The effective annual percentage rate, also called the annual percentage yield, is the annual percentage rate with compounding on loans that are for a fraction of a year. As discussed under compounding, the assumption is that interest is paid on interest that would accumulate for each period during the year. The formula for computing the effective annual percentage rate (EAPR) is:

$$EAPR = (1 + I/P)^P - 1$$

Where : I = Annual (nominal) interest rate

P = Number of periods in the year

Example

Assume the facts above, which were a 90-day, $2,000 note with a 6% interest rate. Substituting, the EAPR would be:

$$EAPR = \left(1 + \frac{.06}{4}\right)^4 - 1 = (1 + .015)^4 - 1 = (1.015)^4 - 1$$

$$EAPR = 1.06136 - 1 = .06136$$

Thus, while the annual percentage rate is 6.08%, the effective annual percentage rate is 6.136%, due to the assumed compounding within the year.

C. **Negative Interest Rate**—Under a traditional (positive) interest rate agreement, a borrower (recipient) pays a lender (provider) interest for the use of funds. Under a negative interest rate agreement, the flow of benefit payment (interest) is reversed: The owner of the funds pays the recipient to hold the funds. Thus, for example, a financial institution would **charge** depositors interest to hold their money on deposit rather than **pay** them interest on those deposits as has traditionally been the case.

Example

Big Bank charges a –.5 (negative) interest rate on deposits made by its largest corporate customers. A corporate client that deposited $1,000,000 would have to pay the bank $5,000 ($1,000,000 · .005) annual interest rather than receiving interest on its deposit.

1. The concept and use of negative interest rates is primarily a monetary policy approach that resulted from the failure of the traditional zero (0.0%) lower limit to central banks' interest rate to adequately stimulate economic activity.
2. In theory, the use of a negative interest rate by central banks would encourage businesses and individuals to spend, lend, or invest their funds rather than pay to have those funds held by a financial institution.
3. Since negative interest rates are primarily a monetary policy issue, they are covered in the "Money, Banking and Monetary/Fiscal Policy" lesson in the "Economic Concepts and Analysis" area.

V. **Term Structure of Interest Rates**—The term structure of interest rates describes the relationship between long-term interest rates and short-term interest rates.

A. The relationship is commonly plotted on a graph with the interest (yield) plotted on the vertical axis and time plotted on the horizontal axis.

B. The resulting plot is called a "yield curve" and is used to illustrate the level of interest rates for various durations (lengths of time) as of a point in time.

C. At a point in time a yield curve may take one of the following forms:

1. **Normal yield curve**—an upward sloping curve in which short-term rates are less than intermediate-term rates, which are less than long-term rates.
   a. Historically, this curve reflects the most common relationship between short-term and long-term rates.
   b. Long-term rates are normally higher than short-term rates because the longer period exposes securities to a greater interest rate risk; if interest rates increase, the value of outstanding fixed-rate securities will decline.
   c. Normal yield curve example:

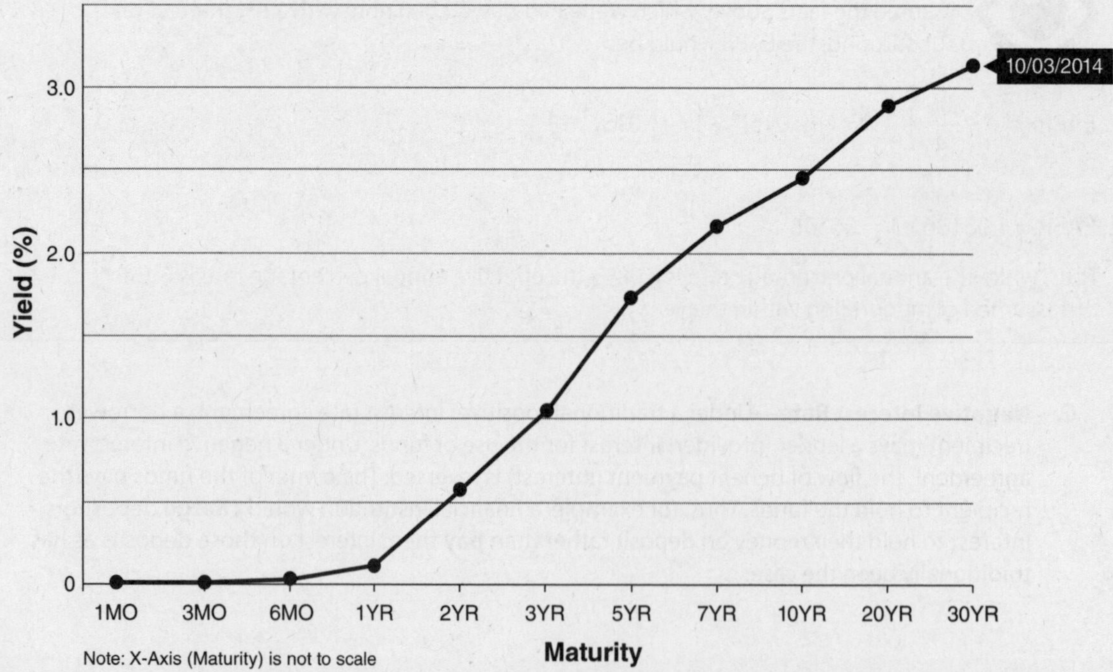

d. The normal yield curve above is as of October 3, 2014, and shows the yield as of that date on securities ranging from 1 month to maturity (approaching 0.0% yield) to 30 years to maturity (about 3.1% yield).

2. Other forms of yield curves

a. Inverted (or abnormal) yield curve—A downward-sloping curve reflecting that short-term rates are greater than intermediate-term rates, which are greater than long-term rates.

b. Flat yield curve—A horizontal curve reflecting that short-term, intermediate-term, and long-term rates are about the same.

c. Humped yield curve—A curve that increases and then decreases reflecting that intermediate-term rates are higher than both short-term and long-term rates.

Financial Valuation

Introduction to Financial Valuation

Financial valuation is the process of assigning an estimated monetary worth to an item—asset, liability, equity, or an entire entity. Valuation has many uses in finance and accounting. This lesson defines valuation and value concepts, and it describes the uses and characteristics of valuation. In addition, the kinds of inputs used for valuation purposes and their relative importance, as well as possible approaches to valuation, are identified.

After studying this lesson, you should be able to:

1. Define various relevant value-related terms.
2. Identify various uses of valuation for business purposes.
3. Describe the characteristics of value and valuation.
4. Identify the kinds and describe the relative importance of inputs used for valuation purposes.
5. Identify and describe the alternative approaches that can be used in the valuation process.

I. **Definitions**
   A. **Valuation**—The process of assigning worth or value to something.
   B. **Financial Valuation**—The process of estimating the fair value (market value) of an asset (investments, intangible assets, etc.), a liability (warranty obligations, bonds, etc.), equity (preferred stock, common stock, etc.) or a business enterprise.
   C. **Accounting Fair Value**—The price received to sell an asset or paid to transfer a liability in an orderly transaction between market participants.

II. **Uses**—Valuation is required in many business contexts, including, among others:
   A. **Recognition of Assets and Liabilities**
   B. **Investment Analysis**
   C. **Capital Budgeting**
   D. **Business Acquisitions (Mergers and Acquisitions)**
   E. **Assessment of Closely Held Businesses**
   F. **Tax Determinations**
   G. **Buy/Sell Agreements**

III. **Characteristics**—Whatever the purpose of valuation in a business context, certain characteristics apply in carrying out the valuation process:
   A. Most valuation has elements of both science (objective characteristics) and art (subjective characteristics):
      1. **Science**—As a science, valuation involves the use of quantitative data and techniques, as well as financial models and other techniques to develop estimates of value.
      2. **Art**—As an art, valuation incorporates a qualitative dimension and the use of professional judgment, including an understanding of the purpose and context of a valuation, the selection of appropriate quantitative techniques and data, and, ultimately, the assignment of a value.
   B. For business purposes, value is measured in money.

C. The determination of value is for a specific item, which may be:

1. **A separate asset, liability or equity item**—A financial instrument, an operating asset, a bond, or common stock, for example.
2. **A group of assets or liabilities**—A portfolio of financial instruments, a capital project, a group of operating assets (e.g., a division or brand), or an entire business entity as a going concern, for example.

D. The determination of value takes into account the attributes of the item being valued, including its condition and location.

E. The determination of value is as of a particular point in time.

F. The quality of an estimate of value depends on the quality of the assumptions and inputs used, the appropriateness of the techniques used for measurement, and the judgment applied.

IV. Input Characteristics—U.S. GAAP provides a framework for prioritizing or ranking the quality of inputs used in fair value determination. It identifies three levels:

A. Level 1—The highest level:

1. Inputs in this level are unadjusted quoted prices in active markets for assets or liabilities identical to those being valued that the entity can obtain at the measurement date; all such inputs are observable in a market.
2. Quoted prices in an active market provide the most reliable evidence of fair value and should be used when available.

B. Level 2—The middle level:

1. Inputs in this level are observable for assets or liabilities, either directly or indirectly, other than quoted prices described in level 1, above, and include:
   - **a.** Quoted prices for **similar** assets or liabilities in active markets
   - **b.** Quoted prices for identical or similar assets or liabilities in markets that are **not active markets** and in which there are few relevant transactions, prices are not current or vary substantially, or for which little information is publicly available
   - **c.** Inputs, other than quoted prices, that are observable for the assets or liabilities being valued, including, for example, interest rates, yield curves, credit risks, and default rates
   - **d.** Inputs derived principally from, or corroborated by, observable market data by correlations or other means
2. Depending on the circumstances specific to the asset or liability being valued, these inputs when applied may need to be adjusted for factors such as condition, location, and the level of activity in the relevant market.

C. Level 3—The lowest level:

1. Inputs in this level are unobservable for the assets or liabilities being valued and should be used to determine fair value only to the extent observable inputs are not available;
2. When unobservable inputs are used, they should reflect the entity's assumptions about what market participants would assume and should be developed based on the best information and data available in the circumstances.

V. Valuation Approaches—U.S. GAAP also specifies three broad approaches that can be used to develop a fair value; these approaches are applicable to financial valuation in general:

A. Market Approach (also Called the Sales Comparison Approach)—Uses prices and other relevant information generated by market transactions involving assets or liabilities that are identical or comparable to those being valued.

1. This approach is based on the premise that a market participant will not pay more than it costs to purchase a similar item.

B. Income Approach—Uses valuation techniques to convert future amounts of economic benefits or sacrifices of economic benefits to determine what those future amounts are worth as of the valuation date.

1. Typically converts future cash flows or earnings amounts using models, including:
   a. Discounted cash flows
   b. Option pricing models
   c. Earnings capitalization models
2. This approach is based on the premise that a market participant is willing to pay the present value of the future economic benefits to acquire an item.

C. Cost Approach—Uses valuation techniques to determine the amount required to acquire or construct a substitute item (replacement cost or reproduction cost).

1. Use of this approach is more limited than the market approach or the income approach.
2. Use would be especially appropriate for valuing specialized types of assets.

Valuation Techniques—General

A number of methods and techniques can be used in carrying out the valuation process. This lesson identifies and describes the general kinds of methods, inputs, and sources available in establishing value.

After studying this lesson, you should be able to:

1. Identify the nature of the inputs that are appropriate at each of the three levels of inputs used for valuation purposes.
2. Identify specific kinds and sources of data that are relevant to each level of input used.
3. Identify some of the items that may be valued using specific kinds of inputs.
4. Select and apply inputs for the valuation for specific purposes.

I. **Introduction**—Various valuation methods, techniques, and models are used in finance and accounting. The most significant of those are presented here using the U.S. GAAP hierarchy of inputs as a framework for presentation.

II. **Level 1**—Quoted market prices in active markets for identical assets or liabilities.

   A. These values would consist of prices from exchange-traded markets and dealer markets for identical assets or liabilities as those being valued.

   B. Examples of markets include public markets, including stock markets, bond markets, commodities markets, and currency markets, as well as dealer markets (e.g., over the counter markets).

   C. Since the quoted market price is for an identical asset or liability, adjustments to the quoted prices are not appropriate in establishing value.

   D. Quoted market prices would be appropriate for valuing exchange-traded investments, futures contracts, actively traded bonds, actively traded debt, commodities, and the like.

III. **Level 2**—Inputs other than those in level 1 that are either directly or indirectly observable are used for valuing an item, including:

   A. Quoted prices for **similar** assets or liabilities in **active markets** are used for valuing an item.

      1. These inputs consist of quoted market prices for assets or liabilities similar to those being valued.
      2. The market may be any of those identified above as active markets.
      3. Examples would include:
         a. The valuation of common stock of a public company that is restricted from sale by SEC requirements but for which there are shares publicly traded in an active market
         b. The valuation of a receive-fixed, pay-variable interest rate swap contract based on a LIBOR swap rate

   B. Quoted prices for **identical** assets or liabilities in markets that are **inactive** are used for valuing an item.

      1. These inputs would consist of quoted market prices for assets or liabilities identical to those being valued, but in a stock, commodities or other market in which there is little interest shown by potential investors, resulting in few trades.
      2. The market, for example, may be a brokered market for unrestricted securities and may apply to, for example, such instruments as private label, mortgage-backed securities, collateralized debt obligations, and certain municipal bonds.

C. Quoted prices for **similar** assets or liabilities in markets that are **inactive** are used for valuing an item.

1. These inputs would consist of quoted market prices for assets or liabilities similar to those being valued in stock, commodities or other markets in which there is little interest shown by potential investors, resulting in few trades.

2. The market, for example, may be a brokered market for residential or commercial real estate and may apply to apartment developments, shopping malls, office buildings, and the like.

D. Inputs other than quoted prices that are observable are used for valuing an item.

1. These inputs would consist of observable measures, other than quoted prices, that are relevant to the assets or liabilities being valued.

2. These inputs would include, for example, interest rates, yield curves, credit risks and default rates, and may apply to secondary market loans or currency swaps.

E. Inputs not directly observable, but derived principally from, or corroborated by, observable market data are used for valuing an item.

1. These inputs would use market data and be developed by correlation or other means to be useful in valuing an asset or liability.

2. The inputs would include, for example, the use of multiples of earnings, revenues or similar performance measures to value a business enterprise.

3. An example would include the valuation of a building using the price per square foot from transactions involving comparable buildings in similar locations.

IV. Level 3—Inputs are unobservable and based on an entity's assumptions. Estimates are used for valuing an item.

A. These inputs are based primarily on an entity's assumptions, estimates and data, and not on external, market-based inputs.

B. These inputs consist of things like expected cash flows, expected life or residual value, expected volatility, expected inflation, and the like.

C. The use of these inputs may be appropriate in valuing, for example, asset retirement obligations, mortgage servicing rights, capital projects, closely held businesses, and the like.

Valuation Techniques—CAPM

One of the widely used techniques in business valuation is the capital asset pricing model (CAPM). The CAPM model uses a measure of systematic risk in establishing an appropriate rate of return for investments in assets. This lesson describes CAPM, presents the CAPM formula, illustrates its use, and identifies the assumptions, limitations, and uses of CAPM.

After studying this lesson, you should be able to:

1. Describe CAPM and how it is used.
2. Understand the basic CAPM formula, including the role and meaning of *beta*.
3. Calculate required rates of return using CAPM.
4. Identify the assumption and limitations of CAPM.

I. Introduction

Definition
Capital Asset Pricing Model (CAPM): An economic model that determines the relationship between risk and expected return and uses that measure in valuing securities, portfolios, capital projects and other assets.

A. CAPM incorporates both the time value of money and the element of risk:

1. The time value of money is incorporated as the risk-free rate of return
2. The element of risk is incorporated in a risk measure called "beta"

B. CAPM recognizes that the expected rate of return on an investment (e.g., stock, portfolio, capital project, etc.) must provide for (and at least be equal to) the rate on a risk-free investment plus a premium for the risk inherent in the investment.

1. If an investment is expected to provide a rate of return (RR) equal to or greater than the computed rate using CAPM, the investment is economically feasible.
2. If an investment is expected to provide a rate of return (RR) less than that computed using the CAPM formula, the investment is not economically feasible, and should not be undertaken.

II. CAPM Formula

A. The basic CAPM formula is expressed as:

$$RR = RFR + \beta\,(ERR - RFR)$$

Where:

RR = Required rate of return; the minimum rate of return that must be earned on an investment (e.g., stock, portfolio, capital project, etc.) to provide for (and at least be equal to) the rate on a risk-free investment plus a premium for the risk inherent in the particular investment

RFR = Risk-free rate of return; a measure of the time value of money, which in the United States is generally measured by the rate (yield) on U.S. government bonds

β = Beta of the investment; a measure of volatility, as described below

ERR = Expected rate of return for a benchmark for the asset class (type of asset) being valued

B. CAPM example

Example

1. Assume the following:

   Risk-free rate (RFR) = 3%

   Beta (β) = 2

   Expected rate (ERR) = 10%

2. Then:

   Required rate (RR) = RFR + β (ERR – RFR)

   RR = .03 + 2(.10 – .03)

   RR = .03 + 2(.07)

   RR = .03 + .14

   RR = 0.17 (or 17%)

Thus, given the assumed facts, the required rate of return for the assumed investment is 17%.

C. Beta described

1. Beta is a measure of the systematic risk as reflected by the volatility of an investment.
2. Technically, it is computed as:

Beta (β) = (Standard deviation of an asset [a] / Standard deviation of asset class benchmark [b]) × Coefficient of correlation of a and b

3. **Beta (β) value significance**
   - **a.** β = 1, then an investment price (value) moves in line with the asset class benchmark for that investment; the investment has average systematic risk.
   - **b.** β > 1, then an investment price (value) moves greater than the asset class benchmark for that investment; the investment has higher systematic risk—the investment is more volatile than the benchmark for the asset class.
     - **i.** In the example, above, β = 2 says that the assumed asset is more volatile (more risky) than the benchmark for its asset class; therefore, the required rate of return (17%) is significantly more than the benchmark rate (10%).
   - **c.** β < 1, then an investment price (value) moves less than the asset class benchmark for that investment; the investment has lower systematic risk—the investment is less volatile than the benchmark for the asset class.

d. Additional example:

Examples

Assume:

Risk-free rate = 3%

Benchmark rate = 7%

Excess market return = 4% (Market benchmark rate – Risk-free rate = Premium)

1. If β = 1 for an asset, the excess rate of return (premium) for the asset is 4% (1.0 × .04) and its total required rate of return is 7% (3% + 4%).
2. If β = .80 for an asset, the excess rate of return (premium) for the asset is 3.2% (.80 × .04) and its total required rate of return is 6.2% (3% + 3.2%).
3. If β = 2.0 for an asset, the excess rate of return (premium) for the asset is 8% (2.0 × .04) and its total required rate of return is 11% (3% + 8%).

III. Plotting of CAPM—The following graph shows the plotted slope of β under three assumptions as to its value:

A. When β = 1, a percentage change in an asset class benchmark return (i.e., a market) produces the same percentage change in an individual asset (e.g., a stock) of the same asset class.

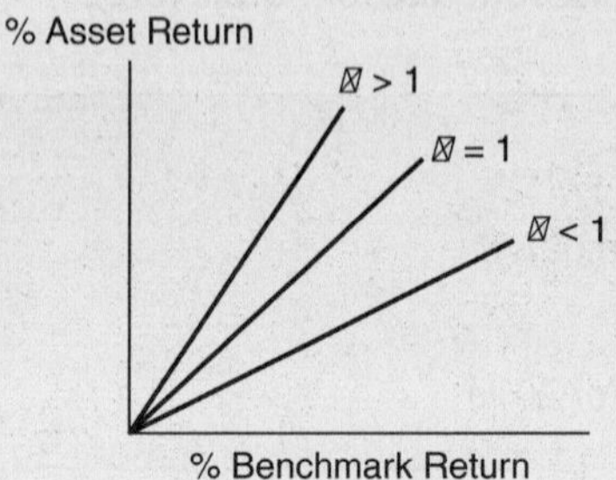

B. When β > 1, a percentage change in an asset class benchmark return produces a greater than equal change in an individual asset of the same asset class.

C. When β < 1, a percentage change in an asset class benchmark return produces a less than equal change in an individual asset of the same asset class.

IV. CAPM Assumptions and Limitations—CAPM is based on a number of assumptions, some of which are more significant to the outcome than others. Some of the most significant assumptions and limitations of CAPM are:

A. All investors are assumed to have equal access to all investments and all investors are assumed to be using a one period time horizon.

B. It is assumed that asset risk is measured solely by its variance from the asset class benchmark.

C. It is assumed that there are no external cost—commissions, taxes, etc.

D. It is assumed that there are no restrictions on borrowing or lending at the risk-free rate of return; all parties are assumed to be able to do so.

E. It is assumed that there is a market for all asset classes and, therefore, a market benchmark; to the extent there is not a market or a benchmark for a particular asset class, CAPM cannot be used.

F. It uses historical data, which may not be appropriate in calculating future expected returns.

V. CAPM Uses—CAPM provides a required rate of return (discount rate) that can be used in determining the value of a variety of assets. For example, it can be used in

A. Analysis of Securities—establishing a required rate of return for securities valuation. A key factor in the analysis of securities for investment purposes is the level of risk associated with the security. The higher the level of risk, the higher the rate of return required by an investor.

1. Generally, the required rate of return on an investment can be used as the discount rate applied to future cash flows for valuation purposes.
2. Because CAPM uses beta as a measure of the relative (undiversifiable) risk of an investment compared to that of a larger market, it can be used to establish a required rate of return (discount rate) for securities valuation.
3. Specifically, the lower the beta of a security, the lower the risk of that security when compared with the larger market risk. Thus, when appropriately used, CAPM provides an easy way to compare risk levels between securities.

B. Corporate Investment in Capital Projects—establishing hurdle rates (or discount rates) for capital projects.

1. In this case, the determination of a discount rate using CAPM would involve using the following (with assumed values as shown for illustration purposes):
   a. Company beta or industry beta as surrogate for the project beta = 1.50
   b. The risk-free rate of return = 8%
   c. An asset class benchmark = 16%
2. Calculation of required discount rate (or hurdle rate):

$$RR = RFR + \beta(ERR - RFR)$$
$$RR = .08 + 1.50(.16 - .08)$$
$$RR = .08 + 1.50(.08)$$
$$RR = .08 + .12 = .20 \text{ (or 20\%)}$$

3. The 20% would be used as the discount rate in the computation of the net present value (NPV) of a capital project. (Note: The net present value (NPV) method and other capital budgeting methods are covered in detail in the next topic.)

C. Establishing fair compensation for a regulated monopoly.

Valuation Techniques—Option Pricing

One of the most difficult financial instruments to value has been options—the right to buy or sell an asset. To address that issue, special option pricing models have been developed. This lesson defines options and the factors that play a role in establishing the value of an option. It also identifies and describes two of the most common option pricing models—the Black Scholes model and the binomial pricing model.

After studying this lesson, you should be able to:

1. Define an option and differentiate major types.
2. Identify the factors that affect the value of an option and the role of these factors.
3. Describe the Black Scholes and binomial option pricing models.

I. Introduction

A. Definition

Option: A contract that entitles the owner (holder) to buy (call option) or sell (put option) an asset (e.g., stock) at a stated price within a specified period. Financial options are a form of derivative instrument (contract).

1. Under terms of an American-style option, the option can be exercised any time prior to expiration.
2. Under terms of a European-style option, the option can be exercised only at the expiration (maturity) date.

B. Valuing Options

1. An option may or may not have value.
2. Valuing an option, including determining it has no value, is based on six factors:
   - **a.** Current stock price relative to the exercise price of the option—The difference between the current price and the exercise price affects the value of the option. The impact of the difference depends on whether the option is a call option or a put option.
     - **i.** Call option (a contract that gives the right to buy)—A current price above the exercise (or strike) price increases the option value; the option is considered "in the money." The greater the excess, the greater the option value.
     - **ii.** Put option (a contract that give the right to sell)—A current price below the exercise price increases the option value; the option is considered "in the money." The lower the current price relative to the exercise price, the greater the option value.
   - **b.** Time to the expiration of the option—The longer the time to expiration, the greater the option value (because there is a longer time for the price of the stock to go up).
   - **c.** The risk-free rate of return in the market—The higher the risk-free rate, the greater the option value.
   - **d.** A measure of risk for the optioned security, such as standard deviation—The larger the standard deviation, the greater the option value (because the price of the stock is more volatile; goes up higher and down further than its market changes).
   - **e.** Exercise price
   - **f.** Dividend payment on the optioned stock—The smaller the dividend payments, the greater the option value (because more earnings are being retained).
3. There is a direct relationship between these factors and the fair value of an option.

II. Black–Scholes Model

A. The original Black–Scholes model was developed to value options under specific conditions; thus, it is appropriate for

1. European call options, which permit exercise only at the expiration date
2. Options for stocks that pay no dividends
3. Options for stocks whose price increases in small increments
4. Discounting the exercise price using the risk-free rate, which is assumed to remain constant

B. As with other models used to estimate fair value of an option, the Black–Scholes method uses the six factors cited above. The advantage of the Black–Scholes model is the addition of two elements:

1. Probability factors for:
   - **a.** The likelihood that the price of the stock will pay off within the time to expiration, and
   - **b.** The likelihood that the option will be exercised.
2. Discounting of the exercise price

C. Many of the limitations (condition constraints) in the original Black–Scholes model have been overcome by subsequent modifications, so that today **modified** Black–Scholes models are widely used in valuing options.

D. The underlying theory of the Black–Scholes method and the related computation can be somewhat complex. Therefore, its use is best carried out using computer applications.

III. Binomial Option Pricing Model (BOPM)

A. The binomial option pricing model (BOPM) is a generalizable numerical method for the valuation of options.

1. The BOPM uses a "tree" to estimate value at a number of time points between the valuation date and the expiration of the option.
2. Each time point where the tree "branches" represents a possible price for the underlying stock at that time.
3. Valuation is performed iteratively, starting at each of the final nodes (those that may be reached at the time of expiration), and then working backwards through the tree towards the first node (valuation date).
4. The value computed at each stage is the value of the option at that point in time, including the single value at the valuation date.

B. BOPM Process

1. The BOPM process consists of three basic steps:
   - **a.** Generate a price tree.
   - **b.** Calculate the option value at each tree end node.
   - **c.** Sequentially calculate the option value at each preceding node (tree branch).
2. The process can be illustrated using a simple one-year option:
   - **a.** Assume an option for a share of stock that expires in one year and has an exercise price of $100. An evaluation estimates that at the end of the year the underlying stock could have a price as high as $120 and as low as $80.

b. These facts can be represented graphically as follows:

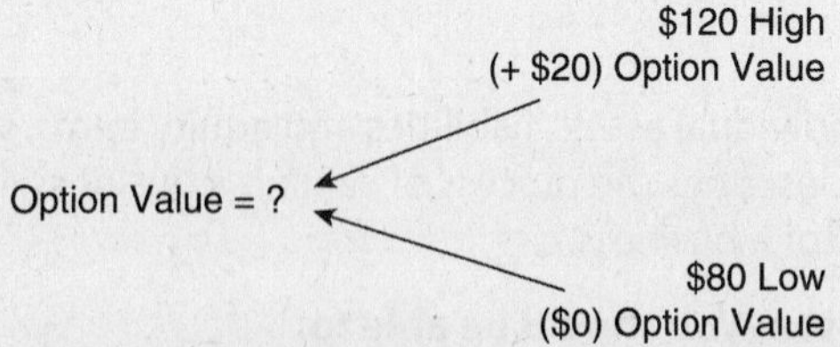

c. Probabilities are assigned to each of the possible outcomes to develop an expected value for the option.

> Assume that a .60 probability is assigned to the $120 high value and a .40 probability (1.00 – .60) is assigned to the $80 low value. The entity's cost of funds is 10%.
>
> Expected Value = [(.60 × $20) + (.40 × $0)]/1.10
>
> = [$12 + $ 0]/1.10
>
> Option Value = $12/1.10 = $10.91

d. While the one-period model is an extreme simplification of the use of the binomial option pricing model, it illustrates the approach. In practice the entire time period of the option would be divided into multiple subperiods, with the expected outcome of each period being the input for the prior period.

e. The binomial option pricing model can be used for American-style options, which permit exercise any time up to the expiration date, and when the underlying stock pays dividends, which the original Black–Scholes model does not accommodate.

Valuation Techniques—Business Entity

In addition to valuing individual assets, liabilities and equity items, valuing an entire business entity may be needed. This lesson describes the process of valuing a business, including the approaches available for estimating the value of a business.

After studying this lesson, you should be able to:

1. Define business valuation and describe the business valuation process.
2. Describe the types of financial statement analysis relevant to a business valuation.
3. Identify and describe the approaches that may be used to determine the value of a business.
4. Apply a number of valuation techniques, including: a) discounted cash flows; b) capitalization of earnings; c) earnings multiples; and d) free cash flow.
5. Describe various forms of business combination and the role of valuation in carrying out a business combination.

I. Introduction

A. Definition

Business Valuation: The estimation of the economic value of a business entity or portion thereof.

1. The valuation may be for an entire business entity or for a portion (fractional share) of an entity.
2. When an entity is publicly traded in an active market, its value can be determined by its market capitalization, its total value in the market, which is a direct measure of its fair value. Thus, the prime concern is the valuation of non-public entities.

B. The valuation would be used to determine the cash price that would be received upon the sale of a business interest or for related purposes, including for:

1. Buy-sell agreements
2. Business combinations (mergers and acquisitions)
3. Estate purposes

II. Business Valuation Process

A. The valuation of a business should be carried out according to a process, including:

1. Establishing standards and premise of the valuation
2. Assessment of the economic environment of the business
3. Analysis of financial statements
4. Formulation of valuation

B. Standards and Premise of Valuation—The first element in a business valuation process is to establish the standards and premise of the value to be developed, which establishes the reasons for and circumstances surrounding the business valuation.

1. The standards of value establishes the conditions under which the business will be valued. For example:
   a. Is the valuation legally or otherwise mandated, or
   b. Is it at the request of a business owner, or
   c. Is it at the mutual request of a business owner and a prospective buyer, or
   d. Is it in connection with a business combination?

2. The premise of value establishes any assumptions to be used in the valuation. For example:
    a. Will the business continue in its entirety as a going concern, or
    b. Will the business be merged into the acquiring firm, or
    c. Will the assets be separately sold?

C. Economic Environment Assessment

1. The broadest issue of concern in establishing the value of a business is the economic environment(s) in which it operates.
2. The nature of the macro and local environments and the status of the industry in which the business operates should be determined as the larger context for valuing a specific business.

D. Financial Statement Analysis

D. Financial Statement Analysis—Once the implications of the operating environment and industry on the valuation process are understood, the financial statements of the entity being valued should be analyzed; that analysis might include:

1. **Common-size analysis**—Converting dollar amounts on the financial statements to percentages for comparison over time and with other entities.
    a. Common-size income statement would show all individual items of revenue, expense, gain and loss as a percentage of total revenues (or net revenues).
    b. Common-size balance sheet would show all individual items of assets, liabilities, and equity as a percentage of total assets.
2. **Trend analysis**—Determining the changes over time in major financial measures, including revenues, profits/losses, ownership interest and dividends/withdrawals.
3. **Ratio analysis**—Determining important ratios and other measures to assess changes over time and to compare with other entities in the industry.
4. **Adjustments**—Making adjustments to the basic financial statements to better reflect normal, on-going operations (normalization) or to better facilitate comparisons with other entities; such adjustments might include, for example:
    a. The elimination of non-operating assets
    b. The elimination of non-recurring items
    c. The elimination of differences in accounting treatments (e.g., accelerated depreciation versus straight-line depreciation)

E. Formulation of Valuation

1. With an understanding of the economic and industry environment and the outcomes of financial statement and related analysis, alternative methods may be used to assign a value to the business. The alternative approaches are:
    a. Market approach
    b. Income approach
    c. Asset approach

III. Business Valuation Approaches

A. Market Approach (for Business Valuation)

1. This approach determines the value of an entity by comparing it to other entities with similar characteristics in the same industry, in the same market(s), of the same size, with highly similar product lines, similar risks, and other factors.

2. Characteristics

   a. This approach is often called the "guideline public company method."

   b. The market value of a publicly traded entity is used as the basis for establishing the value of a highly comparable entity.

   c. Similar to the comparable sales method used in real estate appraisals.

3. **Discounts/adjustments**—The market approach provides a means of valuing an entire entity, but adjustments may be needed when determining the value of a portion (or fractional share) of the business ownership or when the business interest may lack marketability.

   a. **Share of business entity**

      i. Controlling interest exists when an owner (investor) has greater than 50% ownership of an entity's voting rights, in which case the controlling interest can elect the board of directors who, in turn, can control all aspects of an entity's operation. A greater-than-50% ownership occurs when there is a business combinations.

      ii. Minority interest exists when an owner (investor) has less than 50% ownership of an entity's voting rights, in which case the minority interest is not able to exercise control over the entity and the value of the ownership should be discounted relative to the value assigned to the controlling interest (a non-controlling discount).

   b. **Lack of marketability**—Marketability is the ability to convert an asset, in this case an ownership interest in a business, into cash with a high degree of certainty as to the proceeds.

      i. A publicly traded entity is likely to be more marketable than a privately held entity.

      ii. Because publicly traded entities are more marketable than privately held entities, they are worth more.

      iii. The value of a business ownership interest that lacks marketability must be discounted from what a comparable publicly traded entity would be worth; the discount could be substantial.

      iv. The appropriate level of discount is a matter of professional judgment; some statistics show it should be between 30% and 55%.

4. **Disadvantages of market approach**

   a. Difficulty in identifying publicly traded entities which are highly comparable to non-publicly traded entities.

   b. Nonpublic entity ownership is less liquid than publicly traded shares, which may make it difficult to determine the liquidity discount necessary.

B. Income Approach (for Business Valuation)

1. This approach determines the fair value of an entity by calculating the net present value of the benefit stream generated by the entity; the resulting net present value is the value of the entity.

   a. Net present value is calculated by applying a discount rate or capitalization rate to the benefit stream provided by the entity (i.e., its cash flows, earnings, etc.).

   b. The discount or capitalization rate used is the yield (return) needed to attract investors, given the risk associated with the investment.

2. **Alternative income approaches**—There are a number of income approaches that are used; four of the most significant are described here: discounted cash flows, capitalization of earnings, multiples, and free cash flow.

   a. **Discounted cash flows**—Uses discounted future cash flows to get their net present value.

      i. Future cash flows consist of both expected future inflows and outflows.

- **ii.** The discount rate used may be based on:
  - **1.** The weighted-average cost of capital (WACC)
  - **2.** The capital asset pricing model (CAPM)
  - **3.** (Both as previously described)
- **iii.** The discounted cash flow method will be used and illustrated in the next topic, "Capital Budgeting."

b. **Capitalization of earnings**—Applies a capitalization rate to the earnings of an entity to determine the value of the entity.

- **i.** Net income (or other measure of earnings) is divided by an assumed or desired rate of return to obtain the value of the entity that generated the earnings.
- **ii.** Simple example:

Example

This example assumes no future growth and disregards inflation.

An entity expects to earn $100,000 and the rate of return required for the level of risk is 20%.

Capitalized value = $100,000/.20 = $500,000

The value of the business would be $500,000.

Notice that a $500,000 investment earning at the rate of 20% would provide a $100,000 return.

Example

This example assumes a 4% growth rate and a 3% inflation rate.

An entity expects to earn $100,000 and the rate of return required for the level of risk is 20%

Capitalized Value = Expected Earnings/[Discount Rate – (Growth Rate + Inflation Rate)]

Capitalized Value = $100,000/[.20 – (.04 + .03)]

Capitalized Value = $100,000/.13 = $769,231

The value of the business would be $769,231

c. **Earnings multiples**—Applies a multiple factor to the earnings of an entity to determine the value of the entity

- **i.** A multiple attempts to capture many of an entity's operating and financial characteristics in a single number, which can be multiplied by a measure of earnings (or other factors) to get an entity's value.
- **ii.** The multiple is, in effect, the same as the rate used above to capitalize earnings.
  - **1.** A capitalization rate of 20% would be the same as a multiple of 5 (100%/20% = 5).
  - **2.** When using the capitalization rate, as shown above, the rate is divided into earnings to get a value; when using the multiple, the multiple is multiplied by the earnings to get a value.

- **iii.** Multiples can be developed for a number of financial statement relationships, some of which are considered enterprise multiples and some of which are considered equity multiple.
- **iv.** Enterprise multiples provide a value for the entity as a whole, not just the value of the common shareholders interest. Computing these multiple requires using:
    1. The value of the enterprise (EV) in the numerator; that is, the sum of equity market value, debt, and other liabilities (the amount of liquid assets may be subtracted)
    2. The value of enterprise earnings before interest, depreciation, and amortization (EBITDA) in the denominator
    3. Thus, the equation is: EV/EBITDA
- **v.** Equity multiples provide a value for the equity holders' interest, not for the enterprise as a whole. Computing these multiples requires using:
    1. The market value of the equity in the numerator
    2. A measure of earnings (or other measure) in the denominator
    3. The most commonly used equity measure is based on the price-to-earnings ratio (P/E ratio).
- **vi.** P/E ratio
    1. The P/E ratio (multiple) is computed as: Market price/Earnings per Share.
    2. Market price is the per share price of a stock in the market.
    3. Earnings per share is provided in the financial statements, but an earnings per share based on projected earnings usually is more appropriate, as is making adjustments for non-operating and finance items.
- **vii.** PEG ratio
    1. PEG is a variation of the P/E multiple which provides comparisons when growth varies across entities.
    2. PEG is computed as (P/E)/EPS growth rate.
    3. PEG permits easier comparisons between entities in different stages of development and is especially appropriate for firms in fast growing industries (e.g., technology).
- **viii.** Developing an appropriate earnings-based multiple for valuation or comparison requires:
    1. Determining an appropriate group of comparable companies
    2. Developing forecasts of earnings to use in the calculation; future expected earnings are a better measure than historic earnings
    3. Carefully analyzing and adjusting forward-looking earnings to eliminate non-operating or non-recurring items
    4. Insuring that the values in the numerator and the denominator are consistent with each other
- **ix.** A number of other multiples can be developed for an entity and may be appropriate in certain circumstances, including, for example:
    1. Book value multiple = Market value/Book value
    2. Revenue value multiple = Market value/Revenue

x. Using multiples for valuation

1. A multiple (or multiples) derived from a set of similar or comparable public entities can be used to estimate the value of a private entity or the ownership interest in such an entity.
2. Highly comparable entities with the same multiples would be expected to have the same value.
3. Therefore, if a set of highly comparable public entities, for example, have a P/E multiple of 15 (i.e., the value of the firm is 15 times earnings), and then the comparable private entity would be expected to have a value 15 times its earnings.
4. By multiplying the multiple by the basis on which the multiple was developed (e.g., 15 times earnings), the value of an entity can be derived.

xi. Multiple choice and characteristics

1. The choice of an appropriate multiple for valuation purposes depends on the nature of the business. Valuing an entity in a capital-intensive industry, for example, probably would employ a different multiple than would be used in valuing a consulting firm, which may have little capital investment.
2. Entities with higher growth, lower risk and higher payout ratios would be expected to have higher multiples of earnings, book value price to equity, or book value to revenue than entities with the opposite characteristics.
3. Because of differences in underlying fundamentals over time and between countries, multiples computed over time or between countries are less likely to be reliable measures.

d. Free Cash Flow

i. Free cash flow is the cash that an entity generates after the cash flow expended or amortized to maintain or expand its capital asset base.

1. Free cash flow provides financing that enables an entity to pursue opportunities, including new product undertakings, acquisitions, debt reduction, and the like.

Free cash flow is calculated as:

	Net Income
+	Depreciation/Amortization
−	Capital Expenditures
±	Changes in Working Capital
=	Free Cash Flow

ii. The use of free cash flow is a variation on the use of discounted cash flow, described above, but uses a different measure of cash flow.

iii. Free cash flow may be an appropriate means of measuring value, especially in the following cases:

1. Entities with no dividend history or for which dividends are not reflective of earnings
2. Entities with a number of years of reliable free cash flow

iv. The value of an entity would be determined by computing the present value of future free cash flow using an appropriate discount rate (as illustrated above in the discounted cash flow approach).

C. Asset Approach (for Business Valuation)

1. This approach determines the fair value of an entity by adding the values of the individual assets that comprise the business.
   a. The underlying premise is that no rational investor would pay more for an entity than the sum of its component or similar net assets.
   b. The fair value of each individual asset (and, where appropriate, liability) is determined and the sum of those values (or net values) establishes a value for the business entity.
2. Determining the value of individual assets will require the use of another basic valuation technique, for example, an income approach, a market approach, or a cost approach.
   a. Under this approach, the value of certain assets (e.g., intangible assets) may be difficult or impossible to determine independent of the overall entity.
3. The use of the asset approach is more appropriate in some circumstances than in others:
   a. It is less likely to be appropriate in valuing a going concern.
   b. It is less likely to be appropriate in valuing a non-controlling fractional interest in an entity.
   c. It is more likely to be appropriate when an entity is liquidating (going out of business).
   d. It is more likely to be appropriate when an entity has nominal cash flows and/or earnings.

IV. Business Valuation and Business Combinations

A. For corporations, business valuation is commonly used in conjunction with business combinations. A business combination occurs when an existing or newly formed business entity either:
   1. Acquires a group of net assets that constitute a business (e.g., a division or product line)
   2. Acquires equity interest in another entity and obtains control of that entity

B. Business combinations may take one of three legal (or statutory) forms:
   1. **Merger**—One preexisting entity acquires either a group of assets that constitute a business or controlling equity interest of another preexisting entity and "collapses" the acquired assets or entity into the acquiring entity.
      a. In this form of combination, the acquired assets or entity cease to exist separate from the acquiring entity.
      b. Only the acquiring entity remains; the assets and liabilities of the acquired entity have been merged into the acquiring entity.
   2. **Consolidation**—A new entity is formed to consolidate (combine) the net assets or the equity interest of two (or more) preexisting entities, which cease to exist.
      a. In this form of combination, only the new entity exists after the combination. The assets and liabilities of the preexisting entities are combined to form the new entity.
      b. The preexisting entities cease to exist as legal entities; only the new entity remains as a legal entity.
   3. **Acquisition**—One preexisting entity acquires controlling equity interest of another preexisting entity and both entities continue to exist and operate as separate legal entities.
      a. In this form of combination, one entity acquires more than 50% of the voting stock of another entity but does not "collapse" that entity; it continues to exist.
      b. The acquiring entity becomes the "parent" of the acquired "subsidiary."
      c. In virtually all such cases, consolidated financial statements will be required.
      d. Many present-day corporations operate as a subsidiary of a higher-level parent corporation.

C. Reasons for and Valuation of Business Combinations

1. Because most business combinations involve public companies, existing market value (a Level 1 input) provides a "starting point" for valuing a business combination. For business combinations that do not involve a publicly traded entity, methods previously described may be use to develop a base valuation.
2. Those "starting point" or base valuations likely will need to be adjusted to recognize the financial effects of the reason (or reasons) for the business combination.
3. The reasons for a business combination and the effect on valuation may include, among others:
    a. **Expected synergies**—The potential that the performance and value of the combining of firms will be greater than the firms operating separately, resulting in financial benefit to the shareholders
    b. **Economies of scale**—The combined companies can operate at a larger scale and with reduced fixed cost when compared to the sum of the separate operations, thus increase profit margins
    c. **Reduce competition**—The desire to eliminate a competitor and in the process acquire larger market share, which may enable the acquiring firm to have more control of the prices of its good/service
    d. **Diversification**—The addition of new goods/services to offerings or the movement into new geographical areas, either of which may tend to dampen variations in the acquiring firms revenues and earnings
    e. **Supply chain control** (also called vertical combination)—The acquisition of a supplier or a customer so as to gain greater control over the supply chain for goods or services and thus reduce costs and improve efficiency by such things as better coordination, decreased transportation expenses, and reduced turnaround time
    f. **Bargain purchase**—The acquired firm may be perceived as being undervalued by the market and, thus, present a bargain investment opportunity for the acquiring firm
4. The ultimate objective of all of these reasons, and others, for effecting a business combination is to improve the financial performance of the entity (or entities).

D. The value associated with the reason or reasons for a business combination provides a basis for adjusting the market value of the acquired entity. Thus, they enter into determining the total value to be assigned to the combination.

E. For accounting purposes, the total value of the combination (the purchase price) must be allocated to recording all identifiable assets acquired (including any identifiable intangible assets), liabilities assumed, and noncontrolling interest (if any) at fair value as of the date of the combination.

1. Fair values for individual assets and liabilities may be determined using the market approach, the income approach, or the cost approach, as previously described.
2. If the purchase price (business valuation) exceeds the net fair value assigned to identifiable items, an intangible asset "goodwill" is recognized for the difference.
3. If the purchase price (business valuation) is less than the net fair value assigned to identifiable items, an extraordinary gain is recognized for the difference.

Note: Accounting for business combinations is covered in detail in the Financial Accounting and Reporting (FAR) section of the course.

Hedging and Derivatives

Hedging is a strategy for managing certain kinds of risks. This lesson identifies the kinds of risks that are commonly hedged and some ways and kinds of instruments (tools) used to carry out the hedging, primarily derivatives. Common risks that can be hedged are described, and how they can be hedged is illustrated. In addition, the use of derivatives for speculative purposes is described.

After studying this lesson, you should be able to:

1. Describe hedging, the common risks that can be hedged, and the common instruments that are used to carry out hedging.
2. Assess how a given risk can be hedged, including the appropriate approach and instrument to be used and what position should be taken.
3. Define and describe what constitutes a derivative instrument and the determination of the value of a derivative instrument.
4. Describe how derivatives can be used for speculation.

I. **Overview**—Hedging is a risk management strategy which involves using offsetting (or counter) transactions so that a loss on one transaction would be offset (at least in part) by a gain on another transaction (or vice versa).

   A. You would "hedge a bet" by offsetting a possible loss from betting on one team to win by also betting on the other team to win.

   B. You would hedge against a possible loss in inventory value by entering into a contract to sell comparable inventory at a fixed price (set now) for future delivery.

   C. While hedging is used to reduce risk, it also reduces profit potential.

II. **Hedging Elements**—Hedging involves two basic elements:

   A. **Hedged Item**—The recognized asset, recognized liability, commitment, or planned transaction that is at risk of loss. It is the possible loss on the hedged item that is hedged.

   B. **Hedging Instrument**—The contract or other arrangement that is entered into to mitigate or eliminate the risk of loss associated with the hedged item. Derivatives are the primary instrument used for hedging.

III. **Common Hedged Items (Risks)**—The number and kinds of items that can be hedged is extensive. The most commonly hedged items include:

   A. **Inventory/Commodity Prices**—Risk that the price of an inventory/a commodity (e.g., raw material, energy, good for resale, etc.) will change and adversely affect inventory/commodity values and profit margins

Examples

1. ***Risk to Future Purchase of Inventory***—Hedge the risk that market price changes in inventory will adversely affect the cost of inventory to be acquired in the future. For example, if the price of an input to the production process increased significantly, the firm may not be able to pass that increase cost to its customers, resulting in a decrease in its profit margins.

Similarly, if a company has a contract to acquire inventory under a firm purchase commitment, a decline in the market price of that inventory would result in a loss. For example, the value of inventory to be acquired under a firm, fixed-price contract would be adversely affected if the market price of the inventory decreased before the delivery date of the inventory (i.e., a loss would be recognized as the difference between the contract price and the lower market price at delivery date).

2. ***Risk to Existing Inventory***—Hedge the risk that the value of existing inventory will decrease as a result of changes in market prices. For example, the value of inventory held for future sale would be adversely affected by a decline in its market value, resulting in a lower of cost or market write down recognized as a loss in the period of decline.

B. **Foreign Currency Exchange Rates**—Risk that the exchange rate between currencies will change such that the value of revenues, expenses, assets, or liabilities expressed in a foreign currency will be adversely affected when converted to the domestic currency.

Examples

1. ***Transaction Risk***—Hedge the risk of exchange rate changes reducing the dollar value of a receivable denominated (to be settled) in a foreign currency. For example, a receivable denominated in a foreign currency will result in collection of a fixed number of foreign currency units, but the dollar value of those units will vary with changes in the exchange rate between that foreign currency and the dollar.
2. ***Transaction Risk***—Hedge the risk that the dollar value of an investment in a foreign subsidiary (operation) will fluctuate as a result of exchange rate changes. For example, translation (conversion from foreign currency units to dollars) of accounts on the financial statements of a foreign subsidiary requires use of changing exchange rates, which subject the account value carried by the parent in dollars to fluctuate solely as a result of exchange rate changes.

C. **Interest Rates**—Risk that an increase in the market rate of interest will adversely affect either the value of an existing fixed-rate interest investment or the cost of interest on variable-rate debt.

Examples

1. ***Risk to Value of Investment***—Interest rate risk to an investment in fixed-rate debt results from the fact that as the market rate of interest increases, the value of outstanding fixed-rate debt instruments decreases. This occurs because with higher interest rates available in the market, investors will reduce what they are willing to pay for outstanding debt (that has a lower interest rate) to a level that provides a return equal to the current market rate of interest. Such a decline will reduce the value of outstanding investments in fixed-rate debt.
2. ***Risk to Cost of Borrowing***—Interest rate risk to outstanding variable-rate debt results from the fact that as the market rate of interest increases, the cost of debt (interest expense) to the borrower increases.

D. **Credit (Default) Risk**—Risk that the issuer of debt will default (i.e., fail to make payments as due), which would result in the investor suffering a loss

Example

Risk of Issuer Default

Hedge the risk that an investment in bonds will not be repaid by the issuer of the bonds, resulting in a loss to the investor of the entire investment.

IV. Common Hedging Instruments—The most common type of instrument used for financial hedging is the derivative.

A. A **derivative** is a financial instrument (contract) with all three of the following elements:

1. It has one or more underlyings and one or more notional amounts.

a. An **underlying** is a specified price, rate, or other variable (e.g., a stock price, a commodity price, an interest rate, a foreign exchange rate, etc.).

b. A **notional amount** is a specified unit of measure (e.g., shares of stock, pounds or bushels of a commodity, number of currency units, etc.).

2. A derivative requires no initial net investment or one that is smaller than would be required for other types of similar contracts.

3. The terms of a derivative require or permit a net settlement; the derivative can be settled for cash or an asset readily convertible to cash in lieu of physical delivery of the subject of the contract.

4. The value or settlement amount of a derivative is the amount determined by the multiplication of the notional amount and the underlying. (e.g., shares of stock multiplied by the price per share).

B. Derivative Instruments—The number and kinds of derivative instruments that may be used for hedging is extensive. The most commonly used derivatives for hedging include:

1. Futures contracts—Contracts to deliver or receive a commodity, foreign currency, or other asset in the future at a price set now.

a. Futures contracts are executed through a clearinghouse (futures exchange).

b. They are standardized in that the underlying commodity and the commodity's quality, quantity, and delivery are prespecified in the contract.

c. Because futures contracts are traded on an exchange, margin requirements, marking to market, and margin calls apply, and settlement occurs daily.

Example
A wheat farmer may enter into a contract to sell a standard quantity of wheat for delivery in the future at a price set at the time of the contract. The contract would eliminate the risk that wheat prices will fall prior to the delivery date, but it also limits what the farmer will receive for the wheat if prices increase.

2. Forward contracts—Contracts to deliver or receive a commodity, foreign currency, or other asset in the future at a price set now.

a. Forward contracts are executed directly between the contracting parties, not through a clearinghouse/ exchange like futures contracts.

b. Because they are negotiated contracts, forward contracts can be customized to any commodity, amount, and delivery date.

c. Forward contracts are settled only at the end of the contract.

Example
A user of wheat as an input commodity may enter into a forward contract to buy wheat for delivery in the future at a price set at the time of the contract. This would assure the buyer that its cost of wheat at the end of the contract would be fixed. But it would also preclude buying that wheat at a lower price if the market price declines by the delivery date.

3. **Option contracts**—Contracts between a buyer and seller that give the buyer of the option the right to buy (call option) or sell (put option) a particular asset in the future at a price set now (known as the strike price).
    a. Option contracts give the buyer the right to buy or sell a particular asset but do not require the option holder to do so. Thus, the option holder will exercise the option only if it is economically favorable to do so.
    b. Option contracts are traded either on an exchange (exchange-traded options) or over the counter as contracts negotiated between parties.

Example
An investor expects the market price of a particular stock to go up over the next month but is concerned about the possible adverse effects of macroeconomic conditions on the entire market. The investor may buy an option contract to purchase the stock (a call option) at a future date at a price set now. If the price of the stock increases above the strike price, the investor would exercise the option; if the price does not increase, the investor would not exercise the option.

4. **Swap contracts**—Contracts between a buyer and seller by which they agree to exchange cash flows (typically related to interest), currencies, commodities, or risks.
    a. Swap contracts are executed directly between the contracting parties, not through a clearinghouse/exchange.
    b. Because they are negotiated contracts, swap contracts may be executed for any amount or length of time.
    c. For cash flow swaps, the parties normally do not exchange the principals involved, only the cash flows, which are typically associated with interest.

Example
A debtor with variable-rate debt outstanding may be concerned that the market rate of interest will increase and increase its cost of servicing its debt (i.e., interest expense). An interest rate swap contract would enable the debtor with variable-rate payments to hedge its interest rate exposure (that the variable rate will increase) by receiving a variable rate from a counterparty in exchange for paying the counterparty a fixed rate. Note that if the market rate goes up, the debtor will both pay a higher interest and receive a higher interest, so that its net cost is the amount of the fixed interest payment.

V. **Hedging Instruments Applied to Hedged Items**—When applied to items at risk, hedging instruments eliminate or mitigate certain risk associated with the hedged item. Using some of the kinds of hedged item examples described above, the following show how each of the risk in those examples may be hedged using a hedging instrument (or instruments).

Note
Accounting for derivatives is covered in detail in the Financial Accounting and Reporting (FAR) section of CPAexcel.

A. **Commodity/Inventory Hedges**

1. **Example with hedge—risk to firm commitment to buy inventory (or commodity)**—Hedge the risk that market price changes will adversely affect the cost of inventory to be acquired through a firm contract to buy the inventory. For example, the value of cotton inventory to be acquired under a firm, fixed-price contract would be adversely affected if the market price of the cotton decreased before the delivery (i.e., a loss would be recognized as

the difference between the contract price and the market price at delivery). In order to protect against the changes in the fair value of the firm commitment, the company could enter into a futures contract to sell cotton. Any loss on the inventory value would be offset by a gain in the value of the futures contract (and vice versa).

Example

Silver Fox Manufacturing makes silver dinnerware and bases its sales price to retailers on the price of silver at the time of sale. When the market (spot) price of silver is $19 per ounce, Silver Fox enters into a firm commitment contract with Deep Mine for the purchase of 100,000 ounces of silver for delivery in six months at $20 per ounce. Silver Fox is concerned that the market price of silver will decline below $20 per ounce during the commitment period, which would result in it recognizing a loss on the purchase. To hedge that possibility, Silver Fox enters into a forward contract to sell 100,000 ounces of silver for delivery in six months at $20 per ounce. At the end of the six-month commitment period, silver is selling in the spot market for $21 per ounce.

Silver Fox will recognize a gain on its acquisition of silver from Deep Mine calculated as 100,000 ounces × ($21 – $20) = $100,000.

Silver Fox will recognize a loss on its forward contract of $100,000, the 100,000 ounces times the $1 per ounce excess of its cost ($21) to cover its contract to sell over it sales price ($20).

Although in this example Silver Fox would have been better off without the forward contract, the gain and loss exactly offset each other, providing Silver Fox certainty as to the cost of its silver inventory.

2. **Example with hedge—risk to existing inventory**—Hedge the risk that the value of inventory accounted for using lower of cost or market will decrease as a result of changes in market prices. For example, the value of inventory held for future sale would be adversely affected by a decline in its value, resulting in a write-down recognized as a loss in the period of decline. In order to hedge the risk of loss due to inventory write-down, the firm could enter into a forward contract or a put option contract to sell the inventory at a future date. Any loss on the decline in inventory value would be offset by a gain in the value of the forward contract or put option.

Example

Hedgehog Inc. acquired inventory at a cost of $100,000 which it expects to sell in four to six months. To hedge the possibility of a decrease in inventory value prior to its sale, Hedgehog enters into a forward contract to sell an equivalent inventory at the end of three months. Assume that three months later the inventory has a value of $80,000. Hedgehog will recognize a $20,000 lower of cost or market write-down loss on its inventory but will recognize a $20,000 gain on the value of its forward contract. Specifically, it can acquire the inventory for $80,000 that it has a forward contract to sell for $100,000.

B. Foreign Currency Hedges

1. **Example with hedge—transaction risk**—A receivable denominated in a foreign currency will result in collection of a fixed number of foreign currency units, but the dollar value of those units will vary with changes in the exchange rate between that foreign currency and the dollar. A U.S. company could enter into a forward contract now to sell those foreign currency units when received in the future and thus hedge the receivable.

Example

U.S.A. Providers Inc. sells components to a Japanese manufacturer on account with terms of net 90. The obligation is denominated (to be settled) in 105,000 yen. U.S.A. Providers will receive a known number of yen (105,000), but over the three-month credit period, the dollar value of that yen will rise or fall, depending on changes in the exchange rate between the dollar and the yen. U.S.A. Providers can lock in the dollar value of the yen it will receive by entering into forward contract to sell 105,000 yen in three months. If the dollar strengthens relative to the yen during the three-month period, U.S.A. Providers will receive fewer dollars for the yen it receives from collecting the receivable (a dollar loss), but it will recognize an equivalent gain on its contract to sell yen at the price established three months earlier.

2. **Example of hedge—translation risk**—Hedge the risk that the dollar value of an investment in a foreign subsidiary (operation) will fluctuate as a result of exchange rate changes. For example, translation (conversion from foreign currency units to dollars) of accounts on the financial statements of the foreign subsidiary requires use of changing exchange rates, which subject the accounts carried on the parent's books to fluctuate solely as a result of exchange rate changes. The U.S. parent could (1) borrow in the foreign currency of the subsidiary (a liability) to offset (hedge) the effects of changes in the exchange rate on conversion of the financial statements (a net asset), or (2) acquire a foreign currency forward contract to offset (hedge) the effects of changes in the exchange rate on the conversion of the financial statements (a net asset).

Examples

1. Farco Inc. has a foreign operation that is heavily invested in assets. It is concerned that when it translates the financial statements of its foreign operation, an appreciation of the dollar against the foreign currency will result in its asset dollar values being greatly reduced. To hedge that possibility, Farco could incur foreign currency liabilities (e.g., incur foreign debt) so that its foreign liabilities approximate its foreign assets. By having an approximate matching of assets and liabilities, upon translation into dollars, any loss (or gain) on the value of the translated assets will be offset by a gain (or loss) on the value of translated liabilities.
2. Red, White and Blue (RWB) Inc. has a 100% owned subsidiary, EuCo, located in France. Because of the nature of its business, EuCo has a high level of current assets and few current liabilities. EuCo maintains its accounts in euros, which RWB translates to dollars for consolidated financial statement purposes. RWB is concerned that the euro will decline in value against the dollar over the next few months, resulting in a lower dollar value of the translated net assets of EuCo. RWB decides to hedge this translation risk by entering into a forward contract. RWB estimates that its net asset exposure as of the next balance sheet date will be 100,000 euros. Therefore, RWB enters into a forward contract to sell 100,000 euros as of the next balance sheet date. If the dollar declines against the euro, the value of the forward contract will increase (because after the decline RWB could buy the euros at the lower dollar cost and sell them at the higher contracted amount). So, while the decline in the dollar versus the euro would result in assets being converted to a lower dollar value, that decline would be offset by the increase in value of the forward contract.

C. Interest Rate Hedges

1. **Risk to value of investment**—Interest rate risk to an investment in fixed-rate debt results from the fact that as the market rate of interest increases, the value of outstanding fixed-rate debt instruments decreases. This occurs because with higher interest rates available in the market, investors will reduce what they are willing to pay for outstanding debt (that has a lower interest rate) to a level that provides a return equal to the market rate of interest. Such a decline will reduce the value of outstanding investments in fixed-rate debt.

Example

A firm can hedge its risk of market rate interest increases adversely affecting the value of its investment by using forward/futures contracts, swap contracts, or option contracts.

a. If a forward or futures contract is used, a contract to sell the investment at a price set at the present with delivery in the future could be used.

b. If an interest rate swap contract is used, the fixed-rate debt would be swapped with a counterparty for variable-rate payment.

c. If an option contract is used, a put option (option to sell) would be acquired, which gives the investor the right to sell its investment at some future time at a price set now.

Example

Risk to Cost of Borrowing

Interest rate risk to outstanding variable-rate debt results from the fact that as the market rate of interest increases, the cost of debt (interest expense) to the borrower increases. A firm can hedge its cost of borrowing with variable-interest debt by:

1. **Using a forward/futures contract**—If interest rates increase, the forward/futures prices will fall. The firm could sell a forward/futures contract now at the current (high price) and buy a forward/futures contract later (at the lower price) to satisfy its sell obligation. The resulting gain will offset (in part at least) the higher interest expense on the variable-interest debt.
2. **Using an interest rate swap**—The firm could enter into an interest rate swap, which would be a contract to exchange a stream of cash flows from interest. The firm with the variable-interest debt would swap its potentially variable stream of interest payments for a fixed stream of interest payments.

D. **Credit (Default) Risk Hedge—Credit (Default) Risk**—Risk that the issuer of debt will default, which would result in the investor suffering a loss. A firm can hedge credit risk using a credit default swap (CDS), which involves the transfer of the credit risk on debt between parties. In return for a fee, the seller of the CDS contract assumes the credit risk that the buyer (who owns the underlying debt) does not wish to carry. If the issuer of the debt defaults, the buyer receives compensation for its loss from the seller of the CDS, very much like buying an insurance policy.

Example

Assume Dover Inc. invests $5,000,000 in the five-year, 8% bonds of Junkie Inc. Because of changes in market conditions (e.g., weak economic performance, increasing price of oil, etc.), Dover becomes concerned about the possibility of Junkie having to default on it bonds. Dover could buy a credit default swap (CDS) in the amount of $5,000,000 to cover the potential loss from default. Assume the fee is 2.0%. Dover would pay $100,000 per year for the CDS ($5,000,000 × .02).

If Junkie does not default, the coverage would have cost Dover $500,000 (5 years × $100,000), which would reduce its total income from the investment.

If, however, Junkie defaults, Dover will receive the full $5,000,000 maturity value of the bonds from the seller of the CDS.

VI. Hedging Summary—Hedging provides a means of mitigating (reducing) or eliminating certain risks associated with assets, liabilities, revenues, expenses, cash flows, and other items.

A. General Guideline—Typically, hedging is undertaken to either protect against an increase or a decrease in value of the hedged item. As a general rule:

1. **Hedging an increase** in the hedged item is carried out by buying a futures/forward contract or call option and selling the contract or exercising the option to derive the hedging benefit of an increased price.
2. **Hedging a decrease** in the hedged item is carried out by selling a futures/forward contract or buying a put option and buying in the future (at a decreased price) to cover the contract.

B. Hedging involves both costs and risks:

1. **Costs** associated with hedging may include:
   - **a.** Reduced profit derived from the hedged item as a result of hedging that turns out to be unnecessary (i.e., the price paid to avoid uncertainty)
   - **b.** Loss of benefit from a possible favorable change in the price of the hedged item
   - **c.** Difference between spot rates/forward rates and bid/asked prices
   - **d.** Fees charged for execution of contracts
   - **e.** Internal administrative cost of executing, monitoring and managing hedging activity
2. **Risks** associated with hedging may include:
   - **a. Credit risk**—The risk that the counterparty to a contract fails to meet its contractual obligations. This risk is less likely for contracts executed through an exchange than for negotiated contracts.
   - **b. Market risk**—The risk of loss from adverse changes in market factors that affect the hedged item.
   - **c. Basis risk**—The risk of loss from ineffectiveness of the hedge that results when offsetting investments do not experience price changes in entirely opposite directions as expected. Basis is the ultimate difference between the value of the hedged item and the value of the hedging instrument.

VII. Derivatives and Speculation—While derivatives are major instruments used for hedging, they also can be used for speculation.

A. Speculation has as its purpose the making of a profit, unlike hedging, which has as its purpose the offsetting of gains and losses so as to achieve greater certainty as to value.

B. Investors may use derivatives to speculate on the direction that a security, commodity, or other item will move.

Example

An investor believes the stock of ABC Inc. will increase in value. Rather than buy the stock and hold it, the investor may buy a call option, which gives the investor the option to buy the stock in the future at a price set now. The cost of the option is a fraction of the cost of buying the stock. If the stock price increases above the contracted exercise (strike) price during the term of the option, the investor will exercise the option and recognize a profit as the difference between the strike price and the higher market price. If the stock price does not increase above the strike price, the investor will not exercise the option and will lose the cost of payment for the option.

Capital Budgeting

Introduction and Project Risk

Capital budgeting is concerned with the acquisition and financing of long-term (or capital) asset investments. Making capital budgeting decisions involves assessing both the risks inherent in long-term undertakings and the likely rewards (or returns) to be derived from those undertakings. This lesson defines and describes capital budgeting and considers the nature and role of risk and reward in the capital budgeting process.

After studying this lesson, you should be able to:

1. Define capital budgeting.
2. Define risk and identify the risks associated with capital project evaluation.
3. Identify the ways project risk can be mitigated.
4. Describe the relationship between: a) risk and reward and b) the cost of capital and capital budgeting.

I. Capital Budgeting

A. In order to be successful in a competitive environment, an entity must have a more or less continuous stream of new undertakings or projects. Identifying and implementing profitable projects is essential if a firm is to grow and survive in the long run. This section is concerned with the kinds of decisions involved in considering new undertakings or projects, including the risk-reward relationship inherent in new undertakings.

B. Capital budgeting is the process of measuring, evaluating, and selecting long-term investment opportunities. These opportunities are typically in the form of projects or programs being considered by a firm and almost always would involve significant cost and extend over many periods. Depending on the entity, such projects may include the routine acquisition of new property, plant, and equipment, changing a production process, adding new products or services, establishing new locations, or other similar undertakings. All of the various kinds of projects and programs undertaken by an entity over time largely determine its current resources and operations, as well as its ongoing success or failure. Therefore, effective capital budgeting is essential to every successful organization.

II. Project Risk and Reward Considerations

A. Inherent in every project considered are elements of risk and reward. Risk is the possibility of loss or other unfavorable results that derives from the uncertainty implicit in future outcomes.

B. Definition of Risk

1. Risk is defined in technical models in terms of the deviation of actual returns from expected returns. (A number of technical risk and return models are used to measure market risk, especially as it applies to securities investments, including the capital asset pricing model, the arbitrage pricing model, the multi-factor model, and the regression model.) The risks associated with investment in a project or similar undertaking result from a number of uncertainties, some of which are specific to the undertaking and some of which relate more to the larger market (macroeconomic) environment. A particular project may be at risk from the following:
   - **a.** Incomplete or incorrect analysis of the project, including failure to incorporate revenue or cost elements or misestimation of those elements
   - **b.** Unanticipated actions of customers, suppliers, and competitors, including changing prices of resources, and the advent of new technology
   - **c.** Unanticipated changes in laws, regulations, or other political changes
   - **d.** Unanticipated macroeconomic changes, including changes in interest rates, inflation/deflation rates, tax rates, and currency exchange rates

C. Reducing Risk

1. For a large firm, certain risks associated with individual projects are mitigated by having a large number of diverse projects (a portfolio of projects) which span multiple periods. In effect, having a diverse portfolio of projects reduces the aggregate risk to the firm in much the same manner that diversification of securities holdings reduces the risk in a securities investment portfolio. Like diversification of securities holdings, diversification of projects seeks to reduce risk by having multiple investments that are not highly correlated with each other so that the positive performance of some investments (projects or securities) will offset the negative performance of other investments. The reduced risk that results from a large, diverse portfolio of projects results because:
   - **a.** With a large number of projects, each individual project accounts for a relatively small percentage of total undertakings, thus any unexpected outcome will have only a small impact on the total firm results.
   - **b.** With a large number of diverse projects, the unfavorable outcomes experienced by some projects are more likely to be offset by favorable outcomes experienced by other projects.
2. The risks that result from the uncertainty associated with the evaluation of individual projects can be addressed in a number of ways. The most important of these approaches is discussed in the "Ranking Projects" lesson, after we have considered each of the alternative evaluation approaches.
3. On the other hand, certain risks are likely to impact most projects in the same manner.

Example
The risk associated with an increase in interest rates would apply similarly to all long-term projects. An unanticipated increase in interest rates would tend to result in lower returns from all long-term projects. In most cases, risks derived from the macroeconomic environment cannot be reduced by project diversification.

4. Identifying and assessing the risks inherent in a project, especially those risks not reduced by diversification, are essential in determining an appropriate expected reward (or return) from a project. The expected return on a project must be sufficient to cover the expected net cost of the project and provide a profit sufficient to meet the returns demanded by those who provide the firm's capital-creditors and shareholders. Just as the return demanded by those who provide capital will vary with the perceived risk associated with their investment in the firm, so also will the expected return required on projects vary with the perceived risk associated with each project considered by the firm.

D. The Risk-Reward Relationship

1. The risk-reward relationship is familiar: the greater the perceived risk, the greater the expected reward. Thus, the relationship between risk and reward is positive and can be shown graphically as:

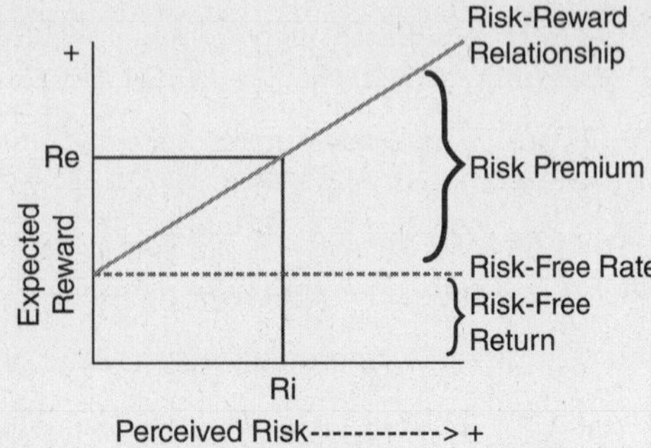

2. As the above graph shows, there is a risk-free rate of return expected on every investment. This rate reflects the reward expected for the deferred current consumption that results from making an investment. In the United States, the risk-free rate of return normally is measured by the rates on U.S. Treasury securities (bills and notes). Investors or firms could earn the rates paid on these securities without incurring the risk associated with commercial securities or with project undertakings. The return expected above the risk-free rate, called the "risk premium," depends on the perceived risk inherent in an investment opportunity-securities, projects, or other. In the graph above, if the level of risk is perceived to be Ri (Risk) on the horizontal axis, the expected return is Re (Return) on the vertical axis. At higher levels of expected risk, a higher return would be expected, and at lower levels of expected risk, a lower return would be expected.

3. The relationship between a firm's projects and the sources of the firm's capital that funds those projects provides a basis for establishing the rate of return required on its project undertakings. The interrelationship between a firm's undertakings and its sources of capital can be illustrated as follows:

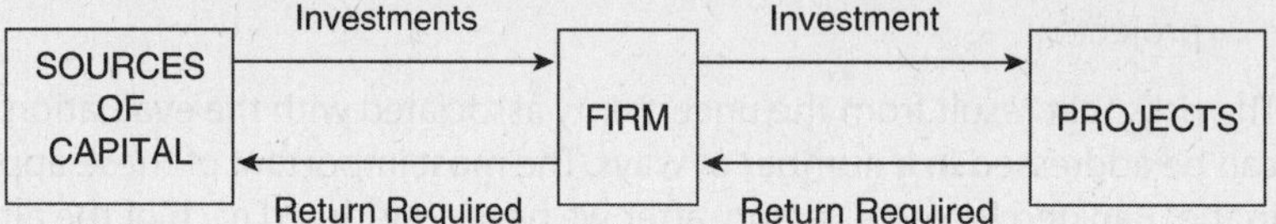

4. As the illustration shows, the rate of return required in order to attract and maintain capital funding determines the rate of return that must be earned on projects by the firm. The rate of return required to attract and maintain capital is the cost of capital to the firm and that cost of capital is the rate the firm must earn on its investment in projects, often called the hurdle rate. Unless a firm is able to earn an adequate rate of return on the aggregate of its undertakings, it cannot attract and maintain capital.

5. Beta (as described in the lesson "Valuation Techniques—CAPM") is a measure of systematic risk. In the context of capital budgeting, the beta of a project is a measure of the relative riskiness of that project. For a firm, the weighted average beta of all its project investments is a measure of the firm's total risk of projects. And, because the return to investors in the firm (its sources of capital, as shown in the diagram above) is dependent on the returns earned by the firm's projects, the weighted average beta of the firm's projects is a measure of investor risk.

E. Discount/Hurdle Rate

1. As described in the "Cost Concepts" lesson, while the cost of capital can be determined for each element of capital (e.g., long-term notes, bonds, preferred stock, common stock, etc.), it is usually appropriate to calculate and use the weighted average cost of capital.

   Specifically, the cost of capital for each element is weighted by the proportion of total capital provided by each element. The resulting weighted average is the rate of return that a firm must expect to earn on a project it undertakes. In evaluating projects, that rate is called the hurdle rate or discount rate.

Evaluation Techniques

Introduction and the Payback Period Approach

Successful capital investments are essential to the success of a business. Therefore, accurate evaluation of potential capital projects is critical. The payback period approach is one of the basic techniques for assessing the economic feasibility of capital projects. This lesson identifies the techniques for evaluating and comparing potential capital projects; it also describes and illustrates the use of one of these techniques, the payback period approach, including the advantages and disadvantages associated with its use.

After studying this lesson, you should be able to:

1. Identify the primary techniques for assessing capital projects.
2. Identify the primary technique for ranking capital projects.
3. Describe the payback period approach to capital project evaluation.
4. Compute the payback period for a given project.
5. Describe the advantages and disadvantages of the payback period approach.

I. **Introduction**—This and the following lessons consider various techniques for evaluating capital budgeting opportunities.

   A. Six different techniques will be described and illustrated, and the advantages and disadvantages will be summarized. The techniques to be considered are:

      1. Payback period approach
      2. Discounted payback period approach
      3. Accounting rate of return approach
      4. Net present value approach
      5. Internal rate of return approach
      6. Profitability index approach

   B. The first five approaches are used primarily to decide whether to accept or reject a project based on the economic feasibility of the project. The last technique, the profitability index approach, is particularly useful in ranking acceptable projects.

II. **Payback Period Approach**

   A. The payback period approach to assessing a capital project determines the number of years (or other periods) needed to recover the initial cash investment in the project and compares the resulting time with a pre-established maximum payback period. If the expected payback period for a project is equal to or less than the pre-established maximum, the project is deemed acceptable; otherwise, it would be considered unacceptable.

   B. The following example is used to illustrate this analysis:

      1. A firm is considering a project with an initial cash outlay of $250,000 and no residual value. The project is expected to provide five years of new cash flows as follows:

Year 1	$ 50,000
Year 2	75,000
Year 3	75,000
Year 4	75,000
Year 5	25,000
TOTAL	$300,000

2. The firm's maximum payback period is three years.

C. **Analysis**—With a three-year maximum payback period, this project would not be acceptable. The total expected cash inflow over the first three years of the project is:

Year 1	$50,000
Year 2	75,000
Year 3	75,000
TOTAL	$200,000 less than initial cash outlay $250,000 = Reject

D. **Specific Considerations**

1. **Working capital**—Working capital consists of current assets (cash, accounts receivable, inventory, supplies, etc.) and current liabilities (accounts payable, wages payable, etc.). Many long-term projects will both require an investment in working capital (current assets) and derive the benefits of new current liabilities. The difference between an increase in current assets and the benefit derived from an increase in current liabilities is the net investment in working capital for a project.
   a. That net working capital investment is a required cost of a project and should be recognized as a cash outflow, usually at the beginning of the project, in the analysis of a project. For example, in the analysis of a project, in addition to the fixed asset costs (land, building, furniture/fixtures, etc.), new working capital in the form of cash (change fund, operating funds, etc.), accounts receivable, inventory and current payables may be required. The net cost of (amounts tied up in) those working capital items would be a cash outflow required of the project and included in the project analysis.
   b. For a project with a limited expected life, the net working capital investment is normally liquidated at the end of the project and should be treated as a cash inflow, measured at its present value, in the analysis of a project. However, for the payback period approach to project evaluation, the residual value of a net working capital investment normally is not considered because that approach considers cash flows only until the point at which the initial cost of the project is recovered. If the project recovers the initial investment within the preestablished maximum period, any cash flow associated with the working capital residual value after that maximum period is not relevant.
2. **Depreciation**—Depreciation expense does not create a cash flow; it is the yearly (or other period) allocation of the cash flow that occurred when a project's assets were acquired. Because depreciation expense (per se) does not create a cash flow, it is not considered in the determination of the payback period (an approach which is based on cash flows).
   a. However, to the extent depreciation expense is deductible for income tax purposes, it saves taxes and the cash outflow that would be required to pay those taxes. That cash outflow savings, called a "tax shield," is considered in determining the payback period.
   b. For example, if $100 of tax deductible depreciation expense occurs during a year and the firm's tax rate is 30%, the tax shield would be .30 × $100 = $30, the amount of cash that would be saved as a result of the tax deductibility of the depreciation expense. That $30 would be recognized as a cash inflow (savings) for each period it occurred.
3. **Residual (salvage) value**—The residual value associated with a capital project normally is not considered in the payback period approach to project evaluation because that approach considers cash flows only until the point at which the initial cost of the project is recovered. If the project recovers the initial investment within the pre-established maximum period, any cash flow associated with the project residual value after that maximum period is not relevant.

III. Advantages and Disadvantages of the Payback Period Approach—The payback period method uses expected cash flow, (not expected accounting net income), the cash flows are not discounted, and they do not consider the results after the maximum payback period.

A. Advantages

1. Easy to understand and use
2. Useful in evaluating liquidity of a project (i.e., how quickly cash is recovered)
3. Establishing a short maximum period reduces uncertainty

B. Disadvantages

1. Ignores the time value of money (i.e., present value of the future cash flows)
2. Ignores cash flows received after the payback period (including any cash flow from the residual value of the project)
3. Does not measure total project profitability
4. Maximum payback period may be arbitrary

IV. Conclusion—Because of the serious disadvantages associated with the payback period method, its most appropriate use is in preliminary screening of projects or when used in conjunction with other evaluation methods.

Discounted Payback Period Approach

The discounted payback period approach to assessing the economic feasibility of capital projects is a variation of the basic payback period approach that takes the time value of money into account. This lesson describes and illustrates the discounted payback period approach, and identifies the advantages and disadvantages associated with its use.

After studying this lesson, you should be able to:

1. Describe the discounted payback period approach to capital project evaluation.
2. Compute the discounted payback period for a given project.
3. Describe the advantages and disadvantages of the discounted payback period approach.

I. **Discounted Payback Period Method**—The discounted payback period method is a variation of the payback period approach, which takes the time value of money into account. It does so by discounting the expected future cash flows to their present value and uses the present values to determine the length of time required to recover the initial investment. Because the present value of the cash flows will be less than their future (nominal) values, the discounted payback period will be longer than the undiscounted payback period.

   A. Using the five-year cash flows shown below (second column), discount factors assuming 6%, and a maximum payback period of three years, the analysis would be:

Year	Cash Flow	PV Factor	PV Amount	Sum of PVs
1	$ 50,000	.943	$ 47,150	$ 47,150
2	75,000	.890	66,750	113,900
3	75,000	.840	63,000	176,900
4	75,000	.792	59,400	236,300
5	25,000	.747	18,675	254,975
TOTALS	$300,000		$254,975	

   B. The present value of cash inflows expected over the first three years, the maximum payback period for the firm, is $176,900, less than the initial cash outlay of $250,000. Thus, the project would be rejected. Notice that the three-year cash flows under the undiscounted and discounted payback period methods are different:

Undiscounted	$200,000
Discounted	176,900

   C. The discounted cash flows would take a longer period to recapture a given initial cash outlay than the undiscounted cash flows.

   D. **Specific Considerations**

      1. **Working capital**—Working capital consists of current assets (cash, accounts receivable, inventory, supplies, etc.) and current liabilities (accounts payable, wages payable, etc.). Many long-term projects will both require an investment in working capital (current assets) and derive the benefits of new current liabilities. The difference between an increase in current assets and the benefit derived from an increase in current liabilities is the net investment in working capital for a project.

a. That net working capital investment is a required cost of a project and should be recognized as a cash outflow, usually at the beginning of the project, in the analysis of a project. For example, in the analysis of a project, in addition to the fixed asset costs (land, building, furniture/fixtures, etc), new working capital in the form of cash (change fund, operating funds, etc.), accounts receivable, inventory, and current payables may be required. The net cost of those working capital items would be a cash outflow required of the project and included in the project analysis.

b. For a project with a limited expected life, the net working capital investment is normally liquidated at the end of the project and should be treated as a cash inflow, measured at its present value, in the analysis of a project. However, for the discounted payback period approach to project evaluation, the residual value of a net working capital investment normally is not considered because that approach considers cash flows only until the point at which the initial cost of the project is recovered. If the project recovers the initial investment within the preestablished maximum period, any cash flow associated with the working capital residual value after that maximum period is not relevant.

2. **Depreciation**—Depreciation expense does not create a cash flow; it is the allocation of the cash flow that occurred when a project's assets were acquired. Because depreciation expense (per se) does not create a cash flow, it is not considered in the determination of the discounted payback period (an approach which is based on cash flows).

   a. However, to the extent depreciation expense is deductible for income tax purposes, it saves taxes and the cash outflow that would be required to pay those taxes. That cash outflow savings, called a "tax shield," is considered in determining the discounted payback period.

   b. For example, if $100 of tax deductible depreciation expense occurs during a year and the firm's tax rate is 30%, the tax shield would be .30 × $100 = $30, the amount of cash that would be saved as a result of the tax deductibility of the depreciation expense. That $30, discounted to its present value, would be recognized as a cash inflow (savings) for each period it occurred.

3. **Residual (salvage) value**—The residual value associated with a capital project normally is not considered in the discounted payback period approach to project evaluation because that approach considers cash flows only until the point at which the initial cost of the project is recovered. If the project recovers the initial investment within the preestablished maximum period, any cash flow associated with the project residual value after that maximum period is not relevant.

E. **Advantages and Disadvantages**—The advantages and disadvantages of the discounted payback period method are the same as for the undiscounted payback period method, except that the use of time value of money becomes an advantage, not a disadvantage. Like all methods that use time value of money concepts, it is subject to the uncertainty associated with assuming an interest rate applicable to future periods.

Accounting Rate of Return Approach

The accounting rate of return approach uses accounting-based values to assess the economic feasibility of capital projects. This lesson describes and illustrates the accounting rate of return approach. It additionally identifies the advantages and disadvantages associated with its use.

After studying this lesson, you should be able to:

1. Describe the accounting rate of return approach to capital budgeting evaluation.
2. Compute the accounting rate of return for a given project.
3. Describe the advantages and disadvantages of the accounting rate of return approach.

I. Accounting Rate of Return

Definition
The Accounting Rate of Return (also called the Simple Rate of Return) Method: Assesses a project by measuring the expected annual incremental accounting income from the project as a percentage of the initial (or average) investment.

A. Expressed as a formula, the accounting rate of return (ARR) would be calculated as:

ARR = (Average Annual Incremental Revenues – Average Annual Incremental Expenses) / Initial (or Average) Investment

B. Both incremental revenues and incremental expenses in the numerator are as determined by accrual accounting. If the average amount invested in the project were used in the denominator, rather than the full initial investment, it would be computed as the average book value of the asset over its life.

C. Specific Considerations

1. **Working capital**—Working capital consists of current assets (cash, accounts receivable, inventory, supplies, etc.) and current liabilities (accounts payable, wages payable, etc.). Many long-term projects will both require an investment in working capital (current assets) and derive the benefits of new current liabilities. The difference between an increase in current assets and the benefit derived from an increase in current liabilities is the net investment in working capital for a project.

   A net working capital investment would not enter into the determination of incremental net income (the numerator) over the life of a project, so it would not affect the ARR determination. A net working capital investment would enter into the amount of the investment (or average investment), the denominator used in the ARR determination. A net working capital investment would increase the amount of the initial investment. Specifically, the amount of a net investment in working capital would be added to the investment in fixed assets in determining either the initial investment or the average investment over the life of the project.

2. **Depreciation**—Depreciation expense is explicitly recognized under the accounting rate of return approach.
   a. While all of the other methods of evaluation are based on measuring cash flows, this method is based on expected accounting revenues and expenses, including depreciation expense. Thus, the accounting rate of return approach is the only approach that recognizes depreciation expense per se.
   b. Because the ARR approach explicitly recognizes depreciation expense, the choice of depreciation method used by a firm will affect the accounting income and, therefore, the ARR (i.e., percentage rate).
   c. The possible use of different depreciation methods may be considered a disadvantage of the ARR method. It is a compatibility issue firm's should recognize.

3. **Income taxes**—Income tax expenses are explicitly recognized under the accounting rate of return approach. Because it is based on expected accounting revenues and expenses, expected income tax expenses would be taken into account in computing the net increment in accounting income. Because the full amount of expected tax expense enters into determining the net increment in accounting income, the tax effect is taken into account in full; the issue of "tax shield" (a cash flow concept) is not relevant.
4. **Residual (salvage) value**
   a. Conceptually, the residual value associated with a capital project should be taken into account in determining incremental income (the numerator) to the extent that residual value is expected to generate an increase in accounting income (from a gain) or a decrease accounting income (from incurring a loss) upon disposal. Practically, however, it is difficult to estimate such an amount at the beginning of a project; therefore, it is usually ignored in measuring accounting income for a project.
   b. When the average investment in a project is used (the denominator), the residual value is taken into account in the determination of the average investment. That average would be determined as:

Average investment = [Initial investment (+ Net working capital, if any) + Residual value] / 2

Note: That is basically: (Beginning investment + Ending investment) / 2

D. The following assumptions are used to illustrate the analysis, assuming the initial investment is used:

1. A firm is considering a project with an initial cash outlay of $250,000 and no residual value. The project is expected to provide incremental net income (Revenues – Expenses) over the next five years of the following amounts:

Year 1	$ 12,000
Year 2	18,000
Year 3	26,000
Year 4	24,000
Year 5	20,000
TOTAL	$100,000

2. The average expected incremental net income is: $100,000 / 5 years = $20,000. Therefore:

ARR = $20,000 / $250,000 = 8.0% ARR

3. The resulting 8.0% would be the expected annual rate of return on the project. If the average amount invested were used as the denominator, it would be a much lower denominator (depending on the depreciation method used) and the accounting rate of return would be much higher. The determined rate could be compared to a preestablished rate to determine whether he project is acceptable.

II. Advantages and Disadvantages of the Accounting Rate of Return

A. Advantages

1. Easy to understand and use
2. Consistent with financial statement values
3. Considers entire life and results of project

B. Disadvantages

1. Ignores the time value of money (i.e., present value of future net profits or losses)
2. Uses accrual accounting values, not cash flows
3. Use of different depreciation methods will give different results for projects

Net Present Value Approach

The net present value approach is one of two major methods of assessing the economic feasibility of capital projects that take into account the time value of money. This lesson describes and illustrates the net present value approach, and identifies the advantages and disadvantages associated with its use.

After studying this lesson, you should be able to:

1. Describe the net present value approach to capital budgeting evaluation.
2. Compute the net present value for a given project.
3. Describe the advantages and disadvantages of the net present value approach.

I. Net Present Value

Definition
Net Present Value Approach: Assesses projects by comparing the present value of the expected cash inflows (revenues/savings/residual value/etc.) of the project with the expected cash outflows (initial cash investment/other payments) of the project.

A. The present value (PV) of expected cash inflows is determined by discounting those flows to their present value using the firm's cost of capital as the discount rate (also called the "hurdle rate"). The present value (PV) of expected cash outflows includes the initial cash investment in the project (which is at present value) and any subsequent costs of the project. Cash outflows subsequent to initiation of the project would be discounted using the same discount rate as cash inflows. The difference between the resulting present value of cash inflows and the present value of cash outflows is the net present value of the project. If the net present value is zero or positive, the project is deemed economically acceptable; if the net present value is negative, the project is deemed unacceptable.

B. Specific Considerations

1. **Working capital**—Working capital consists of current assets (cash, accounts receivable, inventory, supplies, etc.) and current liabilities (accounts payable, wages payable, etc.). Many long-term projects will both require an investment in working capital (current assets) and derive the benefits of new current liabilities. The difference between an increase in current assets and the benefit derived from an increase in current liabilities is the net investment in working capital for a project.
   - **a.** That net working capital investment is a required cost of a project and should be recognized as a cash outflow, usually at the beginning of the project, in the analysis of a project.
   - **b.** For a project with a limited expected life, the net working capital investment is normally liquidated at the end of the project and should be treated as a cash inflow, measured at its present value, in the analysis of a project.
   - **c.** For example, in the analysis of a project, in addition to the fixed asset costs (land, building, furniture/fixtures, etc.), new working capital in the form of cash (change fund, operating funds, etc.), accounts receivable, inventory, and current payables may be required. The net investment in those working capital items would be a cash outflow required of the project and included in the project analysis. If the project is expected to have a limited life, the working capital items will be liquidated at the end of the project, which returns their value to the firm. That future return of working capital should be recognized as a cash inflow, at its present value, in analysis of the project.

2. **Depreciation**—Depreciation expense does not create a cash flow; it is the allocation of the cash flow that occurred when a project's assets were acquired. Because depreciation expense (per se) does not create a cash flow, it is not considered in the determination of the net present value (an approach which is based on cash flows).
   a. However, to the extent depreciation expense is deductible for income tax purposes, it saves taxes and the cash outflow to pay those taxes. That cash outflow savings, called a "tax shield," is considered in determining the net present value.
   b. For example, if $100 of tax deductible depreciation expense occurs during a year and the firm's tax rate is 30%, the tax shield would be .30 × $100 = $30, the amount of cash that would be saved as a result of the tax deductibility of the depreciation expense. That $30, discounted to its present value, would be recognized as a cash inflow (savings) for each period it occurred.
3. **Residual (salvage) value**—The residual value associated with a capital project is considered in the net present value approach. Any residual value expected at the end of the project life would be discounted to its present value and treated as a positive value in the determination of net present value. Conversely, if it is expected that an additional disposal cost would be incurred at the end of the project life, that cost would be discounted to its present value and treated as a negative value in the determination of net present value.

II. Using the facts given in the prior lesson and assuming the firm's cost of capital at 6%, the analysis would be:

Year	Cash Flow	PV Factor	PV Amount	Sum of PVs
1	$ 50,000	.943	$ 47,150	$ 47,150
2	75,000	.890	66,750	113,900
3	75,000	.840	63,000	176,900
4	75,000	.792	59,400	236,300
5	25,000	.747	18,675	254,975
TOTALS	$300,000		$254,975	

III. The present value of (all) cash inflows is $254,975, and the cost of the initial investment in the project is $250,000. Therefore:

PV of Cash Flows	$254,975
Initial Investment	250,000
Net Present Value	$ 4,975

IV. Since the net present value of the project is estimated to be $4,975, the project should be accepted. Notice, unlike the prior payback period methods, which only consider the results during the maximum payback period, the net present value method considers the entire period (life) of the project.

Note
The most common NPV exam question asks you to determine NPV. However, some questions give you the NPV and ask you to calculate cash inflows or cash outflows. You should note that if you have any two of the three factors (NPV, PV of cash inflows, PV of cash outflows), using the equation given above, you can determine the third factor using simple algebra.

Example
A firm acquired a new machine that it expects to have a 5-year life and no residual value. The machine is expected to provide after tax cash inflows of $100,000 per year for each year of its 5-year life. The firm's hurdle rate is 10% and present value factors are:

PV of an annuity for 5 years at 10%	3.7908
PV of a single amount at the end of 5 years at 10%	.6209

If the acquisition of the new machine has a positive net present value of $15,000, what was the cost of the machine?

NPV = PV cash inflows – PV cash outflows

$15,000 = ($100,000 × 3.7908) – Cost of machine (C)

C = $379,080 – $15,000; C = $364,080, the cost of the new machine

V. Advantages and Disadvantages of the Net Present Value Method

A. Advantages

1. Recognizes the time value of money (i.e., present value of the future cash flows)
2. Relates project rate of return to cost of capital
3. Considers the entire life and results of the project
4. Easier to compute than the internal rate of return method (the other discounted cash flow method)

VI. Disadvantages

1. Requires estimation of cash flows over the entire life of the project, which could be very long
2. Assumes that the cash flows resulting from new revenues or cost savings are immediately reinvested at the hurdle rate of return (i.e., the discount rate used to compute present values)

Internal Rate of Return Approach

Like the net present value approach, the internal rate of return approach takes the time value of money into account in assessing the economic feasibility of capital projects. This lesson describes and illustrates the internal rate of return approach, and identifies the advantages and disadvantages associated with its use.

After studying this lesson, you should be able to:

1. Describe the internal rate of return approach to capital budgeting evaluation.
2. Compute the internal rate of return for a given project.
3. Describe the advantages and disadvantages of the internal rate of return approach.

I. Internal Rate of Return

Definition

The Internal Rate of Return (also called the Time Adjusted Rate of Return) Method: Evaluates a project by determining the discount rate that equates the present value of the project's future cash inflows with the present value of the project's cash outflows. The rate so determined is the rate of return earned by the project.

A. Conceptually and mathematically, the internal rate of return method is directly related to the net present value method. Whereas the net present value method uses an assumed discount rate to determine whether the present value of a project is positive or not, the internal rate of return computes the discount rate (rate of return) that would make the present value of the project's cash flows equal to zero. Both approaches (NPV and IRR) will always result in the same accept or reject outcome.

B. Once the IRR is determined, it would be compared with the firm's (or other unit's) cost of capital or other measure of desired rate of return. If the IRR equals or is greater than the minimum acceptable rate of return, it would be financially acceptable.

C. Special Considerations

1. **Working capital**—Working capital consists of current assets (cash, accounts receivable, inventory, supplies, etc.) and current liabilities (accounts payable, wages payable, etc.). Many long-term projects will both require an investment in working capital (current assets) and derive the benefits of new current liabilities. The difference between an increase in current assets and the benefit derived from an increase in current liabilities is the net investment in working capital for a project.
   - **a.** That net working capital investment is a required cost of a project and should be recognized as a cash outflow, usually at the beginning of the project, in the analysis of a project.
   - **b.** For a project with a limited expected life, the net working capital investment is normally liquidated at the end of the project and should be treated as a cash inflow, measured at its present value, in the analysis of a project.
   - **c.** For example, in the analysis of a project, in addition to the fixed asset costs (land, building, furniture/fixtures, etc.), new working capital in the form of cash (change fund, operating funds, etc.), accounts receivable, inventory and current payables may be required. The net investment in those working capital items would be a cash outflow required of the project and included in the project analysis. If the project is expected to have a limited life and the working capital items will be liquidated at the end of the project, the working capital value will be returned to the firm. That future return of working capital should be recognized as a cash inflow, at its present value, in analysis of the project.

2. **Depreciation**—Depreciation expense does not create a cash flow; it is the allocation of the cash flow that occurred when a project's assets were acquired. Because depreciation expense (per se) does not create a cash flow, it is not considered in the determination of the internal rate of return approach (an approach which is based on cash flows).

   However, to the extent depreciation expense is deductible for income tax purposes, it saves taxes and the cash outflow to pay those taxes. That cash outflow savings, called a "tax shield," is considered in determining the internal rate of return.

   For example, if $100 of tax deductible depreciation expense occurs during a year and the firm's tax rate is 30%, the tax shield would be .30 × $100 = $30, the amount of cash that would be saved as a result of the tax deductibility of the depreciation expense. That $30, discounted to its present value, would be recognized as a cash inflow (savings) for each period it occurred.

3. **Residual (salvage) value**—The residual value associated with a capital project is considered in the internal rate of return approach. Any residual value expected at the end of the project life would be discounted to its present value and treated as a positive value in the determination of the internal rate of return. Conversely, if it is expected that an additional disposal cost would be incurred at the end of the project life, that cost would be discounted to its present value and treated as a negative value (cash outflow) in the determination of the internal rate of return.

II. Calculation of Internal Rate of Return

A. The calculation of a project's exact internal rate of return is best done with a financial calculator. In the absence of a financial calculator, the determination of the internal rate of return will require interpolation and trial and error.

B. The determination of a project's cash flow, including the treatment of depreciation and salvage value, is the same as under the NPV approach.

C. Assuming an even cash flow over the life of a project, the determination of the internal rate of return begins by solving the equation:

> Annual cash inflow (or Savings) × PV factor = Investment cost, or
>
> PV factor = Investment cost / Annual cash inflow (or Savings)

D. Using the investment cost and expected annual cash inflow, the present value factor can be determined. Next, the resulting present value factor would be related to an interest (discount) rate for the time period of the project. Only by rare coincidence will the exact calculated present value for the number of periods be found on a present value table. Therefore, it will be necessary to interpolate to determine the exact internal rate of return.

III. Illustration—The following assumptions are used to illustrate the process:

A. A firm is considering a project with an initial cost of $37,500 and no residual value. The project is expected to save the firm $10,000 per year over its five-year life. The following values were extracted from a present value of an annuity table for five periods:

Rate	8%	10%	12%	14%	16%
5 Periods	3.993	3.791	3.605	3.433	3.274

$$\text{PV factor} = \frac{\text{Initial cost}}{\text{Annual savings}} = \frac{\$37{,}500}{\$10{,}000} = 3.750 \text{ PV Factor}$$

B. On the annuity table, the present value factor closest to 3.750 is 3.791. Since 3.750 is less than 3.791, but greater than the next listed value, 3.605, the exact internal rate of return is greater than 10%, but less than 12%.

C. That rate can be determined using interpolation as follows:

Interest Rate	Present Value Factors	
10%	3.791	3.791
IRR (?)		3.750
12%	3.605	______
Difference	.186	.041

D. The true internal rate of return is 10% plus .041/.186 of the 2% difference between 10% and 12%. The **calculation** would be:

IRR = 10% + (.041/.186) .02 =

= 10% + (.2204) .02 =

= 10% + .0044 = 10.44% IRR

E. The determination of the internal rate of return is especially difficult when the cash flows from the project are not even over the life of the project. Unless a computer program is used, the calculation of the internal rate of return when all future cash flows are positive but uneven requires a trial and error approach. You begin by picking a likely rate and then determining the resulting net present value. If the computed net present value is more or less than zero, the rate is iteratively adjusted until a zero net present value is found. The corresponding rate used is the internal rate of return. When future cash flows are both positive and negative, the internal rate of return method can result in multiple solutions and it should not be used in that case.

IV. Advantages and Disadvantages of the Internal Rate of Return Method

A. Advantages

1. Recognizes the time value of money (i.e., present value of the future cash flows)
2. Considers entire life and results of the project
3. Meaning of resulting rate is intuitive

B. Disadvantages

1. Difficult to compute
2. Requires estimation of cash flows over the entire life of the project, which could be very long
3. Requires that all future cash flows be of the same direction, either positive or negative
4. Assumes immediate reinvestment of cash flows resulting from new revenues or cost savings at the project's internal rate of return (Note: This is different from the net present value–NPV–approach, which assumes reinvestment of cash flows resulting from new revenues or cost savings at the hurdle [discount] rate used.)
5. Limited usefulness when comparing projects of different sizes (initial costs), with different length lives, or with different timing of cash flows.

V. Modified Internal Rate of Return (MIRR)

A. MIRR is a variation of the conventional IRR.

B. Whereas the IRR assumes that cash inflows from a project are continuously reinvested at the computed IRR, the MIRR assumes that positive cash inflows are reinvested at the firm's reinvestment rate and the cash outflows are discounted at the firm's cost of capital.

C. Specifically, the calculation is:

1. Determine the future value of the cash inflows using the firm's reinvestment rate (the rate of return at which cash flows can be reinvested).
2. Determine the present value of the cash outflows using the firm's cost of capital.
3. Apply the following formula to get the MIRR:

$$\text{MIRR} = \sqrt[n]{\frac{FV(\text{positive cash flows, reinvestment rate})}{-FV(\text{negative cash flows, finance rate})}} - 1$$

D. Unlike the IRR, the MIRR can be used when a project has both positive and negative cash flows.

Ranking Projects

Once economically feasible projects are identified, acceptable projects need to be ranked in terms of desirability. While the net present value and internal rate of return approaches provide a measure of relative attractiveness, neither takes into account the relative cost of each project. This lesson considers the profitability index, a measure designed to rank projects in terms of economic desirability.

After studying this lesson, you should be able to:

1. Describe the profitability index approach to ranking capital projects.
2. Compute the profitability index for given projects.
3. Rank projects using the profitability index.
4. Describe the equivalent annual annuity approach to ranking capital projects.
5. Describe the step in applying the equivalent annual annuity approach.
6. Describe and apply certain approachs to dealing with uncertainty in capital project evaluation.

I. **Profitability Index**—The profitability index (PI), also called the cost/benefit ratio or present value index, provides a way of ranking projects by taking into account both cash flow benefit expected from each project and the cost of each project.

   A. The PI determines the benefit-to-cost ratio of a project (or other investment) by computing the value provided per unit (dollar) of investment in a project.

   B. The PI for each project may be computed using either the present value of future cash inflows or the net present value (NPV = net of cash inflows and outflows, including the initial project cost) of a project, with either of these values divided by the initial project cost.

      1. When the present value of future cash inflows is used, the PI for each project would be computed as:

PI = PV of Cash inflows / Project cost

         a. A project would be economically feasible (and logically acceptable) only if the PI ≥ 1; otherwise, the present value of cash inflows would be less than the cost of the project.

         b. The resulting percentage index (≥ 1) for each project can be used to rank projects. The higher the percentage, the higher the rank of the project.

      2. When the net present value (NPV) is used, the PI for each project would be computed as:

PI = Net present value / Project cost

         a. A project would be economically feasible if the NPV is zero or positive (present value of expected cash inflows is equal to or greater than the present value of expected outflows). Thus, the resulting PI would be ≥ 0, which means the project is providing value at least equal to the discount rate used (e.g., WACC).

b. The resulting percentage index (≥ 0) for each project can be used to rank projects. The higher the percentage, the higher the rank of the project.

II. Illustration

A. The following illustrates the determination of the profitability index (PI) for two projects being considered using assumed values for PV (or, alternately, NPV):

Project A: PV (or NPV) = $60,000 / Initial cost = $50,000 = 1.20 PI

Project B: PV (or NPV) = $110,000 / Initial cost = $100,000 = 1.10 PI

1. Based just on present values (PV) or net present values (NPV), Project B ($110,000) would be ranked higher than Project A ($60,000), but when the amount of the initial investment is taken into account, Project A has a higher profitability index (PI = 1.20) than Project B (PI = 1.10). That result comes about because of the much lower initial investment cost of Project A.

III. Equivalent Annual Annuity Approach—The **equal annual annuity** (EAA) approach provides a means of comparing projects, especially those with unequal lives.

A. The EAA calculates the constant annual cash flow generated by a project over its entire life as if it was an annuity and uses the present value of that cash flow as a basis for comparing projects.

B. The EAA is calculated for each project in the following manner:

1. The NPV for each project is determined.
2. For each project the annual cash flows that when discounted (at the cost of capital or other discount rate) for the life of the project exactly equals the NPV of the project; the dollar amount so determined is the EAA for a project.

   a. The formula used to compute the EAA would be:

   EAA = [r(NPV)] / [1 – (1 + r)– n]

   Where: r = discount rate
   NPV = net present value
   n = number of periods

   b. The formula for the above calculation is readily available as a computer application and on financial calculators.

3. The project with the highest EAA is the most desirable project to pursue.

IV. Capital Budgeting Risks—Because capital budgeting analysis uses projections and assumptions, there is a risk that the actual outcomes may vary from the results of the analysis. A number of techniques have been developed to incorporate uncertainty and to measure risks in a project analysis. Those techniques include:

A. Probability Assignment—Under this approach, probabilities are assigned to possible outcomes. These probabilities may be assigned based on past experience, industry-wide measures, forecasts, simulation, or other bases. Once possible outcomes have been identified and probabilities have been assigned, an expected value can be determined.

Examples

1. Assigning probabilities to cash inflows

PV of Possible Cash Inflows	Probability of Each Cash Flow	Expected Value (EV)
$ 125,000 (pessimistic)	.20	$25,000
150,000 (most likely)	.60	90,000
200,000 (optimistic)	.20	40,000
	1.00	$155,000

2. The computed $155,000 is a probability adjusted estimate of the cash inflows to be received from the project. Note: It is $5,000 more than the most likely value estimate.
3. Using expected value data, management also can determine the standard deviation (an estimate of how each expected outcome differs from the mean) and the coefficient of correlation (which provides a measure of risk that is normalized for the size [amount] of the investment).

B. **Risk-Adjusted Discount Rates**—Under this approach to addressing uncertainty in project assessment, different discount rates are used for projects with different levels of risk. For a project with higher or lower than normal risk, a higher or lower discount rate would be used.

C. **Time-Adjusted Discount Rates**—Under this approach, cash flows associated with the later years of a long-term project are discounted at a higher rate than cash flows of the earlier years. This use of a higher discount rate for later years reflects the increased uncertainty in making longer-term projections.

D. **Sensitivity Analysis**—Under this approach, the most likely set of assumptions is used to compute the most likely outcome. Then one of the assumptions is changed, and the resulting outcome is determined. This process of changing one assumption at a time is repeated until the effect of changing each major assumption separately on the final outcome is known. This process allows management to consider how sensitive the outcome is to each major assumption.

E. **Scenario Analysis**—This approach is similar to sensitivity analysis except that rather than changing one assumption (variable) at a time, multiple related assumptions are changed simultaneously. This enables management to determine the range of possible outcomes that might occur.

F. **Other Risk Consideration Approaches**—In addition to the foregoing approaches for recognizing and measuring risk inherent in project analysis, firms might also employ:

1. Simulation
2. Decision-tree analysis

V. **Summary**—When ranking acceptable capital projects, methods based on discounted values are much better than methods that do not incorporate the time value of money. The net present value method and, especially the profitability index derived using net present value and the initial project cost, generally are preferable to other methods. In the final analysis, however, some degree of subjectivity is likely to enter into deciding which projects will be implemented.

A. Once capital budgeting (project investment) decisions have been made, the impact of these plans must be built into other affected budgets. For example, a planned new project may have implications for sales revenue, production costs, and cash flows, in addition to asset acquisition.

B. Once initiated, a project should be monitored frequently to ensure that it continues to meet the entity's requirements for acceptability.

Capital Project Ranking Decisions

Because firms have practical limitations on the number of capital projects they can undertake, they will select acceptable projects based on their relative economic value to the firm. This lesson considers the need for ranking capital projects and the appropriateness of each of the evaluation approaches considered in prior lessons as a means of ranking projects.

After studying this lesson, you should be able to:

1. Describe project ranking and why it occurs.
2. Describe how each of the project evaluation techniques can be used for ranking projects.

I. Introduction

A. The above lessons covering the payback period approach through the internal rate of return approach consider the evaluation of possible projects to determine whether a project is economically feasible for a firm to undertake. The resulting decision is to either accept or reject a project. Theoretically, a firm and its investors would benefit if the firm pursues all projects that meet its acceptability requirements, especially when the net present value and internal rate of return methods are used. In practice, however, a firm will limit the number of projects undertaken, especially in the short run.

B. This limitation on projects, called capital rationing, may occur for a number of reasons, including:

1. The firm does not have access to sufficient funds to take on all its acceptable projects.
2. The firm may not have sufficient management capacity to take on all its acceptable projects.
3. Firm management may believe market conditions are too unstable to commit to all acceptable projects.

C. When management decides to limit the economically acceptable projects it will undertake, it will select projects based on some ranking of the projects. In addition, project ranking will be used in any case in which projects are mutually exclusive—selecting one, rules out selecting others. For example, if a firm has determined two or more alternative acceptable projects to revamp a production process, only one of these alternatives will be implemented. The project selected should be based on a ranking of projects using established criteria. Use of each of the accept-reject decision approaches described above in making ranking decisions will be discussed. In addition, the use of a profitability index for ranking will be described.

II. Payback Period and Ranking—The limitations inherent in the payback period method of making the project accept-reject decision also limit its usefulness in ranking projects. Recall, the major limitations of this method are its failure to consider the time value of money (i.e., it does not discount future cash flows) and its failure to consider economic results after the payback period. Therefore, use of the payback period method to rank projects would place them in order of how quickly invested capital would be recovered (measured in nominal dollars), and not their relative economic value to the firm. Relative payback periods may be important, however, when liquidity issues are a major concern to a firm, since the payback period measures how quickly an investment will be recovered.

III. Discounted Payback Period and Ranking—Like the payback period method, this method evaluates a project based on how quickly an investment will be recovered. Unlike the payback period approach which uses nominal cash flows, the discounted payback period method discounts future cash flows and uses the discounted present value to determine the payback period. Because it uses discounted values it is better than the undiscounted payback period approach, but for ranking purposes it fails to consider the total economic performance of a project. It only measures the outcome up until the initial investment is recovered. Use of this method for ranking would be appropriate only when liquidity issues are a major concern.

IV. Accounting Rate of Return and Ranking—The accounting rate of return uses estimated future accrual-based net income and the cost of the investment (or average cost of the investment) to develop a rate of return on the investment. Because the computation uses nominal accrual-based net income, and not discounted cash flows, its use in ranking projects would ignore the time value of money and would not take into account the impact of different net incomes earned in different future periods. For example, two projects with the same accounting rate of return, based on average expected net incomes, may have very different timings of those incomes.

V. Net Present Value and Ranking

A. The net present value of a project is derived by discounting future cash inflows (or savings) and determining whether the resulting present value is more or less than the cost of the investment and any other cash outflows. If the net present value is zero or positive, the project is economically feasible; if the net present value is negative, the project should be rejected. Because the net present value approach uses discounted cash flows, it provides a means of ranking projects in terms of a comparable dollar value of each project. For example, other things being equal, the project with the highest positive net present value would be ranked first, the second highest positive value ranked second, and so on.

B. While the net present value method enables not only a basis for accepting or rejecting a project, but also a useful ranking of projects, it does not address the issue of differences in initial cost of each project. This issue is addressed by the use of a profitability index, which is described below. Despite this issue, ranking projects by the level of their positive net present values is usually a preferred basis.

VI. Internal Rate of Return and Ranking

A. Like the net present value approach, the internal rate of return method incorporates the present value of future cash flows. Specifically, it determines the rate of return inherent in a project by determining the discount rate that equates the present value of the inflows with the present value of the outflows of the project. Furthermore, like the net present value method, the internal rate of return used to identify acceptable projects can also rank them. But, also like the NPV approach, it does not address the issue of differences in initial cost of each project, which is addressed by the profitability index. If the IRR method is used to rank projects, the project with the highest internal rate of return would be ranked first, the second highest rate next, and so on. However, when comparing projects of very different sizes (initial costs), different life-spans or different timings of cash flows, the rankings resulting from using IRR (the rates) may not indicated the most desirable project.

B. While both the NPV and IRR approaches will result in the same accept or reject outcome, differences between the methodologies used in the two approaches can result in different rankings for a given set of projects. These ranking may be different depending on:

1. Project size
2. Timing of cash flows
3. Project life-span

VII. Profitability Index and Ranking—While the other methods discussed above are primarily concerned with determining the economic feasibility of capital projects, the profitability index method is primarily intended for use in ranking projects. It does so by taking into account both the present value and the cost of each project. Specifically, the index results from dividing the net present value of the project by the initial cost of the project. As a result of that division, if present value of cash inflows is used an index of 1.0 is logically the lowest acceptable outcome. If net present value is used an index equal to or greater than 0 (zero) would be the lowest feasible value. As values on the profitability index increase, so does the financial attractiveness of the proposed project.

VIII. Equivalent Annual Annuity and Ranking—Like the profitability index, this method is designed to rank projects. It ranks projects by the present value of an annuity that exactly equals the net present value of each project. The larger the annuity amount, the higher the ranking of the project when comparing projects. This method is particularly appropriate when ranking projects with different expected lives. While the equivalent annual annuity method is more complicated to compute than the profitability index, there are computer and financial calculator applications designed to perform the calculation.

IX. Summary

A. In summary, when ranking acceptable capital projects, methods based on discounted values are much better than methods that do not incorporate the time value of money. The net present value method and, especially the profitability index derived using net present value and the initial project cost, generally are preferable to other methods. In the final analysis, however, some degree of subjectivity is likely to enter into deciding which projects will be implemented.

B. Once capital budgeting (project investment) decisions have been made, the impact of these plans must be built into other affected budgets. For example, a planned new project may have implications for sales revenue, production costs, and cash flows, in addition to asset acquisition. Further, once a project is initiated, it should be monitored frequently to assure that it continues to meet the entity's requirements for acceptability.

Financing Options

Introduction and Financial/Capital Structure

All activities and undertakings of an entity, including capital projects, must be financed. A variety of both short-term and long-term potential sources is available to most firms. This lesson introduces the need for financing and distinguishes between financial and capital structures and the nature of financing provided by each.

After studying this lesson, you should be able to:

1. Define and distinguish financial structure and capital structure.
2. Describe financial structure and capital structure in the context of an accounting balance sheet.

I. Introduction

A. Once the projects and activities to be undertaken are determined, a firm must separately decide how those undertakings will be financed. This relationship and requirement exist from the inception of a firm and they continue throughout its operating life.

B. This section on Financing Options defines an entity's financial and capital structure, identifies various means of short-term and long-term financing and the advantages and disadvantages of each means of financing, summarizes the cost of capital concepts, and outlines guidelines for making appropriate financing decisions in different circumstances.

II. Financial Structure and Capital Structure

A. From an accounting perspective, all items of liabilities and owners' equity are sources of financing an entity's assets, and therefore its operations. While accounts payable and common stock equity may be significantly different in terms of amount, duration, and other characteristics, each is nonetheless a source of funds for carrying out the activities of the entity. The mix of all elements of liabilities and owners' equity constitutes a firm's financial structure. The concept of capital structure is less inclusive. It includes only the long-term sources of financing, that is, long-term debt and owners' equity. The elements of and relationships between financial structure and capital structure can be illustrated using a typical balance sheet format:

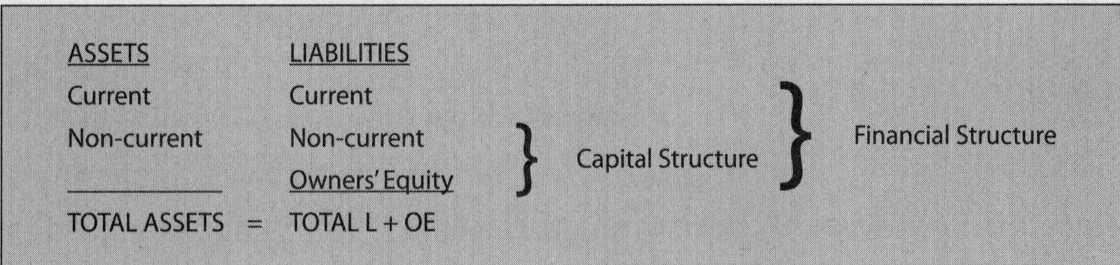

B. Thus, financial structure is a more inclusive concept and measure than capital structure. While all elements of financial structure are sources of an entity's financing, only the elements of capital structure provide long-term financing.

Short-Term (Working Capital) Financing

Introduction to Short-Term Financing

Short-term financing is comprised of sources that provide funding for a period of one year or less. This lesson describes short-term financing and identifies the primary current assets and liabilities used for short-term financing. Detailed coverage in subsequent lessons includes each of the major items identified in this lesson.

After studying this lesson, you should be able to:

1. Define short-term financing.
2. Identify major forms of short-term financing.

I. Short-Term (Working Capital) Financing

A. Like the accounting definition of current liabilities, the concept of short-term financing generally applies to obligations that will become due within one year. Therefore, items which are considered current liabilities also are considered forms of short-term financing. In addition, current assets which can be used to secure financing would be forms of short-term financing. The primary forms of short-term financing include:

1. Trade accounts payable
2. Accrued accounts payable (e.g., wages, taxes, etc.)
3. Short-term notes payable
4. Line of credit, revolving credit, and letter of credit
5. Commercial paper
6. Pledging accounts receivable
7. Factoring accounts receivable
8. Inventory secured loans

B. Each of these forms of financing is described and discussed in the following lessons.

Payables

Among the most common forms of short-term financing are the various payables due within one year or less. This lesson considers three of those, including trade accounts payable, accrued accounts payable, and short-term notes payable. Each of these forms of payable is described and the advantages and disadvantages as a form of financing are identified.

After studying this lesson, you should be able to:

1. Describe how accounts payable, accrued accounts payable, and short-term loans provide financing.
2. Describe the advantages and disadvantages of each of these forms of financing.

I. Trade Accounts Payable

A. Financing through trade accounts payable occurs in the normal course of business as a firm routinely buys goods or services on credit from its suppliers. The credit derived from trade accounts normally is not secured, in that no assets are pledged as collateral, but rather depend on the borrowers ability and willingness to pay the obligation when due. Financing certain acquisitions (e.g., supplies and inventory) through trade accounts is a highly flexible source of short-term financing—the level of financing goes up concurrent with the purchase of the goods or service. This sort of financing that occurs automatically in the carrying out of day-to-day operations, as happens with many general short-term payables, is called "spontaneous financing."

B. Often, trade credit is extended with the offer of a cash discount for early payment of an obligation. These offers would be incorporated as part of the credit terms and generally are expressed as a percentage of the amount of the obligation. For example, credit terms of "2/10, n/30" offer a 2% discount if the bill is paid within 10 days, otherwise the full amount is due within 30 days. Other discount rates and discount periods are common. The annual effective rate of interest implicit in such cash discount offers shows that effective cash management would take advantage of most cash discount offers. For example, the effective annual percentage rate (APR) of not taking an offer of "2/10, n/30" is almost 37%, calculated as follows using $1.00 (100%) as the amount of the obligation:

$$APR = [(\text{Discount Lost} / \text{Principal}) \times 1] / \text{Time Fraction of Year}$$

$$APR = [(.02/.98) \times 1]/(20/360) = .0204 \times (360/20)$$

$$APR = .0204 \times 18 = 36.73\%$$

C. The principal is the amount that would have been paid if the discount were taken. (Even if $1.00 were used as the principal, rather than $0.98, the APR would be .02 × 18 = 36.0%.)

D. The advantages and disadvantages of using trade accounts payable for financing can be summarized as:

1. Advantages

- **a.** Ease of use—little legal documentation required
- **b.** Flexible—expands and contracts with needs (purchases)
- **c.** Interest normally not charged
- **d.** Unsecured—no assets pledged as collateral
- **e.** Discount often offered for early payment

2. **Disadvantages**
   a. Requires payment in the short-term
   b. Higher effective cost if discounts not taken
   c. Use-specific—finances only assets acquired through trade accounts

II. Accrued Accounts Payable

A. Accrued accounts payable result from benefits or cash received for the related unpaid obligation. Thus, they are very much like trade accounts payable in their financing implications. Common examples are:

1. Salaries and wages payable
2. Taxes payable
3. Unearned revenue (collected in advance)

B. To the extent that there is a timing difference between when the benefit (or cash) is received and when the related obligation is satisfied, the cost or funds involved provide temporary (short-term) financing to the entity. For example, if salaried employees are paid once a month, they effectively are making a recurring one-month loan to the firm, which accumulates to the total monthly pay for all salaried employees. (The technical amount would be the average salaries for the month.) For a large firm, the resulting amount of financing would be significant. A similar effect occurs from taxes and revenues collected prior to payment or satisfaction of the obligation.

C. The advantages and disadvantages are similar to those for trade accounts payable, including:

1. **Advantages**
   a. Ease of use—occurs in the normal course of business
   b. Flexible—expands and contracts with activity
   c. Unsecured—no assets pledged (though taxing authorities have a specific legal claim)
2. **Disadvantages**
   a. Requires satisfaction in the short term
   b. Certain sources are use specific—only finances benefits acquired through accrued accounts (e.g., salaries)

III. Short-Term Notes Payable

A. Short-term notes payable result from borrowing, usually from a commercial bank, with repayment due in one year or less. These borrowings are typically for a designated purpose, require a promissory note be given, and carry a rate of interest determined by the credit rating of the borrower. Although a promissory note (a legally enforceable promise to pay) is required, short-term notes generally are unsecured, unless the borrower's credit rating dictates the lender require security. The interest rate usually will be expressed as a rate (or points) above the prime rate (or a similar benchmark). For example, the rate may be expressed as "1.00% over prime."

B. In addition to the interest cost associated with short-term notes, the borrower also may be required to maintain a compensating balance with the lending institution. A compensating balance is an amount that the borrower maintains in a demand deposit account with the lender as a condition of the loan (or for other bank services). The amount required is usually expressed as a percentage of the loan (or other factor) and increases the effective cost of the loan.

C. A special form of note is a "structured note." Although most commonly associated with intermediate or long-term instruments, structured short-term notes are possible. A structured short-term note (or other short-term or long-term structured security) is one whose cash flows (borrower's/issuer's payment obligation and lender's/investor's return) are contingent on changes in the value of an underlying interest rate, stock index, commodity price or other factor. As an example: A small oil company borrows using a one-year note with the interest rate on the borrowing tied to the price of oil. Because the cash flows depend on the value of an underlying, structured notes and other structured securities are derivatives.

D. The advantages and disadvantages of short term notes for financing purposes are:

1. **Advantages**
   - **a.** Commonly available for creditworthy firms
   - **b.** Flexible—amounts and periods (within one year) can be varied with needs
   - **c.** Unsecured—no assets pledged as collateral
   - **d.** Provides cash
   - **e.** Short maturity permits refinancing at lower cost if interest rates decline
2. **Disadvantages**
   - **a.** Poor credit rating results in high interest (and possibility of security required)
   - **b.** Requires satisfaction in the short-term
   - **c.** A required compensating balance increases cost and reduces effective funds available
   - **d.** Refinancing at higher rates may be necessary if interest rates increase

Standby Credit and Commercial Paper

Standby credit makes funds available from a lender for a specific amount, usually for a specified period of time, and often to be available under certain conditions. This lesson covers several forms of standby credit, including line of credit, revolving credit, and letter of credit. It also covers commercial paper as a form of financing.

After studying this lesson, you should be able to:

1. Define and describe the following forms of short-term financing: a) line of credit; b) revolving credit; c) letter of credit; and d) commercial paper.
2. Identify the advantages and disadvantages of: a) stand-by credit and b) commercial paper.

I. Line of Credit/Revolving Credit/Letter of Credit

Definition
Line of Credit: An informal agreement between a borrower and a financial institution whereby the financial institution agrees to a maximum amount of credit that it will extend to the borrower at any one time.

A. Generally, the agreement is good only for the prospective borrower's fiscal year and, although the agreement is not legally binding on the financial institution, provides the firm reasonable assurance that the agreed upon financing will be available. Like a short-term note, a line of credit is generally unsecured, has an interest rate that is indexed to the prime rate (or other benchmark), and may require a compensating balance. Unlike a short-term note, however, a line of credit usually is not arranged for a specific purpose, but rather for a more general use. For example, it might be available "to meet working capital requirements."

Definition
Revolving Credit Agreement: Like a line of credit, but it is in the context of a legal agreement between the borrower and the financial institution.

B. Borrowings under such agreements are generally unsecured and have the same interest, maturity, and compensating balance requirements as a line of credit.

Definition
Letter of Credit: A conditional commitment by a bank to pay a third party in accordance with specified terms and commitments.

C. For example, payment may be made to a third party (e.g., a supplier) upon submission of proof that goods have been shipped. Use of a letter of credit provides assurance of funding to the third party without the borrowing firm having to pay in advance of shipment of goods. Letters of credit are frequently used in connection with foreign transactions.

D. The advantages and disadvantages of line of credit, revolving credit, and letter of credit are:

1. **Advantages**
   - **a.** Commonly available for creditworthy firms
   - **b.** Highly flexible—credit used (debt incurred) only when needed

c. Unsecured—no assets pledged as collateral

d. Line of credit and revolving credit provide cash for general use

2. **Disadvantages**

a. Poor credit rating results in high interest (and possibly security)

b. Typically involve a fee

c. Requires satisfaction in the short term

d. A required compensating balance increases cost and reduces effective funds available.

e. Line of credit does not legally obligate the financial institution

II. Commercial Paper

> **Definition**
> *Commercial Paper:* Short-term unsecured promissory notes sold by large, highly creditworthy firms as a form of short-term financing.

A. By convention, these notes are for 270 days or less (otherwise, SEC registration is required), with most being for six months or less. Commercial paper may be sold with interest discounted (deducted up front) or to pay interest over the (short) life of the note or at its maturity, and may be sold directly to investors or through a dealer. The effective interest rate is typically less than the cost of borrowing through a commercial bank.

B. The advantages and disadvantages associated with the use of commercial paper for financing are:

1. **Advantages**

a. Interest rate is generally lower than other short-term sources.

b. Larger amount of funds can be obtained through multiple commercial paper notes than would be available through a single financial institution.

c. Compensating balances are not required.

d. Unsecured—no assets are pledged as collateral

e. Provides cash for general use

2. **Disadvantages**

a. Only available to most creditworthy firms

b. Requires satisfaction in the short-term, usually of a large amount

c. Lacks flexibility of extension or other accommodation available in bank loans

Receivables and Inventory

Sources of financing for a firm include certain non-cash current assets. This lesson considers the ways accounts receivable and inventory can provide financing, either by being converted to cash or serving as security for borrowing.

After studying this lesson, you should be able to:

1. Define and describe pledging accounts receivable as a form of short-term financing and the advantages and disadvantages of pledging accounts receivable.
2. Define and describe factoring accounts receivable as a form of short-term financing and the advantages and disadvantages of factoring accounts receivable.
3. Describe the use of inventory as security for short-term financing and the advantages and disadvantages of using inventory secured loans.
4. Identify and describe different forms of securing inventory as collateral for short-term financing.

I. Pledging Accounts Receivable

A. Financing through pledging accounts receivable uses a current asset—trade accounts receivable—as security for short-term borrowings. Specifically, the firm pledges some or all of its accounts receivable as collateral for a short-term loan from a commercial bank or finance company. If the terms of agreement between the firm and the lender provide that all accounts receivable are pledged without regard to or an analysis of the collectability of individual accounts, the lender will lend a smaller portion of the face value of receivables than if only specific accounts with known risk are pledged. For example, a maximum loan of only 70% of receivables may be made when simply all receivables are pledged, but as much as 90% of face value may be loaned on receivables that have been determined to be creditworthy. The rate of interest on loans secured by accounts receivable will typically range from 2% above prime and up. In addition, a fee based on the face value of the receivables is usually charged.

B. The advantages and disadvantages of using pledged accounts receivable to secure a loan are:

1. **Advantages**
   - a. Commonly available
   - b. Flexible—as new receivables occur, they are available as security
   - c. Compensating balances are not required.
   - d. Provides cash for general use
   - e. Lender may assume billing and collection services
2. **Disadvantages**
   - a. Accounts are committed to lender.
   - b. Cost may be greater than certain other sources of short-term financing.
   - c. Requires repayment in the short term

II. Factoring Accounts Receivable

A. Factoring accounts receivable is the sale of accounts receivable to a commercial bank or other financial institution (called a "factor"). Actual payment to the firm for its accounts receivable may occur at various times between the date of sale and collection of the receivables. The funds received can then be used for financing of other assets or used for other purposes. The terms of the sale may be:

> Without Recourse—the factor bears the risk associated with collectibility (unless fraud is involved).
>
> With Recourse—the factor has recourse against the firm for some or all of the risk associated with uncollectibility.

B. The factor charges a fee (factor's fee) based on the creditworthiness and length of maturity of the receivables, and the extent to which the factor assumes risk of uncollectibility.

C. The advantages and disadvantages of factoring accounts receivable are:

1. **Advantages**
    a. Commonly available
    b. Flexible: as new accounts receivable occur, they are available for sale
    c. Compensating balances are not required.
    d. Provides cash for general use
    e. Buyer generally assumes billing and collection responsibilities.

2. **Disadvantages**
    a. Cost may be greater than certain other sources of short-term financing
    b. If sold with recourse, firm may have ongoing risk
    c. Sale of their accounts may alienate customers

III. Inventory Secured Loans

A. With an inventory secured loan a firm pledges all or part of its inventory as collateral for a short-term loan. The amount that can be borrowed depends on the value and marketability of the inventory. Different arrangements for inventory secured loans provide different treatment of the inventory and different levels of security for the lender:

1. **Floating lien agreement**—The borrower gives a lien against all of its inventory to the lender, but retains control of its inventory, which it continuously sells and replaces.
2. **Chattel mortgage agreement**—The borrower gives a lien against specifically identified inventory and retains control of the inventory, but cannot sell it without the lender's approval.
3. **Field warehouse agreement**—The inventory used as collateral remains at the firm's warehouse, placed under the control of an independent third-party and held as security.
4. **Terminal warehouse agreement**—The inventory used as collateral is moved to a public warehouse where it is held as security.

B. The cost of using inventory secured loans for financing will depend on several factors, including the nature of the inventory used as collateral, the credit standing of the borrower, and the specific type of security agreement. The typical interest rate is 2% above prime and up, and may involve other fees.

C. The advantages and disadvantages of using inventory to secure short-term financing are similar to those for pledging accounts receivable. They include:

1. **Advantages**
    a. Commonly available for certain inventories (e.g., oil, wheat, etc.)
    b. Flexible—as new inventories are obtained, they are available as security
    c. Compensating balances are not required.
    d. Provides cash for general use

2. **Disadvantages**
    a. Pledged inventory may not be available when needed.
    b. Cost can be greater than certain other sources of short-term financing.
    c. Requires repayment in the short term
    d. Not available for certain inventory

IV. This lesson identified and described the most common forms of short-term financing. Because these forms of financing have to be satisfied in the near term, generally they are not appropriate for financing capital projects. Nevertheless, they provide an important role in the overall financing of a firm's total assets and operations.

Long-Term (Capital) Financing

Introduction to Long-Term Financing

Long-term financing is comprised of sources that provide funding for periods greater than one year and includes both debt and equity instruments. This lesson describes long-term financing and identifies the primary forms of long-term financing. Subsequent lessons provide consideration of each of the forms of long-term financing.

After studying this lesson, you should be able to:

1. Define and describe long-term financing.
2. Identify the primary forms of long-term financing.

I. Long-Term (Capital) Financing

A. Long-term financing comprises the sources of funds used by a firm that do not mature within one year. A distinction is sometimes made between intermediate-term and long-term financing. In that case, intermediate-term financing is taken as sources of financing that mature in more than one year but less than ten years, and long-term financing is taken as sources of financing that extend beyond ten years, including shareholders' equity. Since the different sources may overlap those two time periods, the discussion here treats both categories as long term and makes note of the likely term of each source. Furthermore, treating all sources of funding that are not short term as a group is consistent with distinguishing those sources, which constitute capital structure (as contrasted with financial structure) of a firm.

B. Because long-term financing provides the major source of funding for most firms and because the length of commitment associated with these sources is by definition for a long period of time, a firm should carefully consider the alternative sources of long-term financing and the relative proportion of each it will employ. The cost associated with each source and the relative dollar amount of each source used will determine the firm's weighted average cost of capital that, as we discussed earlier, will determine which undertakings are economically feasible for the firm to pursue. The primary forms of long-term financing would include:

1. Long-term notes
2. Financial (capital) leases
3. Bonds
4. Preferred stock
5. Common stock

C. Each of these forms of financing is discussed in the following lessons.

Long-Term Notes and Financial Leases

Two common forms of long-term debt financing are notes and financial leases. This lesson describes the use of each of these sources and identifies the advantages and disadvantages associated with the use of each.

After studying this lesson, you should be able to:

1. Describe the use of long-term notes for long-term financing, including: a) the common restrictive covenants associated with long-term notes and b) the advantages and disadvantages of using long-term notes for long-term financing.
2. Describe the use of financial leases for long-term financing, including: a) a comparison between the use of purchase and leasing alternatives and b) the advantages and disadvantages of financial leasing for long-term financing.
3. Define the meaning of lease characteristics, including: a) net leases and b) net-net leases.

I. Long-Term Notes

A. Long-term notes typically are used for borrowings normally of from one to ten years, but some may be of longer duration. These borrowings usually are repaid in periodic installments over the life of the loan and usually are secured by a mortgage on equipment or real estate. In addition to requiring collateral, long-term notes often contain restrictive covenants that impose restrictions on the borrower so as to reduce the likelihood of default. Such covenants commonly place restrictions on:

1. **Maintaining certain working capital conditions**—For example, maintaining a minimum dollar amount of working capital or a minimum working capital ratio.
2. **Additional incurrence of debt**—Requiring lender approval before taking on additional long-term debt, including such as might arise through financial leases.
3. **Frequency and nature of financial information**—Requiring the borrower to provide periodic financial statements and related disclosures, perhaps with an audit report.
4. **Management changes**—Requiring lender approval before certain changes in key personnel are made.

B. The cost of financing through use of a long-term note will depend on a number of factors, including the general level of interest in the market, the creditworthiness of the firm borrowing and the nature and value of any collateral, and will be expressed as a function of the prime interest rate (or other benchmark). Therefore, during the life of the note, the rate of interest will fluctuate as the prime rate changes.

C. A special form of note is a "structured note." A structured note (or other structured security) is one whose cash flows (borrower's/issuer's payment obligation and lender's/investor's return) are contingent on changes in the value of an underlying interest rate, stock index, commodity price or other factor. As an example: A transportation company borrows using a five-year note with the interest rate on the borrowing tied to a transportation stock index. Because the cash flows are dependent on the value of an underlying, structured notes and other structured securities are derivatives.

D. The advantages and disadvantages associated with the use of Long-Term notes include:

1. **Advantages**
   - **a.** Commonly available for creditworthy firms
   - **b.** Provides long-term financing, often with periodic repayment
2. **Disadvantages**
   - **a.** Poor credit ratings result in higher interest rates, greater security requirements, and more restrictive covenants.
   - **b.** Violation of restrictive covenants triggers serious consequences, including technical default.

II. Financial Leases

A. Leasing, rather than buying, is an alternative way of financing the acquisition of certain assets. When leasing is an option for acquiring assets in a capital budgeting project, evaluation of the project has to take into account the different costs associated with each alternative for financing the project assets—buying and leasing. Therefore, the analysis would need to determine:

1. Whether the proposed project is economically feasible if assets are purchased; and

2. Whether the proposed project is economically feasible if assets are leased.

B. Several possible outcomes of the analysis are possible:

1. **Reject**—If neither analysis shows that the project is economically feasible, the project would be rejected.

2. **Purchase**—The project should be accepted using asset purchase if:

   a. The traditional capital budgeting analysis (e.g., net present value using the cost of capital) shows the project to be economically feasible, but the leasing-based analysis does not.

   b. Both analyses show the project to be economically feasible, but the traditional purchase analysis shows a better "return."

3. **Lease**—The project should be accepted using asset leasing if:

   a. The leasing-based analysis shows the project to be economically feasible, but the traditional capital budgeting analysis does not.

   b. Both analyses show the project to be economically feasible, but the leasing-based analysis shows a better "return."

C. **In analyzing the alternatives,** leasing may be the better option as a result of lower cost of leasing. That is, the lessor can provide the asset at a lower cost than if the lessee purchased the asset. This may occur because the lessor has efficiencies, lower interest rates, or tax advantages that the lessee does not have. In addition to being justified on a strictly economic basis, leasing is sometimes used for more subjective reasons, including flexibility and convenience.

D. From a financial management perspective, if leasing were used, the lease would be considered a financial lease, as opposed to an operating lease. While the classifications used in finance (financial and operating) are similar to the concepts of capital leases and operating leases used in accounting, there are some differences. A financial lease is a legally enforceable, non-cancelable contract under which the lessee commits to making a series of payments to the owner of the asset (lessor) for the use of the asset over the period of the lease. Thus, for financial analysis purposes, whether the lease is, in effect, a sale—the concept underlying the designation for capital lease in accounting—is not relevant. Practically, however, both categories (financial and capital) reflect the same consequence for financing—the use of an asset is acquired at the present with the cost being incurred over multiple future periods. (In both finance and accounting, operating leases are considered more like renting than a means of financing asset acquisition and are not particularly relevant here).

E. In finance, leases are described as being **net leases** or **net-net leases** to identify which costs of the asset are the responsibility of the lessee. In a net lease, the lessee assumes the cost associated with ownership during the period of the lease. Normally, these costs are referred to in accounting as executory costs and include maintenance, taxes, and insurance. In a net-net lease, the lessee is responsible for not only the executory costs, but also a pre-established residual value. The particular nature—lease, net lease, or net-net lease—will affect the cost of the lease to the lessee and, therefore, the viability and benefits of leasing.

F. The advantages and disadvantages associated with leasing are:

1. **Advantages**

   a. Limited immediate cash outlay

   b. Possible lower cost than purchasing, resulting primarily from lessor efficiencies, lower interest rates, or tax savings, some of which are "passed on" to the lessee

c. The resulting debt (lease payment) is specific to the amount needed.

d. Possibility of scheduling payments to coincide with cash flows

e. No (or fewer) restrictive agreements than incurring certain other debt

2. **Disadvantages**

a. Not all assets are commonly available for lease.

b. Lease financing is asset specific—funds are not available for general use.

c. Lease terms may prove different than the period of asset usefulness.

d. Often chosen for reasons other than economic justification

Bonds

One of the most common forms of obtaining long-term debt financing for large corporations is through the issuance of bonds, which can provide large amounts of funding for long periods. This lesson defines and describes bonds, bond characteristics, bond valuation, and bond yields. It concludes with a summary of the advantages and disadvantages associated with the use of bonds for financing purposes

After studying this lesson, you should be able to:

1. Define bonds, and describe bond characteristics and types of bonds based on the nature of security provided.
2. Define and compute the determination of a bond's selling price.
3. Define and compute a bond's a) current yield and b) yield to maturity.
4. Describe the effects of changes in the market rate of interest on bond values.
5. Describe the advantages and disadvantages of using bonds for long-term financing.

I. Introduction

A. Debt financing can be obtained through either the private market or the public market:

1. The private market includes loans from financial institutions or through private placement using unregistered instruments, typically through insurance companies or pension funds.
2. The public market involves the sale of SEC-registered instruments (bonds) in the market.

Definition
Bonds: Long-term promissory notes wherein the borrower, in return for buyers'/lenders' funds, promises to pay the bondholders a fixed amount of interest each year and to repay the face value of the note at maturity.

B. While most bonds have some common characteristics, there are differences between certain kinds of bonds. Common characteristics include:

1. **Indenture**—the bond contract
2. **Par value or face value**—the "principal" that will be returned at maturity, most commonly $1,000 per bond
3. **Coupon rate of interest**—the annual interest rate printed on the bond and paid on par value
4. **Maturity**—the time at which the issuer repays the par value to the bondholders

II. Major Differences

A. Security—A major difference in bonds is whether the bond issue is secured by collateral.

Definitions
Debenture bonds: Unsecured; no specific asset is designated as collateral. These bonds are considered to have more risk and, therefore, must provide a greater return than secured bonds.

Secured bonds: Have specific assets (e.g., machinery and equipment) designated as collateral for the bonds.

Mortgage bonds: Secured by a lien on real property (e.g., land and building).

B. Callability (also Called Redeemability)—Callable bonds provide that the bonds can be redeemed (bought back) by the issuer prior to maturity.

1. Callable bonds are most commonly used to enable the issuing firm to call in outstanding bonds if the market rate of interest declines significantly below the interest being paid on the outstanding bonds. By calling in high-interest outstanding bonds, and issuing new bonds at the current lower interest rate, the firm can reduce its interest expense.
2. Bonds issued with a callable feature usually pay a higher rate of interest than comparable bonds without a call feature. The higher interest rate compensates the holder for the risk that the bonds will be called before maturity and the investor will be faced with reinvesting at a lower rate of interest.
3. Bonds issued with a callable feature also may provide that the issuer pay a premium (over par or face value) at the time it calls the bonds.

C. Convertibility—Convertible bonds provide that the bond holder has the option of converting the bonds into a specified number of shares of equity (stock) of the issuing company. Investors in convertible bonds will exercise the option to convert if the market price of the stock increases.

1. Bonds issued with a convertible feature usually pay a lower rate of interest than comparable bonds without a convertible feature. This lower interest rate results from the value of the holder's option to convert the bonds into stock.
2. Convertible bonds also may contain a call provision, which would permit the issuing company to call the bonds so as to limit the up-side potential recognized by the bond holders.

D. Zero-Coupon Bonds—Debt security (bond) that does not pay interest during its life; there are no (zero) coupons to submit for interest payments. These bonds provide a profit to investors by selling at a deep discount (i.e., amount less than maturity value) and paying full face value when redeemed at maturity. Because they provide payment only at maturity, the market price tends to fluctuate more than that of coupon bonds.

E. Floating Rate Bonds—Debt security (bond) that pays a rate of interest that fluctuates over the life of the instrument. Typically, the rate of interest paid is tied to a macroeconomic benchmark rate such as the prime rate, the U.S. Treasury Bill rate, LIBOR (London Interbank Offered Rate), the federal funds rate or similar rate, plus a spread (which is a constant amount). For example, the rate might be quoted as "prime rate (which varies) + .50% (which remains constant)." Because the rate of interest paid "floats" (increase or decrease) with changes in a macroeconomic benchmark, the bonds tend to maintain their market value as the market rate of interest changes.

F. Eurobonds—Debt security (bond) payable in the borrower's currency but sold outside the borrower's country. For example, a U.S. firm (issuer) might issue bonds payable in dollars but sold in another country. Because the registration and disclosure requirements are less than in the U.S., the bond can be issued at lower costs than in the U.S.

III. Cost of Bond Financing—The cost of financing with bonds (and other debt) is the stated interest rate less the tax savings from the tax deductibility of interest expense.

A. Cost of debt = Interest rate × (1.0 – Marginal tax rate)

IV. Bond Values

A. Because a very large number of bonds, each with a par value of (say) $1,000, can be issued, very large sums can be raised through bond issues. While the par value of each bond may be $1,000, the cash proceeds received upon issuing the bonds will depend on the relationship between the coupon interest rate (on the face of the bond) and investors' required rate of return when the bonds are issued. The investors' required rate of return would be based primarily on the return available from other investment opportunities in the market with comparable perceived risk (i.e., the investors' opportunity cost). If the investors' required rate—the market rate—is more than the coupon rate, the bonds will sell at less that par (i.e., at a discount); if the market rate is less than the coupon rate, the bonds will sell at more than par (i.e., at a premium).

B. The determination of a bond's selling price at issue and the determination of a bond's market value during its life is a function of the present value of its future cash flows. Bonds have two cash flows:

1. **Periodic interest**—Discounted as the present value of an annuity
2. **Maturity face value**—Discounted as the present value of a single amount

C. Both cash flows would be discounted using the market (investors') required rate of return at the time, which reflects the market's assessment of the risk inherent in the bond issue and rates available through other comparable investments.

Example

Assume $10,000 in bonds outstanding that pay semiannual interest at 6% coupon rate, maturing in six years, and the market rate of interest is currently 5%.

1. **PV of periodic interest**—An annuity of 12 payments (6 years × semiannual) at $300 per payment ($10,000 × .06 × 1/2) discounted at the market rate of interest .025 (.05 × ½). The table factor for annuity with 12 periods at .025 = 10.26. Thus, the present value of interests payments is $300 × 10.26 = $3,078.
2. **PV of maturity value**—A single amount to be received in 12 periods at the market rate of interest .025. The table factor for a single amount with 12 periods at .025 = .7436. Thus, the present value of the maturity value is $10,000 × .7436 = $7,436.
3. The current value of the bonds is $3,078 + $7,436 = $10,514.

V. Bond Yields

A. Two measures of rates associated with bonds are noteworthy: current yield and yield to maturity.

1. **Current yield (CY)**

Definition

Current Yield: The ratio of annual interest payments to the current market price of the bond. Assuming a $1,000, 6% bond currently selling for $900, the current yield (CY) would be computed as:

CY = Annual Coupon Interest / Current Market Price

CY = ($1,000 × .06) / $900 = $60 / $900 = 6.67

a. Thus, while the coupon rate is 6%, the current yield based on the current price is 6.67%. As the market price of the bonds changes, so too will the current yield.

2. **Yield to maturity (expected rate of return)**

Definition

Yield to Maturity (also called the Expected Rate of Return): The rate of return required by investors as implied by the current market price of the bonds is the yield to maturity.

a. Changes in the market price of an outstanding bond reflect changes in the rate of return expected on those bonds. Determining the yield to maturity is done by determining the discount rate that equates the present value of future cash flows from the bond issue with the current price of the bonds. That rate is the rate of return currently expected by bondholders. The process of determining that rate is identical to the process of determining the internal rate of return on a capital project. In the absence of a financial calculator or computer, the process is one of trial and error, and interpolation using present value tables.

b. As the bondholders' current expected rate of return, **the yield to maturity is an important measure of the firm's current cost of debt capital**.

VI. Term Structure of Interest Rates—The term structure of interest rates (also called the yield curve) shows the current yield to maturity (rate of return) on bonds of similar quality that have different lengths of times until maturity. The term structure is commonly plotted with interest rates on the vertical (Y) axis and time until maturity (i.e., "term") on the horizontal (X) axis.

A. Because **changes in the market rate of interest** cause the price of bonds to change inversely (i.e., as market rates of interest go up, the value of bonds goes down, or vice versa), investors in bonds face a (market) interest rate risk. Furthermore, longer-term fixed-rate debt (like bonds) has greater risk than shorter-term debt because, with a longer holding period, there is a greater possibility that an increase in the market rate of interest will occur and result in a decline in the value of the debt. Therefore, the longer the term of bonds, the greater the maturity premium and, therefore, the higher the required rate of return.

B. Consequently, the term structure curve (yield curve) is normally upward sloping from lower left to upper right, showing that the rate of return increases as the term (life) of the debt increases. This is called a "normal yield curve."

C. If the plotted term structure curve shows that short-term interest rates are higher than long-term rates, it shows that the rate of return decreases as the term of the debt increases. This is called an "inverted yield curve."

D. If the plotted term structure curve shows little or no change over time, it is called a "flat yield curve."

> **Note**
> *The term structure of interest rates was covered in detail in the "Interest Rate Concepts and Calculations" lesson.*

VII. Structured Bonds—Structured bonds provide that either the periodic interest payments or the value at maturity varies with changes in one or more underlyings, which might include specified stock or bond market indexes, commodity prices, currency exchange rates, or other factors. Because the value (cash flows) of period interest payments or the value at maturity depends on change in an underlying, structured bonds are derivative instruments—they derive their value from the value of the underlying. Callable bonds, which give the issuer the ability to redeem the bonds before maturity, are a simple possible example of a structured bond because the call option embedded in the bond may provide for payment of a call premium based on an underlying. Convertible bonds are also a simple example of a structured bond because the holder has the option to convert the bonds to stock, the value of which may change, thus changing the value at conversion.

VIII. Advantages and Disadvantages—Advantages and disadvantages associated with the use of bonds for financing purposes can include:

A. Advantages

1. A source of large sums of capital
2. Does not dilute ownership or earnings per share
3. Interest payments are tax deductible

B. Disadvantages

1. Required periodic interest payments—default can result in bankruptcy
2. Required principal repayment at maturity—default can result in bankruptcy
3. May require security and/or have restrictive covenants

Preferred Stock

Two types of equity instruments commonly used for long-term financing are preferred stock and common stock. As the term implies, preferred stock offers "preferences" to shareholders that are not provided to common shareholders. This lesson considers the characteristics of preferred stock, the valuation of and returns on preferred stock, and the advantages and disadvantages associated with the use of preferred stock for financing purposes.

After studying this lesson, you should be able to:

1. Define preferred stock and describe preferred stock characteristics.
2. Define and compute for preferred stock: (a) current theoretical value, (b) expected rate of return, and (c) cost of financing using preferred stock.
3. Describe the advantages and disadvantages of using preferred stock for long-term financing.

I. Preferred Stock

Definition
Preferred Stock: A class of ownership in a corporation that has a priority claim on its assets and earnings before common stock, generally with a dividend that must be paid out before dividends to common shareholders are paid.

A. Preferred stock grants an ownership interest in a corporation that has preference claims not held by common stock shareholders. Commonly, those preference claims give preferred shareholders a priority claim to income distributions (dividends) and to assets upon liquidation of the firm.

B. Although preferred stock grants an ownership interest in the firm, it is frequently described as having characteristics of both bonds and common stock.

1. It is like bonds in that the dividend amount, like interest, is expected and limited in amount and generally preferred stock does not have voting rights.
2. It is **like common stock** in that it:
   - **a.** Grants ownership interest
   - **b.** Has no maturity date
   - **c.** Does not require dividends be paid
   - **d.** Provides that dividends paid are not an expense and are not tax deductible
   - **e.** Has liability that is limited to the amount of the investment
3. **Unlike common stock**, for which there are few variations in features, preferred stock may have a variety of characteristics, including:
   - **a.** A firm can have different classes or types of preferred stock with different characteristics and different preferences.
   - **b.** Cumulative/noncumulative feature to distinguish whether dividends not paid in any year accumulate and require payment before payment of common dividends.
   - **c.** Participating/nonparticipating feature to distinguish whether preferred shareholders receive dividends in excess of the stated preference rate.
   - **d.** Protective provisions to protect preferred shareholders' interest. For example, the right to vote under certain circumstances or the requirement for a preferred stock sinking fund.

e. Convertible/nonconvertible feature to distinguish whether preferred stock shareholders can exchange preferred stock for common stock according to a specified exchange rate.

f. Call provision, which gives the firm the right to buy back the preferred stock, normally at a premium.

II. Preferred Stock Values

A. Because of its preference claim to dividends, for financial valuation and analytical purposes, preferred stock is treated very much like bonds. Like bonds, the value of preferred stock is the present value of expected future cash flows. Whereas bonds have two forms of future cash flow (interest and principal at maturity), dividends are the only primary stream of future cash flows for preferred stocks. Furthermore, while bonds have a maturity, preferred stock may be outstanding indefinitely. Therefore, the elements used to estimate the value of preferred stock are:

1. Estimated future annual dividends
2. Discount rate in the form of investors' required rate of return
3. An assumption that the dividend stream will exist in perpetuity

B. Using the assumed elements, the theoretical value of a share of preferred stock (PSV) can be calculated as:

PSV = Annual Dividend / Required Rate of Return

C. For example, if the annual dividend is $4.00 and preferred investors expect an 8% return, the implied value of the preferred stock would be:

PSV = $4.00 /.08 = $50.00

III. Preferred Stock Rate of Return

A. Like bondholders, preferred stockholders have a rate of return they expect to earn on their investment. That currently expected rate of return can be derived using two directly determinable elements:

1. Annual dividend
2. Market price

B. Using these elements, the expected rate of return (PSER) can be calculated as:

PSER = Annual Dividend / Market Price

C. Assuming an annual dividend of $4.00 and a current market price of $52.00, the calculation would be:

PSER = $4.00 / $52.00 = .077 = 7.7%

D. Thus, based on the current market price, the currently expected rate of return on the preferred stock is 7.7%.

IV. Cost of Financing with Preferred Stock

A. **Outstanding Preferred Stock**—Since the annual dividend is "fixed" and the market price will change to reflect changes in market perceptions of the stock, the expected rate of return (computed above) reflects the rate investors currently require to invest in the stock. That rate is a measure of the firm's current cost of outstanding preferred stock capital.

B. New Preferred Stock—The cost of newly issued preferred stock is determined by dividing the annual dividend by the issue price, including any premium or discount.

Example

Assume 1,000 shares that pay an $8.00 per year dividend (.08 × $100 par) are issued for $102,500 (at a premium). The cost of the newly issued shares is

$8,000/$102,500 = 7.8%
(less than the stated rate of 8% because the proceeds exceed par).

V. Advantages and Disadvantages—The advantages and disadvantages associated with the use of preferred stock for financing include:

A. Advantages

1. No legally required periodic payments; default cannot result from failure to pay dividends
2. Generally a lower cost of capital than common stock
3. Generally does not bestow voting rights
4. No maturity date
5. No security required

B. Disadvantages

1. Dividend expectations are high.
2. Dividend payments are not tax deductible.
3. If triggered, protective provisions may be onerous.
4. Generally, a higher cost of capital than bonds.

Common Stock

Common stock is the basic form of long-term equity financing for corporations. This lesson considers the characteristics of common stock, the valuation and returns on common stock, and the advantages and disadvantages associated with the use of common stock for financing purposes. In addition, this lesson considers the use of "crowdfunding" as a means of issuing equity securities, with special consideration of the regulatory requirements when using crowdfunding to acquire equity financing.

After studying this lesson, you should be able to:

1. Define common stock and describe common stock characteristics.
2. Define and compute common stock's: (a) current theoretical value and (b) expected rate of return.
3. Describe the advantages and disadvantages of using common stock for long-term financing.
4. Define crowdfunding and identify the major limitations and requirements when using crowdfunding for issuing equity securities.

I. Common Stock Characteristics

A. Common stock represents the basic ownership interest in a corporation. Unlike preferred stock, the characteristics of common stock are fairly uniform. While it is possible in some jurisdictions to have more than one class of common stock with different rights, regulatory and other requirements virtually preclude more than one class of common stock. Characteristics of common stock include:

1. **Limited liability**—Common shareholders' liability is limited to their investment.
2. **Residual claim to income and assets**—Common shareholders' claim to income and assets on liquidation comes after the claims of creditors and preferred shareholders.
3. **Right to vote**—For directors, auditors and changes to the corporate charter. A temporary power of attorney, called a proxy, can be used to delegate that right.
4. **Preemptive right**—The right of first refusal to acquire a proportionate share of any new common stock issued

B. The fact that common shareholders have only a residual claim to income (and assets on liquidation) adds an element of risk, often referred to as financial risk, for the common shareholder. While the common shareholders are entitled to all income remaining after other capital sources (creditors and preferred shareholders) have received interest and dividends, they bear the risk of weak earnings. As a consequence, the cost of common stock capital is usually higher than that of either bonds or preferred stock.

II. Common Stock Value

A. As with other sources of capital, the value of common stock is the present value of expected cash flows; for common stockholders that includes expected dividends and stock price appreciation (a consideration generally not encountered with preferred stock). Thus, if an assumption is made that a share of common stock is to be acquired and held for only one year, the current value of that share should be the sum of:

1. Present value of dividends expected during the one-year holding period discounted at the investor's required rate of return and
2. Present value of the expected stock market price at the end of the one-year holding period discounted at the investor's required rate of return.

B. When considering an investment for multiple holding periods, expectations about future dividends, and especially future stock market prices, becomes much less certain. One way to address that uncertainty in financial analysis is by assuming that dividends grow indefinitely at a constant rate. The constant growth in dividends is assumed to incorporate both dividends distributed and growth in stock value. Under that assumption, the current value of common stock (CSV) can be computed as:

CSV = Dividend in 1st Year / (Required Rate of Return – Growth Rate)

Example

Assume an expected dividend of $2.10, an expected indefinite dividend growth of 5% annually and a required rate of return of 8%, the resulting value of the common stock would be:

CSV = $2.10 / (8% – 5%) = $2.10 / .03 = $70.00

III. Common Stock Expected Return

A. Under the assumption that dividends are expected to grow at a constant rate indefinitely into the future (in perpetuity) and that the stock market price is reflected by that dividend growth rate, the expected rate of return (CSER) for a prospective current investor (marginal investor) can be computed as:

CSER = (Dividend in 1st Year / Market Price) + Growth Rate

Example

Assuming an expected dividend of $2.10, a growth rate of 5% and a current market price of $70.00, the calculation would be:

CSER = ($2.10 / $70.00) + .05

CSER = 03 + .05 = .08 = 8%

Thus, the marginal investor with a required rate of return of 8% would be willing to pay $70.00 per share, the current market price of the stock.

IV. Cost of Financing with Common Stock

A. The expected return (computed above) is the current cost of financing through the use of existing (outstanding) common stock.

B. Other approaches to estimating the cost of outstanding common stock include:

1. Capital asset pricing model (CAPM), as previously described and illustrated
2. Arbitrage pricing model
3. Bond-yield-plus approach

C. The cost of capital through the issuance of new common stock would be expected to be higher due to flotation costs (i.e., the costs associated with issuing the new securities).

1. Flotation costs reduce the proceeds received and, therefore, increase the cost of financing.
2. Using the facts in the example above and assuming the same $70 sellng price, but with a $5 per share flotation cost, the calculation would be:

   CSER = [$2.10/($70 – $5)] + .05

   CSER = ($2.10/$65) + .05

   CSER = .032 + .05 = .082 (8.2%)—the cost of the new issue

D. **Retained Earnings**—In addition, since common stockholders have a residual claim to income, and retained earnings are largely residual income, the expected rate of return on common stock also reflects the implicit cost of internal financing—that is, the cost of using retained earnings rather than distributing them in the form of dividends. The cost of capital for retained earnings (for which there are no flotation costs) would be less than the cost of capital for issuing new common stock due to the flotation costs of issuing such new securities.

V. Expected Return versus Historic Return

- **A.** The expected (*ex ante*) rate of return is different than the historic (*ex post*) rate of return.
- **B.** The total historic rate of return on common stock (and on other investments) is the total dollar return earned since acquisition divided by original cost of the investment. For common stock, the total dollar return would consist of both dividends received and the change in the market price of the stock since it was acquired.
- **C.** The historic or expected return on a portfolio of common stocks (or other investment) is the weighted average of the historic/expected return on the investments in the portfolio.

VI. Advantages and Disadvantages—The advantages and disadvantages associated with the use of common stock financing include:

- **A. Advantages**
  - **1.** No legally required periodic payments. Default cannot result from failure to pay dividends
  - **2.** No maturity date
  - **3.** No security required
- **B. Disadvantages**
  - **1.** Generally a higher cost of capital than other sources
  - **2.** Dividends paid are not tax deductible.
  - **3.** Additional shares issued dilute ownership and earnings.

VII. Raising Equity through Crowdfunding

- **A.** Crowdfunding is the raising of funds for an undertaking (e.g., business venture, project, etc.) by obtaining many small amounts from a large number of sources, typically accomplished through Internet solicitation.
  - **1.** U.S. securities regulations historically have precluded the sale (issue) of equity securities through the use of crowdfunding.
  - **2.** In October 2015, the SEC adopted rules, as required by Title III of the 2012 JOBS Act, that permit companies to offer and sell equity securities through crowdfunding.
- **B. Crowdfunding Regulations**—The regulations adopted by the SEC permit the use of crowdfunding for the sale of equity securities subject to certain limits and requirements imposed on both companies seeking crowdfunding and investors.
  - **1. Company-related requirements**—For companies seeking crowdfunding, the rules:
    - **a.** Preclude the use of crowdfunding by certain entities, including non-U.S. companies, companies that must report under the Exchange Act, companies that have no specific business plan, companies that plan to merge with or acquire another unspecified company, certain investment companies, and companies that fail to comply with SEC reporting requirements
    - **b.** Require all crowdfunding transactions take place through an SEC-registered broker-dealer or funding portal
    - **c.** Limit the amount a company may raise through crowdfunding during any 12-month period to a maximum of $1 million
    - **d.** Require certain reporting by the company, including information about the business, the intended use of funds raised, the security price and the total offering amount; a

discussion of the company's financial condition and disclosure of its financial statements; information about officers, directors, owners of 20% or more of the company and certain related party transactions

2. **Investor-related requirements**—For investors participating in crowdfunding, the rules:

    a. Limit the amount an individual investor may invest in offerings to:

        i. If the investor's annual income or net worth is less than $100,000, the greater of:

        > $2,000, or

        > 5% of the lesser of their annual income or net worth

        ii. If the investor's annual income or net worth is equal to or greater than $100,000, 10% of the lesser of their annual income or net worth

    b. Limit the maximum amount an investor may invest in all crowdfunding equity offerings during a 12-month period to $100,000

    c. Generally imposes a one-year holding requirement before the securities may be resold

Cost of Capital and Financing Strategies

Capital structure consists of long-term sources of financing. Each of those sources has a cost associated with its use. A number of factors determine the cost of each element of capital. This lesson summarizes factors that enter into that determination and then identifies guidelines for appropriate financing strategies.

After studying this lesson, you should be able to:

1. Identify and describe factors that influence the cost of capital.
2. Identify and describe the guidelines appropriate in developing financial strategies.

I. Cost of Capital—Summary Concepts and Relationships

A. Long-term financing is provided by those sources of capital funding that do not mature within one year. Thus, these sources include long-term notes, financial leases, bonds, preferred stock and common stock (including retained earnings), as well as variations (hybrids) of these kinds of securities. Although computed differently, the cost of obtaining capital from each of these sources is the rate of return that each source requires, which is based on the returns available from other comparable investments in the market—the investors' opportunity cost. While the cost of each element of capital will be unique for each firm, some of the general relationships that influence these costs can be identified:

1. **Macroeconomic conditions**—Includes market conditions and expectations concerning economic factors such as interest rates, tax rates, and inflation/deflation rates. Increasing interest rates, tax rates and inflation, or expectation thereof, will result in a higher cost of capital.
2. **Past performance of the firm**—Reflects management's operating and financial decisions and the riskiness associated with those decisions. The greater the inferred risk inherent in past performance, the higher the risk premium required and, therefore, the cost of capital.
3. **Amount of financing**—Recognizes that the larger the absolute amount of financing sought, the higher the cost of capital.
4. **Relative level of debt financing**—Recognizes that at some level of debt financing increasing financing sought through debt will increase the cost of marginal debt and result in increasing the cost of capital.
5. **Debt maturity**—Recognizes that the longer the maturity of debt, the higher the cost of capital. The longer the debt, the greater the risk of interest rate changes, thus, lenders charge a maturity premium for that risk.
6. **Debt security**—Recognizes that the greater the value of collateral relative to the amount of debt, the lower the interest rate, or cost of capital.

B. Historic Rates of Return

1. Rates of return earned historically by investors on various forms of investment provide insight into the relative average cost of each element of capital over long periods of time. For example, one study (Ibbotson & Sinquefield) shows the following long-run annual rates of return:

Security Type	Annual Rate of Return
Long-Term Corporate Bonds	5.9%
Common Stock	12.3
Common Stock—Small Firms	17.6 (Others have shown as low as 12.7%)

2. Since preferred stock has characteristics of both bonds and common stock, the rate of return on preferred stock reasonably could be expected to be greater than that of bonds, but less than that of common stock.

II. Financing, Leverage and Business Risk—The mix of capital financing affects not only the cost of capital but also the business risk of the firm. Financial leverage is a measure of risk as the level of debt financing increases.

A. In a business context, leverage is the use of borrowing, cost structure, or other arrangement to increase the potential benefit derived from an undertaking, operation, or position. Two types of leverage are common in financial management:

1. **Operating leverage**—Measures the degree to which a firm incurs fixed cost in its operations.

   a. If fixed cost are high, a significant decrease in sales can dramatically affect operating results. Therefore, all other things equal, the greater a firm's fixed cost, the greater its business risk.

   b. On the other hand, if sales increase for a firm with a high degree of operating leverage, there will be a larger increase in return on equity.

   c. The following formula is used to compute the degree of operating leverage (DOL):

   DOL = % change in operating income/% change in unit volume

   d. Notice that the numerator uses operating income, which does not consider financing expense.

2. **Financial leverage**—Measures the extent to which a firm uses debt financing.

   a. Generally, debt is a less costly form of financing than equity; therefore, a firm would like to use as much debt financing as is reasonable so as to produce higher returns to shareholders.

   b. However, as more and more debt is issued, the risk associated with it increases. This increases the cost (interest rate) on additional debt to compensate lenders for the increased risk. It also increases the risk to shareholders that the interest payments and/or principal repayment cannot be met.

   c. The following formula is used to compute the degree of financial leverage (DFL):

   DFL = % change in EPS/% change in EBIT

   Where: EPS = Earnings per share

   EBIT = Earnings before interest and taxes

III. Financing Strategies

A. At any point in time, a firm's historic financing strategy is evident in its balance sheet. The assets show the results of the firm's accumulated investment in projects and other undertakings, and the liabilities and shareholders' equity sections show how the firm's undertakings have been financed. For any new undertaking the firm generally will have several alternative means of financing it. Although the best financing alternative will depend on all the facts and circumstances existing at the time, certain guidelines for appropriate financing strategy exist. These guidelines include:

1. **Hedging principle of financing**—This guideline (also called the principle of self-liquidating debt) holds that long-term or permanent investments in assets should be financed with long-term or permanent sources of capital and short-term needs should be financed with short-term sources of financing. Thus, long-term assets (e.g., property, plant, and equipment, among others) and permanent amounts of current assets (e.g., level of accounts receivable and inventory generally on hand) should be financed with long-term debt or equity. Conversely, temporary investments in assets (e.g., a temporary increase in inventory to meet seasonal demand) should be financed with temporary sources of financing. **The objective of this principle is to match cash flows from assets with the cash requirements need to satisfy the related financing.**

2. **Optimum capital structure objective**—This guideline seeks to minimize a firm's aggregate cost of permanent (long-term) capital financing by using an optimum (or satisfying) mix of debt and equity components. Since a corporation will have common stock, a major issue is how much debt financing it should use relative to its equity financing. As noted above, basic long-term debt financing is less costly than common stock financing. (This is logical, if for no other reason than that the tax shield resulting from debt expense—interest—is tax deductible, while the cost of common stock—dividends—is not.) Therefore, firms will be motivated to use increasing amounts of long-term debt for financing; this is the concept of financial leverage. However, at some level of relative debt the increased risk of default associated with the debt will result in debt investors demanding such a high return (default premium) that the cost of debt may be greater than the cost of common stock. **The objective in structuring the firm's capital mix is to determine the set or sets of capital sources that result in the lowest composite cost of capital for the firm.**
3. **Business risk constraint**—This guideline recognizes that a firm with higher variability in its operating results should limit the extent to which it uses debt financing (i.e., financial leverage). Business risk derives from the uncertainty inherent in the nature of the operations of the business and would be affected by such things as macroeconomic conditions, degree of competition, size, diversification, and operating leverage, etc. This risk is measured in terms of the variability of a firm's expected operating earnings (earnings before interest and taxes, known as EBIT). The higher the variation, the greater the risk. **Firms with a higher level of business risk have an increased chance that operating results may cause default on fixed obligations and, therefore, should use less debt financing than a firm with steady operating results.**
4. **Tax rate benefit effect**—This guideline recognizes that, other things being equal, the higher the tax rate of a firm, the greater the benefit of debt financing. Because the cost of debt—that is, interest—is tax deductible, it generates a tax benefit. **Therefore, the higher the tax rate faced by a firm, the greater the amount of tax saved from the use of debt financing compared to using equity financing.**

B. These guidelines should be taken into account in deciding the nature and mix of resources used by a firm in financing its projects and operations.

IV. Summary—This section has considered the major options available to a firm for financing its capital projects and its ongoing operations. It has considered the nature of a firm's financial and capital structure, the short-term and long-term sources and cost of financing available, and the advantages and disadvantages of each. Finally, guidelines for an effective financing strategy have been identified and described.

Working Capital Management

Introduction to Working Capital Management

As described in earlier lessons, working capital components—current assets and current liabilities—represent sources of short-term financing. Effective management of those working capital elements not only optimizes that financing role, but it also enhances the operating functions of a firm. This lesson defines and describes working capital, the objectives of working capital management, and it identifies elements of working capital to be considered in detail in subsequent lessons.

After studying this lesson, you should be able to:

1. Define working capital and its components.
2. Describe the general objective of working capital management.

I. Working Capital

Definition

Working Capital (also called Net Working Capital): The difference between a firm's current assets and its current liabilities. Expressed in a formula it is: Working Capital = Current Assets – Current Liabilities

II. Current Assets and Current Liabilities—Current assets and current liabilities are considered short-term balance sheet elements, defined for purposes here as follows:

Definitions

Current Assets: Cash and other resources expected to be converted to cash, sold, or consumed within one year.

Current Liabilities: Obligations due to be settled within one year.

III. Definitions—While these definitions are consistent with those used in accounting and the included individual assets and obligations existing at any point in time are considered short-term, the amounts committed to current assets, and the financing provided by current liabilities each include an amount that is permanent in nature. As an example, although inventory is likely to turn over and fluctuate during the year, there will always be some minimum amount of resources invested in inventory. Similarly, trade accounts payable will be paid and new ones incurred during the year, but there is some minimum amount of financing provided by trade payables throughout the year. These minimum amounts are permanent uses (assets) and sources (liabilities) of financing.

IV. Objective—The **objective** in managing working capital is to maintain adequate working capital in order to:

- A. **Meet ongoing operating and financial needs** of the firm, for example:
  1. **Inventory**—To meet production requirements
  2. **Cash**—To meet obligations as they come due.
- B. **Not overinvest** in net working capital (assets) which provide low returns or increase costs, for example:
  1. **Excess idle cash**—which has a low rate of return, if any

2. **Excess accounts receivable**—which do not earn interest
3. **Excess inventory**—which both incurs storage costs and risks becoming obsolete

V. **Management of Net Working Capital**—Provides another illustration of the trade-off between risk and reward in financial management. Sufficient net working capital must be maintained to avoid the risk of interrupting operations and the ability to meet current obligations, but over-investment in net working capital reduces the rewards, which could be recognized by the firm through investment in assets with greater returns.

A. The following lessons discuss the management of the **major elements of working capital including**:

1. Cash
2. Marketable securities
3. Accounts receivable
4. Inventories
5. Current liabilities

B. The focus is on current assets both because of their differences and because the use of current liabilities as a means of short-term financing was discussed in the earlier section. Nevertheless, a summary discussion of the management of current liabilities will conclude this section.

Cash Management

Since cash is pervasive in carrying out business activities, strategies for the management of cash are essential to the short-term stability of a firm and to its long-term prosperity. This lesson describes a number of techniques available for use to accelerate the collection of cash and to control the outflow of cash, the central objectives of cash management.

After studying this lesson, you should be able to:

1. Define cash and describe the basis for determining cash requirements.
2. Describe ways of accelerating and controlling cash inflows.
3. Describe ways of deferring and controlling cash outflows.

I. Introduction to Cash Management (or Treasury Management)

Definition
Cash (the most liquid of assets): Considered to consist of all currency, coins and other demand instruments (checks, money orders, etc.) held either on hand (e.g., day's receipts, change fund, petty cash fund, etc.) or in demand deposit accounts with financial institutions.

A. **Cash Objective**—Since cash (per se) provides little or no return (and will lose real value during inflation), firms seek to maintain a minimum cash balance consistent with meeting its debt and other obligations as they come due. Holding too much cash will result in loss of return to the firm.

B. **Cash Budgets**—The basis for determining a firm's cash needs is its cash budget, which shows expected cash receipts and disbursements for each budget period. If the projected cash balance is higher than the needed amount, management can plan to make investments or pay down existing debt. On the other hand, if a cash shortage is projected, management can either reduce cash requirements, make plans to borrow, or otherwise plan for the shortfall. In order to monitor these cash balances, large firms prepare daily cash reports so that excess cash can be invested and cash shortages provided for. Because management projections of the amount and timing of cash inflows and outflows may prove incorrect, firms must invest in some amount of cash to hedge that uncertainty.

C. **Cash Inflows/Outflows**—Within the context of its target cash balance firms will seek to accelerate cash inflows and defer cash outflows in order to have cash available for a longer period so that it can be invested in higher return projects or undertakings. For example, the claim to cash reflected by accounts receivable does not provide the return to the firm that would result from collecting the account and investing the cash in inventory or a capital undertaking.

In the News—"Cash management tools," says Bob Seiwert, a senior vice president of the American Bankers Association, are designed to help "get the money in quickly but not pay it out until you absolutely have to"—a tried-and-true cash-flow strategy.

(Excerpted from "How to Manage Your Cash Better," *Inc., The Magazine for Growing Companies* [December 2010/January 2011], p. 67.)

II. Accelerating and Controlling Cash Inflows

A. The time between when a firm establishes a claim to cash (e.g., as a result of providing goods or services) and when that cash is available to the firm to reinvest should be as short as possible. As noted above, a claim to cash, whether in the debtor's accounts payable or en route to the firm's bank account, does not provide a return to the firm. Therefore, the firm should establish policies and procedures to reduce this time period, and to simultaneously provide security of the cash.

B. Efforts to encourage prompt payment by debtors will be discussed in the next lesson on accounts receivable management. Here we are concerned with reducing the time from when a customer initiates payment until the cash is available for use by the receiving firm, a time period commonly referred to as (incoming) float. This period of float may be reduced by:

1. **Lockbox system**—Under a lockbox collection system, the firm leases post office boxes in areas where it has a high volume of payments through the mail. Customers remit payment to those post office boxes ("locked boxes"). The firm's bank collects the remittances from the lockboxes and processes and deposits the checks directly to the firm's account(s). The bank then notifies the firm of the sources and amounts collected so that the firm can update its cash and receivables accounts. A lockbox arrangement may reduce the float from seven (or more) days to two or three days, depending on the circumstances.
   - **a.** The resulting benefits are:
     - **i.** Cash is available for use sooner than it would be otherwise.
     - **ii.** The firm's time spent handling collections drops considerably, resulting in less cost and greater security.
     - **iii.** Reduced likelihood of dishonored checks and earlier identification of dishonored checks.
   - **b.** Firms with a high volume of receipts by mail should investigate the use of a lockbox system.
2. **Preauthorized checks**—As the title implies, under this arrangement cash is collected through checks that are authorized in advance. Such an arrangement would be especially appropriate for a firm to consider when its customers pay a fixed amount each period for many periods (e.g., rent or mortgage payments).
   - **a.** The basic process would involve:
     - **i.** Customer's authorization and indemnification agreement with the firm's bank
     - **ii.** Firm builds database with needed information
     - **iii.** Each period the firm prepares an electronic file and deposit slip and sends them to the bank.
     - **iv.** The bank prints checks, deposits funds to the firm's account, and processes checks through the clearing system.
   - **b.** In a more automated process, the bank would process the electronic file through the Automated Clearing House (ACH) network which would reduce the paying party's bank account and credit (add to) the receiving party's bank account, normally within 24 hours.
   - **c.** The use of preauthorized checks has several significant advantages:
     - **i.** Cash is available for use sooner and the amount is highly predictable.
     - **ii.** The firm's handling of collection is reduced considerably, resulting in less cost and greater security than a lockbox arrangement.
     - **iii.** Customers may appreciate not having to deal with periodic bills.
3. **Preauthorized debit/credit card charges**—Under a preauthorized debit or credit charge arrangement, cash is collected by a charge to a debit or credit card that has been authorized in advance. While the process is similar to the use of preauthorized checks, a bank is not a party to the authorization agreement.
   - **a.** The basic process would involve:
     - **i.** Customer provides firm with information and authorization for charges
     - **ii.** Firm charges debit/credit card as provided by authorization
     - **iii.** Firm provides customer with receipt, commonly by e-mail

iv. Firm's card processor submits charge through debit/credit card interchange system to:

1. Firm's bank to recognize amount in firm's account
2. Customer's card issuer to charge customer's account

v. Charged amount shows up on firm's bank statement as deposit and on customer's debit/credit card statement.

b. The use of preauthorized debit/credit cards has the same advantages as the use of preauthorized checks.

4. **Remote deposit**—Remote deposit (also called "Check 21" after the law that authorized its use) is a way to process checks received without sending those physical paper checks to the bank. With remote deposit, the entity receiving a check uses a special scanner to develop a digital image of the checks (called "check truncation," because the processing of the physical paper check stops at that point) and electronically sends the images to its bank where they are processed as a deposit. Among the benefits of remote depositing are:
   a. Elimination of the need to physically deliver paper checks to the bank for deposit
   b. Electronic check images generally clear faster resulting in funds deposited more quickly and bad checks detected sooner.
   c. Process can be integrated with the firm's accounting system (e.g., cash and accounts receivable accounts)
   d. Digital images of processed checks and deposits are available without the need to prepare duplicate paper copies.
5. **Concentration banking**—Concentration banking is used to accelerate the flow of cash to a firm's principal bank. That flow is achieved by having customers remit payment and company units making deposits to banks close to their locations. The funds collected in the multiple local bank accounts are transferred regularly, and often automatically, to the firm's account in its primary (or concentration) bank. The benefits of concentration banking are similar to those resulting from a lockbox arrangement and, in fact, a lockbox system can incorporate concentration banking. The benefits of concentration banking include:
   a. Cash available for use sooner than it would be otherwise.
   b. Excess cash from multiple locations flow to a single account (or bank) for better control and use.
   c. Arrangements can be made with the concentration bank to automatically invest cash in excess of needed amounts.
   d. A variation, called "sweeping" takes excess funds from accounts, even within the same bank, at the end of each work day and either invests those funds for very short periods of time (even overnight) in money market funds or other instruments, or uses them to pay down lines of credit.
6. **Depository transfer checks/official bank checks**
   a. Depository transfer checks, also called "official bank checks," are used to transfer funds between a firm's accounts. Depository transfer checks are unsigned, non-negotiable, and payable only to an account of the firm. For example, in a manual system, at the time a unit of the firm makes a deposit at a local bank, it also prepares and sends a depository transfer check to its principal (and perhaps, concentration) bank. The receiving bank deposits the funds to the firm's account and processes the depository check back to the local bank where funds were deposited by the firm's unit.
   b. As an alternative to traditional processing of depository transfer checks, an automated system exists which transmits the deposit information electronically to the principal bank where the actual check is prepared and processed, and the funds deposited to the firm's

account. Under either the traditional or the automated process, funds normally are not available for the firm to use until the depository transfer check actually clears the local bank.

c. Using depository transfer checks is an efficient way of transferring funds between a firm's banks, especially when an automated transfer system is used. Depository transfer checks may be used in conjunction with a lockbox and/or concentration banking arrangement(s).

7. **Wire transfer**—Wire transfer is an electronic means of transferring funds between banks. The Federal Reserve Bank Wire System and a private wire service operate in the United States. Because it is a relatively expensive method of transferring funds, wire transfers should be used only for large transfers, for example, as a means of moving large sums in a concentration banking arrangement. (See also "Electronic Funds Transfer," below.)

C. **Summary**—This subsection has described the procedures that a firm can use to speed up its collection of cash or the transfer of cash between the firm's banks. The basic purpose of such procedures is to make cash available sooner so that it can be put to work earning a return. The next subsection looks at ways the payment of cash can be deferred and controlled.

III. **Deferring and Controlling Cash Outflows**—The central objectives of deferring and controlling cash outflows are to make cash available to the firm for a longer period and to control cash disbursements. Several methods are identified and described.

A. **Managing the Purchases/Payment Process**

1. This topic recognizes that certain things can be done to conserve cash both before and after obligations are incurred. These include:

a. Establish and use charge accounts rather than paying cash. This would include the use of credit cards, which can be limited in amount and types of purchases permitted.

b. Select suppliers that provide generous deferred payment terms.

c. Do not pay bills before they are due, except to take advantage of discounts offered.

d. Stretch payments, which involves making payments after the established due date. This would be appropriate where it is customary in the industry and where there are no adverse financial affects or where impairment of credit rating would not result.

B. **Remote Disbursing**—Remote disbursing is intended to increase the float on checks used to pay obligations. By increasing the float, cash is available longer to the paying firm. It is accomplished by establishing checking accounts in remote locations and paying bills with checks drawn on those accounts. Therefore, even when the entity being paid receives the payment check in a timely manner, it takes longer for the check to clear the account of the paying firm. Thus, it has use of the funds for a longer period of time. Practically, electronic processing and banking requirements have pretty much eliminated the usefulness of remote banking for delaying account reduction for any significant period of time.

C. **Zero Balance Accounts**

1. The use of zero balance accounts is based on an agreement between the firm and a bank under which the firm has accounts with no real balance. Under one arrangement, checks written on these accounts are processed as usual, resulting in overdrawn accounts, but by agreement with the bank these overdrafts are covered automatically, usually at the end of each day, by transfers from a master account. Thus, at the end of each day, these accounts have no balance.

2. Under a different application of zero balance accounts, after a firm determines an amount to be paid from an account—for example, the monthly payroll—an amount equal to the payments is deposited into the account. Therefore, the account has no real balance since any outstanding checks are exactly equal to the account balance.

3. The benefits of zero balance accounts include:

a. Near elimination of excess cash balances in those accounts

b. Very little administration required, e.g., monitoring and reconciling accounts

c. Possible increase in payment float through use of zero balance accounts in remote banks

D. Payment through Draft—Like a check, a draft is an order to pay. But unlike a check which is drawn on an account of the writer, a draft is drawn on (payable from) an account of a bank (or other entity). In essence, a draft is a form of check that is guaranteed by the bank (or other entity) on which it is drawn.

1. **Common forms of draft include**:

   a. **Bank draft**—An order to pay drawn by a bank on itself or on a correspondent bank with which the issuing bank has an account. These kinds of drafts are used by banks dealing with other banks and are "sold" by banks to customers. When purchased, the customer pays the bank the amount of the draft (plus a fee) and the bank issues the customer a draft (check) drawn on itself or its account with another bank. Thus, the customer has a check that is guaranteed to be paid when presented. Bank drafts can be issued on an:

      i. **Individual basis**—A single draft for a specified amount

      ii. **Automatic basis**—Recurring drafts for a fixed amount issued periodically and charged to a customer's account

   b. **Cashier's check**—An order to pay drawn by a bank's cashier on an account of the bank (but not on the account of another bank). Functions the same way as a bank draft, as described above, except cashier's checks are drawn only on the bank that issues the check and are done only on an individual basis.

   c. **Certified check**—An order to pay in the form of a customer's check that has been "certified" as having the funds by the bank. When a bank certifies a check, it immediately withholds the amount of the check from the writer's account and the check becomes the bank's obligation to pay.

   d. **Money order**—An order to pay a sum of money, often sold by non-bank institutions (e.g., United States Postal Service, Western Union, etc.). Functions the same as a cashier's check, but usually has a limited dollar amount (e.g., $1,000 is a common limit).

2. **Benefits of payments by draft include**:

   a. Provides assurance to the payee that the instrument will be honored for its stated value.

   b. Except for certified checks, drafts do not disclose bank/checking account information to the recipient and, in fact, do not require a checking account.

   c. Automation of bank drafts facilitates the payment of recurring obligations of a fixed amount.

3. **Disadvantage of payments by draft**—The primary disadvantage of payment by draft is that they typically involve a fee that may make their use relatively expensive compared to payment by check.

E. Positive Pay System—These systems are offered by banks as a means of fraud detection for an entity's checking accounts.

1. Under a positive pay system, an entity electronically transmits to its bank a file for the checks it has issued. That file contains the entity's account number, check issue dates, check numbers and check amounts for all checks written.

2. When the entity's checks are presented at the bank for payment, they are compared electronically against the list provided by the entity.

3. If the elements of a check do not exactly match the file presented by the issuing entity, the bank treats the check as an exception item that is held until the issuing firm is contacted.

4. The bank provides the issuing firm, either electronically or by fax, information about the exception item.

5. The issuing firm can then either approve payment of the item or return the check through the banking system.

F. Electronic Funds Transfers (EFTs)—As the title implies, an electronic funds transfer is an electronic means of transferring funds similar to wire transfer, but used in a broader context. Rather than payments occurring through the use of checks or drafts, payments are initiated and processed based on the transfer of computer files between entities.

Example

A company prepares a file of payments to vendors with all applicable information and transmits the file electronically to its bank. The bank then reduces the firm's account and forwards the payments electronically through the Automated Clearing House (ACH) system, which routes payments electronically to the accounts of individual vendors, employees, etc.

1. The advantages of electronic fund transfers include

- **a.** Drastically reduced float, so firms can defer payments until they are due and still ensure payments are received when due.
- **b.** Much of the administration can be routine and integrated with a firm's larger accounting and information system, thus reducing cost and errors.
- **c.** Very low transaction fee costs, especially when compared to traditional check writing and mailing.

G. Summary—This subsection has looked at ways the outflow of cash can be deferred and better controlled so that cash is available for use longer than it would be otherwise and so that lower cost and better security are provided in the management of cash. The next lesson looks at the management of marketable securities, a separate item of working capital.

Short-Term Securities Management

Cash in excess of immediate needs should be "put to work" by investing it to earn a return. Appropriate short-term investment securities require selection in a prudent manner so as not to put the firm's cash position at risk. This lesson describes the objective in choosing short-term investments and identifies a variety of instruments that may be suitable.

After studying this lesson, you should be able to:

1. Identify and describe guidelines for short-term investments.
2. Identify and describe various short-term investment opportunities and instruments.

I. **Temporary Excess Cash**—When a firm has temporary excess cash, it should invest those funds so as to earn a return greater than would be provided by "idle cash." Because the funds so invested will be needed in the near term to satisfy obligations or to invest in planned undertakings, management must be prudent in the use of such investments. The following considerations will be of major concern in selecting short-term investments:

   A. **Safety of Principal**—Investments should have little risk of default by the issuer. Default risk is a measure of the likelihood that the issuer will not be able to make future interest and/or principal payments to a security holder. Temporary investments should be in securities with a low risk of default, U.S. Treasury issues, for example.

   B. **Price Stability**—Investments should not be subject to market price declines that would result in significant losses if the securities were sold for cash. Investments in most debt instruments have an associated interest rate risk, the risk that derives from the relationship between the rate of interest paid by a security and the changing rate of interest in the market. Specifically, the market value of an existing debt instrument varies inversely with changes in the market rate of interest. Thus, the interest rate risk is that the market rate of interest will increase, resulting in a decrease in the market value of an investment. If sold, that investment would incur a loss and, as a result, less cash would be available. Investing in securities that mature in a short period mitigates this risk.

   C. **Marketability/Liquidity**—Investments should be in instruments that have a ready market for converting securities to cash (i.e., liquidating the securities) without incurring undue cost. Thus, thinly traded (e.g., closely held) securities, or those with a high cost of premature conversion (e.g., some certificates of deposit), should be avoided.

   D. **Other Factors**—That may enter into the short-term investment decision, but are usually of much less concern, include:

      1. Taxability—Whether or not the investment income is taxable
      2. Diversification—The extent to which risk is reduced by having multiple investments that are not highly correlated with each other so that the positive performance of some investments will offset the negative performance of other investments
      3. Cost of administering—The cost incurred to make and maintain investments, including brokerage fees, management fees, and custodial fees

II. **Investment Opportunities**—A variety of opportunities is available for short-term investments in what is referred to as the money market. The primary investments in the money market include:

   A. **U.S. Treasury Bills**—Considered virtually risk-free, these direct obligations of the U.S. Government are available in increments of $5,000 with a minimum $10,000 investment. With maturities of 3 months (91 days), 6 months (182 days), and 1 year (365 days), they are periodically available directly through Federal Reserve Banks and they are continuously available in the secondary market. U.S. Treasury Bills provide:

      1. Safety of principal
      2. Price stability if held to (short) maturity
      3. Marketability/liquidity

B. Federal Agency Securities

1. These securities are obligations of a federal government agency (such as the Federal National Mortgage Association ["Fannie Mae"], Federal Home Loan Bank, Federal Land Bank, and others) that are the responsibility of the agency; these securities are not backed by the good faith and credit of the federal government. As a consequence, these securities are perceived as having slightly more risk than Treasury obligations.

2. In addition, they are not as marketable as Treasury obligations. Therefore, the securities of these agencies have slightly higher yields to compensate for the higher default risk and lower marketability. These securities are offered in various denominations and with a wide range of maturities. The secondary market for these securities is good (while the secondary market for Treasury obligations is excellent).

C. Negotiable Certificates of Deposit—These securities are issued by banks in return for a fixed time deposit with the bank. The securities pay a fixed rate of interest and are available in a variety of denominations and maturities. Unlike conventional certificates of deposit, negotiable certificates of deposit can be bought and sold in a secondary market. Therefore, if a holder needs cash before maturity, rather than incurring an interest penalty by "cashing in" the certificate, it can be sold in the secondary market at little or no penalty. These securities offer a high safety of principal and relatively short-term stability, but somewhat less marketability than Treasury or federal agency obligations.

D. Bankers' Acceptances—A banker's acceptance is a draft (or order to pay) drawn on a specific bank by a firm that has an account with the bank. If the bank accepts the draft, it becomes a negotiable debt instrument of the bank and is available for investment. The primary use of bankers' acceptances is in the financing of foreign transactions. Bankers' acceptances are issued in denominations that relate to the value of the transaction for which the acceptance was made. Maturities typically are from 30 days to 180 days. Because acceptances have a higher risk and less marketability than Treasury or Federal agency obligations, they have a higher yield than those securities.

E. Commercial Paper—Commercial paper consists of short-term unsecured promissory notes issued by large, established firms with high credit ratings. Commercial paper is available in a variety of denominations, either directly from the issuing firm or dealers, and can be purchased with maturities from a few days up to 270 days. The secondary market for commercial paper is very limited and is usually restricted to dealers in the paper. Because of the lack of marketability, commercial paper provides a yield greater than other short-term instruments with comparable risk, but usually still less than the prime rate of interest.

F. Repurchase Agreements (Repos)

1. In a repurchase agreement the firm makes an investment (a loan) and simultaneously enters into a commitment to resell the security at the original contract price plus an agreed interest income for the holding period. These agreements are usually for large denominations and have maturities specified in each agreement. The yield available is usually less than available on Treasury bills, but may offer advantages of liquidity and very short maturity.

2. The major benefits of investing in repurchase agreements are:

   a. The time of the agreement (maturity) can be adjusted to any length, including as short as one day.

   b. Since the agreement provides for resale of the investment at the original price (plus interest), the risk of market price declines is avoided.

3. These benefits make repurchase agreements a viable investment option, especially for very short-term uses of excess cash.

III. Investment Assessment—As described above, a firm has a variety of options available for short-term investment opportunities. In selecting from among those opportunities, the firm will consider such factors as safety of principal, price stability and liquidity of the various investments. The objective in considering such factors is to minimize the risk associated with the investment, while seeking to earn a competitive rate of return. Thus, the making of short-term (or long-term) investments illustrates the risk-reward trade-off discussed earlier for capital project investments.

A. The risk-reward relationship reflects that the greater the perceived risk inherent in an opportunity, the greater the reward expected from an investment in the opportunity.

B. In making short-term investments of temporary excess cash, a firm likely will give priority to avoiding risk, rather than maximizing return.

C. **Coefficient of Variation**—One measure used to assess the risk-reward relationship (for either short-term or long-term investments) is the coefficient of variation.

1. The coefficient of variation is a measure of the relative variability (or dispersion) of return values around the mean return; it can be thought of as a measure of the total risk per unit of return.
2. The coefficient of variation ratio is computed as:

Coefficient of variation (CV) = SD/AR

Where: SD = Standard deviation of investment average return (which is a common measure of how much an investment deviates from its average performance; that is, its volatility.)

AR = Average rate of return of investment

Example

The common stock of X Company has a 10% average return with a standard deviation of 20%. What is the coefficient of variation (CV) for X's common stock?

CV = .20/.10

= 2.0

3. The lower an investment's coefficient of variation, the better its total risk-return trade off. If the AR (used as the denominator) is zero or negative, the resulting ratio (coefficient) will not be valid and the CV cannot be used to assess risk for that investment.

D. **Sharpe Ratio**—another measure used to assess the risk-reward relationship (for either short-term or long-term investments) is the Sharpe ratio (or Sharpe index).

1. The Sharpe ratio measures how well the average return on an investment compensates for the risk of the investment; it can be thought of as a measure of the excess return (reward) per unit of risk.
2. The ratio is computed as:

Sharpe ratio = (AR – RR)/SD

Where: AR = Average rate of return of investment

RR = Average risk-free rate of return

SD = Standard deviation of investment average return (which is a common measure of how much an investment deviates from its average performance; that is, its volatility)

Example

The common stock of X Company has a 10% average return with a standard deviation of 20%. The current risk-free rate measured by the return on T-Bills is 2%. What is the Sharpe ratio for X's common stock?

Sharpe ratio = (.10 – .02)/.20

= .08/.20

= .40

3. The greater an investment's Sharpe ratio, the better its risk-adjusted performance. A negative ratio indicates that an investment with no risk would perform better than the investment being analyzed.
4. When used to compare securities or portfolios in the same macroeconomic environment (thus, having the same risk-free rate) and for the same time period, the risk-free rate is often ignored and only the average return used as the numerator in the calculation.
5. In using the Sharpe ratio for a portfolio of securities (i.e., a group of securities taken together), the average return (AR) would be measured using weighted average return for the portfolio and the standard deviation of the excess portfolio returns.
6. In using the Sharpe ratio to analyze security or portfolio returns over a long period of time (or during a shorter period during which returns vary significantly), the geometric mean (average) of the returns should be used instead of a weighted average.

Accounts Receivable Management

Accounts receivable results from a decision to sell goods or services on credit. Management of the resulting receivables requires the adoption of a set of credit and collection policies. This lesson describes the role of accounts receivable and the decisions and processes needed to manage those receivables.

After studying this lesson, you should be able to:

1. Describe the general terms of credit elements that an entity must establish.
2. Describe the means of determining the credit worthiness and credit limits for customers.
3. Describe the ways of monitoring and collecting accounts receivable.
4. Describe the special issues associated with receivables from foreign customers and how to address those issues.
5. Identify the quantitative measures useful in managing accounts receivable.

I. Introduction

A. For many businesses, accounts receivable account for a significant portion of current assets, and in some cases up to 25% of total assets. For these firms, effective management of accounts receivable is essential not only for profitability, but also for viability. For any firm that sells goods or services on account, how it manages its credit and collection process plays a role in the firm's success (or failure).

B. From an accounting perspective, accounts receivable management is concerned with the conditions leading to the recognition of receivables (the debit) and the process that results in eliminating the receivable (the credit). Therefore, this lesson will consider:

1. Establishing general terms of credit
2. Determining customer creditworthiness and setting credit limits
3. Collecting accounts receivable

II. Establishing General Terms of Credit—If sales are to be made on credit, the firm must establish the general terms under which such sales will be made. To a certain extent, for competitive reasons the terms of sale adopted by a firm will need to approximate terms established in its industry. Specific terms of sale decisions to be made include:

A. Total Credit Period—Establishes the maximum period for which credit is extended. Typical industry practice reflects that the length of the credit period relates to the "durability" of goods sold. For example, firms that sell perishable goods (e.g., fresh produce) typically have a shorter credit period than firms that sell more durable goods. This credit period establishes the length of time the firm is expected to finance its sales on credit and for which it must, in turn, have financing.

B. Discount Terms for Early Payment—If a discount is to be offered for early payment of accounts, the discount rate and period must be decided. The combination of the discount rate and period will determine the effective interest rate associated with the discount offered which, in turn, will determine the effectiveness of the discount policy. As we saw in the earlier discussion of trade accounts payable, the effective interest rate on cash discounts not taken usually are significant. For example:

2/10, n/30 = 2% discount if paid within 10 days = 36.7% APR

5/10, n/30 = 5% discount if paid within 10 days = 94.74% APR

1. The rate and period a firm can economically offer depends on the margin realized on its sales and its cost of financing its accounts receivable. Practically, the rate and period will need to be competitive with other firms in the industry.

C. Penalty for Late Payment—Determines the penalty to be assessed if customers don't pay by the final due date, including the length of any "stretch" period before the penalty applies. The penalty should at least cover the cost of financing the accounts receivable for the overdue period.

D. Nature of Credit Sales Documentation—Determines the form of documentation to be required from customers at the time they purchase on account. The most common arrangement is to sell on an open account, that is, an implicit contract documented only by a receipt signed by the buyer. If the amount being charged is very large or if the buyer's credit is suspect, a firm will likely require more formal documentation, such as a commercial draft. If foreign sales are to be made, appropriate processes will have to be decided upon.

III. Determining Customer Creditworthiness and Setting Credit Limits

A. The decisions here are to determine whether a customer can buy on account and, if so, what maximum amount can be charged. In making these decisions it is critical to recognize that the objective is to maximize profits, not to minimize credit losses. A policy that is too stringent will result in a failure to make sales that would be paid, resulting in lower losses on accounts receivable, but also resulting in lost revenues.

B. When a customer is considered for credit, there are two major approaches to determining whether to grant credit and at what level:

1. **Credit-rating service**—A number of firms are in the business of assessing the creditworthiness of individuals and businesses, including Equifax, Experian, TransUnion, and Dun and Bradstreet. Reports from these agencies provide considerable information about a potential credit customer, including a score that reflects relative creditworthiness. Such scores can be used in both making the credit decision and in establishing a credit limit. Other sources of information about prospective credit customers include trade associations, banks, and chambers of commerce, among others.
2. **Financial analysis**—In some cases, a firm may undertake its own analysis of a prospective credit customer. Since this can be an expensive undertaking, it is typically done only by large firms and in special circumstances where the seller wants a more direct understanding of the prospective credit customer. The analysis would rely on information from outside sources, but would incorporate the firm's own analysis, including financial ratios development from the prospect's financial information. Since the consideration is whether to extend short-term credit, the focus of the analysis will be on the prospect's short-term debt-paying ability.

In the News—*Dear Norm, So far this year, three of my customers have gone out of business without a formal bankruptcy proceeding. In each case, the bank—as the secured creditor—has taken all the assets and sold them off, leaving nothing for the trade creditors. If the case had gone to bankruptcy court, we would have gotten at least a portion of what we are owed. If this is a trend, it's going to mean trouble for companies like mine. Is there anything I can do about it? (Roger Cooper, Chief Financial Officer, Spectronics)*

Unfortunately, there are times when somebody else's unfair, unreasonable, or even unethical business practices are simply a cost of doing business. I'm afraid that Roger Cooper's problem with disappearing debtors fall into that category....

So what are his options? Aside from checking Dun & Bradstreet reports, I could think of only two. One is to have his salespeople try to get financial statements from customers before making the sale. You can tell from a company's balance sheet how much debt it has and thus how much credit risk you're taking on its receivables.... Roger's other option was to hire a specialized credit-checking firm that does in-depth analyses of customers' financial situations.

(Adapted from "Street Smarts," by Norm Brodsky in *Inc., The Magazine for Growing Companies*, December 2010/January 2011, p. 40.)

C. Once credit-granting decisions have been made and credit sales have occurred, the final area of accounts receivable management is collection.

IV. Collecting Accounts Receivable

A. The most significant risk faced in selling on credit is that a sale will be made, but not collected. Even with the best of screening processes, a business that sells on account can expect some loss from non-collection. The objective is to keep that post-sale loss to a minimum. To accomplish this, a firm must monitor its accounts receivable and take action where appropriate.

1. **Monitoring accounts receivable**—Collection management needs to monitor accounts receivable both in the aggregate and individually. Assessment of total accounts receivable is done with averages and ratios, including:
   - **a.** Average collection period
   - **b.** Day's sales in accounts receivable
   - **c.** Accounts receivable turnover
   - **d.** Accounts receivable to current or total assets
   - **e.** Bad debt to sales
2. Individual accounts receivable can be assessed using an aging of accounts receivable schedule. Such a schedule shows for each credit customer the amount owed by how long the amount has been due. A typical schedule would take the form:

	Not Due	30 Days Over	60 Days Over	90 Days Over…	Totals
Customer A	$	$	$	$	$

   - **a.** Since the probability of not collecting increases with the age of an amount due, overdue accounts need to be pursued promptly.
3. **Collection action**—When accounts are overdue, effective management requires action be taken, including:
   - **a.** Prompt "past due" billing
   - **b.** Dunning letters (demands for payment) with increasingly serious demands
   - **c.** Use of collection agency
4. These actions are not without a financial and, probably, a goodwill cost. Therefore, each case may need to be decided based on the amount involved and other considerations.

V. International Receivables—Sales on account and other receivables from foreign customers can present special collection issues. International differences in law, culture and customs may increase uncertainty as to the timing and/or collectibility of amounts due. Those differences call for special consideration when making sales or incurring accounts receivable from foreign customers.

A. Collection in Advance—Generally, collection in advance is not a reasonable expectation when making sales to foreign customers. Often, such customers are not comfortable with prepaying for goods or services not yet received. In addition, prepayment may not be feasible from a cash flow perspective. Therefore, purchases on-account are a common and expected option for foreign customers.

B. Open-Account Sales—While sales on account (accounts receivable) are common and generally secure from abuse within certain countries, and especially in the U.S., when used for international sales they can present special collection problems. If payment is not made by a foreign buyer, the domestic seller may face the following problems:

1. Pursuing collection in a foreign country, which may be difficult and costly
2. Dealing with a foreign legal system that may have different standards for such matters
3. There may be an absence of documentation and other support needed to successfully pursue a claim.

C. **Mitigating Foreign Collection Problems**—When sales are made on credit to foreign buyers, the most secure means of assuring collection is through the use of documentary letters of credit or documentary drafts.

1. These methods protect both the seller and the buyer.
2. These methods require that payment be made based on presentation of documents conveying title, and that specific procedures have been followed.
3. A documentary letter of credit adds a bank's promise to pay the exporter to that of the foreign buyer based on the exporter (domestic entity) complying with the terms and conditions of the letter of credit.
4. A documentary draft is handled like a check from a foreign buyer, except that title does not transfer to that buyer until the draft is paid.

Inventory Management

Inventory plays a role in the operation of manufacturing, retail, and most service businesses. Management of the inventory asset is central to these businesses. This lesson identifies and describes alternative inventory systems and presents certain quantitative techniques that can help manage inventory.

After studying this lesson, you should be able to:

1. Identify and describe the characteristics of the two general inventory management systems common in the United States.
2. Identify the benefits of a just-in-time inventory system.
3. Describe and compute: a) economic order quantity and b) reorder point.
4. Identify the quantitative measures useful in managing inventory.

I. Central Issue

A. The central issue in inventory management is to determine and maintain an optimum investment in all inventories. For a manufacturing firm, that includes raw materials, work-in-process, and finished goods; for a retail firm, it is goods for resale. As with other aspects of financial management, inventory management involves a risk-reward trade-off. In this case, the trade-off is between overinvesting in inventory so as to avoid shortages and incurring excessive cost, and underinvesting in inventory to save cost, but incurring the risk of shortages.

B. Two general approaches to systems of inventory management are currently common in the U.S.: the traditional materials requirement planning system and the just-in-time inventory system.

II. Traditional Materials Requirement Planning (MRP) System—This approach to manufacturing and inventory management has been predominant in the U.S. since the 1960 though in many firms it has been replaced by just-in-time systems in recent years. It is characterized by:

A. **Supply Push**—Goods are produced in anticipation of a demand for the goods. Therefore, the characteristics of the products available to the end user have already been decided—colors, features, sizes, etc.

B. **Inventory Buffers**—Because production is in anticipation of sales, inventories are maintained at every level in the process as buffers against unexpected increased demand. If demand is less than production, finished goods inventory accumulates.

C. **Production Characteristics**—MRP is based on long set-up times and long production runs; it is not flexible. It uses specialized labor and function-specific equipment.

D. **Supplier/Purchases Characteristics**—Relationships with suppliers are impersonal with purchases made through bids accepted from many suppliers. The low bid is usually accepted, regardless of the supplier's location. Purchases are normally made in large lots, which may be greater than what is immediately needed.

E. **Quality Management**—Quality standards are set at an acceptable level, allowing for a certain level of defects.

F. **Accounting Issues**—Traditional cost accounting is used with emphasis on job order and processing cost approaches. Multiple inventory accounts are used. Accounting involves complex cost accumulation and allocations, including setting standards, allocating costs, variance analysis and reporting.

III. Just-in-Time Inventory (JIT) Inventory System

A. This approach to manufacturing and inventory management originated in the Japanese auto industry (Toyota) and has been widely adopted in recent years to improve production and, especially, inventory management. As the term implies, the basis of the system is obtaining (supply side) and delivering (sell side) inventory just as or only when it is needed. It is characterized by:

1. **Demand pull**—Goods are produced only when there is an end-user demand. Goods are produced with the characteristics desired by the customer and in the quantity demanded.
2. **Inventory reduction**—The customers' demand pulls inventory through the production process in that each stage produces only what is needed by the next stage and outside purchases are made only as needed. Thus, excess raw materials, work-in-process and, ideally, finished goods inventories are greatly reduced or eliminated.
3. **Production characteristics**—Production occurs in work centers or cells in which the full set of operations to produce a product are carried out. Workers are trained to operate multiple pieces of equipment and robots are used where feasible. Each work center functions like a mini-factory.
4. **Supplier/purchases characteristics**—Close working relationships are developed with a limited number of suppliers to help coordinate operating interrelationships and to help assure timely delivery of quality inputs. The physical distance between supply source and production facilities is minimized. Goods are purchased only in the quantity needed to meet production demand and entered directly in the production process.
5. **Quality management**—Because inventory is squeezed out of every stage of the production process, inputs to the process must be high quality, otherwise a defective input likely would stop production. Therefore, there must be total control of quality of inputs. This is accomplished by working closely with suppliers to insure quality in their production process, as well as implementing quality practices within its own processes.
6. **Accounting issues**—JIT uses simplified cost accounting. It eliminates or combines inventory accounts because inventory is reduced or eliminated. Many more accounts are considered direct cost (e.g., material handling, equipment depreciation, and repairs and maintenance), thus reducing amounts allocated on a somewhat arbitrary basis. The accounting focuses less on variance analysis and more on aggregate measures, including days inventory on hand, return on assets, lead-time, and others.
7. **Summary**—In summary, just-in-time inventory systems and related production processes provide the following financial benefits:
   a. Reduced investment in inventory
   b. Lower cost of inventory transportation, warehousing, insurance, property taxes, and other related costs
   c. Reduced lead time in replenishing product inputs
   d. Lower cost of defects
   e. Less complex and more relevant accounting and performance measures

B. While just-in-time inventory and related production processes can provide significant benefits for many firms, the concepts and practices cannot be used by every firm and will not be appropriate for all processes of some firms. Firms that use a traditional materials requirement planning system or similar large lot production systems will be particularly concerned with the economic order quantity and the appropriate reorder point.

IV. Economic Order Quantity

A. There is a trade-off between inventory ordering cost and inventory carrying cost. Specifically, the larger the quantity ordered, the lower the per unit cost of ordering (clerical, transportation, handling, etc.), but the higher the carrying cost (warehousing, insurance, property taxes, financing costs, etc.). Determining the order size that will minimize total inventory cost is solved using the economic order quantity model. The basis for the model recognizes that:

Total Inventory Cost = Total Order Cost + Total Carrying Cost

1. Further:

Total order cost =	Number of orders	×	Per order cost
or, =	(Total units for period/order size)	×	Per order cost
or, =	T/Q	×	O
Total carrying cost =	Average inventory	×	Per unit carrying cost
or, =	(Order size/2)	×	Per unit carrying cost
or, =	Q/2	×	C

2. Therefore:

$$\text{Total inventory cost} = [(T/Q) \times O] + [(Q/2) \times C]$$

3. By rearranging to solve for Q, the economic order quantity (EOQ), we get:

$$EOQ = \sqrt{\frac{2\ TO}{C}}$$

4. To illustrate the application of this equation, assume the following for a firm's production period:

Total demand for input X = 10,000 units

Per order cost = $100

Per unit carrying cost = $2.00

$$EOQ = \sqrt{\frac{2 \times 10{,}000 \times 100}{2}} = \sqrt{\frac{2{,}000{,}000}{2}} = \sqrt{1{,}000{,}000} =$$

EOQ = 1,000

5. Therefore, the firm should order in lot sizes of 1,000 units to minimize its total cost of inventory acquisition.

B. The following assumptions are inherent in the economic order quantity model:

1. Demand is constant during the period.
2. Unit cost and carrying cost are constant during the period.
3. Delivery is instantaneous (or a safety stock is maintained).

C. To the extent these assumptions do not hold, formula modifications will need to be made.

V. Reorder Point

A. This analysis is concerned with determining the inventory quantity at which goods should be reordered. In a traditional materials requirement planning system, inputs tend to be acquired periodically and in large lots which are used over a long production period. At some remaining quantity new inputs must be ordered so as to be available before the current inventory runs out; that quantity is the reorder point.

B. The quantity at which inventory is reordered must be sufficient to continue production until the new order is delivered—the delivery time stock. In addition, a safety stock is usually maintained to hedge against unforeseen events (e.g., unexpected usage or unusual defects). Therefore, the reorder point can be expressed as:

Reorder Point = Delivery Time Stock + Safety Stock

C. To illustrate the application of this equation, assume the following for a firm:

Example

Annual usage equally over a 50-week year = 300,000 units

Delivery time = 2 weeks

Safety stock = 1,000 units

The weekly usage is: 300,000/50 weeks = 6,000 per week.

Therefore, the reorder point (RP) is:

RP = 6,000 per week × 2 weeks = 12,000 + 1,000 safety = 13,000 units

When the stock drops to 13,000 units, inventory should be reordered.

VI. Supply Chain Management

A. A supply chain is the entire sequence of processes involved in the sourcing, production, and distribution of a good. Every entity that contributes in any way to the final good is part of the supply chain.

B. Supply chain management is concerned with managing the flow of goods, services, information, and finances related to a particular product from the raw material stage through the delivery of the final output to the end user. It involves coordinating and integrating these flows both within and among entities. The primary objective of supply chain management is to meet end-user demand with the most efficient resource usage. Supply chain management often is used in the efficient management of inventory.

C. A key aspect of supply chain management is the sharing of information from final sale back through the supply chain so that all relevant parties are aware of the needs of each subsequent party in the supply chain. The intent of such sharing is to improve processes so as to reduce inventory, time, defects, and costs all along the supply chain.

VII. Inventory Management and Control—Management and control of inventory can be facilitated by the use of certain ratios, including:

A. Inventory turnover

B. Number of days' sales in inventory

C. See the later lessons in the "Ratio and Measures for Working Capital Management" subtopic.

Current Liabilities Management

Major current liabilities including trade accounts payable, accrued accounts payable, and short-term notes, were discussed at length in the section on "Short-Term (Working Capital) Financing." As was noted, current liabilities are forms of short-term financing, which implicitly must be satisfied (paid or restructured), in the short-term, usually using current assets. Although the material presented earlier will not be repeated here, some brief comments will be provided in summary.

After studying this lesson, you should be able to:

1. Describe the general concepts and guidelines related to the use and management of current liabilities.

I. Current Liabilities

A. Major current liabilities including trade accounts payable, accrued accounts payable, and short-term notes, were discussed at length in the "Short-Term (Working Capital) Financing" section. As was noted there, current liabilities are forms of short-term financing, which implicitly must be satisfied (paid or restructured) in the short term, usually using current assets.

B. The material presented earlier will not be repeated here, but some brief comments will summarize that material.

1. **Short-term liabilities**—Short-term liabilities are most appropriately incurred in connection with assets which will generate cash in the short term to repay the liability. This is the essence of the principle of self-liquidating debt, also called the hedging principle of financing.
2. **Permanent amount of financing**—Just as some amount of current assets is a permanent use of financing, some amount of current liabilities provides a permanent amount of financing. For example, to the extent a minimum balance always remains in trade accounts payable, that minimum amount is a form of permanent financing.
3. **Short-term borrowing**—Generally, short-term borrowing does not require collateral and does not impose restrictive covenants.
4. **Early payment**—Discounts offered for early payment of trade accounts payable are usually significant, many with an effective annual interest rate of over 30%, and should be taken if possible.
5. **Effective cost of borrowing**—If current liabilities (e.g., short-term notes, line of credit, etc.) require maintaining a compensating balance (greater than any balance that would otherwise be maintained with the institution), the effective cost of borrowing is greater than the stated cost.
6. **Standby financing**—A line of credit provides an effective means of arranging "standby" financing. The credit is prearranged and can be used when needed, thus reducing the cost associated with any idle borrowing.

II. Working Capital Management Coverage

II. Working Capital Management Coverage—Prior lessons have considered management of the major elements (or accounts) which comprise working capital, including management of:

A. Cash

B. Marketable securities

C. Trade accounts receivable

D. Inventories

E. Current liabilities

III. Working Capital Focus—The focus in prior lessons has been on the financial management of working capital elements, not the accounting for them. The general objective is to manage all of these elements so as to maximize the firm's use of resources and thereby increase its profitability.

Ratios and Measures for Working Capital Management

Introduction to Ratio Analysis

Ratios and related measures can be used to analyze financial and other information of an entity. These ratios and measures quantify relationships between financial and operating items to provide important summary indicators about a firm, which are useful to financial management and others. This lesson defines ratio analysis and points out some important concepts related to the use of ratios. Subsequent lessons cover the ratios and measures most commonly used and that are appropriate for the "Working Capital Management" topic.

This lesson contains supplemental documents:

1. Define ratio analysis, and describe the uses of ratio analysis.
2. Describe and apply the concepts that aid in the determination of ratios.

I. Ratio Analysis Defined

> **Definition**
> *Ratio Analysis*: The development of quantitative relationships between various elements of a firm's financial and other information.

> **Note**
> This and the immediately following lessons provide an introduction to and overview of a variety of ratio concepts. The focus, however, is on those ratios and measures that are particularly useful for financial management purposes, including the management of cash, accounts receivable, inventory, accounts payable, and other financial elements.
>
> A later lesson in the "Operations Measurement" subsection of BEC covers a broader range of ratios and measures, including those particularly useful for general management, investors, and analysts. That coverage includes use of the DuPont approach to assessing return on investment.

II. Ratio Analysis Purpose—Ratio analysis and related measures enable comparisons over time for a firm, across firms (especially within the same industry), and facilitate identifying operating and financial strengths and weaknesses of a firm.

III. Ratio Analysis Concepts—The following concepts are helpful in understanding and using ratio analysis and similar measures:

A. The names given to ratios and other measures usually indicate the elements to be used in the analysis.

> **Example**
> Debt to Equity ratio = Total **Debt** (Liabilities) / Owner's **Equity**

B. The name given to ratios frequently indicates the quantitative function to be performed. The terms "to" and "on" indicate dividing of the first item described by the second item described.

Example
Debt to Equity Ratio = Divide Debt by Equity

Return on Assets = Divide Net Income (the Return) by Assets

C. When using a balance sheet value with an income statement value, you must get the average balance for the balance sheet value. The income statement value is for the year; the balance sheet values are for points in time. Therefore, you need to average the balance sheet items.

Example
Accounts Receivable Turnover
= (Net) Credit Sales / Average (Net) Accounts Receivable (e.g., Beginning + Ending/2)

IV. Ratios and Measure Types—Ratios and related measures can be grouped according to the major purpose or type of measure being analyzed. The major purpose or types of measures fall into the following categories:

A. Liquidity/Solvency

B. Operational Activity

C. Profitability

D. Equity/Investment Leverage

Liquidity/solvency and operational activity ratios and measures are covered in the next lessons. Other types of ratios and measures are covered later in the "Operations Measurement" area.

Liquidity Measures

This lesson considers ratios and measures which assess the liquidity of a firm. Each measure is described and the method of calculation is illustrated.

After studying this lesson, you should be able to:

1. Define liquidity measures.
2. Identify and compute a number of common liquidity measures.

I. Liquidity Measures

Definition
Liquidity (*also known as Solvency*): Measures the ability of the firm to pay its obligations as they become due.

A. These measures are particularly appropriate for use in managing working capital.

II. Major Liquidity Measures

A. **Working Capital**—Measures the extent to which current assets exceed current liabilities and, thus, are uncommitted in the short term. It is expressed as:

Working Capital = Current Assets – Current Liability

B. **Working Capital Ratio** (also known as the current ratio)—Measures the quantitative relationship between current assets and current liabilities in terms of the "number of times" current assets can cover current liabilities. It is computed as:

Working Capital Ratio (WCR) = Current Assets / Current Liabilities

1. The WCR is a widely used measure of a firm's ability to pay its current liabilities.
2. Changes in current assets and/or current liabilities have determinable effects on the WCR:
    a. An increase in current assets (alone) increases the WCR.
    b. A decrease in current assets (alone) decreases the WCR.
    c. An increase in current liabilities (alone) decreases the WCR.
    d. A decrease in current liabilities (alone) increases the WCR.
    e. If the WCR equals 1.00, equal increases or equal decreases in current assets **and** liabilities will not change the WCR; it will remain 1.00.
    f. If the WCR **exceeds** 1.00, then:
        i. Equal increases in current assets **and** liabilities decrease the WCR.

Example
WCR = CA 20,000 / CL 10,000 = 2

WCR = (CA 20,000 + 10,000) / (CL 10,000 + 10,000) = 30,000 / 20,000 = 1.5

ii. Equal decreases in current assets **and** liabilities increase the WCR.

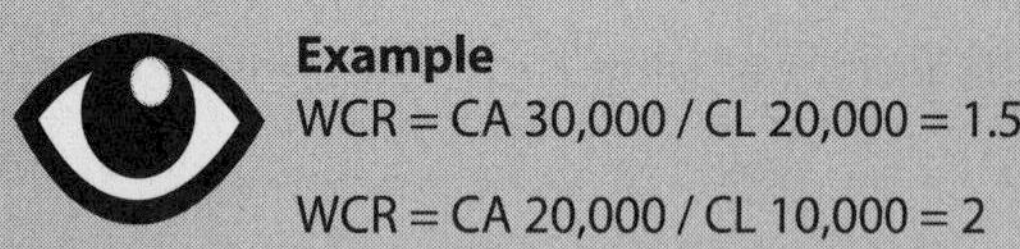

Example
WCR = CA 30,000 / CL 20,000 = 1.5

WCR = CA 20,000 / CL 10,000 = 2

g. If the WCR is **less** than 1.00 then:

i. Equal increases in current assets **and** liabilities increase the WCR.

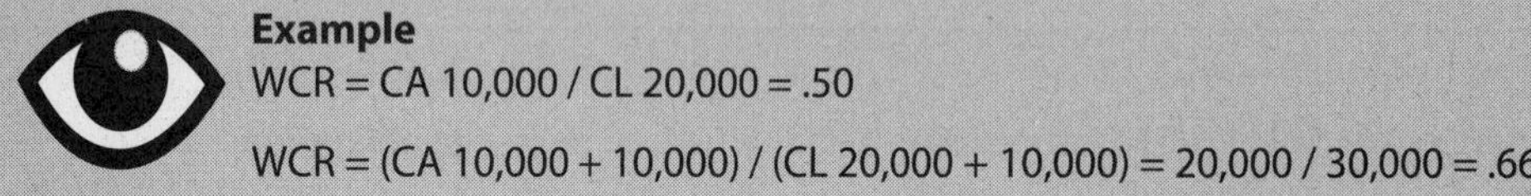

Example
WCR = CA 10,000 / CL 20,000 = .50

WCR = (CA 10,000 + 10,000) / (CL 20,000 + 10,000) = 20,000 / 30,000 = .66

ii. Equal decreases in current assets **and** liabilities decrease the WCR.

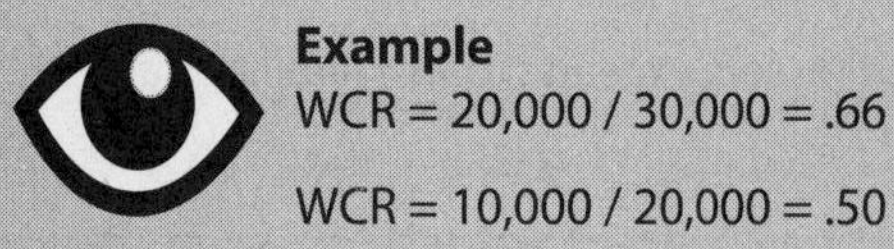

Example
WCR = 20,000 / 30,000 = .66

WCR = 10,000 / 20,000 = .50

C. **Acid Test Ratio** (also known as quick ratio)—Measures the quantitative relationship between highly liquid assets and current liabilities in terms of the "number of times" that cash and assets that can be converted quickly to cash cover current liabilities. It is computed as:

Acid Test Ratio = (Cash + (Net) Receivables + Marketable Securities) / Current Liabilities

D. **Defensive-Interval Ratio**—Measures the quantitative relationship between highly liquid assets and the average daily use of cash in terms of the number of days that cash and assets that can be quickly converted to cash can support operating costs. It is computed as:

Defensive-Interval Ratio =
(Cash + (Net) Receivable + Marketable Securities) / Average Daily Cash Expenditures

E. **Average Collection Period**—Measures the number of days on average it takes an entity to collect its accounts receivable; the average number of days required to convert accounts receivable to cash. It is computed as:

Average Collection Period = (Days in Year × Average Accounts Receivable) / Credit Sale for Period

F. Times Interest Earned Ratio—Measures the ability of current earnings to cover interest payments for a period. It is measured as:

> Times Interest Earned Ratio =
> (Net Income + Interest Expense + Income Tax Expense) / Interest Expense

G. Times Preferred Dividends Earned Ratio—Measures the ability of current earnings to cover preferred dividends for a period. It is computed as:

> Times Preferred Dividends Earned Ratio = Net Income / Annual Preferred Dividend Obligation

Operational Activity Measures

This lesson considers ratios and measures which assess the operational activities of a firm. Each measure is described and the method of calculation illustrated.

After studying this lesson, you should be able to:

1. Define operational activity measures.
2. Identify and compute a number of common operational activity measures.

I. Operational Activity Measures

Definition
Operation Activity Ratios: Measure the efficiency with which a firm carries out its operating activities.

II. Operational Activity Ratios—Operational activity ratios focus on measures that assess the management of accounts receivable, inventory, accounts payable, and related measures including:

A. Accounts Receivable Turnover—Measures the number of times that accounts receivable turnover (are incurred and collected) during a period. Indicates the quality of credit policies (and the resulting receivables) and the efficiency of collection procedures. It is computed as:

Accounts Receivable Turnover =
(Net) Credit Sales / Average (Net) Accounts Receivable (e.g.,(Beginning + Ending) / 2)

B. Number of Days' Sales in Average Receivables—Measures the average number of days required to collect receivables; it is a measure of the average age of receivables. It is computed as:

Number of Days' Sales in Average Receivables = 300 or 360 or 365 (or other measure of business days in a year) / Accounts Receivable Turnover (computed in A, above)

Note
The number of days' sales in average receivables gives the same results as the average collection period measure covered in the prior lesson, "Liquidity Measures." While the two measures result in the same amount (number of days), they are useful for two different purposes.

As covered in the prior lesson, the average collection period focuses on liquidity, that is, how long before accounts receivable can be expected to convert to cash (i.e., be collected). That approach or perspective would be important in cash budgeting, for example.

As covered in this lesson, the number of days' sales in average receivables focuses on how well the granting of credit and the collection of sales on account are being managed. That approach or perspective is important in policy and performance review.

That is why essentially the same measure is presented in both lessons and why the description of them is different.

C. Inventory Turnover—Measures the number of times that inventory turns over (is acquired and sold or used) during a period. Indicates over or under stocking of inventory or obsolete inventory. It is computed as:

Inventory Turnover = Cost of Goods Sold/Average Inventory (e.g.,(Beginning + Ending) / 2)

D. Number of Days' Supply in Inventory (also number of days' sales in inventory)—Measures the number of days inventory is held before it is sold or used. Indicates the efficiency of general inventory management. It is computed as:

Number of Days' Supply in Inventory = 300 or 360 or 365 (or other measure of business days in a year) / Inventory Turnover (computed in C, above)

E. Accounts Payable Turnover—Measures the number of times that accounts payable turn over (are incurred and paid) during a period. Indicates the rate at which an entity pays its average accounts payable and, thereby, how well it manages paying its obligations. It is computed as:

Accounts Payable Turnover = Credit Purchases/Average Accounts Payable (e.g.,(Beginning + Ending) / 2)

1. If the amount of credit purchases is not available, an entity may use cost of goods sold, adjusted by changes in inventory. Thus, that computation of accounts payable turnover would be:

(Cost of Goods Sold + Ending Inventory – Beginning Inventory)/Average Accounts Payable

F. Number of Days' Purchases in Average Payables—Measures the average number of days required to pay accounts payable; it is a measure of the average age of payables. It is computed as:

Number of Days' Purchases in Average Payables = 300 or 360 or 365 (or other measure of business days in a year) / Accounts Payable Turnover (computed in E, above)

G. Capital Turnover—Measures how well the number of times that the average owners' equity is represented by sales (revenue) during a period. It shows how well the entity is using owners' equity to generate revenue. (This is different from return on owners'/shareholders' equity, which uses net income [not revenue] as the numerator.) It is computed as:

Capital Turnover = Annual Sales (or Revenue)/Average Owners' Equity.

H. Operating Cycle Length—Measures the average length of time between the acquisition of inventory and the collection of cash from the sale of that inventory, including the time to collect accounts receivable if sales are made on account.

1. The top half of the following timeline shows the time period that constitutes the **operating cycle** and the related events (transactions) that make up the operating cycle.

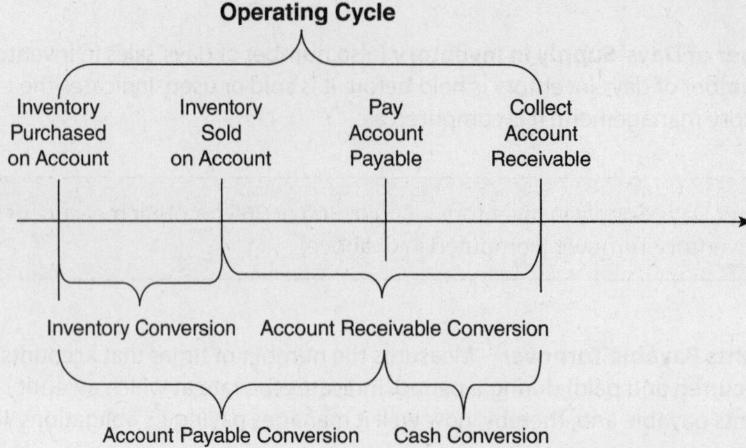

2. The bottom half of the timeline above shows the four conversion periods (or sub-cycles), which are identifiable in the operating cycle. Those component cycles are:
   a. **Inventory conversion cycle**—The (average) period of time from the acquisition of inventory until it is resold (or used). It is measured using the number of days' supply in inventory.
   b. **Accounts receivable cycle**—The (average) period of time from selling inventory on account (recognizing account receivable) until the account is collected (collection of account receivable). It is measured using the number of days' sales in accounts receivable.
   c. **Accounts payable cycle**—The (average) period of time from the purchase of inventory on account (recognizing account payable) until the account is paid (payment of account payable). It is measured using the number of days' purchases in accounts payable.
   d. **Cash conversion cycle**—The (average) period of time between when cash is paid to suppliers (e.g., for inventory) and when cash is collected from customers (including the time to collect accounts receivable, if sales are made on account); it measures the time to go from "cash-back to-cash." Notice that:
      i. The actual cash outflow and inflow establish the start and end of the cash conversion cycle.
      ii. The cash conversion cycle (CCC) can be computed as:

CCC = Inventory Conversion Cycle + Accounts Receivable Conversion Cycle – Accounts Payable Conversion Cycle, or as:

CCC = Operating Cycle – Accounts Payable Conversion Cycle

      i. If any three of the four conversion cycles are known, the fourth conversion cycle can be determined.

Financial Management Risk Concepts—Summary

Throughout this lesson on financial management, several concepts of risk have been identified and described. This section summarizes those concepts so that the elements of risk can be better understood and the differences appreciated.

After studying this lesson, you should be able to:

1. Define various forms of risk and describe the nature/consequences of each.
2. Describe ways certain risk may be mitigated.

I. **Risk**—Risk is the possibility of loss or other unfavorable outcome that results from the uncertainty in future events. Entities face a variety of different kinds of economic risk as they carry out their operating and financing activities. Many of those kinds of risk have been identified and described in earlier sections. This section summarizes those risks and certain other risks not previously identified.

II. **Business Risk**

A. This concept refers to the broad macro-risk a firm faces largely as a result of the relationship between the firm and the environment in which it operates. Thus, the nature and extent of this broad risk factor would be a function of both the nature of the firm and the nature of the environment. The nature of the firm would include the kind of products and services it provides, its cost structure, its financial structure, and all the other elements that make up the total firm, including the specific kinds of risk inherent in the firm. The nature of the environment would include the general economic conditions (e.g., as reflected by business cycles), competition, customer demand, technology, and other major elements of the environment in which the firm operates. The firm's business risk would be embodied in the firm's sensitivity (given its nature) to changes in the general economic environment (given its nature).

B. The various business risk elements faced by a company are frequently classified into two types, diversifiable and nondiversifiable.

1. **Diversifiable risk** (also called unsystematic, firm-specific, or company-unique)—The portion or elements of risk that can be eliminated through diversification of investments. In our discussion of capital budgeting we noted that a firm could mitigate certain risks associated with individual projects by investing in diverse kinds of projects. Similarly, a firm would reduce certain risks associated with its securities investments by diversification of the securities in its portfolio.
2. **Nondiversifiable risk** (also called systematic or market-related)—The portion or elements of risk that cannot be eliminated through diversification of investments. The factors that constitute nondiversifiable risk usually relate to the general economic and political environment. Examples include changes in the general level of interest, new taxes, and inflation/deflation. Since these broad changes affect all firms, diversification of investments does not tend to reduce the risk associated with these factors of the environment.

C. In a sense, the concept of business risk is sufficiently broad to include virtually all operating risks faced by a firm. In fact, for financial analysis purposes this risk is measured by the expected variability in a firm's earnings, before taking into account its interest and taxes (called EBIT—earnings before interest and taxes). Since EBIT reflects all of a firm's results for a period except its cost of borrowing (interest), it measures the expected consequences of all of a firm's operating activities (except debt financing) and the risk inherent in those activities.

III. **Specific Risks**—Various other specific risks are discussed in the following subsections:

A. **Financial Risk**—This is the particular risk faced by the firm's common shareholders that results from the use of debt financing, which requires payment regardless of the firm's operating results, and preferred stock, which requires dividends before returns to common shareholders. The payment of interest reduces earnings available to all shareholders and the payment of preferred dividends reduces the retained earnings available to common shareholders. The existence of these obligations increases the risk to common shareholders that variations in earnings will result in inadequate residual profits to reward common shareholders and could result in insolvency.

B. Default Risk—This is the risk associated with the possibility that the issuer of a security will not be able to make future interest payments and/or principal repayment. In the United States the lowest uncertainty of future payments—the lowest default risk—is ascribed to U.S. Treasury obligations. They are considered to be free of the risk of default (risk-free) and are used as the benchmark when evaluating the default risk of other securities. For securities that are not considered risk-free, a default risk premium is included in establishing the rate of interest appropriate for a security or for evaluation purposes.

C. Interest Rate Risk

1. This is the risk associated with the effects of changes in the market rate of interest on investments. The clearest illustration is provided by the effect of changes in the market rate of interest on long-term debt investments. When debt investments are made, the price paid depends on the market rate of interest for comparable investments at the time. As the market rate of interest subsequently changes, so also does the value of the debt investment—they change inversely, i.e., in opposite directions. Therefore, if the market rate goes up, the value of the outstanding debt goes down. A firm (or individual) that invests in debt has the risk that the market rate of interest will go up, causing the value of the debt to go down, which if sold before maturity would result in a loss.
2. A similar risk exists in other business contexts. For example, in using discounted cash flows for capital budgeting decisions, an interest rate is used (the hurdle rate) based on the expected cost of capital to fund the project. If interest rates change causing a higher cost of capital, the real present value will be less than that assumed. A project that was economically feasible under one interest rate assumption may prove to be unacceptable as a result of an increased interest rate.
3. Generally, the longer the period of an interest-based investment, the greater the perceived risk of the investment. Thus, the interest rate risk associated with a three-month Treasury bill would be less than that of a 20-year bond investment, and the 20-year bond would require a higher interest rate risk premium. Note that Treasury obligations are not interest rate risk-free because the interest rate risk results from the difference between the effective rates paid by an investment and the current rate in the general market.
4. Interest rate risk can be hedged in a number of ways, the most common of which are forward and forward contracts, interest rate swaps and option contracts.
    a. **Forward and futures contracts**—These contracts are agreements to buy or sell a specific asset at a specified price at a future date. Technically, forward and futures contracts differ in how they are executed. Forward contracts are carried out directly between two parties (i.e., "over the counter"), not on an organized exchange, and can be customized between the two parties. Futures contracts are carried out on an organized exchange (futures exchange), and have standardized quantities, time periods, etc. Because they are carried out through an organized exchange, futures contracts provide greater protection against default and liquidity risks than forward contracts carried out directly between two parties.
        i. In hedging interest rate risk of an existing asset or obligation, forward and futures contracts can be used to acquire a security (hedging instrument) whose price also moves with changes in the interest rate, but moves in the opposite direction as that of the item being hedged (hedged item). As a consequence of holding both items, the changes in the prices of the two items caused by changes in the market rate of interest offset each other (at least in part).
        ii. The change in prices of the hedged item and the hedging instrument (forward/futures contract) may not exactly offset each other due to underlying differences in

the instruments (e.g., length of instrument, etc.) or due to changes that are not the result of changes in interest rates (e.g., issuer's crediting rating, etc.). The risk that is not offset and, therefore, remains after the effects of hedging is called basis risk.

Examples

1. An investment security (debt instrument) paying a fixed rate of interest would suffer a loss in value if the market interest rate increases. To offset that possibility, a contract to sell interest rate futures (e.g., a contract to sell Treasury bond futures) would be acquired. A subsequent increase in the market rate of interest would result in a loss on the original investment, but a gain on the interest rate futures contract (i.e., the Treasury bond can be sold at the higher contract price established before the increase in the market rate of interest).
2. A liability (debt) with a variable interest rate would result in a loss (an increase in interest cost) if the market rate of interest increases. To offset that possibility, a contract to sell interest rate futures (e.g., a contract to sell Treasury bill futures) would be acquired. A subsequent increase in the market rate of interest would result in an increase in the interest rate (and interest cost) on the original debt, but a gain on the interest rate futures contract (i.e., the Treasury bill can be sold at the higher contract price established before the increase in the market rate of interest).

b. **Interest rate swaps**—These contracts are agreements between two parties (counterparties) to exchange sets of interest-rate-based future cash flows. Under the terms of the contract, one party agrees to pay a fixed rate of interest and receive a floating rate of interest and the other party agrees to pay a floating rate of interest and receive a fixed rate of interest. The floating rate is based on a benchmark rate such as the prime rate or LIBOR.

Examples

1. An investment in a debt instrument paying a floating rate of interest would suffer a loss in value if the market interest rate decreased. To offset that possibility, an interest rate swap to pay a floating rate and receive a fixed rate could be used. A subsequent decrease in the market rate of interest would result in a decrease in the interest rate (and interest received) on the original investment, but there would be a fixed interest received from the swap (regardless of changes in the market rate).
2. A liability (debt) with a variable interest rate would result in a loss (an increase in interest cost) if the market rate of interest increases. To offset that possibility, an interest rate swap to pay a fixed rate and receive a floating rate could be used. A subsequent increase in the market rate of interest would result in an increase in the interest rate (and interest cost) on the original debt, but there would be an increase in the interest rate (and amount) received from the swap contract.

c. **Option contracts**—These contracts are similar to forward and futures contracts, but provide the buyer the choice (option) of whether or not to buy or sell a specific asset at a specified price on or before a future date, whereas a forward or futures contract requires the parties to execute the buy/sell terms of the contract.

   i. A **call** option (contract) grants the owner the right (but not the obligation) to **buy** some underlying asset.

   ii. A **put** option (contract) grants the owner the right (but not the obligation) to **sell** some underlying asset.

Example

An investment security (debt instrument) paying a fixed rate of interest would suffer a loss in value if the market interest rate increases. Macroeconomic conditions indicate that the market rate of interest will increase prior to sale of the investment, resulting in a loss in value of the security. To offset that possibility, an option contract that allows the sale of the bonds (a put option) would be acquired. If there is a subsequent increase in the market rate of interest, the option contract would allow the sale of the bonds at or near the price established when the option contract was executed.

D. **Inflationary (or Purchasing Power) Risk**—This risk derives from the possibility that a rise in the general price level (inflation) will result in a reduction in the purchasing power of a fixed sum of money. For example, given inflation, the real purchasing power of a future cash flow from a capital project would be less than the nominal purchasing power of that cash flow. Therefore, if inflation is expected to be significant, it may be appropriate to adjust the cash flows and hurdle rate used for the expected inflation. To compensate for expected inflation, an inflation risk premium is included in establishing the rate of interest appropriate for a security or for evaluation purposes.

E. **Liquidation (or Marketability) Risk**

1. This risk derives from the possibility that an asset cannot be readily sold for cash equal to its fair value. Two possible elements are implied:
   a. Inability to sell for cash in the short term
   b. Inability to receive fair value in cash for the asset
2. Mitigating this risk would be especially important when making investments that may need to be converted quickly to cash. To compensate for lack of liquidity, a liquidity risk premium is included in establishing the rate of interest appropriate for a security or for evaluation purposes.

IV. **International Risk**—A firm that has transactions denominated in a foreign currency or operations in a foreign country faces additional risks not faced by a firm that does all of its business domestically. Those risks relate to the different political environment and the use of a different (foreign) currency.

A. **Political Risk**—This risk exists to a greater or lesser extent any time a firm has substantive operations in a country other than its home country. Differences in political climate, governmental processes, business culture and ethics, labor relations, market structures, and other factors all add elements of uncertainty and, therefore, risk to the firm.

B. **Currency Exchange Risk**—This risk derives from changes in exchange rates between currencies. As exchange rates change, so also does the home currency value of transactions and balances that are denominated in the foreign currency. Changes will affect firms in three ways:

1. **Foreign Currency Transaction Risk**—This risk results when a transaction is to be settled in a foreign currency and the exchange rate changes between the date the transaction is initiated and when it is settled. For example, assume a U.S. firm buys from a French firm and agrees to pay the French firm in euros. If the dollar cost of the euro increases between the date the purchase takes place and when the U.S. firm pays its obligation, the U.S. firm will pay more dollars to acquire the required euros. Both payables and receivables denominated (to be settled) in a foreign currency are subject to the currency exchange risk.

2. **Foreign Currency Investment Risk (also Foreign Currency Translation Risk)**—This risk results when a firm has a direct foreign investment. As exchange rates change so also does the home currency value of the foreign investment and its operating results. For example, the dollar value of a foreign subsidiary and its operating results will decrease if the foreign currency weakens against the dollar—the same foreign currency asset value and net income would equal fewer dollars in the parent's balance sheet and income statement.

3. **Foreign Currency Economic Risk**—This risk results when changes in the exchange rate impacts an entity's future international transactions. As **exchange rates** change so also does the home currency value of future transactions denominated in the foreign currency. **Exchange rate changes** may make the future transactions no longer economically viable. For example, the dollar value of future foreign currency revenues may be reduced such that sales would no longer be profitable. Or, the dollar value of future foreign currency expenses may be increased such that costs may be unacceptably high.

Information Technology

Information Technology Governance

Risks and Controls in Computer-Based Accounting-Information Systems

Virtually all accounting systems are now automated. This lesson considers critical issues related to managing the risks of computer-based accounting systems. The lesson also introduces the COBIT model and framework for assessing best practices in IT security and control.

After studying this lesson, you should be able to:

1. Explain the most important risks in a computer-based accounting system.
2. Compare and contrast the risks in manual and computerized accounting systems.
3. Compare and contrast the basic processes of manual and automated accounting systems.

I. Basic Information Processes in Manual and Automated Accounting Systems

- **A. Basic Processes in a Manual AIS**
  1. Journalize—Record entries.
  2. Post—To general ledger.
  3. Summarize—Prepare a trial balance.
- **B. Basic Processes in an Automated AIS**
  1. Input—Record or capture event data in system (input to storage).
  2. Process—Update data storage.
  3. Output—Retrieve master data from storage.
- **C. AIS File Organization**—The accounting records in an AIS fall into four main categories:
  1. Source documents and other data capture records, which may be in manual (e.g., customer order forms, sales invoices, journal vouchers, time cards, etc.) or electronic (e.g., online screen entry, "cookies," auto-fill screens, etc.) form. Where possible, data capture techniques should automate data collection and capture to reduce costs and improve accuracy
  2. Data accumulation records (or journals), such as daily cash receipt summaries, weekly payroll summaries, monthly purchases journals, etc.
  3. Subsidiary ledgers (or registers), such as accounts receivable, accounts payable, and the fixed asset register, etc.
  4. General ledger and financial statement records
- **D.** Very few manual accounting systems still exist. However, in all current computerized systems, humans perform some tasks. Hence, manual controls matter (a lot), even in computer-based systems

II. Risks in Computerized Systems

- **A. Risks in Computer-Based Systems**—Organizational risks depend on management's "risk appetite," and the organization's activities and environment (see the "COSO ERM Model" and "Risk Management Policies and Procedures" lessons). The following risks are heightened with computerized, compared with manual, accounting systems:
  1. Reliance on faulty systems or programs
  2. Unauthorized access to data leading to destruction or wrongful changes, inaccurate recording of transactions, or recording of false or unauthorized transactions

3. Unauthorized changes in master files, systems, or programs
4. Failure to make necessary changes in systems or programs
5. Inappropriate manual intervention
6. Loss of data

B. All organizations using computer-based systems face these risks. Their significance and the degree of control necessary to mitigate them varies across organizations.

III. **Comparison of Risks in Manual versus Computer-Based Transaction Processing Systems**—Although the objectives of controls in manual and computer-based systems are the same, the risks present in the two systems differ; consequently, the control procedures necessary to mitigate these risks also differ. Some of the implications of manual versus computerized systems for internal control are summarized below.

A. **Segregation of Duties**—A fundamental control in manual systems, the segregation of duties, is discussed in the "Risk Management" lesson. In a computerized environment, transaction processing often results in the **combination of functions that are normally separated** in a manual environment. For example, when cash receipts are processed by a cashier, the cash deposit, the cash receipts journal, and the A/R subsidiary ledger are (usually) all updated by a single entry. In a manual environment, at least two of these functions would normally be segregated.

1. In these instances, a well-designed computer system provides a compensating control.

a. Continuing with the cash receipts example: in a manual system, when the same person: (1) records the cash receipt, (2) prepares the bank deposit and (3) updates the customer's account in the accounts receivable ledger, then lapping (i.e., posting Customer A's payment to Customer B's account to cover up the earlier theft of the Customer B's payment) is possible. In an automated system, the computer program prevents this fraud by ensuring that the same customer is identified with the cash receipt, the bank deposit, and the accounts receivable posting.

b. As is also discussed in the "Risk Management" lesson, **segregation of duties (SoD) software** can help identify and resolve segregation of duty conflicts.

B. **Disappearing Audit Trail**—Manual systems depend heavily on a paper audit trail to ensure that transactions are properly authorized and that all transactions are processed. Physical (paper) audit trails are substantially reduced in a computerized environment, particularly in online, real-time systems. (In many batch systems, source documents still exist and provide an excellent paper audit trail.)

1. **Electronic audit trails**—Audit trails are built into better accounting information systems software. These are created by maintaining a file of all of the transactions processed by the system (transaction log file), including the username of the individual who processed the transaction; when properly maintained, electronic audit trails are as effective as paper-based audit trails.

C. **Uniform Transaction Processing**—Computer programs are uniformly executed algorithms—which is not the case with less-reliable humans. Compared with a manual system, processing consistency increases in a computerized environment. Consequently, "clerical" errors (e.g., human arithmetic errors, missed postings) are "virtually" eliminated.

1. In a computerized environment, however, there is increased opportunity for "systemic" errors, such as errors in programming logic. For example, if a programmer inadvertently entered a sales tax rate of 14% instead of 1.4%, all sales transactions would be affected by the error. Proper controls over program development and implementation help prevent these types of errors.

D. **Computer-Initiated Transactions**—Many computerized systems gain efficiency by automatically generating transactions when specified conditions occur. For example, the system may automatically generate a purchase order for a product when the quantity on hand falls below the reorder point. Automated transactions are not subject to the same types of authorization found in manual transactions and may not be as well documented.

1. Automated transactions should be regularly reported and reviewed. Care should be taken to identify transactions that are more frequent or in larger amounts than a predetermined standard.

E. Potential for Increased Errors and Irregularities—Several characteristics of computerized processing act to increase the likelihood that fraud may occur and remain undetected for long periods.

1. Opportunity for **remote access to data** in networked environments increases the likelihood of unauthorized access.
2. **Concentration of information** in computerized systems means that, if system security is breached, the potential for damage is much greater than in manual systems. This risk is greater in cloud-based systems.
3. Decreased human involvement in transaction processing results in **decreased opportunities for observation.**
4. Errors or fraud may occur in the **design or maintenance of application programs.**

F. Potential for Increased Management Review—Computer-based systems increase the availability of raw data and afford more opportunities to perform analytical reviews and produce management reports. Audit procedures are frequently built into the application programs themselves (embedded audit modules) and provide for continuous monitoring of transactions.

1. The opportunities for increased reporting and review of processing statistics can mitigate the additional risks associated with computerized processing.

The COBIT Model of IT Governance and Management

After studying this lesson, you should be able to:

1. Describe the COBIT framework, its purpose and components, and the basic IT processes that it identifies.
2. Describe the four domains of IT activity that are found in the COBIT framework.
3. Identify the seven information criteria found in the COBIT framework.
4. Identify the five IT resources that are found in the COBIT framework.

I. The Control Objectives for Information and Related Technology (COBIT) Framework

A. Introduction

1. Although there are many available models for IT governance, COBIT is a widely used international standard for identifying best practices in IT security and control. COBIT provides management with an information technology (IT) governance model that helps in delivering value from IT processes, and in understanding and managing the risks associated with IT. In addition, COBIT provides a framework that helps align IT with organizational governance.
2. COBIT bridges the gaps between strategic business requirements, accounting control needs, and the delivery of supporting IT. COBIT facilitates IT governance and helps ensure the integrity of information and information systems.
3. COBIT is consistent with, and complements, the control definitions and processes articulated in the COSO and COSO ERM models. The most important differences between COSO and COSO ERM and COBIT are their intended audiences and scope. The COSO and COSO ERM models provide a common internal control language for use by management, boards of directors, and internal and external auditors. In contrast, COBIT focuses on IT controls and is intended for use by IT managers, IT professionals, and internal and external auditors.
4. The COBIT framework is organized around three components:
    a. **Domains and processes**—The IT function is divided into four domains within which 34 basic IT processes reside:
        i. **Planning and organization**—How can IT best contribute to business objectives? Establish a strategic vision for IT. Develop tactics to plan, communicate, and realize the strategic vision.
        ii. **Acquisition and implementation**—How can we acquire, implement, or develop IT solutions that address business objectives and integrate with critical business process?
        iii. **Delivery and support**—How can we best deliver required IT services including operations, security, and training?
        iv. **Monitoring**—How can we best periodically assess IT quality and compliance with control requirements? Monitoring IT processes are identified as particularly relevant for the CPA Exam. The COBIT model identifies four interrelated monitoring processes:
            1. ME1. Monitor and evaluate IT performance—Establish a monitoring approach, including metrics, a reporting process, and a means to identify and correct deficiencies.
            2. ME2. Monitor and evaluate internal control—This is required by the Sarbanes-Oxley Act (SOX) Section 404.
            3. ME3. Ensure regulatory compliance—Identify compliance requirements and evaluate, and report on, the extent of compliance with these requirements.
            4. ME4. Provide IT guidance—Establish an IT governance framework that aligns with the organization's strategy and value delivery program.

b. Effective IT performance management requires a monitoring process. This process includes the following:

i. Information criteria—To have value to the organization, data must have the following properties or attributes:

1. Effectiveness
2. Efficiency
3. Confidentiality
4. Integrity
5. Availability
6. Compliance
7. Reliability

ii. IT resources—Identify the physical resources that comprise the IT system:

1. People
2. Applications
3. Technology
4. Facilities
5. Data

c. More than 300 generic COBIT control objectives are associated with the 34 basic IT processes identified in COBIT. The COBIT model, the components mentioned above, and the 34 basic IT processes are summarized in the following figure:

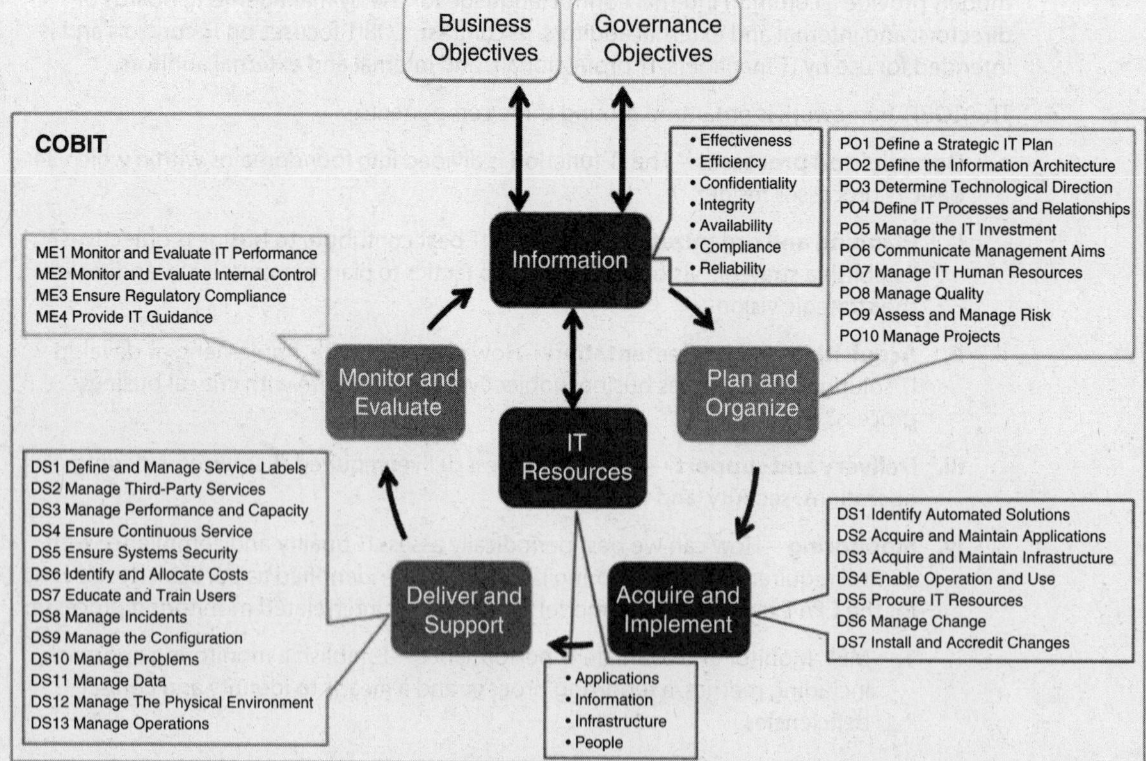

d. Within the figure, items ME1 to ME4 are the processes related to monitoring, items PO1 to PO11 are the processes related to planning and organization, and so on.

e. If you would like to learn more about COBIT, this YouTube video briefly explains more about its purpose and uses:

www.youtube.com/watch?v=bg_GEN8AZA0

Introduction to Enterprise-Wide and Cloud-Based Systems

After studying this lesson, you should be able to:

1. Define enterprise-wide or enterprise resource planning systems.
2. State the goals, components, and typical architecture of ERP systems.
3. Define cloud-based systems.
4. Describe the benefits and risks of cloud-based systems.
5. Identify conditions in which an organization might benefit from implementing an ERP system.
6. Identify conditions in which an organization might benefit from implementing cloud-based systems.

Note
Enterprise-wide and cloud-based systems are increasingly common in CPA Exam questions. On recent exams, these topics are found both in multiple-choice and written communication questions.

I. **Enterprise Architecture**—An organization's enterprise architecture is its effort to understand, manage, and plan for IT assets. An organization's IT security governance plan must articulate with, and be informed by, the organization's enterprise architecture plan.

II. **Enterprise-Wide or Enterprise Resource Planning (ERP) Systems**—ERPs provide transaction processing, management support, and decision-making support in a single, integrated, organization-wide package. By integrating all data and processes of an organization into a unified system, ERPs attempt to manage and eliminate the organizational problem of consolidating information across departments, regions, or divisions.

   A. **Goals of ERP systems:**

      1. **Global visibility**—The integration of all data maintained by the organization into a single database; once the data is in a single database—which binds the whole organization together. Once it is integrated into a single database, the data are available to anyone with appropriate authorization.
      2. **Cost reductions**—Long-run systems maintenance costs are reduced by eliminating the costs associated with maintaining multiple systems.
      3. **Employee empowerment**—Global visibility of information improves lower-level communication and decision making by making all relevant data available to the employee; this empowers the employee and, in turn, makes the organization more agile and competitive in a volatile business environment.
      4. **"Best practices"**—ERP systems processes are based on analysis of the most successful businesses in their industry; by adopting the ERP system, the organization automatically benefits from the implementation of these "best practices."

   B. **Components of an ERP System**—ERP systems are typically purchased in modules (i.e., Sales, Logistics, Planning, Financial Reporting, etc.); ERP vendors design their systems to be purchased as a unit, that is, from a "single source"; however, many organizations pick and choose ERP modules from several vendors according to their perception of how well the ERP model fits with their organization's way of doing business, a practice called choosing the "best of breed."

      1. **Online transaction processing (OLTP) system**—The modules comprising the core business functions: sales, production, purchasing, payroll, financial reporting, etc. These functions collect the operational data for the organization and provide the fundamental motivation for the purchase of an ERP.

2. **Online analytical processing (OLAP) system**—Incorporates data warehouse and data mining capabilities within the ERP.

C. **ERP System Architecture**—ERP systems are typically implemented using a **client/server network** configuration; although early implementations generally utilized proprietary LAN and WAN technologies, current implementations often use Internet-based connections.

1. ERPs may use **two-tiered or three-tiered** architectures; because two-tiered systems combine programs and data on a single server, three-tiered architecture is preferred, particularly in larger systems.

III. **Cloud-Based Systems and Storage**—An organization's decision to deploy cloud-based systems should flow from its enterprise architecture plan which should include consideration of an IT sourcing strategy. An IT sourcing strategy concerns the organization's plan to insource, outsource, or pursue a hybrid strategy (mixed insourcing and outsourcing) in relation to its IT assets.

A. Cloud systems are also called **the cloud, cloud computing, cloud storage**, and **cloud services**. In cloud-based storage, a virtual data pool is created by contracting with a third-party data storage provider. When managed well, such an approach uses outsourcing to gain the benefits of relying on a professionally managed data storage provider. When executed well, this approach can provide a massive, universally accessible data store while minimizing the risks of unauthorized access by intruders, at a reasonable cost. When managed poorly, risks include data loss, system penetration and access by intruders, and failures of internal control, including inadequate monitoring and testing of system risks. Such a system might also include the creation of a virtual private network (VPN) to limit access to the system and encrypt sensitive information.

1. **Cloud service providers (CSPs)**—Vendors who provide cloud services (e.g., Amazon Cloud, Dropbox).

B. **Cloud Deployment Models**

1. **Private cloud**—The cloud infrastructure exists solely for an individual organization.

2. **Community cloud**—A cloud infrastructure that is shared by users in a specific community (e.g., municipal governments, an industry association, related to compliance requirements).

3. **Public cloud**—The cloud infrastructure available to the public or a large industry group (e.g., Dropbox, Amazon Cloud services).

4. **Hybrid cloud**—A cloud that includes two or types of the above types of clouds with partitions between the types of services.

C. **Cloud Service Delivery Models**—Describe the services that a client contracts for:

1. **Infrastructure as a service (IaaS)**—Use of the cloud to access a virtual data center of resources, including a network, computers, and storage. Example: Amazon Web Services and Carbonite.

2. **Platform as a service (PaaS)**—A development environment for creating cloud-based software and programs using cloud-based services. Example: Salesforce.com's Force.com.

3. **Software as a service (SaaS)**—Remote access to software. Office 365, a suite of office productivity programs, is an example of SaaS.

D. **Benefits of Cloud-Based Systems:**

1. **Universal access**—System data is available at any site with Internet access.

2. **Cost reductions**—Long-run systems maintenance costs are reduced by eliminating the costs associated with maintaining multiple systems.

3. **Scalability**—Cloud-based systems are highly scalable, meaning that they grow with an organization. Specifically, organizations can buy only the capabilities and storage that they currently need but can contract for expansion as organizational needs evolve.

4. **Outsourcing and economies of scale**—Cloud-based systems allow organizations to outsource data storage and management to organizations with the capabilities and competencies to manage these facilities. By outsourcing to organizations who specialize in cloud services, economies of scale may be obtained, wherein the cloud provider realizes cost benefits, some of which are passed on to the organization who purchases cloud services. An additional benefit is therefore, obviously, cost savings due to a reduced need for internal IT personnel.
5. **Enterprise-wide integration**—Cloud-based systems can be integrated with enterprise-wide systems to allow the seamless integration of organizations across units and geography. Indeed, some argue that fully realizing the benefits of ERPs requires cloud-based systems.
6. **Deployment speed**—Typically, CSPs can provide services much faster than organizations that attempt to duplicate these services using internal IT departments.

E. Risks of Cloud-Based Systems

1. The risk of data loss and outages is potentially increased by putting all of one's data online with one vendor. In reality however, most large cloud-based vendors store data at multiple sites, meaning that the risks of data loss with cloud-based systems, while important, may not be as great as might be feared.
2. There is an increased risk of system penetration by hackers, crackers, and terrorists when all one's data is stored with one vendor.
3. Cloud-based systems rely on the competence, professionalism, reliability, viability, and transparency of the CSP. Hence, diligence in vendor screening and selection is essential to cloud-computing security and success. In addition, CSPs may be unwilling to divulge details of their operations that auditors (internal or external) require to ensure that an organization's data is stored safely.
4. Data stored in community and public clouds may be vulnerable to actions by other tenants of the CSP. This may create legal issues related to data privacy and data availability.
5. Storing data with a high-profile CSP (e.g., Amazon Cloud) can make one a high-profile target for cyber-attackers.

F. Summary—Despite the risks, many organizations are moving their primary storage to cloud-based systems.

IT Functions and Controls Related to People

After studying this lesson, you should be able to:

1. Identify the critical functions in an IT Department and the desired segregation of these functions.
2. Identify the critical roles within functions in an IT Department.
3. Identify critical controls related to IT personnel: hiring, evaluation, and firing (termination).
4. Give examples of incompatible IT function duties and responsibilities.
5. Match IT risks to incompatible IT function duties and responsibilities.

Administration of a Typical Organizational IT Function

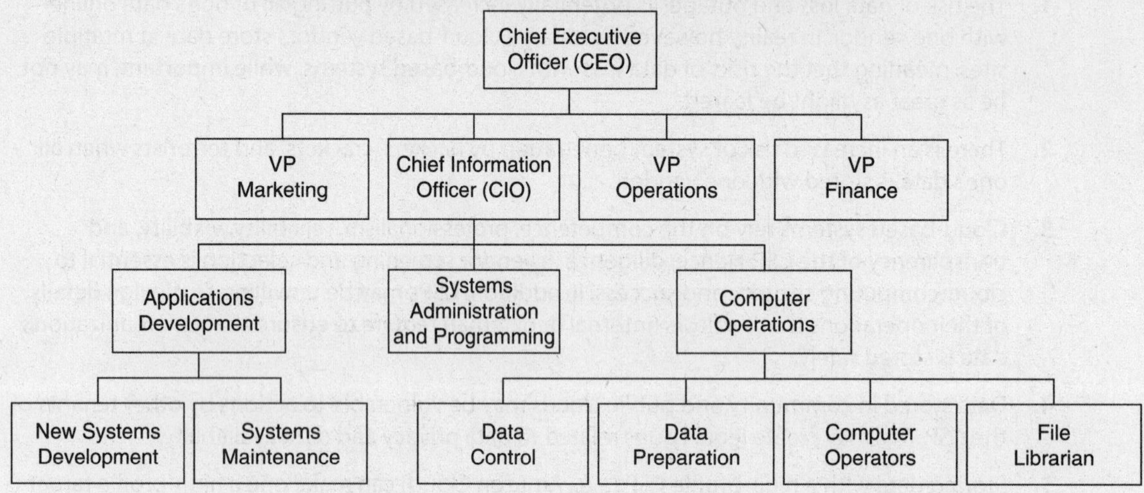

I. **Organizational Structure of the Information Technology (IT) Department**
   A. As illustrated in the above diagram, the chief information officer (CIO) oversees the IT department.
      1. In some organizations the CIO is called the vice president of information technology or the chief technology officer (CTO).
      2. The CIO generally reports to the chief executive officer (CEO).
      3. The CIO is responsible for efficient and effective functions of existing systems and for planning for the development and technical resources for future systems.
      4. The CIO is ultimately in control of hardware and software operations for the entire company.
   B. There are three main functional areas within most IT departments:
      1. **Applications development**
      2. **Systems administration and programming**
      3. **Computer operations**

II. **Segregation of Functions**—The functions in each area must be strictly segregated within the IT department. Without proper segregation of these functions, the effectiveness of additional controls is compromised.

A. The following diagram illustrates this point:

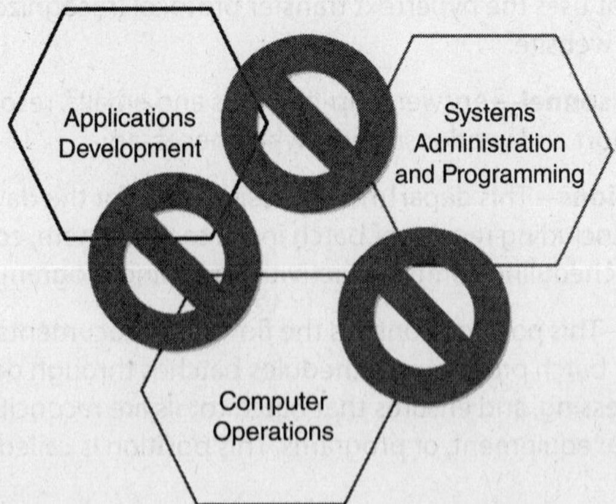

B. **Applications Development**—This department is responsible for creating new end-user computer applications and for maintaining existing applications.

1. **Systems analysts**—Responsible for analyzing and designing computer systems; systems analysts generally lead a team of programmers who complete the actual coding for the system; they also work with end users to define the problem and identify the appropriate solution.
2. **Application programmers**—Work under the direction of the systems analyst to write the actual programs that process data and produce reports.
3. New program development, and maintenance of existing programs, is completed in a "test" or "sandbox" environment using copies of live data and existing programs rather than in the "live" system.

> **Note**
> *The controls listed in this section are all general controls—controls over the IT department as a whole. The majority of the controls are also preventive controls. For example, the segregation of duties inherent in the organizational structure of the IT department prevents employees from making unauthorized changes to program and data files; personnel hiring policies prevent the organization from hiring individual who don't meet management's specifications; and so on.*

C. **Systems Administration and Programming**—This department maintains the computer hardware and computing infrastructure and grants access to system resources.

1. **System administrators**—The database administrator, network administrator, and web administrators are responsible for management activities associated with the system they control. For example, they grant access to their system resources, usually with usernames and passwords. System administrators, by virtue of the influence they wield, **must not be permitted to participate directly in these systems' operations.**
2. **System programmers**—Maintain the various operating systems and related hardware. For example, they are responsible for updating the system for new software releases and installing new hardware. Because their jobs require that they be in direct contact with the production programs and data, it is imperative that they are **not permitted to have access to information about application programs or data files.**
3. **Network managers**—Ensure that all applicable devices link to the organization's networks and that the networks operate securely and continuously.
4. **Security management**—Ensures that all components of the system are secure and protected from all internal and external threats. Responsibilities include security of software and systems and granting appropriate access to systems via user authentication, password setup, and maintenance.

> **Note**
> *Although the adjective "system" applies to system analysts, administrators, and programmers, system analysts are engaged in a different function from system administrators and programmers.*

5. **Web administrators**—Operate and maintain the web servers. (A web server is a software application that uses the hypertext transfer protocol (recognized as http://) to enable the organization's website.

6. **Help desk personnel**—Answer help-line calls and emails, resolve user problems, and obtain technical support and vendor support when necessary.

D. **Computer Operations**—This department is responsible for the day-to-day operations of the computer system, including receipt of batch input to the system, conversion of the data to electronic media, scheduling computer activities, running programs, etc.

1. **Data control**—This position controls the flow of all documents into and out of computer operations; for batch processing, schedules batches through data entry and editing, monitors processing, and ensures that batch totals are reconciled; data control should not access the data, equipment, or programs. This position is called "quality assurance" in some organizations.

2. **Data entry clerk (data conversion operator)**—For systems still using manual data entry (which is rare), this function keys (enters) handwritten or printed records to convert them into electronic media; the data entry clerk should not be responsible for reconciling batch totals, should not run programs, access system output, or have any involvement in application development and programming.

3. **Computer operators**—Responsible for operating the computer: loading program and data files, running the programs, and producing output. Computer operators should not enter data into the system or reconcile control totals for the data they process. (That job belongs to Data Control.)

4. **File librarian**—Files and data not online are usually stored in a secure environment called the **file library**; the file librarian is responsible for maintaining control over the files, checking them in and out only as necessary to support scheduled jobs. The file librarian should not have access to any of the operating equipment or data (unless it has been checked into the library).

E. Functions in the three key functions (i.e., applications development, systems administration and programming, computer operations—should be **strictly segregated.** (This is a bit like the "cannibals and missionaries" problem from computer science and artificial intelligence.) In particular:

1. **Computer operators and data entry personnel**—Should never be allowed to act as programmers.

2. **Systems programmers**—Should never have access to application program documentation.

3. **Data administrators**—Should never have access to computer operations ("live" data).

4. **Application programmers and systems analysts**—Should not have access to computer operations ("live" data).

5. **Application programmers and systems analysts**—Should not control access to data, programs, or computer resources.

F. This matrix illustrates the above segregation of IT functions:

Role	Live System	Application Programming	Systems Programming
Data entry, data control, file librarian	No	No	No
Computer operators	Yes	No	No
Systems programmers	Yes	No	Yes
Application programmers, system analyst, data administrator	No	Yes	No

III. Personnel Policies and Procedures—The competence, loyalty, and integrity of employees are among an organization's most valuable assets. Appropriate personnel policies are critical in hiring and retaining quality employees.

A. Hiring Practices—Applicants should complete detailed employment applications and formal, in-depth employment interviews before hiring. When appropriate, specific education and experience standards should be imposed and verified. All applicants should undergo thorough background checks and verification of academic degrees, work experience, and professional certifications, as well as searches for criminal records.

B. Performance Evaluation—Employees should be evaluated regularly. The evaluation process should provide clear feedback on the employee's overall performance as well as specific strengths and weaknesses. To the extent that there are weaknesses, it is important to provide guidance on how performance can be improved.

C. Employee Handbook—The employee handbook, available to all employees, should state policies related to security and controls, unacceptable conduct, organizational rules and ethics, vacations, overtime, outside employment, emergency procedures, and disciplinary actions for misconduct.

D. Competence—COSO requires that "Management … [should] specify the competence levels for particular jobs and to translate those levels into requisite knowledge and skills. These actions help ensure that competent, but not over-qualified employees serve in appropriate roles with appropriate responsibilities."

E. Firing (Termination)—Clearly, procedures should guide employee departures, regardless of whether the departure is voluntary or involuntary; it is especially important to be careful and thorough when dealing with involuntary terminations of IT personnel who have access to sensitive or proprietary data. In involuntary terminations, the employee's username and keycard should be disabled before notifying the employee of the termination to prevent any attempt to destroy company property. Although this sounds heartless, after notification of an involuntary termination, the terminated employee should be accompanied at all times until escorted out of the building.

F. Other Considerations—Recruiting and retaining highly qualified employees is an important determinant of organizational success. Ensuring that an organization has training and development plans, including training in security and controls, is essential both to employee retention, and to creating a system of internal control.

Role of Information and Technology in Business

IT and Business Strategy

This lesson builds on the CPAexcel lessons on business strategy and market analysis. Begin your study strategy with the "Business Strategy and Market Analysis" module and study this lesson afterward.

After studying this lesson, you should be able to:

1. Describe the role of IT in business strategy.
2. Describe the IT value chain.
3. Describe the value and process of an integrated approach to business strategy, risk management, and managing IT resources.
4. Give examples of how IT is changing business strategy.

I. Introduction to and Review of Business Strategy

A. Every successful organization creates a process to determine what it will do, what is important, and how to do those things that it determines are important. This process is called "**governance**," which is the set of processes and structures, implemented by the board, to oversee the activities of the organization in pursuit of organizational objectives, according to the Institute of Internal Auditor's International Standards for the Professional Practice of Internal Auditing. Two key elements of governance are:

1. **Strategy**
2. **Oversight**

Definitions
Strategy: The sequence of interrelated procedures for determining an entity's long-term goals and identifying the best approaches for achieving those goals

Oversight: The process of managing and monitoring an organization's operations to achieve internal control and effectively manage risks

II. The Problem of IT and Business Strategy

A. Integrating IT investments into an organization's overall business strategy is an ongoing problem for several reasons, including:

1. **Lack of strategic focus**—Many IT investments are bottom-up projects. That is, they originate in business unit needs and may be undertaken without a sense of the organization's overall strategy
2. **Lack of strategic investment**—Because of the bottom-up nature of many IT investments, there is often an overinvestment in existing businesses and inadequate attention to transformative technologies that may be the future of the business.
3. **Inadequate scope and agility**—Because many IT investments are made in business units, and not at a corporate level, the projects may be too small in scope and inadequately scaled to meet changing business needs.

III. The Changing Role of IT in Business Strategy

A. Digitization (i.e., the movement of data to electronic form) and **globalization** (i.e., the integration of cultures and economies due to digitization) have made IT investments central to many businesses' strategy. However, not all of these investments have been effective.

B. Reminder—The CPAExcel lessons on business strategy (see the "Generic Strategies" lesson) argue that there are two basic strategies: product differentiation and cost leadership. IT may influence these strategies in the following ways:

C. Product Differentiation—This strategy involves setting your product apart from your competitors' by offering one that's faster, has enhanced features, and so in. How can IT influence product differentiation?

1. The Internet, as a distribution channel, can create product differentiation. For example, eBay's success was partially built on its ability to create a new market of online products, many of which had been previously available only in specialized markets (e.g., antique Russian watches; all types of Beanie Babies)
2. Many advanced technologies (i.e., lasers, 3-D printers) improve product quality and create differentiation.
3. Many products are increasingly digitized (e.g., books, music) which can both increase quality and reduce costs.
4. Information on the Internet can be changed quickly (versus, e.g., sales obtained by mailed catalogs). Because of this, product life cycles are shorter and product evolution is faster. These changes can be used to create differentiation.

D. Cost Leadership—A low-cost strategy involves offering a cheaper product than your competitors. The low cost is made possible by operating more efficiently. How can IT influence cost leadership?

1. Many companies now use advanced technologies to reduce their costs and improve the efficiency of production and delivery systems.
2. Because the Internet is available to almost everyone, intense price competition can result. The outcome may be that many companies shift away from a low-cost strategy toward a product-differentiation strategy.

IV. Conclusion

A. Many companies have struggled to integrate their strategic planning, risk management, and IT investments because they have failed to see the co-relations of these efforts. Integrating these functions is critical to effective and efficient governance. Hence, these activities should be managed using a comprehensive, overarching, integrated approach. To do otherwise is to create a patchwork approach that will yield undesirable, disparate results.

System Types by Activity

After studying this lesson, you should be able to:

1. Define the goals and components of the types of information systems presented in this lesson.
2. Compare and contrast the features and uses of the types of information systems presented in this lesson.
3. Give examples of the uses of the types of information systems presented in this lesson.

I. **Purposes of IT Systems**—IT systems are often classified according to the types of activities the systems support.

   A. **Operational Systems**—Support the day-to-day activities of the business (purchasing of goods and services, manufacturing activities, sales to customers, cash collections, payroll, etc.).

      1. Are often known as **transaction processing systems (TPS)**.
      2. Operational systems process **nonfinancial transactions** (placing orders for goods, accepting an order from a customer, etc.) and **financial transactions** (billing a customer, receiving payment from a customer, paying employees for services rendered).
      3. Financial transactions **generate debit and credit entries** into the accounts.
      4. Accounting systems are transaction processing systems.

Exam Tip
The definitions of these system types in CPA Exam questions can be vague and imprecise (e.g., distinguishing DSS from ESS). Your goal should be to find the best match, based on your knowledge of the system types and your reasoning processes. For example, a typical question might ask: Which type of system provides this capability? Your goal is to best match the capability to the system type.

   B. **Management Information Systems (MISs)**—Systems designed to **support routine management** problems based primarily on data from transaction processing systems.

      1. MISs support management of daily operations; management issues in this area consist primarily of well-defined, structured problems.
         a. MISs take planning information (budgets, forecasts, etc.) data and compare it to actual results in periodic management reports (summary reports, variance reports, and exception reports).
      2. **Accounting information systems (AISs)**—AISs take the financial data from transaction processing systems and use it to produce financial statements and control reports for management (e.g., accounts receivable aging analysis, product cost reports, etc.); AISs are a **subset of MIS**.

   C. **Decision Support Systems (DSSs)**—DSSs provide information to mid- and upper-level managers to assist them in managing non-routine problems and in long-range planning.

      1. Unlike MISs, **DSSs frequently include external data** in addition to summarized information from the TPS and include significant analytical and statistical capabilities.
      2. **Data-driven DSSs**—Process large amounts of data to find relationships and patterns.
         a. **Data warehousing, which uses data mining,** illustrates data-driven DSSs. These terms are discussed in the lesson "System Types by Data Structure" under the heading "Knowledge Management (KM)," but they are also important to data-driven DSSs.
      3. **Model-driven DSSs**—Feed data into a previously constructed model to predict outcomes. For example, if a company increases its product price, by how much will demand for the product decrease?
      4. **Executive support systems (ESSs) or strategic support systems (SSSs)**—A subset of DSSs especially designed for forecasting and making long-range, strategic decisions; thus, these systems have a greater emphasis on external data.

5. **Group support systems (GSSs)**—Facilitate group collaboration of users' information to generate analyses, recommendations, or solutions. These systems may include functions such as calendars, meeting scheduling, and document sharing.

D. **Knowledge Work Systems**—Facilitate the work activities of professional-level employees (engineers, accountants, attorneys, etc.) by providing information relevant to their day-to-day activities (e.g., how the company has handled specific types of audit exceptions) and/or by automating some of their routine functions (e.g., computer-aided systems engineering [CASE] packages used by programmers to automated some programming functions).

1. Usually exist separately from operational systems, but can be integrated

2. **Office automation systems (OASs)**—Provide similar support to clerical-level employees.

a. Include many of the typical programs found on personal computers: word processing, spreadsheets, end-user databases, etc.

E. **Enterprise Resource Planning Systems (ERPs) or Enterprise-Wide Systems**—ERPs provide transaction processing, management support, and decision-making support in a single, integrated package. See the BEC lesson "Introduction to Enterprise-Wide and Cloud-Based Systems" about these systems.

System Types by Data Structure

After studying this lesson, you should be able to:

1. Contrast flat-file with database approaches to information management.
2. Define a knowledge management system, and identify its key components.
3. Give examples of applications of knowledge management systems.
4. Describe some data activities that may be used in a data warehouse.

I. **Types of IT Systems**—IT systems can also be identified by the way that data is captured and processed.

A. **Flat-File Systems**—Early IT systems used flat-file technology. Flat files are characterized by:

1. **Independent programs and data sets**—Each application develops its own set of data and processing programs; data sharing across applications is accomplished through creation of separate programs that select data records from one application and reformat them so that the data can be incorporated into another application.
2. High degrees of **data redundancy** (multiple instances of the same piece of information; data redundancy can lead to data inconsistency—different values for the same piece of information).
3. Difficulty in achieving **cross-functional reporting** (combining of information from multiple applications in a single report—e.g., a report that combines gender and ethnicity information from the personnel system with hours worked from the payroll system).

Exam Tip
Flat-file systems are sometimes contrasted with database systems. The point of this comparison is usually to highlight the limitations of the former (i.e., flat-file systems) with the capabilities of the latter (i.e., database systems). For questions on this topic, flat-file systems are uniformly "bad" and database systems are uniformly "good."

B. **Database Systems**—Database systems are discussed in greater detail in the "Data Structures, Software, and Databases" lesson

1. To briefly reiterate this content, in a database system, data from related applications is pooled together in logically related files (the database) that can be accessed by multiple applications through a database management system (DBMS).
2. Organizational database systems may exhibit a high level of integration (e.g., a few, large databases) or a low level of integration (e.g., more, smaller databases); the higher the required integration, the lower the amount of data redundancy and the easier it is to achieve cross-functional reporting, i.e., usable, accessible data.

C. **Knowledge Management (KM)**—Knowledge management attempts to ensure that the right information is available at the right time to the right user. Various practices attempt to electronically capture and disseminate information throughout the organization. Knowledge management practices seek specific outcomes, including shared intelligence, improved performance, competitive advantage, and more innovation. Knowledge management includes:

1. **Knowledge base (or knowledgebase)**—A special type of database designed for retrieval of knowledge; this database provides the means to collect and organize the information and develop relationships among information components.
2. **Expert systems (knowledge-based systems)**—A computer program containing subject-specific knowledge derived from experts; the system consists of a set of rules used to analyze information provided by the user of the system; based on the information provided, the system then recommends a course of action.
3. **Data warehouse**—A database designed to archive an organization's operational transactions (sales, purchases, production, payroll, etc.) over a period of years; external data that might be correlated with these transactions, such as economic indicators, stock prices, exchange rates, market share, political issues, weather conditions, and others, can also be incorporated into the data warehouse.

a. **Data mart**—A specialized version of a data warehouse containing data preconfigured to meet the needs of specific departments; companies often support multiple data marts within their organization.

b. Terms associated with data warehouses:

   i. **Drill down**—The ability to move from summary information to more granular information (i.e., viewing an accounts receivable customer balance and drilling down to the invoices and payments which resulted in that balance).

   ii. **Slicing and dicing**—The ability to view a single data item in multiple dimensions; for example, sales might be viewed by product, by region, by time period, by company, etc.

c. **Data mining**—The process of performing statistical analysis and automatically searching large volumes of data to identify patterns and relationships among the data elements. Obviously, the ability to recognize patterns (using heuristics and algorithms) in data is essential to data mining.

Data Structures, Software, and Databases

This lesson introduces, or reviews, computer concepts related to data, hardware, software, and databases. Some of the content of this lesson is covered in the "IT (Computer) Auditing" lesson in the "AUD module" of CPAexcel. Some of the questions from the "IT (Computer) Auditing" lesson in the AUD module of CPAexcel are also useful and relevant to this lesson.

After studying this lesson, you should be able to:

1. Describe the fundamental elements, relations among elements, and structure of computer data.
2. Define and describe: (a) the three categories of computer software, (b) the common types of programming languages, (c) databases and their advantages, (d) the components and controls of database management systems (DBMSs).
3. Give examples of common DBMS controls and match them to the risks that they address.

I. **Data Structures in Accounting Systems**—All information and instructions used in IT systems are executed in binary code (i.e., zeros and ones). This section looks at how the zeros and ones are strung together to create meaning.

   A. **Bit** (binary digit)—An individual zero or 1; the smallest piece of information that can be represented.

   B. **Byte**—A group of (usually) eight bits that are used to represent alphabetic and numeric characters and other symbols (3, g, X, ?, etc.). Several coding systems are used to assign specific bytes to characters; ASCII and EBCIDIC are the two most commonly used coding systems. Each system defines the sequence of zeros and ones that represent each character.

   C. **Field**—A group of characters (bytes) identifying a characteristic of an entity. A data value is a specific value found in a field. Fields can consist of a single character (Y, N) but usually consist of a group of characters. Each field is defined as a specific data type. Date, Text, and Number are common data types.

Entity	Field	Data Value	Data Type
Invoice	Invoice Number	4837	numeric
Customer	Street Address	1034 Rose Ave.	alphanumeric or text
Product	Sale Price	$13.95	currency

The data type determines how programs will treat the characters entered into the field; in a database environment, fields are also known as attributes.

   D. **Record**—A group of related fields (or attributes) describing an individual instance of an entity (a specific invoice, a particular customer, an individual product).

   E. **File**—A collection of records for one specific entity (an invoice file, a customer file, a product file).

      1. In a database environment, files are sometimes called tables.

F. Database—A set of logically related files.

CPA Exam questions sometimes ask you to order data elements by size. The following data hierarchy displays these relationships:

Files: are composed of

Records: are composed of

Fields: are composed of

Data values: are composed of

Bytes (characters): are composed of

Bits: the smallest storage element in a computer system.

Study Tip

Except for "file" the words get longer as the units get bigger:

Bit (**3** characters)

Byte (**4** characters)

Field (**5** characters)

Record (**6** characters)

File (**4** characters)

Database (**8** characters)

II. Software

A. Software—Instructions (i.e., programs) for hardware

B. Computer Software—Divided into three categories: systems software, programming languages, and application software.

C. Systems Software

1. The programs that run the computer and support system management operations. Several of the most frequently encountered types of systems software are
   a. **The operating system**—Interface between the user and the computer hardware.
   b. **Database management systems (DBMS)**—Discussed in the next section.
   c. **Data communications software**—This topic is also discussed in the lesson on "Computer Networks and Data Communication".
   d. **Utility programs**—These programs perform maintenance (e.g., defragging a hard drive, finding and recognizing devices that are attached to a system) tasks.

D. Programming Languages

1. All software is created using programming languages. They consist of **sets of instructions** and a **syntax** that determines how the instructions can be put together. Types and examples of programming languages include:
   a. High-level, general purpose languages, such as the C programming language
   b. Object-oriented languages such as C++, which are used to design modular, reusable software
   c. Integrated development environments, such as Java, which provide templates that can be used to automatically generate code
   d. Hypertext Markup Language (HTML), a tagging language, discussed in the lesson on "The Internet—Structure and Protocols"

e. Scripting languages, such as PERL or Python, which are used to add functionality to web pages

f. Fourth-generation programming languages, which are often used in database systems. An example command might be, "FIND ALL RECORDS WHERE ZIPCODE = 40703."

g. Low-level languages (e.g., assembler or machine) have code that is similar to a computer's instruction set architecture.

E. Application Software

1. The diverse group of end-user programs that accomplish specific user objectives. Can be general purpose (word processors, spreadsheets, databases) or custom-developed for a specific application (e.g., a marketing information system for a clothing designer). May be purchased off the shelf or developed internally.

Definition
Enterprise or Enterprise Resource Planning (ERP) Software: Software for creating an integrated, organization-wide system to support business activities (sales and marketing systems, accounting systems, human resource management systems, etc.). See the "Introduction to Enterprise-Wide and Cloud-Based Systems" lesson for more information.

F. Software Licensing—Organizations should have policies and procedures to ensure that they comply with software copyright law. Failure to do so risks lawsuits and the organization's good name.

III. Databases

A. A Set of Logically Related Files—Most business data is highly inter-related, and consequently, most business data is stored in databases.

B. For example, the following independent flat files could easily be brought together into a database (relationships are represented by arrows):

Customer File<==>Sales Invoice File<==>Product File<==>Purchase Order File<==>Vendor File

C. Databases are characterized by the way the data relationships are established and the way the database is implemented across the organization.

D. The "System Types by Data Structure" lesson describes flat-file systems, which are often contrasted with database systems. Compared to flat-file systems, database systems reduce the amount of redundant data and facilitate data retrieval and reporting.

1. In the context of comparing flat-file versus database systems, redundant data is considered "bad" (i.e., inefficient and ineffective). However, backing up data (see the "Physical Access Controls" lesson) also creates data redundancy. This "planned" data redundancy is an essential control in computerized systems.

E. Database Management System

1. A system for creating and managing a well-structured database. A "middle-ware" program that interacts with the database application and the operating system to define the database, enter transactions into the database, and extract information from the database; the DBMS uses three special languages to accomplish these objectives:

   a. **Data definition language (DDL)**—Allows the definition of tables and fields and relationships among tables.

   b. **Data manipulation language (DML)**—Allows the user to add new records, delete old records, and to update existing records.

c. **Data query language (DQL)**—Allows the user to extract information from the database; most relational databases use structured query language (SQL) to extract the data; some systems provide a graphic interface that essentially allows the user to "drag and drop" fields into a query grid to create a query; these products are usually called **query-by-example (QBE)**.

2. **Database controls**—A DBMS should include the following controls:

   a. **Concurrent access issues management**—For example, to control multiple users attempting to access the same file or record. These are to prevent record change logouts and errors.

   b. **Access controls**—i.e., tables that specify who can access what data within the system. Used to limit access to appropriate users.

   c. **Data definition standards**—For example, to determine and enforce what data elements must be entered and which are optional. These improve and ensure data quality.

   d. **Backup and recovery procedures**—To ensure integrity in the event of system errors or outages. These prevent data loss and corruption.

   e. **Update privileges**—Define who can update the data, and when the data can and should be updated. These are used to control data changes and improve data integrity.

   f. **Data elements and relationships controls**—To ensure data accuracy, completeness, and consistency.

Information Systems Hardware

This lesson introduces, or reviews, computer hardware concepts. Some of this content is also covered in the "Other IT Considerations" lesson in the AUD section of CPAexcel. Many of the questions from the "Other IT Considerations" lesson in the AUD section of CPAexcel are useful and relevant to this lesson.

After studying this lesson, you should be able to:

1. Define and describe the types of, and relations among, computer hardware components.
2. Describe the common types of computers.
3. Give examples of applications of the types of computers.
4. Give examples of applications of the differing types of secondary storage devices.

I. **Computer Hardware**—These are hunks of metal and silicone and plastic. To paraphrase Dave Barry, computer hardware "is the part of the computer that stops working if you spill beer on it." Computer hardware includes the physical equipment in your computer and the equipment that your computer uses to connect to other computers or computer networks. Computer hardware falls into four principal classifications:

   A. **Central Processing Unit (CPU)**—The CPU is the control center of the computer system.

      The CPU has three principal components:

      1. **Control unit**—Interprets program instructions.
      2. **Arithmetic logic unit (ALU)**—Performs arithmetic calculations.
      3. **Primary storage (main memory)**—Stores programs and data while they are in use. It is divided into two main parts:
         a. **Random access memory (RAM)**—Stores data temporarily while it is in process.
         b. **Read-only memory (ROM)**—A semi-permanent data store for instructions that are closely linked to hardware (e.g., "firmware"). Includes portions of the operating system. Hard to change.

   B. **Secondary Storage Devices**—Provide permanent storage for programs and data; depending on their configuration these devices can either be online (the data on the device is available for immediate access by the CPU) or offline (the device is stored in an area where the data is not accessible to the CPU).

      1. **Magnetic disks**—Random access devices: data can be stored on and retrieved from the disk in any order. A common form of secondary storage. Also called "hard disks" or "hard disk drives" (HDDs).
      2. **Magnetic tape**—Magnetic tape is a **sequential access device**: Data is stored in order of the primary record key (i.e., document number, customer number, inventory number, etc.) and is retrieved sequentially; although once used for transaction processing, now mostly used in **data archives**.
      3. **Optical disks**—Use laser technology to "burn" data on the disk (although some rewritable disks use magnetic technology to record data); in general, read-only and write-once optical disks are more stable storage media than magnetic disks; optical disks, like magnetic disks, are random access devices. There are several different types of optical disks.
         a. **RAID (redundant array of independent [previously, inexpensive] disks)**—A technology for storing redundant data on multiple magnetic disks. Its purpose is to reduce the likelihood of data loss.

b. **Solid state drives (SSDs)**—Use microchips to store data and require no moving parts for read/ write operations. SSDs are faster and more expensive per gigabyte than CDs, DVDs, and HDDs. SSDs are increasingly used instead of HDDs in microcomputers, but cost and limited capacity have constrained their adoption. SSDs that are pluggable are often called "thumb drives," "flash drives," or "USB drives" (because they use a USB interface to plug into other devices).

c. **Cloud-based storage**—Also called "Storage as a Service" (SaaS). This type of storage is hosted offsite, typically by third parties, and is accessed via the Internet. See the CPAExcel lesson, "Introduction to Enterprise—Wide and Cloud—Based Systems" on this topic.

C. **Peripherals**—Devices that transfer data to or from the CPU but do not take part in processing data; peripherals are commonly known as input and output devices (I/O devices).

1. **Input devices**—Instruct the CPU and supply data to be processed. Examples include keyboard, mouse, trackball, touch-screen technology, point-of-sale (POS) scanners.
2. **Output devices**—Transfer data from the processing unit to other formats. For example: **printers, plotters, monitors, flat panel displays, cathode ray tube (CRT) displays.**

D. **Common Types of Computers**—Computers are often categorized according to their processing capacity and use.

1. **Supercomputers**—Computers at the leading edge of processing capacity; their definition is constantly changing as the supercomputer of today often becomes the personal computer of tomorrow; generally used for calculation-intensive scientific applications, for example, weather forecasting and climate research.
2. **Mainframe computers**—Powerful computers used by commercial organizations to support mission-critical tasks such as sales and order processing, inventory management, and e-commerce applications. Unlike supercomputers, which tend to support processor-intensive activities (i.e., a small number of highly complex calculations), mainframe computers tend to be input and output (I/O) intensive (i.e., a very large number of simple transactions). Frequently support thousands of simultaneous users.
3. **Servers (high-end and mid-range)**—Computers that are specifically constructed to "serve" thousands of users on a client/server computer network. May have some of the control features of mainframe computers but run slower and cost less.
4. **Personal computers (PCs) or workstations**—Designed for individual users and typically include word processing and spreadsheet software, and, network connectivity to enable people to check their Facebook pages. Sometimes also called a "fat client."
5. **Thin client computers**—Computers with minimal capabilities (e.g., slow processing speed, small amount of storage) that is used to access resources on a network system.
6. **Laptop computers**—Light, portable computers that include a greater risk of theft than a PC or workstation.
7. **Tablet computers**—Lighter and less powerful than laptops but bigger and more powerful than mobile devices.
8. **Mobile computing devices**—Include smartphones, handheld devices, and, increasingly, wearable computing technologies (e.g., Fitbit). Ubiquitous computing devices that, like thin client computers, depend on network connections for their value and power.

Transaction Processing

After studying this lesson, you should be able to:

1. Describe the steps and processes in a typical: (a) manual accounting system, (b) batch processing systems, (c) online, real-time processing system, and (d) data entry and master file updating process.
2. Describe the advantages and disadvantages of batch versus online, real-time processing.
3. Give examples of appropriate and inappropriate applications of batch and ORLT.
4. Give examples of common controls in batch processing systems.
5. Give examples of common controls in OLRT systems.

I. **Transaction Processing**—How are manual and automated accounting systems similar? How do they differ? This lesson reviews manual transaction processing. It then compares and contrasts manual with computerized transaction processing. Some of the documents, validation techniques, and processing procedures used in manual accounting systems carry over to computerized transaction processing systems.

II. **Manual Processing of Accounting Information**—The steps in the classic manual accounting process model are as follows:

   A. A business transaction occurs and is captured on a source document.

   B. Data from the source document is recorded chronologically in a journal (journalizing):

      1. The journal records the complete accounting transaction—the debit and the credit.

   C. Individual debits and credits are copied from the journal to the ledgers (posting); all transactions are posted to the general ledger, and many are also posted to a subsidiary ledger.

      1. **The general ledger**—Classifies transactions by financial statement accounts (cash, inventory, accounts payable, sales revenue, supplies expense, etc.).
      2. **The subsidiary ledgers (subledgers)**—Classify transactions by alternative accounts (e.g., customer accounts, vendor accounts, product accounts). Not all transactions are posted to subledgers: each subledger corresponds to a single general ledger account, and only transactions that affect that account are posted in the subledger. Examples of subledgers include:

         a. **A/R subledger**—Classifies A/R transactions (credit sales and customer payments) by customer

         b. **A/P subledger**—Classifies A/P transactions (credit purchases and payments to vendors) by vendor

         c. **Inventory subledger**—Classifies inventory transactions (product purchases and product sales) by product

   D. The ledgers are used to produce summarized account reports:

      1. The general ledger produces the trial balance and financial statements.
      2. The subsidiary ledgers produce reports consistent with their content (customer A/R balances, vendor A/P balances, etc.).

III. **Computerized Processing of Accounting Information**—In mostly automated accounting systems, transaction data is captured and recorded chronologically; it is then reclassified and summarized by account; finally, the account summaries are used to produce financial statements and other reports.

Files used to record this information correspond roughly to journals and ledgers. However, these activities occur much more quickly in automated than in manual systems.

A. **Data Entry/Data Capture**—When a transaction occurs, the data may be manually recorded on a physical source document and then keyed into the system, or the data may be captured electronically using automated data capture equipment such as bar code readers.

   1. The transaction data is recorded in a **transaction file**:

      a. **Transaction files**—In a computerized environment, they are equivalent to journals in a manual environment.

      b. **Transaction files are temporary files**—Data in the transaction files is periodically purged from the system to improve system performance.

B. **Master File Update**—Data from the transaction files is used to update account balances in the master files. For example, the data from recording a utilities bill payment would be used to increase the balance of the utilities expense account and decrease the balance of the cash account in the general ledger master file.

   1. **Master files** are used to maintain transaction totals by account:

      a. **Master files**—In a computerized environment, they are equivalent to ledgers in a manual environment.

      b. The general ledger and the subsidiary ledgers are all examples of master files.

      c. Master files are **permanent files.** The individual account balances change as transactions are processed but the accounts and master files themselves are never deleted.

C. **System Output**—The master file account balances are used to produce most reports.

   1. The general ledger master file is used to produce the financial statements.

IV. **Processing Methods**—The processing method refers to the way computerized systems capture data and update the master file. Two principal methods are employed:

A. **Batch Processing**—Batch processing is a periodic transaction processing method in which transactions are processed in groups:

   1. Input documents are **collected and grouped** by type of transaction. These groups are called **"batches."** Batches are **processed periodically** (i.e., daily, weekly, monthly, etc.).

   2. Batch processing is accomplished in four steps:

Step 1: Data entry: The transactions data is manually keyed (usually) and recorded in a transactions file.

Step 2: Preliminary edits: The transaction file data is run through an edit program that checks the data for completeness and accuracy; invalid transactions are corrected and re-entered.

Step 3: Sorting: The edited transaction file records are sorted into the same order as the master file.

Step 4: Master file update: The individual debits and credits are used to update the related account balance in the general ledger master file and, if appropriate, in the subsidiary ledger master file.

3. An example of batch processing for an inventory update:

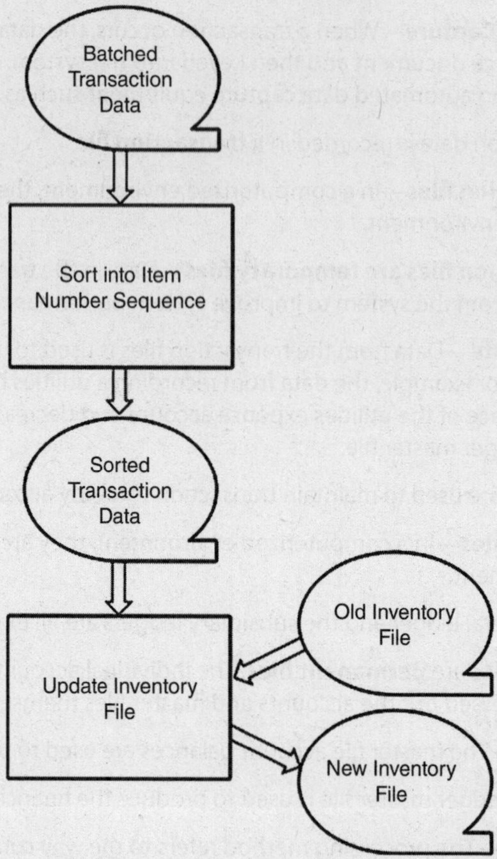

4. **Batch controls**—One or more batch control totals is usually calculated for each batch.

   a. The manually calculated batch control total is compared to computer-generated batch control totals as the batch moves through the update process.

   b. Differences between the two control totals indicate a processing error.

5. Batch processing is a **sequential processing method**—transactions are sorted in order to match the master file being updated.

   a. In some situations, sequential transaction processing can dramatically improve transaction processing efficiency.

6. **Time lags**—An inherent part of batch processing: There is always a time delay between the time the transaction occurs, the time that the transaction is recorded, and the time that the master file is updated. Thus, under batch processing:

   a. The accounting records are not always current.

   b. Detection of transaction errors is delayed.

7. Batch processing is appropriate when:

   a. Transactions occur periodically (e.g., once a week, once a month, etc.).

   b. A significant portion of the master file records will be updated.

   c. Transactions are independent (e.g., no other time-critical activities depend on the transaction in question).

B. Online, Real-Time (OLRT) Processing—OLRT is a continuous, immediate transaction processing method in which transactions are processed individually as they occur.

1. In OLRT processing, transactions are entered and the master files updated as transactions occur.
    a. Requires random access devices such as magnetic disk drives to process transactions.
2. Each transaction goes through all processing steps (data entry, data edit, and master file update) before the next transaction is processed. Thus, under OLRT processing:
    a. The accounting records are always current.
    b. Detection of transaction errors is immediate.
3. Because transactions are processed as they occur, OLRT systems generally require a networked computer system to permit data entered at many locations to update a common set of master files; this means that OLRT systems are more expensive to operate than batch systems.
4. OLRT systems are desirable whenever:
    a. It is critical to have very current information.
    b. Transactions are continuous and interdependent as, for example, when a sales order is received: sales orders are received continuously and, once approved, cause other activities to occur (e.g., picking the goods in the warehouse, shipping the goods to the customer, invoicing the customer).
    c. Transactions are infrequent and few in number. (Batch processing is cost-effective only when a significant number of transactions must be processed.)

C. Point-of-Sale (POS) Systems—POS systems are one of the most commonly encountered data capture systems in the marketplace today. POS systems combine online, real-time processing with automated data capture technology, resulting in a system that is highly accurate, reliable, and timely.

1. POS systems usually consist of a special-purpose computer connected to or integrated with an **electronic cash register**:
    a. Each individual POS system is generally **networked to a central computer** that maintains a database of the products available for sale as well as the financial accounting data.
2. POS systems use **scanners** to capture data encoded on **product bar codes**:
    a. Using scanners provides dramatic increases in **processing efficiency** and **transactions accuracy**.
3. Increased transaction detail and faster available information in a POS system facilitate:
    a. Just-in-time inventory management
    b. Cash flow management
    c. Integration of marketing with production (e.g., build to order or on demand)

Emerging Technologies

Emerging Technologies in AIS

This lesson discusses emerging technologies in AIS and their implications for accounting and accountants. Recent technology advances promise big changes in the risks of and controls in accounting systems.

After studying this lesson, you should be able to:

1. Describe the characteristics of HMDs, automated IT security, recent advances in payment processing systems, and the Internet of things.
2. Give examples of how these emerging technologies can be used to provide strategic advantage, improve risk management, and increase internal control.
3. Give examples of the risks of these emerging technologies to organizations.

Definition
COSO's Principle #11 (out of 17): "The organization selects and develops general control activities over technology to support the achievement of objectives."

This lesson discusses five emerging technologies with the potential to disrupt traditional accounting systems. Knowing about these technologies helps in answering written communication tasks. What better way to impress a CPA Exam grader than to demonstrate your knowledge of emerging AIS technologies?

I. Introduction

- **A.** The technologies presented in this lesson are potentially disruptive for accounting systems. Remember the Internet? Own a cell phone? These are examples of some earlier disruptive technologies.
- **B.** This lesson progresses from technologies that are already widely implemented (e.g., payment processing systems) to those for which implementation is expected (head-mounted displays [HMDs] in 10 to 15 years).

II. Emerging Payment Processing Systems

- **A.** Historically payment services were provided by financial institutions; they were very expensive to sellers.
  - **1.** New vendors and innovations in payment systems (i.e., systems for processing customers' payments for goods and services) are increasingly important drivers of business success.
- **B.** Emerging payment systems are simple to use, cheaper, and seller and user friendly. They can reduce costs and increase online sales.
- **C.** **What Are Payment Systems**?—Credit cards, Apple Pay, Samsung Pay, Walmart Pay, PayPal, Venmo, Amazon "One-Click" payments
- **D.** **Seller Strategies**—Simplify payments for customers, reduce processing fees.
  - **1.** **State of the market**—Many payment options, no clear market winner yet.
  - **2.** **Strategies for simplifying payments**
    - **a.** Reduce customer keystrokes and data entry.
    - **b.** Payment data storage is a customer choice.
    - **c.** "Make payment systems for dummies"—Clarify when payment is processed. Make paying easy.
    - **d.** Market the payment systems—Make it clear to consumers – which methods do we accept?

e. Monitor check-out abandonment rates? Identify check-out problems.

f. Train employees in new systems and methods.

III. Internet of Things (IoT)

A. The Internet of things (IoT) is the widespread connection of electronic devices to the Internet. Recent news reports suggest that hackers are increasingly targeting (i.e., hacking) IoT applications.

1. The result is a real-time data stream that enables the monitoring and control of any device that is electronic. Gartner, an IT research and consulting company, estimates that by 2020 there will be over 26 billion devices connected to the Internet.

2. Directed at physical processes (e.g., consumer applications, manufacturing, mining, energy production, and logistics and distribution)

   a. Receive a real-time data feed from any electronic device

B. Example Applications

1. **Medicine and agriculture**—Real-time data feeds that monitor the status and condition of any living organism (e.g., Fitbit)

2. **Insurance**—Sensory data on road conditions, weather, traffic, driver behavior, etc.

3. **Banking**—Monitor use and status of ATMs, physical security of offices and buildings

4. **Marketing**—Respond in real time to customers' interests and physical proximity

C. Business Implications

1. Transform business processes and models

2. Enables new products (e.g., the Fitbit)

3. New, advanced analytics—track emerging trends and interests

4. New insight into production processes and customers

D. Accounting Implications

1. Automated information collection and data streaming for audits (internal and external) and tax engagements

2. Real-time managerial accounting monitoring data

3. **New skill sets for CPAs**—Managing the IoT and the resulting "big data"

E. Risks

1. **Privacy, intrusive devices**—Previously unimagined data will become available about individuals and their behavior (e.g., medical and financial data)

2. Complexities of data ownership, availability, distribution, storage

3. The creation and management of "big data"

IV. Automated IT Security: Authentication

A. Everyone hates the current state of user access security (i.e., authentication). Memorizing hundreds of passwords, which shouldn't be written down, to authenticate identity is increasingly obsolete in a world in which recognition technologies are accurate, cheap, and readily available.

B. The Goal for User Authentication—Fully integrated, multifactor security, automated systems

1. The adoption of the IoT will lead to increasing use of automated security systems.

2. Authentication in these systems will use multiple identifiers. Identifiers may include:

   a. Biometrics (e.g., fingerprints, iris scans, body scans, facial recognition)

   b. Advanced analytics that identify system use patterns (e.g., typical login times, pressure and force on keyboard and mouse)

c. Objects (e.g., cell phones, key cards)

d. Knowledge (challenge questions)

e. Contextual patterns of use that combine the above identifiers using artificial intelligence (AI).

C. **Risks and Prognosis**

1. Risks include the inevitable failures and shake-outs as vendors and users experiment with new authentication systems.

2. Gartner Reports expects increasing waves of IT security automation that, in 10 to 20 years, will result in the *complete automation* of integrated, multifactor authentication systems.

V. Head-Mounted Displays (HMDs)

A. Twenty years ago no one would have believed how smartphones have changed our lives. Some experts now forecast that, within 20 years, HMDs will similarly dominate the market for immersive communication technologies. One example of an HMD is Google Glass. Some aircraft pilots have been wearing HMDs for many years.

B. **What Is an HMD?**

1. HMDs are display devices that are worn on the head (like glasses) or as a part of a helmet. They include one or two small optical displays.

2. HMDs will be fully or partially "immersive." That is, they will provide augmented (partially) or virtual (fully) reality experiences that immerse the user in a digitized experience (e.g., Google Glass).

3. **Risks**—Digital distraction and information overload

C. **Implications for Accounting**—Ubiquitous computing. Real-time data streaming.

1. Make real-time monitoring more convenient and accessible. Less intrusive than "head-down" devices like smartphones.

2. The Internet of Things will be an important driver of HMD adoption and use. Combining IoT with HMDs creates the possibility for greater flexibility of head movements, lower weight, and easier accessibility to critical visual information and real-time data streaming.

3. **Example Applications**—Monitoring productive processes, financial results, continuous monitoring of critical accounting applications including IT availability and real-time event streaming (e.g., hacks into an accounting system), document retrieval, virtual presence video calling

VI. Gamification

Given the availability of gaming development software, why should learning about accounting, business, auditing, appropriate professional behavior, and control systems be boring?

A. What is it?

1. Gamification is the application of video gaming principles in simulations, or the use of badges and points as motivators, to engage users in learning content that is essential for their jobs.

B. What is its value?

1. Gamification "makes learning fun again" (to paraphrase Donald Trump). It uses psychological principles based in graphics, design, images, motivation, and narrative (stories) to simulate actual scenarios that are relevant to users' jobs.

2. Evidence suggests that users learn and retain more from gamification than traditional learning approaches.

C. Examples of gamification

1. Several CPA firms use gamification to reward employees for engaging in health and wellness

activities. By earning points for healthy, stress-reducing behaviors, employees not only take better care of themselves but also win prizes and rewards for these behaviors.

2. One large CPA firm (RSM) uses gamification to simulate opportunities for employees to build client relationships and to engage in behaviors that promote the firm's brand. Teams of employees compete between offices for points, which convert to donations to winning office local charities.
3. The AICPA created the game" Bank On It" as a fun and engaging way to teach high school students the principles of accounting.
4. A large bank uses IT security and data privacy training provided by *True Office* to train employees in data privacy and compliance. Results indicate that employees both learn more and enjoy the training more with gamification.

VII. Summary

A. This lesson discusses five technologies—emerging payment processing systems, the Internet of Things, automated IT security, head-mounted displays (HMDs), and gamification—that are likely to be disruptive technologies in the next five to 20 years.

Sources

AICPA. 2017. Bank On It website, https://www.startheregoplaces.com/students/games-tools/bank-on-it/.

Baxter, R. J., et al. 2016. "Applying Basic Gamification Techniques to IT Compliance Training: Evidence from the Lab and Field." *Journal of Information Systems* 30, no. 3: 119–133.

Huffman, E. "How Gamification Can Help Engage Millennial Employees," *Journal of Accountancy*, July 16, 2016, http://www.journalofaccountancy.com/newsletters/2016/jul/how-gamification-can-engage-millennial-employees.html#sthash.t8m6TGVA.dpuf

Big Data

This lesson discusses big data—what it is, its value and risks, and its implications for accounting and accountants. Recent technology advances promise big changes in the risks of and controls in accounting systems.

After studying this lesson, you should be able to:

1. Define and describe big data.
2. Give examples of risks and benefits of big data.
3. Identify some possible sources of big data in organizations.
4. Describe the relevance of big data to CPAs.
5. Describe the control considerations to consider in big data initiatives.

Definition
COSO's Principle #11 (out of 17) "The organization selects and develops general control activities over technology to support the achievement of objectives."

I. What Is Big Data?

A. The creation, analysis, storage, and dissemination of extremely large data sets. Such data sets have recently become feasible due to advances in computer storage technologies (e.g., the cloud), advanced data analytics, and massive computing power.

B. Gartner (an IT research and consulting firm) definition: "high volume, velocity, and/or variety information assets that demand new, innovative forms of processing for enhanced decision making, business insights or process optimization."

1. Ubiquitous computing (i.e., smartphones and wearables, e.g., the Fitbit), the Internet of Things, and advances in biometrics (i.e., automated human recognition) are all sources for big data.

C. **Governance**—Organizations must establish a clear governance structure for big data projects.

1. They must consider the responsibilities, scope, and limits of their big data projects.
2. Big data projects require a clear purpose, scope, and plan.
3. Organizations must consider the qualitative characteristics of information in formulating big data plans (see the information criteria section of the "The COBIT Model of IT Governance and Management" lesson for a listing of the qualitative characteristics of information)

D. Big data will result in **expanding** existing data warehouses.

E. **Big Data Analytics and "Smart Data"**

1. **Emerging focuses of big data**—Data mining (discovering data trends), expanded OLAP (online analytical processing)
2. Another name for big data is "smart data," which generally refers to both big data and the use of advanced analytic methods on the data.

F. **Big Data Sources**

1. **Organizational "dark data"**—Data collected from business activities that may be reused in analytics, business relationships, or directly monetized (sold). "Dark data" is also sometimes used as a synonym for "metadata" (i.e., data about data).
2. **Operational and social media data**

II. Value and Risks of Big Data

A. Value—Uses include marketing and sales, operational and financial performance, risk and compliance management, product and service innovation, improving customer experiences and loyalty, data monetization (sales)

B. Risks

1. Privacy
2. Legal issues and prohibited uses (e.g., of medical data and HIPPA)
3. Technology and structure—Where and how will be store and protect it?

C. Example Projects

1. Xerox used big data to reduce attrition at call centers by ~ 20%.
2. The Weather Company and IBM partnered to better manage weather forecasts to improve business performance. The project integrates data from over 100,000 sensors and aircraft and millions of smartphones, buildings, and moving vehicles.
3. Kroger integrates customer data to enable it to improve its product offerings and target offerings to specific sets of customers. As a result, Kroger's is the #1 rated loyalty card program in the industry.

III. Relevance to Accounting and Accountants

A. Possible New Roles for CPAs—Data scientists of financial information

B. Important Applications of Big Data in Auditing, Tax Work, and Risk Analysis

1. E.g., big data analysis of risk of material misstatement of an audit client
2. E.g., big data analysis of our identified risk areas

C. Control Considerations for Big Data Initiatives

1. **Approach and understanding**—Is top management informed of and engaged in the big data initiative. Do they understand its scope and risks?
2. **Data quality**—Does the data collection and storage process result in accurate, reliable, complete, and timely data?
3. **Data confidentiality and privacy**—Does the organization comply with external laws and regulations and its own internal standards for data confidentiality and privacy?
4. **Availability**—Are disaster recovery and event response plans in place and reliable?

IV. Conclusion

A. Big data sets are here and sure to grow in importance.

B. They have varied uses and applications.

C. Users, including accountants and auditors, must consider ethical and legal risks.

D. Users, including accountants and auditors, must consider controls over big data projects.

Bitcoin and Blockchain: Implications for Accounting and Control

After studying this lesson, you should be able to:

1. Define and describe bitcoin and blockchain.
2. Identify and describe some common uses of bitcoin and blockchain.
3. Explain why individuals or businesses would use bitcoin or blockchain.
4. Explain why bitcoin is attractive as a payment means for criminals.
5. Describe some risks and limitations of bitcoin.

I. Bitcoin Introduction

A. What Is bitcoin?

1. Bitcoin is an intangible asset—An intangible asset is an object that has value but not a physical form. Intangible assets include patents, trademarks, copyrights, goodwill (in some cases) and bitcoins. The intangible asset designation is the view of the IRS (i.e., that bitcoins are taxed as "property" not as currency).
   a. One difference in bitcoins from some intangible assets is that bitcoins can be bought, sold, and traded (in contrast, e.g., to goodwill).
   b. Because bitcoin is taxed as property, gains or losses are capital gains or losses.
2. Bitcoin is also "electronic cash" (but remember, bitcoin is taxed by the IRS as property not as a currency). However, unlike most cash, no central government or authority manages bitcoin. It is a peer-to-peer (i.e., decentralized) currency that relies on a database system (called blockchain) to authenticate and validate the audit trail and existence of bitcoins.
3. Bitcoin is a decentralized currency that is not under the control of a government, centralized authority, or financial institution. Bitcoin is the first and most popular "crypto-currency" (i.e., a currency that relies on encryption technology for validation and control). (But remember, bitcoin is taxed as property not as currency.)
4. Bitcoin is also a network, payment, and accounting system. To buy or sell bitcoins, to use them as payments, or to receive them as income, one must have a wallet (much like a bank account) and a connection to a bitcoin exchange.

II. Bitcoin Technology, Benefits, and Risks

A. Technology of Bitcoin

1. Bitcoins are created by "mining," which is basically solving mathematical puzzles requiring dedicated, very fast computers.
2. The network: Accounting for (i.e., tracking) bitcoins operates on a **peer-to-peer network**, which is an alternative to the client-server network discussed in the CPAExcel lesson "Computer Networks and Data Communication." In a peer-to-peer network, any node can communicate with any other node. This is different from a client-server network in which all client computers communicate only with the server.
   a. A peer-to-peer network is decentralized, which is essential to bitcoin's goal of independence of centralized authority, governments, and financial institutions.
   b. Bitcoins are stored in a "blockchain" (i.e., a type of fancy database). Blockchain is the topic of the second part of this lesson.

c. Bitcoin transactions—You send or receive bitcoins with an address, which is like a bank account. Here's an example of a bitcoin address: 2MJf24pNsLuFYk9mJd1dXHkKj9h5YhoEey. Bitcoin addresses are matched to private keys, which need to be kept confidential. If you have both a bitcoin address and the private key for that address, you can make bitcoin payments from that address (note the potential security issue with bitcoins). Of course, you also need an address to send payment, in order to pay by bitcoin.

B. Why Use Bitcoins?

1. Bitcoins are independent of any government or central authority. For those who distrust central authority and love markets (e.g., libertarians), bitcoins are a great alternative to currencies that are controlled by governments.
2. Some users try to make their bitcoin transactions anonymous by using anonymous accounts and exchanges that work to hide users' identity. Imagine the most embarrassing purchase that you have ever made. Now image the receipt for that purchase on the desk or cell phone of your boss, your significant other, or your parents. Everyone has purchases that they don't want to share with the world. Perhaps you are more interested in bitcoin now?
3. Bitcoin transaction costs are cheap. Banks and other financial institutions charge (sometimes large) transactions fees. As of May 2017, the fee for executing a bitcoin transaction is less than $0.01 US. For most merchants, bank card fees start at around 2%. For a large volume of transactions, bitcoins save money for both merchants and consumers.
4. Bitcoin transactions are favorites of criminals and terrorists since they were originally designed to be untraceable. But it is now challenging to make bitcoin transactions untraceable since new methods exist for tracking these transactions. These new tracking methods are used by law enforcement agencies.

C. Bitcoin Risks, According to the Securities and Exchange Commission

1. New investments, including new currencies, have a heightened risk of fraud. Bitcoin investors and users may be targets for fraudsters and criminals.
   a. Example—A bitcoin Ponzi scheme. In July 2013, the Securities and Exchange Commission charged an individual for an alleged bitcoin-related Ponzi scheme. The defendant advertised a bitcoin "investment opportunity," promising investors up to 7% returns *per week*. Instead, the defendant used bitcoins from new investors to pay existing investors.
   b. In 2016, $72M USD was stolen from the world's largest bitcoin exchange (Bitfinex Exchange in Hong Kong). Unsurprisingly, the method used in the hack has not been fully disclosed (since doing so would likely spur others to try the hack).
   c. Some law enforcement officers call bitcoins "bitcons" because of their use in cons and frauds and the frequency with which crooks target bitcoins for theft.
2. Do not expect to recover bitcoin losses from fraud. Ironically, the potential anonymity of bitcoins (which makes them attractive) also makes recovery of losses difficult for law enforcement.
   a. Recovery issues include the difficulty of tracing bitcoin transactions, their international (cross-border) use, the absence of an issuing authority, and the difficulty of seizing or freezing bitcoins.
3. Holding and investing in bitcoins has unique risks.
   a. These include a lack of insurance, a history of extreme price fluctuations (volatility), the possibility of government regulation and restriction of bitcoins (e.g., China, Vietnam, Iceland), and security issues (e.g., bitcoin exchanges may fail—Mt. Gox, a bitcoin exchange, failed after hackers stole bitcoins worth millions).

III. Blockchain Introduction

A. What Is Blockchain?

1. Blockchain is a decentralized, distributed ledger. "Decentralized" and "distributed" mean that anyone in the peer-to-peer "network" (i.e., the people and machines that are allowed access to the ledger) can always log, view, and confirm its validity and accuracy. Simply stated, blockchain is an independent, secure, non-modifiable audit trail of transactions, collected into an open ledger database. It is also an encryption-secured, distributed database of transactions.

2. Blockchain was created as part of the invention of bitcoins to provide a secure, decentralized cryptocurrency tracking system.

3. A blockchain record is an electronic file that consists of "blocks," which document transactions. Each block includes a time and a link to a previous block using a unique code.

4. Because blockchain relies on decentralized users confirming one another's ledgers, it requires adoption by many users to be useful. Hence, blockchain is unlikely to transform business in the short term.

5. The security of blockchain depends on three factors: independent confirmation; asymmetric encryption; and cheap, fast computing capacity. Committing a fraud in the blockchain would require altering a block (i.e., a transaction record). Difficulties in committing this fraud include:

   a. This fraud would require changing *all* copies of the record across the *entire* distributed database. Anyone monitoring the fraudster's blockchain could identify the alteration and the fraud. Game over!

   b. Altering other copies (i.e., those other than the fraudster's) of the blockchain would require acquiring the private keys for *all* other copies of the blockchain. In a large distributed network, this would be impossible.

   c. Cheap, fast computing power makes it easy for networked computers to monitor for attempts to change the blockchain.

For BEC TBS and written communication questions, remember that blockchain is a powerful example of COSO's advocacy of continuous monitoring. Blockchain is an excellent example of a new technology that enables continuous monitoring of the accounting system.

IV. Blockchain Applications, Risks, and Limitations

A. Blockchain Applications (examples are from Blockchain Geeks, undated)

1. Smart contracts—Blockchain enables the enforcement of contracts through mutual block monitoring (e.g.., Ethereum). Imagine that a bank agrees to loan money to a company where the interest rates is tied to the company's financial ratios. Blockchain could make the company's financial data transparent to the bank by embedding the financial data in the blockchain.

2. Internet of Things (IoT)—One likely application of blockchain's "smart contracts" is the Internet of things. Imagine a restaurant supplier who wants to monitor and purchase only chickens that are treated humanely by a chicken farm. With IoT sensors installed on each chicken (monitoring its physiology) and blockchain, the supplier could accept or reject **individual** (!) chickens based on their treatment.

3. Open source payment—Why use financial institutions, and their fees, for payments when a verifiable, open-ledger network is available for these payments? Why not make payments directly between parties? Coming to an economy near you, and soon, are payment systems that rely on blockchain and its peer-to-peer system (e.g., OpenBazaar).

4. Financing and crowdfunding—The previous example also illustrates the use of blockchain for financing. Crowdfunding (e.g., Kickstarter and Gofundme) offers another opportunity for blockchain, including the possibility of crowdfunded start-up operations that are financed by investors investing through blockchain technology.

5. Corporate governance and financial reporting—Imagine a company whose financial records are continuously available to everyone, everywhere, through a blockchain (e.g., in the app

Boardroom). Any recorded issue (is the company making illegal payments to vendors?) could be investigated by anyone with access to the blockchain. If all financial records are available always and everywhere, would we still need external auditors as monitors?

6. Supply chain auditing—Want to monitor whether the T-shirt you bought was made by child labor in Pakistan? Is the diamond your fiancé gave you a blood diamond? Go the company's blockchain and trace its supply chain to its source. The company Provenance offers this service.
7. Predictive analytics—Blockchain can be used to aggregate millions of users' expectations about an event. These predictions can improve forecasting of weather, business outcomes, sporting events, or elections.
8. Identify and access management—Blockchain ledgers can document characteristics of users that enable multifactor identification. With blockchain, users' might need only a single point of identification (e.g., a fingerprint) to link to their permanent record, which could be confirmed by any transaction identifier in the record. Netki is a start-up company that is working to implement such a system. Banks and law enforcement are using similar technologies as a part of anti–money laundering initiatives and "know your customer (KYC)" practices.
9. Auditing and monitoring—The importance of an unassailable transaction record to auditors is perhaps somewhat obvious. If auditors can begin with a transaction record that does not need to be audited, considerable time (and client money) will be saved in internal and external auditing.

B. Risks and Limitations

1. Hacks, cracks, and attacks
   - **a.** The attacks and hacks discussed in the bitcoin section are examples of potential hacks on a blockchain network.
2. Blockchain technology is very complex and relies on sophisticated, advanced encryption and networking technologies.
   - **a.** To crooks and fraudsters, complexity is opportunity. Expect to see several frauds in early blockchain implementations that exploit this complexity.
   - **b.** Complexity means that users can commit what are, after the fact, obvious control errors that lead to large losses. E.g., "I didn't understand that the private key needed to stay private."

V. Summary and Conclusion

A. Bitcoin and, more importantly, blockchain are critical, potentially disruptive technologies for accounting and accountants.

1. Given their potential impact on the practice of accounting, a basic knowledge of these technologies is essential to professional accountants.
2. Large accounting firms (e.g., Deloitte) are investing heavily in exploring blockchain technologies.
3. A basic knowledge of these technologies can impress BEC TBS and written communication graders.

Sources

Babbs, A. "What Is Blockchain and Why Is It Growing in Popularity?" *ARS Technica*, November 6, 2016, https://arstechnica.com/information-technology/2016/11/what-is-blockchain/

Blockchain Geeks, undated. "What Is Blockchain Technology? A Step-by-Step Guide for Beginners." https://blockgeeks.com/guides/what-is-blockchain-technology/

Deloitte. "Blockchain Technology: A Game-Changer in Accounting?" March 2016. https://www2.deloitte.com/content/dam/Deloitte/de/Documents/Innovation/Blockchain_A%20game-changer%20in%20accounting.pdf

Iansiti, M., and K. R. Lakhani. "The Truth About Blockchain," *Harvard Business Review* (January–February 2017). https://hbr.org/2017/01/the-truth-about-blockchain

Securities and Exchange Commission. "Investor Alerts and Bulletins: Investor Alert: Bitcoin and Other Virtual Currency-Related Investments," May 7, 2014. https://www.sec.gov/oiea/investor-alerts-bulletins/investoralertsia_bitcoin.html

Machine Learning and Artificial Intelligence

This lesson introduces a topic that many argue will fundamentally change both accounting practice and professional life: artificial intelligence. It also explores the types of AI systems, their benefits and risks, and some early accounting applications of AI.

After studying this lesson, you should be able to:

1. Define artificial intelligence (AI) and machine learning.
2. Describe the categories of AI.
3. Describe the differing levels of tasks and intelligence of AI systems.
4. Briefly describe the AI applications at Deloitte, KPMG, EY, and PwC.
5. Describe the potential benefits of implementing AI.
6. Describe some short-term, medium-term, and long-term risks of AI.

I. What Is Artificial Intelligence (AI)?

A. Introduction—Will accounting work survive AI?

1. RPA = robotic process automation—this is the replacement of humans with AI and robotics technology
2. Example: Accounting work before and after spreadsheets (1980–2000) (Ip, 2017)
   a. Bookkeeping jobs dropped by ~ one-half (from 2 to 1 million)
   b. Accounting and auditing jobs increased by ~ 100% (from 1 to 2 million)
3. AI and accounting—will we observe similar outcomes from AI as we observed with spreadsheets? Accountants running with (not against) the machines? Increased demand for accountants with technology-enabling skills (e.g., advanced spreadsheet skills, Tableau, R, Python, PERL).

B. Artificial intelligence is the creation of intelligent hardware and software.

1. Most AI systems harvest and use big data. Example: Machine learning systems are of little value without massive data sets to learn from.
2. AI systems demand fast computers.
3. **Categories of AI**
   a. **Machine learning (analysis)**—Systems that use big data to learn rules and categories to enable prediction and classification. For example: neural networks. A common accounting application —classifying journal entries
   b. **Robotics (activity)**—For example: machine-directed welding, controlling production, manufacturing, and distribution processes
   c. **Intelligent agents (engagement)**—Computer "agents" that perform tasks—e.g., data harvesting and cleaning. Can also analyze market trends—e.g., in finding and purchasing airline tickets. Such systems interact with humans (e.g., Siri® on the Apple® iPhone®) and have natural language processing ability.
   d. **Expert systems (analysis and activity)**—Build and apply expertise in a domain. May include machine learning or intelligent agent subsystems.

C. One classification identifies the level of intelligence exhibited by the AI hardware and software. (See the "Types of AI and Their Intelligence Levels" table)

1. Data harvesting and cleaning

a. Includes tasks such as acquiring or extracting data (e.g., pulling it from databases or websites) and cleaning (e.g., putting it in usable form) and validating it (confirming its accuracy). In the next generation of audits, *n* (the sample size) will be "all the data." Why sample when AI technologies make the entire population available for analysis?

Table 1 Types of AI and Their Intelligence Levels

Tasks	Intelligence	Example applications	Example tools and technologies
1. Data harvesting and cleaning	Low	Prepare client information for analysis	Pattern recognition, machine learning
2. Analyzing numbers	Medium	Data analytics—e.g., visualization, prediction	Machine learning, neural networks
3. Analyzing words, images, and sounds	Medium	Analyzing financial statement disclosures, fraud detection	Natural language processing
4. Performing digital tasks	Medium– High	Business process analysis, automated system access controls	Process automation, biometric scanning systems
5. Perform and monitor physical tasks	Medium– High	Audit—Drones observe and count client inventory, robots perform physical tasks	Internet of Things (IoT), video imaging and analysis, industrial robots
6. Self-aware AI	High	Strategic planning and real-time, real-world decision making	None

Source: Adapted from Kokina and Davenport (2017)

2. Analyzing numbers

a. Includes common financial and nonfinancial data analysis using, for example, advanced Excel functions and the Tableau software. For example, Netflix suggests what you should watch next based on quantitative data about your ratings and viewing habits.

3. Analyzing words, images, and sounds

a. Includes the analysis of natural language disclosures in financial statements (e.g., 10-K SEC filings) and from audio files of conference calls (e.g., of CEOs and CFOs presenting and answering questions about their companies). Other examples include analyzing vitas for hiring decisions and Google Translate.

4. Performing digital tasks

a. Includes business process reengineering to improve efficiency and effectiveness. For example, automating security systems to improve recognition and minimize errors through multifactor, automated identification. An area of emerging application. Another example: AI systems have reduced costs by help lawyers and financial analysts review loan contracts (e.g., at JPMorgan Chase).

5. Performing physical tasks

a. Includes applications of robotics and drones, which include both physical devices and IoT sensing and reporting technologies. The most publicized example is self-driving cars.

6. **Self-aware AI**

   a. Does not exist and likely will not exist for 20 to 100 years. Such systems would rival (and eventually exceed?) human intelligence.

II. AI—Accounting Applications—Reported Big 4 Initiatives

A. **KPMG**—Implemented an AI unjt and partnered with IBM Watson™ initiative.

1. IBM Watson is an expert system and natural language processing system (featured on the game show *Jeopardy*).
2. **Example application**—Using AI predictive analytics to help clients identify and manage financial statement risks
3. **So far**—Few updates from KPMG about uses and applications

B. **Deloitte**—Partnering with many vendors to automate specific audit tasks and processes including document review, confirmations, inventory counts, disclosures, predictive risk analytics, and producing and filling client request lists

1. **Example**—Partnering with Kira Systems to do document reviews and extract data from client contracts, leases, employment contracts, invoices, and other documents

C. **PwC**—Halo System analyzes accounting journals for risky transactions and to identify inefficient processes.

1. Automates coding and classification of journal entries
2. Includes a dashboard that displays financial analytic data
3. Includes many traditional analytic tools along with AI-based predictive analytics (e.g., analyses for fraud risk).

D. **EY**—Focused on integrating Big Data and advanced analytics into audit practice.

1. 2017—Launched an AI center in India in early 2017, hired "Global Innovation Artificial Intelligence Leader."
2. Few announced initiatives.

III. AI Benefits and Risks

A. **AI Benefits**

1. Speed, accuracy, and cost. Ability to scale up and speed up applications and to reduce costs. Ability to obtain, clean, and analyze large (all available?) data in real time. Apply AI to robotics, pattern recognition, and complex communication (e.g., natural languages) problems.

B. **Risks of Implementing AI**

1. **Short term**—AI systems often include the biases of their developers. Hence, AI systems must be monitored, reviewed, and validated to identify and correct such biases, which can include:

   1. **Data biases**—Harvesting and creating data sets that omit relevant variables and considerations.
   2. **Prediction biases**—Systems that include biased data will obviously generate biased predictions. In addition, the reasoning built into the system can reflect the biases of developers.
   3. **Learned (or "emergent" or "confirmation") biases**—Smart machines will learn and integrate the biases of those who train them. Hence, machines can be trained to "confirm" the biases of those who train them.

2. **Medium term**

   a. **Lost jobs and disappearing employment**—Some economists and computer scientists argue that many jobs will be lost to AI. Others argue that many jobs will be displaced but not lost.

b. **Legal and ethical issues**—Who is liable when the AI screws up? How can AI systems be integrated into the workforce without disruption? How can privacy be protected when AI systems manage processes? Who monitors the (AI) monitors?

3. **Long term**—The end of humanity? Some experts, including Elon Musk, Bill Gates, and Stephen Hawking, argue that AI may lead to the end of humans, as machines exceed and replace human intelligence and, ultimately, humans (like "SkyNet" in the *Terminator* movie series). These experts argue that AI development should be regulated and controlled.

IV. Implications for Accounting and Auditing Work—Accounting jobs are likely to evolve to include:

A. Partnering with AI to monitor and improve performance and results.

B. Oversight of AI in accounting and auditing tasks. Determining when and how tasks should be automated versus assigned to humans.

C. Developing new and refining existing AI applications.

D. Executing human-only tasks, including:

1. Client relations and interpreting complex financial results and scenarios
2. Tasks that are too narrow or rare to be successfully automated

V. Summary and Conclusion

A. AI and smart machines will change the nature of accounting work over the next 20 years. Opportunities exist within this disruption for accountants to partner with the machines to better serve clients and the public interest.

B. Benefits from AI include scalability, improved service, accuracy (e.g., of predictions), and reduced costs.

C. Risks of AI include bias, employment disruption, and unresolved legal, ethical, and privacy issues.

Sources

Appelbaum, D., and R. A. Nehmer. "Using Drones in Internal and External Audits: An Exploratory Framework." *Journal of Emerging Technologies in Accounting* 14, no. 1 (2017): 99–113.

Davenport, T. H., and J. Kirby. *Only Humans Need Apply: Winners and Losers in the Age of Smart Machines*. New York, NY: Harper Business, 2016.

Ip, G., "We Survived Spreadsheets; We'll Survive AI," *Wall Street Journal*, August 3, 2017, p. A2.

Kokina, J., and T. H. Davenport. "The Emergence of Artificial Intelligence: How Automation Is Changing Auditing." *Journal of Emerging Technologies in Accounting* 14, no. 1 (2017): 115–122.

Williot, B., and W. Andrews. "*A Framework for Applying AI in the Enterprise*." Gartner Reports, 2017. ID G00336031.

Information Security/Availability

Protection of Information

IT Security Principles

The AICPA Assurance Services Executive Committee (ASEC) principles and criteria can be used to evaluate: (1) the controls of a system and (2) the confidentiality and privacy of the information processed by the system. The ASEC specifies five trust services principles, which are the core of this lesson. These principles are attributes of an IT system that support the achievement of management's objectives: security, availability, processing integrity, confidentiality, privacy.

After studying this lesson, you should be able to:

1. Describe the five IT security principles specified by the AICPA Assurance Services Executive Committee (ASEC).
2. Give examples of each of the five IT security principles.
3. Identify the seven categories of criteria that can be used to assess the five IT security principles.
4. Describe the time-based model of controls.
5. Describe a defense-in-depth strategy.
6. Give examples of IT preventive, detective, and corrective controls.

I. **Security**
   - A. Security is the foundation of systems reliability. Security procedures restrict access to authorized users only, protect the confidentiality and privacy of sensitive information, provide integrity of information, and protect against attacks.
   - B. Security is a *top management* issue. Management is responsible for the accuracy of the internal reports and financial statements produced by the organization's information system (IS). Management must certify the accuracy of the financial statements and maintain effective internal controls.

II. **Availability** concerns whether the system is operational and usable as specified in commitments and agreements. This principle relates to whether internal control supports system availability for operations and monitoring.

III. **Processing integrity** concerns the completeness, validity, accuracy, timeliness, and authorization of system processing. Specifically, does the system of internal control help ensure that the system processes information, as intended, without errors or manipulations?

IV. **Confidentiality** concerns whether confidential information is protected consistent with the organization's commitments and agreements.

V. **Privacy** addresses whether the system's collection, use, retention, disclosure, and disposal of personal information conforms to its own commitments and with criteria set forth in generally accepted privacy principles (GAPP). An essential first step in assessing privacy issues is to inventory an organization's relevant data and to understand the laws and regulations to which these data are subject. GAPP includes these 10 subprinciples:
   - A. **Management**—The entity defines documents, communicates, and assigns accountability for its privacy policies and procedures.

B. Notice—The entity tells people about its privacy policies and procedures and explains why personal information is collected, used, retained, and disclosed.

C. Choice and Consent—Give customers and users a choice to opt out (United States) or opt in (Europe) to the collection of their personal information.

D. Collection—The entity collects personal information only for its identified purposes.

E. Use and Retention—The entity uses personal information consistent with its statements about use. It retains personal information only as long as needed or allowed by law or regulations.

F. Access—People can access, review, and update their information.

G. Disclosure to Third Parties—Third parties receive information only according to policy and individual consent.

H. Security for Privacy—Management takes reasonable steps to protect personal information against unauthorized access.

I. Quality—Personal information is accurate, complete, and relevant.

J. Monitoring and Enforcement—Someone monitors the entity's compliance with its privacy policies and procedures and has procedures to address privacy-related complaints and disputes.

VI. Categories of Criteria for Assessing IT Security Principles—The ASEC also specifies the categories of the criteria that can be used (e.g., in an audit or control review engagement) to assess the achievement of the trust services principles. These criteria are organized into seven categories, discussed next, all of which are discussed in other CPAExcel BEC lessons.

A. Organization and Management—The organizational structures and processes for managing and supporting people within its operating units. This includes criteria addressing accountability, integrity, ethical values and qualifications of personnel, and the operational conditions in which they function.

B. Communications—How the organization communicates its policies, processes, procedures, commitments, and requirements to authorized users and other parties engaged with the system.

C. Risk Management, and Design and Implementation of Controls—How the entity:

1. Identifies potential risks that would affect the entity's ability to achieve its objectives
2. Analyzes those risks
3. Develops responses to those risks including the design and implementation of controls and other risk-mitigating actions
4. Conducts ongoing monitoring of risks and the risk management process

D. Control Monitoring—How the entity monitors the system, including the suitability and design and operating effectiveness of the controls, and takes action to address identified deficiencies. This is discussed, in depth, in the COSO control monitoring lessons.

E. Logical and Physical Access Controls—How the entity restricts logical and physical access to the system, provides and removes that access, and prevents unauthorized access to the system.

F. System Operations—How the entity manages the execution of system procedures and detects and mitigates processing deviations, including logical and physical security deviations.

G. Change Management—How the organization identifies the need for changes to the system, manages these changes according to a controlled process, and prevents unauthorized changes from being made.

VII. Preventive, Detective, and Corrective Controls in IT Systems

The categories of preventive, detective, and corrective controls are also important in IT systems and are discussed in the "Types and Limitations of Accounting Controls" lesson. Next we discuss a couple of illustrations of the *application* of these control categories to IT systems. The content below assumes that you can define preventive, detective, and corrective controls.

A. Time-Based Model of Controls

1. Given enough time and resources, most preventive controls can be circumvented. Accordingly, detection and correction must be timely.
2. The time-based model evaluates the effectiveness of an organization's security by measuring and comparing the relationships among the three categories of controls:
   a. P = Time it takes an intruder to break through the organization's preventive controls
   b. D = Time it takes to detect that an attack is in progress
   c. C = Time to respond to the attack
3. If P > (D + C), then security procedures are effective. Otherwise, security is ineffective.

B. Defense-in-Depth—The strategy of implementing multiple layers of controls to avoid having a single point of failure.

1. Computer security involves using a combination of firewalls, passwords, and other preventive procedures to restrict access. Redundancy also applies to detective and corrective controls.
2. Some examples of IT preventive controls used for defense-in-depth include:
   a. Authentication controls to identify the person or device attempting access
   b. Authorization controls to restrict access to authorized users. These controls are implemented with an access control matrix and compatibility tests.
   c. Training in why security measures are important and teach them to use safe computing practices
   d. Physical access controls to protect entry points to the building, to rooms housing computer equipment, to wiring, and to devices such as laptops, cell phones, and PDAs.
   e. Remote access controls include routers, firewalls, and intrusion prevention systems to prevent unauthorized access from remote locations

C. Preventive controls are imperfect, so organizations implement controls to enhance security by monitoring the effectiveness of preventive controls and detecting incidents in which they have been circumvented. Examples of IT detective controls include:

1. **Log analysis (i.e., audit log)**—The process of examining logs that record who accesses the system and the actions they take.
2. **Intrusion detection systems (IDS)**—Automate the monitoring of logs of network traffic permitted to pass through the firewall. The most common analysis is to compare the logs to a database containing patterns of known attacks.
3. **Managerial reports**—Can be created to disclose the organization's performance with respect to the COBIT objectives. Key performance indicators include downtime caused by security incidents, the number of systems with IDS installed, and the time needed to react to security incidents once they are reported.
4. **Security testing**—Include vulnerability scans and penetration testing.

D. Examples of IT Corrective Controls

1. Creation of a computer emergency response team (CERT) to deal with major system incidents
2. A chief security officer with organization-wide responsibility for security
3. **Patch management**—Involves fixing known vulnerabilities and installing the latest updates to antivirus software, firewalls, operating systems, and application programs

Managing Cyber Risk: Part I—Applying COSO Principles to Cyber Risk

At the time of the original COSO internal framework (1992):

- The Internet was a novelty unknown to 99% of the public (in 1992: 14 million users; now > 3 billion users).
- American Online (AOL) had just been released.
- "Cell" phones were bulky and were still only phones (i.e., they were not "smart").
- The release of the first iPhone was 15 years in the future.

This lesson describes how 10 of the 17 COSO principles can be applied to managing cyber risks.

After studying this lesson, you should be able to:

1. Describe how each of the 10 internal control principles in this lesson can be applied to addressing cyber risks.
2. Describe the relationship and roles of preventive, detective, and corrective controls in relation to cyber risks.
3. Describe what, and to whom, an organization should communicate about its cyber risks and controls.

I. Cyber Risk Assessment

A. **Principle 6**—The organization specifies objectives with sufficient clarity to enable the identification and assessment of risks relating to objectives.

   1. Assessing cyber risks should begin with an understanding of which information systems are most valuable to an organization and why they are important to the achievement of the organization's objectives. Unless management understands which systems are critical to organizational objectives and which are not, it will underallocate scarce resources to mission-critical systems and overallocate resources to unimportant systems.
   2. Valuing IT systems requires collaboration and coordination between business unit and IT stakeholders.

B. **Principles 7 and 8—Risk Identification and Fraud**

   1. **Principle 7**—The organization identifies risks to the achievement of its objectives across the entity and analyzes risks in order to determine how the risks should be managed.
   2. **Principle 8**—The organization considers the potential for fraud in assessing risks to the achievement of objectives.
   3. Applying principles 7 and 8 requires an assessment of the likelihood and severity of cyber risk impacts. This initiative should be led by senior management, in collaboration with business and IT stakeholders, and must include individuals with a deep understanding of the organization's cyber risk profile.
   4. Risk identification must consider that cyber-criminals often engineer industry-specific attacks. For example, organized criminals often attack financial institutions and retailers to exploit system vulnerabilities for profit (e.g., credit card data or personally identifiable information [PII]). Alternatively, nation-states or industrial spies might attack the oil and gas industry to steal strategic data about future exploration sites.

C. **Principle 9**—The organization identifies and assesses changes that could significantly impact the system of internal control.

1. Rapidly changing technologies and cyber-criminals' quick adaption to these changes yields new methods of exploiting system vulnerabilities. For example, the changing technologies of the web, mobile, cloud, and social media have increased the risks of exploitation by cyber-criminals. Similarly, outsourcing, offshoring, and third-party contracting (e.g., for cloud storage) expose organizations to potential cyber vulnerabilities that are ultimately outside of the organization's control.

II. Control Activities to Address Cyber Risks

A. **Principle 10**—The organization selects and develops control activities that contribute to the mitigation of risks to the achievement of objectives to acceptable levels.

B. **Principle 11**—The organization selects and develops general control activities over technology to support the achievement of objectives.

C. **Principle 12**—The organization deploys control activities through policies that establish what is expected and procedures that put policies into action.

D. A **defense-in-depth approach**—While cyber risks cannot be avoided, they can be managed through careful design and implementation of appropriate controls. Because cyber breaches are inevitable, control structures should be deployed in a layered approach that prevents intruders from freely roaming the information systems after the initial layers of defense are compromised.

   1. Preventive, detective, and corrective controls are all essential to addressing cyber risks. Well-designed preventive controls may stop attacks from being realized by keeping intruders outside of the organization's internal IT environment and keeping the information systems secure. Additional preventive controls within the internal IT environment may act as obstacles to slow the intruders.

   2. When exploits occur, controls should permit a timely detection of breaches, which enables management to take corrective actions and to assess potential damages as early as possible.

   3. After corrective actions are taken, it is important that management assess the root cause to improve its controls to prevent or detect similar exploits that may occur in the future.

   4. In addition to preventive and detective controls, the control activities deployed to mitigate cyber risks should include a combination of general information technology controls (GITCs) along with other business controls.

E. Control activities related to cyber risks should be mapped to each organizations' objectives and cyber risk profile.

III. Communicating about Cyber Risks and Controls

A. **Principle 13**—The organization obtains or generates and uses relevant, quality information to support the functioning of internal control.

   1. An organization's controls determine the information requirements needed to support the effective monitoring and assessment of these controls. The information requirements of the internal control system will follow from the cyber risk assessment and control design processes described earlier. Formally documenting information requirements (and the related risk analysis and response) helps ensure that processes and controls can be executed consistently with relevant, quality information.

   2. The availability of "big data" (e.g., terabytes of log data related to information systems) can create an information overload problem when communicating about cyber risks. Control system data must be transformed into actionable, high-quality information that informs and communicates about the effectiveness of cyber-related controls.

B. **Principle 14**—The organization internally communicates information, including objectives and responsibilities for internal control, necessary to support the functioning of internal control.

   1. Communication about cyber risks should include all personnel, personnel responsible for managing and monitoring cyber risks and controls, and the board of directors.

a. All personnel

i. People are often called the weakest link in internal control systems. Organization-wide communication should raise awareness and vigilance regarding cyber risks (e.g., what should employees do when they receive an email from a coworker that includes a hyperlink or attachment? What should employees do if they find a USB drive on the floor?).

ii. Cyber-criminals "socially engineer" their attacks to exploit human trust and curiosity.

b. Personnel responsible for managing and monitoring cyber risks and controls

i. Sharing of internal control information among designated personnel will enable relevant personnel to execute their cyber control responsibilities.

ii. Responsible personnel must formally document cyber controls.

c. Board of directors

i. The board must understand critical cyber trends that may influence the organization's ability to achieve its objectives. Complex IT topics must be communicated respectfully and meaningfully to the board.

C. **Principle 15**—The organization communicates with external parties regarding matters affecting the functioning of internal control.

1. External communication about cyber security may be relevant for shareholders, owners, customers, business partners, regulators, financial analysts, government entities, and other external parties.
2. External parties can be useful sources of information about cyber risk assessment and controls (e.g., regulators, industry experts).
3. Some (though surely not all) external parties should be informed about cyber events and cyber control activities (e.g., external auditor).
4. Assistance from cyber risk specialists may be needed to prioritize the deployment of resources against cyber risks.

Managing Cyber Risk: Part II—A Framework for Cybersecurity

After completing this lesson, you should be able to:

1. Describe the purpose of the framework for cybersecurity.
2. Identify and describe the following elements of the framework for cybersecurity: core, profile, and the implementation tiers.
3. Identify and describe the four elements and five functions of the cybersecurity framework.
4. Identify and give examples of the four implementation tiers.
5. Identify and give examples of framework profiles.
6. Identify and give examples of organizational applications of the cybersecurity framework.

I. **Introduction**—The need for a cybersecurity framework

  A. Recent news headlines (e.g., Russia hacking the U.S. election, North Korea hacking and crippling Sony's network) make clear the severity of the threat of cyber risks to national security, public health and safety, and organizational accounting and information systems.

  B. In 2013, then-President Obama issued an executive order to enhance the security and resilience of the U.S. cyber environment. The resulting cyber risk framework was a collaboration between the government and the private sector.

  C. The goals of the framework included creating a common language for understanding, and cost-effective means for managing, organizational cybersecurity risks without imposing regulations. Specifically, the framework provides a means for organizations to:

    1. Describe current cybersecurity and existing risks
    2. Describe target or goal cybersecurity and desired types and levels of risk
    3. Identify and prioritize improvements to cybersecurity
    4. Assess progress toward the cybersecurity goal
    5. Communicate with stakeholders about cybersecurity and risk

  D. The framework complements, but does not replace, existing risk management (e.g., COSO) and cybersecurity (e.g., COBIT) approaches.

  E. Both public (government) and private (business) organizations have responsibilities related to ensuring the U.S. *critical infrastructure*, which is defined as the "systems and assets, … physical or virtual, so vital to the United States that their incapacity or destruction would debilitate security, national economic security, national public health or safety, or any combination of these." National Institute of Standards and Technology, 2014

II. **The framework consists of three parts: the core, the profile, and the implementation tiers.**

  A. **Framework Structure**

    1. The core includes cybersecurity activities, outcomes, and references (i.e., standards and guidelines).
    2. The profiles help align organizational cybersecurity activities with business requirements, risk tolerances, and resources.
    3. The implementation tiers are a way to view and understand alternative approaches to managing cybersecurity risk.

B. The *framework core* is a matrix of four columns or elements by five rows or functions that lists activities (with examples) to achieve specific cybersecurity outcomes. The four core *elements* (functions, categories, subcategories, and references) are types or levels (shown as columns), and the five *functions* or activities (identify, protect, detect, respond, recover) appear in the following figure:

Functions	Categories	Subcategories	References
Identify			
Protect			
Detect			
Respond			
Recover			

Note: this table is reproduced from the framework.

III. The core elements relate to one another.

A. Functions organize basic, high-level cybersecurity activities and include: Identify, Protect, Detect, Respond, and Recover (see descriptions below). They help manage cybersecurity risk by organizing information, enabling risk management, addressing threats, and enabling learning through monitoring.

1. The functions align with existing methods for incident management and help in assessing the value of cybersecurity investments. For example, investments in cybersecurity planning improve responses and recovery, which reduces the effect of cybersecurity events on service quality.

B. Categories are high-level cybersecurity outcomes that link to organizational needs and activities. Examples of categories are: asset management, access control, physical security, and incident detection processes.

C. Subcategories divide categories into specific outcomes of technical and/or management activities. In accounting and auditing terms, these are high-level control goals. Examples include: Identify and catalog external information systems; Protect data at rest; and Investigate notifications from detection systems.

D. (Informative) References are specific standards, guidelines, and practices that provide benchmarks and methods for achieving the control goals (i.e., outcomes) found in the subcategories.

IV. The five core functions (listed here) may be performed periodically or continuously to address evolving cybersecurity risks.

A. Identify—Develop the foundational understanding to manage organizational cybersecurity risk by identifying and assessing organizational systems, assets, data, and capabilities.

1. Identification activities include understanding the business context, the resources that support critical functions, and the related cybersecurity risks. Examples of outcome categories within this function include: asset management, business environment assessment, governance assessment, risk assessment, and risk management strategy.

B. Protect—Develop and implement controls to ensure delivery of critical infrastructure services.

1. The protect function enables preventing, detecting, and correcting cybersecurity events. Examples of outcome categories within this function include: access control, awareness and training, data security, information protection processes and procedures, maintenance, and protective technology.

C. **Detect**—Develop and implement controls to *identify* cybersecurity incidents. This topic is covered in the "Computer Crime, Attack Methods, and Cyber-Incident Response" lesson. Examples of outcome categories within this function include: anomalies and events, security continuous monitoring, and detection processes.

D. **Respond**—Develop and implement controls to *respond* to *detected* cybersecurity events. Examples of outcome categories within this function include: response planning, communications, analysis, mitigation, and security improvements.

E. **Recover**—Develop and implement controls for *building resilience and restoring capabilities or services* impaired due to a cybersecurity event. Examples of outcome categories within this function include: recovery planning, improvements, and communications.

V. Implementation Tiers

A. Implementation tiers identify the degree of control that an organization desires to apply to cybersecurity risk. The tiers range from partial (Tier 1) to adaptive (Tier 4) and describe an increasing degree of rigor and sophistication in cybersecurity risk management and integration with an organization's overall risk management practices.

1. Organizations should determine their desired tier, consistent with organizational goals, feasibility, and cyber risk appetite. Given rapidly changing cyber risks, the assessment of tiers requires frequent attention.

B. The four tier definitions are as follows:

1. Tier 1: Partial

- *Risk Management*—Organizational cybersecurity risk management practices are informal. Risk is managed as ad hoc and reactive. Prioritization of cybersecurity activities may not be directly informed by organizational risk objectives, the threat environment, or business requirements.
- *Integrated Risk Management Program*—Limited awareness of cybersecurity risks with no organization-wide approach to managing cybersecurity risk. Cybersecurity risk management occurs irregularly on a case-by-case basis. Organizational sharing of cybersecurity information is limited.
- *External Participation*—Organization has weak or nonexistent processes to coordinate and collaborate with other entities.

2. Tier 2: Risk Informed

- *Risk Management*—Management approves risk management practices when needed but not as a part of an organizational-wide policy. Prioritization of cybersecurity activities is informed by organizational risk objectives, the threat environment, or business requirements.
- *Integrated Risk Management Program*—While there is some awareness of organizational cybersecurity risk, there is no established, organization-wide approach to managing cybersecurity risk. Risk-informed, management-approved processes and procedures are defined and implemented, and staff have adequate resources for cybersecurity duties. Organizational cybersecurity information sharing is informal and as needed.
- *External Participation*—The organization assesses and understands its cybersecurity roles and risks but has not formalized its capabilities to share information externally.

3. **Tier 3: Repeatable**
   - *Risk Management Process*—The organization's risk management practices are formally approved as policy. Organizational cybersecurity practices are regularly updated based on the application of risk management processes to changes in business requirements and changing threats and evolving technologies.
   - *Integrated Risk Management Program*—Organization-wide management of cybersecurity risk exists. Management has risk-informed policies, processes, and procedures that are defined, implemented, and regularly reviewed. Consistent, effective methods respond to changes in risk. Personnel possess the knowledge and skills to perform their appointed roles and responsibilities.
   - *External Participation*—The organization understands its dependencies and communicates with cyber security partners to enable collaboration and risk-based management in response to incidents.
4. **Tier 4: Adaptive**
   - *Risk Management Process*—The organization adapts its cybersecurity practices based on experience and predictive indicators derived from cybersecurity activities. Continuous improvement processes include advanced cybersecurity technologies and practices. The organization actively adapts to a changing cybersecurity landscape and responds to evolving and sophisticated threats in a timely manner.
   - *Integrated Risk Management Program*—An organization-wide approach to managing cybersecurity risk uses risk-informed policies, processes, and procedures to address cybersecurity events. Cybersecurity risk management is part of the organizational culture and evolves from an awareness of previous activities, information shared by other sources, and continuous awareness of activities on their systems and networks.
   - *External Participation*—The organization manages risk and actively shares information with partners to ensure that accurate, current information is shared to improve collective cybersecurity before a cybersecurity event occurs.

VI. Framework Profiles

A. The framework profile aligns and integrates the functions, categories, and subcategories with the organization's requirements, risk tolerance, and resources. A profile enables organizations to establish a plan for aligning cybersecurity risk with organizational goals. It considers legal and regulatory requirements, industry best practices, and risk appetite. Complex organizations may have multiple profiles, aligned with particular components and recognizing their subunit (e.g., division, branch) needs.

B. Profiles can be developed for both the current and the desired state of cybersecurity. The current profile indicates achieved cybersecurity outcomes. The target profile indicates desired outcomes consistent with cybersecurity risk management goals. Profiles support business requirements and help communicate risk with stakeholders.

C. Comparison of profiles (e.g., current and target) may reveal gaps to address in meeting cybersecurity risk management objectives. Organizational business needs and risk assessment will drive gap reduction priorities. This risk-based approach enables an organization to allocate resources (e.g., staffing, funding) efficiently to achieve cybersecurity goals.

VII. Recommended Framework Applications

A. **Review and Assess Cybersecurity Practices.** The organization asks, "How are we doing?" with respect to cybersecurity and cyber risk, including comparing current cybersecurity activities with those in the core. This review does not replace formal, organization-wide risk management (e.g., guided by COSO). This assessment may reveal a need to strengthen some and reduce other cybersecurity practices and risks. This reprioritizing and repurposing of resources should reduce prioritized cyber risks.

B. **Establish or Improve a Cybersecurity Program.** The following steps illustrate use of the framework to create a new cybersecurity program or improve an existing program. Organizations may repeat these steps as needed.

1. **Prioritize risks and determine scope.** After identifying its mission, objectives, and high-level priorities, the organization makes strategic decisions regarding the scope and purpose of cybersecurity systems and the assets needed to support these objectives.
2. **Link objectives to environment.** The organization identifies its systems and assets, regulatory requirements, and overall risk approach to support its cybersecurity program. It also identifies threats to, and vulnerabilities of, those systems and assets.
3. **Create current profile.** Develop a current profile by indicating which category and subcategory outcomes from the framework core are achieved currently.
4. **Conduct risk assessment.** Guided by the overall risk management process or previous risk assessment, analyze the operational environment to determine the likelihood of a cybersecurity event and its potential impact. Monitor for and consider emerging risks and threats and vulnerable data to understand risk likelihood and impact.
5. **Create a target profile.** Assess framework categories and subcategories to determine desired cybersecurity outcomes. Consider additional categories and subcategories to account for unique organizational risks, as needed (e.g., financial fraud risk in financial institutions). Consider influences and requirements of external stakeholders, such as sector entities, customers, and business partners.
6. **Determine, analyze, and prioritize gaps.** Compare current and target profile to determine gaps. Create a prioritized action plan to address gaps. Determine resources necessary to address gaps.
7. **Implement action plan.** Determine and implement actions to address gaps.

C. **Communicate Cybersecurity Requirements to Stakeholders**

1. Use the framework's common language to communicate requirements among interdependent stakeholders for the delivery of essential critical infrastructure services. Examples include:
   - Create a target profile to share cybersecurity risk management requirements with an external party (e.g., a cloud or Internet service provider or external auditor or regulator).
   - Determine the current cybersecurity state to report results as a part of a control review.
   - Use a target profile to convey required categories and subcategories to an external partner.
   - Within a critical infrastructure sector (e.g., the financial services industry), create a target profile to share as a baseline profile. Use this baseline profile to build tailored, target profiles that are customized to specific organizational members' cyber security risks and goals.

D. **Identify Opportunities to Adapt or Apply New or Revised References**

1. Use the framework to identify opportunities for new or revised standards, guidelines, or practices where additional references would help address emerging risks.
2. For example, an organization implementing a given subcategory, or developing a new subcategory, might discover that there are few relevant informative references for an activity. To address that need, the organization might collaborate with technology leaders or standards bodies to draft, develop, and coordinate standards, guidelines, or practices.

E. Protect Privacy and Civil Liberties

1. Privacy and civil liberty risks arise when personal information is used, collected, processed, maintained, or disclosed in connection with an organization's cybersecurity activities. Examples of activities with potential privacy or civil liberty risks include:
   a. Cybersecurity activities that result in the over-collection or over-retention of personal information (e.g., phone records or medical information)
   b. Disclosure or use of personal information unrelated to cybersecurity activities
   c. Cybersecurity activities that result in denial of service or other similar potentially adverse impacts (e.g., when cybersecurity results in service outages at an airport or secured government building)
2. **Processes for Addressing Privacy and Civil Liberty Risks**
   a. **Governance of cybersecurity risk**
      i. The organization's assessment of cybersecurity risk and responses should consider privacy implications.
      ii. Individuals with cybersecurity-related privacy responsibilities report to appropriate management and receive appropriate training (e.g., in generally accepted privacy principles [GAPP]).
      iii. Organizational processes support compliance of cybersecurity activities with applicable privacy laws, regulations, and constitutional requirements.
      iv. The organization continuously and periodically assesses the privacy implications of its cybersecurity measures and controls.
   b. **Processes for identifying and authorizing individuals to access organizational assets and systems**
      i. Identify and address the privacy implications of data access when such data include collecting, disclosing, or using personal information.
   c. **Awareness and training measures**
      i. Cybersecurity workforce training includes training in organizational privacy policies and relevant privacy regulations.
      ii. The organization informs service providers of the organization's privacy policies and monitors for service providers for compliance with these policies.
   d. **Anomalous activity detection and system and assets monitoring**
      i. The organization conducts privacy reviews of anomalous activity detection and cybersecurity monitoring.
   e. **Response activities, including information sharing or other mitigation efforts**
      i. The organization assesses and addresses whether, when, how, and extent to which personal information is shared outside the organization as part of cybersecurity assessment and monitoring.
      ii. The organization conducts privacy reviews of cybersecurity initiatives.

VIII. Summary and Limitations

A. Cybersecurity is a national security issue and a requirement of almost every organization.

B. The framework for cybersecurity guides organizations in common cybersecurity principles, standards, and best practices. However, it is not tailored to the specific security needs of any single organization. Instead, it provides a common framework to enable organizations to review and assess their cybersecurity programs.

Sources

National Institute of Standards and Technology, "Framework for Improving Critical Infrastructure Cybersecurity," Version 1.0, February 12, 2014; https://www.nist.gov/sites/default/files/documents////draft-cybersecurity-framework-v1.11.pdf

IT Policies

According to COSO, internal control is a dynamic and iterative process that includes policies that reflect management's intentions regarding what is to be done and how. Procedures are actions that implement policies. Together, policies and procedures are essential to organizational control. This lesson describes some IT policies that are important to internal control.

After completing this lesson, you should be able to:

1. Describe the purpose of policies in a system of internal control.
2. Describe the essential elements of a policy.
3. Describe some common IT policies.
4. Describe some methods of monitoring IT policies.
5. Give examples of how specific IT policies can be useful in managing cyber risks.

I. IT policies help to establish a shared organizational understanding of IT and to manage cyber risks effectively. IT policies are administrative controls and boundaries for acceptable IT-related behavior. They can be particularly valuable in decentralized or geographically dispersed entities.

II. All policies, including IT policies:

- **A.** Should be linked to the entity's strategy and objectives
- **B.** Need an owner who is responsible for ensuring that the policy is operating and is updated
- **C.** Need a process for evolving with change
- **D.** Should include a title, purpose, scope and context, statement of responsibilities, and time for updating

III. Important IT Policies

- **A. Values and Service Culture**—What is expected of IT function personnel in their interactions with clients and others
- **B. Contractors, Employees, and Sourcing**—Why, when, and how an entity selects IT human resources from among employees or outside contractors (i.e., an IT sourcing and outsourcing policy)
- **C. Electronic Communications Use**—Policy related to employee use of the Internet, intranet, email, blogs, chat rooms, and telephones
- **D. Use and Connection Policy**—Policy that states the entity's position on the use of personal devices and applications in the workplace and connection to the entity's systems. May also specify (here or in a separate policy) allowable devices and uses of these devices on the entity's systems.
- **E. Procurement**—Policy on the procurement processes for obtaining IT services
- **F. Quality**—Statement of IT performance standards
- **G. Regulatory Compliance**—Statement of regulatory requirements of IT systems (e.g., in banking or investment systems) or related to data privacy
- **H. Security**—Policy related to guarding against physical or electronic threats to IT. May include disaster recovery preparation policies
- **I. Service Management and Operational Service Problem Solving**—Policies for ensuring the quality of live IT services

IV. Policy Monitoring

A. Policies should be monitored for compliance and success.

B. Policy monitoring may include internal auditing staff.

C. Monitoring may be continuous or periodic, depending on policy importance and the risks of noncompliance.

D. Analysis of IT help calls and operational reports can provide evidence of policy noncompliance.

Introduction to E-Business and E-Commerce

The growing importance of e-business and e-commerce is illustrated by the remarkable growth of eBay. In 1997, eBay reported 34,000 registered users and about 4 million auction listings. In 2005, eBay had about 180 million registered users and almost 2 billion auction listings, a growth rate of about 50,000%! This lesson introduces the basic concepts of e-business and e-commerce. It also discusses typical e-business and e-commerce business models and components, and some of the costs and benefits of moving to an e-business model.

After studying this lesson, you should be able to:

1. Define and distinguish e-business from e-commerce.
2. Define and describe the requisites and risks of e-commerce.
3. Identify and discuss typical e-commerce business models.
4. Give examples of e-business and e-commerce.
5. Give examples of conditions that are favorable and unfavorable to e-commerce.
6. Give examples of the e-commerce business models.

I. Definitions

Definition
E-business: The generic name given to any business process that relies on electronic dissemination of information or on automated transaction processing. This lesson distinguishes e-business from e-commerce and describes the benefits, risks, and some common business models of e-commerce.

A. E-business can be conducted within the organization as well as between the organization and its trading partners. Most e-business is conducted via the Internet using web-based technologies, but other processing modes are also included.

Definition
E-commerce: This term is narrower than e-business and is used to refer to transactions between the organization and its trading partners.

B. **Business-to-Business (B2B) E-Commerce**—Involves electronic processing of transactions between businesses and includes electronic data interchange (EDI), supply chain management (SCM), and electronic funds transfer (EFT).

C. **Business-to-Consumer (B2C) E-Commerce**—Involves selling goods and services directly to consumers, almost always using the Internet and web-based technology. B2C e-commerce relies heavily on intermediaries or brokers to facilitate the sales transaction.

D. **Business-to-Employee (B2E)**—Involves the use of web-based technology to share information with, and interact, with an organization's employees, e.g., through portals and intranets.

E. **Business-to-Government (B2G)**—Involves the growing use of web-based technologies to provide, and support, governmental units (e.g., providing property tax data online, paying parking tickets online, online contract bidding).

F. Some of the more pervasive types of e-business and e-commerce are discussed below.

II. **E-Commerce—Requisites and Risks**

A. **Requisites**—E-commerce depends on trusting two parties:

1. **Your trading partners**—Are they honest and are they whom they represent they are? To this point, there is a *New Yorker* magazine cartoon in which two dogs are talking, while one of the dogs is seated at a computer. One dog says to the other, "On the Internet, no one knows that you are a dog."
2. **The site or service provider**—One of the biggest challenges to eBay becoming a global business, for example, was their remarkable ability to convince strangers to trust one another, and, to trust eBay with their personal financial information.

B. **Risks of E-Commerce**

1. **System availability**—Online systems must be stable and availability. This was an early challenge to eBay. In its early days, it asked users to stay off of the system during peak hours!
2. **Security and confidentiality**—Data breaches—for example, the 2013 Target credit and debit card breach—can irreparably harm trust in systems and companies.
3. **Authentication**—Is an online person or company who they say they are? Increasingly, e-commerce sites (e.g., Upwork) include verification of identity as a prerequisite to site use.
4. **Nonrepudiation**—This is, essentially, the existence of an audit trail that renders actions verifiable. Hence, one cannot deny, after a transaction, one's role in it.
5. **Integrity**—Is the system secure from hackers and crackers? Creating a system that is immune to hacks is a formidable undertaking. Even the FBI website has been hacked.

C. **Risks of not Implementing E-Commerce**

1. Your customers find it cheaper and easier to buy online.
2. **Limited growth**—E-commerce offers global reach.
3. **Limited markets**—E-commerce turns what once were small, highly specialized markets (e.g., collecting antique fountain pens) into large, worldwide markets.

III. **E-Commerce Models**—How do companies make money using e-commerce and e-business technologies? Typical e-commerce models include:

A. **Electronic Marketplaces and Exchanges**—These marketplaces bring together buyers and sellers of goods who connect virtually rather than physically to one another. The most common example is probably eBay, but many special-interest marketplaces focus on specific industries, for example buyers and sellers in the chemical industry.

B. **Viral Marketing**—Organizations increasingly attempt to increase brand awareness or generate sales by inducing people to send messages to friends using social networking applications. For example, users of Facebook are familiar with the icon that allows Facebook users to post articles and advertisements on their Facebook pages.

C. **Online Direct Marketing**—Many companies now have large online presences to sell directly to consumers or other businesses. Examples include Amazon, a pioneer in direct online sales, and Walmart, whose virtual presence is an important part of the company's business strategy.

D. **Electronic Tendering Systems**—These tendering or bidding systems allow companies to seek bids for products or services that the organizations wish to purchase. General Electric pioneered tendering systems.

1. Also called "e-procurement systems."

E. **Social Networking/Social Computing—Is** concerned with how people use information systems to connect with others. Examples include instant messaging, wikis, Facebook, Twitter, and other examples that purchasers of this course are likely familiar with. Social networks are social structures composed of nodes, representing individuals or social network resources, that link to one another. **Social network service** examples include Facebook, YouTube, Flickr, and many other emerging sites.

E-Commerce Applications

After studying this lesson, you should be able to:

1. Describe some common e-commerce applications, including CRM, EDI, EFT, and SCM.
2. Give examples of appropriate and inappropriate applications of CRM, EDI, EFT, and SCM.

I. Common E-Commerce Applications Include:

A. **Customer Relationship Management (CRM)**—Technologies used to manage relationships with clients; biographic and transaction information about existing and potential customers is collected and stored in a database; the CRM provides tools to analyze the information and develop personalized marketing plans for individual customers.

1. **Primary objective of a CRM system—**To retain current customers and gain new customers

2. A CRM system includes the technology software designed for current and potential clients that is essentially a database of all data related to customers. Used properly with the right processes, a CRM system can further sales, marketing, and customer service interactions. Common features of CRM software include:

   a. **Sales force automation**—Tracking contacts and follow-ups with customers or potential customers automatically to eliminate duplicate efforts.

   b. **Marketing automation—**Triggering marketing efforts when, for example, new contacts or prospects are entered into the database, such as sending promotional material via email. Also facilitates targeted marketing campaigns to specific customer interests (e.g., Kroger promoting grocery products only to interested customers).

   c. **Customer service automation**—Handling common customer interactions in an automated manner. For example, Internet service providers often have automated, prerecorded troubleshooting for common internet or modem issues.

   d. In addition to automated features, a CRM system provides additional value with the rich data that can be assessed, such as sales history and projections, marketing campaign success, trends, and performance indicators.

B. **Electronic Data Interchange (EDI)**—EDI is computer-to-computer exchange of business data (e.g., purchase orders, confirmations, invoices, etc.) in structured formats allowing direct processing of the data by the receiving system; EDI reduces handling costs and speeds transaction processing compared to traditional paper-based processing.

1. This figure illustrates an EDI exchange:

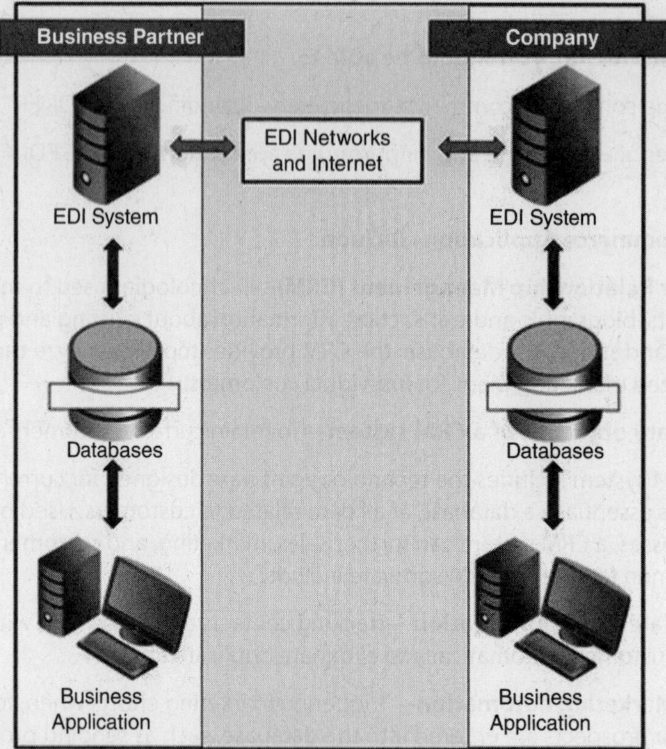

2. EDI requires that **all transactions be submitted in a specified format**; translation software is required to convert transaction data from the internal company data format to the EDI format and vice versa.
   a. The most common specification in the United States is the American National Standards Institute format **ANSI X.12**; internationally, the United Nations EDI for Administration, Commerce and Transport (**UN/EDIFACT**) format is the dominant standard.
3. EDI can be implemented using direct links between the trading partners, through communication intermediaries (called "service bureaus"), through value-added networks (VANs), or over the Internet.
   a. Despite increased interest in web-based EDI using an XML-based standard (RosettaNet is the leading contender for this standard), **the vast majority of EDI transactions are still processed through value-added networks.**
      i. The **well-established audit trails, controls, and security** provided for EDI transactions by VAN are the principal reasons for their continued popularity.
4. EDI costs include the following:
   a. **Costs of change**—Costs associated with locating new business partners who support EDI processing; legal costs associated with modifying and negotiating trading contracts with new and existing business partners and with the communications provider; costs of changing internal policies and procedures to support the new processing model (process reengineering) and employee training.
   b. **Hardware costs**—Often additional hardware such as communications equipment, improved servers, etc., is required.
   c. Costs of **translation software**
   d. Cost of **data transmission**
   e. Costs of **security, audit**, and **control procedures**

C. **Electronic Funds Transfer (EFT)**—A technology for transferring money from one bank account directly to another without the use of paper money or checks; EFT substantially reduces the time and expense required to process checks and credit transactions.

1. Typical examples of EFT services include the following:

    a. **Retail payments**—Such as credit cards, often initiated from POS terminals

    b. **Direct deposit**—Of payroll payments directly into the employee's bank account

    c. **Automated teller machine (ATM) transactions**

    d. **Nonconsumer check collection**—Through the Federal Reserve wire transfer system

2. **EFT service**—Typically provided by a third-party vendor that acts as the intermediary between the company and the banking system:

    a. Transactions are processed by the bank through the Automated Clearing House (ACH) network, the secure transfer system that connects all U.S. financial institutions.

3. **EFT security**—Provided through various types of **data encryption** as transaction information is transferred from the client to the payment server, from the merchant to the payment server, and between the client and merchant.

4. **Token-based payment systems**—Such as electronic cash, smart cards (cash cards), and online payment systems (e.g., PayPal) behave similarly to EFT, but are governed by a different set of rules.

    a. Token-based payment systems can offer anonymity since the cards do not have to be directly connected to a named user.

5. **Electronic wallets**—These are not payment systems, but are simply programs that allow the user to manage his or her existing credit cards, usernames, passwords, and address information in an easy-to-use, centralized location.

D. **Supply Chain Management (SCM)**—The process of planning, implementing, and controlling the operations of the supply chain: the process of transforming raw materials into a finished product and delivering that product to the consumer. Supply chain management incorporates all activities from the purchase and storage of raw materials, through the production process into finished goods through to the point-of-consumption.

1. Here's an illustration of an SCM process:

Supply Chain Activities

RAW MATERIALS
Supplier Network
Enterprise
Marketing
Sourcing
Operations
Logistics
Engineering
Distributive Network
END CONSUMERS

E. **Computer Networks**—Computer networks (see the "Computer Networks and Data Communication" lesson) are essential to e-business, e-commerce, and social computing.

ERM for Cloud Computing

This lesson introduces risk management principles for the cloud computing environment.

After studying this lesson, you should be able to:

1. Describe the often underestimated risks of cloud computing.
2. Describe a strategy for ERM for cloud computing.
3. Identify some important risks of cloud computing and match them to risk responses and controls that help to mitigate these risks.

I. ERM for Cloud Computing

A. Contracting with a cloud service provider can be very easy (e.g., think of what you had to do to sign up to use Dropbox or Amazon Cloud). Because of this, many organizations may contract with a cloud service provider (CSP) without understanding the complexities and risks that come with cloud computing.

1. A risk assessment and analysis must be done before contracting for cloud computing.

a. Most organizations will include senior management and the IT steering committee in this analysis. If the risk is substantial, cloud computing should be a topic for a board of directors discussion.

b. The risk analysis should consider the legal, regulatory, and operational risks of cloud computing.

c. With the exception of an internal, private cloud, cloud computing is a type of IT outsourcing. The risk analysis must consider the increased inherent risk of outsourcing control over some portion of the organization's IT system.

i. Public clouds contain higher inherent risk than do private clouds.

B. ERM for cloud computing begins with clear objectives and a well-structured plan.

1. The cloud computing plan should include a strong cloud governance structure and reporting model, an assessment of internal IT skills, and a well-defined, entity risk appetite.

C. Effective cloud solutions require considering and integrating:

1. The relevant business processes—For example, sales, product development, manufacturing, distribution, procurement, payroll, financing

2. The deployment model—For example, public, hybrid, private

3. The service delivery model—SAAS, PAAS, IAAS (see the introductory lesson on cloud computing for term definitions)

II. Cloud Computing Risks and Responses—This section gives examples of important cloud risks, and, related responses and controls.

A. Risk—Unauthorized Cloud Activity

1. Response—Preventive and detective controls related to unauthorized procurement and use of cloud services

a. Examples

i. A cloud use policy that articulates how, when, and for what uses cloud computing is allowed

ii. A list of approved cloud vendors

iii. A policy that identifies who responsible for authorizing and contracting for cloud services

Example

Controlling Cloud Computing

A small business unit of a large corporation decided to use cloud services to implement a customer relationship management (CRM) system. The unit created the system without consulting senior management or the internal IT organization. After launch, the data included confidential customer and credit card data. As a result, confidential data was stored on a public cloud in violation of the corporation's policies.

B. Risk—Lack of CSP Transparency

1. **Response**—Assessment of the CSP system of internal control
    - a. For example, approved list of cloud vendors includes only vendors who provide sufficient information to enable informed risk assessments of the integrity of CSP operations
    - b. For example, list of required information from CSP related to the type of service provided (i.e., IAAS, SAAS, PAAS)
        - i. Examples of information likely to be required—References for the vendor, information about appropriate usage, performance data, network infrastructure, data center, security, data segregation, and compliance policies

C. Risk—CSP Reliability and Performance

1. **Response**—Effective incident management plan and procedure
    - a. For example, contract with backup CSPs in the event of a system failure with a primary CSP
    - b. For example, implement CSP availability monitoring

D. Risk—Cyber-Attack

1. **Response**—Incident management plan that considers increased likelihood of attack on CSP
    - a. Store only nonessential, nonsensitive data on CSP solution.
    - b. Deploy encryption on all cloud-hosted data.
    - c. Contract with backup CSPs in anticipation of a hack on the primary CSP.

Mobile Device, End-User, and Small Business Computing

After studying this lesson, you should be able to:

1. Describe the unique risks, and strategies for managing these risks, of end-user computing.
2. Describe the unique risks, and strategies for managing these risks, of small-organization computing.
3. Describe the unique risks, and strategies for managing these risks, of mobile devices.
4. Match the risks of mobile devices to strategies for managing these risks.
5. Match the risks of small-organizational computing to strategies for managing these risks.
6. Match the risks of end-user computing to strategies for managing these risks.

I. **End-User and Small Business Computing**—The creation, implementation, and control of systems by end users and in small businesses, can increase control risks compared with systems created and operated by IT professionals in larger, traditional IT environments. End-user and small organizational computing carry unique risks. Though these risks cannot be eliminated, strong compensating controls can substantially improve organizational security and control.

   A. User-developed systems bear unique risks.

      1. Systems developed by non-IT professionals may be created rapidly, without knowledge or application of the systems development methodology.
      2. Testing and documentation may be inadequate or nonexistent.
      3. Control over data may be lost, and the end user may use tools that integrate poorly with the existing organizational systems.
      4. Anyone who has encountered Excel spreadsheets that sprawl and include calculations that cannot, or have not, been verified, is familiar with the perils of end user–developed applications. Recently, two Harvard economists (Carmen Reinhart and Kenneth Rogoff) admitted that their conclusions in a very influential research paper were erroneous. The cause of their error was an end-user–developed spreadsheet that contained errors, and had not been reviewed or checked. Many stories exist of the perils of unverified spreadsheets (e.g., see the European Spreadsheet Risks Interest Group—EuSpRIG).
      5. Management may rely on user-developed systems and files without realizing that they have not been verified and validated.

II. **Characteristics of Small Business Environments**

   A. **Microcomputers** linked to networks are used almost exclusively.

   B. **IT is Outsourced**—There is **no centralized information technology department**.

   C. Because there are too few individuals to provide for segregation of duties (in end-user environments, there is usually only a single individual), **incompatible functions are frequently combined**. It is critical to effective control that the functions of authorization, custody of assets, and record keeping be separated. If essential, the duties of authorization and review/auditing may be combined.

III. **Specific Risks and Controls Related to Small-Organizational Computing**

   A. **Physical Access**—Because personal computers are often found in openly available areas, care should be taken to make sure that doors are locked when offices are open and that removable storage devices (diskettes, CDs, DVDs, flash drives, etc.) are stored in secure locations.

B. **Logical Access**—All machines should require a username and password in order to access the system and should be set to automatically log out of the system when they have not been used for a period of time; networked systems should protect all network available resources from unauthorized access.

C. **Data Backup Procedures**—Company-wide standards for backing up files should be established and enforced; if possible, this process should be centralized and automated through a network; off-site backups must be maintained on an ongoing basis.

D. **Program Development and Implementation**—User-developed programs—which include spreadsheets and databases—should be subject to third-party review and testing to ensure that they operate as expected; copies of the authorized versions of these programs should be separately cataloged and maintained in a secure location.

E. **Data Entry and Report Production**—Since it is common for a single individual to be responsible for all aspects of a transaction, all work should be regularly reviewed by an independent third party.

IV. Additional Strategies for Managing Small-Business Computing Risks

1. Integrate all feasible standard IT controls into the end-user or small business environment.
2. Where possible, additional supervision and/or review should be implemented as a compensating control.
3. If complete segregation of duties (i.e., authorization, record keeping, custody, review/auditing) is impossible, consider combining the authorization and review/auditing functions. This (more limited) segregation of duties is present in the following recommendation.
4. One important compensating control in many small organizations is an actively engaged owner/manager/volunteer who oversees many accounting functions.
    a. Although there are obvious risks to concentrating many accounting functions in a single individual, there are also a few advantages to this approach—specifically, that a single individual is committed to monitoring all accounting activities and transactions.

V. Managing Mobile Devices—The use of mobile computing devices, including iPhones, Androids, and tablet computers (e.g., the iPad and Galaxy) is now ubiquitous. These devices can enhance individual and organizational productivity but also present unique and formidable challenges to IT security and control. Use of these devices is quite recent. BlackBerry devices originated in the early 2000s while the first iPhone was introduced in 2007. Recent devices blur the boundary between mobile devices and computers.

A. **Risk and Security Challenges**

1. **Malicious applications**—Mobile devices are susceptible to malicious applications that contain hidden functionalities to collect and transmit user data to third parties. While only a few examples exist of the successful exploitation of these vulnerabilities, organizations must proactively manage data security to meet these challenges by monitoring emerging security threats in mobile computing. To do otherwise is to allow mobile devices to become electronic Trojan horses that infiltrate the organization and can harvest and transmit data on operations to hackers, crackers, and spies.
2. **Loss and theft**—The ubiquity and portability of mobile devices makes them particularly vulnerable to loss or theft. If a user loses a mobile device that links to an organizational system, and the device is not password protected, then system capabilities must enable blocking the device from accessing organizationally sensitive systems.
3. **Restricting access and permission rights**—Because of the increased risks of loss or theft of mobile devices, it may be desirable to allow users fewer access and permission rights on mobile devices than on desktop devices, or laptops that remain on organizational property. For example, users may be permitted to change some files on desktop devices and to view (but not change) these files on mobile devices (called view-only access).

B. Benefits—Mobile devices enable ubiquitous computing, including integration with enterprise-wide systems and cloud-based storage vendors. Enabling users to connect—using hand-held, mobile devices—to enterprise-wide systems allows for data capture and transmission at point of origin, which can significantly improve information quality.

C. User and Usability Challenges—Redesigning organizational information displays to fit on hand-held, mobile devices poses formidable design challenges. Additional challenges include changing functionalities in the mobile environment (e.g., browser and JavaScript availability), the speed of the mobile network, the computation load of encryption, and user input from a tiny keyboard or from a voice-driven application (e.g., Siri on the iPhone). Such challenges can include requiring a user to type a complex, long password on a tiny touch keyboard where system lockout occurs after two mistaken password entries.

D. User Training—Mobile security training is essential to effective security awareness. Training programs must teach users organizational policies on the use of mobiles, password maintenance procedures, when and how to use (and not use) mobile devices, and procedures in the event a device is lost or stolen.

E. Summary—Despite the formidable security challenges presented by mobile devices, their growing use and integration into organizational systems is inevitable due to their popularity and considerable personal and organizational benefits.

Multi-Location System Structure

After studying this lesson, you should be able to:

1. Describe the advantages and disadvantages of centralized, decentralized, and distributed systems.
2. Give examples of appropriate and inappropriate use of centralized, decentralized, and distributed systems.

I. **Centralized, Decentralized, and Distributed Systems**—Organizations with multiple locations must address the problem of consolidating and coordinating data from the individual locations. The three systems approaches to this issue are as follows:

   A. **Centralized Systems**—Maintain all data and perform all data processing at a central location; remote users may access the centralized data files via a telecommunications channel, but all of the processing is still performed at the central location.

      1. **Advantages**
         a. Better data security once the data is received at the central location
         b. Consistency in processing
      2. **Disadvantages**
         a. **High cost of transmitting**—Large numbers of detailed transactions
         b. **Input/output bottlenecks**—At high traffic times (end of period)
         c. **Slower responses**—To information requests from remote locations

   B. **Decentralized Systems**—Allow each location to maintain its own processing system and data files. In decentralized systems, most of the transaction processing is accomplished at the regional office, and summarized data is sent to the central office. For example, in payroll processing, the regional offices calculate time worked, gross pay, deductions, and net pay for each employee and transmit totals for salary expense, deductions payable, and cash paid to the central database.

      1. **Advantages**
         a. **Cost savings** by reducing the volume of data that must be transmitted to the central location
         b. Reduction of processing power and data storage needs at the central site
         c. Reduce input/output bottlenecks
         d. Better responsiveness to local information needs
      2. **Disadvantages**
         a. Greater potential for security violations because there are more sites to control
         b. Cost of installing and maintaining equipment in multiple locations

   C. **Distributed (or Hybrid) Database Systems**—So named because rather than maintaining a centralized or master database at a central location, the database is distributed across the locations according to organizational and user needs.

      1. **Advantages**
         a. Better communications among the remote locations because they must all be connected to each other in order to distribute the database
         b. More current and complete information
         c. Reduction or elimination of the need to maintain a large, expensive central processing center
      2. **Disadvantages**
         a. Cost of establishing communications among remote locations
         b. Conflicts among the locations when accessing and updating shared data

Computer Networks and Data Communication

This lesson introduces, or reviews, basic principles related to computer networks. This content is needed to understand principles of accounting controls that rely on computer network technology.

After studying this lesson, you should be able to:

1. Describe the two categories of transmission media; provide examples of each of these types of media.
2. Define a network operating system, and describe three configurations of network operating systems.
3. Describe the purpose of communications devices and give examples of these devices.
4. Compare and contrast local area with wide area networks.
5. Describe some common network management tools and reports.
6. Give examples of appropriate and inappropriate uses of public and private networks.
7. Identify the major security and control issues associated with computer networks.
8. Give examples of the network management tools that can be used to monitor computer networks.

I. **Computer Networks and Data Communications**—A computer network consists of two or more computing devices connected by a communications channel to exchange data. The communications channel will use specific devices, and a set of protocols (i.e., standards), to exchange data and share resources among devices.

II. **Uses—What Do Networks Do?**—Common uses and applications of networks include:

A. **File Services**—Enable user sharing of files.

B. **E-mail Services**—Link to e-mail systems.

C. **Print Services**—Enable connections to printers.

D. **Remote Access Capabilities**—Enable connections to remote devices (e.g., a special purpose computer such as a supercomputer).

E. **Directory Services**—Identify what is available on a network.

F. **Network Management**—Functions to control and maintain the network including information about network traffic, access attempts, and errors.

G. **Internet Connection Services**, including:

1. **Dynamic host configuration protocol (DHCP)**—A protocol used to obtain and release IP addresses. This protocol enables computers to connect to an IP-based network such as the Internet.
2. **Domain name system (DNS)**—The system that translates network nodes into IP addresses

III. **Components of a Network**

A. **Nodes**—Any device connected to the network is a node:

1. **Client**—A node, usually a microcomputer, used by end users; a client uses network resources but does not usually supply resources to the network. May be "fat" or "thin" (see the lesson on "Information Systems Hardware").
2. **Server**—A node dedicated to providing services or resources to the rest of the network (e.g., a file server maintains centralized application and data files, a print server provides access to high-quality printers, etc.); servers are indirectly, not directly, used by end users.

The following figure is an example of a simple client/server computer network:

B. Transmissions Media—The communication link between nodes on the network; the link may be one of several types of wired or wireless media. Local area networks (LANs) use dedicated communications lines (i.e., used only by the network); wide area networks (WANs) use public or shared communications lines (i.e., telephone lines, television cables, etc.)

1. Wired communications media

a. Copper or twisted pair

i. Traditionally used for phone connections

ii. The slowest, least secure (e.g., easy to tap) and most subject to interference of the wired media

iii. Recent modifications have, however, improved performance significantly

iv. Least expensive media

v. Performance degrades with cable length

b. Coaxial cable—Similar to the cable used for television, coaxial cable is faster, more secure, and less subject to interference than twisted pair but has a slightly higher cost.

c. Fiber optic cable—Extremely fast and secure, fiber optic cable communications are based on light pulses instead of electrical impulses; therefore, they are not subject to electrical interference and the signal does not degrade over long distances; more expensive to purchase and to install.

2. Wireless communications media

a. Microwave transmission—May use a combination of terrestrial microwave and/or satellite microwave transmission; used primarily by WANs.

b. Wi-Fi or spread-spectrum radio transmission

i. Used in both large networks serving hundreds of users and small home networks

ii. Found in both LANs and WANs

iii. Generally slower than wired systems using coaxial cable or fiber optic cable

c. Bluetooth—Uses the same radio frequencies as Wi-Fi but with lower power consumption resulting in a weaker connection; used to provide a direct communications link between two devices (i.e., a headset and a smartphone, a computer and a printer, etc.).

   d. **Digital cellular (cellular digital packet data, or CDPD)**—Allows transmission of data over the cell phone network; used by WANs.

C. **Network Operating System**—Controls communication over the network and access to network resources:

   1. **Peer-to-peer systems**—All nodes share in communications management; no central controller (server) is required; these systems are relatively simple and inexpensive to implement; used by LANs.

   2. **Client/server systems**—A central machine (the server) presides as the mediator of communication on the network and grants access to network resources; client machines are users of network resources but also perform data processing functions; used by LANs and by the world's largest client—the Internet.

   3. **Hierarchical operating systems**

      a. Use a centralized control point generally referred to as the host computer

      b. The host not only manages communications and access to resources but also often performs most of the data processing.

      c. Nodes connected to these systems often function as dumb terminals which are able to send and receive information but do not actually process the data.

      d. Used by WANs

D. **Communications Devices**—Link networks to other networks and to remote access. Examples include modems, hubs, repeaters, multiplexers, concentrators, bridges, routers, and gateways. You should know that these terms are associated with networks but you don't need to know their specific functions within networks (unless you are an IT auditor).

IV. **Types of Networks**—Networks are characterized by the way that the network is constructed and managed, and by the network's geographic reach.

A. **Local Area Networks (LANs)**—Local area networks were so named because they were originally confined to very limited geographic areas (a floor of a building, a building, or possibly several buildings in very close proximity to each other). With the advent of relatively inexpensive fiber optic cable, local area networks can extend for many miles. For example, many urban school districts have local area networks connecting all of the schools in the district.

B. **Wide Area Networks (WANs)**—Although WANs can vary dramatically in geographic area, most are national or international in scope.

C. **Storage Area Networks (SANs)**—A type of, or variation of, LANs that connect storage devices to servers

D. **Personal Area Networks (PANs)**—Often a home network that links devices used by an individual or family to one another and to the Internet.

V. **Networks, by Ownership**—Networks can also be classified by their ownership and use, which influences their characteristics.

A. **Private**—Network resources are dedicated to a small number of applications or a restricted set of users (e.g., a corporation's network).

   1. Usually use leased telephone lines that are dedicated to the network's use

   2. Traditional EDI systems use a private network.

   3. **Advantages**—Secure, flexible, performance often exceeds that of public networks.

   4. **Disadvantage**—Costly

B. **Public**—Resources are owned by third-party companies and leased to users on a usage basis (also referred to as public switched networks [PSNs]).

   1. Example: What you use when you go to Starbucks, McDonald's, and so on.

2. **Advantages and disadvantage**—In general, the opposite of those for private networks, but a significant disadvantage is that public networks are much less secure. In fact, anyone with basic network skills can read your messages on some less-secure public networks. And how do you know the security features of public networks? You usually don't. Thank goodness that there is so much network traffic, and most of it is uninteresting to hackers and crackers.

3. **Exploding use of public networks**. The availability of public networks is now seen as essential to a geographical area's competitiveness and workforce efficiency.

C. **Cloud Computing/Cloud Services**—A type of public network. See the separate lesson on this topic.

VI. **Network Management Tools**—The following tools and reports help manage, and monitor, an organization's networks:

A. **Response Time Reports**—How fast is the system responding to user commands? Generated reports should indicate average, best, and worst time responses across the system (e.g., by lines or systems).

B. **Downtime Reports**—Which portions of the system were unavailable and for how long?

C. **Online Monitors**—Check transmission accuracy and errors.

D. **Network Monitors**—Display network node status and availability.

E. **Protocol Analyzers**—Diagnostic tools that monitor packet flows across the system. They are useful in diagnosing the volume and nature of network traffic, and in analyzing network performance.

F. **Simple Network Management Protocol (SNMP)**—A software-based, TCP/IP protocol that monitors network performance and security.

G. **Help Desk Reports**—Useful in identifying network problems raised by users and potential violations of network policy by users including employees.

The Internet—Structure and Protocols

This lesson introduces, or reviews, basic principles related to computer networks. This content is needed to understand principles of accounting controls that rely on computer network technology.

After studying this lesson, you should be able to:

1. Identify the acronyms, and purpose, of the core protocols and technologies that underlie and support the Internet.
2. Describe the Internet.
3. Define intranets and extranets.
4. Describe the purpose and uses of XBRL.
5. Describe the purpose of Web 2.0.

I. The Internet—Structure and Protocol

A. A "network of networks"—a global network of millions (or billions) of interconnected computers and computer networks.

B. The world's largest client-server network.

C. End-user access to the Internet is provided by **Internet service providers (ISPs)** that either provide direct connections to the **Internet backbone** (a collection of extremely high-speed, high-capacity communications lines joined together at network access points) or connect to larger ISPs that ultimately provide that connection.

D. A **markup** or **tagging language** specifies how data will be processed or displayed.

E. **Key Internet Protocols**

1. **Transmission Control Protocol/Internet Protocol (TCP/IP)**—Two core network protocols that underlie the Internet.
   a. **Hypertext Transfer Protocol (HTTP)**—The foundation protocol for data transmission on the Internet. Part of the TCP/IP protocol.
   b. **Simple Mail Transfer Protocol (SMTP), Internet Message Access Protocol (IMAP)**—Protocols for e-mail services. Part of the TCP/IP protocol.
   c. In a **packet-switched network**, information is grouped into packets for transmission. TCP/IP is a **packet-switched network** protocol. The Internet is the world's largest **packet-switched network**.
2. **Extensible Markup Language (XML)**—Protocol for encoding (tagging) documents for use on the Internet.
   a. **Extensible Business Reporting Language (XBRL)**—XML-based protocol for encoding and tagging business information. A means to consistently and efficiently identifying the content of business and accounting information in electronic form.
      i. **Extensible** means that users can create taxonomies for specific environments, for example, for taxation reporting, environmental regulation reporting, or automobile manufacturing.
      ii. XBRL is used in filings with the Securities and Exchange Commission that are made available on EDGAR, the SEC's Electronic Data Gathering and Retrieval database.
      iii. Some companies now report their financial statements in both paper and XBRL formats.

3. **Other protocols**

   a. **Hypertext Markup Language (HTML)**—Core language for web pages. The basic building-block protocol for constructing web pages.

   b. **File Transfer Protocol (FTP)**—Used for file transfer applications

   c. **Instant messaging (IM)**—Protocol for instant messaging

   d. **Uniform Resource Locator (URL)**—A protocol for finding a document by typing in an address (e.g., www.azdiamondbacks.com). URLs work like addresses on mail processed by the post office.

   e. **World Wide Web (the web or WWW)**—A framework for accessing linked resources (e.g., documents, pictures, music files, videos, etc.) spread out over the millions of machines all over the Internet

   f. **Web browser**—Client software (e.g., Internet explorer, Firefox, Chrome, Mosaic, etc.) that provides the user with the ability to locate and display web resources

   g. **Web servers**—The software that "serves" (i.e., makes available) web resources to software clients. Web servers (e.g., Apache and Internet Information Server [IIS]) typically run on "server" hardware. However, many computing devices today support their own web server software.

F. **Intranets and extranets**—Intranets and extranets are private (e.g., limited access) networks built using Internet protocols. Therefore, users can access network resources through their web browser rather than a proprietary interface. This substantially reduces training time for users and system development time for programmers. Thus, intranets and extranets are rapidly replacing traditional proprietary LANs and WANs:

1. **Intranets**—Available only to members of the organization (business, school, association); intranets are often used to connect geographically separate LANs within a company.

2. **Extranets**—Intranets that are opened up to permit associates (company suppliers, customers, business partners, etc.) to access data that is relevant to them.

II. **Web 2.0**—The so-called second generation of the web. Refers to web-based collaboration and community-generated content using web-based software tools such as:

A. **Blog**—An asynchronous discussion, or web log, led by a moderator that typically focuses on a single topic. Similar to an electronic bulletin board. An efficient way to share information, views, and opinions.

B. **Wiki**—An information-gathering and knowledge-sharing website developed collaboratively by a community or group, all of whom can freely add, modify, or delete content.

C. **Twitter**—A micro-variation of a blog. Restricts input (tweets) to 140 characters (at the time this lesson was written) common use is to "follow" friends, politicians, and celebrities. Increasingly, companies use Twitter to inform followers and to brand themselves and market their services.

D. **RSS (Really Simple Syndication)/ATOM Feeds**—An easy way to get news and information. An XML application that facilitates the sharing and syndication of website content by subscription. RSS-enabled client software (including most browsers and RSS readers) automatically checks RSS feeds for new website content on a regular basis.

Logical and Physical Access Controls

Logical Access Controls

After studying this lesson, you should be able to:

1. Describe the purpose of logical access controls and some common strategies for managing logical access risks.
2. Identify common identity and authenticity policies and procedures.
3. Describe the purpose of, and common forms of, firewalls.
4. Give examples of common logical access controls and the risks that they help to mitigate.
5. Describe the evolution of authentication technologies.
6. Explain why emerging authentication technologies are superior to current technologies.

I. **Introduction**—The growth of e-commerce and other Internet-based technologies has increased organizational computing risks as a result of network-based exchanges between parties who have no prior contacts, contracts or agreements. This lesson considers controls related to establishing logical access controls, which concern virtual (i.e., nonphysical) means of protecting information assets.

  A. **Logical Access Control**—Most large organizations use **logical access control** software to manage access control. Functions of such systems include managing user profiles, assigning identifications and authentication procedures, logging system and user activities, establishing tables to set access privileges to match users to system resources and applications, and, log and event reporting. Hence, many of the functions and procedures described in this lesson are managed through logical access control software.

  B. **Common Levels of Logical Access Control**

    1. Read or copy
    2. Write, create, update or delete
    3. Execute (run) commands or procedures
    4. A combination of the above privileges

  C. **What Should Logical Access Controls Protect?** The more important information assets of an organization often include data, data dictionaries, telecommunications links, the operating system and system software, domain name servers, libraries and directories, application software and web applications. Logical access controls help protect the integrity of these virtual assets.

II. **Identification and Authorization**—Though controlling physical access to program and data files is a fundamental concern in any IT system, controlling logical access to IT resources—that is, controlling electronic access to data via internal and external networks—is a much larger concern. The primary controls over logical access involve user identification (authentication) and user authorization.

  A. **User Authentication**—The first step in controlling logical access to data is to establish user identification. This is an area of growth and change in IT (see the lesson on "Emerging Technologies in AIS") normally accomplished by creating a username for each authorized user and associating the username with a unique identifier.

    1. The identifier is typically based on:

      a. Something the user *knows* (a logon ID, passwords, personal identification numbers [PINs])

      b. Something the user *has* (smart card, ID badges)

   c. A *physical characteristic* of the user (fingerprints, voiceprints, facial scan)

   d. A user habit that the system detects (e.g., the physical characteristics of the user's touch on the mouse or keyboard; a particular movement on the mouse pad that the user has identified as part of their user profile)

   e. A combination of the above characteristics, called **multifactor authentication**.

2. **Passwords**—Should be memorable to users but hard for hackers to identify. They should "be strong" to resist attempts to crack them. A strong password:

   a. Is at least eight characters long

   b. Includes upper- and lowercase letters, at least one numeral, and at least one special character (where the operating system allows)

   c. Is not easily linked to the user (e.g., spouse's name, pet name, school mascot, etc.).

   d. Should be changed periodically (e.g., every 30 days). This is because passwords may be hacked without user knowledge, meaning that ending an intruder's use of the system requires mandated password changes.

   e. Let's be honest. Passwords are horrible! Within a few years, most IT security experts expect them to be replaced with physical and multifactor authentication. Let us all give thanks for the coming death of the password.

3. **Security tokens**—Include devices that provide "one-time" passwords that must be input by the user as well as "smart cards" that contain additional user identification information and must be read by an input device.

   a. One-time passwords

      i. Used to strengthen the standard password by requiring access to a physical device that displays a new one-time password every 30–60 seconds

      ii. A randomizing algorithm generates the one-time password.

      iii. The user enters this password along with the traditional username and password.

      iv. After receipt, the system recalculates the password and permits or denies access.

   b. **Smart cards and identification badges**—Have **identification information embedded in a magnetic strip on the card** and require the use of additional hardware (a card reader) to read the data into the system. Depending on the system, the user may only need to swipe the card to log onto the system or may need to enter additional information.

4. **Biometric controls**

   a. A physical or behavioral characteristic permits access.

   b. Possible physical biometric identifiers include palms, hand geometry, iris or retina scans, fingerprints, and facial recognition.

   c. Behavior-based biometric identifiers include signature and voice recognition.

   d. **Advantages**: Costs for many systems have dropped dramatically and many recognition devices are small.

   e. **Disadvantages:** Lack of uniqueness, unreliability

5. **Multi-factor authentication**—Since all authentication techniques are individually subject to failure, many organizations require multi-factor authentication procedures—the use of several separate authentication procedures at one time (e.g., username, password, one-time password, and fingerprint). Redundant authentication procedures significantly enhance the authentication process.

B. **Authorization Controls**—The authorization matrix or access control list (ACL) specifies each user's access rights to programs, data entry screens, and reports. The authorization matrix contains a row for each user and columns for each resource available on the system. There are usually several levels of access for each resource, as shown below:

Username	Resource 1	Resource 2	Resource 3	Resource 4
cls56	N	N	A	R
NMever	A	A	N	N
olsen332	R	R	X	R
jparker	X	X	R	R

N = No access
R = Read access only
A = Add, Read
U = Update, Read
X = Add, Update, Delete, Read

III. Firewalls—The purpose of a firewall is to allow legitimate users to use, and to block hackers and others from accessing, system resources. It consists of hardware, or software, or both, that helps detect security problems and enforce security policies on a networked system. A firewall is like a door with a lock for a computer system. It inspects, and when necessary filters, data flows. There are multiple types, and levels, of firewalls:

A. Network

1. Filters data packets based on header information (source and destination IP addresses and communication port)
2. Blocks noncompliant transmissions based on rules in an access control list
3. Very fast (examines headers only)
4. Forwards approved packets to application firewall

B. Application

1. Inspects data packet contents
2. Can perform **deep packet inspection** (detailed packet examination)
3. Controls file and data availability to specific applications

C. Personal—Enables end users to block unwanted network traffic

IV. Additional Logical Access Control Considerations

A. Remote Access Security—With the spread of ubiquitous computing, managing remote access is a critical security consideration in organizations. See the "Mobile Device, End-User, and Small Business Computing" lesson for discussion of policies and procedures related to remote access security.

B. Intrusion Detection Systems (IDSs)—Monitor network systems for unusual traffic.

C. A Honeypot or Honeynet is a server that lures hackers to a decoy system. Its purpose is to identify intruders and provide information to help block them from live systems.

D. IDSs, honeypots, and honeynets complement, and are usually integrated with, firewalls.

Physical Access Controls

After studying this lesson, you should be able to:

1. Identify and describe some important considerations in locating information processing resources and facilities.
2. Identify and describe some important controls related to the physical security of information systems.
3. Identify and describe some important controls related to physical protecting data libraries and programs.
4. Give examples of physical access controls and the risks they help to mitigate.

I. **IT Facilities**—IT facility controls include computer hardware (CPUs, disk and tape drives, printers, communications devices, etc.), software (program files), and data files, as well as the computing infrastructure (network communication media and devices) and the rooms and buildings in which the software, hardware, and files reside. Control over IT facilities involves safeguarding equipment, programs, and data from physical damage.

   A. Possible threats to physical security include fired or disgruntled employees, employees or individuals with substance addictions (e.g., seeking assets to sell or buy drugs), and employees or individuals with severe financial or emotional problems. Remember the **Fraud Triangle** indicators of risk that are discussed in the *Auditing and Attestation* section of CPAExcel.

Exam Tip
The controls listed in this section are all **general controls**: controls over the IT department as a whole. Some of the controls are **preventive controls**. For example, restricting physical access to the IT department prevents unauthorized individuals from gaining physical access to the system.

II. **Physical Location Controls**—Computer operations should be located in facilities that are safe from fire, flood, climate variations (heat, humidity), and unauthorized access. Generally, computer operations are located away from windows (in a building's interior), not on a top floor or basement, and not on a first floor.

   A. The computer room should be **climate controlled** to control and monitor heat and humidity, which can damage equipment and data files. Generally, there should be no opening windows in IT facilities. In addition, the heat generated by large banks of servers must be considered and controlled, and is sometimes redirected to heat buildings.

   B. The system for detecting environmental threats should include **alarm control panels, water and smoke detectors, and manual fire alarms.**

   C. **Fire suppression systems** appropriate for electrical fires should be installed. **Handheld fire extinguishers** should also be available. Although they were once popular, **Halon systems** are now banned due to environmental concerns.

   D. Adequacy of power and backup power systems should be periodically evaluated. Potential electrical system risks include failure (blackout), reduced voltage (brownout), sags, spikes and surges, and **electromagnetic interference (EMI)**.

   E. All physical protection and recovery systems require maintenance and monitoring. Regular inspection by fire departments are both a best practice, and in many cases, required by local, regional, or state laws.

III. **Physical Access**

   A. **Access to the Computer Operations Areas**

      1. Should be restricted to those directly involved in operations. In larger organizations, authorized individuals should be issued, and required to wear, identification badges.

      2. Physical security should include mechanical or electronic door locks, keypad devices, access card readers, security personnel, and surveillance devices.

3. **Social engineering**—Methods used by attackers to fool employees into giving the attackers access to information resources. One form of social engineering concerns physical system access:

   a. In **piggybacking** an unauthorized user slips into a restricted area with an authorized user, following the authorized user's entry.

B. **Data Stored on Magnetic Disks, Tapes, and USB Drives**—Should be protected by a combination of logical and physical controls, including:

1. **External labels**—Used by computer operators, or by smart end users, to visually (physically) identify the disks or USB drives.
2. **Internal labels (sometimes called "header" and "trailer" records, in reference to their origins in magnetic tape)**—Read by the processing program to determine the identity of the data file.
3. **File protection rings or locks**—Physically prevent the media from being overwritten.
4. **Setting file attributes**—Logically restrict the ability of the user to read, write, update, and/or delete records in a file.

C. **Programs and Data Files**—Should be physically secured and under the control of a file librarian in order to protect the programs and data from unauthorized modification. See also the "Program Library, Documentation, and Record Management" lesson.

Encryption and Secure Exchanges

After studying this lesson, you should be able to:

1. Describe the elements, purpose, and basic method of encryption.
2. Describe the purpose and basic method of digital signatures and certificates.
3. Identify the purpose of, and acronyms associated with, secure Internet transmission protocols.
4. Describe, and compare and contrast, symmetric and asymmetric encryption.
5. Describe the purpose and value of virtual private networks (VPNs).
6. Give examples of appropriate and inappropriate uses of symmetric and asymmetric encryption.
7. Describe some emerging models for improving encryption.

I. Introduction

A. The growth in e-commerce and other Internet-based technologies has increased risks from network-based exchanges between unrelated parties.

B. This lesson considers threats and controls related to ensuring the privacy and security of information, and, secure online financial exchanges.

II. Privacy and Security Issues in Networked Systems

A. Encryption—This is the process of converting a plaintext message into a secure-coded form (ciphertext).

1. **Decryption** reverses **encryption** (to read a message). Encryption technology uses a mathematical algorithm to translate **cleartext (plaintext)**—text that can be read and understood—into **ciphertext** (text that has been mathematically scrambled so that its meaning cannot be determined without decryption).
2. Encryption can provide **privacy** (protection of data against unauthorized access) and **authentication** (user identification). It can protect stored (i.e., **data at rest**) or transmitted (i.e., **data in motion**) data and verify the data authenticity.
3. Encryption is an essential but imperfect control. The security of encryption methods rests upon key length and secrecy. Generally, key security declines with use.

B. "Key" Elements of Encryption

1. The **encryption algorithm** is the function or formula that encrypts and decrypts (by reversal) the data.
2. The **encryption key** is the parameter or input into the encryption algorithm that makes the encryption unique. The reader must have the key to decrypt the ciphertext.
3. **Key length** is a determinant of strength. Longer keys are harder to decrypt.

C. Symmetric Encryption

1. Fast, simple, easy and less secure than asymmetric encryption
2. More often used in data stores (i.e., data at rest) since only one party then needs the single algorithm and key
3. Also called single-key encryption, symmetric encryption uses a **single algorithm** to encrypt and decrypt.
4. The sender uses the encryption algorithm to create the ciphertext and sends the encrypted text to the recipient.
5. The sender informs the recipient of the algorithm.
6. The recipient reverses the algorithm to decrypt.

D. Asymmetric Encryption

1. Safer but more complicated than symmetric encryption
2. More often used with data-in-motion
3. Also called public/private-key encryption
4. Uses two paired encryption algorithms to encrypt and decrypt
5. If the **public key** is used to encrypt, the **private key** must be used to decrypt; conversely, if the **private key** is used to encrypt, the **public key** must be used to decrypt.
6. To acquire a public/private key pair, the user applies to a **certificate authority (CA)**:
   a. The CA registers the public key on its server and sends the private key to the user.
   b. When someone wants to communicate securely with the user, he or she accesses the public key from the CA server, encrypts the message, and sends it to the user.
   c. The user then uses the private key to decrypt the message.
   d. The transmission is secure because only the private key can decrypt the message and only the user has access to the private key.

E. Quantum Encryption—Quantum mechanics from physics is emerging as a technology that may revolutionize computing encryption. It uses the physical properties of light (photons) to generate seemingly uncrackable codes.

III. Facilitating Secure Exchanges—E-commerce should occur only with high certainty regarding the **identity** of the trading partners and the **reliability** of the transaction data. Electronic identification methodologies and secure transmission technology are designed to provide such an environment.

A. Digital Signatures

1. An electronic means of identifying a person or entity
2. Use public/private key pair technology to **provide authentication of the sender** and verification of the content of the message.
3. The authentication process is based on the private key.
4. Vulnerable to **man-in-the-middle attacks** in which the sender's private and public key are faked. A digital signature is like the sealing of an envelope with the King's personal wax seal in the days of Kings. A thief may steal, or a forger may duplicate, the King's seal. Therefore, the message from the King, or the e-mail—in the case of digital signatures—may not be from the person who the receiver thinks that it is from, because a thief stole the seal (or the private key).

B. Digital Certificates

1. For transactions requiring a high degree of assurance, a digital certificate provides legally recognized electronic identification of the sender, and, verifies the integrity of the message content.
   a. Based on a **public key infrastructure (PKI)** which specifies protocols for managing and distributing cryptographic keys
   b. In this system, a user requests a certificate from the certificate authority. The certificate author then completes a background check to verify identity before issuing the certificate.
   c. More secure than digital signatures
2. **A certificate authority or certification authority (CA**) manages and issues digital certificates and public keys. The digital certificate certifies the ownership of a public key by the named subject (user) of the certificate. This allows others (relying parties) to rely upon signatures or assertions made by the private key that corresponds to the certified public key.

C. Secure Internet Transmission Protocols

1. Sensitive data sent via the Internet is usually secured by one of two encryption protocols:
   1. **Secure Sockets Layer (SSL)** uses a combination of encryption schemes based on a PKI;
   2. **Secure Hypertext Transfer Protocol (S-HTTP)** directs messages to secure ports using SSL-like cryptography.
2. **Secure Electronic Transactions (SET)**
   - **a.** Developed by VISA and MasterCard. A protocol often used for consumer purchases made via the Internet. Uses multiple encryption schemes based on a PKI.
   - **b.** Used by the merchant (i.e., the intermediary between the bank and customer) to securely transmit payment information and authenticate trading partner identity.
3. **Virtual Private Network (VPN)**—A secure way to connect to a private local area network (LAN) from a remote location, usually through an Internet connection. Uses authentication to identify users and encryption to prevent unauthorized users from intercepting data. Should be part of an organization's remote access security plan.

IV. The Limits and Future of Encryption

A. Encryption must be part of a broader strategy to achieve confidentiality and security. It alone is insufficient. Access controls and strong authentication techniques help, as does limiting, as appropriate, user actions (read, write, change, delete, copy, etc.) when accessing confidential information.

B. Encryption is something of an "arms" race with hackers. IT professionals and researchers are always improving encryption to remain ahead of hackers, who develop improved strategies for breaking encryption.

C. Emerging strategies, currently being researched, for improving encryption include "honey" encryption, where wrong guesses about the encrypting key yield falsified data that looks correct (but isn't), and quantum encryption, where data are encrypted using the perplexing Alice-in-Wonderland–like qualities of quantum computers.

System Disruption/Resolution

Organizational Continuity Planning and Disaster Recovery

This lesson covers two topics: disaster recovery and business continuity planning.

After studying this lesson, you should be able to:

1. Define and describe the purpose and key alternatives of a disaster recovery plan (DRP).
2. Define and describe the purpose of, and steps in, organizational (business) continuity planning.
3. Give examples of the risks of inadequate DRPs.
4. Give examples of the risks of inadequate organizational continuity planning.
5. Compare and contrast a disaster recovery plan with organizational continuity planning.

I. **Organizational (Business) Continuity Planning**—The disaster recovery plan relates to organizational processes and structures that will enable an organization to recover from a disaster.Business (or organizational) continuity management (sometimesabbreviated BCM) is the process of planning for such occurrences and embeddingthis plan in an organization's culture. Hence, BCM is one element of organizational risk management. It consists of identifying events that may threaten an organization's ability to deliverproducts and services, and creating a structure that ensures smooth and continuous operations in the event the identified risks occur. One six-step model of this process (from the Business Continuity Institute) is

   A. **Create a BCM Policy and Program**—Create a framework and structure around which the BCM is created. This includes defining the scope of the BCM plan, identifying roles in this plan, and assigning roles to individuals.

   B. **Understand and Evaluate Organizational Risks**—Identifying the importance of activities and processes is critical to determining needed costs to prevent interruption, and, ensure their restoration in the event of interruption. A business impact analysis (BIA) will identify the maximum tolerable interruption periods by function and organizational activity.

   C. **Determine Business Continuity Strategies**—Having defined the critical activities and tolerable interruption periods, define alternative methods to ensure sustainable delivery of products and services. Key decisions related to the strategy include desired recovery times, distance to recovery facilities, required personnel, supporting technologies, and impact on stakeholders.

   D. **Develop and Implement a BCM Response**—Document and formalize the BCM plan. Define protocols for defining and handling crisis incidents. Create, assign roles to, and train the incident response team(s).

   E. **Exercise, Maintain, and Review the Plan**—Exercising the plan involves testing the required technology, and implementing all aspects of the recovery process. Maintenance and review require updating the plan as business processes and risks evolve.

   F. **Embed the BCM in the Organization's Culture**—Design and deliver education, training and awareness materials that enable effective responses to identified risks. Manage change processes to ensure that the BCM becomes a part of the organization's culture.

G. The following figure illustrates the prioritization of BCP risks by the importance of the function to the organization's mission. Risk prioritization would be part of the second phase of BCM.

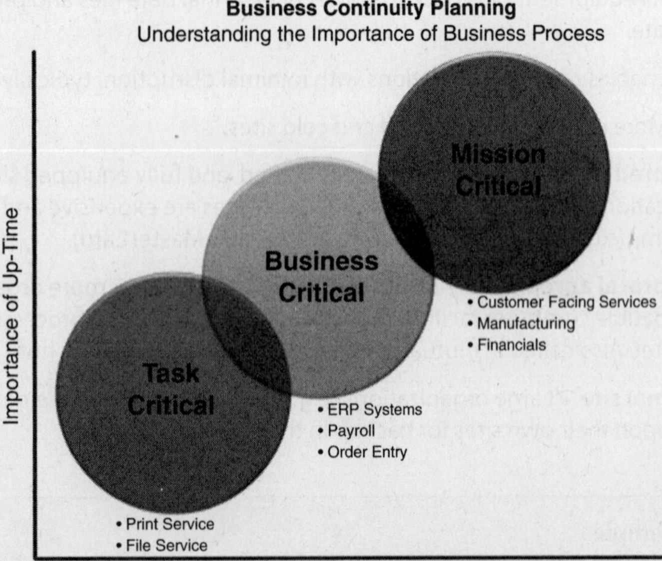

II. Disaster Recovery Plans (DRPs)

A. DRPs enable organizations to recover from disasters and continue operations. They are integral to an organization's system of internal control. DRP processes include maintaining program and data files and enabling transaction processing facilities. In addition to backup data files, DRPs must identify mission-critical tasks and ensure that processing for these tasks can continue with virtually no interruptions, at an affordable cost.

1. Examples of natural disasters include fires, floods, earthquakes, tornadoes, ice storms, and windstorms. Examples of human-induced disasters include terrorist attacks, software failures (e.g., American Airlines recent flight control system failure), power plant failures, and explosions (e.g., Chernobyl), chemical spills, gas leaks, and fires.

B. Two Important Goals of Disaster Recovery Planning

1. The **recovery point objective (RPO**) defines the acceptable amount of data lost in an incident. Typically, it is stated in hours, and defines the regularity of backups. For example, one organization might set an RPO of one minute, meaning that backups would occur every minute, and up to one minute of data might need to be re-entered into the system. Another organization, or the same organization in relation to a less mission-critical system, might set an RPO of six hours.

2. The **recovery time objective (RTO)** defines the acceptable downtime for a system, or, less commonly, of an organization. It specifies the longest acceptable time for a system to be inoperable.

C. Disaster recovery plans are classified by the types of backup facilities, the time required to resume processing, and the organizational relations of the site:

1. **Cold site ("empty shell")**—An off-site location that has all the electrical connections and other physical requirements for data processing, but does not have the actual equipment or files. Cold sites often require one to three days to be made operational. A cold site is the least expensive type of alternative processing facility available to the organization. If on a mobile unit (e.g., a truck bed), it is called a **mobile cold site**.

2. **Warm site**—A location where the business can relocate to after the disaster that is already stocked with computer hardware similar to that of the original site, but does not contain backed-up copies of data and information. If on a mobile unit, it is called a **mobile warm site**.

3. **Hot site**
   a. An off-site location completely equipped to quickly resume data processing.
   b. All equipment plus backup copies of essential data files and programs are often at the site.
   c. Enables resumed operations with minimal disruption, typically within a few hours.
   d. More expensive than warm and cold sites.
4. **Mirrored site**—Fully redundant, fully staffed, and fully equipped site with real-time data replication of mission-critical systems. Such sites are expensive and used for mission-critical systems (e.g., credit card processing at VISA and MasterCard).
5. **Reciprocal agreement**—An agreement between two or more organizations (with compatible computer facilities) to aid each other with data processing needs in the event of a disaster. Also called a "mutual aid pact." May be cold, warm, or hot.
6. **Internal site**—Large organizations (e.g., Walmart) with multiple data processing centers often rely upon their own sites for backup in the event of a disaster.

Example
Mirrored Site
MasterCard maintains a duplicate computer center in Kansas City, Missouri, as an emergency backup to its primary computer center in St. Louis.

Example
Contracting for Disaster Recovery
Rather than build their own backup facilities, many firms contract with disaster recovery firms, such as Comdisco Disaster Recovery Services in Rosemont, Illinois, and SunGard Recovery Services, headquartered in Wayne, Pennsylvania. These disaster recovery firms provide hot sites housing spare computers at locations around the country where subscribing firms can run their critical applications in an emergency.

Backup and Restoration

After studying this lesson, you should be able to:

1. Describe some common backup and restoration methods and procedures.
2. Describe common network-based backup and restoration methods and procedures.
3. Identify which backup and restoration procedures are common in batch versus online processing systems.
4. Give examples of the risks that are addressed by backup and restoration procedures.

I. Backup and Restoration Procedures

A. Formal plans for making and retaining backup copies of data to enable recovering from equipment failures, power failures, and data processing errors.

1. At least one archive should be off-site so that recovery is possible even when a major disaster occurs.
2. Controls over storage libraries mirror those for data processing sites.
3. Decisions regarding backup devices and media should consider vendor (outsourcing) availability, standardization, capacity, speed, and price.
4. Backup procedures may be full (all data), incremental (data changed from a certain time) or differential (data changed since the last full backup).
5. Inventory procedures—An inventory of backups, on and off-site must be maintained that includes, at a minimum, data set name, volume serial number, data created, accounting period, and storage location (e.g., bin).
6. Many organizations outsource responsibility for backup and restoration. Organizations that do not outsource generally purchase software systems that help manage these processes.
7. Restoration procedures should be integrated into the organization's continuity plan.
8. Backup and restoration procedures must be regularly tested and reviewed.

Note
Controls relating to program and data backup files and disaster recovery plans are corrective controls (i.e., controls designed to help correct and recover from previously detected problems).

B. Businesses rely extensively on the concept of **redundant backups**—having multiple backup copies—which means that if one backup fails or if the problem occurred before the last backup, the organization need not rely on a single archived copy.

C. Backup and recovery procedures link to the type of processing employed:

1. **"Grandfather, father, son" system**
   a. A traditional term used to refer to a three-generation backup procedure: the "son" is the newest version of the file; the "father" is one generation back in time, the "grandfather" is two generations back in time;
   b. Associated with batch processing in a magnetic tape environment where a new master file (the "son") was created when the old master file (the "father") was updated.
   c. Sorry for the sexist terminology here; this is probably because in the 1960s, all the IT people in corporations were male. It is interesting that all the voices of computers these days are female (e.g., Siri, Alexa, the Scarlett Johansson movie *Her* where she is the voice of a computer). All those "grandfather" computers apparently gave birth to daughters!

Note
While studying for the CPA Exam, please know the following terms and their "value" designations: System backup is good; data redundancy is bad. (Of course, system backup is data redundancy, but don't get philosophical about this topic until AFTER you pass the CPA Exam.)

2. See the following illustration of a grandfather/father/son approach:

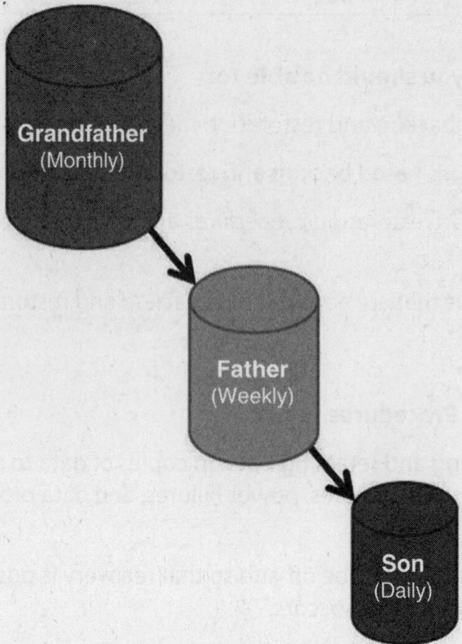

3. **Checkpoint and restart**—Common in batch processing systems, a checkpoint is a point in data processing where processing accuracy is verified; if a problem occurs, one returns to the previous checkpoint instead of returning to the beginning of transaction processing. This saves time and money.
4. **Rollback and recovery**—Common to online, real-time processing; all transactions are written to a transaction log when they are processed; periodic "snapshots" are taken of the master file; when a problem is detected the recovery manager program, starts with the snapshot of the master file and reprocesses all transactions that have occurred since the snapshot was taken.

D. **Network-Based Backup and Restoration**—Network capabilities increasingly provide continuous backup capabilities; such backup facilities are necessary to create fault-tolerant systems (systems that continue to operate properly despite the failure of some components) and high-availability clusters (HACs). HACs are computer clusters designed to improve the availability of services; HACs are common in e-commerce environments where services must be continuously available.

1. **Remote backup service (online backup service)**
    a. An outsourcing service that provides users with an online system for backing up and storing computer files.
    b. Remote backup has several advantages over traditional backup methodologies: the task of creating and maintaining backup files is outsourced; the backups are off-site; some services can operate continuously, backing up each transaction as it occurs.
2. **RAID**—RAID (redundant array of independent disks; originally redundant array of inexpensive disks) stores the same data in different places (thus, redundantly) on multiple hard disks. By placing data on multiple disks, I/O (input/output) operations can overlap in a balanced way, improving performance. Since the use of multiple disks lessens the likelihood of failures, storing data redundantly reduces the risk of system failure.
3. **Storage Area Networks (SANs)**—Replicate data from and to multiple networked sites; data stored on a SAN is immediately available without the need to recover it; this enables a more effective restoration but at a relatively high cost.
4. **Mirroring**
    a. Maintaining an exact copy of a data set to provide multiple sources of the same information
    b. Mirrored sites are most frequently used in e-commerce for load balancing—distributing excess demand from the primary site to the mirrored.
    c. A high-cost, high-reliability approach that is common in e-commerce.

Computer Crime, Attack Methods, and Cyber-Incident Response

After studying this lesson, you should be able to:

1. Describe the common sources, goals, and types of computer crimes.
2. Describe the common methods used to attack computers and information systems.
3. Describe a common approach to responding to cyber-incidents.
4. Give examples of the goals of computer criminals.
5. Give examples of strategies that are useful in mitigating computer crime and discuss their usefulness.

I. **Computer Crimes and System Attacks**

A. **Introduction**—Computers and information systems may be either the means or the objects of computer crimes. This lesson describes common types of computer crimes and methods of attacking computers. It also discusses protocols for responding to cyber-incidents (i.e., security breaches).

II. **Computer Crimes**—Computer crimes involve the use of the computer to break the law including gaining unlawful access to computer resources. Computer crime categories include:

A. **Computer or System as Target**—A perpetrator may use a computer to deny others the use or services of a computer system or network. Examples include denial of service (DoS) attacks and hacking.

B. **Computer as Subject**—A perpetrator may unlawfully gain access to many computers on a network and use these computers to perpetrate attacks on other computers. Examples include a distributed denial of service attack (just described) or the use of malware (i.e., programs that exploit system and user vulnerabilities) to gain access to computers and networks.

C. **Computer as Tool**—A perpetrator unlawfully uses a computer or network to gain access to data or resources (other than the computer itself). Examples include fraud, unauthorized access breaches, phishing, and installing key loggers.

D. **Computer as Symbol/User as Target**—A variation on the computer-as-tool crime. Here, a perpetrator deceives a user to obtain access to confidential information. Examples—social engineering methods including phishing, fake website, and spam mail.

III. **Who Commits Cyber-Crimes?** The categories of computer criminals include:

A. **Nation-States and Spies**—Some foreign nations (e.g., China, Russia?) seek intellectual property and trade secrets for military and competitive advantage.

B. **Industrial Spies**—Organizations seek intellectual property and trade secrets for competitive advantage.

C. **Organized Criminals**—Organized crime engages in computer crime for profit (e.g., blackmails that threaten to harm data resources).

D. **Hacktivists**—Those who make social or political statements by stealing or publishing an organization's sensitive information (e.g., WikiLeaks).

E. **Hackers**—Some individuals commit cyber-crimes for fun and for the challenge of breaking into others' systems. Hackers can be "good person" or "white hat" hackers as well as "bad person" or "black hat" hackers.

IV. **Computer and System Attack Methods**—Some of the more common logical (not physical facility) attack methods appear below. We consider physical facility attack methods in a separate lesson.

A. **Access Issues**—These concern issues gaining access to computing resources.

1. **Back door or trapdoor**—A software program that allows an unauthorized user to gain access to the system by sidestepping the normal logon procedures. Historically, programmers used back doors to facilitate quick access to systems under development. If left in a system or installed by a hacker, they enable unauthorized access.
2. **Botnets (or zombie computers)**—A collection of computers under the control of a perpetrator that is used to perpetrate DoS, adware, spyware, and spam attacks.
3. **Eavesdropping**—The unauthorized interception of a private communication, such as a phone call, email, or instant message transmission.
4. **Hacking or cracking**—Malicious or criminal unauthorized penetration of computer systems and networks.
5. **Hijacking**—An attacker takes control of the system, network, or communication.
6. **Identity theft**—Using someone else's identity (e.g., Social Security number) to create credit cards, establish loans, or enter into other transactions.
7. **Keystroke loggers**—Software that records keystrokes (e.g., to steal passwords or logon information).
8. **Man-in-the-middle attack**—A perpetrator establishes a connection between two devices and then pretends to be each party, thereby intercepting and interfering with messages between the parties (e.g., to steal passwords or credit card information).
    a. **Packet sniffing**—Programs called packet sniffers capture packets of data as they move across a computer network. While administrators use packet sniffing to monitor network performance or troubleshoot problems with network communications, hackers also use these tools to capture usernames and passwords, IP addresses, and other information that can help them break into the network. Packet sniffing on a computer network is similar to wiretapping a phone line. This is one form of a man-in-the-middle attack.
9. **Masquerading or impersonation**—Pretending to have authorization to enter a secure online location.
10. **Password crackers**—Once a username has been identified, hackers can use password-cracking software to generate many potential passwords and use them to gain access. Password cracker programs are most effective with weak passwords (i.e., passwords with fewer than eight characters, that use one letter case, or that do not require numbers or special symbols).
11. **Phishing**—A deceptive request for information delivered via email. The email asks the recipient to either respond to the email or visit a website and provide authentication information. You probably get several phishing queries every week.
12. **Phreaking**—A form of hacking on telephone communications (e.g., tapping into a conversation or getting phone services for free).
13. **Session masquerading and hijacking**—Masquerading occurs when an attacker identifies an IP address (usually through packet sniffing) and then attempts to use that address to gain access to the network. If the masquerade is successful, then the hacker has hijacked the session—gained access to the session under the guise of another user.
14. **Malicious software (malware)**—Programs that exploit system and user vulnerabilities to gain access to the computer; there are many types of malware.
15. **Social engineering or spoofing**—Using deceit or deception to gain logical access to the system. The deception is to persuade employees to provide usernames and passwords to the system. These deceptive requests may be delivered verbally or through email, text messaging, or social networking sites. Fraudsters may spoof by faking an identity (e.g., a company or friend) or an email (e.g., pretending to be your bank or a friend of yours) or by creating a website that mimics a real website.
16. **Spyware**—Adware that watches a user's computer activity without proper consent, reporting the information to the creator of the spyware software.

17. **Trojan horse**—A malicious program hidden inside a seemingly benign file. Frequently used to insert back doors into a system (see above).

18. **War chalking, driving, and walking**—Multiple methods for identifying access points in order to gain unlawful access to wireless networks.

B. Service issues concern efforts to block users' access to computing resources.

1. **Denial of service (DoS) attack**—Rather than attempting to gain unauthorized access to IT resources, some attackers threaten the system by preventing legitimate users from accessing the system. Perpetrators instigate these attacks, using one or many computers, to flood a server with access requests that cannot be completed. These include ransom and blackmail DoS attacks in which the criminal threatens to deny service unless the user pays a ransom or engages in a specific act (e.g., grants access to their system).

2. **Email bombing or spamming**—Attacking a computer by sending thousands or millions of identical emails to the address.

C. Data issues concern efforts to inappropriately access or change data.

1. **Data diddling**—Changing data in an unauthorized manner (forgery) either before or during input into the computer system (e.g., changing credit ratings or fixing salaries).

2. **Data leakage**—Uncontrolled or unauthorized transmission of classified information from a data center or computer system to outside parties (e.g., remote employees increase the risk of data leakage if networks are unsecure).

D. Asset, data, and hardware destruction and misuse damage or destroy assets and resources.

1. **Logic bomb**—An unauthorized program planted in the system; the logic bomb lies dormant until the occurrence of a specified event or time (e.g., a specific date, the elimination of an employee from active employee status).

2. **Salami fraud**—Taking a small amount of money from many accounts using a variety of rounding methods

3. **Software piracy**—Unauthorized copying of software

4. **Spam**—Unsolicited mass emailings; the volume of spam can make systems unusable

5. **Superzapping**—The use of powerful software to access secure information while bypassing normal controls

6. **Virus**—An unauthorized program, usually introduced through an email attachment, that copies itself to files in the user's system; these programs may actively damage data, or they may be benign.

7. **Worm**—Similar to viruses except that worms attempt to replicate themselves across multiple computer systems. Worms generally try to accomplish this by activating the system's email client and sending multiple emails. Worms generally exist *inside* of other files; unlike viruses, they are not stand-alone programs.

V. Cyber-Incident Responses

A. A cyber-incident is a violation of an organization's security policy (Source: Software Engineering Institute, Carnegie Mellon University). The well-managed organization will have a cyber-incident protocol (i.e., response and action plan) as a part of its business continuity plan. This protocol will specify the level of the incident.

B. An action plan for a cyber-incident will likely include:

1. Planning for and testing of the protocol including specification of the response team

2. Event detection procedures

3. Event logging procedures (i.e., who, what, where, when, and how). For example, verifying that a claimed event occurred, describing the event, the systems affected, and the period of outages.

4. Triage and incident analysis, including a severity classification of the level of the event (e.g., from a minor to a crisis event) with a set of actions following from the event's classification. Will also include an assessment of the likelihood of repetition and a search of information sources regarding the incident.
5. Containment and removal of threats
6. Decision and action regarding event announcement or secrecy
7. Recovery from incidents
8. Closure
9. Event reporting
10. Monitoring and system revisions, as needed

VI. Strategies for Preventing and Detecting Computer Crime

A. Given the importance of information assets, organizations must invest to protect and defend their information systems. Strategies for decreasing the likelihood of crime and reducing losses include:

1. **Make crime harder (i.e., less likely)**—By creating an ethical culture, adopting an appropriate organizational structure, requiring active oversight, assigning authority and responsibility, assessing risk, developing security policies, implementing human resource policies, supervising employees effectively, training employees, requiring vacations, implementing development and acquisition controls, and prosecuting fraud perpetrators vigorously.
2. **Increase the costs (difficulty) of crime**—By designing strong internal controls, segregating duties, restricting access, requiring appropriate authorizations, utilizing documentation, safeguarding assets, requiring independent checks on performance, implementing computer-based controls, encrypting data, and fixing software vulnerabilities.
3. **Improve detection methods**—By creating an audit trail, conducting periodic audits, installing fraud detection software, implementing a fraud hotline, employing a computer security officer, monitoring system activities, and using intrusion detection systems.
4. **Reduce fraud losses**—By maintaining adequate insurance, developing disaster recovery plans, backing up data and programs, and using software to monitor system activity and recover from fraud.

Processing Integrity (Input/Processing/Output Controls)

Program Library, Documentation, and Record Management

After studying this lesson, you should be able to :

1. Describe the source program library management system (SPLMS) and its role in controlling application development.
2. Describe the four types and levels of documentation, their value, and to whom they hold valuable.
3. Describe the basic elements in a record retention and destruction system.
4. Give examples of the value of quality documentation to organizations.
5. Give examples of the conditions under which each type of documentation would be valuable.
6. Describe the conditions under which records must be retained versus the conditions under which they must be destroyed.

I. Program Library, Documentation, and Record Management

- **A.** Source code programs are normally maintained in a library under secure storage (the source program library, or SPL) that is maintained by a file librarian. The library, or an archive of the library, should be off-site and built to withstand fires, floods, and other natural disasters. It (obviously) must also include the same logical and physical controls as are built into the organization's other data processing and storage sites.
- **B.** When new programs are developed or old programs modified, the SPLMS manages the migration from the **application development test environment to the active production library**.
- **C.** The SPLMS ensures that only valid changes are made to the system by checking for all necessary authorizations and, for program modifications, by comparing the new source code to the old source code. Only after verification does the program migrate to the SPL.
- **D.** Authorized versions of major programs should be maintained in a secure, off-site location. (The external auditor frequently maintains these files.)

II. Purpose of Documentation

- **A. Documentation of the Accounting System is Required**
  1. By law, for example in the Foreign Corrupt Practices Act, and SOX
  2. To build and evaluate complex systems
  3. For training
  4. For creating sustainable/survivable systems
  5. For auditing (internal and external)
  6. For process (re)engineering

III. Levels of Documentation—Four levels of documentation should be maintained; documentation at each level generally includes flowcharts and narrative descriptions.

- **A. Systems Documentation**—Overviews the program and data files, processing logic and interactions with each other's programs and systems; often includes narrative descriptions, flowcharts, and data flow diagrams; used primarily by systems developers; can be useful to auditors.

B. Program Documentation—A detailed analysis of the input data, the program logic, and the data output; consists of program flowcharts, source code listings, record layouts, etc.; used primarily by programmers; **program documentation is an important resource if the original programmer is unavailable**.

C. Operator Documentation (Also Called the "Run Manual")—In large computer systems, operator documentation provides information necessary to execute the program such as the required equipment, data files and computer supplies, execution commands, error messages, verification procedures, and expected output; used exclusively by the computer operators.

D. User Documentation—Describes the system from the point of view of the end user; provides instructions on how and when to submit data and request reports, procedures for verifying the accuracy of the data and correcting errors.

> **Note**
> All of the preceding controls are general and preventive.

IV. Forms of Documentation—Multiple forms of documentation facilitate the process of creating, documenting, evaluating, and auditing accounting systems. Important forms of documentation include the following:

A. Questionnaires—Ask about use of specific procedures.

B. Narratives—Text descriptions of processes.

C. Data Flow Diagrams (DFDs)

1. Portray business processes, stores of data, and flows of data among those elements
2. Often used in developing new systems
3. Use simple, user-friendly symbols (unlike flowcharts)
4. For example, a DFD for the delivery of goods to a customer would include a symbol for the warehouse from which the goods are shipped and a symbol representing the customer. It would not show details, such as computer processing and paper output.

D. Flowcharts

1. For example, system flowcharts, present a comprehensive picture of the management, operations, information systems, and process controls embodied in business processes.
2. Often used to evaluate controls in a system
3. Too complicated and technical for some users. DFDs are easier to understand.

E. Entity-Relationship (E-R) Diagrams—Model relationships between entities and data in accounting systems.

F. Decision Tables—Depict logical relationships in a processing system by identifying the decision points and processing alternatives that derive from those decision points.

V. Record Retention and Destruction

A. Source documents, preferably in electronic form, must be retained as required by organizational policy, business needs, external or internal audit requirements, or applicable law (e.g., the IRS or HIPAA) or regulation.

B. Organizations must have a plan to ensure that retained records are kept confidential and secure often under the logical control of the originating departments.

C. In some cases, laws, regulations, or good business practices require the regular, systematic destruction of old records (e.g., medical or credit histories, juvenile or criminal records). Record destruction must follow a systematic, controlled process and must not be haphazard (e.g., thrown into a dumpster).

1. For example, privacy laws in about 31 U.S. states require that personal records be destroyed after a fixed time period.

Input and Origination Controls

After studying this lesson, you should be able to:

1. Match input controls to the risks that they will mitigate.
2. Give examples of the risks of inadequate input controls.
3. Explain the difference between input and origination controls.
4. Describe the most important input application controls.

I. Introduction

A. Application controls concern the accuracy, validity, and completeness of data processing in specific application programs. They can be placed in one of three categories:

1. **Input and origination controls**—Control over data entry and data origination process
2. **Processing and file controls**—Controls over processing and files, including the master file update process
3. **Output controls**—Control over the production of reports
4. This lesson covers input and origination controls; the next lesson covers processing, file, and output. In CPAexcel, these controls, i.e., input, processing, file, and output, appear under the heading of IT Development as a reminder that such controls should be considered in designing new systems.

B. Processing methodology (batch processing versus online, real-time processing) can impact the selection of application controls as not all controls work with batch and online, real-time processing systems.

> **Exam Tip**
> When answering questions about application controls, the processing method (batch or OLRT) is an important determinant of the correct answer.

II. Input Controls—(Also known as programmed controls, edit checks, or automated controls.)

A. **Introduction**—Ensure that the transactions entered into the system meet the following control objectives:

1. **Valid**—All transactions are appropriately authorized; no fictitious transactions are present; no duplicate transactions are included.
2. **Complete**—All transactions have been captured; there are no missing transactions.
3. **Accurate**—All data has been correctly transcribed, all account codes are valid; all data fields are present; all data values are appropriate.

B. There are more input than processing and output controls.

1. This is due in part to the importance of correct input data: if data is incorrectly input, then subsequent uses of the data are compromised (i.e., GIGO: garbage in, garbage out).
2. The abundance of input controls is also because, historically, many errors occur in the (manual) input phase: the processing and output phases are largely controlled by computer programs that, when properly developed and tested, are not susceptible to errors.
3. Increasingly, the best input control is to automate data entry (i.e., to not have a (manual) input process. Hence, the growing use of the term "origination" to replace "input" to reflect the automation of what was once, a primarily manual "inputting" process.

C. Here are some important input controls:

1. **Missing data check**—The simplest type of test available: checks only to see that something has been entered into the field.

2. **Field check (data type/data format check)**—Verifies that the data entered is of an acceptable type—alphabetic, numeric, a certain number of characters, etc.
3. **Limit test**—Checks to see that a numeric field does not exceed a specified value; for example, the number of hours worked per week is not greater than 60. There are several variations of limit tests:
    a. **Range tests**—Validate upper and lower limits; for example, the price per gallon cannot be less than $4.00 or greater than $10.00.
    b. **Sign tests**—Verify that numeric data has the appropriate sign (positive or negative); for example, the quantity purchased cannot be negative.
4. **Valid code test (validity test)**—Checks to make sure that each account code entered into the system is a valid (existing) code; this control does not ensure that the code is *correct*, merely that it exists.
    a. In a database system, this is called **referential integrity** (e.g., an important control to prevent the creation of fake entities, vendors, customers, employees).
5. **Check digit**—Designed to ensure that each account code entered into the system is **both valid and correct**. The check digit is a number created by applying an arithmetic algorithm to the digits of a number, for example, a customer's account code. The algorithm yields a single digit appended to the end of the code. Whenever the account code (including check digit) is entered, the computer recalculates the check digit and compares the calculated check digit to the digit entered. If the digits fail to match, then there is an error in the code, and processing is halted.
    a. A highly reliable method for ensuring that the correct code has been entered
    b. A parity check (from the data controls lesson) is one form of a check digit

Example

A Practical Example of Check Digits

The final digit in an International Standard Book Number (ISBN) is a check digit that confirms the accuracy of the other digits. There are also check digits in many credit card numbers and patient (e.g., the Mayo Clinic) and customer numbers.

6. **Reasonableness check (logic test)**—Checks to see that data in two or more fields is consistent. For example, a rate of pay value of "$3,500" and a pay period value of "hourly" may be valid values for the fields when the fields are viewed independently; however, the combination (an hourly pay rate of $3,500) is not valid.
7. **Sequence check**—Verifies that all items in a numerical sequence (check numbers, invoice numbers, etc.) are present. This check is the most commonly used control for validating processing completeness.
8. **Key verification**—The rekeying (i.e., retyping) of critical data in the transaction, followed by a comparison of the two keyings. For example, in a batch environment, one operator keys in all of the data for the transactions while a second operator rekeys all of the account codes and amounts. The system compares the results and reports any differences. Key verification is generally found in batch systems, but can be used in online real-time environments as well. As a second example, consider the process required to change a password: enter the old password, enter the new password, and then re-enter (i.e., key verify) the new password. This is a wasteful procedure that we all hope dies soon.
9. **Closed loop verification**—Helps ensure that a valid and correct account code has been entered; after the code is entered, this system looks up and displays additional information about the selected code. For example, the operator enters a customer code, and the system displays the customer's name and address. Available only in online real-time systems.

10. **Batch control totals**—Manually calculated totals of various fields of the documents in a batch. Batch totals are compared to computer-calculated totals and are used to ensure the accuracy and completeness of data entry. Batch control totals are available, of course, only for batch processing systems or applications.

    a. **Financial totals**—Totals of a currency field that result in meaningful totals, such as the dollar amounts of checks. (Note that the total of the hourly rates of pay for all employees, e.g., is not a financial total because the summation has no accounting-system meaning.)

    b. **Hash totals**—Totals of a field, usually an account code field, for which the total has no logical meaning, such as a total of customer account numbers in a batch of invoices.

    c. **Record counts**—Count of the number of documents in a batch or the number of lines on the documents in a batch.

11. **Preprinted forms and preformatted screens**—Reduce the likelihood of data entry errors by organizing input data logically: when the position and alignment of data fields on a data entry screens matches the organization of the fields on the source document, data entry is faster, and there are fewer errors.

12. **Default values**—Pre-supplied (pre-filled) data values for a field when that value can be reasonably predicted; for example, when entering sales data, the sales order date is usually the current date; fields using default values generate fewer errors than other fields.

13. **Automated data capture**—Use of automated equipment such as bar code scanners to reduce the amount of manual data entry; reducing human involvement reduces the number of errors in the system.

Processing, File, and Output Controls

After studying this lesson, you should be able to:

1. Describe the most important application controls related to processing, files, and outputs.
2. Match processing, file, and output controls to the risks that they mitigate.

I. Introduction

A. **Application controls** concern the accuracy, validity, and completeness of data processing in specific application programs. They can be placed in one of three categories:

1. **Input and origination controls**—Control over data and origination entry process
2. **Processing and file controls**—Controls over processing and files, including the master file update process
3. **Output controls**—Control over the production of reports

B. This lesson covers processing, files, and output controls; the previous lesson covered input and origination controls.

C. Processing methodology (batch processing versus online, real-time processing) can impact the selection of application controls as not all controls work with batch and online, real-time processing systems.

> **Exam Tip**
> When answering questions about application controls, an important determinant of the correct answer is the processing method.

II. Processing Controls—Controls designed to ensure that master file updates are completed accurately and completely. Controls also serve to detect unauthorized transactions entered into the system and maintain processing integrity.

A. **Run-to-Run Controls**—Use comparisons to monitor the batch as it moves from one programmed procedure (run) to another; totals of processed transactions are reconciled to batch totals—any difference indicates an error. Also called "control totals."

B. **Internal Labels ("Header" and "Trailer" Records)**—Used primarily in batch processing, electronic file identification allows the update program to determine that the correct file is being used for the update process.

C. **Audit Trail Controls**—Each transaction is written to a transaction log as the transaction is processed; the transaction logs become an electronic audit trail allowing the transaction to be traced through each stage of processing; electronic transaction logs constitute the principal audit trail for online, real-time systems.

III. Types of Files

A. Accounting systems typically include the following four file types:

1. **Master files** are updated by postings to transaction files.
2. **Standing data** is a subcategory of master file that consists of infrequently changing master files (e.g., fixed assets, supplier names and addresses)
3. **Transaction files** are the basis for updating master files.
4. **System control parameter files** determine the workings, including error characteristics and bounds, of system runs.

B. A primary goal of data control is to ensure that access, change, or destruction of data and storage media is **authorized**.

IV. File Controls—Some additional file controls that are not discussed in other lessons include:

A. **Parity Check (Parity Bit)**—A zero or 1 included in a byte of information that makes the sum of bits either odd or even; for example, using odd parity, the parity check bit for this byte of data:

001101

is zero because the sum of the digits in the byte is 3, an odd number.

Had the bit been as follows:

101101

the sum of the digits would be 4, and the parity bit would have been 1.

1. Parity checks are one application of "check digits" (i.e., self-confirming numbers).

B. **Read after Write Check**—Verifies that data was written correctly to disk by reading what was just written and comparing it to the source.

C. **Echo Check**—Verifies that transmission between devices is accurate by "echoing back" the received transmission from the receiving device to the sending unit.

D. **Error Reporting and Resolution**—Controls to ensure that generated errors are reported and resolved by individuals who are independent of the initiation of transactions (**segregation of duties**).

E. **Boundary Protection**—Sort of a computer traffic cop. When multiple programs and/or users are running simultaneously and sharing the same resource (usually the primary memory of a CPU), boundary protection prevents program instructions and data from one program from overwriting the program instructions or data from another program.

F. **Internal Labels ("Header" and "Trailer" Records)**—Used primarily in batch processing, electronic file identification allows the update program to determine that the correct file is being used for the update process. Read by the system. Very important for removable storage.

G. **External Labels**—Labels on removable storage that are read by humans.

H. **Version Control**—Procedures and software to ensure that the correct file version is used in processing (e.g., for transaction files).

I. **File Access and Updating Controls**—These controls ensure that only authorized, valid users can access and update files.

J. **Output Controls**—Ensure that computer reports are **accurate** and are **distributed only as authorized.**

   1. **Spooling (print queue) controls**—Jobs sent to a printer that cannot be printed immediately are spooled—stored temporarily on disk—while waiting to be printed; access to this temporary storage must be controlled to prevent unauthorized access to the files.
   2. **Disposal of aborted print jobs**—Reports are sometimes damaged during the printing or bursting (i.e., separation of continuous feed paper along perforation lines) process; since the damaged reports may contain sensitive data, they should be disposed of using secure disposal techniques.
   3. **Distribution of reports**—Data control is responsible for ensuring that reports are maintained in a secure environment before distribution and that only authorized recipients receive the reports; a distribution log is generally maintained to record transfer of the reports to the recipients.
   4. **End user controls**—For particularly critical control totals, or where end users have created systems, perform checks of processing totals and reconciling report totals to separately maintained records. This is also sometimes called one-to-one checking.
   5. **Logging and archiving of forms, data and programs**—Should be in a secure, off-site location.
   6. **Record retention and disposal**—This is discussed in the "Program Library, Documentation, and Record Management" lesson.

Accounting System Cycles

The Accounting System Cycle: Introduction

After studying this lesson, you should be able to

1. For accounting cycles as categories of activity:
   - **a.** Describe the accounting cycle as a set of interrelated cycles that are grouped into categories.
   - **b.** Describe the major activities of each accounting cycle.
2. For the accounting cycle as a set of accounting procedures:
   - **a.** Describe the accounting cycle as a set of procedures that begin with business transactions.
   - **b.** Describe the sequence of activities (procedures) in the accounting cycle.
3. Describe some controls and risks that occur across all accounting cycles.
4. Match controls that are common across accounting cycles to the risks to which they relate.
5. Evaluate controls and risks that are common across accounting cycle in an entity's system of internal control.

This lesson discusses the accounting cycle, which has two meanings, both of which will be explored in this lesson. It also discusses some general risks and procedures in accounting systems that are common to all cycles.

I. Introduction: What Is the Accounting Cycle?

- **A.** The accounting system accumulates and reports information that is relevant to the financial position of an entity. Transactions are one relevant piece of information for an accounting system. A transaction is an economic agreement between two entities to exchange goods or services *or* any other event that can be measured in economic terms by an organization (e.g., selling goods to customers or depreciating equipment).
- **B.** The term "accounting cycle" is used in two different ways—as a way to categorize business and accounting activities and as a set of accounting procedures to accumulate and report information.

II. The Accounting Cycle as a Set of Accounting Procedures

- **A.** This is the simple way to characterize the accounting cycle. Students usually learn this view in their first accounting class. In this view, the accounting cycle is the competent, timely execution of the following procedures:
  1. Analyze transactions and business documents.
  2. Journalize transactions.
  3. Post journal entries to accounts.
  4. Determine account balances and prepare a trial balance.
  5. Journalize and post adjusting entries.
  6. Prepare financial statements and reports.
  7. Journalize and post closing entries.
  8. Balance the accounts and prepare a post-closing trial balance.
  9. Repeat.

B. Another, even simpler way to characterize the activities of an accounting system is as a set of data processing steps:

1. Data capture (input) (steps 1 and 2 above and the journalizing parts of steps 5 and 7)
2. Data storage and data processing (steps 3–5 and 7 and 8 above)
3. Information output/reporting (step 6)

III. The Accounting Cycle as a Way to Categorize Business and Accounting Activities

A. This is the more complicated, and interesting, way to characterize the accounting cycle. Students typically learn this view in their first accounting systems class.

B. Many business activities are paired in give-get exchanges. The basic exchanges can be grouped into five major transaction cycles or modules or business activity:

1. **Revenue cycle**—Interactions with customers (give goods; get cash)
2. **Expenditure cycle**—Interactions with suppliers (give cash; get goods)
3. **Production cycle**—Give labor and raw materials; get finished product.
4. **Human resources/payroll cycle**—Hire, use, and develop labor; give cash and benefits.
5. **General ledger, reporting, financing cycle**—Give cash; get cash; report financial outcomes.

C. Thousands of transactions occur within each cycle, but there are relatively few **types** of transactions in a cycle. Every transaction cycle relates to other cycles. For example:

1. The revenue cycle receives finished goods from the production cycle, provides funds to the financing cycle, and provides data to the general ledger and reporting system.
2. The expenditure cycle gets funds from the financing cycle, provides raw materials to the production cycle, and provides data to the general ledger and reporting system.
3. The production cycle gets raw materials from the expenditure cycle, gets labor from the human resources/payroll cycle, provides finished goods to the revenue cycle, and provides data to the general ledger and reporting system.
4. The human resources/payroll cycle gets funds from the financing cycle, provides labor to the production cycle, and provides data to the general ledger and reporting system.
5. The financing cycle gets funds from the revenue cycle, provides funds to the expenditure and human resources/payroll cycles, and provides data to the general ledger and reporting system.
6. The general ledger and reporting system gets data from all of the cycles and provides information for internal and external users.

D. Many accounting software packages implement the different transaction cycles as separate modules. For example, different ERP systems group somewhat differing activities together into modules or cycles.

1. Not every organization needs every module. For example, retail companies don't have a production cycle.
2. Some organizations may need extra modules. For example, a not-for-profit organization or a medical services company may have a "revenue" cycle that looks very different from that of a retailer or manufacturing company.
3. The implementation of each transaction cycle can differ significantly across organizations.

E. The goal of the accounting system is to create logical groupings of activities, organizational activities, that generate financial information which is useful to managing and controlling the entity.

IV. Risks that Are Common Across Cycles—Some risks are general to accounting systems. These include:

- **A.** Loss, Alteration, or Unauthorized Disclosure of Data
  - **1.** This risk and related controls are discussed in several other BEC lessons (e.g., file backups, file labels, access controls, modification of default settings on ERP systems to increase security, encryption, and secure transmissions).
- **B.** The accounting system is not functioning as required by law, regulation, or organizational policy.
  - **1.** This risk, and related controls, are discussed in the lessons on monitoring internal controls.

V. Control Goals that Are Common Across Cycles—These goals are also discussed in lessons in the Auditing and Attestation (AUD) section of CPAExcel.

- **A.** All transactions are properly authorized.
- **B.** All recorded transactions are valid.
- **C.** All valid and authorized transactions are recorded.
- **D.** All transactions are recorded accurately.
- **E.** Assets are safeguarded from loss or theft.
- **F.** Business activities are performed efficiently and effectively.
- **G.** The organization complies with all applicable laws and regulations.
- **H.** All financial disclosures are full and fair.
- **I.** Accurate data is available when needed.

Revenue Cycle

Businesses sell goods or services. Nonprofit organizations solicit and receive donations. These activities are core activities of the revenue cycle, the focus of which is to sell items (or receive pledges for donations) and to collect payments (on receivables or pledges).

After studying this lesson, you should be able to:

1. Describe the purpose of the revenue cycle.
2. Describe the major activities of the revenue cycle.
3. Identify some important forms/documents of the revenue cycle.
4. Identify some important risks and controls of the revenue cycle.
5. Match controls to the risks to which they relate.
6. Evaluate the controls and risks in an entity's system of internal control.

I. Core Activities of the Revenue Cycle

A. Sales

1. Receive customer orders (see "Emerging Technologies in AIS" lesson related to emerging payment systems).
2. Approve customer credit/sales authorization.

B. Physical (or Virtual) Custody of Products or Services

1. Fill the order and prepare for shipping (if a physical merchandise).
2. Ship or deliver the product.

C. Accounts Receivables

1. Bill (if needed).
2. Manage receivables (e.g., returns and allowances, determine collectability of accounts).

D. Cash

1. Collection and receipt of payments.
2. Reconciliations.

II. Inherent Risks of the Revenue Cycle

A. Revenue Recognition—Is that revenue real?

1. To be recognized in the financial statements, revenue must be realized or realizable and earned.
2. Many revenue cycle frauds concern booking faked revenue or booking revenue prematurely. In a typical fraud, a company will prematurely record revenue (e.g., the MiniScribe Corp. fraud).
3. Another revenue cycle fraud is the creation of fictitious customers who "buy" things (hence the goods are "delivered") but never pay for them.

B. Are Those Receivables Collectible?

1. Estimating the collectibility of receivables is sub jective. Where there is subjectivity, management may be inclined to err on the side that is in its self-interest.
2. An important revenue cycle fraud is "sales" to fictitious customers where the receivables are then written off.

C. Customer Returns and Allowances

1. Estimating returns and allowances, particularly for new products or technologies, requires that management make subjective estimates.

III. Relevant Stakeholders

A. Customers—Who, obviously, buy products or services

1. Establishing that customers exist and are granted credit appropriately are important controls in the revenue cycle

B. Outbound Logistics Providers—Ship goods to customers.

IV. Important Revenue Cycle Forms (in Electronic Systems), Documents (in Paper Systems), and Files

A. See the table at the end of this lesson.

B. Vocabulary Word—Lading

1. **Archaic noun**—The action or process of loading a ship or other vessel with cargo
2. **Used in a sentence**—"After much sweat and toil, and Bill dropping a crate on his foot, the lading of the cargo ship was complete, and it set sail for New Jersey."
3. **Why you should learn this word**
   a. Imagine sweaty, heavyset men loading a cargo of freshly cut green bananas onto a ship in St. Lucia, in the Caribbean, among swaying palm trees. Picture this scene, and you'll also remember that the foreman of these men must have a **bill of lading** (see the table at the end of this lesson for definition).

V. Accounting and Business Risks in the Revenue Cycle

A. Sales Issues

1. **Customer abandons order before completion.**
   a. See the "Emerging Technologies in AIS" lesson on emerging payment processing methods for ways to reduce abandonment of orders.
2. **High payment processing fees.**
   a. See the "Emerging Technologies in AIS" lesson on payment processing methods for ways to reduce payment processing fees.
3. **Incomplete or inaccurate customer orders.**
   a. Automate data entry. Make the purchasing process "idiot proof" (i.e., very easy to understand).
   b. Data input controls including:
      i. Completeness checks
      ii. Automatic lookup of reference data like customer addresses
      iii. Reasonableness tests comparing quantity ordered to past history
   c. Password or biometrics control over terminals to ensure that sales are authorized by the sales department.
   d. Input controls (see separate lesson on "Input and Origination Controls")
4. **Faked sales or sales inconsistent with policy.**
   a. Controls include appropriate authorization evidenced by the receipt of a signed purchase order (or digital signatures).
   b. Required evidence of existence of customer
      i. Controls—Confirmation and review of customer files

B. Receivables and Account Issues

1. **Grant credit to undeserving customers e.g., with poor credit**—Controls include:
   a. Hiring vendors to determine credit status (e.g., credit card and bank cards are examples of this strategy)
   b. Establish credit-granting process, *that are independent of sales.*
      i. Attempt to address the risk of collusion in sales and credit granting—an important fraud prevention strategy to prevent credit sales in violation of company policy.
   c. Cash-only businesses reduce sales by reducing uncollectible receivables, since, if one has no credit sales, one's uncollectible accounts = 0!
2. **Failure to bill customers**—Controls include:
   a. Segregation of duties in shipping and billing functions
   b. Sequentially pre-numbered sales orders, which enables identification of missing sales orders when matching to billings
   c. Picking tickets, packing slips, and sales invoices
3. **Receivables inappropriately written off**—Controls include:
   a. Segregation of duties—Individual independent of sales and cash receipts should be authorized to write off accounts
   b. Access to terminal/system to write-off accounts restricted by password, device, or biometrics
4. **Other billing errors**—Controls include:
   a. Pricing based on price list master file
      i. Confirm accuracy of price lists (this can be very complicated).
      ii. Check quantities on packing slip against quantities on sales order.
      iii. Utilize bar code and RFID scanners to eliminate data entry and reduce errors.
5. **Other errors in customer accounts**—Controls include:
   a. Conduct edit checks (see lesson on "Input and Origination Controls").
   b. **Batch processing controls**—Reconcile batch totals to detect posting errors; compare number of accounts updated with number of checks received.
   c. Independent reconciliations of customer accounts to source records; monthly customer statements
   d. Independently confirming receivables (e.g., by internal or external auditors)

C. Shipping Issues

1. **Shipping errors**—Ever receive the wrong item from eBay or Amazon? Were you happy? Controls over such errors include:
   a. Online shipping systems that check quantities shipped; bar code scanners and RFID tags to record picking and shipping
   b. **Application controls**—These include field checks and completeness tests; postponing printing of the packing slip and bill of lading until verification of accuracy of shipment.

D. Cash and Cash Receipt Issues—Theft of Cash. This is not good. Controls include:

1. **Segregation of duties**
   a. For example, two people opening emails/mail together
   b. Remittance data is sent to the accounts receivable clerk while cash and checks are sent to the cashier.

c. Prompt documentation and restrictive endorsements of remittances

d. Reconcile total credits to accounts receivable total debits to cash.

e. Send a copy of the remittance list to independent party (internal auditing) to compare with validated deposit slips and bank statements.

f. Send monthly statements to customers.

g. Cash registers automatically record cash received

h. Make a daily bank deposit of all remittances.

i. Perform independent bank reconciliations.

Important Revenue Cycle Files, Forms, and Documents

File, Form or Document	Purpose	Comments and Controls
Customer or sales order	Document order, including items, prices, and stock numbers	
Credit check files	Document granting or denial of credit	Review for compliance, accuracy, and completeness.
Aged trial balance	Document receivables and give evidence of collectibility	Are receivables collectible? Are they timely?
Picking list (physical goods)	Items to be pulled from warehouse	Increasingly automated and use bar code or RFID tagging
Packing list (physical goods)	Contents to be shipped	Increasingly automated and use bar code or RFID tagging
Bill of lading (physical goods)	Specifies terms of shipment Legal document between the shipper (e.g., company that makes a product) and the carrier detailing the type, quantity and destination of carried goods Also, a receipt for shipment when the goods are delivered	Can help in determining date goods were sold (cutoff) Can also match received goods to bill of lading (which specifies shipped goods) to confirm receipt
Customer invoice	Client's bill	Useful in documenting existence of customer and receivable
Remittance advice	Helps match payments to invoices.	Sent by customer to selling company. Often used in complex billing cases (e.g., medicine and Medicare, large construction projects).
Deposit slip/cash receipts listing	Document bank deposit and cash receipts.	Determine completeness of deposit and of cash receipt.
Customer statements (monthly)	Document orders and payments.	Determine billings and collections (accuracy and existence). Useful in documenting existence of customer and receivable

Expenditure Cycle

Buying stuff is fun. Paying for it is not. Bills, bills, bills. You have them. You hate them. So do businesses. When you buy stuff, you have to pay for it. Bummer. But hey, you need the stuff and so do businesses. Organizations exist to generate value for their stakeholders. The expenditure cycle is about efficiently and effectively buying things (called acquisition, procurement, or purchasing), paying for them (payments), and having them delivered (virtually or physically—call inbound logistics; getting stuff from "there" to "here").

After studying this lesson, you should be able to:

1. Describe the purpose of the expenditure cycle.
2. Describe the major activities of the expenditure cycle.
3. Identify some important forms/documents of the expenditure cycle.
4. Identify some important risks and controls of the expenditure cycle.
5. Match controls to the risks to which they relate.
6. Evaluate the controls and risks in an entity's system of internal control.

I. **Core Activities**

   A. **Request and Authorize Purchase**

      1. Request goods and services.
      2. Authorize purchase.

   B. **Acquire Goods**

      1. Purchase goods/services.

   C. **Take Custody and Pay for Goods**

      1. Receive goods and services.
      2. Disburse cash.

   D. **Return Needed?** If so, return it and document the return.

II. **Inherent Risks**

   A. An organization buys something. Should it be capitalized or expensed?

      1. In some cases, management has some discretion, according to standards, regarding when purchased items should be capitalized or expensed.
      2. Abuses of this discretion: An important part of the WorldCom fraud was capitalizing expenses (i.e., inappropriately recording expenses as assets).

   B. Do we have unrecorded liabilities?

      1. For example, do we have obligations (e.g., loans) to major shareholders or officers that are unrecorded?

III. **Relevant Stakeholders**

   A. **Suppliers**—Supply products or services.

      1. Establishing that suppliers exist and that their bills are legitimate and accurate are important controls.

   B. **Inbound Logistics Providers**—Deliver needed goods or services (e.g., FedEx, Air Express, rail companies).

IV. Important Forms (in Electronic Systems), Documents (in Paper Systems), and Files

A. See the table at the end of this lesson.

V. Accounting and Business Risks and Controls

A. Request and Authorize Purchase

1. Cash through vendor frauds (usually) is perpetrated within the organization.
   a. Need strong controls over vendor creation to avoid fictitious vendors.
2. Ordering unneeded or authorized goods or services.
   a. Requires a formal process for authorizing the purchase of goods and services (example of unauthorized ordering is purchasing cloud computing services without the knowledge of IT or senior management; see "Emerging Technologies in AIS" lesson)
   b. Integrated system (ERP) should track all orders and receipts.

B. Acquire Goods

1. Potential issues in acquiring goods include purchasing goods at inflated prices, of inferior quality, from unauthorized suppliers; paying kickbacks (gifts from suppliers to purchasing agents)
   a. Require purchasing agents to disclose relationships.
   b. Use only approved suppliers.
   c. Control system specifies acceptable relationships to and gifts from suppliers.
   d. Periodically review (monitor) purchases and purchase orders.

C. Take Custody

1. Issues in taking custody of goods include receiving unordered or defective goods; errors and omissions in counting goods received; receiving invoices for goods never ordered or received.
   a. Institute separation of duties in receipt of goods versus other expenditure cycle procedures.
   b. Utilize automated receiving system (bar code or RFID scans).
   c. Utilize automated matching and monitoring of purchase order to goods received.

D. Pay for Goods

1. Issues in paying for goods include errors in vendor invoices (usually in their, not your, favor); paying the same invoice multiple times; paying for goods not received; recording and posting errors in accounts payable.
   a. Match received items to vendor invoices/budgetary controls and monitoring of costs compared to expected costs.
   b. Use voucher system to authorize payment of invoices that are tracked through inspection process.
2. Failing to take available purchase discounts
   a. Automate payment processes/monitor discounts taken and forgone.
3. Misappropriating checks, e-checks, cash, or EFTs
   a. Segregation of duties for payment preparation and approvals; vendor creation controls; processing controls over EFTs; see "Risk Management Policies and Procedures" lessons.

E. Return of Goods Needed?—If so, return goods and document the return.

1. Tracking returns, particularly in retail sales, can be critical. Some major frauds were perpetrated through purchasing goods and returning them, in collusion with employees, to get both a refund and the goods.

Important Cycle Files, Forms, and Documents

File, Form, or Document	Purpose	Comments and Controls
Check or e-check	Pay vendor for what we bought.	Often automated for small amounts. Larger amounts require more authorization and documentation.
EFT (electronic funds transfers)	Should be documented through payment system and either bank or financial institution processing	Important control to ensure that only authorized EFTs are processed
Purchase order or requisition	Specify items ordered, freight terms, shipping address, and other information for vendor.	Formally requests a supplier to sell and deliver specified products at designated prices. Often automated, including in EDI systems
Receiving report	Were goods received and in good condition (an inspection report)?	Document receipt and condition of goods received. Documents delivery, date, shipper, supplier, and purchase order number.
Vendor invoices	Request payment from customer.	
Voucher or voucher package	Purchase order and receiving report	Accounts payable (AP) department indicates accounts debited and credited, who authorized and reviewed the purchase.
Open purchase orders	Purchases not yet received (and therefore not yet recorded)	Useful in testing for liabilities, recorded and unrecorded
Accounts (vouchers) payable balances	Whom do we owe? What do we owe them?	Useful in testing for liabilities, recorded and unrecorded

Production Cycle

Some organizations make physical goods and hold them in inventory, potentially as raw materials, goods in process, or finished goods. The production cycle is concerned with manufacturing physical products. Some aspects, risks, and controls of this cycle also apply to virtual (digital) products.

This cycle also includes consideration of the management of fixed assets, which may be a part of a production cycle. It also includes considerations of managing inventory. The acquisition of and payment for goods is considered in the expenditure cycle. Processing information about the goods acquired is input into the production cycle.

After studying this lesson, you should be able to:

1. Describe the purpose of the production cycle.
2. Describe the major activities of the production cycle.
3. Identify some important forms/documents of the production cycle.
4. Identify some important risks and controls of the production cycle.
5. Match controls to the risks to which they relate.
6. Evaluate the controls and risks in an entity's system of internal control.

I. Core Activities

A. Forecast Sales/Plan Production/Product Design/Authorize Production

1. Manufacturing resource planning (MRP) and just-in-time (JIT) manufacturing systems help forecast materials needs and plan production
2. The master production schedule (MPS) specifies how much of each product to produce and when to produce it.
3. A production order authorizes manufacturing.

B. Move Raw Materials into Production

1. Materials requisition authorizes moving materials from storeroom to production.

C. Production Process

1. Receive raw materials into production.
2. Production processes vary greatly by product and level of technology:
   a. **Computer-integrated manufacturing (CIM)**—The use of IT to fully or partially automate the production process can dramatically change the production process.
   b. Many production processes are now partially or fully integrated with robotics (i.e., the use of robots to execute production tasks).
3. Manage cost accounting processes.
   a. See the "Manufacturing Costs" lesson to review cost accounting for manufacturing costs

D. Complete Production Process and Deliver Goods

II. Inherent Risks

A. Inventory Manipulations

1. Many, many frauds include inflated or falsified inventory values. For example, the Phar-Mor Drugs fraud was built on overstating inventory values and generating falsified profits as a result. Phar-Mor sustained the fraud because auditors told them, in advance, at which stores

they would inspect inventory. Phar-Mor then made sure that the audited stores (and *only* the audited stores) had sufficient inventory.

B. Inventory Mark-Downs

1. Has obsolete inventory been written down to its true (reduced) value? Do our monitoring processes include periodic reviews to assess the value of inventory?

III. Relevant Stakeholders

A. Production Workers—Make the stuff that we sell.

1. Please see the "HR and Payroll Cycle" lesson.

B. Raw Materials Suppliers

1. As in the expenditure cycle, establishing that suppliers exist and that their bills are legitimate and accurate are important concerns.

IV. Important Forms (in Electronic Systems), Documents (in Paper Systems), and Files

A. See the table at the end of this lesson.

V. Accounting and Business Risks and Controls—Inventory

A. Manage inventory levels to avoid stock-outs (lost sales) and too much inventory (carrying costs).

1. Increasing use of just-in-time methods (see the "Inventory Management" lesson).
2. Accurate inventory control and sales forecasting systems; online, real-time inventory systems; periodic physical counts of inventory; and regular review of sales forecasts to make adjustments. Use of a perpetual inventory system; use of techniques such as just-in-time, economic order quantity, and reorder points as methods of managing inventory:heavy reliance on technology to determine when and how much to order.

B. Inventory Theft or Destruction—Controls include:

1. Physically securing inventory and restricting access; may include security staff and electronic surveillance
2. Documentation of inventory transfers
3. Releasing inventory for shipping only with approved sales orders
4. Accountability—Employees handling inventory should sign the documents or enter their codes online to ensure accountability.
5. Wireless communication and RFID tags provide real-time tracking.
6. Periodic counts of inventory, increasingly by RFID tags (a near-continuous control)
7. Insurance (self-insurance or third-party)

VI. Accounting and Business Risks and Controls—Fixed Assets

A. Major asset acquisitions are approved, as appropriate, and supplied by approved vendors.

1. Major asset acquisitions approved by board (or top management, as appropriate) and properly controlled through capital budgeting techniques.

B. Fixed assets exist, are properly valued, and haven't been stolen.

1. Detailed records document assets and accumulated depreciation.
2. Depreciation is properly calculated and posted.
3. Retirements are approved by an appropriate level of management.
4. Property disposition follows approved, documented procedures (and not a couple of good ol' boys and apickup truck hauling off that old tractor to their place on a Sunday afternoon).

5. There is physical control and security over assets to prevent theft (e.g., security guards, electronic surveillance).
6. Individuals who are otherwise independent of property, plant, and equipment (e.g., internal auditors) perform periodic physical inspection of plant and equipment.

C. Written policies for capitalization versus expensing decisions exist and are followed and monitored.

D. Under- or Over-Investment in Fixed Assets

1. A comprehensive system for monitoring fixed asset ownership, warranties, and repairs exists and links to the production planning system.
2. The budgetary system is integrated with the fixed asset system.

E. Fixed Asset Theft or Destruction

1. See control list related to theft or destruction of inventory—Many of these procedures are relevant for fixed assets.

Important Files, Forms, and Documents

File, Form, or Document	Purpose	Comments and Controls
Bill of materials	Specifies part number, description, and quantity of each component used in making finished product	Can be matched to goods produced to detect over- or underuse of materials
Master production schedule	Plan indicating how much of each product to produce and when to produce it	Result from sales forecasts and from production design and planning process
Materials requisition or materials transfer ticket	Authorize moving raw materials from storeroom to production.	Match to physical materials received in production for agreement
Move tickets	Identify parts to be transferred, their destination, and the time of transfer. Often now integrated into automated systems that scan parts	May be a part of a scanning or RFID system
Operations list	Sequence of steps in making a product, which equipment to use, and how long each step requires	Used when multiple production processes exist
Inventory reports	For raw materials, goods in process, finished goods	May be online or (less often now) on paper

HR and Payroll Cycle

People—You love them. You can't live without them. Neither can organizations. The human resources management (HR) and payroll cycle concerns managing workers. But as a character in Jean Paul Sartre's play, *No Exit*, says, "Hell is other people." Or at least managing them can be. Sometimes people do bad things. How can we prevent, detect, and correct these bad things? Let's find out.

After studying this lesson, you should be able to:

1. Evaluate the controls and risks in an entity's system of internal control.
2. Describe the major activities of the HR and payroll cycle.
3. Identify some important forms/documents for the HR and payroll cycle.
4. Identify some important risks and controls for the HR and payroll cycle.
5. Match controls to the risks to which they relate.
6. Evaluate the controls and risks in an entity's system of internal control.

I. Core Activities

- **A. Recruiting and Hiring Employees**
- **B. Training and Developing Employees' Skills**
- **C. Supervision and Job Assignments**
  1. E.g., Timekeeping
- **D. Salaries and Benefits**
  1. Compensation (payroll)
  2. Employee benefits (e.g., medical, health, and life insurance, parking, fitness centers)
  3. Taxes on wages and benefits (leading to withholdings and lots of accounting complexities)
  4. Vacations and time off
- **E. Monitoring and Evaluation**
  1. Performance evaluation
- **F. Transitions**
  1. Discharging employees, due to voluntary or involuntary termination
  2. Facilitating employee retirement

II. Inherent Risks

- **A.** Fictitious or "ghost" employees don't just occur in ghost stories. Hiring people who don't exist can be a fraud perpetrated by another employee who most decidedly **does** exist and who is getting undeserved resources (money or assets).
- **B.** Many famous frauds have occurred when employees are terminated but remain on the payroll and their checks (or EFTs) are endorsed or received by mountebanks (i.e., people who trick others out of their money).

C. There are, usually, very good controls over underpaying people—the people themselves! Very often, however, if we overpay people, they won't say anything, which is why controls relating to overpaying employees are much more important than controls related to underpaying people.

III. Relevant Stakeholders

A. Employees (obviously)

1. Establishing that employees exist and that their bills, paid salaries, and benefits are legitimate and accurate are important concerns.

B. HR service providers, including health maintenance organizations, financial services companies, retirement companies, banks, credit unions, and life insurance companies

C. Federal and state governments, to which wage-related taxes usually are owed. Failure to pay, and the theft of, payroll taxes is a common area of fraud in small organizations.

IV. Important Forms (in Electronic Systems), Documents (in Paper Systems), and Files

a. See table later in the lesson.

V. Accounting and Business Risks and Controls

A. Recruiting and Hiring Employees

1. Hiring unqualified or illegal employees—Follow law, regulation, and organizational procedures for hiring.

2. Distinguish (according to law) employees from independent contractors.

B. Training and Developing Employees' Skills

1. Retaining high-performing employees is critical to the success of most organizations (e.g., public accounting). Organizations need plans and policies to enable this.

C. Supervision and Job Assignments

1. **Timekeeping**—Increasingly automated (e.g., scanned badge readers). Automating this function generally improves controls by reducing segregation of duties concerns.

D. Salaries and Benefits

1. Compensation

a. Payroll activities require:

1. Maintaining and updating master payroll file
2. Updating tax rates and deductions, (often) computing time and attendance
3. Preparing and distributing payroll
4. Calculating employer-paid benefits and taxes
5. Disbursing payroll taxes, deductions, and benefit costs

b. Compensation may be based on hours, self-reports, commissions, fixed salaries, or bonuses.

2. Payroll accounting

a. Often outsourced, which can be an effective segregation of duties in a critical area of control

b. Should be paid by direct deposit as an accounting control and a convenience to employees (*no checks*, if possible). Issuing checks generally reduces accounting controls compared to direct deposits.

c. Payroll department should validate and periodically monitor employee records.

d. **Control goals**—All payroll transactions must have proper authorization, be valid, be recorded, and be accurate.

3. **Segregation of duties**
   a. If there is a low level of automation, try to segregate the following functions: timekeeping, payroll preparation, personnel management, and paycheck distribution.
   b. Generally, the more automation, the less the need for segregation of duties.
   c. Outsourcing payroll functions, in a smaller organization, can improve controls by increasing segregation of duties.

E. Monitoring and Evaluation

1. **Performance evaluation**—Should be regular, systematic, unbiased, and follow organization's policies

F. Transitions

1. **Discharging employees**—Due to voluntary or involuntary termination
   a. In some cases, must be "pack up your things and be gone in an hour"
2. **Facilitating employee retirement**
   a. Follow organization's policies and procedures, which, of course, indicates that the organization needs such policies.

Important Cycle Files, Forms, and Documents

Document	Purpose	Comments and Controls
Cumulative earnings register	Accumulates year-to-date gross pay, net pay, and deductions by employee	Should be reviewed to match to pay rates and by supervisors to confirm overtime and regular hours (as appropriate)
Workforce inventory	List of employees by department	Useful in tracing to payroll records and identifying that these are real humans Important to review and monitor to ensure terminations are posted in a timely manner
Position control report	List of each position, job qualifications, budgeted salary, and position status (e.g., filled or vacant)	
Skills inventory report	List of employees and current skills	
U.S. Form 941	Employer's quarterly federal tax return (showing all wages subject to tax and amounts withheld for income tax and FICA)	
U.S. Form W-2	Report of wages and withholdings for each employee	Often now posted to website
U.S. Form W-3	Summary of all W-2 forms	
U.S. Form 1-99-Misc	Report of income paid to independent contractors	Note distinction between employees and independent contracts
Other compliance reports	Report compliance data related to regulatory provisions, state and local tax reports, etc.	State or other regulatory agencies may require compliance reports

Example

COSO Example: Payroll Monitoring

The company—Approximately 90% of the employees of a medium-size manufacturing company are at plant sites. The company implemented a new payroll software and workflow to review and approve payroll. All biweekly payrolls are reviewed in detail at the plant sites and submitted to the payroll department. The corporate payroll manager reviews plant payrolls for unusual fluctuations, such as increase/decrease in employee headcount, excessive overtime, and so on. Any identified fluctuations are reviewed and require sufficient response and support prior to payroll processing.

The fraud—This control enabled the corporate payroll manager to identify repeated excessive overtime payments to the plant accountant, which occurred outside the normal monthly plant closing cycle. Further investigation revealed that the plant accountant had falsified overtime hours.

The take-away—Improving on the review of indirect information (i.e., excessive and unexpected overtime) fluctuations enabled this organization to identify a control deficiency and fraud in an area typically considered to be of low to moderate fraud risk.

General Ledger, Reporting, and Financing Cycle

Generating timely, accurate financial reports is an essential organizational activity. The general ledger, reporting, and financing cycle activities are concerned with generating the financing needed in an organization (financing cycle) and completing accounting activities that enable the generating of financial reports.

After studying this lesson, you should be able to:

1. Describe the purpose of the general ledger, reporting, and financing cycle.
2. Describe the major activities of the general ledger, reporting, and financing cycle.
3. Identify some important forms/documents of the general ledger, reporting, and financing cycle.
4. Identify some important risks and controls of the general ledger, reporting, and financing cycle.
5. Match controls to the risks to which they relate.
6. Evaluate the controls and risks in an entity's system of internal control.

I. Core Activities

A. Receive Inputs

1. The other cycles generate transactions that flow to the general ledger.
2. **Financing and investing**—Receive information about financing and investing activities.
3. **Budgeting**—The budget department provides budget numbers, primarily for managerial accounting reports.

B. Create and Post Adjusting Entries

C. Reporting

1. Prepare financial statements (e.g., balance sheet, income statement, statement of cash flows).
2. Produce managerial reports.

II. Inherent Risks

A. Lease accounting, loan covenants and related-party transactions can be problematic in relation to financing activities.

1. Enron created hundreds of sketchy (dubious) special-purpose entities to enable supposed joint ventures with other companies. Their primary purpose was to loot the organization and to hide money from creditors, investors, and auditors.
2. Do we have obligations (e.g., loans) to major shareholders or officers that are unrecorded?

B. Financial statement fraud

1. Unusual or unjustified manual adjusting entries may be an indicator of management attempting to "manage" earnings.

III. Relevant Stakeholders

A. Creditors, Shareholders, Regulators, External Auditors—For financial reporting

IV. Important Forms (in Electronic Systems), Documents (in Paper Systems), and Files

A. See the table later in this lesson.

V. Accounting and Business Risks and Controls

A. Controls over This Cycle

1. Well-designed system of internal control, segregation of duties, a reliable, automated accounting system, and competent accounting personnel
2. Accounting policies and procedures must be approved, documented, and consistent with law, regulations, and organizational policies.
3. Investment and financing activities must be approved, documented, and consistent with law, regulations, and organizational policies.

B. Journal Entry Risks

1. Incorrect or fraudulent journal entries (e.g., to the wrong accounts) or unbalanced entries
2. Transactions not recorded or not posted
3. Inadequate authorization for journal entries
4. Imbalances between debit and credit balance accounts

C. Control and Subsidiary Account Risks

1. Control accounts out-of-balance with subsidiary ledgers.

D. Financial reporting

1. Financial reports are inaccurate, unreliable, or not timely.

Important Cycle Files, Forms, and Documents

File, Form, or Document	Purpose
General ledger	Structure for accumulating accounting information based on the chart of accounts, which is the listing of accounts available for recording accounting entries
General journal	Journal for recording non-routine, including closing and reversing entries; very important to review non-routine entries for error and/or fraud (see the second example below)
Financial statements	Report on the financial condition of the entity
Managerial accounting reports	Reports used internally in managing the entity
Compliance reports	Reports for governmental agencies to comply with laws or regulations (e.g., related to environmental impact, securities)
Control and subsidiary accounts	Subsidiary accounts maintain the details but in the aggregate, sum to control account balance (e.g., accounts receivable control and subsidiary accounts, fixed asset control and subsidiary accounts).

Example

COSO Monitoring Example 1

Goal and procedure—To help manage financial reporting risks, an international consumer products company developed a detailed description of the roles and responsibilities of journal-entry preparers, detail reviewers, and secondary reviewers. The organization then developed a matrix of key journal entries (i.e., those with direct financial statement impact, primarily for the major functional corporate areas including tax, accounting, treasury, legal, etc.), and compared that matrix to the policy.

Analysis and result—This analysis revealed that, in several complex areas, the organization had inadequate journal-entry review. The organization developed a plan for each identified deficiency—mandating the formal sign-off by the preparer, detail reviewer, and secondary reviewer for each key journal entry.

Example

COSO Monitoring Example 2

Goal—To determine if management had implemented effective monitoring procedures over certain identified risks, the audit committee of a small, global manufacturing company directed internal audit to perform specific annual reviews.

Focus—One area of specific concern was manual journal entries, with a particular focus on potential management override activities. Internal audit's review includes basic information, such as the number, dollar amount, preparer, business unit, and timing relative to month- and quarter-end.

Analysis—This analysis included more in-depth information, such as:

- Reasonableness of significant entries (e.g., manual entries in traditionally automated accounts such as inventory)
- Review of the appropriateness of the individual performing the journal entry (e.g., senior executives or unauthorized personnel)
- Review of the frequency of journal entries, particularly relevant to management authorization levels, identification of journal entries without descriptions, and potentially fraudulent entries

The organization created a profile of potential fraudulent entries from management override frauds that were perpetuated at other companies. Internal audit statistically compares the manual journal entries against this profile.

Systems Development and Maintenance

System Development and Implementation

We need a new information system. Should we build it using internal staff or should we buy it (i.e., buy packaged software or hire someone else to build it)? How should we manage the process to ensure that,unlike many software projects, the project is completed on time, on budget, and works as promised? This lesson discusses these issues.

After studying this lesson, you should be able to:

1. Describe the purpose, roles, and stages of the typical systems development life cycle.
2. Describe the work processes and goals of each of the seven development stages.
3. Give examples of the reasons why systems development projects often fail.
4. Give examples of the activities at each stage of the systems development life cycle.
5. Give examples of the roles that accountants may play in systems development.
6. Describe some alternative models of systems development, including why and when they may be used.

I. **Sourcing Decisions**—In some cases, an organization's IT strategy will indicate that it intends to build (i.e., develop) or buy software within certain domains or units. If such a strategy exists, it will indicate a preference that business applications development is insourced (i.e., an internal development process) or outsourced (i.e., purchased from someone else). The systems development life cycle (SDLC) framework (though not each step) applies to either insourced or outsourced development processes.

II. **Developing Business Applications**—The importance, and potential negative consequences, of systems development is evident in the many large-scale systems failures that have cost organizations millions of dollars (e.g., the Denver airport baggage system, ERP at Hershey's, the Bank of America Trust Department). Developing a functioning computer system, on time, and on budget requires communication and coordination among multiple groups of people with very different points of view and priorities. Without a clear plan for defining, developing, testing, and implementing the system, it is perilously easy to end up with a system that fails to meet its objectives and must be scrapped. The systems development life cycle is designed to provide this plan.

III. **Purpose of the Systems Development Life Cycle (SDLC) Method**—The systems development life cycle provides a structured approach to the systems development process by:

   A. Identifying the key roles in the development process and defining their responsibilities

   B. Establishing a set of critical activities to measure progress toward the desired result

   C. Requiring project review and approval at critical points throughout the development process. Before moving forward to each stage of the SDLC, formal approval for the previous stage should occur and be documented.

IV. **Roles in the SDLC Method**—Each party to the development process must review the system and sign off, as appropriate, at stages of development. This helps to ensure that the system will perform as intended and be accepted by the end users. Principal roles in the SDLC include the following:

   A. **IT Steering Committee**—Members of the committee are selected from functional areas across the organization, including the IT Department; the committee's principal duty is to approve and prioritize systems proposals for development.

B. Lead Systems Analyst—The manager of the programming team:

1. Usually responsible for all direct contact with the end user
2. Often responsible for developing the overall programming logic and functionality

C. Application Programmers—The team of programmers who, under direction of the lead analyst, are responsible for writing and testing the program.

D. End Users—The employees who will use the program to accomplish their work tasks using the developed system:

1. Responsible for identifying the problem to be addressed and approving the proposed solution to the problem, often also work closely with programmers during the development process

V. Stages in, and Risks to, the SDLC Method—Riskier systems development projects use newer technologies or have a poorly defined (i.e., sketchy) design structure. In the SDLC method, program development proceeds through an orderly series of steps. At the end of each step, all of the involved parties (typically the lead systems analyst, the end user, and a representative from the IT administration or the IT steering committee) sign a report of activities completed in that step to indicate their review and approval. The seven steps in the SDLC method are:

> **Note**
> *There are several variations of these steps, some with more and some with fewer stages.*

A. Stage 1—Planning and Feasibility Study—When an application proposal is submitted for consideration, the proposal is evaluated in terms of three aspects:

1. **Technical feasibility**—Is it possible to implement a successful solution given the limits currently faced by the IT department? Alternatively, can we hire someone, given our budget, to build the system?
2. **Economic feasibility**—Even if the application can be developed, should it be developed? Are the potential benefits greater than the anticipated cost?
3. **Operational feasibility**—Given the status of other systems and people within the organization, how well will the proposed system work?
4. After establishing feasibility, **a project plan** is developed; the project plan establishes:
   a. **Critical success factors**—The things that the project must complete in order to succeed.
   b. **Project scope**—A high-level view of what the project will accomplish.
   c. **Project milestones and responsibilities**—The major steps in the process, the timing of those steps, and identification of the individuals responsible for each step.

B. Stage 2—Analysis—During this phase, the systems analysts work with end users to understand the business process and document the requirements of the system; the collaboration of IT personnel and end users to define the system is known as joint application development (JAD).

1. **Requirements definition**—The requirements definition formally identifies the tasks and performance goals that the system must accomplish; this definition serves as the framework for system design and development.
   a. All parties sign off on the requirements definition to signify their agreement with the project's goals and processes.

C. Stage 3—Design—During the design phase, the technical specifications of the system are established; the design specification has three primary components:

1. **Conceptual design**—The first step of design process, called conceptual design, is to summarize the goal, structure, data flows, resource requirements, systems documentation, and preliminary design of the system.
2. **Technical architecture specification**—Identifies the hardware, systems software, and networking technology on which the system will run.
3. **Systems model**—Uses graphical models (flowcharts, etc.) to describe the interaction of systems processes and components; defines the interface between the user and the system by creating menu and screen formats for the entire system.

D. Stage 4—Development—During this phase, programmers use the systems design specifications to develop the program and data files:

1. The hardware and IT infrastructure identified during the design phase are purchased during the development phase.
2. The development process must be carefully monitored to ensure compatibility among all systems components as correcting of errors becomes much costlier after this phase.

E. Stage 5—Testing—The system is evaluated to determine whether it meets the specifications identified in the requirements definition.

1. Testing procedures must project expected results and **compare actual results with expectations:**
   a. Test items should confirm correct handling of **correct data, and, data that includes errors.**
2. Testing most be performed at multiple levels to ensure correct intra- and inter-system operation:
   a. **Individual processing unit**—Provides assurance that each piece of the system works properly.
   b. **System testing**—Provides assurance that all of the system modules work together.
   c. **Inter-system testing**—Provides assurance that the system interfaces correctly with related systems.
   d. **User acceptance testing**—Provides assurance that the system can accomplish its stated objectives with the business environment, and that users will use the delivered system.

F. Stage 6—Implementation—Before the new system is moved into production, existing data must be converted to the new system format, and users must be trained on the new system; implementation of the new system may occur in one of four ways:

1. **Parallel implementation**—The new system and the old system are run concurrently until it is clear that the new system is working properly.
2. Direct cutover, **"cold turkey," "plunge," or "big bang" implementation**—The old system is dropped and the new system put in place all at once. This is risky but fast (except when it fails —in which case it is *slower*).
3. **Phased implementation**—Instead of implementing the complete system across the entire organization, the system is divided into modules that are brought on line one or two at a time.
4. **Pilot implementation**—Similar to phased implementation except, rather than dividing the system into modules, the users are divided into smaller groups and are trained on the new system one group at a time:

G. Stage 7—Maintenance—Monitoring the system to ensure that it is working properly and updating the programs and/or procedures to reflect changing needs:

1. **User support groups and help desks**—Provide forums for maintaining the system at high performance levels and for identifying problems and the need for changes.
2. All updates and additions to the system should be subject to the same structured development process as the original program.

3. Here is a "waterfall" visual summary of these stages:

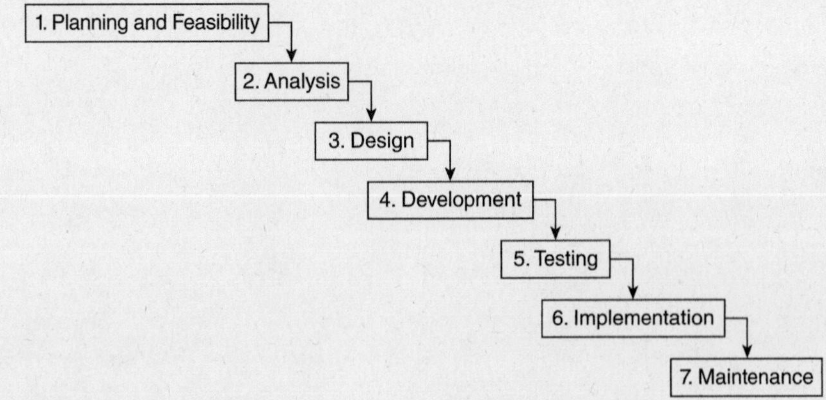

VI. Systems Development Failures—A recent survey indicates that companies complete about 37% of large IT projects on time and only 42% on budget. Why do systems projects so often fail? Common reasons include:

1. Lack of senior management knowledge of, and support and involvement in, major IT projects
2. Difficulty in specifying the requirements
3. Emerging technologies (hardware and software) that may not work as the vendor claims
4. Lack of standardized project management and standardized methodologies
5. Resistance to change; lack of proper "change management." Change management is integral to training and user acceptance
6. Scope and project creep. The size of the project is underestimated and grows as users ask "Can it do this?"
7. Lack of user participation and support
8. Inadequate testing and training. Training should be just-in-time (prior to use) and be at full-load service levels.
9. Poor project management—underestimation of time, resources, scope

VII. Accountant's Involvement in IS Development

A. Accounting and auditing skills are useful in cost/benefit and life cycle cost analyses of IT projects.

B. Possess combined knowledge of IT, general business, accounting, and internal control along with communication skills to ensure new system(s) meet the needs of the users

C. Types of accountants who may participate in system development: system specialist, consultant, staff accountant, internal or independent auditor

VIII. Alternative System Development Processes

A. Smaller, more innovative projects may use more rapid iteration processes, such as:

1. **Prototyping**—An iterative development process focusing on user requirements and implementing portions of the proposed system. Prototypes are nothing more than "screenshots" that evolve, through iterations, into a functioning system.
2. **Rapid application development (RAD)**—An iterative development process using prototypes and automated systems development tools (i.e., PowerBuilder and Visual Basic) to speed and structure the development process.

B. **Modular development** is an alternative model for project organization. In modular development, the system proceeds by developing and installing one subsystem (of an entire company system) at a time. Examples of modules might include order entry, sales, and cash receipts.

Operations Management

Financial and Nonfinancial Measures of Performance

Quality Management

After studying this lesson, you should be able to:

1. Explain the difference between quality of design and quality of conformance and describe why both definitions are important.
2. Recognize the four types of quality costs and describe the types of cost included in each type.

I. What Is Quality?

A. The concept of quality as used in total quality management (TQM) often differs from the traditional concept of quality. "Quality" is most commonly used to refer to "grade." For example, a platinum bracelet is usually considered to be of higher quality than a silver bracelet, and a Mercedes is usually considered to be a higher-quality vehicle than a Ford.

B. However, in TQM, the concept of quality has to do with **how well the item meets its design specifications**. That is, does it perform as it is expected to perform? Using this concept of quality, a car that is designed to have high fuel economy but not a lot of power (as defined by its ability to go from zero to 60 miles per hour in a specified number of seconds) and meets those objectives without experiencing any other significant failures is a much higher quality vehicle than a high-end sports car that has a lot of power but is plagued by constant engine problems and so is often under repair. This concept of quality is known as **"quality of conformance."**

Definition
Quality of Conformance: Refers to the degree to which a product meets its design specifications and/or customer expectations.

C. TQM relies on quality of conformance as evidenced by the fact that the TQM philosophy includes measuring results frequently. That is, if results are measured frequently, then certain expectations are considered in evaluating the results. Quality of conformance (or conformance to specifications) is more certain. On the other hand, conformance to a product design that the customer does not want is destined to fail. Therefore, quality of design is also important. Thus, quality addresses two perspectives in TQM:

1. Failure to execute the product design as specified.
2. Failure to design the product appropriately; **quality of design** is defined as **meeting or exceeding the needs and wants of customers.**

D. The customer's perception of quality depends on both high quality of conformance and high quality of design. Thus, TQM attempts to satisfy both of these definitions of quality.

Exam Tip
There is likely to be at least one question about TQM in Operations Management, and it is likely to ask the candidate to match a cost of quality (e.g., cost of using better-quality materials, cost of scrap, cost of sales returns, etc.) with its appropriate category (i.e., prevention costs, appraisal costs, internal failure costs, or external failure costs).

II. Cost of Quality

A. The costs incurred by an organization to ensure that its products and/or services have a high quality of conformance are known as costs of quality.

B. Cost of quality is based on the philosophy that failures have an underlying cause, prevention is cheaper than failures, and cost of quality performance can be measured. Cost of quality consists of four components—(1) prevention cost, (2) appraisal cost, (3) internal failure cost, and (4) external failure cost. Each of these categories is explained in detail below.

1. **Prevention cost**—The cost of prevention is the cost of any quality activity designed to help do the job right the first time. Examples of prevention cost include:
   - **a.** Quality engineering
   - **b.** Quality training
   - **c.** Quality circles
   - **d.** Statistical process control activities
   - **e.** Supervision of prevention activities
   - **f.** Quality data gathering, analysis, and reporting
   - **g.** Quality improvement projects
   - **h.** Technical support provided to suppliers
   - **i.** Audits of the effectiveness of the quality system
2. **Appraisal cost**—The cost of quality control including testing and inspection. It involves any activity designed to appraise, test, or check for defective products. Examples of appraisal costs include:
   - **a.** Testing and inspection of incoming materials
   - **b.** Testing and inspection of in-process goods
   - **c.** Final product testing and inspection
   - **d.** Supplies used in testing and inspection
   - **e.** Supervision of testing and inspection activities
   - **f.** Depreciation of test equipment
   - **g.** Maintenance of test equipment
   - **h.** Plant utilities in the inspection area
   - **i.** Field testing and appraisal at customer site
3. **Internal failure cost**—The costs incurred when substandard products are produced but discovered before shipment to the customer. Examples of internal failure costs include:
   - **a.** Scrap
   - **b.** Spoilage
   - **c.** Rework
   - **d.** Rework labor and overhead
   - **e.** Reinspection of reworked products
   - **f.** Retesting of reworked products
   - **g.** Downtime caused by quality problems
   - **h.** Disposal of defective products
   - **i.** Analysis of the cause of defects in production
   - **j.** Reentering data because of keying errors
   - **k.** Debugging software errors

4. **External failure cost.** The cost incurred for products that do not meet requirements of the customer and have reached the customer. Examples of external failure costs include:
   a. Cost of field servicing and handling complaints
   b. Warranty repairs and replacements
   c. Product recalls
   d. Liability arising from defective products
   e. Returns and allowances arising from quality problems
   f. Lost sales arising from reputation for poor quality

III. Total Cost of Quality and Quality Cost Behavior

A. An organization's total cost of quality is the sum of its prevention, appraisal, internal failure, and external failure costs. There is inverse trade-off between the cost of failure (internal or external), and the cost of prevention and appraisal in determining the total quality of conformance:

1. When the **overall quality of conformance is low**, more of the total cost of quality is typically related to **cost of failure**. For example, a manufacturer substitutes a lower-quality power cord connection on one of its products with the result that, after a short period of use, the power cords break, rendering the product unusable. This problem causes the quality of conformance for the product to be lower and the cost of external failure to be higher.

2. **Increases in the cost of prevention** and the **cost of appraisal** are usually accompanied by **decreases in the cost of failure** and **increases in the quality of conformance.** Continuing with the power cord example, if the manufacturer increased the amount of testing completed before the product was shipped, more defective products would be discovered. This would **increase the cost of internal failure** but **decrease the cost of external failure**. Since the cost of an external failure is normally greater per unit than the cost of an internal failure (i.e., it is less expensive to identify a faulty product before it has left the factory than to replace or refund a faulty product in the hands of a consumer or distributor), the **overall cost of failure decreases.**

   a. An even more effective method of reducing the overall cost of failure is to increase efforts to **prevent** failures. Although increasing product quality testing (costs of appraisal) saves the difference between the cost of an internal failure and an external failure, the testing itself incurs additional costs and does nothing to increase the product's overall quality of conformance. On the other hand, increased spending on prevention potentially both reduces the cost of failure and increases the quality of conformance. Returning to the power cord example, if the company increases the quality of the power cord connection (thus, making the product less likely to fail) and makes no changes to product testing, the costs of failure due to this problem can perhaps be eliminated completely and the quality of conformance is greatly improved. In general, **the cost of prevention is both less than the cost of appraisal and less than the cost of failure.**

IV. Six-Sigma Quality—What Is Six-Sigma?

Definition
Six Sigma: A statistical measure expressing how close a product comes to its quality goal. One-sigma means 68% of products are acceptable; three-sigma means 99.7% of products are acceptable. Six-sigma is 99.999997% perfect: 3.4 defects per million parts.

A. Six-Sigma Black Belts must attend a minimum of four months of training in statistical and other quality improvement methods. Six-Sigma black belts are experts in the Six-Sigma methodology. They learn and demonstrate proficiency in the DMAIC methodology and statistical process control (SPC) techniques within that methodology. DMAIC is the structured methodology for process improvement within the Six-Sigma framework. It stands for **D**efine, **M**easure, **A**nalyze, **I**mprove, and **C**ontrol.

V. Quality Tools and Methods

A. Total Quality Control (TQC)—The application of quality principles to all company activities. Also known as total quality management (TQM).

B. Continuous Improvement and Kaizen Continuous Improvement (CI) seeks continual improvement of machinery, materials, labor, and production methods, through various means including suggestions and ideas from employees and customers.

Definitions

Kaizen: The Japanese art of continuous improvement. It is a philosophy of continuous improvement of working practices that underlies total quality management and just-in-time business techniques.

PDCA (Plan-Do-Check-Act) also called the Deming Wheel: Focuses on the sequential and continual nature of the CI process.

Cause-and-effect (fishbone or Ishikawa) diagrams: Identify the potential causes of defects. Four categories of potential causes of failure are: human factors, methods and design factors, machine-related factors, and materials and components factors. Cause-and-effect diagrams are used to systematically list the different causes that can be attributed to a problem (or an effect). Such diagrams can aid in identifying the reasons why a process goes out of control.

Pareto chart: A bar graph that ranks causes of process variations by the degree of impact on quality. The Pareto chart is a specialized version of a histogram that ranks the categories in the chart from most frequent to least frequent. A related concept, the **Pareto Principle,** states that 80% of the problems come from 20% of the causes. The Pareto Principle states: "Not all of the causes of a particular phenomenon occur with the same frequency or with the same impact."

Control charts: Statistical plots derived from measuring factory processes; they help detect "process drift," or deviation, before it generates defects. Control charts also help spot inherent variations in manufacturing processes that designers must account for to achieve "robust design."

Robust design: A discipline for making designs "production-proof" by building in tolerances for manufacturing variables that are known to be unavoidable.

Poka-yoke (mistake-proofing): Poka-yoke involves making the workplace mistake-proof. For example, a machine fitted with guide rails permits a part to be worked on in just one way.

Balanced Scorecard and Benchmarking

After studying this lesson, you should be able to:

1. Recognize the critical success factors, tactics, and performance measures that would be appropriately categorized for each of the BSC perspectives.
2. Describe the steps necessary to create a BSC.
3. Recognize the common performance measures included in each BSC category.
4. Recognize the features of a good BSC, pitfalls to be avoided during implementation, and common problems with metric choices.
5. Define benchmarking, and describe the steps and important features involved with benchmarking.
6. Describe the four perspectives of the balanced scorecard (BSC).

I. Introduction

A. This topic demonstrates how value creation can be linked to strategy using the balanced scorecard and other initiatives.

II. Balanced Scorecard

A. The **balanced scorecard (BSC)** translates an organization's mission and strategy into a comprehensive set of performance metrics.

B. The BSC does *not* focus solely on financial metrics.

C. The BSC highlights both nonfinancial and financial metrics that an organization can use to measure strategic progress.

III. Balanced Scorecard Perspectives

A. The BSC is viewed from the following four perspectives:

1. **Financial**—Specific measures of financial performance
2. **Customer**—Performance related to targeted customer and market segments
3. **Internal business processes**—Performance of the internal operations that create value (i.e., new product development, production, distribution, and after-the-sale customer service)
4. **Learning, innovation, and growth**—Performance characteristics of the company's personnel and abilities to adapt and respond to change (e.g., employee skills, employee training and certification, employee morale, and employee empowerment)

B. These classifications facilitate evaluation of the organization's fundamental resources—its people, its processes, and its customers—in relation to its financial performance.

C. Different strategies call for different scorecards. Within each of the four classifications, the organization identifies its:

1. **Strategic goals**
2. **Critical success factors**
3. **Tactics**
4. **Performance measures**

Example

Marfu Manufacturing, a producer of kitchen and bathroom countertops, has decided to pursue a strategy of high quality and product innovation and has identified the following critical success factors, tactics, and performance measures related to this strategy:

	Critical Success Factor	Tactic	Performance Measure
Financial Perspective	Maintain high margins while gradually growing	Gradually phase out low margin jobs	Percentage of jobs with margins over 50%
Customer Perspective	Develop a high level of customer recognition as a cutting edge design firm	Maintain a high profile through participation in design competitions	Number of competitions entered; number of awards won
Internal Business Processes Perspective	Execute designs with an extremely high level of craftsmanship	Develop quality specifications for each job and evaluate at project completion	Number of quality inspection problems noted per job
Learning, Innovation, and Growth Perspective	Attract and retain highly qualified, innovative designers	Promote employee development through continued education and support of professional certification activities	Percentage of design employees who have acquired professional certifications

D. Effective scorecards are designed so that the **tactics that promote achievement of strategic goals in one area support achievement of strategic goals in other areas.** For example:

1. Aggressive hiring of employees with strong research and development skills (a tactic from the Learning, Innovation, and Growth perspective) should result in more new and improved products (a strategic goal from the Internal Business Processes perspective).
2. New and improved products should help the company penetrate new markets (a strategic goal from the Customer perspective).
3. Penetration of new markets should lead to additional revenues, which should improve financial performance (a strategic goal from the Financial perspective).

IV. Creating the Balanced Scorecard

A. The first step in creating a balanced scorecard is to identify the organization's strategic objectives in each of the four areas. Once the objectives have been determined, **SWOT analysis** (see the lesson on Introduction to Business Strategy and Market Analysis) is used to identify the critical success factors necessary for the organization to achieve its strategic objectives within each of the four perspectives.

B. The organization must then develop operational tactics—courses of action—designed to achieve the goals specified by the critical success factors. Finally, performance measures must be developed for each tactic to determine whether the tactics have been successfully implemented.

C. Common performance measures include:

1. **Financial**—Gross profit margin, sales growth, profitability per job or product, stock price, achievement of cash flow goals, and any of the standard financial ratios (inventory turnover, return on investment, current ratio, etc.)
2. **Customer**—Market share, product returns as a percentage of sales, number of new customers, percentage of repeat customers, customer satisfaction as measured by customer surveys, customer complaints, sales trends, etc.

3. **Internal Business Processes**—Percentage of production downtime, **delivery cycle time** (time between order and delivery), **manufacturing cycle time/throughput** (the time required to turn raw materials into completed products), **manufacturing cycle efficiency** (ratio of time required for nonvalue-adding activities to the total manufacturing cycle time), standard cost variances, product defect rate, amount of scrap and rework

4. **Learning, Innovation, and Growth**—Percentage of employees with professional certifications, hours of training per employee, number of new products developed, employee turnover, number of customer requests for specific designers, percentage of project proposals accepted, and employee satisfaction levels. Here are some additional examples:

Balanced Scorecard

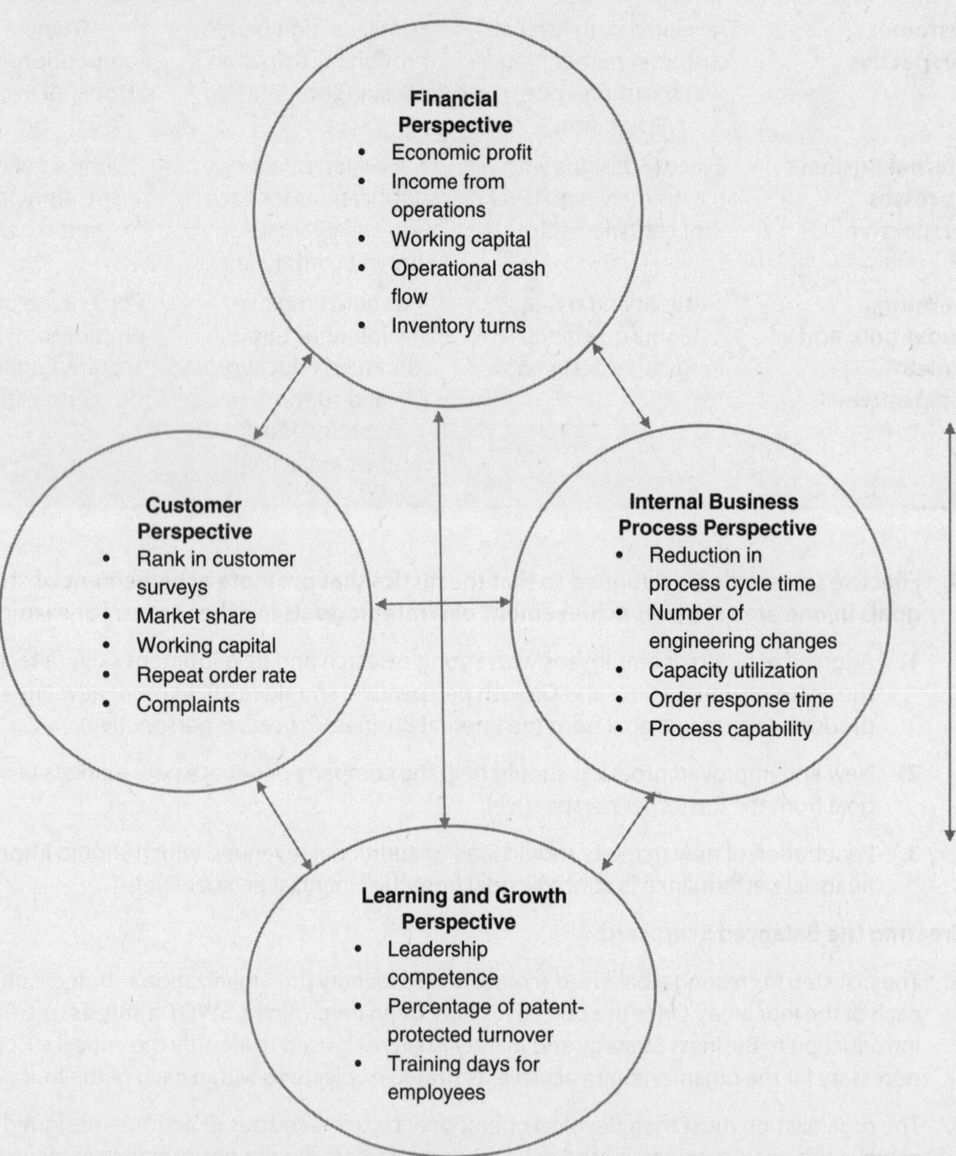

Source: Copyright 2002, *Strategic Finance*, published by the Institute of Management Accountants (IMA), Montvale, NJ, www.imanet.org. Used with permission.

Exam Tip

Most balanced scorecard questions on the CPA Exam are expected to ask the candidate to identify performance measures associated with one of the four classifications or, conversely, to identify the classification in which a particular performance measure would be found.

Definitions of the manufacturing performance measures listed in the Internal Business Processes section (delivery cycle time, manufacturing cycle time, and manufacturing cycle efficiency) may sometimes appear in CPA Exam questions.

V. Features of a Good Balanced Scorecard

A. Articulates a company's strategy by trying to map a sequence of cause-and-effect relationships through metrics

B. Assists in communicating the strategy to all members of the organization by translating the strategy into a coherent and linked set of measurable operational targets

C. Limits the number of measures used by identifying only the most critical ones (Kaplan and Norton suggest a total of 15 to 20)

D. Highlights suboptimal trade-offs that managers may make

VI. Pitfalls That Should Be Avoided When Implementing a Balanced Scorecard

A. Do not assume the cause-and-effect linkages are precise.

B. Do not seek improvements across all measures all the time.

C. Do not use only objective measures on the scorecard.

D. Do not fail to consider both costs and benefits of initiatives such as spending on information technology and research and development.

E. Do not ignore nonfinancial metrics when evaluating managers and employees.

VII. Common Problems with Metric Choices

A. Items chosen leave out important criteria (e.g., both speed and quality are important but can often be traded off, so measuring one without the other will encourage dysfunctional results).

B. The metric may be either too broad or too specific.

VIII. Benchmarking

A. **Benchmarking**—Is a technique of organizational self-assessment via internal and external comparison to sources of excellence in performance. In other words, you try to find someone who is doing it better than you and attempt to emulate their performance!

B. **Benchmarking Should Be Done Systematically**—Identify companies that are best-in-class performers, and then:

1. Measure and compare your performance to them.
2. Attempt to determine drivers of performance.
3. Establish goals.
4. Formulate a plan to increase performance compatible with strategy.

C. **Important Points and Features of Benchmarking**

1. A company can't be the best at everything. Benchmarking should be done in the key areas that create a unique competitive advantage as determined by the company's distinctive competencies.
2. Because best practices change over time, benchmarking should be an ongoing process within the organization. In this way, benchmarking supports continuous learning and improvement. Priorities for benchmarking can change over time—expect this.
3. Don't try to focus on improving in every benchmark all the time.

D. Benchmarking is one tool that can be used to help create an atmosphere that supports a **learning organization**. Learning organizations are able to remain competitive in volatile environments because of their **ability to evaluate and interpret information** and their **willingness to embrace change**. Learning organizations are characterized by flexibility—a willingness to adopt new ideas and new processes—and efficiency in the acquisition and distribution of information. Human capital is especially important in learning organizations, as it is the source of the organization's creativity and vitality.

Competitive Analysis

After studying this lesson, you should be able to:

1. Calculate important conventional financial performance metrics, including the DuPont version of return on investment and residual income.
2. Recognize the concept of value-based management.
3. Calculate economic value added (EVA), weighted-average cost of capital, and cash flow return on investment (CFROI), and describe their features.
4. Recognize prevalent value-based management (VBM) themes and concepts.
5. Calculate the price elasticity of demand and understand how it is used to analyze the effects of substitute and complementary products.
6. Describe target pricing and calculate markups.

I. **Conventional Financial Performance Metrics**—These metrics have been around for many years and often tend to focus on external capital market analysis elements such as income and the investment base.

A. Return on Investment (ROI) = Net Income / Total Assets

DuPont Formula = Return on Sales (ROS) × Asset Turnover

Where:

ROS = Net Income / Sales

Asset Turnover = Sales / Total Assets

1. The DuPont approach to ROI separates ROI into two parts for analysis. The two pieces allow a separate evaluation of profitability as a percentage of sales and the efficiency with which assets were utilized to generate those sales. Multiplying the two parts together results in ROI.

Example

A company is concerned that although profitability is comparable with competitors, their return results have been poor. The company has a new building with a significant degree of excess/idle capacity. The industry average ROI is 20%, with average profit margins of 10%. The company posted the following results for the current year: income of $80,000; sales of $700,000; and assets of $530,000. How can the company explain the difference between profitability versus return?

Profit Margin × Asset Turnover = Return on Investment

(Net Income / Sales) × (Sales / Total Assets) = ROI

($80,000 / $700,000) × ($700,000 / $530,000) = ROI

11.43% × 1.32 = 15.1%

The profit margin of 11.43% is actually better than the industry average of 10%. However, the efficiency with which assets were used (as shown by the asset turnover) at 1.32 turns is lagging the industry average of two turns. Note: The industry average turnover can be found by dividing the ROI of 20% by the profit margin of 10%.

2. The focus on ROI is consistent with the approach taken by external financial analysts making ROI a very important performance metric by which companies are evaluated. However, for internal purposes, ROI suffers from potential accrual distortions and its vulnerability to the diluted hurdle rate problem.

Example

Diluted Hurdle Rate

A manager (with incentive compensation based on ROI) has four assets with an average return (ROI) of 28%. The manager has idle cash to invest in a project that is expected to achieve a return of 25%. The company has a hurdle rate (i.e., required minimum return target) of 20%.

Conclusion: The manager will be unwilling to invest in a project earning any amount less than the current 28% because it would dilute (i.e., reduce) the average return on the total. This manager's preferred decision is bad for the company since, if the decision is up to the manager, the cash will remain unused, rather than generating a return. The diluted hurdle rate problem is associated with virtually all metrics expressed as rates.

B. Residual Income (RI) = Operating Income – Required Rate of Return (Invested Capital)

C. Residual income (RI) is a general form of economic profit. Economic profit differs from accounting income in that it recognizes the cost of capital. RI has often been used as an alternative to ROI to preclude the diluted hurdle rate problem by expressing the return on investment in terms of dollars rather than a rate.

Example

A company has a hurdle rate for investments of 20% and is considering basing the manager's bonus on return on either investment (ROI) or residual income (RI). The manager has achieved an impressive level of performance with an average cumulative return so far of 32%. A prospective investment of $1,000,000 is being considered that is estimated to earn $300,000 in profits. Which metric should be used (i.e., ROI or RI) and why?

The ROI is 30% = $300,000 / $1,000,000. This amount clearly exceeds the hurdle rate established for the manager of 20%, but if the manager's bonus is based on ROI, the manager has no personal incentive to make the investment since it would bring down (i.e., dilute) the current average return achieved of 32%. Thus, what's good for the company is not good for the manager personally. Residual income would be calculated as $100,000 = $300,000 – .2 ($1,000,000). The RI result provides a positive outcome where the income earned exceeds the cost of capital. Thus, with RI the manager and the company both are incentivized to make the investment. This is an outcome that provides goal congruence for the manager and organization.

Note

There are multiple ways of calculating residual income in the sense that some sources suggest using net income or net operating profit after tax (NOPAT) instead of operating income as shown above. The required rate of return is also referred to as the minimum required rate of return but can be equal to whatever management decides. Invested capital is usually total assets, but again can be modified to suit the needs of the user. This is why RI is referred to as a "general" form of economic profit.

II. Value-Based Management (VBM)—Refers to relatively new financial metrics and processes for using them. The most popular VBM metrics and their creators include economic value added (EVA)—Stern Stewart & Company, and cash flow return on investment (CFROI)—Boston Consulting Group.

Exam Tip

Economic value added is perhaps especially important because it is mentioned more than once in the detailed content specification outline.

A. EVA = NOPAT – WACC (Total Assets – Current Liabilities)

1. NOPAT = net operating profit after tax; WACC = weighted average cost of capital

Definition
WACC: Summarizes the overall cost of capital based on the weighted proportion of debt versus equity after reducing the cost of debt by the marginal tax rate.

Example
For a firm that has $40 million in debt costing 10%, $60 million in owners' equity costing 14%, and a marginal tax rate of 40%, the WACC would be

10.8% = 40/100(10%)(1 – .4) + 60/100(14%).

2. EVA is an **economic profit** (EP) metric and a **specific form of residual income**. Like other forms of residual income, EVA is stated in dollars.
3. EVA is **often used for incentive compensation and investor relations.** This is likely due to the emphasis on the use of income (first part of the equation) exceeding the cost of capital (second part of the equation) in measuring wealth creation.
4. EVA suffers from its origins in **accrual-based** NOPAT and the difficulty in defining the nature of economic profit (i.e., economic profit is not cash-based, but it is often adjusted such that it is not strictly accrual-based either).

B. CFROI = (CFO – ED) / Cash Invested

1. For CFROI, economic depreciation (ED) is defined as the annual cash investment required to replace fixed assets; CFO is cash flow from operations.
2. CFROI is a **cash-based** metric that is designed to compute the real internal rate of return on a company's assets and is stated as a **rate.**
3. CFO – ED is designed to approximate free cash flow (FCF), which is approximately equal to cash flow from operations (CFO) less net investment in fixed assets. This amount represents cash that is potentially distributable to shareholders.
4. CFROI is often used for **incentive compensation, valuation, and capital budgeting**. This is likely due to the emphasis on cash flow and the wide acceptance of cash flow for these purposes.
5. CFROI suffers from the weaknesses inherent in **rate-based** metrics (i.e., diluted hurdle rate problem and the potential difficulty in applying rates to analysis where negative cash flows are involved).

Exam Tip
Candidates are not expected to be asked to calculate CFROI but should be aware of the conceptual trade-offs of cash-based metrics versus economic profit-type metrics like EVA. Candidates should expect to be required to calculate EVA.

C. Prevalent VBM Themes and Concepts

1. **Accrual-based metrics are discredited**—This is because accrual-based concepts are designed to fulfill external reporting goals (e.g., consistency, conservatism, and matching) rather than provide economic substance.
2. **Cost of capital is increasingly emphasized**—This emphasizes the economic income view that cost of capital is important in the evaluation of wealth creation.
3. **Shareholders and shareholder value as the primary element of interest is common**—This is about the importance of enhancing and protecting shareholder wealth.
4. **Relating VBM to strategy and making linkages to drivers of success are important**—This recognizes the importance of causality and value drivers as related to strategic planning and execution (i.e., understanding causal performance linkages).

III. Price Elasticity Analysis

A. By definition, the **price elasticity of demand** is the percentage change in quantity demanded divided by the percentage change in price.

$$\text{Price Elasticity of Demand} = \frac{\%\Delta Q}{\%\Delta P}$$

A price is considered elastic if the price elasticity of demand is greater than 1 and inelastic if the elasticity of demand is less than 1.

B. Price elasticity is often tested using the concept of substitute and complementary products. Effects of substitute and complementary products are generally as follows: If products A and B are **substitutes**, an increase in the price of A will cause an increase in the demand for B. If products A and B are **complements**, an increase in the price of A will cause a decrease in the demand for product B.

Example

The cost of playing golf versus the cost of playing tennis behave as products that are substitutes. As the cost of playing golf increases, the demand for tennis (i.e., an alternative to golf) increases. Tennis balls and tennis rackets are products that behave as complements. As the price for tennis balls increases, the demand for tennis rackets decreases.

C. Revenue is the result of both price and volume. If prices are relatively elastic (i.e., price **elasticity** > 1), then an increase in price will tend to decrease volume, making the resulting increase/decrease in revenue uncertain. If prices are relatively **inelastic** (i.e., price elasticity < 1), then an increase in price will tend to increase revenue as volume remains unaffected.

IV. Target Pricing and Markups—The key to properly analyzing markups is to understand what the markup is based on. Sometimes the markup is based on a percentage of cost or a specific type of cost (e.g., direct cost). Other times the markup is based on revenue. Thus, the candidate must focus on specific language that communicates the basis for the markup.

Example

Given a sales target of 1,000 units, direct costs of $50 per unit, and total costs of $80,000, what is the target price necessary to achieve a 25% profit margin on direct costs?

In this case, the markup is based on **direct costs**. Thus, the desired profit is determined based on 25% of $50,000 = $12,500. Given that total costs are $80,000, the necessary price to achieve a total profit of $12,500 would be based on the equation:

Price (1,000 units) – $80,000 = $12,500

Price (1,000 units) = $92,500

Price = $92.50

Given the same set of facts above, what is the target price necessary to achieve a 20% profit margin on sales?

Here the markup is based on **sales**. Unfortunately, the sales number is not disclosed in the problem. But we do know the following: Sales – $80,000 = .20 (sales). Thus, to find price we have:

Price (1,000 units) – $80,000 = .20 (Price) (1,000 units)

80 (Price) (1,000 units) = $80,000

800 (Price) = $80,000

Price = $100.00

Ratio Analysis

After studying this lesson, you should be able to:

1. Calculate important metrics and margins involving profitability, return, asset utilization, liquidity, debt risk, and market ratios.
2. Classify different metrics into appropriate categories of use (e.g., liquidity v. asset utilization).
3. Recognize the purpose of each type of metric category as well as the purpose of each metric.
4. Properly interpret the results of the various metrics.

I. **Profitability and Return Metrics**—The focus here is on margins, return metrics, profitability, and residual income. These are generally conventional financial metrics typically related to external financial reporting.

   A. **Gross Margin = Revenue – Cost of Goods Sold**—This is a conventional metric that reflects profitability prior to the recognition of period expenses (i.e., selling and general/administrative expenses).

   B. **Contribution Margin = Revenue – Variable Expenses**—This is a metric primarily related to internal decision making. Contribution margin (as opposed to gross margin) focuses on cost behavior so that management can evaluate the consequences on profitability and the break-even point of alternative decision scenarios.

Example

Traditional Format Income Statement		Contribution Format Income Statement	
Sales	$20,000,000	Sales	$20,000,000
Cost of Goods Sold	12,000,000	Variable Costs	7,000,000
Gross Margin (GM)	8,000,000	Contribution Margin (CM)	13,000,000
S, G, & A Expenses	3,000,000	Fixed Expenses	8,000,000
Operating Income	$ 5,000,000	Operating Income	$ 5,000,000

The income statements above reflect the traditional, gross margin (GM), and contribution margin (CM) formats. The traditional (GM) format is typical with absorption costing, which is required for external (SEC and IRS) financial and tax reporting. This reflects the classification of costs by manufacturing/nonmanufacturing. The CM format reflects classification by operational cost behavior (i.e., variable/fixed). The CM format is desirable for planning purposes since cost behavior allows management to examine what revenue and cost items are expected to change given different cost-volume-profit results.

Note

Although the traditional format above is consistent with absorption costing and the contribution format is consistent with variable costing, the difference between gross margin and contribution margin presentation is merely a format issue.

   C. **Operating Profit Margin = Operating Income / Sales**—This is a useful metric for determining comparable performance without considering potential confounding interest and tax effects that usually have little to do with operations.

Note
Operating income and earnings before interest and taxes (EBIT) are considered the same thing.

D. **Profit Margin or Return on Sales = Net Income / Net Sales**—This metric expresses the ability of revenue to generate profits and is an important external financial evaluation metric. As presented by the DuPont formula, profit margin or return on sales multiplied by capital or asset turnover is equal to return on investment.

E. **Return Metrics (Return on Investment)**—These metrics are traditionally some of the most widely reported metrics used for providing an overall summary of externally reported financial results. There are several common variations of return, but all present some type of income divided by some type of investment base. Return on investment, return on assets, return on equity, and return on common equity are names that are quite common.

Note
Any one specific ratio often varies slightly in format from one text to another. Thus, it is important to know the general structure of the ratio and be prepared to calculate each as required based on the information given.

Return on Investment or Return on Assets = Net Income / Total Assets

Return on Equity or Return on Common Equity = Net Income / Common Stockholders' Equity

F. **DuPont Version of Return on Investment**

DuPont Formula = Return on Sales (ROS) × Asset Turnover

Where:

Profit Margin or ROS = Net Income / Sales

Capital or Asset Turnover = Sales / Total Assets

The DuPont approach to ROI separates ROI into two parts for analysis. The two pieces allow a separate evaluation of profitability as a percentage of sales and the efficiency with which assets were utilized to generate those sales. Multiplying the two parts together results in ROI.

G. **Residual Income = Operating Income – Required Rate of Return (Invested Capital)**

1. Residual income (RI) is a general form of economic profit. Economic profit differs from accounting income in that it recognizes the cost of capital. RI is often used as an alternative to ROI to preclude the diluted hurdle rate problem by expressing the return on investment in terms of dollars rather than a rate.

Note
The DuPont formula analysis and residual income are covered in detail in the "Competitive Analysis" lesson.

II. **Asset Utilization**—The metrics below are referred to alternatively as asset activity or asset management ratios and examine the efficiency with which assets are used to maintain and generate wealth.

A. **Receivables Turnover = Sales on Account / Average Accounts Receivable**—This metric provides data on the frequency with which (on average) receivables are collected.

B. **Days' Sales in Receivables or Average Collection Period = Average Accounts Receivable / Average Sales per Day**—Similar to receivable turnover, this provides an indication of the average length of the receivables collection period.

C. **Inventory Turnover = Cost of Goods Sold / Average Inventory**—This metric provides an indication of how quickly investment in inventory is being recovered.

D. **Fixed Asset Turnover = Sales / Average Net Fixed Asset**—This metric provides an indication of how efficiently productive assets are generating sales. This metric multiplied by the profit margin (resulting in a return on sales ratio) equals return on investment as used in DuPont analysis (covered in the "Competitive Analysis" lesson).

E. **Note**—Where turnover ratios are required, they are always structured such that the name of the ratio comprises the denominator in some form (i.e., it's "turned over" so that it's on the bottom). For example, "asset" turnover is sales / assets, "inventory" turnover is CGS / inventory, and "receivables" turnover is sales / receivables.

   1. Also, turnover ratios are related to their companion income statement accounts. For example, receivables turnover is related to sales and inventory is related to cost of goods sold, so these are the numerator accounts used, respectively.

III. **Liquidity**—Often referred to as measures of short-term solvency, these ratios are used to evaluate an enterprise's ability to meet its short-term obligations.

A. **Current Ratio = Current Assets / Current Liabilities**—This ratio measures the same concept that working capital does. The current ratio provides a comparison that is useful for standardizing working capital data when comparing organizations of differing sizes.

B. **Quick Ratio or Acid Test Ratio = (Current Assets – Inventory) / Current Liabilities**—This metric removes inventory since inventory is often less liquid than other current assets, such as short-term investments and receivables. Also, inventory may be valued at liquidation value only when a company is in distress making it less appropriate for meeting current obligations.

IV. **Debt Utilization (risk)**—These metrics provide measures of balance sheet risk (i.e., in terms of financial leverage). An enterprise is considered more leveraged, and thus more risky, if it has a comparatively high amount of debt versus owners' equity. Risk from debt is due to the required obligation to pay interest regularly on long-term debt. Owners' equity financing is less risky than financing with debt since the periodic payment of dividends is not required.

A. Debt to Total Assets = Total Debt / Total Assets

B. Debt to Equity = Total Debt / Total Owners' Equity

Note

Debt to Total Assets and Debt to Equity are generally balance sheet–based measures of leverage (i.e., the degree to which assets are being financed by debt) as a measure of risk. Analysts generally prefer one metric or the other, but both are designed to measure the same concept.

C. **Times Interest Earned—Operating Income / Interest Expense.** This approach measures the enterprise's ability to service its debt obligations by measuring the ability to make regular interest payments based on earnings. This reflects risk on the income statement.

V. **Market Ratios**—Market ratios are used to evaluate the value of the enterprise as based on capital market reflections of stock price as related to earnings and book value.

A. **Price Earnings (PE) Ratio**—Market Price per Share / Earnings per Share

B. **Market-to-Book Ratio**—Market Value per Share / Book Value per Share

VI. **Additional Ratios**

A. **Return on Owners' (All Stockholders') Equity**—Measures the rate of return (earnings) on all stockholders' investment

B. **Return on Common Stockholders' Equity**—Measures the rate of return (earnings) on common stockholders' equity

Return on C/S Equity = Net Income – Preferred Dividend (obligation for the period only)/Average Common Stockholders' Equity (e.g., Beginning + Ending/2)

C. **Earnings per Share (EPS—Basic Formula)**—Measures the income earned per (average) share of common stock. Indicates ability to pay dividends to common shareholders. It is computed as:

EPS (Basic) = Net Income – Preferred Dividends (obligation for the period only) / Weighted Average Number of Shares Outstanding

D. **Price-Earnings Ratio (P/E Ratio)**—Measures the price of a share of common stock relative to its latest earnings per share. Indicates a measure of how the market values the stock, especially when compared with other stocks. It is also called the "multiple"—how many times EPS is built into the market price of the stock. It is computed as:

P/E Ratio (the "Multiple") = Market Price for a Common Share / Earnings per (Common) Share (EPS)

E. **Common Stock Dividends Payout Rate**—Measures the extent (percentage) of earnings distributed to common shareholders. It is computed as:

1. Total basis:

C/S Dividend Payout Rate = Cash Dividends to Common Shareholders / Net Income to Common Shareholder

2. Per share basis:

C/S Dividend Payout Rate = Cash Dividends per Common Share / Earnings per Common Share

F. **Common Stock Yield**—Measures the rate of return (yield) per share of common stock. It is measured as:

Common Stock Yield = Dividend per Common Share / Market Price per Common Share

Risk Management

After studying this lesson, you should be able to:

1. List and describe the types of risk and explain how each type is best controlled.
2. List and explain the systematic ways to reduce risk within an organization's operational and strategic structure.
3. List and explain the different types of cost and revenue control that contribute to risk management.

I. **Uncertainty and Risk Management**—There are **multiple approaches** to managing risk, and there are **multiple types of risk** to be managed. Items in each of these categories should be adequately understood and married together to provide a comprehensive approach to risk management.

   A. Management must identify the different types of risk and uncertainty that are relevant and determine their impact as a first step in determining the appropriate approach to risk management.

   B. Management should then identify the different methods that are available for mitigating or eliminating risk to the organization given the types of risk and uncertainty present.

II. **Types of Risk**

   A. **Strategic Risk**—This type of risk occurs as a consequence of the specific and overall action plans to achieve the organization's mission. This includes general market approaches (e.g., cost leadership versus differentiation) and the changing nature of the competitive environment. Strategic and market risk is relatively long-term and can be managed by continually assessing the competitive space in which the organization operates. This includes employing SWOT analysis (i.e., strengths, weaknesses, opportunities, and threats) with an emphasis on weaknesses and threats. Externally, this could include assessing the state of the economy, analyzing the competitive landscape, and determining and optimizing organizational structure. Internally, assessment might include threats to safeguarding assets, ensuring business continuity, and maintaining operational flexibility.

      1. Strategic risk is best controlled by rigorous forecasting and planning, optimizing operating leverage (i.e., proportion of fixed and variable costs), and cost and revenue control. These items fall under the category of "business" risk.

      2. Common tools used here include forecasting, exponential smoothing (uses only historical data points in prediction), and sensitivity analysis.

   B. **Operational Risk**—This type of risk is more short-term in nature and involves daily implementation issues. Specific aspects of operational risk include **process** risk, **shared services** risk, **foreign/off-shore** operations risk, and **credit/default** risk.

      1. Operational risk is best controlled by exceptional execution of the strategic plan. This is often enhanced by attention to customer credit checks, quality, employee training, and management expertise. This type of risk is also properly categorized as "business" risk.

   C. **Market Risk**—This type of risk is associated with large-scale economic events or natural disasters that, to some extent, influence all companies. This is often discussed in the context of volatility. Market risk is considered systematic or nondiversifiable risk.

      1. Market risk can be controlled to some degree by insurance for specific hazard risk, but economic events often cannot be controlled. Thus, companies must assess their exposure to economic downturns and use sensitivity analysis to evaluate their position.

   D. **Various Financial or Non-Operational Risk**—There are many different types of risk included here such as interest rate risk (including price and reinvestment risk), portfolio risk, credit/default risk (note: both financial and operational), liquidity risk, and exchange rate risk. Definitions of these risk types and approaches to mitigating them are covered in more detail in the "Operations Management" section.

III. Methods for Dealing with Risk—Although controlling for strategic and operational risk has been explained in general, there are several systematic ways to reduce risk within an organization's operational and strategic structure as shown below.

A. Modify the structure of the income statement as needed to **determine** the most appropriate **operating leverage approach** to mitigating/eliminating uncertainty.

1. Increasing the proportion of fixed costs increases potential for both higher returns and higher risk due to increased leverage. Thus, using operational leverage involves effectively making a trade-off between risk and return.

2. The enhanced **risk** of having too much fixed costs is based on the risk of not being able to reach the break-even point. The more fixed costs, the harder it is to break even.

3. The enhanced **return** aspect of high leverage is that given low variable costs, the contribution margin per unit is higher. Thus, once the fixed costs are covered (i.e., the break-even point is reached) each unit sold delivers a relatively higher amount of contribution margin per unit.

4. Operating leverage can often be reduced by leasing assets rather than buying them or by considering outsourcing arrangements to minimize fixed costs.

B. Provide **contingency planning** for disaster recovery and business continuity. This type of risk is covered in more detail in part four of the planning and measurement section. Often these issues are addressed by safeguarding equipment, building in redundancy and backup procedures, and using insurance.

C. Use **hedging** and **diversification** to overcome defined levels of excessive exposure.

1. Hedging can mean matching maturities of instruments as well as offsetting the risk by using options and futures contracts. While both are good practices, the latter is emphasized for mitigating/eliminating specific risk exposure.

2. Hedging is often used to offset **foreign currency exchange rate risk** as well as to offset fluctuations in the price of **commodities** over time.

3. Buying options and futures contracts secures the right to purchase the underlying item at a specified price in the future, thus offsetting price risk.

4. Diversification reduces **portfolio risk** but does not completely offset it as a hedging arrangement does. Nevertheless, diversification is quite beneficial for reducing **unsystematic risk** given differing directional volatility from multiple investment instruments.

D. Use **insurance** contracts to provide for risk mitigation or elimination of risk in some cases.

1. Insurance is used to deal with peril and hazard. Peril is something specific that causes a loss, while hazard is a condition that may lead to a loss.

2. Insurance provides for what is known as **pure risk**. This type of risk is characterized by the possibility of either breaking even or losing, but never increasing profits. Other types of risk are known as **speculative risks**.

3. Insurance is commonly used where a specific type of **risk of loss** is involved. This includes personal, property, liability, business interruption, and the failure of others.

4. Often companies (and individuals) purchase **umbrella insurance** in addition to insuring specific types of potential hazard. These policies often cover a variety of potential loss types but relate to liability and other potential deficiencies for which specific policies are potentially limited in their adequacy of coverage.

E. Evaluate uncertainty involved with estimating future costs and revenues. Cost and revenue planning and control can also be included as an important part of a comprehensive risk management plan.

IV. Cost and Revenue Control—Wherever items are within the control of management and excessive risk levels are impinging on important areas of the enterprise, cost and revenue control become extremely important.

A. **Cost avoidance** is the most common way to avoid unnecessary costs and involves finding acceptable alternatives to managing spending for high-cost items and/or not spending for unnecessary goods and services. Cost avoidance is a quicker way to increase profitability than enhancing revenue (but maybe not better) since increasing revenue typically involves at least some increases in proportional costs as well.

B. Attempts to **increase revenue** are often closely linked to strategic objectives and present a longer-term consideration than most cost reduction efforts. For example, compnies can try to increase revenue by increasing the quality of the goods/services provided, but this can take a considerable amount of time.

C. Distinguishing between **committed and discretionary** costs is one way to determine which costs are considered essential and which costs are considered perhaps beneficial but not absolutely necessary. The terms committed and discretionary costs are subject to definition, and this issue is vulnerable to multiple perspectives. The more objectively management behaves toward approaching these definitions, the more likely they are to achieve important distinctions.

D. The distinction between committed and discretionary costs should be related to conformance with **organizational strategy**. The importance of funding specific activities should be related to the achievement of the organization's goals.

E. Often included in the discretionary category are costs related to maintenance, training, advertising, and research and development. The committed cost category is typically related to costs of clearly defined input-output relationships that cannot be omitted without threatening the strategic objectives of the organization. Generally, essential cost initiatives should be determined based on committed costs.

F. One way to control discretionary costs is to establish authority for approval to spend up to a specified amount. Another way to control spending is to require that the spending demonstrate that it supports defined organizational objectives.

Performance Improvement Tools

After studying this lesson, you should be able to:

1. Recognize how the theory of constraints can be used to optimize constrained resources.
2. Explain how the theory of constraints optimizes product mix decisions under conditions of constrained resources.
3. Describe the philosophy and structure of lean manufacturing, and distinguish how it is different from craft and mass production processes.
4. Describe the common philosophy lean manufacturing shares with just-in-time, total quality management, and continuous improvement.
5. Explain why unit costs are lower with lean production than with other manufacturing approaches.
6. Describe the basic concept of the demand flow approach and its relationship to lean manufacturing.
7. Describe the goal of the Six Sigma continuous improvement approach, list its five steps, and recognize the DMAIC roadmap approach to increase and sustain quality.

I. Theory of Constraints

A. The theory of constraints identifies strategies to maximize income when the organization is faced with **bottleneck operations**. A bottleneck operation occurs when the **work to be performed exceeds the capacity of the production facilities.** Over the short run, revenue is maximized by maximizing the contribution margin of the constrained resource.

B. Revenue can also be improved by finding ways to relax the constraint. The following are commonly used methods of relaxing the constraint (eliminating the bottleneck):

1. Re-engineer the production process to make it more efficient.
2. Re-engineer the product to make it simpler to produce.
3. Eliminate nonvalue-added activities at the bottleneck operation.
4. Work overtime at the bottleneck operation.
5. Outsource some or all production at the bottleneck operation.

C. **Product Mix Decisions under Constrained Resources**—In instances when production capacity is insufficient to meet demand, producing the item that **maximizes the contribution margin per unit of the constrained resource** and maximizes profitability for the organization.

Example

Fusion Foods produces two organic cereals: Granola Gems and Mixed Grain Magic. Cost data for the two products is shown below:

	Granola Gems	Mixed Grain Magic
Sales Price (per 1 lb. bag)	$5.00	$7.00
Variable costs:		
Direct materials	$1.50	$1.85
Direct labor	$1.00	$1.25
Variable overhead	$1.50	$1.95
Variable selling and administrative	$0.50	$1.00
Total variable costs:	$4.50	$6.00
Total Contribution Margin:	$0.50	$1.00
Contribution Margin as a Percentage of Sales Price	10%	14.2%

Although Fusion can sell as much of either of the types of cereals as it can produce, its baking ovens can only be run 12 hours per day, constraining the quantity of product that Fusion can produce. The baking ovens can process 72 pounds of Granola Gems in one hour; however, they can only process 30 lbs of Mixed Grain Magic in one hour. What product (or products) should Fusion produce?

Although Mixed Grain Magic is the more profitable of the two products in terms of unit contribution margin ($1.00) and contribution margin percentage (14.2%), using all of the production capacity to produce Mixed Grain Magic will not maximize revenue. Why not? Because the amount of cereal that can be processed in a day is constrained by the amount of oven time available and Mixed Grain Magic requires over twice as much oven time than Granola Gems.

To determine which product to produce, we must determine the **contribution margin per hour of oven time:**

	Granola Gems	Mixed Grain Magic
Contribution margin per unit:	$0.50	$1.00
Number of pounds per oven hour	× 72 lbs.	× 30 lbs.
Contribution margin per hour	$36/hour	$30.00

Despite its smaller unit contribution margin, Granola Gems provides a higher total contribution margin than Mixed Grain Magic because of its higher contribution margin per unit of the constrained resource.

Exam Tip

Production decisions under constrained resources are expected to be tested regularly, though not heavily, on the CPA Exam. In these questions, it is each product's **contribution margin per unit of the constrained resource** that determines profitability, not the product's individual unit contribution margin.

II. Lean Manufacturing

A. Lean manufacturing strives for perfection in quality and removes layers of waste to support continuous improvement. According to the Lean Enterprise Institute, Lean is a business system for organizing and managing product development, operations, suppliers, and customer relations. Businesses and other organizations use lean principles, practices, and tools to create precise customer value—goods and services with higher quality and fewer defects—with less human effort, less space, less capital, and less time than the traditional system of mass production.

B. Lean production is also known by several other names including flexible manufacturing, mass customization, and agile production. The lean production approach belies (shows to be false) the traditional belief that costs are primarily driven by production volume. Process design is shown to have a significant impact on cost reduction.

C. Comparing and contrasting different types of production processes is helpful to understanding the differences in the lean manufacturing approach:

1. **Craft**—A small number of a high variety of unique (i.e., customized or one-of-a-kind) products usually with simple tools or technology and highly skilled labor. Traditional cost accounting systems used with this approach typically involve job costing.
2. **Mass**—Making a large number of standardized or identical products usually with dedicated (i.e., single-purpose), often automated or otherwise sophisticated machinery, and unskilled labor. Traditional cost accounting systems used with this approach typically involve process costing.
3. **Lean**—Making small batches of a high variety of unique products usually with automated or otherwise sophisticated machinery and highly skilled labor (usually cross-trained). Thus, lean production blends the features of craft and mass production processes.

D. **Lean Principles**—can be applied to all functions within an organization and include the following:

1. Identify all steps in the value stream for each product family, eliminating steps that do not create value.
2. Make the value-creating steps occur in tight sequence so the product will flow smoothly toward the customer.
3. As flow is introduced, let customers pull value from the next upstream activity.
4. As value is specified, value streams are identified, wasted steps are removed, and flow and pull are introduced: begin the process again and continue it until a state of perfection is reached in which perfect value is created with no waste.

E. Toyota is given substantial credit for the development of lean production. This production method is not necessarily better for all firms. It is critically important that production processes be chosen based on the appropriateness of the environment in which it is used. Observe the **structural differences between mass and lean producers**:

1. **Inflexible versus flexible equipment**—Mass production typically uses dedicated or single-purpose equipment. Lean production uses flexible multi-use equipment.
2. **High versus low setup time**—Equipment in mass production typically requires a high setup time.
3. **Low versus high labor skill**—Mass production typically requires a low labor skill level because of the presence of labor specialization (workers do one task only). This avoids costly training and the need for workers to thoroughly understand the production process. Lean production requires a flexible, skilled work force. Workers usually work in "U" shaped work cells with equipment that can perform a variety of tasks. Cell workers do their own setups, operate all cell equipment, move materials, control quality, and perform routine equipment maintenance. Investment in worker training is significant.

F. Many of the features of lean manufacturing are similar to or share a common philosophy with just-in-time, total quality management, and continuous improvement. For example, in a lean environment:

1. Workers are "empowered."
2. The organization seeks a close relationship with suppliers.
3. The organization maintains a close relationship with customers (i.e., extensive direct contact and information sharing, working with customers to give them what they want—especially in providing greater variety).

4. Product design engineers work "concurrently" with process design engineers, service engineers, production line workers, and others to ensure that products are easy to make, assemble, ship, and repair.

G. **Why Unit Costs are Lower with Lean Production**

1. Production flexibility is greater (small, perhaps different, batches are economically feasible due to lower setup times).
2. Line employees do their own setups, move their own materials, control their own quality, and perform their own routine equipment maintenance. The need for additional, specially trained employees is eliminated.
3. The number of suppliers is lower, reducing the number of transactions. Other related costs are reduced as well (e.g., soliciting bids, holding inventory). Quality generally is increased since the suppliers tend to have a better understanding of the organization to which they supply goods.
4. A more sophisticated relationship is recognized among costs and their causes or "drivers." Lean producers know that volume is not the major factor affecting cost. They search for drivers of cost by analyzing the tasks (i.e., processes or activities) performed and the resources (i.e., costs) consumed by those tasks.

H. The **demand flow approach, or demand flow technology (DFT)**, uses mathematical methods to link materials, time, and resources based on continuous flow planning. The objective is to link process flows and manage those flows based on customer demand.

1. According to Wikipedia and other historical archives, DFT was initially used to complement just-in-time, which used a pull-based approach (i.e., driven to actual customer demand) via Kanban (i.e., a visual signal from downstream production to indicate the need for work to a prior work station).
2. DFT was introduced as a way for American manufacturers to adopt Japanese production techniques, while trying to avoid cultural conflicts in applying Japanese business methods in an American context.
3. More recently, DFT has come to be seen as a complementary tool for facilitating lean manufacturing. Demand flow technology is promoted as a method particularly suitable for high-mix, low-volume manufacturing.

III. Six Sigma

A. Six Sigma is a continuous improvement approach designed to systematically reduce defects by recognizing that (1) the overall yield of a group of related processes is much lower than the yields of the individual processes; and (2) the total cost of a product or service is directly related to the defect rate.

B. The name, Six Sigma, reflects a level of quality that is nearly perfect. Considering a normal distribution and the fact that the term sigma indicates standard deviation, Six Sigma implies that no defective observations would be present until after six standard deviations from the mean (i.e., only 3.4 defects per million units produced or outside of 99.999966% of production).

Areas Under the Normal Curve

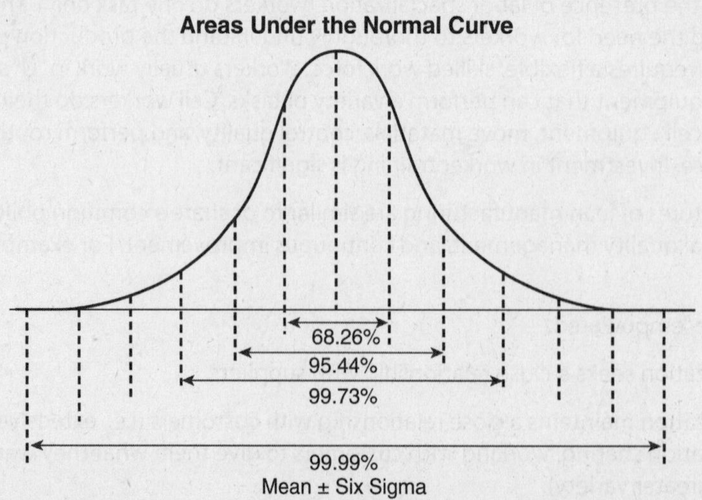

C. Six Sigma involves five steps:

1. **Define the business**—Business goals, objectives, processes, team responsibilities, resources, scope of operations, and quality definitions
2. **Measure the processes**—Defects per unit, defects per million opportunities, and production yield. Note that all defects are counted (not just the number of defective units)
3. **Analyze the process**—Analysis is done to determine the root cause of defects. Tools commonly used with total quality management (TQM) such as Pareto diagrams (histograms) and/or Ishikawa (fishbone) diagrams are used to identify potential causes of defects.
4. **Improve the process**—This involves (1) design experiments and (2) change management to allow statistical exploration of relationships to reveal how to improve quality levels. Once determined, training, policy, and procedures are adjusted to achieve the desired change.
5. **Control**—TQM-type quality tools (e.g., control charts, run charts) are used to achieve sustained improvement in operational quality.

D. Six Sigma prescribes the DMAIC roadmap acronym, which provides a detailed list of steps and tools to increase and sustain quality. These include:

1. **D**efine customers and their requirements.
2. **M**easure defects and other metrics.
3. **A**nalyze to determine root cause of failures and the sources of variation.
4. **I**mprove through experimentation.
5. **C**ontrol results using TQM statistical process control tools (e.g., control charts).

Note
Some would say that Six Sigma provides nothing new in the way of quality efforts and appears to be very consistent with TQM philosophies.

Cost Accounting

Manufacturing Costs

After studying this lesson, you should be able to:

1. Classify product costs and period costs.
2. Identify manufacturing costs.
3. Distinguish direct costs from indirect costs.
4. Distinguish prime costs from conversion costs.

I. Cost Terminology

A. Two fundamental cost classifications exist within a manufacturing organization: product costs and period costs.

1. **Product costs**—Can be associated with the production of specific revenues (i.e., cost of goods sold). They generally attach to physical product units and are expensed in the period in which the goods are sold. Product costs are also known as **inventoriable** costs or **manufacturing** costs.
2. **Period costs**—Cannot be matched with specific revenues (i.e., accountant's salary) and are expensed in the period incurred. These costs are also called **selling and administrative** costs.

B. This division of costs can be seen in the format of the income statement:

Net Sales	
– Cost of Goods Sold	*(product costs)*
= Gross Profit	
– Selling and Administrative Expenses	*(period costs)*
= Net Profit (Loss)	

II. Manufacturing (or Inventoriable) Costs—Include all costs associated with the manufacturing of a product split. Manufacturing costs are split into the "three factors of production," which are:

A. Direct Material—The cost of significant raw materials and components that are directly incorporated in the finished product. For example, direct material costs of a leather briefcase include cost of leather (raw material) as well as buckles and zippers (purchased components).

B. Direct Labor—The wages and salaries paid for work that directly converts raw materials into a finished product. Continuing with our leather briefcase example, the direct labor costs associated with the manufacture of a leather briefcase include wages paid to workers who cut the leather, finish the leather, and sew the briefcase.

C. Factory Overhead—The cost of indirect labor, indirect materials, and other manufacturing costs other than direct material and direct labor that are necessary to support the production process but are not easily traceable to the finished product. For example, factory overhead associated with production of a leather briefcase includes salaries paid to the production line supervisors, wages paid to mechanics who maintain the equipment, wages paid to custodians who maintain the factory, thread used to sew the briefcase together, electricity used to power the equipment and provide lighting to the factory, and depreciation on the factory building and equipment.

1. Factory overhead can be **variable** (the total cost changes with the quantity produced) or **fixed** (the total cost remains the same regardless of the quantity produced, within reasonable limits). In the example above, the cost of thread is variable overhead because with the production of more briefcases, more thread is used; the depreciation on the factory building is fixed because the depreciation stays the same regardless of how many briefcases are produced.
2. In highly automated manufacturing environments, direct labor costs are frequently so insignificant a part of total production costs that they are not separately tracked but simply added to factory overhead costs.

III. Other Manufacturing Cost Classifications—Several other ways of classifying costs are tested on the CPA Exam.

A. Direct Costs and Indirect Costs—This classification looks at the behavior of the cost in regard to how it is traced to the product:

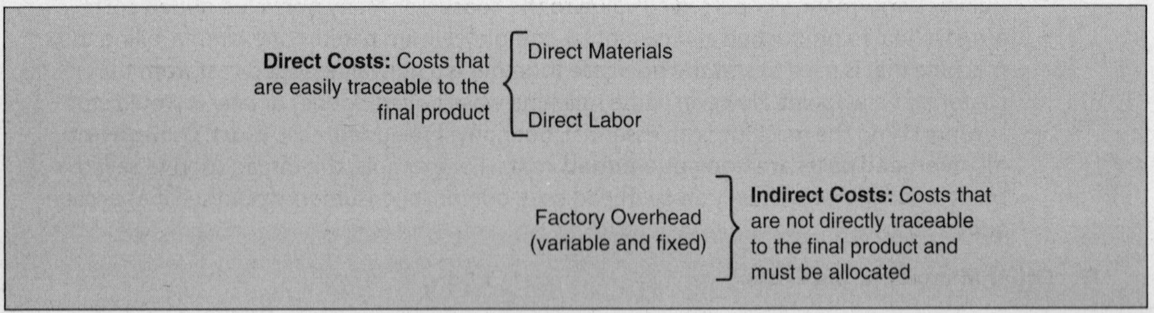

B. Direct Costs—Costs that can be traced to specific units of production. Direct materials are actually incorporated into the product. Direct labor is comprised of the salary costs of workers who fabricate the product.

C. Indirect Costs—(Note: the term "indirect costs" is often treated synonymously with the term "manufacturing overhead.") Necessary costs of the manufacturing process that cannot be easily associated with specific units. These include all manufacturing costs other than direct material and direct labor. Indirect materials such as custodial and maintenance supplies, depreciation, and scrap are also overhead. Indirect labor including salaries for supervisors, custodians, and maintenance and repair personnel are overhead as well. Indirect costs can be either variable (e.g., supplies) or fixed (e.g., depreciation).

1. Note that the distinction between direct and indirect costs is often one of convenience or feasibility. Traditional cost allocation classifies many costs as indirect because they are insignificant or not feasible to trace to products. For example, the cost of thread used to sew a briefcase together could be calculated and assigned to the briefcase as a direct cost. However, because the cost of the thread is so insignificant, it is usually treated as an indirect cost and allocated to each briefcase along with other overhead. (Note: Most companies allocate all overhead costs, but as an exception to the diagram above some variable overhead costs can be traced directly to production. Although accuracy can be increased by this treatment, this distinction will likely not be tested.)

D. Prime Costs and Conversion Costs—Prime costs are direct labor and direct materials, while conversion costs are direct labor and manufacturing overhead. You can think of prime costs as being the "primary" costs (i.e., direct materials and direct labor) of the product. You can think of conversion costs as the "costs of converting" direct materials into a product by using direct labor and overhead.

Exam Tip
Direct labor is included as a prime cost and as a conversion cost. This overlap in classifications is likely to be tested on the exam.

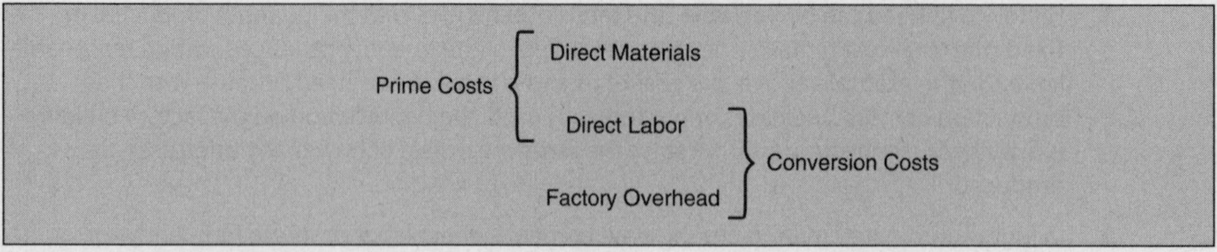

E. Value-Added Costs and Nonvalue-Added Costs

1. **Value-added costs**—Product costs that enhance the value of the product in the eyes of the consumer. Most direct costs are value-added costs. Continuing with the briefcase example, the leather that the briefcase is made of and the labor required to cut the pieces and sew them together are value-added costs.

2. **Nonvalue-added costs**—Costs that could be eliminated without deterioration of product quality, performance, or perceived value to the consumer. Many nonvalue-added costs are essential to production and cannot be completely eliminated. For example, oiling the machine that is used to sew the briefcase together is a nonvalue-added cost from the customer's viewpoint. However, if the machine wasn't oiled, sooner or later it would stop sewing. Oiling the machine is an essential, but nonvalue-added, cost. **Most, though not all, overhead costs are nonvalue-added costs.** For example, the thread used to sew the briefcase together is usually an overhead cost, but most consumers would see it as a value-added cost.

F. Other Manufacturing Costs

1. **Marginal cost or revenue**—Additional cost or revenue resulting from one more unit of output

2. **Accounting cost**—Explicit costs that are "accounted for," typically as evidenced by an entry in a fundamental book or accounting record (e.g., the general ledger)

3. **Average fixed cost**—Decreases as volume increases (subject to the relevant range).

4. **Average variable cost**—Increases as volume increases (subject to the relevant range).

5. **Committed cost**—Cannot be avoided in the current accounting time period (the opposite of discretionary costs).

6. **Discretionary cost**—May or may not be included in the budget and can be considered avoidable as determined by a decision maker with the authority to do so (opposite of committed cost).

Spoilage, Cost, and Inventory Flow

After studying this lesson, you should be able to:

1. Distinguish between normal and abnormal spoilage and scrap.
2. Describe the different types of inventories and the cost flow from inventory and manufacturing accounts to cost of goods sold.
3. Analyze and calculate cost flows using the schedule of cost of goods manufactured and the cost of goods sold.

I. Spoilage and Scrap

A. Some spoilage and scrap may be **normal**—that is, it is unavoidable as part of the manufacturing process. Normal spoilage is included with other costs as an inventoriable product cost.

B. Spoilage and scrap may also be **abnormal,** such as when it is due to carelessness or inefficiency. Abnormal spoilage is separated and deducted as a period expense in the calculation of net income.

1. **Responsibility for scrap**—Normal spoilage is part of the production process and is therefore an uncontrollable cost. Abnormal spoilage is due to production inefficiencies and is a controllable cost. Since managers should only be held responsible for controllable costs, managers should be held responsible for abnormal spoilage, but not for normal spoilage.
2. **Sale of scrap**—If the amount of scrap is immaterial, any monies received from the sale of scrap can be used to reduce factory overhead, and thereby reduce Cost of Goods Sold. Alternatively, if the value of scrap is significant and is saleable, it can be treated as "other sales" in the revenue category.

II. Flow of Costs and Inventory Valuation

Flow of Costs and Inventory Valuation—Companies use one of several cost flow assumptions (LIFO, FIFO, weighted average) to assign inventory costs to ending inventory and cost of goods sold. For retail companies who buy products for resale, this is a fairly straightforward process. For manufacturing companies, however, the addition of raw materials inventory and work-in-process inventory makes the process more complex.

A. **Wholesale and Retail Organizations**—Since these organizations purchase the items that they sell, their inventory calculations are relatively simple. Under the periodic inventory method, inventory is counted at the end of the period and valued, typically using FIFO, LIFO, or weighted average cost flow assumptions. The ending inventory valuation is then subtracted from Goods Available for Sale (the value of the beginning inventory plus purchases) to determine Cost of Goods Sold:

+	Beginning Inventory	
+	<u>Purchases (net)</u>	
=	Goods Available for Sale	
–	<u>Ending Inventory</u>	***reported on the B.S.***
=	Cost of Goods Sold	***appears as a line item on the I.S.***

1. This analysis format, which is sometimes called "account analysis" format because it allows you to analyze the debits and credits of any account, is essentially the same format as is used for the Schedule of Cost of Goods Sold.

B. Manufacturing Organizations

1. Manufacturing organizations maintain three inventories instead of one:
   a. Raw Materials
   b. Work-in-Process
   c. Finished Goods
2. Costs flow from Raw Materials Inventory through Work-in-Process Inventory and into Finished Goods Inventory. As items are sold, costs flow from Finished Goods Inventory into Cost of Goods Sold. The ending balances of the three inventories are added together and reported as a single line item on the Balance Sheet. Cost of Goods Sold appears as a line item on the Income Statement. The analysis of the three inventory accounts is shown on two schedules:

Schedule	***Inventory Accounts Analyzed***
Cost of Goods Manufactured	Raw Materials and Work-in-Process
Cost of Goods Sold	**Finished Goods**

C. Schedule of Cost of Goods Manufactured—This schedule calculates the dollar value of the goods that were completed during the period and transferred to finished goods. It is primarily an analysis of the Work-In-Process account (Beginning Balance + Total Manufacturing Costs – Ending Balance = Cost of Goods Manufactured), but it is sometimes complicated by calculations related to the Direct Materials Inventory. The basic format is as follows:

+ Beg. Value WIP
+ Current Period Additions:
  + Direct Materials*
  + Direct Labor
  + Overhead
– Ending Value WIP
= Cost of Goods Manufactured -> to additions to Finished Goods Inventory

*The current period direct materials costs are calculated by analyzing the Direct Materials Inventory account:

+ Beg. Direct Materials
+ Purchases (net)
= Direct Materials Available for Use
– Ending Direct Materials
= Direct Materials Used -> to Direct Materials line on schedule of cost of goods manufactured

D. Schedule of Cost of Goods Sold—This schedule is produced by analyzing the Finished Goods Inventory. It calculates the Cost of Goods Sold:

	Beginning Finished Goods	
+	Cost of Goods Manufactured	-> from the Schedule of CGM
	Goods Available for Sale	
–	Ending Finished Goods	
=	Cost of Goods Sold	-> appears as a line item on the I.S.

Example

Kingman Enterprises produces custom period furniture for Victorian homes. The following information is available concerning Kingman's production activities during the past quarter:

Inventory	Beg. Value	Purchases/Additions	End. Value
Direct Materials	$120,000	$800,000	$100,000
Work-in-Process	$180,000	Direct Materials:	$120,000
		Direct Labor:	$120,000
		Overhead Applied:	$700,000
Finished Goods	$250,000	Cost of Goods Manufactured:	$350,000

Given this information, calculate the Cost of Goods Manufactured and the Cost of Goods Sold.

Step 1: Calculate the raw materials used during the period:

+	Beg. Direct Materials	+ $120,000
+	Purchases (net)	+ $800,000
=	Materials Available for Use	+ $920,000
–	Ending Direct Materials	– $100,000
=	Direct Materials Used	= $820,000

Step 2: Calculate the cost of goods manufactured:

+	Beginning Value WIP		$180,000
+	Current Period Additions:		
	+ Direct Materials Used	+ $820,000	
	+ Direct Labor	+ $120,000	
	+ Overhead Applied	+ $700,000	
			$1,640,000
	= Total Manufacturing Costs		$1,820,000
–	Ending Value WIP		$ 120,000
=	Cost of Goods Manufactured		$1,700,000

Step 3: Calculate the cost of goods sold:

	Beginning Finished Goods	+ $250,000
+	Cost of Goods Manufactured	+ $1,700,000
	Goods Available for Sale	= $1,950,000
–	Ending Finished Goods	– $350,000
=	Cost of Goods Sold	= $1,600,000

Exam Tip

Be sure that you thoroughly understand the account analysis formats used in this example. The examiners are likely to make these questions more difficult by giving you the Cost of Goods Sold or Cost of Goods Manufactured and asking you for one of the intermediate amounts (e.g., the Ending WIP Inventory value or the Direct Labor added during the period). If you understand the format of the analysis, these types of questions are easy to answer by simply filling in the blanks and solving for the unknowns.

E. The complete CGS/CGM format is shown below. Also, as the arrows show, you should notice how something from each of the sections sends something to the next section. For example, the first section for direct materials moves direct materials used to the next section. You should also notice that sections 1, 3, and 4 are all essentially the same format. This should make it easier to memorize the format.

Cost of Goods Sold/Cost of Goods Manufactured Statement Format

1. Beginning Inventory Direct Materials
   + Direct Materials Purchased
   = Direct Materials Available
   – Ending Inventory Direct Materials
   = Direct Materials Used →

2. Direct Materials Used ←
   + Direct Labor
   + Overhead
   = Total Manufacturing Costs →

3. Beginning Inventory Work in Process
   + Total Manufacturing Costs ←
   = Work in Process Available
   – Ending Inventory Work in Process
   = Cost of Goods Manufactured →

4. Beginning Inventory Finished Goods
   + Cost of Goods Manufactured ←
   = Goods Available for Sale
   – Ending Inventory Finished Goods
   = Cost of Goods Sold

Cost Behavior Patterns

Cost behavior patterns allow us to predict how costs change in response to changes in production or sales. A thorough understanding of cost behavior is necessary in order to perform cost-volume-profit analysis and to prepare production and sales budgets. Cost behavior is consistently tested on the CPA exam—both directly and as part of other topics.

After studying this lesson, you should be able to:

1. Describe the nature of fixed and variable costs and the importance of the relevant range in defining these concepts.
2. Explain how to use the high-low method in calculations involving cost prediction.

I. Costs

A. By analyzing the way costs behave when production and/or sales volume changes, we can predict total costs and estimate profit. However, very few costs behave consistently across a wide range of production or sales volumes: At some point, economies or diseconomies of scale will cause the cost behavior to change. Because of this, all discussions of cost behavior must take place within the concept of a relevant range. A **relevant range** is a range of production volumes where:

1. The range of activity for which the assumptions of cost behavior reasonably hold true; and
2. The range of activity over which the company plans to operate.
3. If (1) is true but (2) is not, then the analysis will not be relevant to the company. If (2) is true but (1) is not, then the assumptions of the model are not satisfied making the analysis invalid.

B. All cost behavior patterns are valid only within a relevant range. We will discuss the concept of a relevant range in more detail in conjunction with cost-volume-profit analysis.

II. Fixed vs. Variable Costs

A. Costs can be separated into two principal behavior patterns.

1. **Fixed costs**—Remain constant in total regardless of production volume. Because of this, **fixed costs** *per unit* **vary**—increasing when production decreases and decreasing when production increases.
2. **Variable costs**—Vary in total, in direct proportion to changes in production volume. **Variable costs** *per unit* **remain constant** regardless of production volume.

B. **Total cost**—Is the sum of fixed costs and variable costs. As such, total costs take on characteristics from both component costs: **total costs per unit vary** with changes in production because fixed costs per unit vary with changes in production; **total costs in total vary** with changes in production because variable costs vary in total with changes in production.

Exam Tip

You should expect to see many CPA Exam questions that ask about the relationship between fixed costs, variable costs, and total costs and changes in production volume. The examiners may also use the fact that the unit cost relationships and total cost relationships are different to confuse the candidate. For example, a question about fixed costs, which remain constant *in total* over changes in production volume, might ask if the fixed cost *per unit* remains constant when production volume changes. The following matrix may help keep these relationships straight:

	Behavior When Production Volume Changes	
	Unit Costs	**Total Costs**
Fixed Costs	Vary	Constant
Variable Costs	Constant	Vary
Total Costs	Vary	Vary

Question
Stanford Machining planned production of 180,000 units this year. Fixed costs were estimated to be $220,000; total variable costs were estimated to be $540,000. Actual production was 150,000. How would you expect the total fixed costs and total variable costs to change because of the change in production volume? What about the unit fixed costs and unit variable costs?

Answer:
Total fixed costs and *unit* variable costs would not change because of the change in production volume (see matrix above). *Unit* fixed costs would increase from $1.22 (220,000/180,000) to $1.47 (220,000/150,000) and total variable costs would decrease from $540,000 to $450,000 ((540,000/180,000) × 150,000).

III. Other Cost Classifications—Many costs exhibit both fixed and variable cost characteristics.

- **A. Step-Variable Costs**—Remain constant in *total* over a small range of production levels, but vary with larger changes in production volume. Supervisory salaries, utility costs, and shipping costs often behave in this fashion.
- **B. Mixed Costs (Also Known as Semi-Variable Costs)**—Have a fixed component and a variable component. The variable component causes them to vary in total with changes in volume. The fixed component, however, prevents them from varying in direct proportion to the change in volume.

Example
Carpenter Corporation leases a copier from a local office supply company. Under the contract, Carpenter pays a base fee of $800 per month for the copier and an additional $0.015 for each copy over 50,000 per month. This is a mixed cost with an $800 fixed cost and a variable cost of $0.015 for the additional copies.

IV. Predicting Costs

A. High-Low Method

1. When predicting the behavior of a total cost or a mixed cost, the high-low method provides a rough estimate of the fixed cost and the variable cost components. Although a more precise cost prediction can be obtained using regression analysis, the high-low method provides a quick, easy cost estimate.
2. The basic concept underlying this method is that when total manufacturing costs change in response to changes in production volume, the changes are, by definition, caused by variable costs.
   - **a.** By calculating the change in total costs between two production volume extremes (the high value and the low value), the total change in variable costs can be isolated.
   - **b.** The unit variable cost can then be determined by dividing the change in total costs by the difference in units produced.
   - **c.** Once the unit variable cost is determined, total fixed costs can be identified by calculating the total variable cost at a specified production volume (e.g., multiply unit variable cost by the number of units produced) and subtracting it from the total cost.

Exam Tip
Although the high-low method typically receives little emphasis in academic studies of managerial accounting, it is likely to be a covered topic on the CPA Exam.

B. Using the High-Low Method—To identify fixed and variable cost components using the high-low method:

1. From the range of production volumes presented, select the period with the highest production and the period with the lowest production.
2. **Note**—Do **not** use highest and lowest *costs*. **Always** use *production volume*.
3. Calculate the **difference in units produced** at the highest and the lowest levels of production.
4. Calculate the **difference in costs** at the highest and the lowest levels of production.
5. **Divide the difference in costs by the difference in units**—This is your estimated variable cost per unit.
6. Find total variable costs by multiplying the **estimated variable cost per unit by the actual number of units produced** at either the high or the low level of production.
7. Subtract the **total variable costs from the total cost** to determine fixed costs.
8. You can now estimate total costs at any production level by multiplying the production in units times the variable cost per unit and adding it to the total fixed costs.

Example

Milkenson Industries reported the following production volumes and costs:

Production	Cost
150,000 units	$375,000
225,000 units	$525,000

What are the fixed and variable costs of production for 250,000 units?

Steps 1–4: ($525,000 – $375,000) / (225,000 – 150,000) = $2.00 variable cost per unit

Steps 4–5: $375,000 – ($2.00 × 150,000 units) = $75,000 fixed costs

or

$525,000 – ($2.00 × 225,000 units) = $75,000 fixed costs

Steps 5–7: ($2.00 × 250,000 units) + $75,000 = $575,000 total costs

Answer: $500,000 variable costs and $75,000 fixed costs

Cost-Volume-Profit Analysis

After studying this lesson, you should be able to:

1. Define the basic breakeven analysis formula and the contribution margin approach to the calculation of the breakeven point.
2. Define contribution margin, and explain how it is used in the calculation of breakeven units.
3. Define the contribution margin ratio, and explain how it is used in the calculation of breakeven units.
4. Describe how to use ratios of income statement elements in calculations involving the contribution margin ratio.
5. Explain how to integrate targeted profit calculations into the contribution margin approach.
6. List and describe the assumptions that constrain the cost-volume-profit model.
7. Demonstrate how to use standard and alternative breakeven charts to analyze cost-volume-profit relationships.

I. Cost-Volume-Profit (Breakeven) Analysis

A. Breakeven is defined as the sales level at which sales revenues exactly offset total costs, both fixed and variable. Note that total costs include period costs (selling and administrative costs) as well as product (manufacturing) costs. The breakeven point is usually expressed in sales units or in sales dollars.

B. **Basic Formula**—The following formula helps define a breakeven point. All other formulas can be derived from this basic formula.

(Quantity × Sales Price) = Fixed Costs + (Quantity × Variable Costs per Unit)

C. It is, however, generally more difficult to use than the contribution margin approach formulas discussed below and is not recommended for use on CPA Exam questions.

II. Using the Contribution Margin per Unit Approach to Calculate Breakeven in Units

A. The contribution margin represents the **portion of revenues which are available to cover fixed costs**. It is calculated as follows:

Sales Revenue – Variable Costs = Contribution Margin

B. The contribution margin can be expressed on a per unit basis:

Sales Price per Unit – Variable Costs per Unit = Contribution Margin per Unit

C. Since the contribution margin per unit represents the amount that the sale of an individual unit contributes to covering fixed costs, it provides an easy way to calculate the number of units necessary to break even.

Example

Consider an item with a unit sales price of $1.50 and a variable cost per unit of $1.00. The unit contribution margin is $0.50 per unit ($1.50 – $1.00). If fixed costs are $5,000, then we know that we have to sell 10,000 units in order to cover fixed costs and break even ($5,000/$0.50)

The following formula expresses this relationship:

Breakeven Point in Units = Total Fixed Costs/Contribution Margin per Unit

Exam Tip

CPA Exam questions will likely require you to calculate the unit sales price and variable costs by dividing total sales revenue and total variable costs by the number of units sold. If you are given total dollars, be sure to look for the number of units sold. You may also need to separately identify total variable costs and fixed costs.

Question

Markson Corporation posted sales of $2,000,000 on a sales volume of 50,000 units. Total costs were $1,700,000, of which $800,000 were fixed costs. What is the breakeven point in units?

Answer:

Sales price per unit:	$2,000,000 / 50,000 =	+ $40
Variable cost per unit:	($1,700,000 – 800,000) / 50,000 =	$18
	Contribution margin per unit =	$22
Breakeven point in units:	$800,000 / $22 = 36,364 units	

III. Using the Contribution Margin per Unit Approach to Calculate Breakeven in Sales Dollars

A. If unit information is available, breakeven point in sales dollars can easily be calculated by calculating the breakeven point in units and then multiplying the number of units by the sales price per unit.

Question

Parker Corporation sells a product for $15. Variable costs per unit are $5. Fixed costs are $700,000. What is Parker's breakeven point in sales dollars?

Answer:

Contribution margin per unit: $15 – $5 = $10

Breakeven point in units = $700,000/ $10 = 70,000 units

Breakeven point in sales dollars = 70,000 × $15 = $1,050,000

IV. Using the Contribution Margin Ratio Approach to Calculate Breakeven in Sales Dollars

A. Sometimes no unit sales price or unit variable cost information is available. In these cases, it is not possible to calculate the breakeven point in units. It is, however, still possible to calculate the breakeven point in sales dollars, but a slightly different approach must be used.

B. When no unit information is available, but total sales revenue, total variable costs, and total fixed costs are known, the breakeven point in sales dollars can be determined by calculating the contribution margin ratio. The contribution margin ratio represents the **percentage of each sales dollar that is available to cover fixed costs.**

C. For example, if total sales are $100 and variable costs are $40, then the contribution margin is $60. This means that for every $100 of sales, $60 is available to cover fixed costs.

D. If we **express the contribution margin as a ratio (or percentage) of sales dollars**, then we can say that 60% ($60/$100) of each sales dollar is available to cover fixed costs. If total fixed costs are $300, then we can calculate the number of sales dollars necessary to cover fixed costs and break even as:

(Breakeven sales × 60%) – \$300 fixed costs	=	\$0
Breakeven sales × 60%	=	\$300
Breakeven sales	=	\$300 / .60
Breakeven sales	=	\$500

E. To check to see if the answer is correct, verify that when variable costs and fixed costs are deducted from breakeven sales, the net income is zero:

+ Breakeven sales	+	\$500	100%
– Variable costs	–	\$200	40%
= Contribution margin	=	\$300	60%
– Fixed costs	–	<u>\$300</u>	
= Net income	=	<u>\$0</u>	

F. The contribution margin per unit formula used to calculate breakeven in units can be modified to calculate breakeven in sales dollars using the contribution margin ratio as follows:

Breakeven Point in Sales Dollars = Total Fixed Costs / Contribution Margin Ratio

Where:

Contribution Margin Ratio = Contribution Margin / Sales Revenue

Question
Given the following facts, calculate breakeven in sales dollars:

Sales Revenue	\$120,000
Variable Costs:	\$90,000
Fixed Costs:	\$40,000

Answer:

Breakeven point in sales dollars = <u>\$40,000</u>
25% *

Breakeven point in sales dollars = \$160,000

Where:

* Contribution Margin Ratio = <u>\$120,000 – \$90,000</u>
\$120,000

= <u>\$30,000</u>
\$120,000

= 25%

V. Multiple Product Analysis—Sometimes breakeven analysis will require calculations that involve a product mix rather than just one product. In that case we can use either a weighted-average approach or a composite (sometimes called a basket or package) approach to calculate a breakeven point for each of the products. As with single-product calculations, we can calculate a breakeven in either units or dollars. Perhaps the most intuitive approach is the composite method. This is because we mostly use the same process to solving the problems as we do with single-product scenarios.

Example

Consider a company that has two products A and B. We assume that the sales mix of these two products is constant. Let's say that the company sells twice as many products of product A as product B and other facts are as follows:

	Product A	**Product B**
Price	\$10	\$30
Variable Costs per unit	\$5	\$10

Total fixed costs are \$600,000 and the total number of products of all types that the company intends to sell is 36,000.

Question:

What is the breakeven point in units for each of products A and B?

Answer:

We are given the sales mix and contribution margin (CM) of each product. From this we can create a composite unit. Fixed costs are treated as common to both products and the individual contribution margins are multiplied by the sales mix and summed to create the composite CM. Individual breakeven points are derived by multiplying the mix by the composite units.

Product A has a CM of \$5 = \$10 – \$5; product B has a CM of \$20 = \$30 – \$10. Product A's CM of \$5 is multiplied by the mix of 2 to get \$10, and Product B's CM of \$20 is multiplied by the mix of 1 to get \$20. Then the two amounts are summed (\$10 + \$20) to get a composite CM of \$30. Using the breakeven formula of fixed costs divided by CM we find a composite breakeven point of 20,000 composite units = \$600,000/\$30. The composite units of 20,000 are multiplied by their respective mix values of 2 and 1 to arrive at individual product breakeven units of 40,000 for A and 20,000 for B.

VI. An Alternative Way of Looking at the Contribution Margin Ratio

A. Although the calculations are the same, many people find that using the common-size income statement format to calculate the contribution margin ratio makes it easier to solve these questions. The common-size format was shown in the initial example in this section and is repeated below:

+ Breakeven Sales	+	\$500	100%
– Variable Costs	–	\$200	40%
= Contribution Margin	=	\$300	60%

B. The common-size format expresses variable costs and the contribution margin as a percentage of sales. Sales is always 100%. When using this technique, you calculate the variable costs as a percentage of sales and then subtract to find the contribution margin as a percentage of sales—the contribution margin ratio.

C. Consider the following question: If sales are $750,000 and variable costs are $300,000, what is the contribution margin ratio? Start by setting up the common-size income statement format and calculate the contribution margin:

		Amount	%
+ Sales	+	$750	100%
– Variable Costs	–	$300	???%
= Contribution Margin	=	$450	???%

Next, calculate variable costs as a percentage of sales:

		Amount	%	
+ Sales	+	$750	100%	
– Variable Costs	–	$300	**40%**	<= $300 / $750
= Contribution Margin	=	$450	???%	

Then subtract to calculate the contribution margin as a percentage of sale—the contribution margin ratio:

		Amount	%
+ Sales	+	$750	100%
– Variable Costs	–	$300	40%
= Contribution Margin	=	$450	60%

You can then use the contribution margin ratio in the breakeven sales dollars formula to calculate breakeven.

Question

Martin Brothers has sales of $400,000, variable costs of $80,000, and fixed costs of $20,000. What is Martin Brothers' breakeven point in sales dollars?

Answer:

First, use the common-size format to solve for the contribution margin ratio:

		Amount	%
+ Sales	+	$400	100%
– Variable Costs	–	80	20%
= Contribution Margin	=	$320	80%

Next, use the formula for breakeven in sales dollars to calculate breakeven sales:

$$\text{Breakeven Point in Sales Dollars} = \frac{\$20{,}000}{80\%}$$

$$\text{Breakeven Point in Sales Dollars} = \$25{,}000$$

Exam Tip

As mentioned in the introduction to this section, virtually all breakeven questions involving calculations can be solved by using one of the two formulas using the contribution margin approach:

Breakeven Units = Fixed Costs / Contribution Margin per Unit

Breakeven in Sales Dollars = Fixed Costs / Contribution Margin Ratio

We expect a significant number of questions on breakeven analysis on the exam, so be sure that you know these formulas!

VII. Complicating Issues

A. The examiners may sometimes add additional factors to complicate breakeven questions and ask conceptual questions about breakeven.

B. Margin of Safety—This indicates the difference between the current sales level and the breakeven point. That is, the margin of safety indicates how much revenue can decrease before operating income becomes negative. Similar to breakeven or profit, margin of safety can be expressed in either units or dollars. For example, if sales are currently 200,000 units and the breakeven point is 150,000 units, the margin of safety would be 50,000 units. Alternatively, where sales are $180,000 and the breakeven point is $110,000, the margin of safety would be $70,000.

C. Targeted Profit—When a targeted profit beyond breakeven is specified, simply add this amount to the fixed cost in the numerator. You can think about the contribution margin on the denominator as having to cover all items in the numerator. This is exactly the same formula as breakeven, but at the breakeven level there is no profit (i.e., only fixed costs are covered by CM).

Sales in Units = (Fixed Costs + **Targeted Profit**) / Contribution Margin per Unit

1. The difference between budgeted or actual sales (in units or in dollars) and breakeven sales (in units or in dollars) is known as the margin of safety.

Question

Bexar Enterprises sells a piece of equipment for $1,000 per unit. Variable costs per unit are $500. If total fixed costs are $10,000 and Bexar wants to earn a profit of $200,000, what amount of unit sales is needed to reach this targeted profit?

Answer:

$$\text{Breakeven in units} = \frac{\$10,000 + \$200,000}{\$1,000 - \$500}$$
$$= \frac{\$210,000}{\$500}$$
$$= 420\ \textit{units}$$

D. Underlying Assumptions—In order to perform breakeven analysis, certain assumptions must hold true. First of all, for breakeven analysis to be relevant and useful, the analysis must be restricted to a relevant range of activity, so that model assumptions are at least approximately satisfied, namely: **fixed costs, unit variable costs, and price must behave as constants.** In addition:

1. **All relationships are linear**. (Note: This is why there are always straight lines, never curved lines, on breakeven charts.)
2. When multiple products are sold, the **product mix remains constant**. (Note: This is not a restrictive assumption of the model, but this condition is widely assumed in practice for problems on the CPA Exam.)
3. There are **no changes in inventory levels;** that is, the number of units sold equals the number of units produced.
   a. **Total costs can be divided** into a **fixed** component and a component that is **variable** with respect to the level of output.
   b. **Volume** is the **only driver** of costs and revenues.
   c. The model applies to operating income (i.e., the CVP model is a **before-tax model**).

Note

Again—assumptions are relevant since they only apply to a relevant range (the volume over which assumptions of the model are expected to be valid, and the volume over which operations are reasonably expected to take place).

VIII. Graphic Interpretations

A. Exam questions are likely to include diagrams of the behavior of individual costs, revenues and costs, and even budgeted revenues and costs. Candidates should expect to be required to identify lines, areas, or points on the graphs (e.g., fixed costs, breakeven point, profits, losses, etc.) or explain the causes or effects of changes in lines (e.g., what caused a change in the slope of the total costs line, what is the significance of a flatter revenue line, etc.).

B. The breakeven chart shown below is familiar to most candidates and may occasionally be used on the CPA Exam.

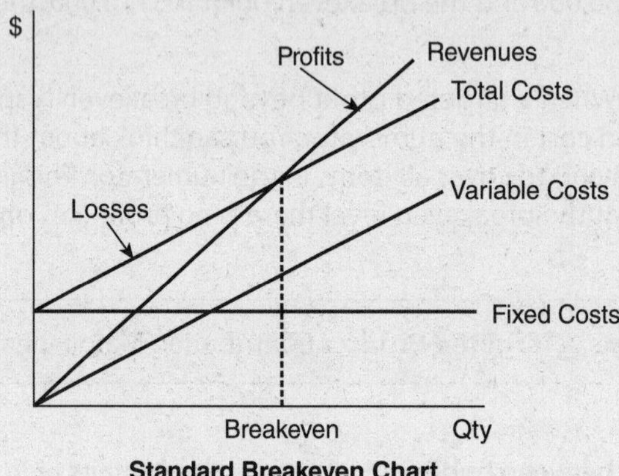

Standard Breakeven Chart

C. The following variation on the breakeven chart is likely to appear on the CPA Exam. This chart eliminates the separate display of a fixed costs line. Fixed costs are represented by the difference between total costs and variable costs, which is, by definition, fixed costs:

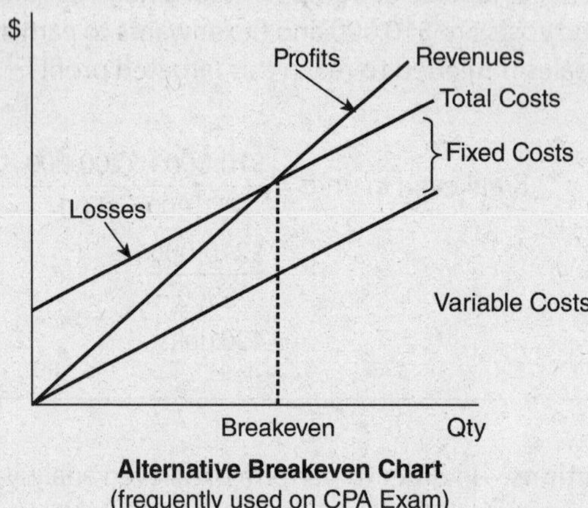

Alternative Breakeven Chart
(frequently used on CPA Exam)

D. Volume-Profit Chart

1. Another variation of the breakeven chart graphs profits (revenues less variable costs and fixed costs) instead of separately graphing revenues, fixed costs, variable costs, and total costs. In this graph, **the slope of the profit line is equal to the contribution margin**: for each unit sold, income increases by the amount of the contribution margin per unit.

2. When no units are sold, the loss is equal to fixed costs. As units are sold, losses decrease by the contribution margin times the number of units sold. At the point where the profit line crosses the x-axis, profits are zero. This is the breakeven point.

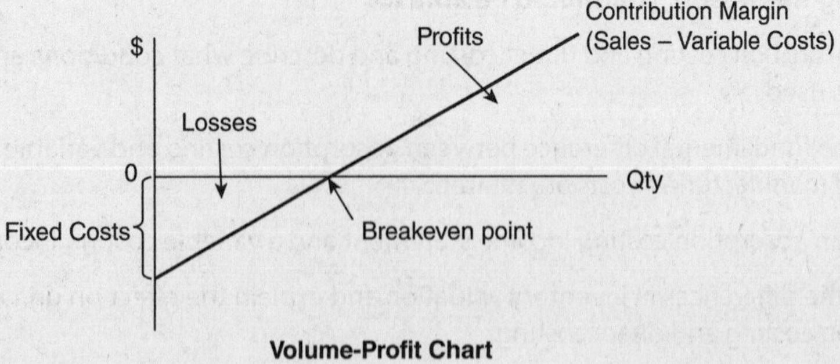

Volume-Profit Chart

3. A few additional observations about the volume-profit chart:

   a. The flatter the line, the smaller the contribution margin per unit.

   b. When comparing profit lines for multiple years and assuming that the sales price has not changed, variable costs per unit for the steeper line are less than variable costs per unit for the flatter line. Steeper lines indicate larger contribution margins; if the sales price is constant, then variable costs must be relatively smaller.

   c. Changes in the profit line's y-intercept indicate changes in fixed costs.

Note

For problems involving taxes and after-tax income, remember: The CVP model is a before-tax or operating income–based model. If you remember this, conversion to after-tax or net income is easy. Merely perform the necessary calculations while using operating income and then convert to after-tax as require.

Exam Tip

The CPA Exam is likely to test CVP by requiring the candidate to determine the breakeven point or income after changing one of the variables involved. We predict that questions will often change something and ask you to determine the effect on those. The effect on income (i.e., increase or decrease) is almost always opposite that of the effect on the breakeven point. The only exception to that is where the only change that is made involves an increase or decrease in quantity. In this instance, income will go up or down but the breakeven point will remain the same.

Absorption and Direct Costing

After studying this lesson, you should be able to:

1. Define absorption costing and direct costing and describe what conditions are present when each method is used.
2. Explain the fundamental difference between absorption costing and variable costing in terms of how fixed manufacturing costs are treated.
3. Contrast an absorption costing income statement and a variable costing income statement.
4. Contrast the differences in inventory valuation and explain the effect on unit costs when comparing absorption costing and direct costing.
5. Describe how to reconcile the difference in income between absorption costing and direct costing.

I. Two Methods

A. Absorption and direct costing are two methods of assigning manufacturing costs to inventory.

Definitions
Absorption Costing: Assigns all three factors of production (direct material, direct labor, and both fixed and variable manufacturing overhead) to inventory.

Direct Costing (also known as *variable costing*): Assigns only variable manufacturing costs (direct material, direct labor, but only variable manufacturing overhead) to inventory.

1. Absorption costing is required for external reporting purposes. This is currently true for both external financial reporting and reporting to the IRS.
2. Direct costing is frequently used for internal decision-making but *cannot* be used for external reporting.

II. Income Statement Cost Classifications

A. A manufacturing company's income statement typically displays two types of costs: product costs and period costs (or, alternatively, **manufacturing costs** and **selling and administrative costs**). To highlight the differences between absorption costing and direct costing, these two cost categories are **further decomposed into two additional groups** depending on whether the costs are **variable or fixed.**

1. **Variable manufacturing costs**
    a. **Direct material**—Materials that are feasibly traceable to the final product
    b. **Direct labor**—Wages paid to employees involved in the primary conversion of direct materials to finished goods
    c. **Variable factory overhead**—Variable manufacturing costs other than direct material and direct labor (e.g., supplies, utilities, repairs, etc.)
2. **Fixed manufacturing costs**
    a. **Fixed factory overhead**—Fixed manufacturing costs (e.g., depreciation on factory buildings and equipment, manufacturing supervisory salaries and wages, property taxes and insurance on the factory, etc.)

3. **Variable selling and administrative costs**
    a. **Selling costs**—Variable costs associated with selling the good or service (e.g., freight out, sales commissions, etc.)
    b. **Administrative costs**—Fixed costs associated with the administrative functions of an organization (e.g., office supplies, office utilities, advertising, etc.)
4. **Fixed selling and administrative costs**
    a. **Selling costs**—Fixed costs associated with selling the good or service (e.g., sales representatives' salaries, depreciation on sales-related equipment, etc.)
    b. **Administrative costs**—Fixed costs associated with the administrative functions of an organization (e.g., officers' salaries; depreciation, property taxes, and insurance on office building, and etc.)

B. The principal difference between the absorption model and the direct costing model rests on **which costs are assigned to products:**
1. The **absorption** model assigns **all manufacturing costs** to products.
2. The direct model assigns **only variable manufacturing costs** to products.

C. The following graphic details the distribution of costs under each method. Notice that the manufacturing overhead costs are split into a variable and a fixed component, and that under direct costing, while the variable overhead is included as a product cost, the fixed overhead is not:

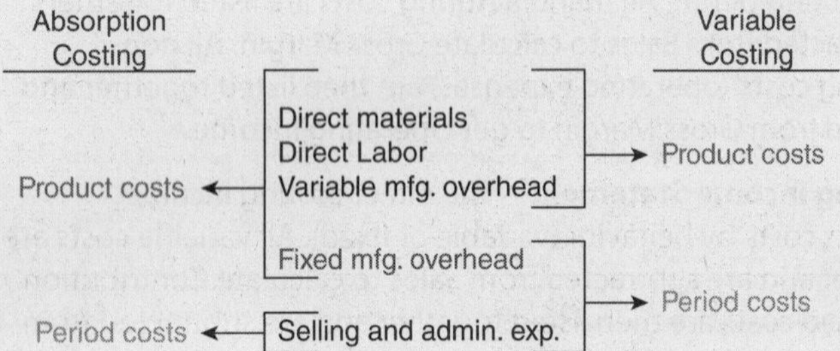

Example

Clark Corp. reported the following manufacturing costs:

Direct materials and direct labor	$700,000
Other variable manufacturing costs	100,000
Depreciation of factory building and manufacturing equipment	80,000
Other fixed manufacturing overhead	18,000

Based on this information, determine the product (inventoriable) costs under absorption costing and direct costing.

Product Costs	**Absorption Costing**	**Direct Costing**
Direct materials and direct labor	$700,000	$700,000
Other variable manufacturing costs	100,000	100,000
Depreciation of factory building and manufacturing equipment	80,000	
Other fixed manufacturing overhead	18,000	
Total inventoriable costs	$898,000	$800,000

III. Income Statement Format

A. Income statements can be prepared using full absorption and direct costing. The methods use different terminology and have different formats.

B. **Absorption Costing Income Statement**—The absorption costing income statement lists its product costs, including the fixed manufacturing costs, "above the line" and subtracts the product costs from Sales to calculate Gross Margin.

+ Sales		
– Variable Manufacturing Costs	—>	*for units sold*
<u>– Fixed Manufacturing Costs</u>	—>	*for units sold*
= **Gross Margin**		
– Variable Selling and Administrative	—>	*for units sold only*
<u>– Fixed Selling and Administrative</u>	—>	*always for total costs*
= **Operating Income**		

C. The absorption costing income statement lists costs by whether they are manufacturing or not. All manufacturing costs are listed together and are subtracted from Sales to calculate Gross Margin. All non-manufacturing costs (operating expenses) are then listed together and are subtracted from Gross Margin to get Operating Income.

D. **Direct Costing Income Statement**—The direct costing income statement lists costs by behavior (variable or fixed). All variable costs are listed together and are subtracted from Sales to calculate Contribution Margin. All fixed costs are then listed together and are subtracted from Contribution Margin to get Operating Income.

Note
All selling and administrative costs are treated as period costs regardless of whether the absorption or variable costing method is used.

Sales		
– Variable Manufacturing Costs	—>	*only for* ***units sold***
<u>– Variable Selling and Administrative Costs</u>	—>	*only for* ***units sold***
= **Contribution Margin**		
– Fixed Manufacturing Costs	—>	*always for total* **cost**
<u>– Fixed Selling and Administrative</u>	—>	*always for* **total cost**
= Operating Income		

Note
Although variable selling and administrative costs are listed along with the variable manufacturing costs (direct material, direct labor, variable manufacturing overhead) and are subtracted from sales to arrive at the contribution margin, the **variable selling and administrative costs are *not* product costs and are *not* considered part of Cost of Goods Sold**. Instead, they are always recognized as a period cost and are completely expensed each period. Fixed Manufacturing Costs are treated as period costs.

Example

Waylen Manufacturing produced and sold 200,000 espresso makers during the year for $40 each. Manufacturing and selling costs were as follows:

Direct materials and direct labor	$4,000,000
Variable manufacturing overhead	900,000
Fixed manufacturing overhead	200,000
Variable selling costs	500,000
Fixed selling costs	100,000

What was Waylen's contribution margin?

$8,000,000	Sales (200,000 × $40)
–4,000,000	Direct materials and direct labor
– 900,000	Variable manufacturing overhead
– 500,000	Variable selling costs
$2,600,000	Contribution margin

What were the inventoriable costs per unit under direct (variable) costing?

$4,000,000	Direct materials and direct labor
+ 900,000	Variable manufacturing overhead
$4,900,000	Inventoriable (product) costs
/ 200,000	units
= $24.50	per unit

E. **Effect of Product Costing Model on Operating Income**—Absorption costing and direct costing assign different costs to inventory. Since direct costing does not include fixed manufacturing costs as part of product cost, the **inventory valuation under absorption costing will always be greater than the inventory valuation under direct costing**. From an external reporting point of view, **direct costing *understates* assets on the balance sheet**.

Example

Brown Manufacturing uses direct costing for internal reporting. During the current year they reported the following costs related to the production of 1 million units:

Direct Materials	$500,000
Direct Labor	80,000
Variable Factory Overhead	100,000
Fixed Factory Overhead	120,000

Under direct costing, their unit cost is $0.68:

Unit product cost = ($500,000 + $80,000 + $100,000)/1,000,000

= $680,000/1,000,000

Under absorption costing their unit cost is $0.80:

Unit product cost = ($500,000 + $80,000 + $100,000 + $120,000)/1,000,000

= $800,000/1,000,000

F. Income Reconciliation—Explaining the difference in income between absorption costing and variable costing.

1. Because absorption costing and direct costing assign different costs to products, there may be a difference in income reported under the two methods. However, absorption costing and direct costing do not always produce different incomes. **When the number of units sold equals the number of units produced, absorption costing and direct costing produce identical incomes.** (Note: This assumes that fixed cost per unit remains the same from one period to the next.)
2. The difference between the two measures of income is due to the different treatment of fixed manufacturing costs. Direct costing deducts all fixed manufacturing costs as a lump-sum period cost when calculating income. Absorption costing assigns fixed manufacturing costs to products and therefore only deducts fixed manufacturing costs when the units are sold.
3. Depending on whether the units sold are greater than or less than the units produced, the fixed manufacturing overhead deducted under absorption costing may be greater or less than the fixed manufacturing overhead deducted under direct costing.
4. The difference can be calculated as:

Ending Inventory Units × Fixed Cost Per Unit – Beginning Inventory Units × Fixed Cost Per Unit

   a. This equation is known as the "income reconciliation rule" and is expected to be widely tested on the CPA Exam.

Example

Assume ending inventory is 5,000 units with a fixed cost per unit of $10; and beginning inventory is 2,000 units with a fixed cost per unit of $10. What is the difference in income between direct costing and absorption costing?

Answer:	5,000 × $10 = $50,000
less	2,000 × $10 = $20,000
AC income > DC income by	$30,000

G. In general:

When:	**Then:**
Units Sold = Units Produced	Absorption Costing N.I. = Direct Costing N.I.
Units Sold > Units Produced	Absorption Costing N.I. < Direct Costing N.I.
Units Sold < Units Produced	Absorption Costing N.I. > Direct Costing N.I.

IV. Comprehensive Example

Example

The following facts are assumed in the income statement examples.

Production costs:

Variable Manufacturing Costs:	$40,000
Fixed Manufacturing Costs:	$10,000
Variable Selling and Administrative Costs:	$20,000
Fixed Selling and Administrative Costs:	$10,000

Production volume: 100,000 units
Sales price per unit: $1.00
Sales volume: Varies with each example

Income statements when sales equal production (assume 100K units sold):

DIRECT I.S.		ABSORPTION I.S.	
Sales	100k	Sales	100k
Variable Manufacturing	40k	Variable Manufacturing	40k
Variable Selling and Admin	20k	Fixed Manufacturing	10k
Contribution Margin	40k	Gross Margin	50k
Fixed Manufacturing	10k	Variable Selling and Admin	20k
Fixed Selling and Admin	10k	Fixed Selling and Admin	10k
Operating Income	20k	Operating Income	20k

Since sales volume equals production volume, there is no change in inventory, and **operating income is equal under both methods.**

Income statements when sales volume is less than production volume (assume 50K units sold):

DIRECT I.S.		ABSORPTION I.S.	
Sales	50k	Sales	50k
Variable Manufacturing	20k	Variable Manufacturing	20k
Variable Selling and Admin	10k	Fixed Manufacturing	5k
Contribution Margin	20k	Gross Margin	25k
Fixed Manufacturing	10k	Variable Selling and Admin	10k
Fixed Selling and Admin	10k	Fixed Selling and Admin	10k
Operating Income	-0-	Operating Income	5k

Since sales volume is less than production volume, inventory levels must increase. Under absorption (full accrual) costing, the units going into inventory include the fixed manufacturing costs. That is, a portion of the fixed manufacturing costs appears on the balance sheet rather than the income statement. Under direct costing, the total fixed manufacturing costs are included on the income statement as a period expense. Therefore, **income under direct costing is smaller than income under absorption costing.**

Income statements when sales volume is greater than production volume (assume 150K units sold):

DIRECT I.S.		ABSORPTION I.S.	
Sales	150k	Sales	150k
Variable Manufacturing	60k	Variable Manufacturing	60k
Variable Selling and Admin	30k	Fixed Manufacturing	15k
Contribution Margin	60k	Gross Margin	75k
Fixed Manufacturing	10k	Variable Selling and Admin	30k
Fixed Selling and Admin	10k	Fixed Selling and Admin	10k
Operating Income	40k	Operating Income	35k

Since sales volume is greater than production volume, inventory levels must decrease. Under absorption (full accrual) costing, the units coming out of inventory include both fixed and variable manufacturing costs. That is, a portion of the fixed manufacturing costs from a prior period is included on the income statement in addition to the fixed manufacturing costs from the current period. Under direct costing, the units coming out of inventory include only the variable manufacturing costs. Only the fixed manufacturing costs for the current period are included on the income statement. Therefore, income under absorption costing is smaller than income under direct (variable) costing.

Job Costing

After studying this lesson, you should be able to:

1. Differentiate the manufacturing environments appropriate for job costing versus process costing.
2. Perform the three steps in allocating overhead using a simple resource driver.
3. Demonstrate the journal entries necessary for applying manufacturing overhead to work-in-process.

I. **Introduction**—Job order costing is used to accumulate costs related to the production of **large, relatively expensive, heterogeneous (custom-ordered) items.** Costing follows the general rules for manufacturing cost flows and is relatively straightforward:

   A. Costs are accumulated in individual work-in-process (WIP) accounts called job order cost sheets, the total of which is accounted for in the WIP control account.

   B. Overhead (OH) is applied based on a predetermined OH rate.

   C. When goods are completed, costs flow on to finished goods and when sold, costs flow into cost of goods sold (COGS).

Note
Job costing is compatible with the use of normal costing, standard costing, and variance analysis.

Example
Mercury Enterprises produces custom surfboards and uses a job order costing system to assign costs to WIP and finished goods inventories. Mercury applies OH to production using a predetermined annual OH rate. The following information is available from Mercury's accounting system for the fiscal year:

Direct labor (DL) costs	$53,500
Direct materials (DMs) issued to production	$45,000
Indirect materials issued to production	$4,000
Manufacturing OH applied	$56,500
Actual manufacturing OH incurred	$67,500

Mercury's beginning WIP inventory was $8,000 and ending WIP inventory was $6,000. What was the cost of jobs completed (i.e., equal to cost of goods manufactured) during the year?

+ Beginning WIP	$ 8,000
+ Direct materials cost	$ 45,000
+ DL costs	$ 53,500
+ Manufacturing OH applied	$ 56,500
= Total manufacturing costs to account for:	$163,000
– Ending WIP	$ 6,000
= Cost of goods manufactured	$157,000

II. **Overhead Allocation**—Direct materials and direct labor are traced to the WIP account, but OH must be allocated to WIP. Since overhead costs are typically not directly traceable to specific units of production, an estimated overhead amount is applied to production based on a predetermined rate. Actual OH costs are accumulated separately. At the end of the period, the applied OH is compared to the actual OH and an entry is made to adjust any difference.

   A. **Predetermined OH Application Rate**—The first step in applying OH to WIP is to calculate the rate that will be used to apply overhead to production. The rate is based on an estimated OH amount divided by an estimated allocation base amount (e.g., machine hours or [DLH]). The measure of activity or volume should have some plausible relationship to the OH charges. For example, if production were highly automated, then machine hours would be a likely choice. Where production is more labor paced, DLH might be a reasonable allocation base.

1. The formula for developing the predetermined overhead rate (POR) is:

POR = Estimated Total OH Costs **/ Estimated** Activity Volume

2. The result of this calculation is the **OH allocation rate** (or **OH application rate**). The OH allocation rate is normally established prior to the beginning of the period. That is, it is a predetermined rate.

Exam Tip
Estimated amounts based on **currently attainable capacity** are always used for this formula, *not* **historical, ideal, or theoretical amounts**. This is likely to be a frequently tested concept on the CMA exam.

B. **Applied OH**—The amount of estimated OH charged to production. Applied OH is calculated by multiplying the POROH by the actual number of units used in production (e.g., DLH or machine hours).

1. Applied OH is included in the cost of WIP by the following entry:

DR: Work-in-Process	XXX	
CR: Factory OH Applied		XXX

C. **Actual OH**—The amount actually paid for OH expenses. These costs are initially charged to the specific expense account (i.e., supplies inventory, utilities, maintenance, supervision, etc.) and to the factory OH control account. For example:

DR: Factory OH Control—Utilities Expense	XXX	
CR: Accounts Payable		XXX

D. **Closing Out the OH Accounts**—At the end of the period the factory OH control account (which contains the actual OH costs) and the factory OH applied account (which contains the OH costs that were applied to production using the POROH) are closed out.

1. For example, assume that the actual OH costs were $50,000 and the OH costs applied to production were also $50,000. The following entry would close (zero out) the OH accounts:

DR: Factory OH Applied	$50,000	
CR: Factory OH Control		$50,000

2. Of course, it is unusual for the estimated OH applied to production and the actual OH costs to be equal. Usually there are differences between the amount of applied OH and the amount of actual OH.

   a. **Immaterial differences** between the two amounts are usually allocated to COGS.

   b. If the **difference** is **material**, it should be **prorated to WIP**, **finished goods, and COGS** based on their respective ending balances.

Exam Tip
The treatment of material differences between actual and applied OH is likely to be tested on the CPA Exam.

E. Overapplied Factory OH—When more OH costs are applied to products than are actually incurred, factory OH is said to be overapplied. When the accounts are closed at the end of the period, overapplied OH reduces Cogs.

Question
Priceless Products incurs $20,000 in actual OH costs during the period. Using their predetermined OH allocation formula, Priceless applied $21,000 to products as OH costs, resulting in $1,000 of overapplied OH. Priceless regards this amount as immaterial and charges over-/underapplied OH to COGS at the end of the period when the accounts are closed. How will this entry affect COGS?

Answer:
COGS will decrease when the accounts are closed:

DR: Factory OH Applied	$21,000	
CR: Factory OH Control		$20,000
CR: COGS		$ 1,000

F. Underapplied Factory OH—When more OH costs are actually incurred during the period than are applied to products, factory OH is said to be underapplied. When the accounts are closed at the end of the period, underapplied OH increases COGS.

Question
Cost Conscious Products incurs $10,000 in actual OH costs during the period. Using their predetermined OH allocation formula, Cost Conscious applied $9,500 to products as OH costs. If Cost Conscious charges over-/underapplied OH to COGS at the end of the period when the accounts are closed, how will this affect COGS?

Answer:
COGS will increase when the accounts are closed:

DR: Factory OH Applied	$ 9,500	
DR: Cost of Goods Sold	$ 500	
CR: Factory OH Control		$10,000

G. Summary of OH Application—There are **three steps** to allocation of OH and they take place at different times during the year.

1. At the **beginning of the year**, we calculate the **OHPOR**. For example, estimated OH is divided by estimated DLH.
2. **During the year**, we periodically allocate OH by multiplying the OHPOR by the actual units of the allocation base.
3. At the **end of the year** we dispose of over-/underapplied OH by taking the difference between actual OH and applied OH to COGS.

4. Numerical Example

Example

Assume the following data and assume OH is applied based on DLH:

Estimated DLH	$100,000
Estimated OH dollars	200,000
Actual DLH	300,000
Actual OH dollars	400,000

Steps are as follows:

1. Calculate the POR: $200,000 / 100,000 DLH = $2 per DLH

2. Apply OH: $2 (300,000 DLH) = $600,000

3. Dispose of the difference in applied versus actual OH:

$600,000 – $400,000 = $200,000 to COGS

H. Additional Points

1. Make sure that you know **which type of OH** to use in these calculations and when to use them. There are three different types: estimated, applied, and actual.
2. Make sure that you multiply the POR by "ACTUAL" units in Step 2.
3. Make sure you know what happens during the different times of the year and which OH amounts are relevant.
4. The terms *budgeted* and *estimated* mean the same thing. Also, the terms *allocated* and *applied* mean the same thing.
5. Be sure to **memorize** this three-step process. It is one of the most widely used calculations you are likely to see on the CPA Exam.

Process Costing

After studying this lesson, you should be able to:

1. Identify and explain the steps in the solution for process costing calculations.
2. Calculate cost per equivalent unit.
3. Calculate the value of work-in-process inventory and the cost of goods transferred out of work-in-process.
4. Explain the approach for accounting for transferred-in costs.

I. Process Costing—Process costing is used to accumulate costs for **mass-produced, continuous, homogeneous items, which are often small and inexpensive**. Since costs are not accumulated for individual items, the accounting problem becomes one of tracking the number of units moving through the work-in-process (WIP) into finished goods (FG) and allocating the costs incurred to these units on a rational basis. The cost allocation process is complicated because:

   A. There may be partially completed items in beginning and ending inventories.

   B. Each of the three factors of production (labor, material, and overhead) may be at different levels of completion, making it necessary to perform separate calculations for each factor.

   C. Some costs do not occur uniformly across the process; this is particularly true for direct materials (DMs). This is why the two categories of the factors of production indicated are typically DMs and conversion costs (i.e., direct labor [DL] and overhead [OH]). DL and OH are normally included together because they are typically uniformly incurred.

Note
Process costing is compatible with the use of normal costing, standard costing, and variance analysis.

II. Three-Step Solution Process

   A. The following steps walk you all the way through the process of allocating costs to WIP and FG for a single factor of production. Since the three factors of production—raw materials, labor, and OH—do not usually accumulate evenly across the production process, the process must be repeated for each of the three factors of production. The three steps are:

   B. Step 1—Determine equivalent units

      1. Clearly identify the physical flow of units. As units move through the production process, each processing department adds material and conversion costs (i.e., labor, and OH) to WIP. As goods move from department to department through the manufacturing process, these costs accumulate.

      2. At the beginning of each period, the units in beginning WIP are, by definition, only partially complete. The completion rate for beginning WIP inventory reflects the work done "to date," meaning during the prior period. A different percentage of completion is normally associated with each factor of production. During the period, fully completed units are transferred to the next department or to FG. At the end of the period, the units remaining in ending WIP are, by definition, at various stages of completion for each factor of production (i.e., DM and conversion costs).

      3. The next chart summarizes the flow of physical units through a single department's manufacturing process and identifies the percentage of completion of the beginning and ending WIP inventory. For this chart, assume that the following numbers of units and percentages of completion are given:

	Physical Units	% of Completion
+ Units in Beg. WIP	+ 20,000	10%
+ Units Added to Production	+ 30,000	—
= Total Units to Account for	= 50,000	—
− Units in Ending WIP	− 10,000	50%
= Units Transferred to Finished Goods	= 40,000	always 100%

Note
This analysis follows the same "account analysis" format used to create the Schedule of COGS and the schedule of cost of goods manufactured (see the "Manufacturing Costs" lesson). You should provide a column to calculate physical units as shown above and a separate column to calculate EU for each of the two types of factors of production (i.e., DM and conversion costs). The following illustrations use only one factor of production since the approach is the same for both.

4. The first task is to calculate the **physical units** to account for. Here they are given, but often you will have limited information. For example, sometimes you will be given only one of the inventories (either beginning or ending) and have you work backward to figure out total units to account for. Use the logical setup in the chart in Section II.B.3 above to help you do that. To make this easy, you should remember that total units to account for will involve two pieces of information: either (units started + units not started) or (units finished + units not finished).
   - **a.** Beginning inventory represents units not started this period, while units added to production are units started. Adding those two sets of units will always give you total units to account for.
   - **b.** Conversely, if you are given ending inventory, you should understand that "units completed and transferred out" provides units finished, while ending inventory provides units not finished, again providing the total units to account for.
   - **c.** Taking this logical approach will always ensure that you know how many physical units to account for.
5. Calculate EU. The term **equivalent units** (EU) refers to the **number of whole units that could have been produced** during the period in terms of cost incurred. For example, the cost associated with six units that are 50% complete is equivalent to the cost associated with three units that are 100% complete.
6. Because the units in beginning and ending WIP inventory can be at different percentages of completion in terms of cost, **the number of physical units remaining in ending WIP inventory plus the units transferred to FG does not reflect the actual work done.** The fraction of work done on the partially completed units in beginning and ending WIP must be taken into account.
7. Solving for the EU of production will depend on which method is being used: weighted average or first in, first out (FIFO).
   - **a.** Weighted average uses only two categories: goods completed and ending inventory. The format will differ in that weighted average combines prior period work (i.e., beginning inventory) with current period work (units finished this period not in [BI]) to determine "goods completed."
   - **b.** The FIFO method uses three categories, separating (1) beginning inventory from (2) the new or current period completed work (called "units started and finished"), while (3) ending inventory (at least for EU) is treated the same as with weighted average.
8. Using the data introduced, use the format below to organize your computation of physical units and EU for the two methods.

Weighted Average:	Physical	% of Completion Multiplier	Equivalent Units
Goods completed	40,000	100%	40,000
Ending inventory	10,000	50%	5,000
Total	50,000		45,000

FIFO:	Physical	% of Completion Multiplier	Equivalent units
Beginning inventory	20,000	100% – 10% = 90%	18,000
Units started and finished	20,000	100%	20,000
Ending inventory	10,000	50%	5,000
Total	50,000		

9. **You should notice several things about the format presented just above.**
   a. **Physical** units are the same (in total) regardless of the EU method used.
   b. The **question stems** in CMA exam problems stating percentage of completion for the ending inventory EU calculation is likely to be communicated in terms of how much dollar-equivalent work was completed in the **current period**. However, the percentage of completion for beginning inventory is typically stated in terms of how much dollar-equivalent work was completed in the **prior period**. This is often confusing to candidates. To make this easier to understand, think about the fact that the FIFO method is interested in calculating **current-period** information separately from prior-period information. As such, FIFO wants to know the EU of work done on the beginning inventory **this current period**. That is why you are required to use the complement (100% – 10%) in the calculation of beginning inventory EU.
   c. Regarding the percentage of completion multiplier: For the weighted average method, the goods completed amount will always be 100%. For the FIFO method, the *units started and finished* will always be 100%. Ending inventory will be the same equivalent units amount for *both* methods. Physical units will, of course, be the same regardless of the method used to calculate equivalent units.
   d. The ultimate goal in calculating equivalent units is to divide the WIP inventory account between (1) work finished and transferred out and (2) ending WIP inventory.
   e. A T-account can be used to check your work and to help display how these two pieces of WIP are relevant. The following T-account provides an example. We know how the *physical* units are divided from the 50,000 units available shown on the left below, and we will use the EU concept to determine (1) the cost of units transferred out and (2) the value of the ending WIP inventory shown in the T-account.

Note
The term "cost of goods transferred out" is often used in process costing rather than the "cost of goods finished" since the units could be transferred through several departments prior to going to FG inventory. Cost of goods finished would only accurately apply to the last department in the sequence.

WIP Inventory—Physical Units

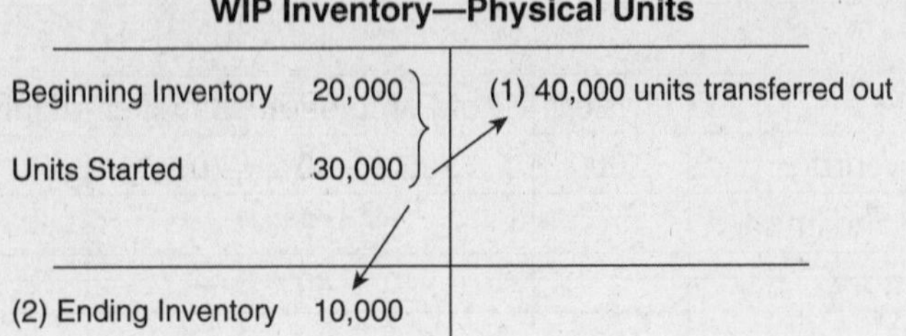

Example

Calculate the equivalent units of production for both the weighted average and the FIFO methods assuming:

Beginning WIP	= 2,000 units, 30% complete
Units started during the period	= 6,000 units
Units transferred out	= 5,000 units
Ending inventory is 40% complete	

Begin by providing the format presented below and inserting all the information we are given that involves no calculations. This includes the **physical** units for beginning inventory and the % of completion. Beginning inventory is 2,000 units at 30% completion, so we insert that information for the FIFO approach (recall that for beginning inventory, we use the complement 1 – 30%). We also know that goods completed and units started and finished are 100%. Goods completed are the same thing as units transferred out because they cannot be transferred out unless they are completed. In addition, we are given the % completion of ending inventory as 40%.

Weighted Average:	Physical	% of Completion Multiplier	Equivalent Units
Goods completed	5,000	100%	
Ending inventory		40%	
Total			

FIFO:	Physical	% of Completion Multiplier	Equivalent Units
Beginning inventory	2,000	100% – 30% = 70%	
Units started and finished		100%	
Ending inventory		40%	
Total			

In this problem, we are not given the ending inventory units, nor are we given the units started and finished. However, we can compute those based on finding the **total units to account for** and working backward. The total units to account for is equal to the sum of all of the units started (6,000 units) and all of the units not started (beginning inventory of 2,000 units), equaling 8,000 units to account for.

Weighted Average:	Physical	% of Completion Multiplier	Equivalent Units
Goods completed	5,000	100%	
Ending inventory		40%	
Total	8,000		

FIFO:	Physical	% of Completion Multiplier	Equivalent Units
Beginning inventory	2,000	100% – 30% = 70%	
Units started and finished		100%	
Ending inventory		40%	
Total	8,000		

Now that we know the physical units to account for, we subtract goods completed of 5,000 units from the total of 8,000 units to determine the ending inventory of 3,000 units. This leaves only the units started and finished to compute, which can be found by subtracting known categories from the total as before to arrive at 3,000 units for units started and finished. Extending these amounts by the multipliers completes the equivalent units calculation as shown.

Weighted Average:	Physical	% of Completion Multiplier	Equivalent Units
Goods completed	5,000	100%	5,000
Ending inventory	3,000	40%	1,200
Total	8,000		6,200

FIFO:	Physical	% of Completion Multiplier	Equivalent Units
Beginning inventory	2,000	1–30%	1,400
Units started and finished	3,000	100%	3,000
Ending inventory	3,000	40%	1,200
Total	8,000		5,600

C. **Step 2**—Determine the cost per equivalent unit.

1. First determine the total costs to account for; the following costs are usually accumulated during the period:
    a. **Beginning WIP costs**—The total costs of production (material, labor, and overhead) that were allocated to the production units during previous periods.
    b. **Transferred-in costs**—The costs of production (material, labor, and overhead) from previous departments that flow with the production items from department to department.
    c. **Current-period costs**—The transfer costs and costs of production (material, labor, and OH) added to the WIP during the current period.
    d. **Total costs to account for**—The total of the beginning WIP costs, the transfer-in costs, and the current period costs. Total costs must be allocated to ending WIP inventory and to FG inventory at the end of the period.

Exam Tip
Costs of units transferred in from a previous department are significant complications that are not likely to be tested on the exam.

2. The type of cost flow assumption used impacts which costs are used to determine the unit price.
    a. **Weighted average cost flow**—Under the weighted-average cost flow assumption, the **beginning WIP inventory costs are added to the current period** costs (including transfer-in costs, if any) before dividing by the EU figure. This process averages the two cost pools together.
    b. **FIFO cost flow**—Under the FIFO cost flow assumption, the costs associated with prior period work on beginning WIP inventory are transferred to FG in their entirety. The current period (equivalent) unit cost is determined by dividing the **current period costs (including transfer-in costs, if any)** by the EU added to production during the current period.

Note
Regardless of the cost flow assumption, all costs must be allocated either to ending WIP inventory or to FG.

Example

Assume that the direct labor costs associated with beginning WIP inventory were $640. An additional $2,600 in DL costs were added during the period.

What is the total cost to be allocated using the weighted-average cost flow assumption? $3,240—the current period costs of $2,600 plus the $640 of costs associated with beginning WIP inventory.

What is the total cost to be allocated using the FIFO cost flow assumption? $2,600—the current period costs; the $640 of costs associated with beginning WIP inventory are transferred to finished goods in their entirety.

3. Calculate the cost per EU. Once the correct EU number and total costs to allocate have been determined (based on the specified cost flow assumption), calculation of the EU cost is straightforward: simply divide the cost to be allocated by the EU.

Example

Continuing with the previous example, the following information has been collected:

Cost Flow Assumption	Equivalent Units	Costs to Allocate
Weighted Average	6,200	$3,240
FIFO	5,600	$2,600

What is the unit cost using the weighted-average cost flow assumption? $0.5226 per unit ($3,240/6,200).

What is the unit cost using the FIFO cost flow assumption? $0.4643 per unit ($2,600/5,600).

D. **Step 3**—Determine (a) cost of goods transferred out of WIP and (b) ending WIP inventory.

1. Use the cost per EU to value the ending WIP inventory and the cost of goods transferred out (recall that this is the ultimate purpose of the two methods). The calculation of **ending inventory** values is straightforward by multiplying the respective cost per EU from each of the two methods by the ending inventory EU:

Weighted average ending WIP inventory $627 = 1,200 ($0.5226).

FIFO ending WIP inventory $557 = 1,200 ($0.4643).

a. Note that although the number of ending WIP inventory equivalent units (1,200 EU) are the same regardless of whether weighted average or FIFO is used, the dollar amounts *will* be different due to the difference in the cost per equivalent unit between the methods.

2. To value the **cost of goods transferred out** for each of the methods, weighted-average is considerably different from FIFO. This is because weighted average averages the two periods' work together while FIFO separately values the cost of goods transferred out by period. For weighted average, **using the table from step 1**, we simply multiply the cost per EU by the goods completed and transferred out (5,000) to provide the final valuation of cost of goods completed.

Weighted Average cost of goods transferred out: $2,613 = 5,000 ($0.5226)

Weighted Average:	Physical	% of Completion Multiplier	Equivalent Units
Goods completed	5,000	100%	5,000
Ending inventory	3,000	40%	1,200
Total	8,000		6,200

3. The calculation for FIFO is similar in that EU are multiplied by the cost per EU for the remaining categories **shown in bold in the table below**, but we must remember that this EU total accounts for the work done in the current period only. Because of this, we must calculate the current period work and add this to the prior period work (beginning inventory amount given to us) to compute the cost of goods transferred out.

Current period work \$2,043 = (1,400 Beginning Inventory + 3,000 Units Started and Finished) = 4,400 EU × \$0.4643 = \$2,043

Plus: Prior period costs \$640 (given)

FIFO cost of goods transferred out \$ = 2,683 = \$2,043 + \$640.

FIFO:	Physical	% of Completion Multiplier	Equivalent Units
Beginning inventory	2,000	100% – 30% = 70%	1,400
Units started and finished	3,000	100%	3,000
Ending inventory	3,000	40%	1,200
Total	8,000		5,600

Study Tip

After calculating these amounts, it is useful to check your work (if you have time) by adding the ending inventory valuation amount to the cost of goods transferred out to determine whether that amount is equal to the total costs to account for. This amount will, in total, be the same for the two methods:

Weighted-average	\$627 WIP + \$2,613 Transferred out = \$3,240
FIFO	\$557 WIP + \$2,683 Transferred out = \$3,240

4. To further illustrate what happened to the amounts, we can again refer to a T-account presentation—this time in dollars rather than units. This requires a separate presentation for the two methods:

Weighted-Average:

WIP Inventory—Weighted-Average Dollars

Debit	Credit
Beginning Inventory \$640 }	\$2,613 Goods completed and transferred out
Production Started \$2,600	
Ending Inventory \$627	

FIFO:

WIP Inventory—FIFO Dollars

Debit	Credit
Beginning Inventory \$640 }	\$2,683 Goods completed and transferred out
Production Started \$2,600	
Ending Inventory \$557	

Joint and By-Product Costing

After studying this lesson, you should be able to:

1. Differentiate the characteristics of joint products from those of by-products and scrap.
2. Recognize terminology related to joint costing, including joint costs, separable costs, and the split-off point.
3. Explain the physical volume, sales value at split-off, and net realizable value methods of joint cost allocation, and perform calculations for each method.
4. Describe the options for the accounting treatment of revenue for by-products.

I. **Joint Products and By-Products are Similar**—They are both the result of a single manufacturing process that yields multiple products. They both face the accounting problem of allocation of the shared costs of production. Two or more products of *significant sales value* are said to be joint products when they:

   A. Are produced from the same set of raw materials; and

   B. Are not separately identifiable until a *split-off point*.

II. **Joint Products Frequently Receive Further Processing After the Split-Off Point**

   A. **Split-Off**—Is the point at which products manufactured through a common process are differentiated and processed separately.

   B. **Separable Costs**—Are additional processing costs incurred beyond the split-off point. Separable costs are attributable to individual products and can be assigned directly.

   C. **Cost Allocation**—Joint costs may be allocated to the joint products in several ways:

      1. **Relative physical volume**—Costs are allocated based on the quantity of products produced. The total volume of all products is established (pounds, feet, gallons, etc.), each product's pro rata share is determined, and the joint costs are allocated based on that proportion.

Question

Joint costs to be allocated: $300,000

	Volume	Proportion	Allocation
Product A	10,000 gal.	_______	_______
Product B	30,000 gal.	_______	_______
Product C	40,000 gal.	_______	_______

Answer:

	Volume	Proportion	Allocation
Product A	10,000 gal.	12.5%	$37,500
Product B	30,000 gal.	37.5%	$112,500
Product C	40,000 gal.	50.0%	$150,000
TOTAL	80,000 gal.	100.0%	$300,000

      2. **Relative sales value at split-off**—Costs are allocated based on the relative sales values of the products either at split-off or after additional processing. When significant markets exist for

the products at the split-off point, the relative sales value of each product at the split-off point can be used to allocate costs.

Question
Joint costs to be allocated: $200,000

	Relative Value	Proportion	Allocation
Product A	$40,000	______	______
Product B	$10,000	______	______
Product C	$50,000	______	______

Answer:

	Relative Value	Proportion	Allocation
Product A	$40,000	40%	$80,000
Product B	$10,000	10%	$20,000
Product C	$50,000	50%	$100,000
TOTAL	$100,000	100%	$200,000

3. **Net realizable value**—Often used when there is no market at split-off, the NRV method uses the ratio of the net realizable value of each product (i.e., final sales value *less any additional separable processing costs* of each product) to the total net realizable value to allocate costs.

Question
Joint costs to be allocated: $200,000

	Ultimate Sales Value	Add'lCosts Beyond Split	Net Realizable Value	Proportion	Allocation
Product A	$ 25,000	$0	______	______	______
Product B	$135,000	$35,000	______	______	______
Product C	$100,000	$25,000	______	______	______

Answer:

	Ultimate Sales Value	Add'l Costs Beyond Split	Net Realizable Value	Proportion	Allocation
Product A	$ 25,000	$0	$25,000	12.5%	$25,000
Product B	$135,000	$35,000	$100,000	50.0%	$100,000
Product C	$100,000	$25,000	$75,000	37.5%	$75,000

III. **By-Products**—By-products differ from joint products in that they have relatively insignificant sales value when compared to the main product(s).

A. **Costing**—Because of their relatively insignificant sales value, by-products usually are not allocated a share of the joint costs of production. However, when by-products are processed beyond split-off, the additional processing costs are assigned to the by-product. These costs reduce the proceeds ultimately recognized from the sale of the by-product.

B. **Net Proceeds from the Sale of By-Products**—Are sometimes used to reduce the cost of the main products.

C. Proceeds—May be recognized in several ways:

1. **Recognize when produced**—The ultimate sales value of the by-product (less any additional costs necessary to sell the by-product) is deducted from the joint cost of the main products *produced* when the by-product is *produced*. This method is preferable as it automatically allocates the cost reductions to cost of goods sold and ending inventory.
2. **Recognize when sold**—When the by-product value is recognized at the time of sale, the net proceeds can be recorded as other revenue, other income, or as a reduction in cost of goods sold.

D. By-Product Examples

Examples

By-Product Cost Treatment as Other Revenue

Where **sales are recorded** for a by-product, the net realizable value from the sale is used to reduce joint costs, and no profit is recognized on sales. Consider the following:

From each batch produced, Sam obtains 1000 gallons of product A, 200 gallons of product B, and 20 gallons of a by-product. The by-product can be sold for $4 per gallon. In this case, management chooses not to assign any cost to the by-product and it is not inventoried. All of the production cost is allocated to the main products A and B, and the by-product's cost is merely recorded as miscellaneous revenue (20 gallons at $4 per gallon = $80). This method is sometimes preferred when the revenue generated by the by-product is insignificant.

By-Product Cost Treatment as a Reduction in Production Cost

Assume the same facts as above except that the by-product value is **recognized at the time of production**. This is the most common scenario if the net realizable value (NRV) is significant. The by-product's NRV ($80) is deducted from the joint products' total cost prior to allocation (i.e., cost is reduced by $80) and by-product inventory would be carried at NRV. Keeping track of by-products with inventory is more important for control when the amount is larger.

Important: Remember that (1) if the by-product is treated as revenue, then there is no effect on the total joint costs; and (2) if the by-product is treated as a reduction in cost of the joint costs, then there will be no cost basis for the by-product and no impact on revenue. Treating the by-product's impact as miscellaneous revenue recognizes the by-product as relatively insignificant.

IV. Scrap—Scrap is a remnant of the production process which has some, but typically comparatively little, recovery value. Scrap is seldom processed beyond the split-off point.

A. The net proceeds from the sale of scrap are used to reduce overhead costs (credit to factory overhead control) or, if material, the sale can be recorded as revenue.

Sales and Direct Cost Variance Analysis

After studying this lesson, you should be able to:

1. Describe standard costing and related concepts in the context of variance analysis.
2. Explain the treatment of variances based on different levels of significance.
3. Calculate revenue variances and direct cost variances, including price/rate and quantity/efficiency variances for direct material and direct labor.
4. Analyze sales variances using quantity and price differences from budgeted amounts.

I. Types of Standards

A. Standards are predetermined or targeted costs. Standards are similar to budgeted amounts stated on a per unit basis, but standards differ from budgets in that they actually appear in general ledger accounts, while budgeted amounts do not. Standards are developed for each factor of production (materials, labor, and overhead) and usually fit into one of two broad categories:

1. **Ideal/theoretical standards**—Ideal standards **presume perfect efficiency and 100% capacity**.
    a. ***Not useful* for control purposes** as they are not practically attainable
2. **Currently attainable standards**—Currently attainable standards are based on **higher than average levels of efficiency**, but are clearly achievable
    a. Typically used for employee motivation, product costing, and budgeting

B. **Some other concepts about variances:**

1. Standards are ***not* only based on historical performance** as this may incorporate past periods' inefficiencies.
2. Standards may be used **by service organizations as well as manufacturing organizations**. They may be used in **both process costing and job-order costing** environments.
3. Standards **may be used to value inventories** (raw materials, WIP, FG) and **cost of goods sold** as long as they:
    a. Are based on currently attainable performance
    b. Do not result in significant variances
4. Variances may also be calculated for sales revenues. Sales variances are based on the **budgeted or planned sales price**.

Exam Tip
Be sure that you understand these conceptual issues since we predict more than half of the variance questions on the CPA Exam will be directed toward the prior points.

II. Variance Calculations

A. Variance analysis analyzes the difference between standard costs and actual costs. When standard costs are used to value inventories, the variance must be written off:

1. **Non-significant variances**—Write off to **CGS**.
2. **Significant variances**—Allocate to ending work-in-process, finished goods, and cost of goods sold.

B. Variance analysis divides the difference between actual costs and standard costs into two parts:

1. Differences due to the **cost of the resource** (price per pound, labor rate per hour, etc.)
2. Differences due to the **quantity used** (gallons, pounds, feet, labor hours, etc.)

C. These variances are given different names depending on the factor of production:

	Differences in Cost	**Differences in Quantity**
Materials	Price Variance*	Usage Variance
Labor	Rate Vari.ance	Efficiency Variance**

*Price variances are often considered to be the responsibility of the purchasing department and are separated from the goods before they enter the production process.

**Although different terminology is sometimes used, price and rate variances are equivalent concepts as are usage and efficiency variances.

Exam Tip
The following method of calculating variances offers an extremely effective and efficient approach to solving variance questions on the CPA Exam. It is, however, quite different from the approach found in most academic texts and courses. The traditional approach to variance analysis is shown in Section VI of this lesson.

D. Variance calculation is a two-step process:

1. Calculate the differences in rates, quantities, and total cost (rate X quantity).
2. Use the differences in rates and quantities to calculate the variances.

III. Step 1: Calculating the Differences—When calculating cost variances, it is best to use the following format:

+ Standard Amount
– Actual Amount
= Difference/Variance

A. When cost variances are calculated in this manner, **negative numbers indicate unfavorable variances and positive numbers indicate favorable variances.**

Example
Mills Company used 80 hours of labor at a cost of $15 per hour to complete 40 steel doors. Based on the company's labor standards for the door, they should have used 85 hours of labor at a cost of $13 per hour to complete the 40 doors. Which of the following correctly states the nature of the variances?

	Efficiency Variance	**Rate Variance**	**Total Variance**
A.	Favorable	Favorable	Favorable
B.	Favorable	Unfavorable	Favorable
C.	Unfavorable	Favorable	Unfavorable
D.	Favorable	Unfavorable	Unfavorable

Answer:

	Quantity		Rate		Total
+ Standard Amount	85	×	$13	=	$1105
– Actual Amount*	80	×	$15	=	$1200
= Difference/Variance	5		($2)		($95)

D is the correct answer:

The positive difference in quantities allowed indicates a favorable quantity variance.

The negative difference in rates indicates an unfavorable rate variance.

The negative difference in the total cost indicates an overall unfavorable variance in total.

B. **A Note about the Standard Quantity**—The "standard quantity" is the "**standard quantity allowed for actual production**." For example, if the standard amount of aluminum required to produce a sheet of siding is 2 lbs. and 50 pieces of siding are produced, then the "standard quantity allowed for actual production" is 100 lbs.

IV. **Step 2: Calculating the Variances**—The differences in rate and quantity are used to calculate the price/rate variance and the usage/efficiency variance as follows:

Price/Rate Variance = Difference in Rates × Actual Quantity

Usage/Efficiency Variance = Difference in Quantities × Standard Rate

Example

Standard materials usage and cost for one unit of Product A is 6 lbs. at $2.00 per lb. Actual units produced were 20 units; 100 lbs. of raw material at a total cost of $225 were used in production. Calculate the materials price and usage variances for Product A.

Answer:

Price/rate variance = ($2.25 – $2.00) 100 lbs. = $25.00 Unfavorable

Usage/efficiency variance = (100 lbs. – 120 lbs.) $2.00 = $40.00 Favorable

Standard Quantity Allowed for Actual Production = 6 lbs. × 20 units = 120 lbs.

Note that the $2.25 actual price was not given in the problem, but was derived from the two related numbers, which were given: 100 lbs. actual quantity used and total price of $225.00

A. **Checking your work**—Notice that the total variance calculated in the analysis format by subtracting total actual costs from total standard costs ($240.00 – $225.00 = $15.00) is the same as the total variance calculated by summing the usage variance and the price variance ($40.00 + ($25.00) = $15.00). When these two independently calculated totals are the same, you can be relatively certain that your calculations are accurate.

Note

Although in this instance we have calculated the price and usage variances together, when price is not controllable by production supervisors, the price variance is frequently removed prior to production and assigned to the department responsible for setting the price, usually purchasing, or personnel (labor rate variances).

Example
Standard labor for one unit is 2 hours at $14.50 per hour. Actual units produced were 15 units; actual labor charges were 40 hours at $14.10 per hour. Calculate the labor rate and efficiency variances for Product A.

Answer:
Rate variance = ($14.10 – $14.50) 40 hrs. = $16.00 Favorable

Efficiency variance = (40 hrs – 30 hrs) $14.50 = $145.00 Unfavorable

Standard Quantity Allowed for Actual Production = 2 hrs. × 15 units = 30 hrs.

Note
Although in this instance we have calculated the rate and efficiency variances together, when the labor rate is not controllable by production supervisors, the rate variance is frequently removed prior to production and assigned to the department responsible for setting the rate, usually personnel.

V. Complicating Factors—Multiple choice questions on the CPA Exam will sometimes complicate these calculations by providing partial information about the standard and actual figures and the related variances. You must use your knowledge of the relationships among these figures to work backwards and provide the answer to the question. Using the format suggested above simplifies these calculations substantially.

Example
Jim Bishop Cabinetry Co.'s records show the following data on labor cost:

Actual rate paid	$14.20 per hour
Standard rate	$14.00 per hour
Standard hours allowed	1,000 hours
Labor efficiency variance	$798.00 unfavorable

What were the actual hours worked?

Answer:
Solving for the unknown in the efficiency variance formula provides the difference between the standard and actual quantity used:

Efficiency Variance: Difference in Quantities = ($798.00) / $14.00 = (57) hours

This difference is substituted back into the analysis format and used to derive the number of actual hours used.

Since (AQ – SQA) SP, (AQ – 1,000 hrs.) $14. Since the labor efficiency variance is unfavorable, that requires that AQ is higher than SQ. Thus, AQ must be SQA of 1,000 hrs. plus 57 hours = 1,057.

VI. Traditional Variance Analysis Format

A. As previously mentioned, most managerial accounting textbooks use a different tool to assist in variance analysis. The tool below should be familiar to most candidates:

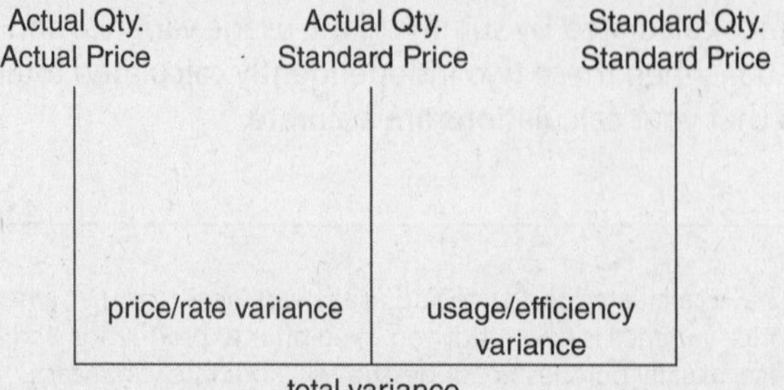

B. The formulas implicit in this model can be stated separately and purely mathematical formulas can be derived to isolate the variances:

Price/rate variance = (AQ × AP) – (AQ × SP)
= AQ (AP – SP)
Usage/efficiency variance = (AQ × SP) – (SQ – SP)
= SP (AQ – SQ)
Total variance **= (AQ × AP) – (SQ × SP)**

Where:

AQ = actual quantity

AP = actual price

SQ = standard quantity

SP = standard price

C. This analysis format takes a different approach to organizing the data, but the concept is the same:

1. Use the analysis tool to organize the data provided in the problem. Then, use the relationships implied by the analysis tool to calculate the variances.

D. We can solve one of the previous examples using this method.

Example
Standard labor for one unit is 2 hours at $14.50 per hour. Actual units produced were 15 units; actual labor charges were 40 hours at $14.10 per hour. Calculate the labor rate and efficiency variances for Product A.

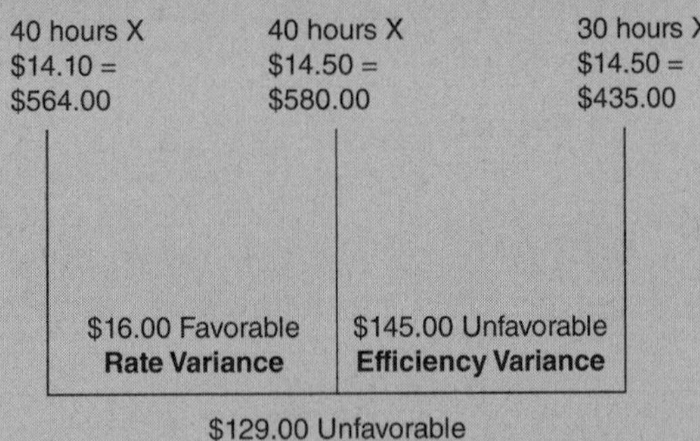

Rate variance = 40 ($14.10 – $14.50)
= 40 (–$0.40)
= ($16.00) Favorable
Efficiency variance = $14.50 (40 – 30)
= $14.50 (10)
= $145.00 Unfavorable
Total variance = ($40 × $14.10) – (30 × $14.50)
= $564.00 – $435.00
= $129.00 Unfavorable

Notice that this technique produces answers identical to the answers derived using the previous model. Use whichever technique works best for you.

VII. Analyzing Sales Variances

A. Although we predict this will not be frequently tested on the exam, questions about sales variances may sometimes appear. Analysis of sales variances can be handled in the same manner as cost variances as long as the following points are observed:

1. **Budgeted or planned sales**—Quantities and prices are used instead of "standard" quantities and prices.
2. **Sales variances work backwards**—When compared to cost variances, that is:
   a. When actual prices are greater than planned prices, favorable variances result (e.g., it is good for people to pay more than you had planned).
   b. When actual quantities sold are greater than planned quantities sold, favorable variances result (e.g., it is good to sell more than you had planned).
3. **Sales variances**—Use slightly different names:
   a. **Sales price variance**—Difference in prices × actual quantity sold.
   b. **Sales quantity variance**—Difference in units × planned unit price.

Example

Mercury Corp.'s master budget showed planned sales revenue of $400,000 on sales of 100,000 units. Actual sales were 90,000 at $4.50 per unit. What were Mercury's sales price, sales quantity, and total sales variances?

Answer:

Sales price variance = ($4.50 – $4.00) 90,000 units = $45,000 Favorable

Sales quantity variance = (90,000 units – 100,000 units) $4.00 = $40,000 Unfavorable

Total variance = $45,000 Favorable – $40,000 Unfavorable = $5,000 Favorable

Overhead Variance Analysis

After studying this lesson, you should be able to:

1. Recognize the differences between overhead variances and direct cost variances.
2. Calculate overhead variances, including spending, volume, and efficiency variances.
3. Recognize the different ways of interpreting the four-way analysis of variances and the variety of aggregation levels used by different companies.

I. Introduction

Exam Tip
Overhead variances are likely to be a fairly light area on the CPA Exam. When questions do appear, they are expected to be conceptual questions about controllability (e.g., which variances is the supervisor actually responsible for) rather than computational questions.

A. The process of analyzing overhead variances is substantially more difficult than analyzing variances related to direct materials and direct labor because:

   1. Some overhead varies with production volume while other overhead is fixed; because of this, separate variances must be calculated for **variable overhead and for fixed overhead.**
   2. Fixed overhead is applied to production based on a specified cost driver; if actual usage of the cost driver differs from planned, **applied overhead costs will change solely as a result of changes in cost driver consumption** (i.e., the variance does not represent true changes in overhead).
   3. While some overhead costs are **controllable** by the production manager, other overhead costs are **uncontrollable** except in the very long run (e.g., depreciation on factory buildings).

B. Recall that both variable and fixed overhead are applied to production based on a single **predetermined overhead application rate:**

> Overhead Application Rate = (Budgeted Variable Overhead + Budgeted Fixed Overhead) / (Budgeted Units of the Allocation Base)

C. Traditionally, the allocation base is a cost driver that is under the control of the production manager (i.e., direct labor hours). If, however, the allocation base is not under the control of the production manager, the **production manager cannot be responsible for overhead variances due solely to the choice of the allocation base.**

D. Variable overhead varies with production volume. It includes indirect costs such as machine supplies, electricity needed for production processes, and incidental manufacturing costs (i.e., the thread used for sewing garments or the screws used in the construction of a piece of furniture). Because the behavior of variable overhead is similar to the behavior of direct manufacturing costs (material and labor), the analysis format used to analyze direct costs can be applied to variable indirect costs:

Question

What are the variable overhead variances for the following?

Bennington City Manufacturing allocates overhead to production based on machine hours. The following information is available regarding its variable overhead for the current quarter:

Variable overhead rate per machine hour:	$0.25
Standard machine hours per unit:	3 hours
Planned production	1,500 units
Planned machine hours (3 hours × 1,500 units)	4,500 hours
Actual machine hours	4,700 hours
Actual units produced	1,700 units
Standard machine hours allowed for actual production (3 hours × 1,700 units)	5,100 hours
Actual variable overhead cost	$1,269

Answer:

	Quantity	×	Rate	=	Total
+ Standard	5,100	×	$0.25	=	$1,275.00
− Actual	4,700	×	$0.27*	=	$1,269.00
= Difference	400		($0.02)		$6.00

*Derived from given information: Actual overhead / Actual quantity

Efficiency Variance: (400) × $0.25 = $100.00 favorable

Spending Variance: ($0.02) × 4,700 = ($94.00) unfavorable

Total Variance = $100.00 + ($94.00) = $6.00 favorable

Exam Tip

Be sure to know the variances for variable overhead and whether they are controllable by the production manager or uncontrollable:

Definitions

Spending Variance: Measures variance due to changes in both rates and quantities of overhead items. It is a controllable variance.

Efficiency Variance: Measures variance due to variations in the efficiency of the base used to allocate overhead (i.e., direct labor hours, machine hours, etc.). As long as the underlying allocation base is under the control of the production manager, it is a controllable variance.

II. Fixed Overhead

A. Fixed Overhead Volume Variance

1. Since fixed overhead does not change with changes in production volume, yet is applied to production based on a unit rate, anytime actual production differs from planned production, a fixed overhead variance results. This variance is known as the **volume variance** and, since it is merely an artifact of the way that we assign fixed overhead to production, it is considered an **uncontrollable** variance.
2. The fixed overhead volume variance is calculated as:

Budgeted Fixed Overhead − (Standard Fixed Overhead Rate × Std. Qty. Allowed for Actual Production)

Example

McGorky Productions has budgeted fixed overhead of $40,000. The fixed overhead is applied to production based on direct labor hours: 0.5 direct abor hours (DLH) are required to produce each unit and the company has budgeted production of 100,000 units. Actual production is 120,000 units.

Fixed Overhead Application Rate	= $40,000 / (100,000 units × .5 DLH per unit)
	= $0.80 per DLH
Standard Quantity Allowed for Actual Production	= 120,000 units × .5 DLH
	= 60,000 DLH
Fixed Overhead Volume Variance	= $40,000 – ($0.80 × 60,000)
	= $40,000 – $48,000
	= $8,000

B. Fixed Overhead Budget Variance

1. Even when actual production is exactly equal to planned production, it is still possible to have fixed overhead variances. The difference between the actual fixed overhead and the budgeted (or planned) fixed overhead is known as the budget variance.
2. The fixed overhead budget variance is calculated as:

Actual Fixed Overhead – Budgeted Fixed Overhead

Example

McGorky Productions' actual fixed overhead is $38,000. Its budgeted fixed overhead is $40,000.

Fixed Overhead Budget Variance = $38,000 – $40,000
= $2,000 favorable

C. A Graphic View of Fixed Overhead Variances

1. The four variances related to manufacturing overhead are illustrated by the graphics below:

   a. **Variable overhead variances**

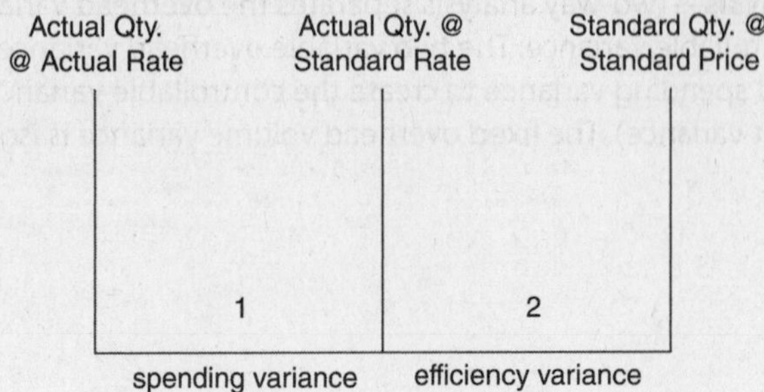

b. Fixed overhead variances

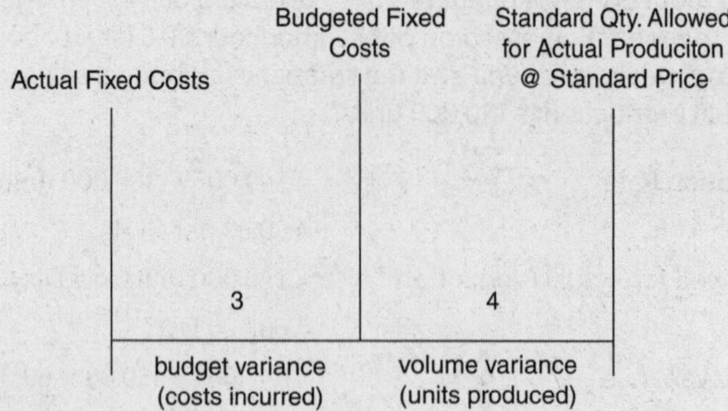

D. Overhead Variances Can Be Difficult to Interpret

1. Because of this difficulty, some companies choose to combine the four basic overhead variances into subtotals that make the numbers easier to evaluate over time. Three combinations are generally found in practice and on the CPA Exam:
   - **a.** Two-way analysis
   - **b.** Three-way analysis
   - **c.** Four-way analysis
2. **Four-way analysis**—Four-way analysis comprises the four variances shown above: the two variable overhead variances (spending variance and efficiency variance) and the two fixed overhead variances (budget variance and volume variance). Four-way analysis provides the most detailed variance information, but it is less commonly used than two-way and three-way analyses because of the difficulty of interpreting the information.
3. **Three-way analysis**—Three-way analysis combines the variable overhead spending variance and the fixed overhead budget (spending) variance into a single variance referred to as the total spending variance.

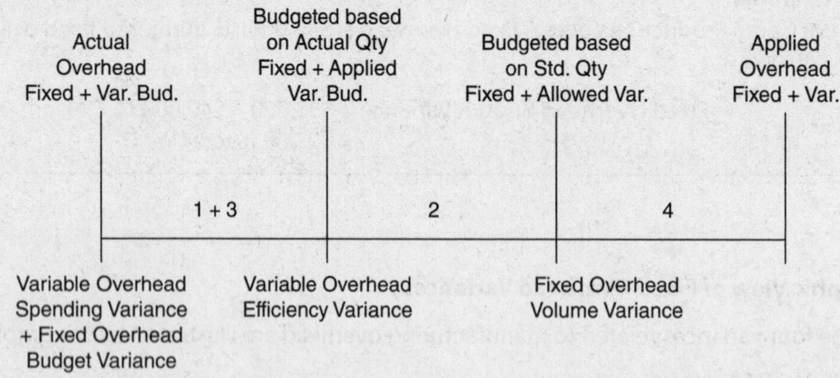

4. **Two-way analysis**—Two-way analysis separates the overhead variances into a controllable and an uncontrollable variance. The two variable overhead variances are combined with the fixed overhead spending variance to create the controllable variance (often referred to as the flexible budget variance). The fixed overhead volume variance is isolated in the uncontrollable variance.

Overhead Variance Analysis

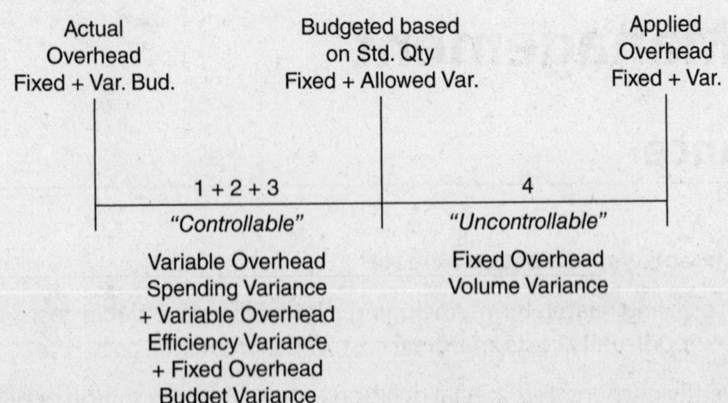

Note
Remember that although the efficiency variance is often controllable, it only reflects variation in units of the allocation base, not variance due to overhead itself.

Process Management

Cost Relevance

After studying this lesson, you should be able to:

1. Define relevant costs and related terms, including avoidable/unavoidable costs, sunk costs, accounting costs, opportunity costs, marginal cost, and incremental cost.
2. Recognize frequently encountered special decisions where the recognition of relevant costs is likely to be tested.
3. Correctly analyze special decisions where relevant costs are used, including sell or process further and keep or drop a product line or segment.

I. Introduction

A. The identification of relevant costs is a critical component in many production decisions: Should we buy a component or make it ourselves? Should we process a product further or sell it now? Should we keep producing a product or drop it?

B. Each possibility is characterized by its own set of costs and associated revenues. Which costs do we need to consider? Must we consider all of them? What if the revenues we lose when choosing one option means that we must forgo another option? The answer is that we must **consider all future factors that differ among alternatives**. Relevant costs and benefits are the future costs and benefits that differ among alternatives.

1. **Avoidable costs**—Costs that can be **eliminated by choosing one alternative over the other**—are relevant costs. **Opportunity costs**—The **benefits that are forgone** when the selection of one course of action precludes another course of action—are also relevant costs.
2. **Unavoidable costs**—Costs that will **remain the same** regardless of which alternative is chosen—are irrelevant to the decision process. Irrelevant costs fall into two general categories:
   a. **Sunk costs**—A sunk cost is a cost that **has already been incurred** and cannot be changed. For example, when deciding whether to buy a new car or keep your current car, the **price paid for the current car is irrelevant** as it occurred in the past and cannot be changed. On the other hand, the **market value of the current car** if you sold it is **relevant** to the decision as it differs between the two alternatives: if you buy the new car, you can sell the current car for its market value; if you keep the current car, you forgo receiving its market value.
   b. **Future costs and benefits that do not differ between alternatives**—Future costs that do not differ between alternatives tend to be fixed costs or allocated costs.

Example
Remington Trucking is considering the purchase of a new delivery truck for $78,000. If they purchase the new truck, they will sell their current truck, which cost them $68,000 two years ago.

General maintenance and insurance on the current truck is approximately $2,800. However, this truck is also due for a major overhaul that will cost $1,500. Straight-line depreciation on the old truck is $8,000 per year.

General maintenance and insurance for the new truck will be approximately the same as for the old truck. If the new truck is purchased, depreciation on it will be $9,000 per year.

Irrelevant costs: When considering whether to purchase the new truck, the $68,000 purchase price is a sunk cost and is irrelevant. The general maintenance and insurance costs are also irrelevant because they are future costs, which do not differ between alternatives.

Relevant costs: The $1,500 cost of the major overhaul on the old truck is an avoidable cost and therefore is relevant (e.g., if the new truck is purchased, the cost of the overhaul can be avoided). The difference in depreciation is relevant but, since depreciation itself is a non-cash item, it is only relevant to the extent that it produces a cash difference due to its effect on income tax liability. The sales value of the current truck and the purchase price of the new truck are also relevant costs as they differ between the two alternatives.

II. Other Cost Concepts

A. **Accounting Costs**—These are costs that can be found in the fundamental books of record (e.g., the general ledger).

B. **Opportunity Costs**—This is the benefit forgone that results from choosing one alternative course of action rather than another (generally, the next-best forgone alternative). Note that some opportunity costs can be approximated from past experience or historical data in the accounting records. But since opportunity costs are forgone, they cannot be fully known without considering decision-specific data. Much of this data is not recorded in the fundamental books of record.

C. In general, **avoidable costs are opportunity costs** and unavoidable costs are not opportunity costs. Opportunity costs generally include **relevant costs**.

D. We often speak of relevant cost concepts while including **relevant revenue** (i.e., relevant costs are merely negative relevant revenues and vice versa).

E. Fixed costs are not equivalent to unavoidable costs. Unavoidable costs cannot be changed while fixed costs can change. Remember that **fixed costs are fixed with respect to output**. For example, utility costs of heating fluctuate constantly with weather conditions and the commodity price per unit of natural gas—but this does not make them variable. Fixed costs are always fixed with regard to the volume of units produced/sold.

F. **Marginal Cost**—This is the cost of producing one more unit. **Incremental cost** is the difference between two decision alternatives.

III. Types of Decisions Using Relevant Costs

A. Several types of decisions involving the identification of relevant costs are frequently encountered. These decisions revolve around:

1. Whether to process a product further or sell it now
2. Whether to keep or drop a product line or company segment
3. Whether to make or buy a product or component
4. Whether to accept or reject a special order

IV. Sell Now or Process Further Decisions

A. This type of decision usually involves processing decisions about joint products, although it can also be applied to processing decisions for a single product. In a joint product environment:

1. Products are not separately identifiable until after the split-off point.
2. The costs incurred up to the split-off point cannot be separated or avoided.

B. When joint products are produced, separate products are identifiable after the split-off point. At that point producers frequently have the option of selling the products immediately or of performing additional processing on some or all of the products before selling them.

C. When making the decision to process a product further or not, **the only relevant facts are the differential future costs and benefits: the separable costs incurred beyond the split-off point, the difference between the revenue that can be earned** at split-off, and the revenue that can be earned after further processing. Joint costs are not relevant.

D. Consider the following example:

1. Chemical Dynamics, Inc. produces three synthetic oils through a joint product production process. Chemical compounds are blended together, heated to 1200 degrees Fahrenheit, and left in vats to cool for two days. At the end of the two days, the three synthetic oils—Algon, Bessite, and Corex—can be separated from the material in the vats. Algon and Corex can be sold immediately after split-off, but Bessite must be processed further before it can be sold. Additionally, Algon and Corex can each be processed further to create more concentrated products (Algon-Extra Duty and Corex-L). Based on the following sales volume, sales price, and cost information, determine which products should be processed further and which should be sold at split-off (you may assume that none of the products can be disposed of as scrap):

		Algon	**Bessite**	**Corex**
Costs incurred up to split-off:				
Cost of raw materials	$40,000			
Cost of production processes	$20,000			
Volume at split-off:		25,000 gal.	20,000 gal.	5,000 gal.
Sales value per gallon at split-off:		$2.00/gal.	n/a	$4.00/gal.
Cost of additional processing:		$15,000	$20,000	$10,000
Volume after additional processing:		20,000 gal.	30,000 gal.	7,000 gal.
Sales value per unit after additional processing:		$3.00/gal.	$6.00/gal.	$4.50/gal.

2. When analyzing this decision, the first step is to eliminate the irrelevant information—the information that does not change. In this example, we can eliminate:
    a. The costs incurred up to split-off (raw materials of $40,000 and production process costs of $20,000) are sunk costs and are therefore not relevant; they have already been incurred and cannot be changed.
    b. The information about Bessite: production volumes, separable processing costs, and unit sales value. Since Bessite *must* be processed further and no other sales or disposal options can be considered, the treatment of Bessite cannot change, so the Bessite data is irrelevant.
3. The relevant costs and benefits, then, are related to Algon and Corex: The revenues realizable and costs incurred at split-off and the revenues realizable and costs incurred if the products are processed further. Each product needs to be considered separately because the highest return may be achieved when one product is sold immediately and the other receives further processing. The costs and benefits for each choice are summarized in the following table:

		Algon		**Corex**	
		Sell at Split-Off	**Process Further**	**Sell at Split-Off**	**Process Further**
Revenues:					
	Price per gallon	$2.00/gal.	$3.00/gal.	$4.00/gal.	$4.50/gal.
	# of gallons	25,000 gal.	20,000 gal.	5,000 gal.	7,000 gal.
Total revenue		$50,000	$60,000	$20,000	$31,500
Additional costs:		- 0 -	$15,000	- 0 -	$10,000
Net realizable value:		$50,000	$45,000	$20,000	$21,500

4. Based on this analysis, it appears that the company should not process Algon further because its net realizable value is less when the goods are processed further. Corex, however, **should** be processed further because its net realizable value is greater when the goods are processed further.

V. Keep or Drop a Product Line (or Business Segment) Decisions

A. When organizations track performance by product line or business segment, they often discover that some products and segments do not perform as well as others and that some may even be operating at a loss. The problem then becomes whether to continue producing the product or segment or to eliminate it.

B. The decision is not as straightforward as it might appear because:

1. Some of the costs charged to the product or segment may not be eliminated if the product or segment is eliminated.
2. Changes in one part of the organization may impact other parts of the organization.
3. There may or may not be alternative uses for the resources freed up by elimination of the product or segment.

Example
Tres Piedres Auto Works is an automobile repair shop that provides brake and transmission service. About a year ago, the shop converted one of its repair bays to an oil change station so that it could offer quick oil change services. Tres Piedres now wants to review the results of this change to determine whether they should keep the oil change facility or convert it back to use for brake and transmission services. The following information is available:

	Brakes	Transmissions	Oil Change
Sales	$190,000	$230,000	$70,000
Costs:			
Variable costs	$114,000	$161,000	$56,000
Fixed costs	$ 28,000	$ 38,000	$22,000
Total costs	$142,000	$199,000	$78,000
Operating income (loss)	$ 48,000	$ 31,000	($ 8,000)

Additional information: If the oil change facility is dropped, the shop will be able to avoid $6,000 in fixed costs related to managing the facility. The shop will also be able to avoid $2,000 in advertising expenses designed to promote the oil change service.

The shop is not operating at capacity, so recovery of the oil change bay if the oil change services were dropped would not increase sales of either brake or transmission services. Quite to the contrary, the manager estimates that brake and transmission service revenues will drop by $3,000 and $7,000, respectively, if the oil change services are dropped.

C. The preceding example contains several elements that are typical of keep or drop a product line decisions.

1. Notice that oil change services **shows a net operating loss.** This is typical of CPA Exam questions in this area. The unsophisticated candidate may quickly assume that dropping a product line that is operating at a loss must necessarily have a positive effect on the company's total net income. However, if the product line revenues are sufficient to cover its avoidable costs, this may not be the case. If the product line's net loss is due to unavoidable costs that have been allocated to it, total net income for the company may be reduced as a result of dropping the "unprofitable" product line.

2. Information is presented regarding variable costs and fixed costs:

   a. In general, **variable costs are avoidable costs.** If we do not provide oil change services, the variable costs related to the oil change services will not be incurred.

   b. **Fixed costs** are usually a **mix of avoidable costs and unavoidable costs.** In this instance, it appears that $6,000 of the $22,000 in fixed costs attributed to the oil change activity are avoidable, leaving $16,000 in unavoidable fixed costs.

3. Information is usually provided regarding **miscellaneous differential costs and revenues.** For example, if the oil change services are dropped, revenues for other services will actually decrease by $10,000 total as a result of lost synergies between the services provided. Additionally, $2,000 in advertising costs can also be avoided. Note that it is quite usual for the examiners to list these costs in addition to the other fixed and variable costs in hopes of causing the candidate to be confused as to whether the costs are included in the fixed and variable cost totals or not: **In the vast majority of cases, these items are *in addition to* the other costs (or revenues).**

D. To determine whether the oil change services should be kept or dropped, you will need to compare the total operating income with oil change services to the total operating income without oil change services. A typical analysis format for these types of decisions is shown below:

	Total with Oil Change	Total without Oil Change	Difference Favorable (Unfavorable)
Sales	$490,000	$410,000	($80,000)
Costs:			
Variable costs	$331,000	$268,300	$62,700
Fixed costs	$ 88,000	$ 82,000	$ 6,000
Total operating costs	$419,000	$350,300	$68,700
Other costs	$2,000	- 0 -	$2,000
Operating income (loss)	$69,000	$59,700	($9,300)

E. Analysis of the changes in revenues and expenses reveals that, despite the net loss attributed to oil change services, the company will be **$9,300 *worse off*** if it drops the oil change services. This is in part because the oil change revenues are greater than the avoidable costs associated with the revenues ($70,000 – ($56,000 + $6,000 + $2,000) = $6,000) and in part because the synergy between the oil change services and the other services offered was such that an additional $3,300 decrease in operating income ($10,000 decrease in brake and transmission service revenues less $6,700 in related cost savings) would occur if the oil change services were eliminated.

Exam Tip
The scenario described in the previous example (e.g., the line that may be dropped initially shows a net loss but further analysis reveals that the line contributes positively to the organization's total performance) is expected to be common to many CPA Exam questions in this area.

F. While some candidates prefer to perform the complete analysis as shown above, others prefer to look only at the **differential analysis**:

	Differences Favorable (Unfavorable)
Sales	($80,000)
Costs:	
Variable costs	$62,700
Fixed costs	$6,000
Total operating costs:	$68,700
Other costs	$2,000
Operating income (loss)	($9,300)

G. The results of the two analysis formats are the same, of course, but many candidates find it easier to look at only the differences.

Special Decisions

After studying this lesson, you should be able to:

1. Recognize frequently encountered special decisions where the recognition of relevant costs is likely to be tested.
2. Correctly analyze special decisions where relevant costs are used, including whether to make or buy a product or component and whether to accept or reject a special order.

I. Accept or Reject a Special Order

A. Special orders, whether for products or for services, require us to think differently about costs and prices specifically because they are "special" orders: **one-time opportunities that are not part of the organization's ongoing business**. Normally, products are priced to cover "full" costs—not just variable production costs but fixed overhead and selling and administrative costs as well. All costs must be covered if the organization is to survive. Special orders, however, are not subject to this constraint. Since fixed overhead and selling and administrative costs have already been covered by regular product sales, they do not need to be considered when pricing special orders.

B. Special-order decisions are usually short-term, profit-maximizing decisions. For these decisions, **the only relevant costs are the costs directly attributable to the special order** and, if the company is operating at capacity, the **opportunity costs** associated with production that must be canceled in order to complete the special order. Strategic considerations may also come into play if accepting the special order has the potential to compromise or, alternatively, promote management's objectives outside of profit maximization. For example, a company might be willing to accept a special order from a customer who represented a market segment that the company was trying to penetrate even if the company lost money on the special order.

C. **Considering a Special Order when There Is Excess Capacity**. If the special order can be completed using existing capacity, only sales revenues and the variable costs of producing the order need be considered.

Example

Marpro Industries produces an electronic flytrap that has proven to be very successful. Marpro plans to produce and sell 100,000 flytraps at $70 each during the upcoming year. The cost of producing and selling each flytrap is:

Direct materials	$25.00
Direct labor	$12.50
Variable manufacturing overhead	$7.00
Fixed manufacturing overhead	$4.00
Variable selling and administrative expense	$3.50
Fixed selling and administrative expenses	$4.50
Total cost per unit:	$56.50

A company that manages horseback riding stables for several ranch resorts has asked Marpro to build 1,000 custom flytraps for their use at a price of $55 apiece. Marpro estimates that the design and retooling costs associated with the customization would cost $3,000. In addition, direct materials cost would increase to $27.00 per unit, variable manufacturing overhead would decrease to $6.50 per unit, and variable selling and administrative expenses would decrease to $1.00 per unit. The order would not affect sales of their standard flytrap and could be produced using existing excess capacity.

Since the special-order price is already less than the cost of a standard flytrap, Marpro initially rejected the order. However, they are now having second thoughts and want to reevaluate the special-order request. Should Marpro take the special order?

Answer:
When considering whether to take a special order, the only relevant costs are the costs directly attributable to the order. In this case, the $3,000 design and retooling cost must be considered as well as the direct unit costs:

Direct materials	$27.00
Direct labor	$12.50
Variable manufacturing overhead	$6.50
Variable selling and administrative expense	$1.00
Cost per unit:	$47.00

Special-order revenue (1,000 × $55)	$55,000
Less: special order unit costs (1,000 × $47)	($47,000)
Less: design and re-tooling costs for the order*	($3,000)
Net profit on the special order	$5,000

*The design and retooling costs could also have been expressed as $3.00 per unit ($3,000/1,000 units) and added to the other unit costs.

Note that the fixed manufacturing overhead and fixed selling and administrative costs have been eliminated from the special-order analysis because they do not change as a result of accepting the special order. Based on this analysis, Marpro should accept the special order as it will increase profits by $5,000.

D. Considering a Special Order when There Is *No* Excess Capacity

1. When no excess capacity exists, acceptance of a special order means that other units must be removed from the production schedule to make room for the special order. The **forgone profits** related to the units that were removed from production represent an **opportunity cost** and must be included in the profitability analysis of the special order.

Example
Consider the same facts as in the preceding example except assume that in order to produce the special order, Marpro will have to eliminate production of 1,500 of its standard flytraps. The relevant costs and benefits associated with the production and sale of the 1,500 standard flytraps are:

Direct materials	$25.00
Direct labor	$12.50
Variable manufacturing overhead	$7.00
Variable selling and administrative expense	$3.50
Total relevant cost per unit:	$48.00

Revenue for 1,500 standard units:	$105,000
Less: relevant costs for 1,500 standard units:	($72,000)
Net profit for the 1,500 standard units	$33,000

Note that the fixed costs allocated to the standard flytraps are unavoidable and, thus, irrelevant: They will remain the same regardless of whether the standard units or the special-order units are produced.

Based on this analysis, the special order would not be accepted when there is no excess capacity. The special order would contribute a total of $5,000 profit to the firm, but the regular sale of the 1,500 standard units would contribute a much larger amount: $33,000. The company would be $28,000 better off ($33,000 – $5,000) by rejecting the special order.

An alternative way of incorporating the opportunity cost associated with the 1,500 standard units into the analysis is to include the opportunity cost as one of the cost factors associated with the special order

Direct materials	$27.00
Direct labor	$12.50
Variable manufacturing overhead	$6.50
Variable selling and administrative expense	$1.00
Cost per unit:	$47.00

Special-order revenue (1,000 × $55)	$55,000
Less: special-order unit costs (1,000 × $47)	($47,000)
Less: design and retooling costs for the order	($3,000)
Less: opportunity cost ($33,000)	($33,000)
Net loss on the special order	($28,000)

Exam Tip

CPA Exam questions may sometimes take this approach to the treatment of opportunity costs. In these cases, it is important to remember that the opportunity cost of the forgone option is added to the costs of the option under consideration.

II. Make or Buy a Product or Component

A. Many organizations prefer to make their own product components rather than purchase them from external suppliers in order to maintain control of production quality and supply. In recent years, however, globalization and increasing price competition have caused many organizations to outsource component production: Suppliers that specialize in large-scale production of a particular component can often provide the component at a lower cost than the organization can produce it.

B. The decision of whether to outsource production—to make or buy a component—is based on comparative analysis of the external purchase costs and the relevant costs of internal production.

Example

Ozone Boards produces handcrafted surfboards. In order to maintain high quality, Ozone has traditionally built all of the board components themselves. Recently, costs associated with production of the board blanks that serve as the foundation of the board have increased substantially due to environmental concerns about some of the chemicals used in production of the blanks. Ozone reports the following costs associated with blank production:

Direct materials	$15.00
Direct labor	$20.00
Variable manufacturing overhead	$10.00
Fixed manufacturing overhead	$13.00
Total cost per unit:	$58.00

Ozone's production schedule requires production of 2,000 blanks per year. A company specializing in the production of board blanks has offered to sell Ozone 2,000 blanks per year at a cost of $48 per blank. Ozone has investigated the supplier and their product and is satisfied that they can produce and deliver a blank that meets Ozone's specifications. Ozone estimates that it will be able to avoid $4,000 in fixed manufacturing overhead costs if it purchases the board blanks instead of producing them. Should Ozone outsource production of the board blanks?

Answer:
In order to compare the cost of internally produced board blanks with purchased blanks, all irrelevant costs (i.e., costs that continue regardless of whether the boards are produced internally or purchased from an external source) must be eliminated from the costs associated with the internally produced blanks. In this instance, total fixed manufacturing overhead costs are $26,000 ($13 per unit × 2,000 units) when the blanks are produced internally. However, if the production of the blanks is outsourced, $4,000 of those costs can be avoided: $22,000 ($22,000/2,000 units = $11.00 per unit) of the fixed manufacturing costs are irrelevant. When comparing the cost of internal production to the cost of purchasing the units from an external source, only the $4,000 of costs ($4,000/2,000 units = $2.00 per unit) that can be eliminated if production is outsourced are relevant production costs.

This leads to the following analysis:

	Make	Buy
Direct materials	$15.00	
Direct labor	$20.00	
Variable manufacturing overhead	$10.00	
Avoidable fixed manufacturing overhead ($4,000/2,000 units)	$2.00	
Cost per unit:	$47.00	$48.00
Total costs (unit cost × 2,000 units)	$94,000	$96,000
Difference in favor of producing blanks internally	$2,000	

When only the relevant costs of producing the blanks internally are considered, it becomes clear that Ozone is slightly better off financially when it produces the blanks internally instead of outsourcing them.

With that said, note that strategic considerations may enter into the analysis. For example, concerns over potential environmental liabilities if Ozone continues to produce the blanks internally might cause the company to decide that the $2,000 difference in costs was not sufficient to justify the risks associated with internal production of the blanks. Whenever possible, strategic concerns should be quantified and included in the analysis.

Transfer Pricing

After studying this lesson, you should be able to:

1. Define transfer pricing and recognize the three major approaches to transfer pricing (market, cost, and negotiated) along with the features of each approach.
2. Explain the goal congruence issue that is a central problem for transfer pricing.
3. Describe the general transfer pricing rule.
4. Explain the importance of capacity in determining an appropriate transfer price.
5. Recognize the advantage and disadvantage of using dual pricing.
6. Explain how transfer pricing can be used to reduce tax liability.

I. Introduction

A. When one division of a manufacturing organization supplies components or materials to another division, the **price charged by the selling division to the buying division** is known as the **transfer price**. Transfer prices are usually determined by one of the following methods:

Definitions

Market price: The price the purchasing unit would have to pay on the open market.

Cost-based price: One of several variations on the selling units' cost of production: variable cost, full cost, cost "plus" (a percentage or a fixed amount).

Negotiated price: A price that is mutually agreeable to both the selling and purchasing unit.

B. In decentralized organizations, the determination of the transfer price is problematic because the managers of the buying and selling departments each seek to maximize their own departmental revenues and minimize their own departmental costs. When both managers **act in their individual best interests, the organization as a whole may suffer resulting in suboptimization**. The existence of suboptimal decision-making usually indicates a problem with management's incentive and reward structure known as **goal incongruence.** Goal incongruence exists when **actions encouraged by the reward structure of a department conflict with goals for other departments or the organization as a whole**.

C. For this reason, senior management usually establishes the methodology for setting internal transfer prices in such a way as to promote **goal congruence**. Goal congruence occurs when the **department and division managers make decisions that are consistent with the goals and objectives of the organization as a whole**. Tax and production capacity issues can also complicate the transfer pricing decision.

Exam Tip
Candidates should be sure to know the definitions of *goal congruence, goal incongruence,* and suboptimization. These definitions may sometimes be tested directly but are also used as distractors in other questions.

II. General Transfer Pricing Rule

A. The following transfer pricing rule helps to ensure goal congruence among department and divisional managers:

Transfer Price per Unit = Additional Outlay Cost per Unit + Opportunity Cost per Unit

B. The Additional Outlay Cost—Includes the variable production costs incurred by the selling unit (raw materials, direct labor, and variable factory overhead) plus any additional costs incurred by the selling unit (storage costs, transportation costs, and administrative selling costs).

C. Opportunity Cost—Is the **benefit that is forgone as a result of selling internally** rather than externally. Depending on the sales volume and production capacity of the selling unit, there may or may not be an opportunity cost associated with the internal transfer of the goods.

1. **Selling unit is operating at full capacity**—When the selling unit is both producing at full capacity and selling all that it produces, the opportunity cost per unit is equal to the revenue given up if the unit is sold internally less the additional outlay incurred in the production and sale of the unit:

Opportunity Cost per Unit = Selling Price per Unit – Additional Outlay Cost per Unit

Example

Trotter Parts Supplier, Inc. has two production divisions. Division A produces Component X, which is used by Division B. Division A pays $8.00 in direct materials, direct labor, and variable factory overhead to produce a unit of Component X, which sells to external customers for $14.00 per unit. Based on this information, the opportunity cost associated with a unit of Component X is:

Opportunity cost = $14.00 – $8.00 = $6.00

And the transfer price should be:

Transfer price = $8.00 + $6.00 = $14.00

In other words, when the selling unit is operating at full capacity and can sell all that it can produce, the transfer price should be equal to the market price. A transfer price that is less than market price is demotivating for the selling division's manager because that division's return is decreased for every unit sold internally instead of externally.

Note

Market price is the "theoretically correct" transfer price.

D. Selling Unit is Operating at Less than Full Capacity—The picture changes when Division A is producing at less than full capacity and has met all of its sales demand. If Division A produces additional units to sell to Division B, no opportunity cost is incurred because no external sales opportunities were forgone: opportunity cost equals zero. The transfer price under these conditions is:

Transfer Price = $8.00 + $0.00 = $8.00

E. That is, when the selling division has excess production capacity, **the transfer price should be equal to the additional costs incurred to produce each unit.** However, because this price provides no additional return to the selling division for units sold internally, most selling units find it unacceptable. In practice, this price usually serves as the lower threshold in a transfer price negotiation or as the basis for cost-based pricing.

III. Negotiated Transfer Prices

A. In keeping with the concept of decentralization, many organizations permit the buying and selling divisions to negotiate the transfer price directly. The buying division's maximum price will be equal to the minimum price for the item on the open market. The selling division's minimum price will be equal to: 1) its direct costs if it has excess capacity; or 2) its market price if it does not have excess capacity. When no external markets exist for the component being transferred, negotiations are typically based on standard costs and divisional profitability considerations.

B. Although negotiated transfer prices can work well when divisions are on equal footing and when managers are well-informed and cooperative, oftentimes this is not the case. When division managers focus primarily on their own profits or are simply not effective negotiators, negotiated transfer prices can lead to divisional strife and run counter to the organization's efforts to create goal congruence among its divisions.

IV. Cost-Based Pricing

A. Under cost-based pricing, the transfer cost is determined by the selling division's production costs. Although cost-based pricing is subject to significant inherent limitations, as long as the selling unit has excess capacity and standard costs are used to set the price, it is a simple, easy-to-understand method to set transfer prices that is used extensively in practice. Several variations on cost-based pricing are common.

1. **Variable cost pricing**—The transfer price is set at the variable costs incurred by the selling division to produce and sell the unit to the purchasing division. In general, these are direct materials costs, direct labor costs, variable factory overhead costs, and variable selling and administrative costs. Note that **the transfer price should always be based on standard costs** rather than actual costs: using actual costs to set the transfer price allows manufacturing inefficiencies to be passed on to the purchasing division and provides no incentive to the selling division to control costs.

    a. Although variable cost pricing is generally attractive to the purchasing division, it does not appropriately motivate the selling division since it only covers the cost of production and does not provide any profit to the selling division.

2. **Full-cost (absorption) pricing**—An allocated portion of the fixed costs of the selling division is added to the product's variable costs to determine the transfer price. Although this price usually has some appeal to both the selling division (it receives some "extra" money to cover fixed costs) and the purchasing division (full absorption cost is likely to be less than the market price), it is problematic for the organization as a whole. Why? Because **the fixed costs allocated to the product by the selling division become variable costs to the purchasing division** as well as to any other divisions who receive the product subsequent to the original purchasing division. When fixed costs are treated like variable costs, any analysis that uses these costs to value earning opportunities will tend to understate profitability.

Example

Tree House Restaurant runs a catering business in addition to its dine-in restaurant. The two businesses are treated as separate divisions in which the catering business buys products from the restaurant business and then resells them.

The catering business recently had an opportunity to cater a 500-plate luncheon for $7.00 per plate, but rejected the offer because it was not high enough to cover the $5.00 transfer price of the food plus the catering business' additional out-of-pocket costs of $2.50 per plate. The catering manager later discovered that the $5.00 transfer cost included $1.50 of allocated fixed costs and that the actual out-of-pocket cost of producing each plate was only $3.50.

Had the catering job been accepted, the restaurant as a whole would have been $500 better off ($7.00 – ($3.50 + $2.50) = $1.00 contribution margin per plate × 500 plates).

3. **Cost-plus pricing**—The transfer price is based on the selling division's additional costs per unit plus either a fixed dollar amount or a fixed percentage of the cost. Cost-plus pricing has the same advantages and disadvantages as full-cost (absorption) pricing: Although it is simple and easily understood, the inclusion of an arbitrary charge as part of the unit cost to the purchasing division may lead to suboptimal decisions later on.

V. Dual Pricing

A. Dual pricing is an attempt to eliminate the internal conflicts associated with transfer prices by giving both the buying and selling divisions the price that "works best" for them:

1. **The selling division**—Uses the market price as its transfer (out) price: this eliminates the potential for the selling division to see a decrease in its returns just because it sells products internally instead of externally.

2. **The purchasing division**—Uses standard variable costs as its transfer (in) price: this enhances the usefulness of product costs for decision-making purposes and eliminates the need for the purchasing division to "share profits" with the selling division by agreeing to a transfer price above cost.

B. Unfortunately, by giving both the buying and selling divisions prices that enhance their profitability, much of the value of pricing as an incentive for divisions to control costs is lost.

VI. Other Considerations

A. Transfer pricing can be a useful tool in promoting goal congruence among organizational divisions, but when production takes place in an international environment, it can be an even more **important tool for reducing tax liability**. Because taxes and import duties vary substantially among countries, the transfer price used to value products as they flow across national boundaries can have a significant effect on the amount of taxes and duties paid. In some domestic instances, transfers of goods across state boundaries can create a similar effect. When these factors enter into play, transfer prices are usually determined by the tax accountant rather than the divisional or corporate managers.

Activity-Based Costing and Process Management

After studying this lesson, you should be able to:

1. Describe how activity-based costing differs from traditional volume-based approaches to costing.
2. Recognize and explain activity-based costing terminology.
3. Explain the effects of adoption of activity-based costing from traditional costing approaches.
4. Describe the key objectives of process management.
5. Describe business process reengineering (BPR) and explain how it differs from incrementally reducing non-value added activities.
6. Identify the central features of outsourcing, shared services, and off-shore operations and describe the risks involved with each.
7. Perform necessary calculations to allocate factory overhead using activity-based costing.

I. Costing

A. Activity-based costing (ABC) is a method of assigning overhead (indirect) costs to products. It is an alternative to the **traditional, volume-based** approach of accumulating large amounts of overhead in a **single pool** and **assigning the costs across all products based on the labor dollars, labor hours, or some other generic allocation base**. The volume-based approach, while simple, does not accurately reflect the true relationship between the products produced and the costs incurred as it systematically over-assigns costs to some products and under-assigns costs to others.

B. By closely focusing on the causes of costs, ABC is better able to identify the cost of an activity and to more accurately associate activities with the products that require them. This has the potential to significantly improve the accuracy of the resulting product cost. Improved costing accuracy leads to improved pricing and other decisions that depend on the accuracy of costs. In addition, managers can potentially improve their understanding of processes and how they consume resources.

II. Activity-Based Costing Terminology

Definitions

Activities: Procedures that comprise work.

Cost drivers: Measures that are closely correlated with the way an activity accumulates costs; i.e., the cost driver for production line setup costs might be the number of machines that have to be set up; cost drivers are the basis by which costs are assigned to products (direct labor hours, machine hours, occupancy percentages, etc.).

Cost center: An area where costs are accumulated and then distributed to products, for example accounts payable, product design, and marketing.

Cost pools: A group of costs that are associated with a specific cost center.

Value-added activities: Processes that contribute to the product's ultimate value; includes items such as design and packaging in addition to direct conversion of direct materials into finished goods.

Nonvalue-added activities: Processes that do not contribute to the product's value; includes items such as moving materials and more obvious activities such as rework; cost reductions can be achieved by reducing or eliminating nonvalue-added activities.

III. Activity-Based Costing Characteristics

A. Activity-based costing begins by identifying activities. Activities form the building blocks of an ABC system because **activities consume resources**. Activities are commonly grouped into one of four categories:

1. **Unit-level activities**—Activities that must be performed for every product unit; for example, using a machine to polish a silver tray or boxing up an item for delivery.
2. **Batch-level activities**—Activities that must be performed for each batch of products produced; examples include setting up the production equipment for the batch and running random quality inspections of items in the batch.
3. **Product-sustaining-level activities**—Activities that are necessary to support the product line as a whole such as advertising and engineering activities.
4. **Facility-(general-operations) level activities**—Activities that are necessary to support the plant that produces the products; for example, plant manager salaries, property taxes, and insurance.

B. Once activities have been identified, overhead costs are assigned to them. The costs assigned to a particular activity comprise an **activity cost pool**. The next step is to identify **cost drivers** that can be used to allocate the costs to products. When the cost pools created in an ABC system are compared to the cost pools created in a traditional, volume-based costing system, ABC results in a **larger number of smaller cost pools that can be more closely aligned to products.**

IV. Effects of Adoption of Activity-Based Costing

A. Because of the way activity-based costing identifies and allocates costs, organizations that adopt activity-based costing tend to have:

1. More **precise measures of cost**
2. More **cost pools**
3. More **allocation bases** (e.g., multiple causes for costs to occur)

B. Activity-based costing can be used:

1. With **job order** and **process costing** systems
2. With **standard costing** and **variance analysis**
3. For **service businesses** as well as manufacturers

C. In general, compared to traditional, volume-based costing, activity-based costing tends to **shift costs away from high volume, simple products to lower volume, complex products.**

> **Exam Tip**
> The items listed here in "Effects of Adoption of Activity-Based Costing" are likely to be the most heavily tested concepts in activity-based costing.

V. Volume-Based Calculation Example

A. YRU Overhead, Inc. currently uses a plant-wide, volume-based approach to manufacturing overhead (OH) allocation. However, they are considering switching to activity-based costing (ABC) for purposes of overhead allocation to increase the cost accuracy. They would like to see a comparison of the two approaches. These are shown below:

B. **Volume-Based Allocation**

1. For the current volume-based approach, YRU uses a predetermined factory overhead rate based on direct labor hours (DLH). For the current year, YRU budgeted overhead of $600,000 based on a volume of 100,000 DLH. Actual overhead amounted to $650,000 with actual DLH totaling 110,000. Given this information, YRU would allocate factory overhead as follows:

   a. **Step 1**—The predetermined rate is based on budgeted OH divided by budgeted DLH. The allocation rate would be calculated as $600,000 / 100,000 DLH = $6 per DLH. This happens at the beginning of the year.

b. **Step 2**—During the year, and using the predetermined rate of $6 per DLH, overhead is allocated to Work-In-Process by multiplying the rate by the actual units of the allocation base: $6 × 110,000 = $660,000.

C. **Activity-Based Costing Allocation**

1. Developing the ABC overhead rates is similar to the volume-based approach. However, based on ABC, YRU has decided to develop four different activities and rates. They do this by placing the overhead into four different cost pools based on the budgeted cost of overhead relevant to four important activities in the factory. The activities, cost pools, costs, and their amounts are shown below.

Activities	Cost Driver	Budgeted Cost	Budgeted Activity	Actual Activity
Moves	Distance of Moves	$ 40,000	500 miles	400 miles
Setups	Number of Setups	$ 60,000	300 setups	280 setups
Disposal	Lbs. of Disposal	$180,000	90,000 lbs.	100,000 lbs.
Batches	Number of Batches	$320,000	1000 batches	800 batches
Total Cost		$600,000		

2. **Note**: The total budgeted cost is the same as the volume-based example at $600,000. In general, the two steps to perform the allocation are also the same, but for the ABC option they must be repeated for all of the four activities and then totaled.

3. **Step 1**—The four allocation rates are determined by dividing the budgeted cost in each category by the budgeted activity. This yields the following rates:

Moves	$40,000/500 miles = $80 per mile
Setups	$60,000/300 setups = $200 per setup
Disposal	$180,000/90,000 lbs. = $2 per lb.
Batches	$320,000/1,000 batches = $320 per batch

4. **Step 2**—The $600,000 of total overhead is allocated to Work-In-Process by multiplying the four predetermined rates by the actual activity levels for each of the activities as follows:

Moves	$80 per mile × 400 miles = $32,000
Setups	$200 per setup × 280 setups = $56,000
Disposal	$2 per lb. × 100,000 lbs. = $200,000
Batches	$320 per batch × 800 batches = $256,000
Total Allocated Cost = $544,000	

5. **Note:** Although the total cost budgeted was $600,000, the total allocated overhead was determined to be $544,000 for the ABC option. This difference is appropriate for activity-based costing and should be expected. The difference is due to a distinction between overhead used versus overhead supplied. This difference is not likely to be tested on the exam.

VI. Process Management

A. Process management involves activity analysis **to achieve an understanding of the work that takes place in an organization**. Fundamentally, process management recognizes that managers often focus on managing processes, while accountants often focus on managing costs. This disconnect prevents a proper understanding of work processes by accountants and the related cost management by managers.

B. Processes can be defined as **a series of activities conducted to accomplish a defined objective**. This implies that a process uses resource inputs to achieve the organization's outputs. Some people refer to this broadly as activity-based management (ABM). ABM is a term that was popularized in the 1980s along with a focus on ABC, but ABM shifts the purpose from increasing costing accuracy (i.e., ABC) to process management (i.e., ABM).

C. The key objectives of process management are to:

1. **Increase manager understanding** of the cause-and-effect relationships involved between processes and the resources they consume
2. **Promote the elimination of waste** to help achieve managerial objectives

D. Process management **highlights interdependencies** across functional business areas by focusing on the processes that cut across business silos, following the input-output relationships as the transformation of inputs to outputs is accomplished by the various processes in the organization. Process management also supports the view that process knowledge and the **continuous improvement** of processes are important. Identifying nonvalue-added activities is a major goal for improvement once an essential understanding of processes is achieved.

E. **Business process reengineering (BPR)**—Reengineering is a process-analysis approach that typically results in radical change. This is a different approach from incrementally reducing and eliminating nonvalue-added activities, and otherwise improving processes. BPR is an effort to make an extreme transformation by analyzing and considering all aspects of current processes for the purpose of making sweeping improvements.

VII. Outsourcing, Shared Services, and Off-Shore Operations

A. **Outsourcing**—This can be defined as contracting a business process to an external provider.

1. There are many reasons for outsourcing, but perhaps the most popular include **lower costs** and/or **higher quality** achieved through lower cost companies that specialize or have great expertise in a certain process, and using **risk-shifting** strategies that involve restructuring the nature of the costs (usually from fixed to variable) or shifting the burden of managing excess capacity to the supplier.
2. The biggest **risk** of outsourcing a particular process is the **risk to quality** due to a decreased amount of control over the process (i.e., limited to the terms of the contract). This could involve defect-prone operations, poor communication regarding the required specifications, or the principal-agent problem (i.e., moral hazard: where the agent deviates from contractual terms because the principal cannot readily observe the agent's actions).

B. **Shared Service**—One part of an organization provides an essential business process that previously had been provided by multiple parts of that same organization. Sometimes confused with merely centralizing operations, the shared-service provider often operates as an internal business.

1. The main purpose of shared services is to provide a process in a more effective and more efficient manner that lowers cost.
2. Although costs often go down with shared services, the risks to converting a process to a shared service include: the cost of moving or restructuring operations; the reduction of service specificity to the needs of specialized processes; and the possibility of less-timely delivery.

C. Offshore Operations—A process is moved to a different country. The movement can be to either an internal or external provider. The distinction between outsourcing and offshoring is that **outsourcing** is always outside of the company (but may or may not be outside the country), while **offshoring** is always outside of the country (but may or may not be outside the company).

1. Offshoring is almost always **due to cost savings** by gaining access to lower cost economies. Upstream phases of the value chain (e.g., R&D) are processes that are not often offshored due to the lack of access to high skills in areas that have cheap labor. Production and service processes are those most often offshored.
2. **Risks** typically involve language or cultural issues and difficulty protecting intellectual property rights in some foreign countries.

Planning Techniques

Budgeting

After studying this lesson, you should be able to:

1. Describe the master budget and the separate parts of the master budget and differentiate a master budget from a flexible budget.
2. Describe the budgeting process from sales forecasting through the various individual budgets that comprise the master budget.
3. Calculate a production/purchases budget, cash budget, and flexible budget.
4. Describe different types of budgets and budgeting concepts, including participative budgets, rolling budgets, zero-base budgets, and budgetary slack.

I. **The Master Budget**—Is a comprehensive plan for the overall activities of a company. The master budget is developed for a specified level of activity: It is a static budget. A static budget is a budget that does not change when actual sales differ from planned sales.

II. **The Master Budget is Composed of Several Coordinated Parts**

A. **Operating Budget**—The operating budget forecasts the results of operations: sales, production expenses, and selling and administrative expenses. The principal budgets found within the operating budget are:

1. Sales budget
2. Production budget
3. Production cost budgets (direct materials, labor, and overhead budgets)
4. Selling and administrative expense budget

B. **Financial Budget**—The financial budget forecasts cash flows and projects the financial statements that will result from operations. The financial budget consists of the:

1. Cash budget
2. Budgeted (or pro-forma) income statement
3. Budgeted (or pro-forma) balance sheet

C. **Capital Expenditures Budget**—The capital expenditures budget projects expenditures related to the acquisition or construction of capital (fixed) assets. Since acquisition of capital assets often requires an extended planning horizon, the capital expenditures budget often spans multiple fiscal periods.

Exam Tip
To the extent the questions on the CPA Exam address specific budgets as opposed to the master budget and the flexible budget, the budgets most likely to be tested are the sales budget, the production/purchases budget, and the cash budget.

III. **Budgeting Process**

A. **Operating Budget**

1. **Sales forecast**—The budgeting process begins with a **sales forecast**. The sales forecast is based on information obtained from both internal and external sources and provides estimates of sales in dollars and in units. These estimates flow forward to the sales budget.
2. **Sales budget**—The sales budget forecasts **planned sales in dollars and in units**, usually on a monthly or quarterly basis. The production budget and many of the items in the selling and administrative expenses budget are based on information from the sales budget.
3. **Production budget**—The production budget projects the **production quantities needed to support sales and provide for the specified quantity of ending inventory**. Its projections

are based on unit sales information from the sales budget, current inventory levels, and desired ending inventory levels. The data from the production budget flows forward to the production costs budgets.

4. **Production costs budgets**—A budget is prepared for each of the three factors of production: a **direct materials budget, a direct labor budget, and an overhead budget**. The budgets are based on unit production information provided by the production budget and, for direct materials, information about current and desired ending inventory levels. The data from the production costs budgets flow forward to the cash budget.
5. **Selling and administrative expense budget**—The selling and administrative expense budget lists the budget expenses for areas outside of manufacturing. Although some items on this budget are tied to the sales budget, most of the information comes from individual department managers as approved by management or by use of the percentage of sales method. The percentage of sales method **determines the expense amount by expressing the expense as a "percentage of sales."** The percentage of sales method is also used in the cash budget to estimate the amount of cash sales.

B. Financial Budgets

1. **Cash budget**—The cash budget projects cash receipts, cash disbursements, and ending cash balance by analyzing:
   a. **Anticipated operating receipts**—Information is derived from the sales budget, and from historical information about customer payment characteristics. The principal items of information include:
      i. Cash sales
      ii. Credit sales and accounts receivable collections.
   b. **Anticipated operating expenditures**—Estimates of expenditures are derived from the production costs budgets, the selling and administrative expense budget and from the company's vendor and employee payment policies. The principal items of information include:
      i. Costs and expenses
      ii. Purchases on account and accounts payable disbursements
   c. **Anticipated capital expenditures**—The capital expenditures budget provides information on planned expenditures for capital assets.
2. **Financing and investing activities**—Based on minimum cash balance requirements specified by management, the amount of cash that must be borrowed or may be invested is determined.

Exam Tip

You should expect cash budget questions to appear frequently on the exam and are likely to include analysis of the cash effects of increases and/or decreases in receivables and payables. The following matrix summarizes these effects:

Cash Effect of Changes in Receivables and Payables

	Receivables	**Payables**
Decrease	*Cash Increases*	*Cash Decreases*
Increase	*Cash Decreases*	*Cash Increases*

Question:

Browning Company anticipates cash sales of $300,000 and cash expenditures of $220,000 this month. Browning also expects that its Accounts Receivable and Accounts Payable balances will decrease by $50,000 and $40,000, respectively. If Browning's current cash balance is $150,000, what is its projected cash balance at the end of the month?

Answer:

+ Current Cash Balance	+ $150,000
+ Cash Sales	+ $300,000
− Cash Expenditures	− $220,000
+ Decrease in A/R	+ $50,000
− Decrease in A/P	− $40,000
= Projected Ending Cash Balance	= $240,000

3. **Budgeted financial statements (pro forma income statement and pro forma balance sheet)**—The budgeted financial statements use information from the operating budgets, the cash budget, and the capital expenditures budget to project the results of operation and financial position at the end of the period.

IV. Production/Purchases Budgets

A. Production/purchases budgets are common on the CPA Exam. The example below provides a set of two questions that are the most common to those asked about production and purchases budgets. When illustrating how to solve these problems we use the cost of goods sold/cost of goods manufactured statements. These statements are something that each candidate should already know. If so, then learning new budgeting statement formats are unnecessary.

B. The production budget must be done first. The production budget establishes how many units must be produced to achieve projected sales volume and inventory level targets. These targets can be modeled quantitatively without using costs. This is why in the statement below you see that the "cost" designations have been eliminated (i.e., to reflect only units). Once production volume is established (usually the objective of the production budget question), then the materials budget can be constructed.

C. Once the production budget has been completed, based on the production needed (in units), an appropriate number of material units must be purchased to satisfy the production required. This is the connection between the production budget and the purchases budget and is reflected by the arrows shown on the left side of the statement below.

D. Sometimes these budgets require dollar values that follow the units required to be produced and purchased. This is not a problem if the unit flows have been properly followed. Then all that is required is to value those units based on the costs per unit given in the question data.

Example

In calculating production and purchases budgets, **use what you already know**. There is no point in creating a new format for the budget that is different from the CGS/CGM format—just find the answer!

Sales budget in units	
January	70
February	90
March	50
April	60

	January	February	March
Beg. Inv—Finished	27	27	
GM = Production	(70)	78	
Goods Available	97	105	
− Ending Inv—Finished	27	15	
Goods Sold	70	90	50
		(.3*90)	(.3*50)
Beg. Inv—Direct	-0-	10	
+ Direct Materials	150	(156)	
Direct Materials	150	166	
− Ending Inv—Direct	10	10	
Direct Materials Used	140	156	
	(70*2)	(78*2)	

Beginning inventory for the year is 27 units. Ending inventory for each month should be 30% of the next month's sales.

How many units should the company **produce** in January?

a. 106

b. 90

c. **70**

d. 78

How many units of direct material (DM) should the company **purchase** in February if each FG unit takes 2 units of DM, they have no beginning inventory in January and they want to maintain an inventory of 10 DM units?

a. 90

b. 106

c. 73

d. **156**

V. Other Budgets and Terms

A. Participative Budgets—Allow subordinates to participate in establishing budget targets. Widely considered a positive behavioral approach, participative budgeting can (1) increase the accuracy of the budget by providing additional information that subordinates bring to the table, and (2) increase perceptions of ownership of the budget targets on behalf of the subordinates.

B. Strategic Budgeting—Implies a long-range view to planning based on the identification of action plans to achieve the company's goals and, ultimately, its mission. Many issues are considered, including a comprehensive internal and external analysis, competitive and economic analysis, and an assessment of various types of risk. Note that strategic budgets are easy to detect since terminology is always oriented to the "big-picture" (e.g., long-range, inside and outside the organization, large investments, economics, competitive opportunities/threats, assessment of distinctive competencies, and market risks).

Exam Tip
Strategic budgeting has become a more popular term in recent years. This may increase the likelihood of seeing more questions on this topic on future exams.

C. A Rolling Budget—Is an incremental budget that adds the current period and drops the oldest period. *Kaizen* (continuous improvement) type companies typically use rolling budgets and de-emphasize past performance in budgeting since results are "expected" to continuously improve.

D. Zero-Base Budgeting—Is a process of starting over each budget period and justifying each item budgeted. This requires additional work over an incremental approach but may provide more accuracy. This process forces managers to carefully think about their expenditures in hopes of reducing or eliminating the cost of unnecessary items.

E. Budgetary Slack—Occurs when managers attempt to build in a cushion for spending and revenue in case targets are not met. The use of slack results in a conservative budget as opposed to the most probable or accurate budget. The risk of managers building slack into their budgets is increased where budget targets are used in evaluation of individual performance and incentive compensation.

VI. Flexible Budget

A. Unlike the master budget, a flexible budget **adjusts revenues and some costs** when actual sales volume is different from planned sales volume. This makes it easier to analyze actual performance because the actual revenues and costs can be compared to the expected revenues and costs at **the actual level of sales activity**. The following adjustments are typical:

1. Revenue is adjusted by multiplying the actual quantity times the sales price.
2. Total variable costs are adjusted by multiplying the actual quantity times the variable cost per unit.
3. Total fixed costs remain the same as long as volume remains within a relevant range, which is normally the case on CPA Exam questions.

Example
Grenwich's master budget anticipated the following revenues, costs, and net income related to a lawn sprinkler they produce:

Master Budget	
Sales (10,000 units @ $15 per unit)	$150,000
Variable manufacturing costs ($5 per unit)	– 50,000
Variable selling and administrative costs ($1 per unit)	– 10,000
Contribution margin	$ 90,000
Fixed manufacturing costs ($2 per unit)	– 20,000
Fixed selling and administrative costs	– 20,000
Operating Income	$ 50,000

Flexible Budget	
Sales (12,000 units @ $15 per unit)	$180,000
Variable manufacturing costs ($5 per unit)	– 60,000
Variable selling and administrative costs ($1 per unit)	– 12,000
Contribution margin	$108,000
Fixed manufacturing costs ($2 per unit)	– 20,000
Fixed selling and administrative costs (total does not change)	– 20,000
Operating Income	$ 68,000

B. **Differences between the flexible budget and the master budget** are known as **sales activity variances** or **volume variances.**

Forecasting Techniques

After studying this lesson, you should be able to:

1. Explain the features of probability and expected value, and calculate the expected value of a particular outcome.
2. Explain dispersion, correlation, and related terminology, including the correlation coefficient (R) and the coefficient of determination (R^2).
3. Explain the components of the regression equation and calculate the predicted forecast values using the regression equation.
4. Describe joint probability and calculate the joint probability of a particular event.

I. Probability and Expected Value

A. Probability analysis is used to determine the likelihood of a specific event occurring when several outcomes are possible. A probability for each outcome is assessed. The probability of a **particular outcome is always between 0 (never) and 1 (always).** The sum of the probabilities associated with the possible outcomes is always 1. (A sum less than one indicates that an outcome has been omitted from the analysis or a probability has been improperly assessed.)

B. The **expected value** is the **long-run average outcome**. Expected value is determined by calculating the **weighted average of the outcomes**: multiply the value of each outcome by its probability and then sum the results.

Example

The useful life of a machine is not known, but there is a 20% probability of a 5-year life, a 50% probability of a 6-year life and a 30% probability of a 7-year life. What is the expected life of the machine?

Years Life		Probability	Expected Value
5	×	.2	= 1.0 years
6	×	.5	= 3.0 years
7	×	.3	= 2.1 years
		1	6.1 years expected life

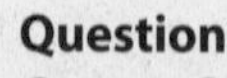

Question:

Gensco Corp. is preparing to develop a new product that requires an investment of $500,000. Gensco believes that if it develops the product there is a 75% chance that it will be able to sell the product to a manufacturer at a profit of $1,000,000. Legal issues are such that if it is unable to sell the product at this price, it will not sell the product at all. What is the expected value of the project?

Answer:

	Profit/Loss	Probability	Expected Value
Profit if product sells:	$1,000,000	75%	$750,000
Loss if product fails to sell	($500,000)	25%	($125,000)
Expected Value		100%	$625,000

Exam Tip
Always check to ensure that your probabilities total 100% (or 1, if you use decimals to represent probabilities). Questions such as this one that state the probability of one event (e.g., the product sells) but do not explicitly mention the second event (e.g., the product doesn't sell) are very common.`

II. Joint Probability

A. Joint probability is the probability of an event occurring given that another event has already occurred. The joint probability is determined by multiplying the probability of the first event by the conditional probability of the second event.

B. CPA Exam questions often use joint probability calculations to assess the likelihood of a particular combination of events occurring (this technique is frequently used in auditing to assess the likelihood of error occurrence). To calculate the probability of a specific combination of events from a set of event combinations:

1. For each combination of events, multiple the probability of the first event by the conditional probability of the second event.
2. Sum the results for all the event combinations.
3. Divide each result for each event combination by the total of all the event combinations to determine the probability of a particular event combination occurring.
4. Sum the probabilities for each event combination to ensure that the total is 1 (or 100%).

Question:
The following information pertains to three order processing centers operated by the Deming Co.:

Office	Percentage of orders handled	Percentage of errors
Northwest	30%	4%
Central	50%	2%
South	20%	8%

If an error is made, what is the likelihood that it will be made in the Central Office?

Answer:

Office	Percentage of orders handled	Percentage of errors	Combined rate	Divide individual rate by total		Probability of error
Northwest	.30	.04	.012	.012/.038	=	.316
Central	.50	.02	.010	.010/.038	=	.263
South	.20	.08	.016	.016/.038	=	.421
	1.00		.038			1.000

Given that an error is made, there is a 26.3% chance that the error will be made at the Central Office.

III. Variance Analysis—Variance analysis measures the **dispersion of values around the expected value** (the **mean** or **average value**).

A. The **smaller the variance**, the **more tightly clustered** the observations around the expected value.

B. Smaller variances are usually associated with less risk.

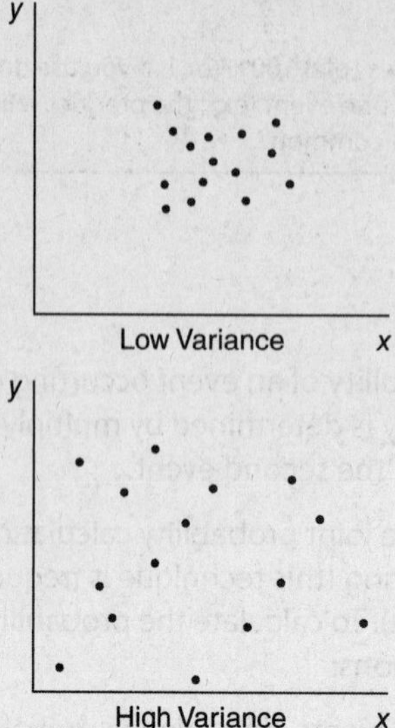

Low Variance

High Variance

IV. Correlation Analysis

A. Correlation analysis measures the strength of the relationship between two or more variables: a dependent variable (a value that changes in response to changes in related values) and one or more independent variables (values that change, but not in response to changes in other variables in the equation). The **correlation coefficient (R)** measures the **strength of the relationship** between the dependent and independent variables. The correlation coefficient can have **values from −1 to 1** where:

1. 1 indicates perfect positive correlation (as *x* increases, so does *y*).
2. −1 indicates perfect negative correlation (as *x* increases, *y* decreases).
3. 0 indicates no correlation (you cannot predict the value of *y* from the value of *x*).

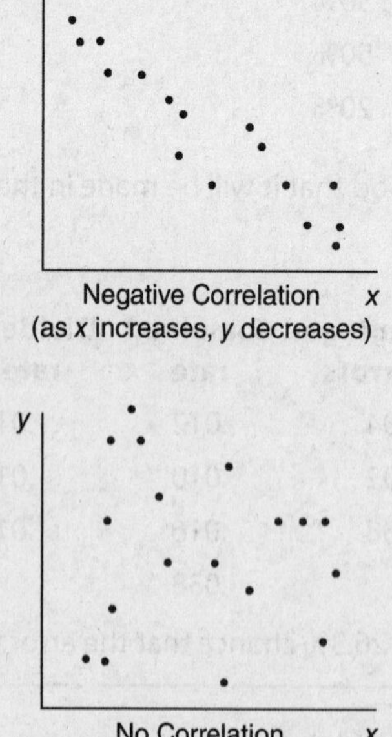

Negative Correlation
(as *x* increases, *y* decreases)

No Correlation
(no relationship between behavior of *x* and behavior of *y*)

B. The **coefficient of determination, identified as R^2 (R-squared)**, indicates the degree to which the behavior of the independent variable predicts the dependent variable. The coefficient of determination is calculated by squaring the correlation coefficient. R^2 can take on **values from 0 to 1**.

1. The closer R^2 is to 1, the **better the independent variable predicts the behavior of the dependent variable**.

Exam Tip
Be sure to understand the relationship between the Coefficient of Determination (R^2) and the Correlation Coefficient (R). The examiners are likely to ask questions about these two measures.

Question:
Bates Company has evaluated two activities for consideration as cost drivers for several manufacturing costs. Regression analysis has produced the following results:

Activity A		**Activity B**	
Y-Intercept:	60	*Y*-Intercept:	35
B:	4.20	B:	3.5
R^2	.81	R^2	.65

Choose the activity which best predicts the manufacturing costs and construct the regression equation:

Answer:
Activity A with an R^2 of .81 is the best predictor: $Y = 60 + 4.2X$

V. Regression Analysis

A. Regression analysis predicts the value of one factor (the dependent variable) based on the value of one or more other factors (the independent variables).

1. **Simple regression**—A regression with one independent variable
2. **Multiple regression**—A regression with several independent variables

B. Linear regression analysis is frequently used in cost accounting to evaluate the strength of the relationship between costs and cost drivers. Regression analysis **does *not* establish cause and effect—it merely indicates a relationship**.

Exam Tip
Regression analysis is likely to be a frequently tested area on the CPA Exam, with perhaps as much as one or two questions appearing on every exam. Questions are not expected to be difficult and are usually confined to defining elements in the regression equation and evaluating the significance of values for the Correlation Coefficient (R) and/or the Coefficient of Determination (R^2).

C. **Regression Equation**—The relationship between the dependent and independent variables is expressed in the regression equation, which takes the following form:

$y = A + Bx$

where: y = dependent variable

A = the y-intercept

B = the slope of the line

x = independent variable

1. The regression equation can be shown graphically:

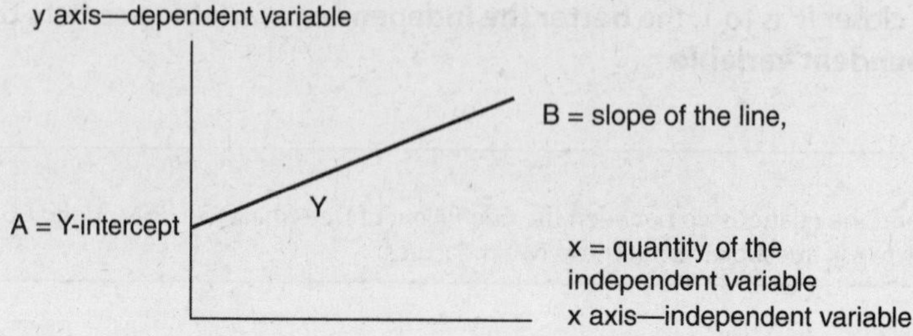

D. Cost Equation—The relationship between fixed costs, variable costs, and total costs can be expressed in the regression equation:

$y = A + Bx$

where: y = total costs (dependent variable)

A = fixed costs (the *y*-intercept)

B = variable cost per unit (the slope of the line)

x = number of units (independent variable)

OR

Total Costs = Fixed Costs + (Variable Cost Per Unit × Number of Units)

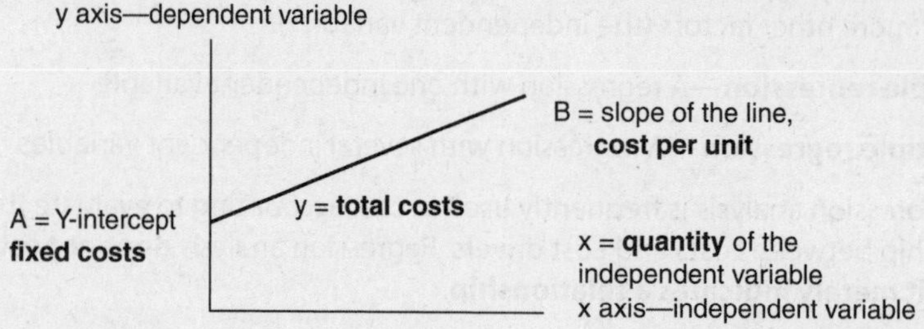

Index

Q

R

S

T